R&D FOR INDUSTRY

R&D for Industry

A century of technical innovation
at Alcoa

MARGARET B. W. GRAHAM
and BETTYE H. PRUITT

The right of the
University of Cambridge
to print and sell
all manner of books
was granted by
Henry VIII in 1534.
The University has printed
and published continuously
since 1584.

CAMBRIDGE UNIVERSITY PRESS

CAMBRIDGE
NEW YORK   PORT CHESTER
MELBOURNE   SYDNEY

Published by the Press Syndicate of the University of Cambridge
The Pitt Building, Trumpington Street, Cambridge CB2 1RP
40 West 20th Street, New York, NY 10011, USA
10 Stamford Road, Oakleigh, Melbourne 3166, Australia

© Cambridge University Press 1990

First published 1990

Printed in the United States of America

Library of Congress Cataloging-in-Publication Data

Graham, Margaret B. W.
R&D for industry : a century of technical innovation at Alcoa /
Margaret B. W. Graham and Bettye H. Pruitt.
p. cm.
Includes bibliographical references.
ISBN 0-521-39413-9
1. Aluminum Company of America – History. 2. Aluminum industry and
trade – United States – Technological innovations – History.
3. Research, Industrial – United States – History. I. Pruitt, Bettye
Hobbs. II. Title. III. Title: R and D for industry.
HD9539.A64A733 1990
338.7′669722′0973 – dc20   90-1420

British Library Cataloguing in Publication Data

Graham, Margaret B. W.
R & D for industry : a century of technical innovation at
Alcoa.
1. United States. Aluminium industries : Alcoa, history
I. Title II. Pruitt, Bettye H.
338.76737220973

ISBN 0–521–39413–9 hardback

Contents

Preface

When we began this history of R&D at Alcoa, in the mid-1980s, we expected that its natural audience would consist mainly of Alcoans past and present, historians of business and technology, and members of other R&D communities around the country. While we have been writing, the subject of R&D and manufacturing has begun to attract wider attention, and we hope that this book will be of interest to those who are concerned about the decline in manufacturing innovation.

The decade of the 1980s has been a time of growing public awareness that industry in the United States has paid far too little attention to the deterioration of its productive capabilities and has been neglecting process innovation. Alcoa, as a mainstream American manufacturing company, has devoted more of its energies to linked process and product innovation than many other American manufacturing companies and has invested far more heavily in R&D than have other metals companies. The history of R&D at Alcoa helps to explain how American manufacturing achieved preeminence during and after World War II, but it also helps us to understand why American manufacturing has gone through a time of troubles in the past two decades. It is apparent from this company's experience that the national climate for R&D, though mediated by the unique character and policies of individual companies, has changed over time from fostering the linkage between R&D and manufacturing to making the linkages more difficult to achieve.

This book grew out of a larger history project conducted by The Winthrop Group, Inc., for Alcoa in preparation for the company's centennial in 1988. As Alcoa approached its second century, its managers were aware that they were facing a period of strategic change as dramatic and as challenging as any in their history. Aluminum production worldwide was expanding rapidly. Basic aluminum was available on the commodity markets, and new structural materials were emerging to challenge aluminum on many fronts. The steel industry in the United States had suffered a precipitous decline in the early 1980s, and Alcoa managers had reason to be proud that their investment in the future had kept them from participating in that decline, even though they shared many of its problems. Earlier than many, and without their backs to the wall, Alcoans were taking a fresh look at their business and what they needed to do to rejuvenate it.

The Alcoa Laboratories had reason to view this period of change as an opportunity. Like R&D laboratories all over the country in the mid-1980s, Alcoa Laboratories was being asked to come up with strategic solutions after more than a decade during which it had been relegated to a position on the strategic sidelines. This meant a new identity for the Laboratories. Changing identities and renewing institutions required self-examination. During the late 1970s, Alcoa Laboratories had been increasing its contacts with the outside world and learning to see itself as others saw it. What it saw was a company with a long history of innovation that had defined itself as technologically mature, and a Laboratory that had lost its sense of direction, if not its sense of purpose, as a consequence. This recognition posed important questions, some of them historical. How had the organization arrived at such a point? What aspects of its traditional identity were strengths to be preserved? What prized traditions should be promoted, and what should be let go? One way to answer some of these questions was to examine the Laboratories' history and its relation both to the company and to the scientific community at large.

As historians of technology and business, we welcomed the chance to write the Alcoa Laboratories history. It promised to fill in a missing part of the record of American industry, the role of R&D in the continuous process industries. Alcoa had preserved its history in valuable corporate and laboratory archives. Moreover, it was our impression that Alcoans were willing to take an objective look at themselves, using their history not as a means to dwell on past successes and achievements but as a springboard to the future. That sense of Alcoa as a place where history would be used constructively has been strengthened over the past few years. We owe appreciation to many Alcoans not only for their assistance but also for their tolerance and sense of fairness.

Throughout the book we have tried to present not just the story of an organization, but also the story of the people who worked within it and helped to shape it. In a study spanning an entire century, such an effort requires focusing on a few individuals, while others whose contributions have been equally as great go without mention. In writing about fields such as R&D, where teamwork is important, such exclusions are as regrettable as they are unavoidable. We hope that Alcoans who read the book will find that, overall, it accurately depicts the history as they understand it and will forgive our inability to give recognition to all who deserve it. Writing history is an act of selection, and though many people have helped us in our effort to achieve accuracy and balance, we alone bear responsibility for the selection process that took place.

It is impossible to mention everyone who has helped us over more than four years of research and writing, but still we must do the best we can to express our appreciation. We could hardly have scratched the surface of Alcoa's rich archival material without the assistance of its professional archivists and librarians. In particular, we wish to thank Kristin Henson at Alcoa Archives, Virgie Jo Sapp, William Frank, Pam DiNardo, Marian Ansani, Earl Mounts, Mary Ann Perfetti, Audrey Farah, and their colleagues in the library and offices at Alcoa Laboratories, and Jack Mulley at Alcoa Records Storage Center. Elizabeth Altman, a free-lance historian, did much of the photographic research, working with Virgie Jo Sapp and Kristin Henson in their respective archives. All of the photographs, unless otherwise attributed, are courtesy of Alcoa. Special thanks go to Nick Kotow for preparing Appendix C on classic research papers and to David Thomas and Vicki Shaner for preparing the graphic illustrations. A second rich source of material was comprised by the many retired Alcoans who contributed their time, their personal files in some cases, and their memories. Too numerous to list here, a list of their interviews is contained in Appendix D. We thank them not only for their generosity but also for giving us the pleasure of glimpsing a very different era in the life of American business.

We wish especially to thank Peter Bridenbaugh, Wayne

Binger, David Brownlee, James Dowd, Howard Dunn, William Frank, Edward Foote, Philip Morton, and Robert Spear for their valuable reading and comments on portions of the manuscript. Our outside reader, David Allison of the National Museum of American History, made many good suggestions that helped to strengthen the structure of the book. Among our colleagues at The Winthrop Group, Inc., our principal reader was George Smith, author of Alcoa's centennial history, *From Monopoly to Competition: The Transformations of Alcoa, 1888–1986* (1988). Judith Gurney, our free-lance editor, gave us many hours of her valuable attention; Lauren Meader did photographic research outside Alcoa. We are grateful, too, for the attention at Cambridge University Press of Frank Smith and Russell Hahn. Finally, we owe a great deal to Louis Galambos of Johns Hopkins University and the Eisenhower Papers Project for his incisive commentary on the text and for his stimulating responses to the intellectual themes raised therein.

Introduction

Industrial research and development (R&D) as a corporate activity, and aluminum as an industrial material, have both existed for roughly a century. Their juxtaposition is no mere chronological coincidence. America's "aluminum century" originated in a scientific revolution that was as important to the nation's industrial life as the American Revolution of the previous century was to its political life. That century is culminating in a period of renewal that may extend both the technology and the industry far into the next century.

During the years 1880–1920 American business underwent a sudden, all-embracing transformation. As the fast-growing extensive economy of a frontier society gave way to the slower-growing intensive economy of an industrial nation, Americans discovered a need for new institutions. Hierarchical companies emerged to give the nation a greater measure of economic security and the kinds of technical and organizational innovations that would sustain economic growth over the long run. The scientific revolution led to an industrial transformation because it was linked to the growth of large corporate enterprise and a professional managerial culture. A powerful symbol of that linkage was the modern industrial research laboratory.[1]

Two science-based industries, the electrical and the chemical, were in the vanguard of the scientific revolution in business. Both emerged as high-growth industries in the United States and abroad around 1880, and both hit their stride by World War I.[2] These industries, which included such subsidiary businesses as photography, paints and dyestuffs, and electric railways, served a dual purpose. In addition to becoming significant economic forces in their own right, they helped to transform many existing industries by providing them with new sources of power,

1

new inputs, new techniques, and sophisticated technical expertise.[3] Steel, glass, rubber, and automobiles all were either altered
or regenerated by the infusion of scientifically trained people,
improved and stimulated by scientific discovery, and rational-
ized by modern management.[4]

Companies in these vanguard industries, which formed the
durable core of the industrial economy, also led the way in
setting up corporate research laboratories in the first decade of
the twentieth century. Although there had been numerous industrial laboratories in the United States before 1900, most had
been "works laboratories," for testing and control at production
sites. The corporate laboratory began integrating activities
from different parts of the organization, pursuing generic technologies (known as "general research"), and transferring technology around the corporate system. Through the corporate
laboratory, technical information became one of the exploitable
assets of the science-based enterprise.[5]

Metals companies, especially the giants of steel, participated
in this industrial transformation in some ways, but not in others. Regenerated by the adoption of new reduction processes
for metals production, these firms became large, integrated,
and scientifically managed. But metalworking, or metallurgy
(the term that referred first to the art, and then considerably
later to the science, of metal fabrication), continued to be dominated by a strong craft tradition that for decades resisted the
infusion of scientific techniques. In the transition from craft-
based to science-based metallurgy it was the nonferrous metals
that led the way, and the most progressive among them was
aluminum.[6]

THE NEED FOR ALUMINUM R&D

In the United States the production of primary aluminum on
an industrial scale had its start with the founding in 1888 of
the Pittsburgh Reduction Company, later named the Aluminum Company of America (Alcoa). Wholly dependent on the
dynamo to power its proprietary electrolytic smelting process,
Alcoa emerged as the first significant electrochemical business.
It was also the catalyst for the formation of many others. The
company would have preferred, like the electrochemical producers of chlorine or abrasives, to confine its activities to the

production of intermediate products – primary metal and chemical by-products. But the marketplace would not oblige. Alcoa had to create demand for its metal by devising aluminum products and then developing the metalworking processes by which other companies could fabricate them.[7]

As a result, Alcoa led other metals companies in seeking scientific solutions to the problems of both metalmaking and metalworking. Its efforts to master its primary processes and to develop large-volume applications for aluminum led the company to establish an integrated R&D organization and to set out to build an aluminum knowledge base from which it could begin to practice metallurgy less as an art and more as a science. It made that investment and assumed its risks confident that because it was the sole primary producer of aluminum in the United States, any investment in R&D would benefit Alcoa either directly or indirectly by helping its customers, the fabricators of aluminum products. By taking on research, including fundamental research, as a formal corporate activity, the company took control of aluminum technology in the United States as it could not have done if it had left the development of aluminum science to other research performers – the independent and government laboratories and the universities.[8]

THE INDUSTRIALIZATION OF R&D

Because of its nature, the industrial laboratory is an institution suspended between two worlds – that of industry and the marketplace, on the one hand, and that of the scientific professions, on the other. It is the ability of this institution to maintain creative contact between the scientific knowledge builders and the problem solvers of industry that makes it peculiarly valuable to the corporation. Yet the tension between these two worlds has been a constant source of managerial difficulty as industrial R&D has evolved within large integrated firms. To understand this evolution it is useful to look at the early history of R&D at the German chemical company, Bayer A.G., a history that has been well documented in an essay by Georg Meyer-Thurow. The stages of R&D progress at Bayer can be seen to compose a pattern of evolution. That pattern has been repeated, with variations, in the R&D laboratories of many major companies in the United States, including Alcoa.[9]

Bayer was originally a manufacturer of dyestuffs. Its first stage of technical development was what we shall call its external or *borrowing* phase. During those two decades, it depended on a variety of sources outside the firm for most of its technical information. Because the underlying technology was still in its formative phase, those sources often were unreliable. Bayer derived its earliest production processes from the work of scientist-entrepreneurs who in the 1860s defined the technology, in part by building bridges between emerging academic theory in chemistry and industrial practice. Toward the latter part of that early stage, in the 1870s, Bayer hired scientists and engineers from other related industries who brought with them experience-based science and know-how. The company also sponsored research in universities on a sporadic basis, but it did not set up its own in-house research facilities because that was regarded as too risky and too expensive.

The second phase of Bayer's R&D development involved *internalization* of these technical resources. Beginning in 1878, Bayer hired Ph.D. scientists out of universities and set them up in primitive works laboratories throughout the company to do product testing and process control, with some research on the side. Over time, their research function became more and more separated from their other activities, and they were allowed to follow up, in an increasingly systematic way, generic opportunities identified in the course of studying the immediate problems they were attempting to solve.

In stage three, which can be characterized as *institutionalization,* Bayer set up its own large central laboratory to pursue the many fundamental research questions that had by then become well defined. That laboratory, which opened in 1891, was the envy of the universities and was regarded as a model facility for chemical research. During the 1890s, Bayer developed an effective set of management policies to coordinate the application of its research findings. That effort was aided by Ph.D. engineers who, by the 1890s, were being trained in German universities for the first time.

After 1900, when Bayer had achieved a fully integrated and fully institutionalized corporate research structure, the firm entered a fourth stage, characterized by a higher degree of *specialization.* During that phase, the company's R&D organization turned increasingly inward. Bayer was technically so self-

sufficient that its researchers no longer needed to rely on outside sources of technology, either academic or industrial. Its
external activities consisted in urging Germany's universities to
teach more advanced courses in the particular applied sciences
it wanted its professionals to command. As Bayer's research
personnel and research functions became more specialized,
the company set up laboratories linked to particular phases of
production. That elaboration of the R&D function created an
even greater need for effective coordination, both within the
R&D organization among its constituent parts and between
R&D and the other parts of the company. Toward the end of
that fourth phase, Bayer began hiring personnel largely on the
basis of their ability to cooperate in this system, rather than for
their scientific competence.

Stage five, which was reached around 1910, can be called
routinization. By that time, the typical form of innovation pursued by Bayer R&D involved small product and process changes.
The company had complete control of its innovation process,
and the results were quite predictable, but also relatively inconse-
quential. Increasingly, researchers were cut off from the outside
world, forbidden to publish, and subjugated to the dictates of
immediate commercial utility. Because of the low standing to
which the research organization sank, research became a dead-
end career. Scientists and engineers hired out of German universities insisted on going into production, not research. The folly
of that situation became apparent when in 1909 Bayer invested
heavily in a new process to produce artificial rubber and failed.
Efforts to penetrate new chemical markets also met with failure
in that period. In short, Meyer-Thurow's account of the evolution of R&D at Bayer indicates that on the eve of World War I,
the routinization of invention had undermined both the R&D
community and the company's use of technology to enter new
markets.

Ultimately, Bayer overcame the rigidities of its pre–World
War I R&D structure. Indeed, it was Bayer's R&D efforts in
product-line diversification, especially in pharmaceuticals, that
led to the company's subsequent emergence as a diversified
giant on a worldwide scale. We can infer that there was, in
effect, a further, *renewal* stage in the history of its R&D organization. The stages of development derived from the Bayer experience give us a simple but useful framework for analyzing the

organizational evolution of R&D in a firm as it moves through its borrowing phase to internalized, institutionalized, specialized, and routinized patterns of development and eventually to renewal.

THE STAGES OF R&D DEVELOPMENT IN THE NATIONAL CONTEXT

In some companies, R&D simply ceases to be an effective source of strategic opportunity and reverts entirely to a limited technical-support function as these companies either go out of business or diversify into wholly nontechnical channels. In others, renewal occurs, both in the R&D organizations and in the companies themselves. The process of renewal has been studied at an industry level, but the part that R&D has played in that process has rarely been explicitly or directly addressed. Another aspect of renewal that has not received as much attention as it should is the national context for R&D. How individual companies in particular industries acquire technical information and conduct research and how they use science and technology to improve existing businesses or to create new opportunities are profoundly affected by the changing relationships among industrial, educational, and governmental institutions – the society's organizational infrastructure.[10]

At any given point in history, the national infrastructure supporting industrial research has been shaped by professional scientific attitudes toward business and by business attitudes toward science. In the historiography of U.S. industrial R&D, the nature of the relationship between the modern corporation and its in-house scientific professionals – inventors, scientists, and engineers – has traditionally reflected public fears about the relationship between science and industry that existed before World War II. The science–industry connection has been portrayed in the history of R&D as a kind of Faustian pact in which technical personnel recruited from universities and independent laboratories have given up their right to control their own research agendas in exchange for assurances of high pay and a chance to advance in management ranks. According to this interpretation, during the formative era of industrial R&D, from about 1900 to the 1930s, corporate America shaped the technical professions in its own image, dominating the national technical infrastructure to such an extent that even the scientific and engineering departments of universities in the United States became mere handmaidens of industry.[11]

More recently, scholars have argued that scientists did not simply "sell out" to industry. In the aftermath of World War I, thousands of scientific professionals began careers in industry, and the industrial laboratory became the place where the different values of the various scientific disciplines encountered each other and the marketplace, and often clashed. However, over time, R&D professionals worked to overcome their differences and to build relationships between academic and industrial research-performing institutions. In adjusting to industrial life, scientists often had to change the way they did science, but they, in turn, affected the direction of technological change in industry and in the society at large.[12]

Nevertheless, the long-standing fear that industry would deflect scientific fields from their natural courses of inquiry and coopt scientists, to the detriment of society, remained a strong undertone of public discussion through World War II and beyond. That war was a watershed event that, by bringing government into the R&D arena, altered the balance of power between science and industry and transformed the terms of the debate over their proper relationship.[13]

After the war, in which scientists were acknowledged to have played a vital, even decisive role, the scientific professions were in a position to reshape the national infrastructure more fully to reflect their values and to serve their professional interests. Among these were the need to increase the number of stable jobs for the scientifically trained in industry and the desire to raise the level of financial support for research activity. Both of these interests fit neatly into the national agenda for the postwar era. Whereas after World War I the U.S. government had abruptly withdrawn its support from many projects initiated during the war, in the 1950s and 1960s, federal policy was guided by a cold-war imperative to sustain the momentum behind new technologies such as the atom bomb, radar, and the jet engine. Public money for R&D poured into the industrial sector through the Defense Department and other defense-related government agencies.

At the same time, the government continued its policy, begun during the New Deal, of intervening to ensure that no single powerful company, such as RCA in "radio-related" electronics, DuPont in artificial fibers, or Alcoa in aluminum, could dominate its industry, either through monopoly or through control of technology. That meant creating competition, not only in manufacturing capability but also in research. When large amounts of federal funding were pumped into R&D after World War II, trained scientists suddenly were in great demand. They had a broader range of attractive career options and were in a position to negotiate within industry the kind of autonomy they previously had enjoyed in only the best academic settings. It had become the turn of the corporation, not the scientist, to face Faust's dilemma, as lavish federal funding for R&D raised the possibility that "big science" would become the mechanism by which government would coopt big business.[14]

In the postwar decades, American corporations that had previously prevailed on science to serve their interests found science to be an unruly servant. The inability of big science to fulfill the heightened expectations that went along with the financial commitment to R&D turned the late 1960s and 1970s into a period of disenchantment and retrenchment. For over a decade, both government support and industry support for research leveled off, and professionals in industrial laboratories labored under the burden of management attitudes that scorned R&D as a source of strategic opportunity, favoring instead diversification and expansion into international markets.

Since the late 1970s, the national context of corporate R&D has shifted again, reflecting concern over tough competition from industrial rivals in the international arena. Central to the discussion of the need for industrial renewal is the debate over the role that R&D must play in the renewal process. As managers struggle to reharness research in support of corporate strategy, they face the need to set aside both the unproductive hostility toward R&D of the 1970s and the overblown expectations of the era of big science. Those who have seen R&D as a predictable process providing innovation on demand must confront a more complex reality. The nature of this reality may be better understood when viewed in a longer-range historical perspective.

THE HISTORY OF R&D AT ALCOA

The history of Alcoa provides an opportunity to observe the evolution of R&D within a corporation, through the phases we have described, over the course of an entire century. It allows us to examine both the internal dynamic of that evolution and the impact of external factors, specifically the changing national climate for R&D. Moreover, specific aspects of Alcoa's history make it particularly valuable. For example, at the level of national policy, Alcoa's story provides an opportunity to examine the effects of monopoly and of U.S. antitrust policy on R&D. Alcoa also provides an interesting study because it has focused on innovation in processes as much as on product development. Its history allows us to examine in depth the characteristics of process R&D and the problems it poses for research management. Because, in the debate on industrial renewal, there are many who claim that the United States has fallen behind chiefly in manufacturing technology, that is, process technology, Alcoa's experience may be useful in helping us to understand the conditions, both within the firm and in the national context, that have either fostered or inhibited process R&D.[15]

In this book, we attempt to relate changes, both structural and personal, in Alcoa's R&D management to the company's capacity for technological innovation. Each of Parts I–V includes one chapter that describes the organizational development of R&D and a second chapter that provides a case study of one or more innovations central to the life of Alcoa R&D during the period. Chronologically, each part encompasses a distinct era, corresponding to one of the stages introduced in the Bayer model. The case studies illustrate the ways in which the conduct of R&D has varied under changing conditions and examine the relationships between how research was managed and how successful it was in addressing the company's technical problems and needs.

Three themes are entwined in this account of one hundred years of Alcoa R&D. The first is the special nature of process R&D, a problem that is critical to an understanding of the role that R&D can play in the lives of the nation's core manufacturing firms. The second is the role of management and managerial institutions in the evolution of a core technology. When a technology is said to mature, what is it that really matures, the technology or the institutions that are established to nurture it? Third is the theme of the relationship between technology and strategy, a relationship that is always important in science-based companies, whether acknowledged or not. To serve a strategic purpose, each corporate laboratory must offer its company a technical vision, a unique formulation of technological opportunity matched to its peculiar technical capabilities. It is up to the corporation to translate the technical vision into major initiatives for the enterprise.

At Alcoa, as at other companies, the institutional mechanisms and capabilities that have made it possible for its laboratories to be effective agents of innovation have changed dramatically over time. Sometimes the changes have been productive, sometimes not. Poised as we now seem to be on the threshold of a new scientific epoch for industry, it can only be beneficial to comprehend more fully the evolution that has occurred over the long sweep of the past century.

Technical note

The aluminum technology of today is a direct outgrowth of developments that originated a hundred years ago. This introductory overview will provide the technological context for issues that are discussed primarily in their historical context in later chapters. It describes processes as currently practiced and understood, pointing to the evolution of the processes involved and emphasizing those features that have been recurrent in research efforts at various times over the last century. The most important aspects of aluminum technology can be considered under four headings: refining, smelting, fabricating, and alloy development.

REFINING

Among the common metals, aluminum is the most abundant in the earth's crust, and yet it is one of the most difficult to wrest from nature. It cannot be mined in pure form, like gold or silver, because it exists only in combination with other elements. It is most commonly found as a silicate – that is, combined with silicon and oxygen – in rocks such as granite, shale, sandstone, and limestone, but it occurs in other mineral deposits, such as clay. The most useful form, however, is the binary compound aluminum oxide, alumina. Alumina exists naturally in pure form as corundum, but it is most often combined with other elements in a wide variety of rocks and ores.

The aluminous ores that have proved to be of commercial significance have been grouped into the broad class called bauxite, after the French town Les Baux, where it was first identified in 1821. There are many types of grades of bauxite deposited regionally around the world. The basic composition is hydrated aluminum oxide – a compound of alumina and water – with impurities, chiefly ferric oxide (iron plus oxygen) and silica (silicon plus oxygen). The aluminum content of bauxite can vary from 30 to 75 percent, and the levels of impurities also vary. For example, the bauxites around Les Baux contain between 20 and 25 percent ferric oxide, but only 3 to 5 percent silica, while those of the United States are low in ferric oxide, but have 5 to 12 percent silica. These differences in composition have led to different problems in refining and smelting for producers using different sources of raw material.

Much of what is said of aluminum in its natural state can also be said of iron: It does not occur in substantial quantities in pure form and is most economically produced by reduction from its oxide, which is mined as ore. Yet iron can be produced in a blast furnace, with the impurities passing readily into slag. Reduction of aluminum from alumina cannot be accomplished economically by heat, but only through electrolytic reaction, and the impurities tend to alloy with and remain as impurities in the metal. For that reason, a costly refining process is necessary to minimize the level of impurities in the alumina.[1]

In 1887 the Austrian chemist Karl Josef Bayer developed the most economical and widely used alumina refining process. The Bayer process involved five basic steps. *Preparation:* Bauxite is dried and ground to a fine powder. *Digestion:* It is then combined with sodium hydroxide (caustic soda) and agitated in a heated, pressurized container, which causes the alumina to dissolve into solution as sodium aluminate. *Separation:* The next step is to separate out the insoluble impurities. These are silica, which forms the compound sodium aluminum silicate during the digestion phase, and ferric oxide, which colors the residue and gives it its name, "red mud." Originally the separation of impurities was done entirely by filtration through heavy cotton fabric, in filter presses, but current practice is to dilute and decant the Bayer liquor, allowing the heavier red mud to settle out, and filtering only as a final purifying step. *Precipitation:* The filtered liquor is next transferred to large steel tanks, where it is seeded with fine particles of aluminum hydroxide, recycled from a later step of the process. This mixture is cooled slowly over 20 to 80 hours, with constant agitation, causing alumina to precipitate, or solidify, onto the seed particles, thereby forming large crystals that are easily separated from

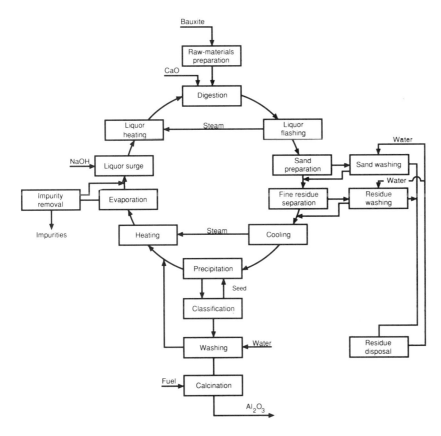

Figure 1. The Bayer process. Source: L. K. Hudson, C. Misra, and K. Wefers, "Aluminum Oxide," *Ullmann's Encyclopedia of Industrial Chemistry* (Weinheim: VCH Verlagsgesellschaft, 1985), vol. A1, p. 567.

the solution. Some of these crystals are returned to the process as seed particles. The rest are washed and then dried, first by causing the liquid to evaporate and then by *calcination* – heating to a high temperature, just below the melting point. The end product is a fine white powder of highly purified alumina. About 10 percent of the alumina produced is marketed as a chemical compound for use in refractories, abrasives, ceramics, fillers, sorbents, and catalyst supports. The rest is used in the production of aluminum.

In the operation of the Bayer process, variables such as the temperature, the rate of temperature change, the level of concentration of the sodium aluminate liquor, and the exact chemical composition of the liquor govern the efficiency of production and the purity and the characteristics of the alumina produced.

The electrolytic smelting process is extremely sensitive to variations in the composition of the input; so the refining step must be carefully controlled in order to keep the stream of production flowing smoothly and the quality of output high. While bauxite is by far the best ore for commercial production, having 50 to 60 percent alumina, a great deal of effort has been expended over the years to develop economical processes for refining lower-grade ores and clay, which are more abundant. Furthermore, because the compositions and characteristics of bauxite vary significantly from region to region, the opening of new mining sites around the world has required adjustments in the refining process.[2] For example, Alcoa could not use the high-silica bauxites of Arkansas economically in the Bayer process until a modification called the "combination process" was developed during World War II. That was because the silica tended to form an insoluble compound with alumina and soda that was carried off in the red mud, causing unacceptable losses of these two key elements.

Refining is an expensive part of aluminum production. The Bayer process requires substantial amounts of energy, typically steam produced by fossil fuel, as well as other inputs – bauxite, caustic soda, lime, and water – that must either be available at hand or be shipped to the refining site. The alumina produced must then be shipped to a smelter, which might, for economic reasons, be located far away. Another consideration is disposal of the process waste, the red mud, which is most often collected in "lakes," where it settles and dehydrates and can be covered over. Innumerable efforts to find productive uses for red mud have proved fruitless. Experimentation with alternatives to the Bayer process and with direct reduction of bauxite, eliminating refining altogether, began when "pure" aluminum was commercialized and has continued ever since, but because of process innovations the commercial viability of the Bayer process has been sustained.[3]

SMELTING

Like the Bayer process, the basic technology for aluminum smelting, the Hall-Héroult process, is a century old, but it has evolved considerably in detail since its invention in 1886, simultaneously by C. M. Hall in the United States and by Paul L. T. Héroult in

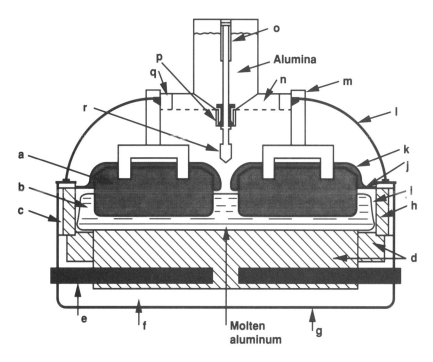

Figure 2. Hall-Héroult reduction cell with prebaked anodes: (a) carbon anode; (b) electrolyte; (c) insulation; (d) carbon lining; (e) current-collector bar;
(f) thermal insulation; (g) steel shell; (h) carbon block; (i) ledge; (j) crust; (k)
alumina cover; (l) removable covers; (m) anode rods; (n) fume collection; (o)
air cylinder; (p) feeder; (q) current supply; (r) crust breaker. Source: William
B. Frank and Warren E. Haupin, "Aluminum," *Ullmann's Encyclopedia*, vol.
A1, p. 466.

France. In current practice, aluminum is produced in an electrolytic cell consisting of a steel shell lined with baked carbon.
Alumina is dissolved in a bath composed primarily of molten
cryolite, a fluoride of aluminum and sodium. Electric current is
introduced through carbon anodes and passes through the bath
to the carbon cathode (the lining), causing the alumina to decom-
pose. As the cell operates, molten aluminum collects on the carbon lining and acts as cathode. It is siphoned off periodically.
The oxygen from the alumina is deposited on the anodes, which
are gradually consumed in the production of carbon dioxide.[4]

It is not possible, using the Hall-Héroult process, to produce
aluminum of purity higher than 99.90 percent. The most commonly used process for refining aluminum to higher purity is the
Hoopes process, conceived by William Hoopes in 1901 and developed by Alcoa's research organization in 1919. The Hoopes pro-

cess is also electrolytic and can produce aluminum up to 99.98 percent pure. Current is passed through a cell containing three liquid layers, kept separate by virtue of their different densities: The bottom layer consists of an aluminum-copper alloy; the middle layer is an electrolyte that is lighter than the alloy but heavier than the top layer, which is pure aluminum. The bottom layer acts as anode, the top layer as cathode, and pure aluminum is transported upward and separated electrochemically from the other elements in the alloy layer. The high-purity aluminum obtained through this extra step is necessary for making certain high-strength alloys whose properties depend on close control of impurity levels. It has also been essential in research, allowing the properties and behavior of aluminum and its alloys to be studied without the confounding effects of impurities.[5]

The evolution of the Hall-Héroult process, like that of the Bayer process, has involved improvements in the quality of output and a continual drive toward greater efficiency. In relative terms, the most stable element of the process has been the cryolite bath. Cryolite occurs naturally only in Greenland; so the aluminum industry has relied on synthetic cryolite since the earliest days of commercial production. This was originally made as a by-product of the Bayer process by combining sodium aluminate with hydrofluoric acid, but with today's technology it is produced as a waste product of the reduction cells. The discovery that alumina would dissolve in molten cryolite to form an electrolyte was critical to the Hall-Héroult breakthrough. Since then, progress has been measured in gradual improvements in cell efficiency achieved by fine-tuning the bath composition and optimizing cell design.[6]

Smelting-cell efficiency has also been improved by innovations in the production and use of carbon electrodes. The technology for producing high-quality carbons from petroleum or coal coke was available to Hall and Héroult at the time of their inventions. But only through experimentation and study of the process was it learned that the former was best for making anodes, because it had a low ash content and therefore contributed fewer impurities, while the latter was superior for carbon-cell lining material, because it resisted attack by the sodium that built up in the electrolyte during operation. After that, development efforts focused largely on improvements in equipment for forming and baking carbons of better quality and longer life.[7]

Anode consumption has been a long-standing concern because of the costly disruption of smelting operations necessitated by replacement of anode stubs. In the 1930s the aluminum industry adapted carbon technology from ferroalloy furnaces: the Soderberg electrode, a continuous, self-baking anode introduced as a paste. In addition to minimizing the cost and labor involved in frequent replacement of anodes, this innovation led to improved environmental conditions because it permitted complete enclosure of the pots and also permitted larger anode sizes and hence larger pot sizes, with the attendant economies of scale. Soderberg pots were installed in the most modern plants built during World War II, but they have since been superseded by prebaked anode pots as a result of advances made in the 1970s and 1980s.[8]

Advances in these and other aspects of the Hall-Héroult process over the years have effected substantial gains in efficiency. It is necessary to distinguish, however, between energy efficiency and the efficiency of the process as a whole. In theory, 100 percent efficiency for the Hall-Héroult process would result in production of three-fourths of a pound of aluminum per hour, using a current of 1,000 amperes. In practice, this productivity rate, called "current efficiency," was improved from around 70 percent in Hall's day to 93 percent in the 1960s, largely through increases in the sizes of pots and in pot amperage, from less than 6,000 to 250,000 amperes. Energy efficiency (kilowatts of power consumed per pound of aluminum produced) also benefits from increases in the scale of operation, but productivity can be pushed at the expense of energy efficiency by increasing the current density, the ratio between the current flowing through the cell and the area within the cell. That was the strategy pursued by American producers until the energy crisis of the 1970s, in contrast to the strategy of the Europeans, who had long been accustomed to high energy costs. In the last 15 years, the focus, both in Hall-Héroult process innovation and in the development of competing processes, has been on achieving a balance between productivity (current efficiencies better than 96 percent) and high energy efficiency.[9]

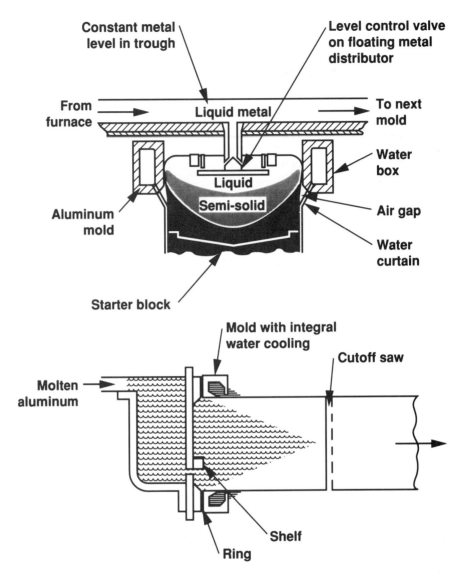

Figure 3. Vertical and horizontal DC casting. Source: J. Paul Lyle and Douglas A. Granger, "Aluminum Alloys," *Ullmann's Encyclopedia*, Vol. A1, p. 495.

FABRICATING PROCESSES

Molten aluminum from the smelting cell can be poured directly into ingot molds or alloyed with other metals before casting. In either case, aluminum typically is cast into ingots by the direct-chill (DC) process. Molten metal is formed in a short mold with a movable bottom. The ingot forms a solid outer shell as it is cooled initially in the mold; then it continues to solidify as it is pushed out beyond the mold and is sprayed directly with water or other quench liquid. As the ingot grows, the bottom of the mold is pushed downward in a vertical casting unit, or outward in a horizontal unit. The process can be operated continuously if sections of the ingot are sawed off and removed as it emerges from the mold. Prior to the development of DC casting in the late 1930s, ingots of about 110 pounds were typically cast in tilt molds; today, DC-cast ingots of 40,000 pounds are not unusual.[10]

In addition to permitting the casting of large ingots, the DC process brought about significant improvements in ingot quality because of its rapid cooling rate, which has a beneficial effect on the internal structure of the metal. For many years poor ingot quality was a perennial problem and a major roadblock to production of high-quality sheet. Its underlying cause is the highly absorptive character of aluminum that causes it to pick up impurities, both from the reduction bath and from the lining of the melting crucible, as well as hydrogen gas from the air. R&D showed that ingot quality could be improved by careful handling and temperature control of the molten metal and by fluxing with gas, but the definitive solution to this problem was found only in the 1970s with the development of filtering and other purification techniques.[11]

Another problem that has plagued the industry, particularly in the area of ingot casting, is the hazard of explosions resulting from contact between molten aluminum and water. DC casting equipment had to be designed to avoid such contact as much as possible. In addition, steps were taken to minimize the hazards through the use of coatings that would inhibit explosive reactions in case of molten-metal "bleedout," through careful operating procedures that would minimize the risk of accidental introduction of moisture into molten aluminum, and through development of protective clothing for cast-shop operatives.[12]

Once cast into ingot, aluminum can be transported to fabricating facilities, where it is processed in a variety of ways. The largest ingots are rolled into plate or sheet – the former is thicker than one-fourth inch, the latter thinner. Ingots are scalped, the surfaces shaved off and made smooth, before rolling. Then they are heated and passed repeatedly between heavy rollers until they reach the thickness of plate. Greater reductions, to sheet or even further to foil, are made in cold-

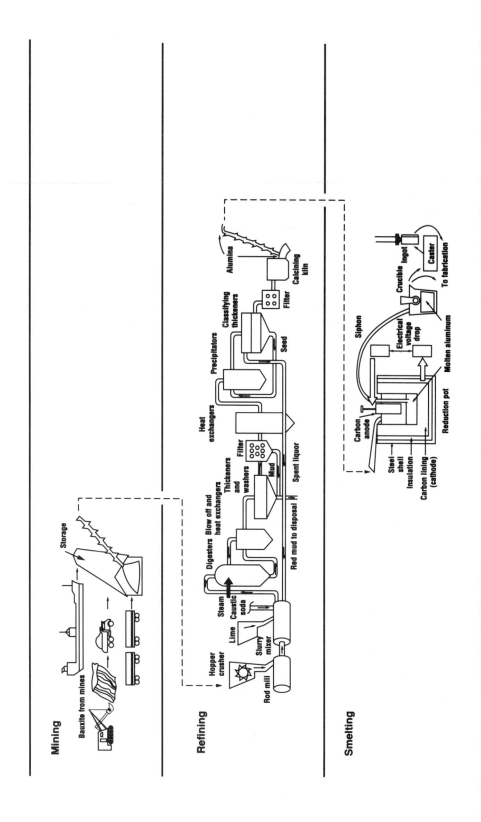

Mining

Bauxite from mines

Storage

Refining

Hopper crusher

Rod mill

Slurry mixer

Lime

Caustic soda

Steam

Digesters

Blow off and heat exchangers

Thickeners and washers

Filter

Mud

Red mud to disposal

Spent liquor

Heat exchangers

Precipitators

Classifying thickeners

Seed

Filter

Calcining kiln

Alumina

Smelting

Carbon anode

Steel shell

Insulation

Carbon lining (cathode)

Reduction pot

Molten aluminum

Electrical voltage drop

Siphon

Crucible

Ingot

Caster

To fabrication

20

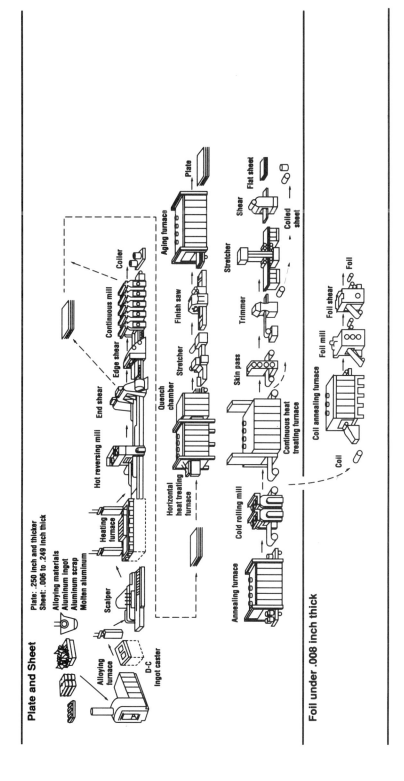

Figure 4. Aluminum production from mining through fabrication. Source: Aluminum Company of America.

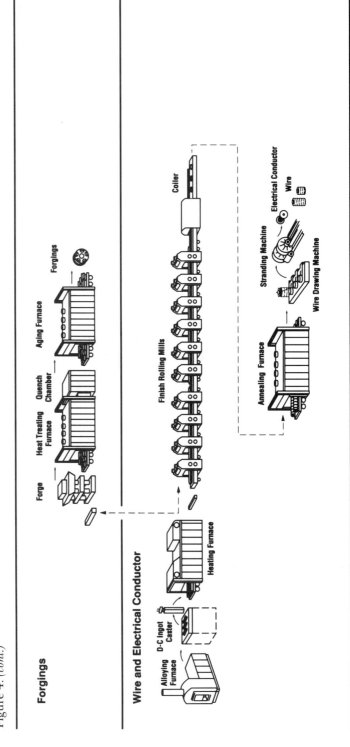

Figure 4. (cont.)

22

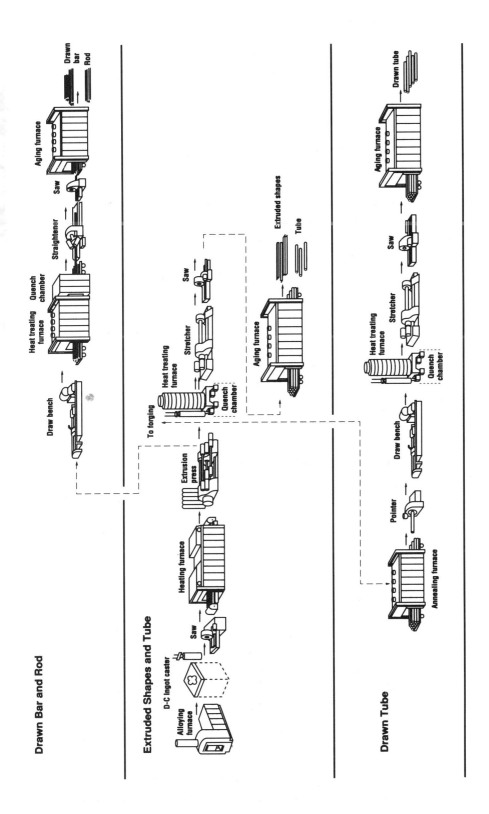

23

rolling mills. It is after rolling that plate and sheet of high-strength alloys are heat-treated, quenched, and age-hardened.

Shapes other than sheet and plate are made from ingot by forging, drawing, and extrusion. Forging involves heating the metal enough to make it workable, then either hammering or pressing it into a die. Aluminum wire, rod, and bar are produced by drawing. This requires initial reduction of the ingot by rolling or extrusion; then the metal is drawn through a succession of smaller and smaller dies, until the desired diameter is reached. Extrusions are made by heating the alloy to temperatures between 400°C and 500°C – temperatures high enough to make it plastic – and forcing it through a die. The metal emerges on the other side having taken the shape of the die, often a highly complex configuration. No other metal can match aluminum's extrudability.

Another important fabricating process for aluminum is casting: molten metal poured or forced into molds of sand, plaster, cast iron, or steel. There are different requirements for casting alloys than for wrought alloys, both because the process demands greater fluidity and because in many common applications, such as engine parts, castings must retain their critical characteristics despite changes in temperature. As a result, the development of casting alloys has proceeded independently, though in tandem with alloy development for other applications. The early application of x-ray technology to quality control in casting plants was an asset that enabled alloy developers in this field to make significant contributions, both in new alloys and in basic understanding of alloy characteristics and behavior.

ALLOY DEVELOPMENT

The tremendous growth of the aluminum industry since its relatively late beginning is attributable largely to the unique characteristics of the metal that permit its fabrication in so many different ways, as well as to its peculiar properties, which often are enhanced by combining it with other metals to form alloys.

There are eight aluminum-alloy systems of commercial significance. Four of these, which are based on copper, zinc, magnesium silicide, or (in the newest generation of alloys) lithium as the major alloying element, achieve their desirable properties through a process of heat treatment, rapid cooling or "quenching," and age hardening. These are the highest-strength aluminum alloys, used almost exclusively in aerospace applications. Other alloys – those containing silicon, manganese, or magnesium, for example – have lower strength but develop other desirable characteristics without heat treatment.

The high-strength, heat-treatable alloys have represented the most advanced aluminum technology since the initial breakthrough in 1909, the development of the aluminum-copper alloy Duralumin by German metallurgist Alfred Wilm. Applied immediately in aircraft construction, they have always had high visibility and a powerful, well-informed customer constituency. Hence, though they are costly and difficult to fabricate, efforts to produce strong alloys have continued and have led to many significant innovations in the plants. Fundamental research has been a constant and indispensable feature of alloy development, promising better control over final properties through greater understanding of the phenomenon of age hardening. Similarly, work on high-strength alloys has spearheaded and dominated the study of corrosion mechanisms and methods of preventing corrosion. The whole field of mechanical testing has also, to a great extent, developed around the need to establish the properties and design criteria of these alloys.

All aspects of aluminum production, process and product, have, over the century, required a great deal of research and experimentation, both to develop these suitable methods and to understand the characteristics of the metal well enough to envision new applications for it. It is largely for this reason that R&D has played such a central role in the history of Alcoa and of the aluminum industry as a whole.

PART I

The protected era, 1888–1909

1

Practical scientists

Charles Martin Hall arrived at the Pittsburgh Testing Laboratory in 1888 a discouraged young man. After a year spent working at the Cowles Electric Smelting and Aluminum Company, then the leading aluminum-producing establishment in the United States, he had failed to prove to the Cowles brothers' satisfaction the commercial feasibility of his invention, an electrolytic process for producing pure aluminum. The Cowleses had a good business in the electrothermal production of aluminum bronze, an alloy of aluminum and copper. Recognizing in Hall's idea a potentially competitive alternative, they had allowed him to demonstrate his process at their Lockport, New York, facility. Several false starts later they must have decided that the neophyte inventor gave them little cause for worry, as they sent him packing without investing in his process as he had hoped.[1]

Hall had already been rejected by the investors he had approached in Cleveland, Boston, and New York, all places where enterprises based on chemistry, electricity, and combinations of the two were taking shape. On the advice of Romaine Coles, a metallurgist employed by the Cowleses, Hall journeyed to Pittsburgh and sought out the owners of the Pittsburgh Testing Laboratory (PTL) for advice and for leads.

The contrast between the Cowles facility and the PTL must have struck Hall rather forcibly when he landed at the latter as a refugee from the Cowles Lockport works. The Cowles brothers, born and raised in Cleveland, and prominent members of that electrochemical center, were cosmopolitan metallurgists with strong ties to the European metallurgical community. Their achievements in developing the electrothermal process for making aluminum gave them wide renown in the international metal-

lurgical establishment of the late nineteenth century. Associated
in their work, as consulting chemist, was Charles Mabery, professor at Cleveland's Case School of Applied Science. Alfred Cowles
had studied in Germany, and both brothers' accomplishments
were followed closely in broadly distributed scientific journals,
such as the *Journal of the Franklin Institute* and *Scientific American*.
When Hall contracted to join the Cowleses, they had recently
invested the sizable sum of $300,000 in their Lockport facility,
which was located near Niagara on the river and boasted the
largest dynamo in the world at the time, made by Cleveland's
Brush Electric Company.[2]

Although the PTL was a modest little establishment compared with the impressive new Cowles works, Pittsburgh, like
Cleveland, was one of several localities where the new science-
based industries were forming in the last decades of the nineteenth century. Smallman Street, where the PTL was located,
was a microcosm of the new industrial world. It ran for two
miles along the southern bank of the Allegheny River, a two-
block-wide section bisected by the Pennsylvania Railroad track.
Located on that narrow strip were a Carnegie steel plant, the
Parks Steel Works, and a Westinghouse machine shop, in addition to many other machine shops, forges, steel mills, and scattered tenements. All of the businesses in this district were of
fairly small scale by the standards of even 20 years later, but
many were potential users of the testing services the PTL was
set up to provide.[3]

This time, Hall found he had come to the right place. Within
a few months of his arrival, a new offshoot enterprise, the Pittsburgh Reduction Company (PRC), was formed by a handful of
hopeful young investors well connected in steel. The PRC set
up a pilot plant on the PTL premises and began the first commercial production of "pure" aluminum, using Hall's electrolytic smelting process.[4]

Unlike the Cowles brothers, the PRC founders, led by transplanted Bostonian Alfred E. Hunt, had no stake in a competing
aluminum technology to impede their vision. Moreover, drawing on their experience with the steel industry, they imagined
markets for aluminum of an entirely different nature and scale.
They knew that an immediate need for "pure" aluminum existed in steelmaking, where aluminum was known to be a corrective for porosity, and they anticipated that when produced at a

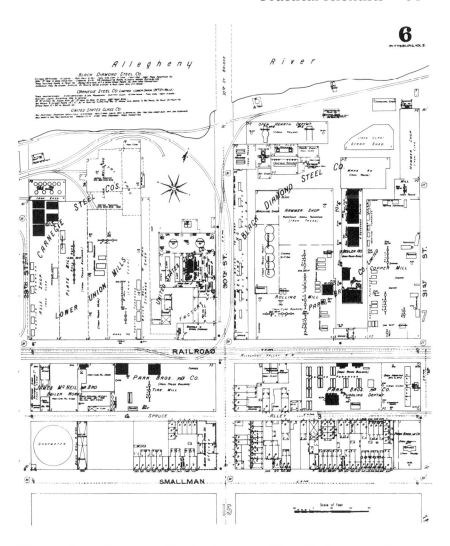

The Smallman Street neighborhood, where Alfred E. Hunt and George Clapp set up their Pittsburgh Testing Laboratory, was at the heart of Pittsburgh's industrial district in the late 1880s and 1890s. Shown here is an insurance map of the area surrounding the Black Diamond Company, where Alfred E. Hunt worked on arriving in Pittsburgh. Also shown are parts of the Carnegie Steel Company lower mill and of the Park Brothers and Company works. The map shows machine and hammer shops, the rolling mill, a copper mill, and a long block of tenement housing overlooked by the open-hearth furnace at one end and separated only by a small alley from the Puddling Department with its puddling furnaces. (From the Sanborn Insurance Map of Pittsburgh of 1895, courtesy of the Library of Congress.)

reasonable cost, aluminum would also find ready markets as a substitute for other metals. Over the next two decades they proved themselves right about the existence of a sizable market, but wrong about its composition.

By 1909, when their patent protection ran out, the PRC, renamed the Aluminum Company of America, had reduced the price of its basic product, primary aluminum ingot, by 96 percent through the exploitation of economies of scale and control of critical inputs – alumina, carbon, and electricity. Large, stable markets for aluminum had been created through the company's efforts. Yet many of these were not replacements for other metals but new applications, generated in other emerging science-based industries or in older, growing industries transformed by the scientific revolution. They included transmission wire for electric utilities and for electric streetcars, ingot to be cast into parts for bicycles, automobiles, and trolleys, tubing for chemicals and petroleum works, and feedstock for some of the many new chemical enterprises.[5]

To a great extent it was the commercial vision of the PRC steel men, with their drive for productivity and their access to capital, that accomplished this transformation. They were out to replicate in aluminum what they had recently seen accomplished with spectacular results in steel through application of the Bessemer and open-hearth processes.[6] But in aluminum, another kind of vision – a technical vision – was also needed, involving a synthesis of the technological opportunity that changing scientific knowledge and technical know-how offered to the new enterprise. It was not enough to introduce a powerful new invention and then leave the rest to craftsmen. Mass production of aluminum depended on the systematic investigation of physical principles and the application of this knowledge in ways that went far beyond the role of scientific knowledge in steel. In the PRC's early years, Charles Martin Hall's unfolding understanding of the process he had discovered, and of the ancillary processes that were combined with it, provided the necessary technical vision. Hall's outlook was pragmatic, oriented toward problem-solving, not theory, and somewhat risk-averse – in short, a good balance for the expansive entrepreneurial men he joined in building the enterprise.[7]

What none of the PRC investors anticipated, as promoters of new inventions rarely do, were the drawbacks of their new material, weaknesses that would emerge only after the mass-produced metal was in use. Many of its desirable properties were well known before aluminum became an industrial metal. Its light weight, silvery appearance, thermal and electrical conductivity, ease of working, resistance to acid, and imperviousness to tarnish and corrosion made pure aluminum immensely attractive in comparison with the best steel available at the time. Aluminum also seemed a likely replacement for nonferrous metals, such as copper, that blackened or tarnished readily. In practice, however, it was difficult to realize the full benefit of these properties. Successful manufacture of aluminum products required metal with low levels of impurities, posing unforeseen problems of quality control in primary production. Although aluminum could be formed as readily as other metals, more easily in most cases, fabrication typically required significant alterations in familiar metalworking machinery and practice. Its susceptibility to heat made aluminum difficult to weld and solder, and its propensity to electrolytic (or galvanic) action made it susceptible to corrosion when in contact with other metals.[8]

None of these problems was readily addressed by the metallurgical methods available to steel. As a result, aluminum manufacturing eventually became a hybrid industry in all senses of the term. To achieve their goals, the aluminum producers needed people educated in the emerging sciences of electrochemistry and physical metallurgy, and they had to borrow ingot-casting and metalworking practices from sources throughout the metals world. In the early decades, the PRC also borrowed heavily from its major customers, the electrical and chemical companies. Important consumers of aluminum, these industries supplied the chemicals, equipment, and electrical power necessary for aluminum production. Moreover, these science-based enterprises provided the most crucial inputs – the knowledge, the know-how, and the experienced personnel to apply these to aluminum processes.

Ultimately, aluminum products would combine some of the best properties that existed in several other materials, but to realize these, aluminum would impose on those who commercialized it, and even on those who used it, a dependence on science greater than that for the common metals. Because of this, the success of the enterprise continued to depend not just

A view looking north around midday over Pittsburgh's North Side at the turn of the century gives an idea of what conditions were like on a clear day in the area where the Pittsburgh Reduction Company commenced operations. (Courtesy of the Carnegie Library of Pittsburgh.)

on the bold strategic vision of financial men and entrepreneurs, but equally on the vision of practical scientists – men who could grasp the many technical problems and devise solutions to them, drawing on the evolving state of electrochemical and metallurgical knowledge to do so.[9]

ORIGINS AND ANTECEDENTS

Its Pittsburgh birthplace was an important factor in Alcoa's identity. Pittsburgh's many attractions – coal, other raw materials, and ready access to all forms of transportation – made it a major industrial center even before the scientific revolution. Aside from aluminum, its industries were not those born of electrochemical processes, but rather those rejuvenated by such processes. It was the home of almost all the continuous-process industries – steel, glass, petroleum, and chemicals – and it financed many more. It was in Pittsburgh in 1876 that Andrew

Carnegie built a huge new Bessemer converter that, in conjunction with the rapid adoption of the open-hearth furnace, would revolutionize the steel industry in a few short decades. Pittsburgh was also the headquarters for Westinghouse, which in 1886 entered the electrical business, after manufacturing transportation equipment, and became one of the large manufacturing companies that would supply the equipment to electrify the entire continent. Both Carnegie Steel and the Westinghouse Electric and Manufacturing Company were to play important roles in the early history of Alcoa.

There is no doubt that its proximity to Pittsburgh's sources of industrial know-how had much to do with the PRC's rapid growth and development. The workshop-cum-laboratory of the PTL was typical of a new form of organization that sprang up in a number of electrochemical centers around the country in the late nineteenth century.[10] The Cowles Lockport works was one of these, and others existed in Cleveland (the Brush Electric Light and Power Company) and in Niagara (the Niagara Research Laboratory). As one contemporary observer described them, these companies were incubators for the electrochemical industry:

Such organizations as research companies, formed explicitly to combine research with practical application, are novelties in the industrial world which have originated with, and are almost peculiar to, electrochemistry. They invent, investigate, and develop electrochemical processes, and furnish facilities to would-be experimenters whose ideas might otherwise remain stillborn.[11]

The Cowleses used their aluminum bronze business to finance other experimental activities in metallurgy and electrothermal processes, particularly electric furnace technology. In fact, the Cowleses eventually produced, in small quantity, many new products that later would become the bases for major enterprises – artificial abrasives, alkalies, calcium carbide, and ferroalloys – as well as "pure" aluminum. Yet they did not commercialize any of these products themselves.[12]

The PTL's founders were men of larger aspirations. Alfred Hunt and George Clapp were men in their thirties, close to Hall's age, but with vastly more experience in industrial life than Hall, who had lived an almost cloistered existence up to then. Both Hunt and Clapp had undergone practical scientific training.

Charles M. Hall (ca. 1890).

Hunt, with a degree in mining and engineering from the Massachusetts Institute of Technology, had worked his way up in the New England steel industry as a chemist and mining engineer before moving to Pittsburgh, where there was greater demand for his expertise in open-hearth-furnace technology. Clapp was a metallurgist, active in Pittsburgh's growing community of professional chemists. Although industrialists and financiers such as Andrew Carnegie, Henry Clay Frick, and the Mellon brothers were financing Pittsburgh's second industrial transformation, it was the younger, better-educated men like Hunt and Clapp who were making it happen.[13]

It was Hall's good fortune that the Cowleses had not taken up his patent option. Although later, in the light of competition from the PRC, the Cowleses clearly realized the value of the patent they had allowed to get away, it was unlikely, in the absence of competition, that they would have backed the developing Hall process with the energy and the resources it needed to become a high-growth business. The U.S. chemical industry with which they identified at the time continued until after World War I to be composed of small, fragmented, and specialized companies. Hall needed promoters with more patience, deeper pockets, and broader vision than the Cowleses.[14]

The PRC was a better match in other ways too. Hall brought the Cowles brothers little that they did not already have, aside from his invention, but the PRC could not have operated without him. Though unconnected to mainstream metallurgy, and inexperienced in industry, Hall was the PRC's chief expert in electrochemical processes. With the respect and support of his new colleagues, he proved to be a resourceful electrochemist with a genius for inventing equipment. The characteristic that set Hall apart from many other inventors was his openness to involvement in the entrepreneurial side of the business. It was probably this practical side to Hall's character, his willingness to take seriously the demands of a growing business and to subordinate his work to its needs, that accounted for Hall's astonishing success. Even in a time that was marked by meteoric rises and the amassing of large fortunes, Hall's story was noteworthy. His original invention became the stuff of American legend, winning him the largest fortune ever produced by one U.S. patent. Hall's stake in Alcoa when he died in 1914 was worth close to $30 million.[15]

An idealized drawing of the first building housing the Pittsburgh Reduction Company, located at Smallman Street and 32nd Street.

THE CRITICAL PATENT

In his patent application of July 1886, Hall described his invention as "the electrolysis of a solution of alumina in a fused fluoride salt of aluminum." The originality of his concept lay in the combination of several key elements. The choice of alumina, the cheapest pure compound of aluminum and oxygen, and of the fluoride solvent, sodium cryolite, was crucial. The stable solution formed by reaction between the solvent and the alumina, serving as an electrolyte, allowed the process to operate continuously: Through electrolysis, the aluminum was separated, settling at the bottom of the crucible, and oxygen was released. As the cell could be continuously fed with alumina, there was no breakdown of the cryolite. Hall had embarked on the course of experimentation that pointed him in the right direction while he was still at college. His mentor in chemistry at Oberlin, Frank Fanning Jewett, had studied in Germany and was able to instruct Hall concerning work done on aluminum in Europe as well as in the United States. Working in a small home laboratory with primitive equipment, Hall had hit upon his invention while pursuing his own postgraduate program of re-search.[16] Aluminum, which does not occur in a free state in nature, had first been isolated by the German chemist Wohler and then produced in small quantities by the noted French scientist Sainte-Claire Deville in 1854. Deville used an expensive sodium process to release the metal through chemical reaction, but the golden rewards that awaited the inventor who could find a cheaper process were widely anticipated. Most of those who followed Deville's lead tried to reduce the price of sodium to cheapen the new electrochemical process. By the 1880s, a new process for making sodium introduced by an American, Hamilton Castner, had reduced the price of sodium to the point that a few producers were willing to invest in aluminum production. At that time, the existing pure-aluminum busi-nesses worldwide, indeed all businesses then dealing in exotic nonferrous metals, were small in scale, most producing a few thousand pounds of metal per year.[17]

Had Hall been more in touch with what was going on in industry while he was a student, he would have realized that he was not as far ahead of the pack in primary processes for alumi-num reduction as he thought.[18] No sooner had Hall located his Pittsburgh backers than correspondence concerning his own patent application revealed that a Frenchman, Paul L. T. Héroult, had put together roughly the same set of elements to the same purpose.[19]

Patent holding was an even more uncertain business before the turn of the century than it has since become. In an interfer-ence proceeding between the Hall and Héroult applications, the U.S. Patent Office ruled in favor of Hall because Héroult had failed to file the required "Preliminary Statement." Hall's patent was granted in April 1889. This turned out to be only the first of many hurdles that Hall would have to overcome to protect the exclusivity of the enterprise he was helping to cre-ate. Another relevant patent application pending at the time was filed by an American inventor, Charles S. Bradley. As early as 1883, Bradley had filed a broad application covering the entire process of "fusing ores" by means of an electric arc, using electrolysis. He had even cited the decomposition of cryolite as an ore of aluminum as his example. Perhaps it was a sign of the chaotic state of the overburdened U.S. Patent Office that the

Certificate for United States patent no. 400,766, granted to Charles M. Hall for the process of reducing aluminum by electrolysis. The fortune he realized from this patent made him, at his death in 1914, the wealthiest U.S. inventor to have a fortune based on a single patent.

Bradley patents, denied once, and delayed altogether for eight years, were in fact finally granted in 1891 and 1892.[20]

Meanwhile, the Cowles brothers had continued experimenting with Hall's general set of elements for aluminum electrolysis. From what they had observed of Hall's experiments on their premises, and from their own efforts, they put together the foundation for a patent suit that was intended to put the PRC out of business. When that failed, and the PRC's declining prices brought about an overnight collapse in their aluminum bronze business, the Cowleses resorted to producing pure aluminum using what had officially become the Hall-Héroult process. When, in turn, the PRC went to court to restrain them from competing with the new process in pure aluminum, the Cowleses responded with a further legal campaign of their own. They proved, in fact, to be a litigious pair, also getting embroiled in a suit with Acheson, another erstwhile aluminum seeker who became the founder of Carborundum.[21]

The suits and countersuits that ensued between the Cowleses and the PRC continued for over a decade, with awards and adverse judgments falling first one way and then the other. The Cowleses' chief weapon in the dispute was that, by a complicated series of maneuvers, they had succeeded in gaining control of the Bradley patents. These were deemed to cover a crucial operating detail of the Hall process: the use of heat generated by the electric current passing through the crucible to maintain the molten solution of alumina and cryolite.

Ultimately, a legal settlement was reached that in some ways benefited both disputants, though the hapless Bradley not at all. When back-to-back decisions in 1901 and 1903 made it impossible for either party to the dispute to produce aluminum without violating a crucial patent held by the other, the two companies came to terms. The PRC paid a sum less than the $3 million it had originally been ordered to pay, partially offset by the earlier judgment against the Cowleses for nearly $300,000, in return for a license to use the Bradley patents. The Cowleses, who were the only serious potential competitors to the PRC on the horizon, agreed not to reenter the business of producing pure aluminum.

Though costly to the PRC, the settlement had two positive consequences. Not only were the Cowleses blocked from producing aluminum again, but the rights to the Bradley patents ex-

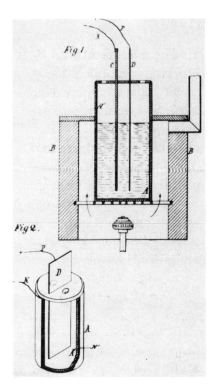

A comparison of the Hall patent illustration above and a drawing of the Héroult apparatus taken from *Scientific American* (Supplement No. 753, June 7, 1890, pp. 12024–5) below reveals important differences between the two approaches. Hall's concepts (Fig. 1) shows a melting pot (*A*) with a protective carbon lining (*A′*) placed in a furnace (*B*). Electrodes *C* and *D* conduct the current. The modification in Fig. 2 shows only one separate electrode (*N*), and the carbon lining (*A′*) acts as the negative electrode. The fixture on a stem suggests an external heating source, and there is little or no insulation to hold in the heat. The Héroult apparatus shows separately wired positive and negative electrodes (+ and −) and a thick layer of insulation around the pot. It shows no external heat source.

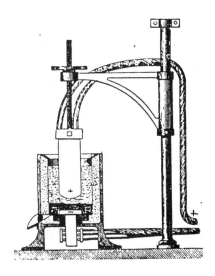

tended by three years the PRC's period of protection, until 1909. Because that took them through a period of national business prosperity, when new entrants might have been tempted to challenge the PRC monopoly, and into a severe downturn, when they certainly would not, it was an important reprieve.[22]

In two senses, the PRC was protected by the Hall patent. On the one hand, it prevented potential domestic competitors from entering the primary production of aluminum until the original enterprise had achieved a scale and level of integration that made the business unassailable. On the other, for a time it allowed the PRC to operate without worrying about keeping up with the advancing state of European know-how in aluminum.

REDUCTION COMES OF AGE

The prototype plant that the PRC set up on Smallman Street was equipped with a 125-horsepower engine with two dynamos made by Westinghouse, a few crucibles or "reduction pots," as they came to be called, and little else. Managing that early smelting process, which called for keeping the primitive generators going, monitoring the pots, and removing the aluminum, involved what one recent commentator has called "titanic efforts."[23]

It fell to Hall to be the superintendent of this operation, a role for which his previous experience had not prepared him. Justly admired for his obvious technical ability, Hall had not the first idea how to hire metalworkers or how to keep a plant going. He never did develop the common touch, but fortunately he was joined by Arthur Vining Davis, a young Amherst-educated friend of the Hunt family who displayed an affinity for shop-floor production. It was another complementary arrangement. Davis became not only Hall's close associate in running the new operation but also his lifelong friend and partner.

Arthur Vining Davis.

It took Hall and Davis from October, when the PRC was formed, until Thanksgiving Day, 1888, to pour the first ingot. From then on, the plant needed to be operated continuously, for whenever the place shut down, as it must often have done in the first uncertain days of operation, the pots would "freeze," leaving unusable metal to be dug out and discarded. Hall and Davis divided the day into 12-hour shifts, eventually hiring a night superintendent to spell them and two "furnace men" to

A view of the Smallman Street works interior featuring the 125-horsepower steam engine and twin dynamos that provided electricity to the aluminum smelter, probably reconstructed for Alcoa's 50th anniversary.

tend the reduction pots. An alert work force was important in these circumstances, but such workers were hard to come by and even harder to keep in the unpleasant and quite evidently unwholesome working conditions. The output of 30 to 50 pounds per day, which was all the plant could produce in the first few months, was only a fraction of the hoped-for output of 250 pounds per day.

Less than two years later, the picture had changed quite drastically. Output had reached over 350 pounds per day, and the little pilot plant was already becoming something of an industrial marvel. In October 1890, Pittsburgh held an industrial exhibition that attracted many foreign visitors. For one international party of mining engineers touring the eastern United States, the PRC was one of the highlights on a two-week tour. Other stops included the Altoona workshops of the Pennsylvania Railroad, the modern steelworks of Harrisburg, Johnstown, where the flood of the previous year had "engulfed 3,000 people," and the new twin engineering wonders: the Davis Island Dam and the Ohio Connecting Bridge on the Ohio River.[24]

Drawing of the first working Hall cells at the PRC, showing cast-iron "pots" with anodes suspended on wires attached to a horizontal copper bus. Empty ingot molds in front of the first two pots show how small the original ingots were.

In its first few years of operation, the PRC's process of making aluminum was in a state of continual change. As with any experimental operation, the process required constant watching and tinkering. Scaling up the operation and reducing costs involved a primitive form of process R&D, trying out new pot designs and sizes, new system configurations, new compositions for the various chemical elements such as the bath and the anode, and frequent adjustments of the electricity supply. Among other discoveries, experimentation soon revealed that the external heat source that Hall had used at first was superfluous when the size of the pots was increased. The sufficiency of the internal heat generated by the chemical reaction itself was a point that Hall had earlier disputed with the Cowleses, one that they would use against him in their patent suits.

Amateurish of management, primitively equipped, and evil-smelling from smoke and fumes, the little pilot plant on Smallman Street nevertheless performed admirably the functions required of it; by 1891 it had the basic outlines of all future aluminum production processes. Though the process was to change drastically in size, power supply, and inputs and to be improved in countless incremental ways in the next few years, the configuration that had been worked out at

Smallman Street managed in a remarkably short time to produce aluminum in enough volume and quality, at a low
enough price (two dollars per pound), to attract its first set of
regular customers, and also to attract a new set of investors.
Some of the early investors had proved restive when the predicted reduction in price did not produce the rush of buyers
they had envisioned. Fortunately, at that point new investors
with much greater resources appeared to propel the PRC to its
next level of output.

The Mellon brothers, owners of the Mellon bank in Pittsburgh, stepped in to help the PRC move to a more efficient
production site. They were just embarking on a plan to diversify their investments by taking controlling positions in entrepreneurial companies when they were approached by the PRC
owners for a loan. Rightly seeing the PRC as the sort of high-
potential venture they had in mind, the Mellons put up $1
million, found a suitable factory site, and provided the financial
and organizational know-how to back the company's first full-
scale operation. Mellon sponsorship was to be a lasting asset to
the company, for the Mellons, whose other interests included
most of the continuous-process industries of the day, did not
confine themselves to venture capitalism. The infusion of Mellon cash and managerial expertise led to the PRC's transformation into a more formally structured organization. Later the
Mellons would also take an active role in developing the state of
the research infrastructure, especially in the area of industrial
chemistry.

The full-scale plant completed in 1891 was located in New
Kensington, on the Allegheny River 16 miles from Pittsburgh,
with good access to fuel supplies and good transportation for
incoming ore supplies and outgoing metal. The steam-powered facility had another Westinghouse engine supporting 12
dynamos. It was anything but grand, but New Kensington
was economically a vast improvement on Smallman Street,
and the price of aluminum quickly dropped to $1.20 per
pound.[25]

As a site for smelting, New Kensington, with coal-fired steam
as its energy source, was only a stopgap measure. In 1893 the
PRC became the first company to buy power from the new
Niagara Power Company and to locate a large plant at Niagara
Falls, thereby doubling the company's smelting capacity by

Map of New Kensington in 1891. The second Pittsburgh Reduction Company works were set up in New Kensington in 1893 when the company needed space to expand its operations. The new works was located in the left foreground along the river at the site of the Brownsville Plate Glass Company (faintly numbered 29).

1896. The hydroelectric economies were so dramatic that the company quickly built a second Niagara plant and moved all its smelting to upstate New York.

Achievement of scale allowed the smelting operation itself to stabilize. In 1900, Professor Joseph Richards, pioneering electrochemist and metallurgist at Lehigh University, pronounced the aluminum smelting process fully developed. With respect to "pure metallurgy – that is, reduction and refining," he told an audience at Philadelphia's Franklin Institute, "there is little to report." In fact,

> about all there is to be said is that during the last few years all the items of expense of the process have been gradually notched down – bauxite is being mixed and prepared better and more cheaply; its conversion into alumina is probably improved; electrolytic carbons are being made cheaper and more durable; electric power is being obtained more cheaply, and, finally, the doubling and doubling again of the size of the works has reduced correspondingly the cost of superintendence and office expenses.[26]

The PRC's Alfred E. Hunt made the same claim, supplying his personal account of the chief discoveries that his company had made in eight years of operation and five years of systematic testing and experimentation. Bauxite, he reported, was

Offices of the Pittsburgh Reduction Company when it moved to New Kensington.

clearly the best ore to use for alumina recovery, and the secret to economic refining was bauxite supplies with as low a silica content as possible. Hall had also discovered that adding another metal salt, such as calcium fluoride, to cryolite would increase the efficiency (measured in output per unit of electricity) of the smelting process by reducing caking. Of course, the power supply was an overwhelming economic factor, and only those companies that had uninterrupted hydroelectric supplies were likely to be able to run their plants in the year-long, round-the-clock manner that made low-cost aluminum production possible.[27]

Unable to anticipate further significant cost reductions from increasing scale alone, the company tried a new strategic direction. It integrated into other process-related activities to reduce costs further and to gain improved control of its inputs. Using electric furnace technology that Hall had patented, by 1894 the PRC began to manufacture its own supply of carbon electrodes from petroleum coke. By 1896, the stable state of the new large-scale facilities had paved the way for the company to pursue other markets for its product. The PRC was producing more aluminum than all the rest of the world producers together, quoting a stable price of 35 cents per pound for its output. As the prices of competing metals rose toward the end of the century, a whole new set of customers were ready to give aluminum a chance. These included bicycle and automobile makers, for lightweight parts, and an especially important category of customer, electric utilities, for aluminum conductor wire. It was to get and keep this market that the company would launch its first sustained program of research on the product side, which would result ultimately in the development of ACSR ("aluminum conductor steel-reinforced").

DEVELOPMENT OF NEW MARKETS

Alfred E. Hunt.

Long before the economics of the basic smelting process had been fully worked out, Alfred Hunt, in consultation with his Mellon backers, designed an explicit strategy for the PRC. Following the example of British Aluminium, at that time the most fully integrated aluminum producer, he intended that the company should take maximum advantage of the time left under patent protection by expanding and integrating still further both horizontally and vertically. Hunt hoped that by increasing capacity and decreasing the cost of aluminum as quickly as possible, the company could compete directly against common metals in established markets, avoiding the painful uncertainties of creating new markets.[28]

The strategy was implemented on the process side, but without the hoped-for results. The reason for this disappointment was clear. Substituting a new material in existing markets required the supplier to offer potential customers product knowledge equal to their knowledge of the materials already in use. Like most other companies in the emerging electrochemicals industry, the PRC concentrated its technical efforts during the first two decades mostly on the process side, defining itself primarily as an intermediate-product producer. Through experimentation and testing, the PRC's chemists and mining engineers assembled and documented a store of know-how adequate to operate their process profitably.[29]

Product-oriented research was a different matter. Not only

did the PRC lack the expertise, but the state of metallurgical knowledge in general, before 1900, simply would not support extensive efforts. The link between the chemical properties of the material and their physical manifestations was missing. As S. K. Colby, later Alcoa's vice-president in charge of sales, noted,

> hammer-and-tongs, cut-and-try methods were all that were possible. A chemical laboratory for checking quality was the extent of the technical control. Mechanical testing was farmed out to testing bureaus. If a salesman complained that an experimental lot of sheet was too hard or too soft to suit a customer's requirements, the mill production had to be slowed up for more samples. If wire failed in use, some new alloy was tried.[30]

It was an age when uniform standards were just beginning to be set for American manufacturing, as they soon would be set in Germany. One way for a manufacturer to dominate a market, then as now, was to offer the most useful information and to persuade customers to adopt his product as standard. It was up to individual manufacturers, therefore, to see that useful information about their products was made available in a form that customers would recognize and accept.[31] Although there was no hard-and-fast division of technical domains in the PRC, Hunt and Hall tended to divide the internal and the external technical activities between them. Hunt, the metallurgist, and the much more outgoing of the two, handled the marketing, while Hall, the electrochemist, concentrated on the process side, the technical support for operations. Hunt, who had closer ties to the metallurgical community and to the marketplace, provided the PRC's information conduit to the outside world, putting out data about the company's process and product.

The PRC's first steady customer was the steel industry, exploiting aluminum's possibilities as a deoxidizing agent for steel. A small amount of aluminum, in the form of an aluminum "pill," added to molten steel was known to combat the pockmarks caused by too much oxygen in the metal coming out of the open-hearth furnace. There was also a small market for pure aluminum as an alloying element with other metals.

After that, new customers for aluminum were not easy to find. Following the first drastic price reduction (a drop from 10 dollars to 2 dollars per pound), only makers of instrument and machine parts, for which aluminum's light weight and ease of working were valued, showed any interest. For the former, reliable information was of little interest because quality was of little concern, while the latter were sufficiently sophisticated, technically, to acquire the knowledge they needed themselves if the properties were sufficiently attractive. Makers of novelty items such as commemorative medals and souvenirs purchased small quantities of the metal, as did producers of "fancy goods," such as trays, tea balls, combs, and picture frames. But these were unreliable customers.

Repeated missionary visits to foundries, rolling mills, and wire-drawing plants, many in the Smallman Street neighborhood, failed to persuade these higher-volume metal fabricators to try out aluminum. Aluminum's working characteristics were so different from those of metals with a higher melting point that craftsmen skilled in other forms of metalworking would not touch it. It was clear to them that equipment and methods would have to be specially adapted in some way. Annealing furnaces, for instance, had to be made to operate reliably at lower temperatures and within narrower ranges of temperature. There was no information base sufficient to suggest how these modifications should be done.[32]

During the first decade of the PRC's existence, Hall took on any technical task that was needed, whether it was within his own area of expertise or not. While the New Kensington works chemist handled the routine testing, Hall directed studies of aluminum working and alumina processing. He turned his hand to the design of rolling equipment.[33] He looked into the special requirements of the PRC's customers and scrutinized the methods of its suppliers. He even did empirical product research on alloy composition, adding different metals to aluminum in varying amounts to achieve a metal with superior casting and working characteristics. By 1897, thanks to the efforts of PRC staff, *Aluminum World* could recommend different lubricants for working aluminum (Vaseline, coal oil, water), along with various modifications to be made to tools used in stamping, drawing, milling, and shearing aluminum. As James C. McGuire, a PRC agent writing in *Aluminum World,* noted

and so it will appear that when these changes can be made in any factory so that aluminum articles can be manufactured practically by the same tools . . . it is merely a question of time when the growth and development of the aluminum business promises to be both constant and steady. . . .[34]

In pursuit of this vision of industrial order and reliability, Hall and his staff of one chemist and one or two laboratory assistants let it be known that they were conducting a research program that they regarded as scientific. They took pains to contrast their work with what they implied were the more haphazard efforts of "other inventors," among whom they evidently numbered even Thomas Edison, whose pronouncements never failed to attract sensational coverage in the press. When Edison announced, in 1896, his intention to "go deeply into the art of hardening aluminum" after he had assessed the full value of x-rays as a research tool, *Aluminum World* informed its readers:

The Pittsburgh Reduction Company has been scientifically studying the tempering of aluminum for a year or more, and when the company has succeeded in accomplishing this end, the readers of this paper shall be the first ones to learn of it, as well as the experiments in this direction of Edison and other inventors.[35]

When disseminating partial research-based information alone failed to create a broader group of users, the PRC began to do its own small-scale fabrication to demonstrate aluminum's broader possibilities. At Smallman Street the company acquired some crude rolling equipment, and A. V. Davis experimented with rolling out sheets of aluminum for hollowware, particularly aluminum tea kettles. No longer needed as the company's main smelting facility once the Niagara Falls plants were built, New Kensington became a fabricating facility, with the old small-scale smelters used for experimental purposes. By the mid-1890s, the PRC had at New Kensington a forge, tube mills, rolling mills, and a significant casting operation, all process technologies borrowed from other metals industries, which it proceeded to adapt for working aluminum. The plant also incorporated a small laboratory employing a professional chemist. This two-story wooden shed became works laboratory, development laboratory, and research laboratory for the PRC's fabricating operations.

Eventually the PRC succeeded in interesting a few marginal enterprises in producing cookware. The aluminum tea kettle

Mechanical finishing of aluminum pans at a cookware operation in New Kensington around 1905. (From *Alcoa in Westmoreland County*, copyright 1986 by Alcoa Laboratories.)

and utensil market grew to consume 30 percent of PRC's output by the turn of the century. But this particular set of customers proved to be a mixed blessing. These small producers fabricated items of rather poor quality and gave the new metal such a bad reputation that the company management had to devote much of its energy to educating these producers. In the end, no amount of information was enough to improve the practices of these small fabricators, and in 1895 the PRC entered the cookware business itself to supply a heavy-duty line of cast-aluminum cookware called Wearever, which was sold door-to-door.[36]

It was only in 1900 that a few industrial customers began to do more to organize the product side of the business. The Delaware Metal Refinery of Philadelphia, for instance, started at that time to offer nine grades of aluminum alloys, noting that these were

made after the formulas and under the direction of its superintendent, Mr. Joseph Richards. . . . The idea which Mr. Richards had in view in producing them is to provide a series of perfectly reliable and uniform alloys, from a very hard, rather brittle alloy, to a strong, tough, softer alloy, thus furnishing a complete series adaptable for the most varied applications.[37]

An important part of the PRC's market development was establishing testing procedures and publishing the results. James Handy, the PTL chemist, adapted for aluminum and its alloys the laboratory methods he used in testing for the steel industry. By 1895 these laboratory methods had been widely published and had added considerably both to the meager stock of available knowledge about aluminum and to the accepted methods for accumulating knowledge about it. Industry journals and professional technical publications cited Handy's work and that of Herr Regelsberger of the Aluminum Industrie Action Gesellschaft as the two main sources of reliable data about aluminum.[38]

Alfred Hunt issued a handbook in 1897 containing much of the data the PRC had amassed in both laboratory and workshop. The first part of the book contained chemical and physical information about aluminum, while the second part presented tables, charts, and lists of gauges that were described as useful to all mechanical engineers and machinists whether they were concerned with aluminum or not. *Aluminum World* praised the book as "the best compendium of information relating to aluminum and the working of the same that has ever appeared in print."[39]

The PRC made it a regular practice to publish its technical information in *Aluminum World,* which it helped to sponsor – "A Journal for Manufacturers of Aluminum and its Alloys, Dealers in Aluminum Goods, and for the Metal Industry in General, with Special Reference to the Reduction of Ores by Electricity." The magazine was a technical almanac, collecting, explaining, and often translating U.S. and European technical and market information. It reported new aluminum products as they appeared as imports or in exhibitions, encouraging domestic fabricators to copy and sell them more cheaply in the United States. Finally, it published annual reports of all aluminum producers, as well as information about production methods used by foundries and fabricators. Yet the more difficult task was to reach the broader public with accurate information and to try to encourage trial by users, which would provide better user information.

The Aluminum World
And Brass and Bronze Industries.

A JOURNAL FOR MANUFACTURERS OF ALUMINUM AND ITS ALLOYS, DEALERS IN ALUMINUM GOODS, AND FOR THE BRASS, BRONZE AND METAL INDUSTRIES IN GENERAL, WITH SPECIAL REFERENCE TO THE REDUCTION OF ORES BY ELECTRICITY.

Entered at the New York Post Office as Second-Class Matter.

VOL. VII   NEW YORK, JULY, 1901.   No. 10.

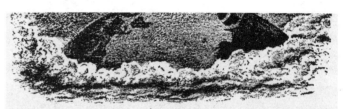

THE ALUMINUM WORLD
AND
Brass and Copper Industries

·. Published Monthly at

47 ANN STREET, NEW YORK.

PALMER H. LANGDON,   -   -   -   Publisher.
ERWIN S. SPERRY,   -   -   Special Contributor.

Subscriptions, Advertisements and News will be received at the following offices:

PHILADELPHIA—Drexel Building......JANNEY, STEINMETZ & CO.
MINNEAPOLIS, MINN., 305 Nicollet Avenue............J. H. HEISSER
BOSTON—172 High Street............ ... .E. L. RUGG
PROVIDENCE, R. I.—125 Eddy Street.... ....E. C. NICKERSON
SAN FRANCISCO, CAL.—300 California Street.........JOHN MARTIN
MONTREAL, CANADA—214 St. James Street...C. T. CHRISTIE & CO.
LONDON, ENGLAND—127 Farringdon Road..........LOUIS LEAKEY

Subscription Rates.—One Dollar per year in advance.
Foreign Subscription, Two Dollars.   Single Copies, Ten Cents.

Advertising Rates on application.

Please remit by Express Order, Post Office Order or Draft on New York, made payable to THE ALUMINUM WORLD.

Address all communications,

THE ALUMINUM WORLD,
47 ANN STREET,
NEW YORK.

NEW YORK, JANUARY, 1902.

Two examples of the *Aluminum World* masthead show how a complex of aluminum-related industries had developed by the turn of the century.

In other countries, that was beginning to happen under government sponsorship, and it seemed to Alfred Hunt that the U.S. Navy would make an excellent sponsor of aluminum usage in the United States.[40]

THE *DEFENDER* EXPERIENCE

No incident revealed the aluminum enterprise's limitations more painfully than Alfred Hunt's highly visible attempt to attract the attention of the U.S. Navy as a customer. Hunt launched a persistent campaign to try to convince the U.S. Navy's Bureau of Construction and Repair to adopt aluminum for its new boats. The superstructures of naval vessels, which required large amounts of metal, seemed a natural application for aluminum's combination of light weight and strength. Reports from abroad showed that aluminum was being used for lifeboats, and several foreign governments were known to be experimenting with the new metal in other marine applications. The America's Cup races offered Hunt an ideal opportunity to attract the navy's attention. Through his wealthy connections, Hunt arranged for the PRC to supply aluminum for the superstructure of *Defender,* a yacht designed by the famous Danish boatbuilder Nathaniel Herreshoff. A consortium of industrialists, including J. P. Morgan and Cornelius Vanderbilt, was having the yacht built to compete in the races off Newport in 1896. "The *Defender* is going to win that cup and aluminum is going to win the race for supremacy in the metal world," trumpeted *Aluminum World.*[41]

The popular press heaped scorn on the project. The *New York World* predicted that salt water would corrode the boat, which it erroneously reported to be made of an alloy composed of 96 percent nickel and 4 percent aluminum. In the pages of *Aluminum World,* Hunt countered this misinformation, which was only too indicative of how little the public knew about aluminum in general. The actual formulation of 96 percent pure aluminum, he wrote, made this material highly resistant to corrosion.

Yet the frustrating reality was that the navy, when asked, wanted nothing to do with aluminum for boat construction. James C. McGuire, the PRC's agent in New York, complained of unwarranted navy conservatism. Pointing to foreign government ventures, he remarked that "it is only reasonable to sup-

The *Defender*, a yacht fitted with an aluminum-plated superstructure, was designed and built by Nathaniel Herreshoff, sponsored by a consortium of wealthy investors led by J. P. Morgan and Cornelius Vanderbilt. It triumphed over Lord Dunraven's yacht *Valkyrie* in the America's Cup yacht races on September 7, 10, and 12, 1895. (Courtesy of the Hart Nautical Collections, MIT Museum.)

pose that these governments know what they are about and are proceeding with some degree of intelligence, after experiments which they have considered satisfactory." The need to resort to the "reasonable" assumption that overseas governments were basing their decisions on experimental data indicated to some that the PRC as yet had no reliable data of its own to cite.[42]

For the PRC, fabricating the rolled plates for the *Defender* was a major technical challenge. It was accomplished only with the help of borrowed facilities. The PRC rolled out the largest aluminum plates and angles ever produced on mills at a Carnegie steel plant.[43]

Defender, with its aluminum superstructure, went on to triumph in the races. But winning supremacy for aluminum was another matter. Publicly, U.S. Navy officials still flatly resisted any idea of adopting the new material for naval vessels. However, the navy had not ignored the new metal altogether. In 1897, a thoughtful paper presented to the U.S. Naval Institute by an assistant secretary of the navy assigned to the Bureau of Construction and Repair revealed that it was observing closely *Defender*'s condition after a period of use. The results bore out the navy's conservative approach, for after a year of exposure to salt water, *Defender* exhibited clear signs of corrosion. Considering this experience, as well as other experiments, the paper noted that

at the present stage, structural aluminum is materially more subject to corrosion than steel. . . . This feature of inferiority must therefore be regarded as subject to further amelioration from increase of knowledge and selection in the preparation of the alloys and from improvement in conditions of insulation and protection.[44]

Although its relative plasticity placed aluminum far ahead of steel in resistance to repeated dynamic forces, and its lightness made it highly desirable, its excessive tendency to galvanic action would have to be corrected "through increase of knowledge and experiment in precautions and higher perfection in manufacture." Until impermeable coatings could be found, the paper continued, aluminum's inferiority in this respect would disqualify it for use anywhere that it might be exposed to salt water and spray. Nevertheless, in the long run, the metal was conceded to have an important mission for the serious marine architect. It was simply "not utopian."

One of the PRC's greatest needs was to discover the causes of aluminum's most vexing problem: corrosion in the presence of other metals. For some time to come, corrosion, that "dread disease of the metal realm," would destroy aluminum's chances of competing with steel for many structural purposes. On naval vessels, for instance, the metal was relegated to cookware and cabin furniture. Having the limitations of aluminum displayed so publicly by the *Defender,* it was difficult to induce users to try it and thus difficult to marshal the hard evidence needed to solve the problem. The inadequacies of the metallurgical knowledge base and PRC's consequent inability to do serious metallurgical research delayed this effort until after World War I. But some forms of experimental activity were feasible sooner, as the climate for research improved in the country at large.[45]

THE TECHNICAL INFRASTRUCTURE

When the PRC needed technical expertise that was beyond the competence of its in-house personnel, it consulted with the handful of professors in universities and colleges who took an interest in applied science – the Columbia College School of Mines, Cornell University, the Massachusetts Institute of Technology, and Lehigh University. Such academic–industrial linkages became more common after 1900 throughout the burgeoning electrochemical industries, but in the mid-1890s it was still a matter of attracting individual scientists with general knowledge to take a special interest in the specific problems of aluminum. Opportunities for fruitful alliances were limited in the United States, where advance-degree programs in all forms of science and engineering were very new, and serious students still felt obliged to study in Germany. When *Aluminum World* arranged for Heinrich Ries of the Columbia College of Mines to write a regular feature called "Work in the Laboratory," which reported the results of experimentation taking place in college and industrial laboratories, it was apparent that this one column could easily devote a fair amount of space to all items worthy of mention.[46]

The PRC formed ties with a few individual professors in order to promote greater academic interest in nonferrous metallurgy. But it was not easy to attract applied scientists, or trained engineers interested in metals, away from ferrous metallurgy, where larger markets made the opportunities seem much greater. The PRC funded special student projects in mining engineering and applied chemistry. In 1897, one of the Hunt sons studying at Sibley College, Cornell, worked with Professor W. F. Durand on his aluminum-zinc alloys, and these were later offered for sale by the PRC as the Sibley alloy.[47]

The most sustained relationship the company had with any academic consultant was with Professor Joseph Richards, who began working with Hall in 1891 and helped him to inaugurate a program of systematic experimentation in electrolysis, the first fundamental research that the PRC had undertaken. Among other things, they experimented with a soluble anode made of carbon containing aluminum.[48]

Richards, whose father was an English metallurgist of the old school, personified the transformation that metallurgy was then undergoing from a craft into a science. The son had started out working with his father at the Delaware Metal Refinery, but after being stricken with lead poisoning, one of the many hazards of working with the smelting process in the days of primitive equipment and poor ventilation, he attended Lehigh and became that university's first Ph.D. recipient in metallurgy. In 1897–8 he studied in Heidelberg and Freiburg.[49]

Like most of his academic contemporaries, Richards lectured and wrote on a wide array of topics related to metallurgy and electrochemistry. Too little was known at the time about nonferrous metallurgy, or even metallurgy in general, to justify a full-time specialist. He taught courses in blowpiping and mining as well as metallurgy. Much of his published work involved translations from German and Italian. Perhaps 10 percent dealt specifically with aluminum. In 1887, Richards published the first of three editions of his book *Aluminium,* a comprehensive treatise on all aspects of the history, characteristics, and methods of producing and working the new metal. Richards's association with the PRC provided him with the only existing opportunity to gain firsthand experience with emerging technology in this leading branch of the electrochemical industry in the United States, and after 1891 his writing about aluminum drew heavily on his PRC consulting. Richards played an active role in helping to turn the new electrochemical center in Niagara into a practical scientific community.[50]

Professor Joseph W. Richards. (From R. D. Billinger, "America's Pioneer Press Agent for Aluminum – J. W. Richards," *Journal of Chemical Education,* June 1937, p. 253.)

ELECTROCHEMISTRY IN NIAGARA

One of the greatest concentrations of useful technical expertise after 1900 was to be found in Niagara, where the PRC and numerous other companies operated electrochemical plants. As Joseph Richards observed in a speech to the American Chemical Society, aluminum not only led the other electrochemical businesses in industrial development but also in a sense, was "the mother of most of them" Many were direct offshoots of early attempts to produce aluminum. Several were subsidiaries of the Cowles Electric Smelting and Aluminum Company, and others were foreign-owned enterprises. They included E. G. Acheson's Carborundum Company, Castner's Niagara Electro-Chemical Company, founded by a consortium of European chemical concerns to manufacture sodium using the Castner

The Pittsburgh Reduction Company was the first large user of Niagara power when it relocated its smelting operations to the banks of the Niagara River in 1895. The artist's rendering above shows the upper works of the PRC adjacent to the Niagara Falls Power Company and the two houses of the lower works spanning the cliff face. The photograph below shows Alcoa's upper Niagara works as it looked before it shut down in the 1940s.

Charles M. Hall (standing right) socializing with friends, Alcoa managers William Hoopes (lower left) and Safford K. Colby (prone, foreground) among them, in Niagara, 1902. The other guests were Mr. Sellers (top left) and his niece, Gertrude Palmer (seated left), whom Hall admired, H. T. Colby (seated center), Grace Austin (seated right), Mrs. Hoopes (lower center), an unknown woman friend (lower right), and little Suzanne Colby behind her father.

process, the Union Carbide Company, and the Ampere Electrochemical Company, which specialized in investigating and developing new processes.[51]

The thriving new electrochemical industry was operated by a community of technologists that quickly took on its own professional identity. The openness of the group in the early days, and the easy flow of ideas, reflected the interdependence of the business and their tendency to specialize rather than compete with each other. The Niagara area soon had the most active chapter of the new American Electrochemical Society. This professional society, formed under the leadership of Joseph Richards in Philadelphia in 1901, patterned itself on the American Chemical Society and the American Institute of Electrical Engineers. It was an association of academics and professionals, with a starting membership of 250 men well known in scientific and engineering circles. The same year, a scientific and trade jour-

Leadership: **Alfred E. Hunt, president**
                   Charles M. Hall, first vice-president
                   George H. Clapp, second vice-president
                   Arthur Vining Davis, secretary and general manager

No of Employees: 260

Primary production: 3 million pounds

Locations: ▲ New Kensington, PA

                △ Niagara Falls, NY

Figure 1.1. Corporate facts, 1898.

nal was established, called *Electro-chemical Industry.* Although well connected with the more scientific side of the electrochemical world and with universities like Columbia and Lehigh, its membership was not at all theoretically oriented. Perhaps because of the heavily capital-intensive nature of the businesses in Niagara, the Electrochemical Society was strongly influenced by the shop culture of mechanical engineering. That orientation may have accounted for the rivalry that soon sprang up between the Niagara center and the Cleveland center, which was very strong metallurgically.[52]

The Electrochemical Society provided Charles Martin Hall with a rare social outlet. Hall, who had been somewhat of a loner in Pittsburgh, well known for spending most of his nonworking time either reading the *Encyclopaedia Britannica* or playing the piano, became a charter member of the society and an enthusiastic participant in its activities. In 1895 he moved his primary residence and his small personal laboratory to Niagara.[53]

In Pittsburgh, the professional scientific community organized a little later. A Pittsburgh chapter of the American Chemical Society was formed in 1906, and several of the PRC's technical staff became active members. About the same time, the Carnegie Institute of Technology set up a metallurgy department under Professor Frederick Crabtree, at first oriented almost exclusively toward iron and steel. The Mellons also began to take an interest in promoting industrial research at the University of Pittsburgh. In 1910 they endowed the university's Mellon Institute for research into process industries, and in 1913 this became the first university institute in the country devoted to industrial research. All of these developments im-

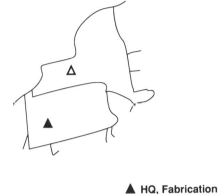

▲ HQ, Fabrication
△ Smelting

Figure 1.2. Corporate locations, 1898.

proved the climate for professional development in the PRC's major regional locations and paved the way for sharing of ideas so necessary to sustain technological momentum in non-ferrous metallurgy.[54]

A PROFESSIONAL TECHNICAL STAFF

The year 1900 is generally taken to mark the beginning of the professional era in the United States, and it was certainly so for the PRC. In 1899, Alfred Hunt died on a military expedition to Cuba. His death was not only a personal loss to his entrepreneurial colleagues but also a critical blow to the decade-old company at a time when it needed to draw heavily on outside sources of technical knowledge. Hunt left the company with an ambitious and well-conceived strategy for expansion, but with severely diminished technical leadership to carry it out. His son Richard, though destined to follow his father in the company, was then only just finishing his metallurgical training at Cornell.

Hunt's external technical role, in particular, required a substitute. It was Hunt who had travelled abroad to see what European aluminum companies were doing, Hunt who had written the articles in *Aluminum World*, Hunt who had arranged for new facilities and committed the company to taking high-profile risks such as that involving the *Defender*. A. V. Davis would be an able successor to Hunt as manager, and he would prove to be equally venturesome, but he was not a technologist, and his growing responsibilities in other areas made it impossible for him to take over the full range of external technical activities that Hunt had performed.

For Hall, as head of the company's technical operations, Hunt's death made it a matter of urgency to hire additional technical professionals. He was not the sort to cultivate wide-ranging technical relationships outside his own areas of expertise, and the size and variety of technical demands required by Hunt's strategy were far greater than he could handle alone. The company had plans for several new additions to the PRC business, growing out of the integration strategy, that placed new technical demands on management. Before 1900, it had relied chiefly on consulting engineers for expertise in building new facilities and solving major engineering problems, a practice common in the steel industry. But as PRC's technical needs multiplied, Hall needed more than the help of a few low-level technicians, if only to coordinate the activities of independent consultants.

Beginning in late 1899, the PRC assembled a group of experienced technical experts, predominantly trained engineers, to carry forward the plans Hunt had devised. Hunt's death certainly focused the urgent need, but Hall may also have been motivated to act quickly by a general move in industry to hire the best available talent away from universities and consulting engineering firms, for that was the year that General Electric set up its new corporate laboratory in Schenectady, and a few other large corporations would soon follow suit. The people chosen by Hall and Davis to be the first high-level technical professionals outside the firm's founders came from the communities in which the PRC had close connections, through Hall's electrochemical network in Niagara, and from the Pittsburgh professional network.

The challenges faced by the new professional technical staff were daunting. In 1900 the PRC set up facilities to produce its own alumina in order to gain greater control over the supply and the quality of inputs to its chemically exacting process. Through its Georgia Mining Company subsidiary, it already owned its own bauxite supplies, which were extracted and shipped to the Pennsylvania Salt Company to be refined. The PRC set up a pilot operation at New Kensington to refine alumina from bauxite, and when the process was developed, it purchased a site at East St. Louis, Illinois, where it built its own refinery. Alumina from East St. Louis soon was sufficiently superior in quality to alumina refined by the Pennsylvania Salt Company for the PRC's smelting works to request that all its supplies come from East St. Louis. In 1903, a large new reduction plant was built at Massena, New York, powered by the St. Lawrence Power Company. This independent supplier was soon purchased by the PRC as part of a policy to control its own power supplies. Two years later, the original carbon-electrode plant at Niagara was replaced with a facility large enough to supply all of the company's needs.[55]

In 1907 the PRC became the Aluminum Company of America (Alcoa), thus officially acknowledging that the scope of its activities embraced far more than the reduction process. Indeed, two years later its activities expanded to include an interest in a group of foundries and fabricators that the company helped to bring together as the Aluminum Castings Company (ACC), run by Edmund E. Allyne. The ACC had operations in Cleveland, Buffalo, and Detroit, thus putting it in close proximity not only to one of the major sources of metallurgical expertise in the country (Case Institute in Cleveland) but also to several of the leading automobile and airplane companies that were using cast-aluminum parts. In 1909, Alcoa also acquired outright an aluminum bronze powder plant in Dover, New Jersey, and about the same time it took a 50 percent share in a fabrication company that it had helped to organize, the Aluminum Casting Company of Cleveland. The spreading interests of Alcoa necessitated dealings with a whole new set of technically based industries and introduced a broadened set of technical problems.[56]

William Whitten and H. C. Peffer, both chemical engineers, Edwin Fickes, a civil engineer, and William Hoopes, an electrical engineer, joined the company in rapid succession between 1899 and 1901. The PRC hired these engineers to staff specific projects. Whitten and Peffer both worked on the alumina refining operation while it was in the pilot phase at New Kensington. Later, Whitten left the company, ultimately to work for DuPont, and Peffer became superintendent of the new refinery when it moved to East St. Louis. Fickes and Hoopes stayed on afterward as permanent technical staff, with management responsibilities at the corporate level.[57]

Three engineers played key roles in forming the technical

structures of the PRC (and then Alcoa) and in linking the company to the outside world. Edwin Fickes was the first member of this triumvirate of technologists who would eventually take over the management of the company's technical affairs. A graduate of Rensselaer Polytechnic Institute, Fickes joined the PRC in 1899 to manage the planning for its latest expansion in Niagara. Within a year, he became chief engineer of the company, with responsibilities for all building, engineering, design, and repair, with offices at the New Kensington works.

His previous experience gave him ideal qualifications to be the designer and builder of many of the PRC's large-scale processes. For six years after his graduation he had supervised construction of all kinds of structures, from bridges over the Ohio River to mills for various heavy industrial concerns in the Pittsburgh area. Prior to joining the PRC, he had spent two years designing and estimating power stations for F. S. Pearson, the firm that had planned and executed the first phase of the PRC's expansion. Pearson was an international consulting engineering firm with headquarters in New York and operations in Europe, Australia, and South America. Fickes would later find that early international experience useful as he gradually became responsible for coordinating the PRC's external technical activities during one of the most intensely international periods of its organizational life. For more than a decade he spent much of his time abroad, finding new sources of raw materials, examining other producers' facilities, and evaluating overseas opportunities in aluminum.[58]

William Hoopes, the second member of the triumvirate, was the PRC's first electrical engineer. A contemporary of Joseph Richards at Lehigh (class of 1886), Hoopes spent the first decade of his career in several areas of the booming electrical industry, building and operating electric lighting plants and electric railways. Coming to Pittsburgh, he worked for a year at Westinghouse before joining the PRC in 1899 as chief electrical engineer.

Hoopes's work was far more localized and more oriented toward the company's internal technical operations than that of Fickes, but in his two decades at Alcoa he also acquired an international reputation, primarily for several important inventions, including ACSR and the Hoopes refining process.

Five years after Fickes and Hoopes joined the company, the

hiring of Earl Blough as chief chemist and metallurgist completed the technologists' triumvirate. Blough had taught physics and chemistry at the high-school level after graduating from
Indiana University. He became interested in industrial chemistry through a summer job as chemist at the Oliver Mining Company and then spent three years doing graduate study in engineering and metallurgy at Cornell prior to coming to the PRC
in 1905.

Blough, who was hired to head a staff of six chemists in New
Kensington, reported directly to Hoopes. His laboratory was
the first under the expanded structure to be centrally funded as
a corporate laboratory serving other facilities besides New Kensington. In 1907, Blough undertook a corporate project on
improving the casting practices at the PRC's main foundry, doing small-scale production and testing in a laboratory furnace,
and comparing his results with the larger-scale results achieved
at the foundry. It was Blough who would be responsible for
establishing the company's first metallurgical function. He
worked to raise the standard of analytical work done at the
company's three main laboratories – New Kensington, East St.
Louis, and Massena – and, on a smaller scale, at other works.
Later he introduced uniform testing standards for control of
metal production at all Alcoa smelting plants.

Together, Fickes, Hoopes, and Blough would take Alcoa
through a short but intense period of international activity.
Apart from their own original contributions, attested by the
patents they received, their most important collective contribution would be to turn the company into an expert borrower of
technology from overseas. During their first decade in the company, however, all three men took their technical direction
from Hall.[59]

HALL AND DIRECTED RESEARCH

Charles Martin Hall remained the senior technical executive
throughout this period and did not relinquish his dominance of
Alcoa's technical program to the newcomers. Even after 1902,
when he was in Niagara Falls, New York, and they were based
in New Kensington and Pittsburgh, he continued to be involved
and in control, coordinating the others' activities from his base
in Niagara through heavy correspondence and occasional visits

Charles M. Hall before he took ill, at the Hall family home in Oberlin, Ohio, in 1906.

to the several laboratories. As a major stockholder in the PRC and a personal friend of A. V. Davis, Hall operated with a fair degree of autonomy. He was frequently called upon for troubleshooting when customers had problems, and he often travelled with Davis to negotiate the purchase of new sites for plants and facilities. Aside from the work he did for the company, Hall continued his own line of experimentation in his personal laboratory, aided by a chemist whose salary he paid himself. In 1904 he wrote to his brother, "I am still working on my enormous scheme for making the rare metals of the platinum group from such things as iron and nickel." Having set aside his own interests in favor of solving the company's process problems for the first 15 years of the PRC's existence, he now considered himself free to work on problems that interested him. This would not have posed difficulties for the company if he had stepped aside to let the professionals take over his central role of technical coordination, but he was slow to relinquish control even when circumstances seemed to dictate his withdrawal. In 1909, Hall endured the first episode of what was to be an extended bout with leukemia. Though he underwent surgery and was not expected to live, his health eventually improved, and he survived for five more years.[60]

Hall's last major technical effort was to seek out the best refining process. After the basic reduction process had been stabilized, he turned his attention toward the ore refining processes. Alumina was a very expensive part of the process, two pounds of alumina being used for each pound of aluminum produced; so reducing the cost of alumina by direct reduction of aluminous ores was an objective several aluminum concerns were pursuing at the time. Recognizing the importance of this effort, Hunt had authorized Hall to do intensive work on his idea for a process that would allow for direct reduction of bauxite in the reduction pots, thus eliminating the costly intermediate step of refining alumina.[61]

European aluminum producers had already adopted a refining process for alumina developed in 1887 by Austrian chemist Karl Josef Bayer. In 1896, *Aluminum World* reported the use of this process at the Ludwigshafen plant of Gebruder Giulini on the Rhine.[62] When the PRC set up its own refining operation in East St. Louis, it chose not to invest in a Bayer license but to develop its own process. Hall was intent on finding a means of avoiding the intermediate use of alumina altogether, and he therefore treated the process used at East St. Louis as a temporary measure. Two years of development showed that his first concept for direct reduction would not work. When he ended up in 1899 with a form of alumina that sank to the bottom of the bath, he finally gave up. Though it was close to the time that the Bayer patent was due to run out, Alcoa purchased a license for the process and modified it for use in East St. Louis.[63] Meanwhile, Hall filed for another patent for an electrothermal approach to producing alumina known as the "Hall dry process," so called because it did not extract the alumina in aqueous solution as earlier processes had done but subjected the original ore to high temperatures in a direct furnace, reducing the impurities to a metallic state and separating them from the molten pure alumina. The dry process consumed several more years of development and large sums of money in a pilot operation at New Kensington before it was abandoned as unworkable. Later it would be picked up and commercialized by the company's research organization.[64]

Along with continuing experiments on his own dry process, Hall evaluated, and in some instances pushed for the adoption of, processes borrowed from outside the company, both from local inventors and from abroad. These included the Keogh process for extracting alumina from bauxite and the Ladd process for taking alumina from clay. Bauxite deposits were not abundant in the United States, and the possibility of using clays containing alumina was attractive. But the problem of using technologies acquired from outside was that the company was reluctant to reveal to outsiders enough about its own processes to enable it to transfer its technologies developed elsewhere. Moreover, the costs of licensing other processes could be prohibitive. In the end, bauxite, with its 50 to 60 percent alumina concentration, was economically so much superior that the idea of using clays was shelved to a later date. Both Hoopes and Blough aided Hall in these efforts.

Hall's later comments to C. B. Fox, head of the East St. Louis operation, suggest that he eventually came to view it as a mistake that the PRC attempted to "make" rather than "buy" its own refining technology during the first decade of the new century. In 1909 he abandoned his own efforts to find alternative approaches to producing suitable alumina and began a major new effort to better adapt the Bayer process for use at East St. Louis. He regretted that he had not sooner become adept at purchasing technology:

If we are going to use the Bayer Process, it seems to me we ought to investigate the process to its fullest extent, and in the form in which it is used by other manufacturers. I do not want to see us make again the mistake which we did before – i.e. of underestimating the advantages of the process which our competitors were using. We really ought to have known all about the Bayer Process as soon as the Bayer patents expired, which was five or six years ago, and not have gone along working our own process with the idea that it was superior, without really knowing.[65]

Hall's illness prevented him from being the one to put his new plan into action. During the year he was incapacitated it was left to Fickes and Hoopes to oversee the implementation of the Bayer process, modified for American bauxites. The new operation, which involved digesting the bauxite under pressure with hot sodium hydroxide to form a solution of sodium aluminate, began on a trial basis in 1909, running in parallel with the refining approach that had been used previously.[66]

The lesson Hall chose to learn from his frustrating experience with refining was not to waste money on in-house technology when it could be acquired at lower cost elsewhere. Another lesson might have been that large sums of money were wasted for want of an adequate knowledge base. Such a knowledge base was now attainable, as Bayer's work in Germany clearly demonstrated. The German head start with industrial research was beginning to pay off and would continue to do so. Finding American substitute processes could have had major strategic implications, but they would have required more investment in research, on a grander scale, than Hall was willing to make.[67]

At the same time, Alcoa's lack of a metallurgical knowledge base was becoming a more serious problem as the company succeeded in attracting a broader range of customers. The PRC's small staff of technical experts felt themselves to be lurching from one embarrassing crisis to another. Such crises typically occurred when end products using aluminum developed serious, unanticipated problems in the marketplace. One case in which the PRC's reputation was at stake occurred in 1905–6 when the company sold to Eastman, for a new line of portable

THE PITTSBURGH REDUCTION CO.

KENSINGTON WORKS—TESTING LABORATORY.

Physical Test Report No. 5923   Date Jan 1906

Subject _Manganese Sheet Alloys_

Received _E. B._   From Order No.

For

Grade 12.5% Mn   Annealed at

Cut From	Original Dimensions		After Fracture	Tensile Strength		Elongation in 8" Per Cent.	Reduction of Area Per Cent.	Wrapping Test.	Twist Test.	Conductivity.
	Diameter	Area □"		Breaking Tension	Breaking Tension per sq. in.					
	.081	.081	.0464	2590	31975		43.33	12 gauge	Hard.	
	.0805	.0805	.049	2590	32175		39.10	"	"	"
	.081	.081	.038	2610	32225		53.08	"	"	"
	.0805	.0805	.049	2580	32050		39.10	"	"	"
	.0815	.0815	.046	2625	32150		43.50	"	"	"
	.081	.081	.046	2610	32225		43.20	"	"	"
	.080	.080	.0326	1270	15875	30.08	58.75	12 gauge	Soft.	
	.080	.080	.0341	1245	15560	28.75	57.37	"	"	
	.080	.080	.0355	1270	15875	29.12	56.65	"	"	
	.080	.080	.0324	1250	16000	26.93	59.50	"	"	
	.0805	.0805	.03233	1250	15625	31.75	59.80	"	"	
	.0805	.0805	.0355	1285	16620	24.00	55.96	"	"	
	.0805	.0805	.0333	1255	15690	30.62	55.64	"	"	
	.0395	.0395		1480	37466			18 gauge	Hard	
	.0395	.0395		1410	35692			"	"	"
	.0395	.0395		1395	35316			"	"	"
	.0395	.0395		1460	36970			"	"	"
	.0395	.0395		1470	37220			"	"	"
	.0395	.0395		1480	37466			"	"	"
	.0395	.0395		1480	37460			"	"	"
			Avg		36797					

Test report dated January 1906 for manganese sheet alloys, possibly related to the experimentation into noncorrosive alloys for camera cases conducted by Earl Blough in 1905–1906.

cameras, quantities of an aluminum-zinc-manganese alloy that it believed to be superior for light weight, strength, and ductility. All went well until purchasers of the cameras took them on vacation to hot, humid climates. In these circumstances, the alloy corroded so badly in contact with the leather camera cases that hundreds of irate customers returned their cameras to the makers. Earl Blough, only recently hired as the company chemist, worked frantically to produce a substitute alloy to redeem the PRC's reputation with the camera company. The aluminum-manganese combination Blough and his helpers hit upon seemed to have all the advantages of the earlier alloy, plus corrosion resistance. It resisted corrosion in nine months of exposure in Pittsburgh's Phipps Conservatory and was immediately placed on the market as alloy 3S, which was eventually produced worldwide. Given the conditions in which Blough was working and the caliber of assistance he had at the time, finding such an alloy was a lucky accident.[68]

In another case, customer foundries supplying aluminum crankcases to the automobile industry discovered that the crankcases were shrinking. They demanded that Alcoa produce an improved version of the aluminum-copper alloy that it was supplying. Once again, a happy accident produced an alloy containing a higher percentage of copper that did not shrink when subjected to high engine temperatures. The result was Alcoa 12 or SAE 30, which became a standard alloy supplied for automotive uses. In neither instance had the company been able to find conclusive information freely available from external scientific sources that would solve its problem.[69]

THE PROPOSAL FOR CORPORATE RESEARCH

By the turn of the century it was possible to avoid such problems with new products. Whereas before 1900, technological research in general offered few remedies, by 1909 the picture was changing. Other companies in similar situations, General Electric (1900), Westinghouse (1903), and AT&T (1907), facing the expiration of critical patents or wishing to defend their products and control their markets, had set up research laboratories, sometimes as separate departments, where at least some fundamental research was performed. In addition, DuPont set up two important laboratories at that time, the Eastern Laboratory, founded to study dyes and organic chemicals, and the Experimental Station, established to study the electrolytic process. Goodyear also started an R&D program in 1908.[70]

Most of these corporate laboratories were originally quite small, not much larger than Blough's chemical laboratory. But once started, they tended to grow fast. By 1909, General Electric employed more than a hundred university-trained researchers. The university training was key. Blough's assistants were technicians, capable of carrying out directions, but not able to solve problems themselves or to follow up on promising leads when they saw them. By contrast, the R&D efforts of General Electric, DuPont, and AT&T were led by men of considerable stature in the U.S. scientific community, Ph.D. scientists who had studied in Germany and taught at the Massachusetts Institute of Technology.

Fickes and Hoopes took the view that it was time for Alcoa to follow the lead of the pioneers of corporate research. Convinced of the great need to do a better job of coordinating and standardizing among the different Alcoa operations, they raised the matter in 1909, first with Hall and then with Davis, asking them to consider setting up a full-fledged central research organization. The rationale they gave was the need for an independent technical authority to set corporate product and process standards and to mediate in the increasingly acrimonious disputes between the different Alcoa works over the quality of the materials that passed between them. The opportunity they undoubtedly recognized was the likelihood that a systematic research program into any fruitful area related to their core technologies not only would aid in future problem-solving but also would be likely to uncover promising spin-offs.[71]

It was Hall who blocked the proposal, and his opposition condemned the company to another 10 years without a central research organization. Davis was in favor of the idea, but he was in the habit of deferring to Hall's technical judgment and his controlling interest in the company. Hall's explicit reason was financial. He doubted that the benefits the company would gain would outweigh the cost increases in overhead, equipment, laboratory space, and personnel. Hall may well have had other reasons. His illness in 1909 made it unlikely that he would be able to direct a laboratory himself; that would mean placing in someone else's hands the technical direction of the company. In hindsight, even from 30 years later when Fickes wrote about it, Hall's opposition seemed small-minded.

The research idea was quite new in the United States and was in the process of being rejected by Carnegie Steel because research and pilot facilities to match installations in Europe would be too expensive. There was no certainty that directed scientific research would pay off in a timely manner in a business oriented toward high-volume production of metals. Even General Electric had originally turned down Charles Steinmetz's proposal to establish an electrochemical research center, yielding only later to the argument that protection was needed against Westinghouse's threatening patent position. Alcoa's technical staff could point to no such clear and present danger. Hall could have opposed the proposal on other grounds, such as the small supply of university-trained researchers in the areas Alcoa needed most. There was also some risk that in-house research would bias the company toward its own solutions, as Hall had found in his own experience with the Bayer process.[72]

Nevertheless, coming at the end of Alcoa's protected era, Hall's opposition has to be seen as shortsighted. The policy that it perpetuated, of purchasing all new technologies outside, would turn out to be a costly mistake. Without more depth in technical support, the company lacked the capability to adapt acquired technologies effectively. Moreover, in the new era of competition that Alcoa was about to enter, the kind of metallurgical control Hoopes and Fickes were hoping to provide would be a very serious competitive need. As it turned out, this need became so compelling in the years that followed the patent expiration that Hoopes and Fickes had no problem getting Davis's agreement to start a corporate laboratory after Hall's death.

In effect, Hall, who had been versatile and resourceful in matching the technical capability to the strategic need in the protected era, became a roadblock as it ended. In the years before World War I, the company's strategic needs would be to integrate the system it had put together, making it a smoothly operating and stable entity that would be technologically competitive, and to learn more about the technical nature of the markets that were rapidly becoming more sophisticated. It was Alcoa's technical professionals, tuned in to what was going on in some of the more progressive companies, who offered the technical vision to match the new strategic needs.

The other cost of Hall's decision, one that can never be measured, was the lost opportunity. If the company had had a department dedicated to research before World War I, what might it have accomplished? As the next chapter shows, there was a telling example in the company's own experience – ACSR – the one product program of the protected era that was large enough, and urgent enough, to justify an eight-year research program.

2

Aluminum cable steel-reinforced: crossbred success

Arthur Vining Davis's selling trip to the West Coast in the spring of 1898 resulted in a major coup for the PRC. He returned with an order for 12 carloads of aluminum conductor wire and high hopes for the beginning of a significant business.[1] It was not the kind of replacement market Alfred Hunt had been hoping for, but it was the next best thing, a chance to sell material in a new and rapidly expanding market in a fast-growing area of the country. Transmission wire for electrical high-tension lines promised to be just what was needed to liberate the PRC from its dependence on those small, fractious customers in highly fragmented and volatile markets, the novelty makers and the cookware manufacturers. The electrical industry was much more the sort of enterprise with which the PRC could be comfortable doing business. Highly capital-intensive and technologically sophisticated, it was a mecca for some of the most progressive industrial interests in the country.[2]

The electrical industry was little more than a decade older than aluminum. The first electrical transmission line had been erected in Germany in 1891, using copper wire. In the same year, the pioneering Telluride project was installed in the United States, with Westinghouse engineers conducting extensive field observations on the phenomenon of energy loss called "corona effect," or loss between the lines – the current leakage into the air that was especially likely to develop in the transmission of higher voltages at high altitudes with copper lines.[3]

As long as major technical characteristics remained unresolved, commercial aspects of electrical power installations continued to be matters for trial and conjecture. Standard materials and facility designs had yet to be developed. While operating experience for different materials was unavailable, straight cost was the compelling factor in deciding among alternative line materials. Utilities putting up new transmission lines were willing to give aluminum a try when its price approached parity with copper, which was then selling for 14 cents per pound. Tests showed that slightly less than half the weight in aluminum (47.7 percent), which sold regularly at 33 cents per pound, was needed to produce a wire of equivalent conductivity. The same volume of commercially available aluminum weighted only 30 percent as much as copper, while its conductivity was 63 percent that of copper. Aluminum offered other advantages to utilities facing the immense capital investment of installing transmission networks. Its lighter weight for equivalent conductivity allowed lighter towers and required fewer supports to carry the wire across country.[4]

With its new commercial linkage to electricity, aluminum appeared to be on the road to becoming a common metal. For the first time the PRC found itself winning significant contracts in direct competition with one of the established metals, including sales to the Snoqualmie Falls Power Company in Colorado and the Telluride Power and Transmission Company, in addition to Standard Electric. By the end of 1898, the PRC had already booked sales of 1.3 million pounds of solid-aluminum wire.[5]

The apparent marketing breakthrough quickly turned into a crisis for the PRC, however, one it very nearly proved incapable of handling. Selling aluminum for uses in the electrical industry posed scientific and technical challenges of an order far beyond any that PRC had faced outside the smelting and refining side of its business. As in the case of the *Defender*, these challenges were highly visible. Edwin Fickes, who joined the PRC just as its new transmission-wire business was taking off, remembered the problems with aluminum wire vividly:

The first attempts to use [the aluminum wire] resulted in failures which if not overcome seemed likely to be disastrous to this branch of the company's business. It was found quickly that it could not be made and used like copper; new methods of manufacturing, testing, handling, erection, splicing, all had to be developed without delay, or else the Company would have to leave the electrical transmission business to the copper people.[6]

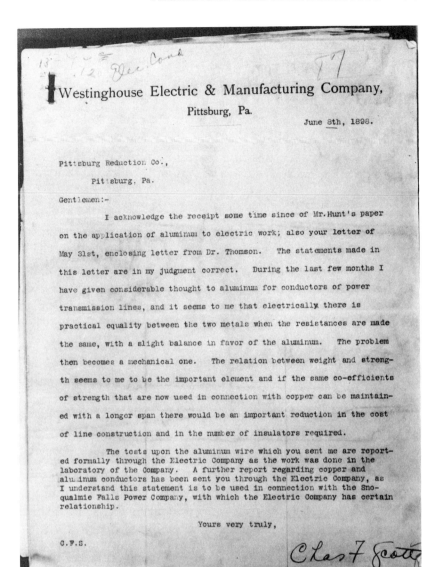

Testimonial letter from Charles F. Scott of Westinghouse Electric and Manufacturing Company ("the Electric Company") attesting to the appropriateness of aluminum for transmission wire, for use by the Pittsburgh Reduction Company management in its efforts to gain a sales contract from the Snoqualmie Falls Power Company, dated June 8, 1898.

TRIAL BY FIRE

The PRC had first investigated the use of aluminum for electrical conductors in 1895, when it arranged for electrical conductivity tests comparing copper and aluminum at Lehigh University and at the Westinghouse laboratories. In that same year it had installed an aluminum bus-bar line at its Niagara Falls works. The company produced its first transmission wire in 1897, drawing it on equipment located at the New Kensington Sheet Mill. The line was to be used in the Chicago stock yards as a substitute for a half-mile length of copper telephone wire, which had had a problem with corrosion from locomotive gases. But applications that justified paying a premium for "pure" aluminum's special corrosion-resistant properties were few in number.

In 1898 the PRC removed the obstacle of cost by offering aluminum wire at the special price of 29 cents per pound (versus the regular price of 33 cents) delivered at the point of consumption. It was this special price that enabled Davis to persuade the Standard Electric Company of California to try aluminum instead of copper for a 46-mile, three-phase line to be installed from Blue Lakes, near Mokelumne Hill, to Stockton in early 1898.[7]

Davis had hoped originally to involve the PRC in the market for transmission wire in a gradual and low-risk way, stimulating intermediate producers to use it, rather than entering the market directly. Once having secured a few substantial contracts from large customers, he had envisioned subcontracting with wire producers to make the new material on their existing equipment. Once they had been introduced to the idea, he expected them to welcome the chance of supplying aluminum wire to what was potentially a vast new market. Except for small quantities of wire that it was already equipped to manufacture, the PRC would produce the aluminum ingot, and the wire makers would do the rest. The PRC stood ready to perform experimental work to back up producers who were working with aluminum for the first time. But when Davis tried to find other companies to help make the aluminum wire he had sold, he found no takers. Companies that produced bronze and copper wire might be somewhat more sophisticated than the novelty and cookware companies, but they were also deeply suspicious of working with a metal that had unfamiliar properties.

Although the PRC offered solid-aluminum wire as part of its product line and had already supplied the #11 (telephone-gauge) wire strung in the Chicago stockyards, its own production capacity for wire when Davis booked the utility sales was nowhere near equal to the new demand. Nor did the company have any way of calculating the strength that would be required for cross-country transmission lines stretched over great heights and long distances and exposed to climatic extremes. The PRC proposed to supply the new utility contracts with what it already had, its strongest available alloy containing approximately 2 percent copper. Unfortunately, the strongest available would turn out to be not nearly strong enough.[8]

To meet the new order, Davis was compelled to purchase more equipment for the New Kensington plant without delay. Initially it was the same equipment used by manufacturers of copper wire – a new rod mill and a three-strand wire-drawing machine (called "Johnny Bull" and ordered from England). Nevertheless, from the start, the PRC met with difficulty fabricating the wire from the aluminum-copper alloy, which was considerably harder to work than was "pure" aluminum. Much of the material had to be scrapped. These manufacturing difficulties paled in comparison with the troubles the customers encountered after delivery.[9]

Once installed in the field, the solid-aluminum wire betrayed some highly dysfunctional characteristics. A line superintendent on one early installation told Charles Martin Hall, who was on a troubleshooting mission, that the new aluminum line was the noisiest he had ever seen. "It would hum and sing in the wind," wrote Hall to Davis, "as you have heard iron telegraph wires, but to a much greater extent." Further reports from the field revealed that the aluminum cables had to be strung with large sags because of their low strength, and the low tension made them vulnerable to wide swings and dancing in high winds. When the weather was cool and very windy, the aluminum wire was all too likely to break and come crashing to the ground. Men coming to repair the line found that it vibrated so violently they could not hold it.[10]

In follow-up tests it was learned that the wire could be expected to vibrate at a frequency almost twice as great as that of copper wire of equal carrying capacity. To combat breakage, customers were finding it necessary to locate their cable supports closer together, offsetting the cost advantages of the aluminum. Under these conditions, customers were not going to realize the supposed economic advantages of using the new metal.

Too little was known about the physical properties of aluminum at that stage for the PRC to be able to explain the wire's failings. Speculation ranged from unfavorable crystalline structure across the wire's axis to minute flaws in the wire caused by faulty production. Whatever the cause, there was no doubt that frequent interruption of service caused by conductor breakage could be catastrophic for the new utilities, and it could also put an end to the sale of aluminum for transmission lines. At great expense, for it involved installing and learning to use new equipment, the PRC moved quickly to increase the strength and reduce the vibration by replacing early installations with multistrand cable, usually seven strands made of pure-aluminum wire.[11]

This time, problems took longer to surface. The new cable showed no tendency to break immediately, and several customers ordered multistrand cable for high-tension wires, among them the Hartford Electric Light Company, which in 1899 constructed a line of seven-strand cable. Several electric-railway companies adopted even heavier cable for electric-railway power feeders. But all sizes of multistrand aluminum cable proved to have another serious weakness, a tendency to develop temporary short circuits in individual strands caused by minute flaws in the aluminum. At best, the short circuits threatened the integrity of the line. They could also produce a dangerous arcing effect that could burn up whole sections of line. Once again, the occasional flaws were traceable to problems in manufacturing. The PRC ingots varied in consistency, displaying weaknesses when made into rod and drawn into wire.[12] No matter how it was configured, pure aluminum alone seemed to lack the inherent strength to withstand the loads imposed by sleet buildup or high winds.

Twenty years later, S. K. Colby summed up the gravity of the situation around 1900 this way:

Few realize the cost to the producing company of this early experience. It is little less than a commercial miracle that the losses involved in the replacement of many of the early lines did not swamp the still struggling industry, and the patient effort to obtain the ultimately successful result was a triumph in introductory sales work and engineering.[13]

Luckily for its conductor-wire business, the PRC was favored in its battle to secure the new market by a general rise in market

Many early installations of aluminum transmission line were in railroad yards and along railway lines. Because railways were large users of electricity and already owned long-distance right-of-ways along their roadbeds, they often became involved in the business of electric power transmission.

prices for other metals in the late 1890s and again after 1904. The PRC was also fortunate in its customers. Electrical engineers were members of a technically astute and versatile fraternity. Founders of a new industry themselves, they were not surprised at the vagaries of another industry in formation. Consulting engineering firms like John Martin of Seattle, San Francisco, and Los Angeles, for instance, willingly cooperated with the PRC to give aluminum a fair trial, and utility customers gave freely their evaluations of the aluminum lines after several years of operation.[14] All recognized that experimentation with aluminum would be worth the effort if the problems could be solved.

Hall readily admitted that the trouble with transmission wires was beyond the scope of his own scientific ability:

Just what happens in a line like this, and in what manner the wire could be broken by vibration caused by the wind, is a problem for a physicist. Can you not refer the matter to some one who could give us a little light on it? Perhaps Mr. Charles F. Scott could do so.[15]

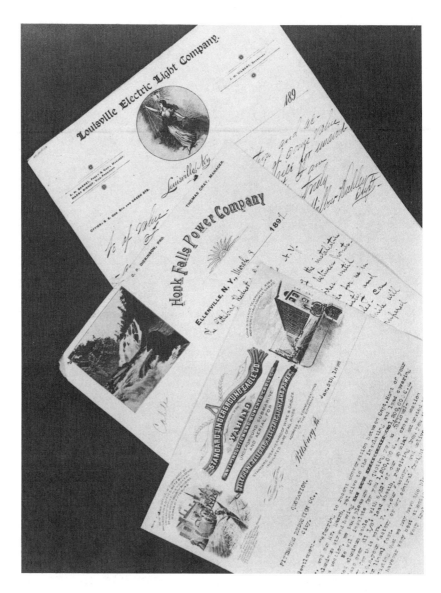

Power company letterheads from 1898 show the wide array of connections the PRC was making in the electric power industry. The vitality of these graphics conveys the aura of industrial progress that attended all aspects of the emerging electric power industry at the turn of the century.

Fortunately, Hall was able to call on Scott and others at Westinghouse, which was heavily involved in investigating the causes of power loss and other transmission failures. The PRC continued to rely on Westinghouse for testing and advice until its transmission-wire business became large enough, and problematic enough, to justify setting up its own electrical testing facilities and hiring its own electrical engineer, William Hoopes.

Apparently it was to solve the problems with conductor wire that the PRC first adopted the committee approach to troubleshooting, which became a common method for managing technology at Alcoa in later years. Representatives of all PRC functions were assembled to consider the transmission-wire problems from their different points of view. Some advocated a return to solid-aluminum wire produced differently, perhaps by extrusion. Others wanted to increase the number of strands in the wire or to concentrate on improving the quality of ingot being produced. Such troubleshooting sessions might help to narrow the problems down, but solutions would require the input of the PRC's recently hired professional engineers. Edwin Fickes was in charge of designing new wire-drawing equipment, and William Hoopes, who had been hired away from Westinghouse, became primarily responsible for what turned out to be a 10-year project to secure the electrical transmission-line business for aluminum.[16]

Hoopes's first project was to tackle the aluminum impurity problem so that thicker strands of wire could be used. Alumina produced by PRC in-house refining was known to have variable amounts of unknown impurities, which had unpredictable effects on the quality of the aluminum produced and on any alloys produced from it. Hoopes and Hall tried out a Hoopes idea for refining aluminum by electrolysis, using a tray of melted impure aluminum as anode. Hall pronounced the process both feasible and novel, certainly worth patenting. But the energy cost was prohibitive, and the equipment never survived to the end of an experiment. Hall decided to abandon the Hoopes approach and concentrate instead on better purification of alumina. However, this work later became the basis for the Hoopes refining process, which did in fact permit the company to produce much purer aluminum.[17]

In 1902, Hoopes travelled to meet with potential aluminum-wire customers on the West Coast. He sent back the discouraging news that aluminum was getting a bad reputation in both Colorado and California. Word came that the PRC's earliest and most loyal aluminum-cable customer, Standard Electric, had just placed an order for 60 miles of copper wire for one of its extensions after a short circuit on one of its small branch

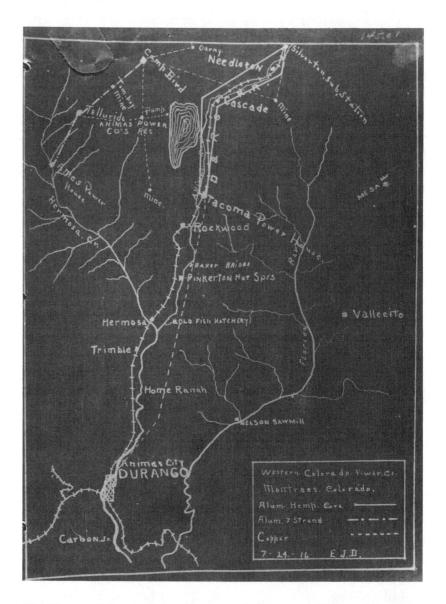

The Western Colorado Power Company tried out several forms of aluminum cable between 1898 and 1905, with mixed results. An Alcoa inspection report of 1916, illustrated by this map, revealed that some of the longer aluminum spans had been replaced with steel and that the customer was entertaining the idea of using copper-clad cable next.

lines had burned off five spans of aluminum wire. That was, said Hoopes, "about the blackest of 'black eyes' we could have received."[18] Upon arrival in Colorado, Hoopes also discovered that a promising customer with whom he had previously spoken had changed his mind and placed an order for 2 million pounds of copper wire because his chief engineer had been reluctant to trust aluminum. Despite tests performed by General Electric that were clearly favorable to aluminum, this engineer had cooked up a spurious set of tests to suggest that aluminum would require towers 20 feet higher than the towers used for copper line. Hoopes's problem was that he had no well-developed data to combat this erroneous information. His only defense against the misleading report was to offer to conduct experiments, which he proposed to do in a day.[19]

Hoopes went further, deciding not to wait for customers to request tests. He persuaded the John Martin Company management to give his material a test if the PRC would supply the cable free of charge. In a letter to Davis, Hoopes wrote that

it is high time that these fusion experiments were made, and very fortunate that we decided not to delay making them, as about 99% of the criticism which is being made upon aluminum is based upon this supposed-to-be fault, and the unfavorable reports have obtained such general circulation that I think it is extremely doubtful whether we shall receive very much business from west of the Rocky Mountains for some time to come.[20]

The fusibility tests Hoopes conducted on the spot to compare the effects of arcs on aluminum and copper wires showed that a major change was needed in the PRC approach. Although there seemed to be little practical difference between the performances of solid aluminum and solid copper when subjected to an arc on a high-tension circuit, the effect of using a multistrand conductor was to cut its resistance to arcs dramatically. Hoopes wrote to Davis in September 1902:

The inference to be drawn from these two conclusions is that it would be preferable to make the conductor solid, if it were possible to do so with safety, and if not, the strands of all conductors for transmission work should be made as large as possible. . . . In short, a good deal of the cable which you have been making in seven strands heretofore had better be made in three strands.[21]

Despite the problems it was having with conductor wire, the PRC made a big commitment of capacity to the wire business when it opened the Massena plant in New York in 1904, for wire cable was one of the major products the plant was designed to produce. Wire for less demanding uses was becoming Alcoa's

One of the earliest aluminum cable installations was in Leavenworth, Kansas, where the Kansas City and Western Railway Company purchased 70 miles of aluminum wire in 1899 and replaced it in 1901 with #2 all-aluminum cable. A 1916 inspection report, illustrated by these photos, revealed that there had been a great many defective joints and that the railway had replaced the high-tension wire with copper before 1911.

fastest-growing product, accounting for 37 percent of the company's total metal output in 1903. By 1904, the entire production facilities for wire, rod, and cable had been moved there from New Kensington, and in 1905 the company obtained its first million-pound cable order for a line from Niagara Falls to Lockport from the Lockport and Ontario Power Company, which went on to place two even larger orders the following year.[22]

With the PRC selling wire cable by the carload, there was considerable incentive to determine the best method of producing it, but Hoopes had difficulty getting cooperation from the plant staffs. Personnel at Massena, struggling to overcome serious blistering problems, were unwilling to experiment with the trade-offs between conductivity and tensile strength and to establish standards for their own wire. They regarded efforts from headquarters to require them to conform to company standards as outright meddling in their affairs. Hoopes persisted, pushing the plant technical staff, over whom he had no direct authority, to do careful tests on the best methods of producing different sizes of wire, taking into consideration the relative effects on strength, elasticity, and conductivity. Eventually his attention to the effects of different methods on the qualities of the aluminum being produced did bring about improvement, but it was slow going, inconsistently observed, and hard to document.[23]

All such experimentation in plants was intensely unpopular. It took time, reduced output, and required the plant staff to do unaccustomed painstaking technical measurements. Manufacturing plants preferred to believe that problems were not of their making, but stemmed from production deficiencies earlier in the process. In nearly every letter he wrote, Hoopes had to invoke A. V. Davis's authority in asking for tests to be performed and trials to be run. Referring to the increasingly acrimonious relations between plants, he wrote to Massena's MacDougall:

Incidentally, Mr. Davis handed me your letter of October 26th to Mr. Falter as bearing upon this subject and in passing remarked that that letter as well as Mr. Falter's letter of October 20th to him were of a kind which he did not believe it was necessary to write and were not particularly helpful to the administration of the company's business.[24]

THE CONDUCTOR RESEARCH PROGRAM

After Hoopes's revealing trip to the West in 1902, he returned determined to find a way to produce a single-strand aluminum cable that would stand up to harsh conditions. Between 1902 and 1910 he conducted what Fickes later called a "big and serious program of research" into the problems of electrical transmission wire. The first five years of the program concentrated on the single-strand objective. After that, Hoopes conceded defeat and turned to the hybrid solution that was to become "aluminum cable steel-reinforced" (ACSR).[25]

By later standards the research program was tiny, consuming perhaps a third of Hoopes's time, assisted by one or two untrained technical assistants and aided by equipment designed by Fickes. It was almost entirely trial and error until a chief chemist and metallurgist, Earl Blough, was hired to do serious analytical work in 1905.

The research conditions could only have been called adverse. Hoopes and Fickes conducted their development work on transmission wire and all other process improvements in an "office" they shared at the New Kensington works. The space had previ-

Edwin S. Fickes.

ously served as the bathroom in the plant manager's living quarters. At first they regarded the bathtub as a nuisance, but then they recognized that it was ideal for developing blueprints. On one side of the office doorway stood Hoopes's equipment for testing electrical conductivity; on the other side a secretary had her desk. In a far corner Fickes worked on building plans and drawings for new equipment. One was the design concept he developed for the seven-strand wire-drawing machine he ordered from a machine-tool builder who supplied equipment to the metals industries. After 1904, whenever Hoopes wanted to try out a new idea, he had to travel from New Kensington to Massena, where the PRC's only production-quality wire-drawing equipment was then located.[26]

From 1902 to 1904 Hoopes tried to improve the initial approach to producing transmission wire out of strong aluminum alloy or heavier "pure" (i.e., 99+ percent) aluminum. In 1904, despairing of aluminum alone and unable to produce alloys that resulted in ingots of adequate consistency, Hoopes came up with the idea of laminated wire, drawn from laminated rod to produce concentric tubular sections of aluminum around a steel core. He applied for a broad patent covering all aspects of his "laminal wire," however it might be produced, but by the time the patent was granted, further experimentation had revealed that a laminated approach would be too expensive. The thickness of the aluminum sections was difficult to control, and it was hard to maintain the identity of the layers during the steps of forging and rolling into rod. Moreover, practical tests of the bimetallic wire showed that the outer aluminum layers broke up in time, taking on the unprepossessing appearance of short tubes strung along a heavy steel wire.[27]

In April 1904, Hoopes tested the possibilities of extrusion, a process for which he also applied for a patent. This new method involved forcing an aluminum rod through progressively smaller dies to achieve the desired thinness of wire. The 1,000-ton vertical extrusion press had to be ordered from the John Robertson Company of Brooklyn, New York, and was duly installed at Massena. After his patent was granted, Hoopes wrote to consult Robertson about his idea of extruding bimetallic wire, to contain a steel core and aluminum casing. Like other machine-tool builders of the time, Robertson was an obvious source of information and expertise, serving as an informal consultant to his customers on fabrication problems.[28]

By November, Hoopes had tired of travelling back and forth between Massena and New Kensington, and Massena's plant superintendent had tired of the inevitable interruptions Hoopes's visits involved. The new machine was installed at New Kensington instead, and the home plant became even more of a de facto experimental facility than before. Much hard experimental work convinced Hoopes and his helpers that extrusion would never work, for "the extruded bimetallic wire idea never proved satisfactory in drawing due to the differences in drawing characteristics between the steel core and aluminum casing." Although that wholly new method of fabrication for aluminum did not solve his immediate problem, the use of extrusion proved to be an important breakthrough on its own account. Aluminum turned out to be especially well suited for extrusion.[29]

Attempts to produce bimetallic wire by different forming processes were also unsuccessful. For example, Hoopes tried to cast molten aluminum around a steel bar. That experiment failed because it proved impossible to establish the right hot-rolling temperatures to turn the resulting stock into rod.

William Hoopes.

FINAL SUCCESS

Despite these problems, Hoopes did not abandon his effort to find alternatives to all-aluminum cable. In 1907, having failed in all other solutions, but convinced that hybrid bimetallic cable would be the only alternative strong enough for certain heavy-duty applications, Hoopes tried a highly controversial method. He developed the cable that became known as ACSR, which had a core of heavy-gauge steel wire wrapped with six strands of aluminum wire. Hoopes applied for a patent on ACSR in 1907, and it was granted the following year. The first ACSR line to be installed replaced an earlier bimetallic line on the property of the Western Ohio Railway Corporation in 1909. It operated at 33,000 volts, using six aluminum wires over one steel.[30]

The timing of Hoopes's invention was fortuitous, coinciding with the end of the PRC's protected era and its emergence as the Aluminum Company of America (Alcoa). Having achieved the scale and integration required for mass production of alumi-

In 1916 the Iowa Railway and Light Company installed the new ACSR at a river crossing near Cedar Rapids. These photographs accompanied the "Record of Electrical Conductor Installation Customer's File."

num at prices competitive with common metals, the company had in hand a product to justify that capacity, one that could compete with a common metal for mass markets. ACSR was an instant success in the market for high-tension lines, and in 1911 the company went into high-volume production. The steel-core, six-strand cable proved to be 57 percent stronger than copper cable and weighed only 80 percent as much. Even with this additional strength, it still cost less than copper cable because of the low price of steel.[31]

Once the cable's special installation characteristics had been worked out to everyone's satisfaction, it became apparent that the properties of ACSR – its larger diameter and lower inductance at the core – had the unforeseen advantage of reducing its susceptibility to the corona effect, a problem the electrical industry had for so long been struggling to solve. This gave ACSR a decisive performance advantage over copper. By 1912, ACSR accounted for 20 percent of annual ingot production, between 7 and 8 million pounds of aluminum sold as wire.[32]

THE DRIVE FOR STANDARDIZATION

Inside the company, the product was less well received. Memories of earlier crises with transmission lines died hard. The works were still being asked to act on Hoopes's say-so, indistinguishable from large-scale trial and error, and there were dire predictions that the steel core would eventually rust. When Hoopes substituted high-grade galvanized steel, opposition only mounted. In addition to the perceived risks they were taking in supplying unproven material to customers, objections to the composite cable arose because it required new and technically demanding procedures from manufacturing and sales alike.[33] To bring the new composite into line with the standards it had set for aluminum, Alcoa had to find some way of setting standards for the steel it purchased. Plants had to test the properties of steel cable they purchased to make sure all lots conformed to their specifications. In February 1911, Hoopes cautioned the plants:

I think we should take careful stress and strain diagrams out of each lot of wire we receive and note on them also the elastic limit shown by the drop of the beam method. In none of the information you have sent me have you been stating the elongation or reduction of area. You should note both of these things and put them on the reports. Incidentally I should like to know about what they are in the present lot of wire you are handling.[34]

The difficulty with conducting these tests was that there were no generally accepted standards for measuring stress and strain. Certainly the plant personnel who were having to do the testing were not aware of any. If they used the stress-and-strain diagram, could they rely on the drop-of-the-beam method? Could the same methods that applied to iron apply to aluminum? As one exasperated plant technician observed to Hoopes, "often times the two are confused and are used interchangeably." Experts were few. Not even the recently established National Bureau of Standards offered any help. The only authority Hoopes could find to cite among experienced testers was the man in charge of the U.S. Army's Watertown Arsenal, which was not only its chief center of materials expertise but also a pioneer in all forms of scientific management techniques.[35]

It was only after several test lines produced at Massena and strung in exposed conditions at other Alcoa locations were shown to have withstood corrosion for four years that ACSR was reluctantly adopted by all wire plants. When A. M. Nutt of Massena's wire laboratory sent Hoopes results, observing that

Two Massena employees standing by reels of transmission cable.

the prototype composite lines showed no diminution in strength after four years, he commented, "I trust the above may bring the steel-cored aluminum cable back to life." It did. Too little conclusive information was available to guarantee to customers that the material would not rust, but so far the results were reassuring. After four years, even nongalvanized steel showed itself to be substantially protected from rusting by the tightly wrapped aluminum envelope. Later, on the basis of nine customer installations, Hoopes sent a circular letter to company locations and to major customers. Tests had been run, he reported, for spans from 200 to 1,000 feet under adverse conditions: a half-inch thickness of sleet, winds of 60 miles per hour, a minimum temperature of −40°F, and a maximum temperature of +110°F. None showed rust or failure.[36]

Meanwhile, standard methods and specifications became more than a matter of internal coordination. As more suppliers gained greater control over their processes, such methods emerged as a competitive necessity. The electrical companies were among the earliest to apply industrial standardization to their products; they, in turn, influenced the buying habits of the utilities. In October 1909, Alcoa lost a big contract in To-

Railroad car adapted to install electrical conductor lines.

ronto to the Wire and Cable Company of Montreal. The reason was price, but Davis decreed that in view of the substantial quality improvements Alcoa's plants had made in production methods, it would be possible and necessary to compete on superior performance. Hoopes wrote:

It has become apparent that we cannot longer pursue the policy we have always pursued heretofore, of having our salesmen obtain the easiest possible specifications, and that our endeavor in the future must be to make our product so much better than the material which can be produced by the Wire and Cable Company or any outsider that we will be able to bid on specifications which they will be unable to meet. . . . It will be necessary, therefore, for you to collect data from the results you already have in your own work, and to obtain additional data by experimenting, so as to be in a position to state, at as early a date as possible, what specifications you will be able to meet. . . . Mr. Davis expects us to beat our competitors by being able to produce goods which they cannot produce.[37]

Hoopes did not confine his efforts with the wire business to the internal tasks of finding substitute processes and improving production practices. A substantial share of his time was devoted to gathering information in support of the sales effort. This included amassing data covering product performance and methods of transmission-line construction. Hoopes experimented with different line designs, including the distance to be maintained between conductors to avoid arcing, and with the use of different metals for fasteners and joints. He engaged the engineering departments of the major electrical companies in dialogue, especially General Electric, whose technical letters he sometimes found it necessary to correct. A letter in 1907 from D. B. Rushmore, an engineer in General Electric's Power and Mining Department, thanked Hoopes for his welcome observations about line construction and observed that "the whole business of high tension transmission construction is yet in a rapidly growing state, and we will probably have to change our ideas a great many times before we settle down to recommendations which are final."[38]

THE IN-HOUSE NEED FOR R&D DEFINED

ACSR was a testimony to the breadth and ingenuity of the small central professional technical staff that Alcoa had assembled. They had designed equipment, devised test methods, and persevered through one disappointing outcome after another, able to draw on a few outside technical experts for advice. It was also an illustration of the community of interest that still existed between the different branches of the electrochemical industry around shared process technologies, for success would not have come to ACSR without considerable outside help in the form of equipment suppliers, consultants, and patient, flexible, and knowledgeable customers. As long as the related electrical and electrochemical industries were in their fluid stages, important transfers of information took place with ease. But institutionalization of R&D in one industry would prefigure comparable developments in the rest. After all companies had developed codified specifications, standard procedures, and formal specialized laboratories, knowledge would flow less freely than it did when more speculative knowledge was accessible from so many sources, through independent and quasi-independent research laboratories, consulting engineers, and equipment suppliers.

There was another, sobering side of the story. ACSR also

provided a vivid demonstration of the company's technical shortcomings. Alcoa had resorted to hybrid solutions for lack of better knowledge about aluminum alloys. The problems with ACSR had betrayed serious production problems at both the refining and smelting stages, as well as the inadequacy of the company's knowledge about aluminum's working properties. By way of comparison, British producers at that time were known to be selling higher-strength pure-aluminum cable for transmission wire. Although that reflected the shorter distances and less severe climatic conditions that the British electrical industry faced, it also showed that British craftsmen working in aluminum fabrication could produce more consistent ingot and that the British industry had access to better knowledge of the working properties of light alloys in general.[39]

Hoopes's problems with the purity of the alumina produced in East St. Louis revealed a gap in know-how similar to the gaps that were evident in processes used for rolling the metal. In fact, control of fabrication processes of all kinds would be severely limited until common standards were developed. If the scientific revolution was really to be consummated at Alcoa, improving the core technologies of the smelting, refining, and fabrication processes would have to be matched by a broad program of methods improvment and process control. That was to take place in the next era, a painful and demanding program that was only reluctantly undertaken under duress of the brief period of intense international competition that preceded World War I.

In short, the chief lesson to be learned from the ACSR experience was that the company needed to maintain more formally organized control over its information so that it would have the ability to generate knowledge in advance of need, or at least as needed. It was the essence of the scientific revolution that improving technology in the narrowest sense was not enough. That was a conclusion that the electrical equipment companies, General Electric and Westinghouse, had already drawn. As the original science-based companies, they had set up in-house research programs and were already becoming pioneers in the various movements for industrial standardization, and they were passing their approaches along. As customers, they were in a position to demand similar methods and procedures from their suppliers. Alcoa either would master its own varied production processes to comply with those demands or would have to forgo their business.

ACSR highlighted one of the costs of any vertical-integration strategy, the tendency for the various parts of a company to blame each other for their problems and the difficulty of assigning clear responsibility under such circumstances. European aluminum companies, which were typically integrated horizontally, but not vertically, did not face these problems to the same degree. The chronic resistance of the Alcoa works to important testing programs, the tendency to blame other parts of the company for failures to meet crucial product specifications, and the obvious need for systematic experimentation and fundamental research on the product side all pointed in the same direction. If ever there was unanimity of Alcoa technical staff opinion on a point, it was this: Ad hoc R&D efforts such as ACSR, done on the side, with no trained and dedicated staff, might allow the company to muddle through in a period when it was still protected by patents, but such primitive methods could not be expected to pass muster in the upcoming competitive era.

The other, more appealing lesson from ACSR was the lesson of serendipity: the tremendous value in pursuing a tough research goal even when the results were different from what had been expected. The push to achieve purer aluminum had germinated the idea that would eventually result in the Hoopes refining process for high-purity aluminum. The search for new metalworking methods for transmission wire ended up making the highly salutary match between aluminum and extrusion, a forming process that would be applied across many products and shapes. And certainly the revenue from ACSR, a market that by 1939 would amount to 48 million pounds of cable annually, earning a profit of about 4.5 cents per pound before tax, was a handsome and long-lasting return on Hoopes's "big and serious program of research." All that was in the future, to be sure, but as the era of patent protection wound to a close, ACSR provided a vivid demonstration to the Alcoa technical community, excepting Hall, of the stream of practical opportunities that could accrue to a systematic program of research applied to primary and metalworking processes alike.[40]

In the short run, only part of this opportunity would be addressed. In 1927, Earl Blough set up a local laboratory at Massena specifically to establish metallurgical control, to collect

View of the Alcoa wire mill at Massena, New York.

information, and to perform routine fatigue testing on ACSR and other aluminum conductors. By that time, Alcoa's centralized R&D organization, the Technical Department, was nearly a decade old. But the more comprehensive and integrated program of the Technical Department era came only after a prolonged period of making do without it, and it required the work of more than a decade to make it effective.[41]

PART II

The first international era,
1909–1928

3

The Technical Department: agent of integration

As between the works superintendents the habit of buck-passing and the writing of acrid and somewhat useless correspondence, even before 1909, was a growing evil. For some time, as opportunity offered, Mr. Hoopes and I each had discussed with Mr. Hall the advantages of having an independent and competent research department which would devote itself to getting at the basic causes of such troubles, finding means to avoid them, ways of improving both output and quality of products, and, last but not least, a laboratory which could be used to set and check standards of quality in a manner acceptable to all concerned. . . . Not having had any success in advancing this idea with Mr. Hall, we tried in August 1909 to interest Mr. Davis.[1]

When its patent protection ran out in 1909, Alcoa had assembled a collection of operations that had the makings of a complete system. But as Fickes and Hoopes ruefully observed, it was anything but an integrated whole at the time. The task during the next era would be to transform a loosely connected and geographically dispersed set of operations into a technological unity. This had to be done in the face of stiff international competition, for the European aluminum producers had been making rapid technological progress.

Until the end of World War I, Alcoa had to depend on a collection of overworked professionals with almost no institutional support to handle its fast-growing and increasingly complex technical responsibility. The company came out of its era of patent protection having slipped behind European practice in a number of areas, and the situation only worsened as it strove to meet direct competition with inadequate expertise. In the postwar period, however, its technical capability was institutionalized. Between 1919 and 1928, Alcoa built a fully devel-

Corporate Facts

Leadership:	Alfred E. Hunt, president Charles M. Hall, first vice-president George H. Clapp, second vice-president Arthur Vining Davis, secretary and general manager Robert E. Withers, treasurer George R. Gibbons, assistant treasurer
No. of Employees:	4013
Primary production:	29.1 million pounds
Locations:	△ Niagara Falls, Massena, NY; Shawinigan Falls, Quebec □ Bauxite, AR ○ East St. Louis, IL ■ New Kensington, PA; Massena, NY; Dover, NJ ▲ New Kensington, PA ▼ New Kensington, PA

Laboratory Facts

Leadership:	Charles M. Hall, vice-president William H. Hoopes, chief electrical engineer Earl Blough, chief chemist
No. of Employees:	6

Figure 3.1. Corporate and laboratory facts, 1909.

oped Technical Department, complete with formal charter, advisory committees, and specialized divisions. In the course of developing its in-house R&D organization, Alcoa caught up with, and in some areas surpassed, its international rivals.

Alcoa's investment in a formal research program constituted an acknowledgment that technological leadership was a more sustainable protection than the exclusivity of a patent or the barrier to entry of heavy capital investment. In the interwar period, Alcoa would face an almost continuous string of government investigations into charges that it illegally monopolized raw materials or manipulated domestic markets. Alcoa's management explained its primary monopoly otherwise, in terms of technological mastery. As S. K. Colby wrote, "few major industries have the advantage of such an intimate knowledge of product, from the raw materials to the final consumer."[2] By the end of Alcoa's first international period, there would be no doubt that it owed this intimate knowledge to its central R&D.

Figure 3.2. Corporate locations, 1909.

PREWAR INTERNATIONAL COMPETITION

The international competition that Alcoa faced with expiration
of its patent protection posed a serious threat on two fronts:
price and quality. The European cartel, which included Alcoa's
Canadian subsidiary, had reestablished itself in 1912 to set a
price for aluminum. Alcoa had participated in an earlier cartel,
starting in 1901, but this time it was forced by the U.S. government to sign a consent decree to stay out of the cartel. Covered
by only a small tariff, foreign aluminum poured into the United
States, undercutting Alcoa's target price of 30 cents per pound.
The result was that in 1913 and 1914, foreign imports of aluminum into the United States equalled 50 percent of domestic
output.[3]

More threatening in the long run than the volume of imported metal was its superior quality. As Alcoa found when it
shipped small amounts abroad, aluminum produced overseas
was far superior to what Alcoa was producing. In its rush to
expand production at the primary end, metal quality had been
neglected. To improve its standard, the company not only had

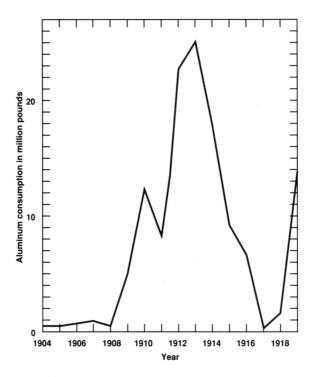

Figure 3.3. Foreign imports of aluminum, 1904–19. Source: "Aluminum Consumption in the United States, 1873–1954," AA.

to coordinate the parts of its integrated production system more effectively but also had to take more disciplined control of its various production processes. Moreover, it had to accomplish this without some of the craft know-how that was available to European metals producers.

In Europe, the frenzied armaments buildup that took place in the decade before World War I forced numerous metallurgical advances in aluminum technology in several different countries. Beginning in 1906, the British National Physical Laboratory (NPL) under Walter Rosenhain pursued an extensive fundamental research program into the composition, physical properties, and working characteristics of metals under the auspices of the Alloy Research Committee of the Institute of Mechanical Engineers. Rosenhain placed heavy stress on performing all metallographic work to the highest standards of accuracy. "Pure materials, as subject of experiment, pure crucibles, well calibrated instruments, patience in readings, careful microscopy are all insisted upon," he wrote early in his tenure at NPL. The findings of the Alloy Research Committee were published in regular reports. Likewise, the British Institute of Metals, founded in 1908, published a journal almost exclusively devoted to the new science of metallurgy. This journal had a long list of subscribers in the United States.[4]

In Germany's Centralstelle für Wissenschaftliche und Technische Forschungen, a government laboratory near Berlin, Alfred Wilm discovered Duralumin, an aluminum alloy that had the strength of mild steel and the potential to revolutionize airplane manufacture and many other structural applications as well. Patented in 1909, it was taken up immediately by several European armaments firms. The metallurgical processes that were used to produce Duralumin – heat treating and age hardening – had long been known in steel, and their application to aluminum held promise that many other new alloys with unusual properties might also be found. Government assistance in European countries arming for war also improved aluminum fabrication processes and the standard of quality for wrought products. Concentrated research efforts in countries that lacked bauxite or some other vital input to aluminum production made new refining technologies available, along with new products such as aluminum bronze powder and aluminum foil, both developed in Germany.[5]

Lacking the stimulus of a big-time armament policy, U.S. industry was pursuing mainly civilian development. New consumers, such as the suppliers of components to the fast-growing automobile industry, who had demanded ever larger amounts of aluminum since 1903–4, required improved performance in many areas. Auto companies, pushing to reduce the weight of their vehicles, sought more and better lightweight aluminum parts of many kinds: housings, crankcases, oil pans. They were particularly interested in alloys with greater thermal stability and workability. Similar criteria applied for aircraft engine parts, where aluminum was proving valuable because light weight was imperative.[6]

HALL AND THE TECHNICAL PROGRAM

Alcoa's small group of technical professionals was losing ground in the attempt to keep up with the diverse demands placed upon it. By 1912, Hall's refusal to approve a central technical organiza-

Automobile parts and body castings were a large and growing market for aluminum in the decade before World War I. These photographs of a finishing operation for Pierce-Arrow fans and body castings in the Trimming Department of the Allyne Brass Foundry Company (above) in Buffalo, New York, and of the highly labor-intensive Pierce-Arrow body molding operation at the Allyne Company in Cleveland (below) were both taken in 1907.

tion was having very evident consequences. In the absence of sorely needed organized R&D at the center, the company had to find other, less efficient ways to meet its technical needs. These expedients led to a growing problem of redundancy of second-rate technical effort.

Hall did not loosen his grip on Alcoa's technical program until his death in 1914. Having denied the request to build a formal corporate R&D organization, he compounded the problem by trying to maintain control when he was no longer physically up to the job. Although he had been out of touch for a period of more than a year, he clearly intended in 1911 to take up where he had left off in important technical decision making. Because of the limitations his illness imposed on him, and the effect it had on his never compliant personality, most of his activities created more difficulties for his subordinates.[7]

Charles Martin Hall at Niagara Falls after the onset of his illness.

Hall conducted much of his work by mail, often from the remote warmer climates – Pasadena, Florida, Bermuda – where he had begun spending the winters. Nevertheless, he demanded detailed reports on the staffing of research positions, on major new projects, and on experiments he had started.[8] When the voluminous reports coming into the central office were not forwarded right away, or when managers did not answer each probing question by return mail, or, as often happened, when experiments were not conducted as he had directed, Hall complained to Moritz and Davis.[9] He wrote lengthy and often sharply critical letters to Charles Fox, head of the East St. Louis works, about the Bayer process; to Edwin Fickes and Charles Moritz, in charge of smelting operations, about plant layouts; to Hoopes about instrumentation; and to Davis about his dealings with the others. Particularly in his last year, the tone of Hall's correspondence became petulant and at times resentful of the people who had taken over his duties. The professional engineers had to go to some lengths to mollify him, especially Hoopes, to whom he took a particular dislike, and whose style of work and decisions he frequently criticized. Only Davis could urge restraint when Hall was being too critical, or taking a favorite point too far, but even Davis would not oppose him.[10]

To compensate for the lack of coordination, Charles Moritz was named operations manager, in 1912, in charge of all reduction plants. In this position, Moritz acted as a buffer between Hall and the works superintendents who were ignoring Hall's instructions. The superintendents clearly considered Hall an impractical crank and resented the disruption any experimental activity caused in their plants. Moritz was empowered to set standards and impose common procedures, a power that at first he had some difficulty exercising. Changes such as these were characteristic of many companies attempting to rationalize their production methods around the turn of the century. Quite a few encountered resistance, and some ran into labor resistance as well.[11]

Often it was not the changes themselves that were unpopular, but the way they were introduced. Moritz wrote to Hall that it was important to go very slowly in the job of establishing uniform practice if he wanted to avoid almost certain mutiny among the works managers. New practices, he suggested, had to be guaranteed to work before they would willingly adopt them. This problem did not particularly concern Hall. When he expressed impatience at one point, Moritz explained that the reduction plants were "not taking kindly" to the direction and orders coming from one source:

I thought that I would give you the facts so that you would better understand why it is a little slow for me to accomplish and show up certain results in a short time, for with the different works operating as they have been – independent of one another – and perhaps not as harmoniously among themselves as they should, it has made it a little difficult for me to handle the situation.[12]

Three major tasks confronted Alcoa's technical staff after the close of the protected era: integration, control, and trial of any competing technologies that might render Alcoa's capital investment prematurely obsolete. Hall was primarily interested in the last of these. He had conceived, in primitive form, most of the processes that were to become central to the modern production of aluminum. In 1909, for instance, he directed an experimental look at water-cooled "open" ingot molds, an idea that would be picked up again in the 1930s to become the direct-chill ingot-casting process. In 1912 he conducted further experiments on his electrically heated carbon-baking furnaces. During his last years he launched a string of projects directed at adapting outside technologies for use by Alcoa. These included devices for raising and lowering the carbon anodes used in French plants, which Hall asked Moritz to investigate, and the

Serpek process, another French innovation that purported to reduce the net cost of alumina through offsetting production of ammonia as a by-product. Hall initiated work on the Serpek process in 1910, and it continued thereafter under Hoopes and Blough. In 1913, Hall even designed a rotary kiln to be used in the process; the following year he sent Blough and Moritz abroad to observe European practice. Ironically, after Hall died, the completion of the agenda he had sketched out would have to await the formation of the research laboratory whose creation he had effectively blocked during his lifetime.[13]

CONTROLLING FOR QUALITY

The particularly vexing problem that occupied all of Alcoa's senior technical personnel in the immediate prewar era was a blister condition that adversely affected the quality of much of the metal Alcoa was producing. This was not a new problem, but international competition had made it vital that it be addressed. In November 1913, Alcoa's London agent, Edward Darling, returned from a trip to Germany with the dispiriting news that in every case the ingots supplied by the Northern Aluminum Company Ltd., Alcoa's Canadian subsidiary, had been judged inferior to ingots supplied by other manufacturers such as Neuhausen, the Swiss company. Germany, which lacked its own bauxite deposits and hydroelectric power and had to rely on limited Swiss primary capacity of German ownership, was a willing buyer of aluminum at that time. Yet Darling reported that six Westphalian rolling mills had rejected all of his samples. He recommended hiring a man from one of the French companies, who, he was sure, could furnish good ingots: "We are absolutely shut out of the German market for rolling ingots at the present time, and we cannot get into this market until we can furnish ingots as well as the German and French ingots."[14]

Edward Darling, first manager of the New Kensington plant and later Alcoa's agent in London.

Blistered sheet was behind the rejections. When annealed and rolled, Alcoa's metal showed quantities of small blisters. All attempts to eliminate this condition had so far failed. In 1909, one Alcoa manager by the name of Fitzgerald resorted to taking the visiting French inventor Paul Héroult out drinking to try to persuade him to shed light on the problem. After "supplying him with about fifteen beers," Fitzgerald had broached the sub-

Nov.6th 1913

ARTHUR DAVIS GRAND HOTEL FLORENCE

CARL BERG NOT SATISFIED ROLLING INGOTS BUT XXXX DEMANDS FURTHER
25 TONS AT ONCE IN GERMANY I WITNESSED CASTING METHODS WHICH AM
MOST DESIROUS TRYING ON PRESENT ORDER TO ACCOMPLISH THIS AND
CLARIFY SITUATION REGARDING PRESENT DELIVERIES DEEM IT ADVISABLE
GO NEWYORK THIS SATURDAY RETURNING IF POSSIBLE NINETEENTH FROM
NEWYORK WIRE IF YOU DO OR DO NOT APPROVE   DARLING

Northern Aluminium Co.Ltd.Caxton House,
S.W.

This telegram from Alcoa's agent in London, E. C. Darling, to Arthur Vining
Davis in Florence came on the heels of the rejection of Alcoa's ingots by Swiss
and German manufacturers. The handwritten notation by Charles Martin
Hall on the bottom of the telegram reads "Mr. Moritz, I agree with what Mr.
Darling [says] about the necessity for doing something to make good rolling
ingots and the futility of trying the same things we have tried in the past. I
think it is clear too that the fault is at least largely in the metal as it comes from
the pots for the reason that Swiss metal when cast by our methods and without
special care makes good sheet. It is especially important for us to improve our
methods on account of our own market in the U.S. as stated by Mr. Davis in
the first letter sent you."

ject with Héroult, but Héroult had kept his secrets to himself. He said only that overcoming the matter of blisters has cost him the hardest year and a half of his life and that the trouble was not in the reduction furnaces.[15]

In 1913, Hall and Blough both suggested experiments to address the problem, but experimentation was difficult. All sample ingots had to be sent from Massena to Blough's laboratory department in New Kensington for remelting and rolling, a process that took two to three weeks. Blough and Moritz set up a small laboratory at Massena to address this and other process control problems, but its capacity was used to the full to cope with ACSR problems alone. By that time, competition for trained research personnel was becoming difficult, as a number of companies hit by foreign competition were hiring researchers. Moritz wrote Hall that he had been able to hire only one, from Western Electric. "I am endeavoring to get several more likely men, but find it hard to get anyone that has had any experience."[16]

Paul H. T. Héroult.

In his New Kensington laboratory, Blough had two assistants. Only one of these was a trained metallurgist, Conrad ("Dutch") Nagel, whom he hired in 1915 and who would later become Alcoa's chief metallurgist. Nagel remembered the period before and during World War I as a time when anyone with metallurgical training could have a field day at Alcoa, with the opportunity to become involved in every part of the company's business. Even the inexperienced Nagel could see that "the company's business activities were 'way ahead' of its technical know-how." The practice of metallurgical R&D was so new that every project entailed first building new equipment for experimentation. In this early generalist phase, a technical worker generally tackled a problem from beginning to end, devising test equipment, pouring and rolling samples.[17]

Attempts to control the blister problem finally led to the broader application of process controls and standards like those Hoopes had introduced for ACSR. Though the new regimen by no means corrected the cause of the problem, which was later found to be gas absorption by the metal during melting, careful control of melting temperature combined with frequent sampling proved to eliminate the symptoms.

Earl Blough took on the difficult task of imposing a common discipline on Alcoa's different production sites through

A view of the smelting operation (ca. 1916) at Massena, New York, shows how likely it was that extraneous material might be introduced into open pots. Carbon anodes like the one in the foreground were easily contaminated, contributing to metal quality problems.

standard testing procedures at several Alcoa plants early in 1914.[18] The adverse information from the field finally gained reluctant compliance from the plants. A letter from Moritz to the Shawinigan works supervisor showed just how bad quality problems could get:

I think that all of us have been more or less careless in our metal shipments, as we have usually shipped practically anything we had on hand, simply with the idea of filling the orders. I personally have always felt this way, but since I have been abroad and had a talk with Mr. Darling and some of his customers, and have also seen the way in which shipments are made, not only by the British Aluminium Company, but by the Aluminium Francaise, I have come to the conclusion that we must brace up and likewise ship our product in better shape. I consequently thoroughly agree with the sentiment expressed by Mr. Darling, that we should inspect all ingot going to customers, to see that it is in A-1 shape and does not contain particles of coke, nails or other extraneous material.[19]

BORROWED TECHNOLOGY

Alcoa's technical staff had its first direct exposure to developments in Europe when Edwin Fickes, sick with exhaustion in

1907, took a rest cure in England, where he "rested" by making new arrangements for Alcoa's overseas marketing, consulting with European experts on bauxite supplies, and surveying recently discovered locations for mining bauxite.[20]

Fickes's first trip abroad for Alcoa inaugurated an intensely cosmopolitan period for the company's senior technical staff. Hoopes, Blough, and Moritz all travelled to Europe before 1914 to learn what they could about rival methods of production and to assess different technologies that were available to license. Picking up useful details simply by observation was difficult because all of the companies jealously guarded their technology before the war, but there was no mistaking the overall conclusion that U.S. practice in metallurgy had fallen far behind. In 1914, the distinguished American chemist and metallurgist George Burgess estimated that the United States was perhaps 10 years behind developments in England.

> The available knowledge concerning the properties of metals and alloys and the dependence of these properties upon what we may call the life-history of these metals, including their pedigree, or preparation and composition, and conditions of birth, or their manufacture, is all too meager, both in quantity and quality.[21]

"Metallurgically speaking," Burgess concluded, the United States was still "a colony of England."

This group picture of Alcoa's senior executives was taken in Alcoa, Tennessee, in 1916, at about the time when the decision was made to seek a director for a corporate laboratory. From left to right: Isaac Glidden Calderwood (superintendent of construction), James W. Rickey (chief hydraulic engineer), Edwin S. Fickes (chief engineer), Arthur Vining Davis (president), Charles B. Fox (manager of alumina), Roy A. Hunt (manager of fabricating), Judge H. Bart Lindsay (local company attorney), and Charles H. Moritz (manager of smelting).

Fortunately, owing to Burgess's efforts, a better standard of metallurgical knowledge and expertise was taking shape in the United States along the lines established by Rosenhain. One of the chief features of these advances was that chemical analysis and physical observation were being linked by the use of new laboratory equipment and instrumentation. Through the study of metal formation and deformation, it was possible to understand with some precision what kinds of chemical compositions, combined with what types of physical working, might be expected to yield certain physical properties and why. In 1913 the National Bureau of Standards (NBS) organized a separate nonferrous-metals research project led by a brilliant young scientist, Paul Merica. It picked up and began to improve on research work that was known to be occurring abroad.[22] These developments by a U.S. government laboratory made it considerably more likely that an in-house metallurgical staff, even if not drawn from the handful of original researchers at work in the United States at the time, would have a reliable knowledge base on which to build.[23]

GROUNDWORK FOR CENTRAL R&D

Charles M. Hall's death in 1914 removed the principal barrier to setting up a central research department in Alcoa. In addition to hiring Nagel to assist Blough at Alcoa's only central research laboratory in 1915, A. V. Davis formed a Research Committee with William Hoopes and Edwin Fickes to plan for an enlarged research laboratory that might find new markets for aluminum through a systematic research program. Davis's job description for the director of this organization called for "an energetic, resourceful, chemical engineer" to set up and direct a corporate research laboratory. It proved difficult to find suitable candidates. After prolonged negotiation, they hired Francis C. Frary, a 33-year-old Ph.D. chemist and practicing chemical engineer, who worked for the Oldbury Electrochemical Company in Niagara. Frary came recommended by Joseph Richards. He combined good academic credentials and some industry experience. After earning both undergraduate and graduate degrees at the University of Minnesota, he had spent a further year of study at Berlin's Technische Hochschule, where he had been exposed to Germany's progress in electrochemistry and to its advanced research climate. He then returned to Minnesota for his Ph.D., awarded in 1912. Among his scientific colleagues he was known as a versatile chemist who was not averse to building equipment and inventing apparatus as he went.[24]

Frary taught industrial chemistry at the University of Minnesota for two years, flirting with an early case of burnout by teaching 15 courses in nine different subjects while conducting experimental research in electrochemistry and metallurgy. During those two years he was successful in producing several hard alloys of lead by electrolysis, through experiments that also served as his introduction to the phenomenon of age hardening. That experience was useful during the war, when the regular supply of lead-hardening antimony was cut off. He left Minnesota because an offer from the Oldbury Electrochemical Company in Niagara attracted him as a chance to do full-time research with good facilities. At Oldbury, Frary became an authority on the production and handling of phosgene. However, he must have found the demand for technical support for operations worse than he expected, or the technical problems less than interesting, for two years later he was receptive to Alcoa's offer.

Alcoa hired Frary on the understanding that he would be given the freedom to design an independent research program. The job was portrayed as the chance to set up a general research laboratory along the lines of the one established at General Electric. A. V. Davis's wish for "enlargement and improvement of commercial use of aluminum" provided an opportunity that Frary described as something that might come once in a generation. Charles Moritz, Alcoa's head of manufacturing, still located at Massena, after his first interview with Frary, noted that "he is very enthusiastic about handling work of an original nature, but not in solving problems that arise from time to time at the Works relating to process control."[25]

With the outbreak of war in Europe, the sudden need to meet demand from the Allies without diverting aluminum from their usual customers sidetracked Hoopes and Davis and delayed the hiring negotiations for six months. Finally, in 1917, A. V. Davis wired Hoopes: "Approve offering Frary five thousand [stop] Services to begin January first." Word quickly spread in the technical community at Massena and in Niagara generally that Alcoa was opening a new laboratory in New Kensington with high-paying jobs. But once again wartime pressures intervened as the United States entered the war. Frary was asked to report to the Edgewood Arsenal near Washington to work on the U.S. chemical-warfare program, developing a facility to produce phosgene. The one-year leave Frary obtained from A. V. Davis was renewed twice before Frary rejoined the company early in 1919.[26]

The delay had certain advantages, for World War I stimulated and expanded U.S. industrial R&D in several different directions that benefited Alcoa and its affiliates, as it did many science-based companies at the time. The most important contributions of the war were clearly defined national goals for science, a temporary government moratorium on patent control, an emergency need for substitute materials that stimulated both chemical and metallurgical research, and a sudden infusion of government funding. The war experience demonstrated the possibilities of an expanded government role in science, but that role would not be taken up in peacetime until much later, when a less centralized, less activist approach was seen to have failed.[27]

Alcoa gained wartime experience with R&D at the government's expense, along with a more complete understanding of its own technical deficiencies. Frary had the experience of putting together a state-of-the-art chemical laboratory at the Edgewood Arsenal, knowing that he would rejoin Alcoa afterward. Meanwhile, a cooperative program with the navy, in which Alcoa learned how to reproduce the German high-strength alloy Duralumin, exposed Blough's process control efforts to a whole new standard of achievement. Most important of all, the Aluminum Castings Company, now 50 percent owned by Alcoa, expanded its Lynite Laboratories into a model for metallurgical laboratories the world over. This Cleveland organization would furnish the core of Alcoa's postwar metallurgical research program.

A PROTOTYPE LABORATORY

The consolidation of several aluminum foundries into the Aluminum Castings Company (ACC) in 1909, in which Alcoa had participated, had allowed the previously separate foundries to pool their collective technical resources. In the period just be-

In 1909 the Aluminum Castings Company, partially owned by Alcoa, absorbed the Allyne Brass Foundry Company, located on East 61st Street in Cleveland. That establishment, shown here in an artist's rendering, became the nucleus of Alcoa's Cleveland operations when Alcoa took it over completely in 1919.

fore the war, aluminum had an excellent chance to supply many important components to the rapidly developing auto industry if it could meet the design challenges. But the combined castings company needed a central technical capability to establish standards and to transfer information learned at any one site to other sites, the same sort of institutional resource Hoopes and Fickes had envisioned for Alcoa. Edward Allyne, president of ACC, authorized the formation of the Lynite Laboratories at company headquarters in Cleveland. Initially set up under production department control, Lynite Laboratories was intended to "function solely and purely as the research and experimental [organ] of the company."[28]

A small research department was created and put in the charge of Zay Jeffries, an instructor at the Case School of Applied Science, who had studied mining and metallurgy at the South Dakota School of Mines and at Harvard. Jeffries had become familiar with some aspects of aluminum castings as a consultant on a new automobile piston design made from Lynite 114, a special ACC alloy.[29]

The new research capability was a secret closely guarded from competitors. The first research office set up shop in a hole-in-the-wall at headquarters equipped with a telephone extension, a few rudimentary pieces of testing equipment, and a newly pur-

chased set of the *Encyclopaedia Britannica*. The "office" soon out-
grew its original quarters and was moved to a "research plant,"
known as Plant R, housed in a separate building. It reported to a
Technical Committee headed by the company's president. Rapidly expanding to employ more than 100 people, including "Metallurgists, Chemists, Metallorgraphists, Physicists, Mechanical
Engineers, Automotive Engineers, experts in testing of materials
and apparatus, and practical experts in various lines of metal
fabrication," it became deeply involved in wartime military development, especially the design, testing, and production problems
associated with the new Liberty aircraft engine. A major metallurgical effort was devoted to adapting Wilm's Duralumin patents
when they became available through the U.S Alien Property
Office for use in castings.

From the beginning, the laboratory's main challenge was to
keep from being overwhelmed by the needs for everyday technical support in operations and sales. Early intentions to have a
research program independent of the immediate needs of current operations were soon all but forgotten under the pressure
of wartime demand. The reality of the situation was quite different from the picture of the laboratory publicized in both the
U.S. and British trade press soon after the war as the model
industrial laboratory devoted entirely to research and experimentation. Even putting Lynite Laboratories in a separate Development Department, designed to concentrate entirely on
new products, did not alleviate the problem of having to do
troubleshooting for ongoing operations. The most that could
be done of a longer-term nature under such circumstances was
to try to carefully document and save reports defining potential
research questions to be followed up in calmer times.[30]

Nevertheless, Lynite Laboratories employed some of the leading technical experts in nonferrous metals in the United States,
and their wartime activities gave them the basis for extremely
important scientific publications in the postwar period. Zay
Jeffries and Robert S. Archer together published a number of
key works on nonferrous metals, including *The Science of Metals*,
which became the accepted university text on metallurgy of the
1920s.[31]

In 1919 the managers of Lynite Laboratories translated what
they had learned about effective structuring of research into an
organization that would better support their original mandate.
In addition to research and experimentation, the laboratory

The Liberty aircraft engine contained a number of critical cast-aluminum parts, including the crankshaft and pistons. Altogether, aluminum parts accounted for as much as one-third the engine weight. The Liberty engine became a major focus of the work of the Aluminum Castings Company just before and during World War I. (Smithsonian Institution, Photograph No. A981.)

The first Liberty engine in flight, August 1917. (Smithsonian Institution, Photograph No. A45344.)

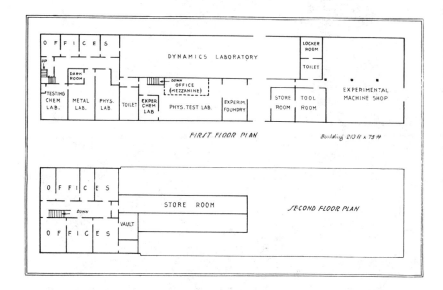

Physical layout of the Lynite Laboratories, widely regarded as a model for metallurgical laboratories. (From *Iron Age*, 17 July 1919, p. 149.)

assumed responsibility for "provision of metallurgical standards." To give it the independence from routine work spelled out in its charter, its three new divisions – Research, Development, and Testing – were all carefully insulated by a Commercial Development Division from interference by the Manufacturing and Distribution Departments, which had enjoyed free run of the premises while the war was on.[32]

These changes were effected just as the bottom fell out of the market for aluminum castings. In this context, Zay Jeffries, head of the laboratory, presented the restructured organization as the source of opportunities for the ACC. In a document entitled "Metallurgical Outlook," he articulated a farsighted technical vision, predicting that, the gloomy outlook notwithstanding, there would be a large market for aluminum in the postwar era. Jeffries rightly saw the question of who would benefit from advancing aluminum technologies as a matter of technical strategy. During the war, many companies and institutions in several countries had gained know-how about the working properties of high-strength aluminum alloys, but that know-how had yet to be captured and explained scientifically. Jeffries identified the know-how that the ACC had acquired about Duralumin as a potential major technical asset, even though the composition

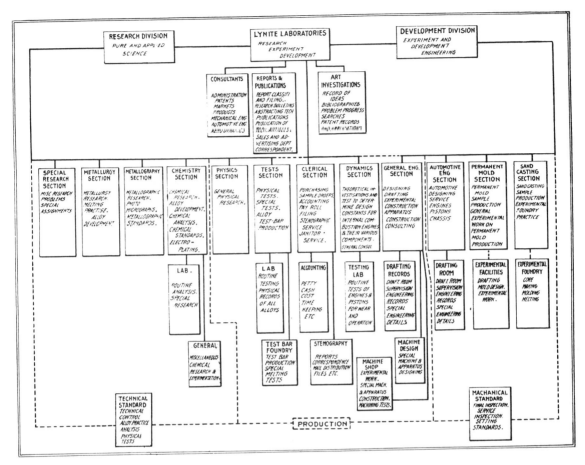

Lynite Laboratories organization chart from 1919. (From *Iron Age*, 17 July 1919, p. 149.)

itself, patented by the Germans, was not proprietary to the company. The ultimate economic value of high-strength aluminum, he predicted, would accrue to those who learned how to turn the art into a science.[33]

At the end of the war, it was uncertain who that would be. Jeffries warned that when the auto companies tried to make their own aluminum parts, as at least some of them were bound to do, they would learn how difficult the metal was to work and would inevitably try to hire away from the metals companies their experienced technical personnel. To avoid the loss of these valuable personnel and their accumulated know-how, the ACC, renamed Aluminum Manufacturers, Inc., would have to do three things: secure control of the Duralumin patents, which Jeffries predicted would not easily be superseded; develop efficient process controls to drive down the cost of the metal; and systematize and codify the knowledge and know-how gained from working with and studying Duralumin.

The Lynite experience had taught Jeffries the difficulties of turning an industrial art into a science. As in so many other businesses converting their operations to mass production at the time, the crucial first step was to set and enforce standards. But documenting the procedures and capturing them for replication elsewhere were also important, Jeffries noted:

We need to write the technology of our business. Just as a system of bookkeeping needs to be so clear that an expert accountant will have no difficulty in determining the methods used, so do our metallurgical processes need to be so accurately described that technical men can control them largely from written descriptions. We have heard that the Manitowoc plant in Wisconsin produced castings very cheaply some years ago. It is my opinion that this plant contributed very little to the Aluminum Manufacturers, Inc., inasmuch as they left no records behind them and consequently what they knew remains with them still or is lost. Our plan is to make our records so complete that others can benefit by them and eventually we must try to reduce the various operations to a science.[34]

It was also crucial not to lose the technical expertise that had been assembled. Unfortunately, the castings business, which had been wildly profitable during the war, was making no money in the immediate postwar period, certainly not enough to support a laboratory employing over 100 people. In 1920, when the automobile market collapsed and Aluminum Manufacturers, Inc., could not pay its Alcoa bills, Alcoa took it over and laid off all but 20 of the laboratory's staff.[35]

The chief value of the Lynite experience was preserved, however. Alcoa kept the modern research facility in Cleveland and also retained in residence there five of the most important members of the research staff, including Jeffries and Archer. Also transferred to Alcoa were the management know-how that had been gained in organizing an effective aluminum laboratory, the process control techniques for high-strength aluminum-alloy production, and the metallurgical know-how gained from working with Duralumin. In 1920, Lynite Laboratories was absorbed in the new Alcoa R&D structure that had only just come into being as the Technical Department.[36]

Alcoa's heaviest period of R&D institution building took place in an international climate of unprecedented ferment and openness in technology and in the context of a major strategic shift for the company. Even though the United States had been an active belligerent for only two years, the effect of World War I on its aluminum business was profound. First, the war created unparalleled opportunities for technological borrowing from overseas companies. Second, new markets appeared in the postwar era, as many new lightweight products made for wartime use turned out to have peacetime applications. On the other hand, heavy overseas demand for aluminum during the war had encouraged the development of a secondary market for scrap aluminum that did not disappear when the war was over. The presence of large amounts of surplus metal in domestic markets diverted management's attention away from its fixation on intermediate capacity and turned attention to the necessity of making money on fabricated products, and hence the need for renewed pioneering.

The demonstration during the war of what concentrated R&D could do changed the U.S. national climate for R&D in nonferrous metals generally. Great strides were made both in building the metallurgical knowledge base and in finding new applications. Government had led the way, but in the postwar era much of that work took place not in government laboratories and universities but in industry.

These developments contrasted sharply with what was going on in England in the postwar period. There the research done on nonferrous metals before and during the war at the NPL, as described in a report by the Alloy Research Committee in 1919, fed into a debate in the nonferrous-metals community that pitted scientists against industry.[37] Walter Rosenhain and others resisted any suggestion that individual companies should set up their own laboratories. They opposed what they termed "the industrialization of science" on the grounds that once hired away into industry, scientists would be diverted from the essential work of creating a sound knowledge base. The clash of cultures – the shop culture of the metalworking craftsman and the school culture of university-trained researchers – was a subject frequently discussed as business leaders urged more effective exploitation of science by industry.[38] Instead, the English metallurgical community supported the idea of setting up institutes, jointly funded by industry and government, to support continued metallurgical research. Despite enthusiastic promotion by industry leaders, the amounts of money actually contributed to this work were disappointingly small. For an industry that had always been extremely secretive, shared research seemed to offer few real appropriable advantages.[39]

In the United States, the demands of the war had demonstrated both the limitations of the current state of the art and the opportunities that could be realized if systematic investigation were undertaken. Science-based companies that had not already done so were moved to establish corporate laboratories, encouraged by the newly formed National Research Council (NRC) to think of industrial research as a patriotic duty, the mark of enlightened corporate leadership. An NRC survey in 1921 found that 350 companies claimed to have some type of dedicated R&D facility, employing a total of over 1,600 technically trained personnel. Many major nonferrous-metals companies were convinced of the necessity to invest in research, and by the early 1920s over 60 manufacturers in the industry maintained research departments and laboratories, and there were also technical personnel attached to smaller companies.[40]

By signing up Francis Frary as research director before the war, Alcoa had stolen a march on other companies bidding for the limited supply of trained research staff. On the eve of his release from military duty, Frary invited the members of Alcoa's Research Committee – Fickes, Hoopes, and Blough – to visit him at his chemical laboratory at Edgewood Arsenal and used the occasion to conduct a brainstorming and planning session for the projected research program. The committee assured Frary that they contemplated a laboratory at Alcoa similar to the one he had shown them at Edgewood.[41]

The Research Committee authorized Frary to hire a strong core for its chemical research team from among the men who had been working with him during the war. The group of chemists Frary brought with him from Edgewood Arsenal – Herman E. Bakken, Dale M. Boothman, Harry V. Churchill, William E. Hoffman, Jr., and Lowell H. Milligan – would remain prominent in the Alcoa technical community for several

Francis Frary at the time he joined Alcoa as director of the Research Bureau.

decades. Having heard the promises made to Frary – an independent research program, modern facilities in a good location, a well-supported staff – they went to what they expected would be temporary assignments until a new research laboratory could be built in an appropriate central location. Several other new staff members for the Technical Department were hired from the NBS, bringing with them the dedication to careful measurement and exacting research procedures developed there in the previous decade. If they went to industry expecting to find better research equipment and better facilities for their work than they could have in universities or in government-supported laboratories after World War I, both groups were at first to be severely disappointed.[42]

FORMATION OF THE TECHNICAL DEPARTMENT

Alcoa's new Technical Department was formed in 1919 as part of a general corporate reorganization that put technical matters on an equal business footing with the other key management functions. Indeed, technology became one of the few functions to be centralized within Alcoa before World War II. The occasion for the reorganization was the transition from prototype to production stage in Alcoa's alloy development program with the navy. This came with the signing of a contract obligating the company to produce a large order of components fabricated from alloy 17S (Alcoa's version of Duralumin) for a proposed naval airship, the *Shenandoah*. So critical was success in this program deemed to be, and so difficult was it of attainment, that an integrated central technical organization combining both metallurgical control and research was considered necessary. Alcoa had not yet taken over the ACC, but A. V. Davis had attended carefully to Jeffries's recommendations about the vital role of the technical community to support participation in emerging aluminum markets.[43]

The Technical Department, headed by William Hoopes until his death in 1925, consisted of two coordinated but largely autonomous bureaus: the Technical Direction Bureau under former chief chemist Earl Blough, and the Research Bureau under Francis C. Frary. The mission A. V. Davis spelled out for the Technical Department as a whole was different from that which the Research Committee had been discussing only a short

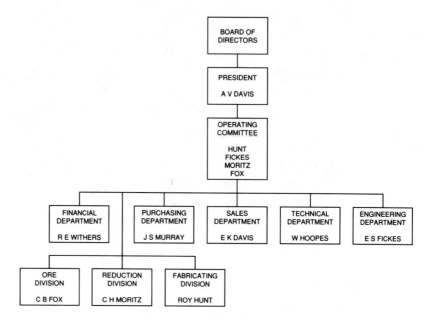

Figure 3.4. Alcoa corporate organization, 1919. Source: AA, env. 1059.

while before. It was to enable the company to make money from fabrication at a time when scrap metal was inundating the market. Davis noted:

I believe that the situation today is entirely different from what it was before the war. At that time we were stressing the manufacture of aluminum and were making our money out of the manufacture of aluminum. We had the theory, in common with our competitors, that it was a good thing to disseminate information in regard to the fabrication or utilization of aluminum in order to increase the consumption of aluminum. Today, however, we find ourselves confronted with the fact that the money which is to be made in the aluminum business is in the fabrication of aluminum. . . . In other words quality is the one thing that is going to enable us to get the jump on our competitors.[44]

To avoid having to pay out excessive royalties or risk expensive lawsuits, Davis also wanted substitutes for 17S. Each part of the Technical Department had to translate these goals into specific program choices, within the constraints of a limited staff, inherited project commitments, and seriously inadequate conditions for research.[45]

The original plan of the Research Committee was that the Technical Department would remain in New Kensington, where

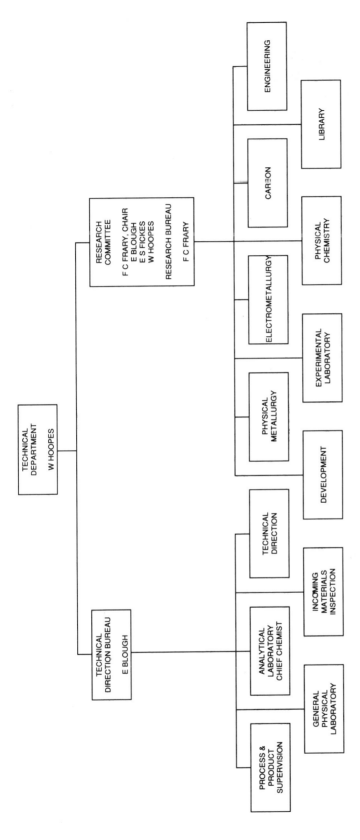

Figure 3.5. Technical Department organization, 1919. Source: AA, env. 1059.

Blough's operation had been, only until a new laboratory could be built at a neutral location. Edwin Fickes recorded the committee's rationale:

> . . . neither Mr. Hoopes nor I wanted the laboratory at any of the works or too closely associated with them, as we feared in time the works where it was situated would become a dominant factor in determining a research policy which would neglect other problems which might be of far greater importance to the Company than those of the single works where the laboratory was located.[46]

Possible sites were Pittsburgh, within easy reach of the Carnegie Institute of Technology and the Mellon Institute, or Edgewater, New Jersey, where Alcoa had recently set up a new mill on the Hudson River. The New Jersey option would place the laboratories in one of the major electrochemical centers of the country, where metal refiners and industrial chemical companies had located, and where Stevens Institute and Columbia University both offered the prospect of a supportive technical community. While the location decision was under discussion, Frary and Blough were encouraged to inspect the new laboratory just built by the New Jersey Zinc Company to "get some ideas."[47]

Unfortunately, a postwar business slump and lingering skepticism on the part of some senior Alcoa managers thwarted the Research Committee. When a downturn in the auto industry in 1920 and 1921 cut Alcoa's sales in half, the apparently simple choice of a location for the new laboratory facility turned into a heated debate, bringing to the surface the second thoughts Alcoa executives were having about their technical priorities. A. V. Davis yielded by degrees to pressure from other Alcoa executives who wanted to avoid additional overhead by locating the research facility at an existing plant site. First he bought extra land at the Edgewater mill site, which was close to New York, though not freestanding, and then he postponed the new laboratory indefinitely. Blough, Frary, and their new staff ended up in ludicrously cramped and inadequate space at the New Kensington works, where they remained for a decade.[48]

THE TECHNICAL DIRECTION BUREAU

The original objective of the Technical Direction Bureau (TDB) was "better aluminum cheaper." Blough and his assistant,

"Dutch" Nagel, were made responsible for improving the routine standards of production and supervising the testing and coordination of metallurgical information. As Hoopes put it to Davis, it was to be "the equivalent of a customer's inspection maintained throughout the process." In practice, this involved putting in place procedures, methods, proper testing equipment, and trained personnel in all Alcoa plants. If the TDB did that task well, it would put itself out of a job. In addition, the TDB was charged with supporting the work of the Research Bureau, making samples and testing when it had equipment or experimental capabilities that the Research Bureau lacked. It was also to serve as the main source of technical information for the Sales Department.[49]

From 1919 on, technical superintendents employed by the TDB Fabrication Division were appointed to work in the plants "rendering whatever assistance possible to the plant management in improving practices" and reporting weekly back to the TDB.[50] These superintendents were the ones who enforced more rigorous standards of control in the plants and who trained plant personnel. Their positions in the field gave them a chance to witness firsthand the kinds of problems that needed to be corrected by nonroutine study and experimentation. From time to time they met in conference and suggested subjects for systematic investigation, such as work on a hot-top ingot mold in 1923. Later, the TDB sent out consulting engineers at the request of plants. Sales support, which was small at first, also took up increasing amounts of time, and in 1923 Blough reported that his group had written 400 letters to the Sales Department in that year alone.[51]

No sooner had the new department been launched than the addition of the experimental mill at New Kensington expanded the original conception of the TDB temporarily from a coordinating function to an operating function. The experimental mill was a small production facility set aside for work on new alloys or small-quantity runs that needed special attention from development personnel. From 1919 to 1922, three-quarters of the TDB's time went to directing the manufacturing development of 17S. Although that left less support for the technical needs of the conventional works as they struggled to adopt common control procedures, it gave members of the TDB staff, many of whom were inexperienced in the manufacture of aluminum, valuable exposure to all the problems of actual production.

An important part of TDB support involved not only testing to ensure that the works were meeting standards but also developing testing equipment rugged enough to stand up to plant use and procedures that would yield accurate results even if performed in haste by barely trained people. Former NBS researcher Richard Templin was hired by the TDB to form a testing division in collaboration with the Research Bureau.[52]

THE CORPORATE AGENDA FOR R&D

In taking over the new Research Bureau, Frary found himself with a task quite different from the task that had existed in 1917. In the postwar company, Frary had to coordinate and control a set of testing facilities widely scattered throughout the company and compete for resources with a development organization of equal influence. One of the difficulties he faced was that he had brought with him a strong group of chemists to study primary processes, but the company was now demanding work on product-related metallurgy. It was not a capricious change in priorities; there was every reason to expect that a flood of imported aluminum would enter the American market when Europeans began paying reparations and repaying war debts. But scientifically trained metallurgists were difficult to find. It was an early demonstration of just how fast technical needs could change in response to wholly uncontrollable short-term market shifts.[53]

Frary also found himself with a set of half-finished projects. One of the costly consequences of not forming a corporate research group sooner was that some expensive purchases of technology had been made abroad that had yet to pay off. Other initiatives, such as the Hall "dry process" for producing alumina and Hoopes's electrolytic cell for refining aluminum, would require more effort if their development was to be completed. Initially, the Research Bureau concentrated on completing the projects Hall had started before his death. Frary took up his early agenda with a Research Committee consisting of Davis and the top technical officers. Even so, he came under criticism from the Operations and Sales Departments, who always wanted to see the Research Bureau devote more attention to their immediate problems.

In view of the heightened interest in metallurgical research and the scarcity of trained researchers, Alcoa was particularly fortunate to inherit the Lynite Laboratories. Even before Aluminum Manufacturers, Inc., was absorbed, it was agreed that Lynite Laboratories would cooperate with the new Research Bureau, and the two groups agreed on a division of the research turf. It was decided that Cleveland would continue its work on castings, forgings, and foundry work, with the goal of catching up with the state of the art in aluminum castings that had been reached by Europeans and by a few specialized domestic competitors. It would also take on the problem of finding a substitute for 17S. The Alcoa Research Bureau itself would deal mainly with primary processes, with some minor attention to wrought alloys, on which Cleveland and New Kensington would collaborate. This arrangement continued when, in 1920, Lynite Laboratories was absorbed into the company as the Cleveland section of the Research Bureau. Faced with his first serious budget cut at that time, Frary reduced the Cleveland establishment to one-fifth its former size. Almost half of the Research Bureau's total research staff in the early years was employed at one or another of three satellite laboratories, located at the company's works in East St. Louis, Badin (North Carolina), and Cleveland.[54]

To placate the operations and sales executives somewhat, representatives of each of those divisions were added to the Research Committee. In 1922 the committee agreed that certain problems would have interdepartmental attention from subcommittees set up on an ad hoc basis to bring in operations and sales people. The first of these was formed to decide on a proposed expansion of the research staff needed to undertake development of silicon alloys, which seemed to offer a possible alternative to Duralumin for some applications. Another subcommittee was charged with addressing problems related to utilization of scrap metal.[55]

The difficulty with all of these committees was that the managers from operating departments who served on them rarely understood the nature and uses of technical information and always had unrealistic expectations of what could be done in short order, and the researchers who served with them had equally unrealistic ideas about what information was available in the typical manufacturing site. The TDB needed no advice on its agenda until after the 17S program was finished. But when it

In the Foreground in the Metallographic Laboratory Is a Precision Potentiometer, Having a Sensitiveness of 0.0000001
Volt.   The misconstructure of aluminum alloys is studied through the metallographer's camera in the left-hand corner.
The specimen is polished and etched and then placed on the stage of the microscope.   The carbon arc lamp on the
bench at the left is for illuminating the object

These photographs of the Lynite Laboratories published in the 17 July 1919
issue of *Iron Age* represent the advanced metallurgical test equipment that the
Alcoa Research Bureau inherited when it absorbed Lynite Laboratories in
1920. The captions are those published with the photographs at the time.

The Channel Construction in the Floor of the Dynamics Laboratories Provides a Bed Plate Practically the Length
of the Room. Floor space is conserved by the overhead location of some of the apparatus, and an Alden absorption dyna-
mometer for rear axle tests is shown in the foreground

A Close View of the 200-Hp. and 500-Hp. Dynamometers and
Their Respective Control Panels on the Switchboard

In Circle, the Weighing System of the Dynamometers. The
scale reads the number of pounds of torque at a 63-in. arm.
and makes horsepower calculation easy

formed its own advisory committee of the same people who advised the Research Bureau, it ran into the same dilemma, a dilemma that had been faced earlier by the Lynite Laboratories: Whether in research or development, there was an unavoidable tension between those facing a demanding marketplace and those shaping the technical capability to support them. The TDB could not possibly expand rapidly enough to handle all of the demands from the various works for routine technical support.[56]

THE RESEARCH BUREAU PROGRAM

Aside from completing unfinished projects, Frary's early research platform focused on his need to build an institution. His objectives were to win credibility by addressing a list of new "live" problems identified by the works managers as critical, to define the state of the art by collecting and translating a base of knowledge about aluminum already available in the literature, mostly European, and to conduct fundamental studies of an academic nature that would extend the existing knowledge base and provide the basis for further applications. Achieving a balance in the pursuit of these objectives would always be the art of the possible, circumscribed by the current concerns of the company and the availability of suitable manpower.[57]

Beginning with a small research force of only six trained researchers and a librarian, Frary set about demonstrating the value of existing knowledge. Sometimes it was a simple matter of finding journal articles or identifying patents that already existed, though Frary's ability to recognize what level of knowledge was readily usable at the works may have been questionable. When Charles Moritz sent Frary a list of subjects that concerned his managers of smelting and carbon plants, for instance, Frary sent him by return mail a synopsis of an article that covered the relationship between bath composition and conductivity from *Revue Metallurgie*.[58]

During its first year, the Research Bureau worked on 51 problems, plus some with the TDB, and answered numerous library requests. As the organization grew, Frary left researchers who were on continuing projects in place. Newcomers were assigned to other projects that could be completed quickly and without too much dependence on outsiders. These included, for instance, determining the causes of variability in the conductivity of wire, an issue raised by the wire mills. Also in this category were experimentation with and study of the reduction process at Badin and Massena and studies of chemical by-products of the Bayer process at East St. Louis.[59]

Frary's main chance to build credibility with the skeptical operations and sales executives was to show financial results, the measurement they understood. The potential cost savings from two or three projects in the primary-process area provided that opportunity. One of his first efforts was to win independence from expensive foreign technologies. In the first two years of work he quickly disposed of the Doremus process for extracting alumina using nitric acid, and he addressed the Serpek process, for which Alcoa was paying a French company

a $100,000 annual license fee without being able to make it
work.

The Serpek process, which became "our major problem for a
number of years," illustrated only too well the dilemma of relying on available technology, and then not providing enough
technical resources to implement it immediately. When Alcoa
first bought the rights to the Serpek process, its prime attraction was that, through furnace treatment of bauxite to produce
aluminum nitride and subsequent digestion of the aluminum
nitride, it produced both high-grade alumina and a by-product,
ammonia, that brought a high price in the prewar period. But
the process was extremely difficult to master, involving very
high temperatures and close temperature control, for which
Alcoa lacked adequate instrumentation. After Hall's death,
Blough had tried it at New Kensington, and then Hoopes at
Massena, but neither could work on it full-time. Although they
did not know it, during the war a government laboratory in
Washington started producing artificial ammonia. After the
war, the General Chemical Company commercialized this process and wiped out the market for high-priced ammonia. Frary
assigned most of his early hires to continuing the Serpek investigation, and he involved the Mellon Institute by assigning one of
his researchers to a fellowship there. He thereby determined
that the Serpek process produced alumina of no better quality
than that produced by the Bayer process, and he decided that
in the absence of additional revenue from ammonia, the Serpek
process did not justify its extra cost.[60]

In addition to stopping unnecessary payments for technology, Frary found other ways to improve the revenue picture. One fruitful discovery, such as the way to make salable
aluminum chloride from dross, or implementation of an improved design for carbon electrodes and the equipment used
to secure them in the smelting pots at Massena, would easily
pay for the entire year's research budget. Another early success was the work done by Junius D. Edwards and Robert
I. Wray to extend the use of aluminum powder for pigment
in paint, work that proved its worth so rapidly that the Logan's Ferry powder works, built for wartime supply of powder for explosives, was able to be converted to this product
soon after the war and quickly found its business exceeding
capacity.[61]

The distinct advantage of concentrating in the areas of smelting and refining was that significant improvements there would have effects on all processes further down the chain. Yet, even as Frary focused on improving the Hall-Héroult and Bayer processes, he hoped for a radical discovery, the same that Hall had sought, a breakthrough that would replace the existing processes and significantly reduce production costs. That was the motivation behind the effort to develop Hoopes's electrolytic refining process on a large scale, with the idea that it could be used to produce commercial-grade aluminum from aluminum-copper alloy, circumventing the costly step of refining bauxite to alumina through the Bayer process. The problems that had plagued the Hoopes cell when he had worked on it under Hall were solved by a thorough investigation of bath composition, completed by Junius Edwards in 1920. After that, a companion process was developed to produce a suitable alloy electrothermally, and in 1923 a pilot plant was set up at Badin for what was now called the Hoopes reduction process. Within a year it was demonstrated that the Hoopes process, though it worked as an additional refining step to produce aluminum of the highest purity, could not be used for direct reduction of bauxite as hoped. By 1924 Frary was ready to state categorically that no viable radical alternatives to the Hall-Héroult process existed. "We have therefore come to the conclusion," he stated, "that our only hopes of reducing the cost of producing aluminum lie in the reduction of the cost of making the ore and in the perfecting and cheapening of the Hall electrolytic reduction process."[62]

This hunt for the elusive radical alternative would reemerge from time to time at Alcoa, and large amounts of time and money would be spent to come to the same conclusion that Frary reached. The work on the Hoopes refining process, however, though falling short of its original radical intent, demonstrated the value of another kind of project, one that would occupy more of the agenda when the easy marks had been exhausted. These were projects that laid the groundwork for future research achievements. Just as the Edwards bath-composition project had been necessary to revive the Hoopes process, so the availability of high-purity (99.9 percent) aluminum was a prerequisite for an accelerated alloy research program.[63]

Meanwhile, at Cleveland, Zay Jeffries and Robert Archer continued their work that focused on product research, while contributing to the fundamental understanding of aluminum-base alloys and of key phenomena such as precipitation hardening. The effort to find a substitute for 17S led to the development of an aluminum-copper-chromium alloy that showed great promise and an improved ferroaluminum alloy with silicon added to reduce the detrimental effects of iron.[64]

Here competitive priorities played a large role in shaping the research program. No Alcoa research location felt the urgency of rapid discovery more than did Cleveland. Building on the fundamental work in metallurgy done in government laboratories before the war, many companies were pushing to develop new alloys. Jeffries had to push ahead with alloy development "so as to anticipate other people in finding and commercializing useful aluminum alloys." He kept in close touch with what information was available both in the United States and abroad, and it was clear that both foreign and local companies were patenting new alloys at a rapid rate. In England, Rosenhain's Y alloys, aluminum-zinc compositions that hardened at room temperature, came into their own in casting shops supplying Rolls-Royce and other automakers. Aluminum-silicon alloys achieved rapid acceptance for auto parts in several European countries, having some very attractive properties, especially resistance to corrosion and thermal stability. Alcoa licensed one modified aluminum-silicon alloy from the French inventor Aladar Pacz.[65]

Alpax or Silumin, as Pacz's alloy containing 13 percent silicon was known in France and Germany, respectively, achieved instant acceptance for sand casting among European automakers. But it took much longer to catch on in the United States. American automakers were more interested in working properties, low machining costs, and regularity of production, and early aluminum-silicon alloys were difficult to work. Another reason for their slow dissemination was that Alcoa preferred to sell products that were fabricated or at least modified in some way, such as through chilling or by heat treating, processes for which Alcoa controlled the patents. In 1923 the aluminum foundry

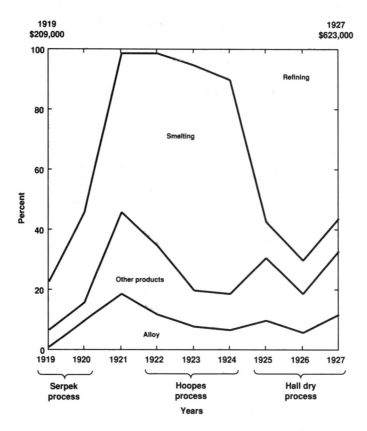

Figure 3.6. Research Bureau program emphasis, 1919–27. Program categories as percentages of total expenditures. Source: Research Bureau annual reports, ALA.

Table 3.1. *Research Bureau (RB) staff locations 1919–28 (end-of-year totals)*

Year	RB Total	New Kensington	Cleveland	Badin	East St. Louis	Massena	Buffalo
1919	28	28					
1920	31	26	5				
1921	17.5	13	4.5				
1922	26	14	5	7			
1923	43	22	4	14	3		
1924	50	30	6	10	4		
1925	55	32	7	12	4		
1926	61	37	7	11	5	1	
1927	66	42	6	10	5	1	2

Source: Alcoa Laboratories History, Vol. 1B, *Alcoa Plant Histories.*

industry had too much capacity, and Alcoa was not anxious to create more competition for itself in that area.[66]

The Cleveland laboratory also took responsibility for perfecting the procedures associated with heat treating and extending the use of these procedures to all Alcoa foundries. They advised on the introduction of new alloys to the foundries and gave advice and training to customer establishments in new foundry techniques. These customers were, of course, also competitors in the castings market. At first, Alcoa's policy was to license alloys for which it owned the rights to all who asked, free of charge. Eventually its policy changed to licensing only foundries that proved themselves qualified to handle the complicated processes involved. At Jeffries's suggestion, Alcoa eventually alleviated the problem of having to train customers in alloy composition and pouring by copying the policy of some French aluminum companies that sold alloys in ingot form. That made it even more important that the Alcoa reduction operations improve their practices. Jeffries noted as late as 1923 that the Massena works, for instance, still sometimes shipped material of terribly wrong proportions, such as a batch of nominally 13 percent silicon alloy that contained 16 percent silicon, or metal rendered so unusable by extraneous iron that the naked eye could detect the error. Another potential source of error in the system, and certainly a major reason for its high costs, was Alcoa's subsidiary, Aluminum Ore Company, the supplier of alumina. It, too, was now receiving attention from the center.[67]

In 1923 a chemical research laboratory was set up at the Aluminum Ore Company in East St. Louis, primarily for the purpose of addressing persistent problems with the Bayer process. One of these was the high consumption of expensive filter cloth, which deteriorated rapidly when the level of heat and the concentration of the digestion liquor were inadequately controlled. Another was inconsistency of the grain or crystal size of the alumina produced. When the crystal structure was too fine, quantities of alumina were lost in the form of dust. Experimental attempts to reduce the cost of the Bayer process that were not based on an understanding of the fundamentals involved invariably caused the quality of the alumina to suffer.

The Aluminum Ore Company on its own could have made money providing its more expensive ore to Alcoa's smelters, but

Alcoa's East St. Louis site, including both the refinery works and the East St. Louis research laboratory.

the company as a whole needed cheaper ore and was willing to invest corporate money in a long-term systematic research program to get it. The laboratory set up to do this work was located at East St. Louis because there was no room at New Kensington. East St. Louis agreed to take ownership of a laboratory devoted to long-term work because the Research Bureau's work on alternatives to the Bayer process had convinced the company that it had to improve the Bayer process economics. However, the special status of the East St. Louis laboratory – a satellite of the Research Bureau, jointly funded by the corporation and one of its major works – would in time give rise to just the kind of organizational ambiguities that Hoopes and Fickes had wished to avoid when they advocated a central, neutral location for corporate R&D.[68]

The shape of the program at East St. Louis reflected the kind of mix between fundamental research directed toward long-term ends and work on more immediate applied problems that would typify the research program at all parts of the Research Bureau after 1923. From 1923 until the mid-1930s the East St.

Louis laboratory (ESL) worked on fundamental problems related to the Bayer process and on finding by-products that would offset the high costs of refining. The "careful study of the whole Bayer Process of dissolving alumina" involved, for example, a study of solubility of alumina in caustic soda at various temperatures and the gathering of the fundamental information necessary for understanding the control of the fineness of the hydrate produced during the precipitation process. In its early years, ESL also worked on recovering soda and making paint from the red-mud residue that resulted from the Bayer process, in addition to work on improving its by-products, such as alumina hydrate for the chemical industry and calcined alumina for abrasives. In 1925, based on its research results, the plant commenced to produce sodium aluminate, trade-named Alcofloc, for use as a water purifier. The sale of this and other by-products expanded rapidly after 1927. Meanwhile, the fundamental study of the solubility of alumina resulted in an "elaborate report" that was used in controlling the East St. Louis operations.[69]

THE 1923 TURNING POINT: REFOCUS ON RESEARCH

The year 1923 marked a critical turning point for the Technical Department. Resources were available, the need was recognized, and conditions were favorable to refocus a significant portion of the entire effort on fundamental research. The company's fortunes had taken a turn for the better as ingot production surpassed wartime levels for the first time. Despite continued increases in foreign imports, it was possible to expect to make money from ingot production. The Research Bureau had resolved, or at least laid to rest, all the problems from the experimental backlog, and the new Research Bureau employees had enough experience in the field to be familiar with the company they had joined and its processes. The TDB's 17S program for the navy had been successfully concluded, leaving the TDB free to pursue full-time its original mandate. The cumulative effect of these achievements was to bring a reconsideration of old research priorities, accompanied by renewed pressure from sales and operations people to get the Research Bureau to focus on matters of concern to them. Chief among these were matters that the TDB had identified as serious gaps in its ability to meet its objective of "better aluminum cheaper."

Earl Blough.

In 1923, in a memo that articulated his personal technical vision, Earl Blough called for a redivision of research responsibilities between the TDB and the Research Bureau. He believed that research in support of metalworking, as opposed to refining and metalmaking, was receiving too little attention. He proposed that the TDB be permitted to go beyond the work of responding to the requests of other organizations and do its own fundamental research on the chemical properties of aluminum and aluminum alloys. The TDB should approach the problem of alloys from an academic viewpoint. "We believe," wrote Blough, "that correct knowledge of the facts involved holds the solution of one of the most important, if not the most important, technical problems confronting the aluminum industry." Similar fundamental work was proposed for the Testing Division, to establish general testing methodology and to acquire necessary basic data. Blough also wanted to extend the program at the experimental mill to look into rolling fundamentals, which he believed to be key to the "very essence of sheet mill operation."[70]

The Blough proposal reflected, in part, issues that had arisen between the TDB and the Research Bureau. Their mutual dependence was difficult for both when they were focusing on the two different sides of the business: the Research Bureau on primary metalmaking and the TDB on metal fabricating and metalworking. The TDB wanted research done at its behest, to serve its problem-solving agenda for the plants. The Research Bureau, in turn, needed the TDB's equipment and skills, especially testing, and it wanted its work to be given higher priority by the TDB.

The TDB was unable to fulfill its original purpose without better technical information, and in any case Blough wanted a more interesting brief. Yet his suggestion was not so much a criticism of the Research Bureau's priorities as it was a call for expansion of effort. Blough asserted that neither his own analytical division nor any other organization in the company was currently equipped to conduct the research needed without reorganization and additional staff. If qualifications were considered, Blough's training and experience as chemist and metallurgist were not as strong as Frary's for metallurgical research, but he had had more exposure to the problem of setting standards in plants. The Research Bureau's Cleveland branch had equally appropriate or perhaps even better skills for such a program, but it was too far away and too small to serve the purpose Blough had in mind: improvement of standards in the wrought-alloy side of the business. Moreover, Cleveland was fully occupied with ongoing work on physical questions: the heat treatment and age hardening of alloys.[71]

The Research Committee deliberated the issues that Blough raised, but came up with a compromise solution, granting him only part of his request. Acknowledging the need for improving the quality of fabricated products, especially sheet, it extended funding for the TDB to expand its work on rolling in the experimental mill. However, the committee reaffirmed the existing division of research and development within the Technical Department. Rather than assign fundamental work in metallurgy to the TDB, it chose to make the program of the Research Bureau more balanced between the two sides of the business, primary production and fabrication, by expanding its metallurgical division. In this way the committee implicitly acknowledged the importance of this research by locating it where immediate demands from operations would be less likely to drive out long-term work. At the same time, it reinforced the interdependence of the Research Bureau and the TDB by creating a Technical Direction Committee, parallel to and with the same membership as the Research Committee. Eventually the Research Bureau obtained some small-scale rolling equipment of its own, which gave its metallurgical division a degree of independence in alloy development. But until that happenend, the R&D program in metallurgy was strictly a cooperative effort.

In accordance with these decisions, in late 1923 the Research Bureau was restructured with a larger staff to create a large metallurgical division under Jeffries, with two sections, one in Cleveland under Archer, the other in New Kensington under Edgar Dix. Dix had been part of the Lynite Laboratories in 1920, but had transferred immediately to the TDB in New Kensington to work on the 17S program. His move to the Research Bureau ensured that the new program in metallurgy would be closely coordinated with both the TDB and the group under Jeffries and Archer in Cleveland and that it would be strongly fundamental in emphasis. With high-purity aluminum becoming available for research purposes from the new Hoopes refining process, conditions were ripe to mount such an initiative.[72]

Unlike the first set of research achievements, for which the groundwork was already in place, systematic work in new alloys was a matter of years rather than months. According to the careful research traditions established by the NBS and rigorously adhered to by the Alcoa researchers, if the chemical compositions of alloys were to be understood in full, they needed to be studied not in isolation but as complete alloy systems. In view of the Research Committee's announced priority, Dix chose silicon alloys as his test case – his first fundamental micrographic study of aluminum-alloy systems. In some ways this high-visibility product was an unfortunate choice, for it quickly focused the obvious conflict of interest between the managers, who wanted "quick and dirty" answers to immediate problems, and the researchers, who were striving for complete understanding of a class of problems. Edward K. Davis, nephew of A. V. Davis and head of Alcoa's Sales Department, complained that by focusing on fundamental study rather than on the working of silicon alloys, Alcoa was leaving its customers in the dark longer than necessary. He blamed Silumin's failure in the United States on the lack of sophistication of U.S. customers who did not know how to make it, and he thought Alcoa should help them. This was not a problem Dix's work was likely to remedy. Davis grumbled to Blough: "It makes one feel cheap to spend so much time in this matter of silumin only to see everybody else [i.e., foundries overseas] make a success of it but us."[73]

On the other hand, Dix's thorough treatment of the silicon-aluminum alloys eventually produced a whole new class of alloys, each with its own special characteristics. Somewhat later, the same work made possible a highly desirable piston design, as well as effective use of silicon alloys for die casting and structural applications.[74]

Another success from Dix's alloy work came in 1927 when he discovered a method of bonding a corrosion-resistant pure-aluminum coating to high-strength-alloy ingot in such a way that it could be rolled into sheet and still retain a uniform coating. This innovation was an outgrowth of a systematic corrosion study begun in 1924 that led to a metallographic study of the mechanism of intergranular corrosion. Dix later noted that his idea for this process was stimulated by experiments in spray-coating alloys with pure aluminum, conducted by Gillett at the NBS; the bonding idea he traced to an accidental discovery reported earlier by Frary when he had tried rolling aluminum alloys between plates of pure aluminum to avoid surface cracking. As with so many individual inventions, it was Dix's insight that two previously unconnected phenomena could be combined for a useful purpose. The product that resulted from his discovery – Alclad sheet – revolutionized aircraft construction, solving the problem of corrosion that had plagued the all-metal aircraft since its inception.[75]

At a more mundane level, the additions to the Research Bureau greatly exacerbated the pressure for space. Frary recalled later that "we had overflowed our quarters down at the plant; we had inherited the stable when the last horse died. We had a shed along there that had been very recently used by the paint staff of the Works and we just couldn't get along." Until new facilities were added or a major redistribution of staff occurred, R&D activities would increasingly be conducted under hardship conditions. That was important, because it was difficult for new work of any kind to be started, or newcomers attracted, when current researchers complained of noisome fumes.[76]

After the first several years of building the organization and establishing its credibility, Frary gained a large measure of autonomy to define his own research program. It was a difficult program to balance because the hybrid nature of the production system required so many forms of technical expertise. The decision to locate metallurgical research directly in the Research Bureau attested to undiminished respect for Frary on the part of the Research Committee and its implicit belief that he possessed the necessary technical objectivity. It also reinforced the Research Bureau's position as a *corporate* research organization, charged with comprehensively addressing long-term work related to all parts of the company, no matter what disciplines were required. Frary's leadership role and his ability to get along with the other parts of the Technical Department became more important when William Hoopes died in 1924. Hoopes's good-natured enthusiasm and problem-solving tenacity were sorely missed by his colleagues, so much so that Frary still paid special tribute to him decades later.[77]

Until 1928, Alcoa was directly involved in international operations. The Research Bureau was responsible for ensuring that Alcoa's foreign works, with different raw materials and different production conditions, had processes that were appropriate

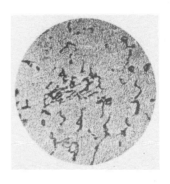

Systematic study of alloys, such as the program on casting alloys conducted at Cleveland, was continually enhanced by improvements in microscopes and the research techniques involved in preparing cross sections of metal for examination. This photomicrograph shows the physical structure of Duralumin, forged, quenched, and heat-treated at 200°C for 2 hours, here shown at ×500 magnification. (From "Delving into Metal Structures," *Iron Age*, 1 April 1926, p. 904.)

for them. It was Frary who handled the external contact. He travelled frequently in the mid-1920s, finding processes that might apply to operations outside the United States and testing out their transferability to domestic operations.

In 1925, Frary redirected the resources of the Research Bureau to revisit the Hall dry process for making alumina. It had little utility for U.S. conditions, though it was suitable for the large new refining and smelting operation in Canada, called Arvida after Arthur Vining Davis. After piloting at Badin in North Carolina, the Hall dry process was pushed along rapidly and installed in full-scale operation at Arvida in 1927. The tariff barriers between Canada and the United States made it uneconomical to import Arvida-produced aluminum, so the dry process "never got anywhere," according to Frary. But for the head of Alcoa's research program, it served an important purpose. The appearance of competitive processes, first the Hoopes reduction process and then the Hall dry process, under development throughout the 1920s, shook the East St. Louis managers out of their complacency and forced them to improve their Bayer process. To Frary, this effect alone was enough to justify the time spent on the dry process. This form of regeneration of old processes – in which technical personnel committed to a particular technology were stimulated by the threat of its replacement to mount R&D programs aimed at major cost savings – might not be counted officially as a payoff to R&D investment, but it was always a potential reward.[78]

During this period, Frary also discovered technologies in Norway that were worthy of further notice. One was the Pedersen process, which involved smelting a mixture of bauxite, limestone, and coke to produce a low-sulfur iron of salable quality, along with a calcium aluminate slag that could be reduced to alumina. This turned out to be less useful in the United States than in Norway, where the iron content of the available bauxite was unusually high, and where Alcoa had an interest in Norsk Aluminum. The second was the Soderberg electrode, already in use in Europe for calcium carbide and ferroalloy production. This electrode was composed of a self-baking carbon paste that could be replenished continuously, eliminating the need for separate carbon baking and the fre-

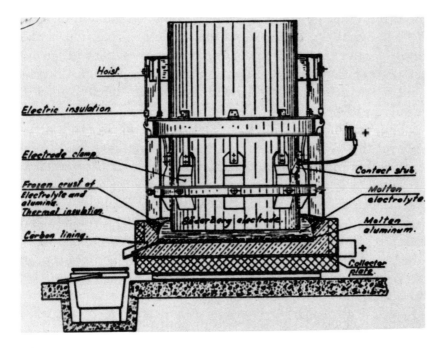

This is a diagram of an early Soderberg electrode. (From M. Sem, J. Sejersted, and O. Bockmann, "Twenty-five Years' Development in the Soderberg System in Aluminum Furnaces," *Electrochemical Society Journal*, vol. 94, November 1948, p. 222.) A 16,000-ampere experimental version of this pot was installed at Alcoa's Badin, North Carolina, plant, challenging the performance of the conventional electrode smelters both in efficiency and in purity of output.

quent replacement of carbon anodes, with its attendant disruption of the smelting process. This innovation was adapted for aluminum smelting by the Operations Department at Badin, funded by the Research Bureau. By 1927, full-scale Soderberg pots had been put into operation in the reduction works at Alcoa, Tennessee.

ACCOMPLISHMENTS AND OMISSIONS

By 1927, Frary was able to claim some significant accomplishments for the Research Bureau, so visible that their value could not be lost on Alcoa's management. He was scrupulous in apportioning credit to the other organizations that had played even the smallest part in the work. But at the same time he was able to give the company's senior executives the powerful sense that he had placed the company in control of its own aluminum technology and of any technologies that might touch on aluminum. This technological protection was a new form of protection, and a more reassuring one, than the patent protection that had run out 20 years earlier. Alcoa was *the* Aluminum Company of America, and in the next era its research organization, suitably housed, would justly be called *the* Aluminum Research Laboratories.

The one thing that might be called a serious research omission in the program of the Technical Department had to do with aluminum for the auto market. After the 1920–1 recession in auto sales, aluminum's share of the growing auto market, especially car bodies, declined steadily. Even in absolute terms, sales for auto construction declined, while steel for bodies and cast iron for crankcases made great inroads. Frary, pointing to the proportionately higher usage of aluminum in the European auto industry, blamed the loss of this critical market on economic factors in the United States:

Cheap gasoline and easy-money conditions among the purchasers in this country have permitted our automobile industry to sacrifice operating economy in favor of a lower first cost, by building heavier cars than the European manufacturers. The use of aluminum to reduce weight and increase mileage per gallon has gone so much further abroad than here that it is estimated that if the American manufacturers should use as much aluminum per car as the European makers do, the automobile industry alone would consume more than the present world's production of this metal.[79]

Business Week reported that Alcoa shifted its emphasis away from trying to sell auto-body sheet toward auto parts and other structural markets in the transportation business after the firm made the mistake, in the early 1920s, of hiring an English auto designer to design a demonstration car, thus alienating the Detroit companies. However, two larger factors seem to have affected the auto market for aluminum, one of which could be attributed to research oversight. The first, for which research was not responsible, was that automakers would not buy material from a single-source supplier. Henry Ford is said to have scrapped much aluminum-working equipment when Alcoa raised its price "once too often." What aluminum he did buy, he purchased either from the scrap market or as ready-made parts from Bohn Bronze Aluminum and Brass Company. General Motors bought relatively little. Some top-of-the-line U.S. automakers, such as Pierce-Arrow, were known for the aluminum in

The Pierce-Arrow, with a cast-aluminum body, that belonged to Charles Martin Hall. The child seated in the car is a neighbor's daughter.

their cars, but the enduring automakers in the United States emphasized low first cost rather than low running cost. The second factor, which was research-related, was the lack of a satisfactory method of welding strong aluminum alloys. Fast, effective, and nondestructive welding was essential to the U.S. car industry of the 1920s, with its growing emphasis on mass production, but Alcoa did not develop the necessary technique until the 1940s.[80]

At one point, Alcoa purchased the American Auto Body Company to make a more concerted assault on that market, but the Research Bureau did almost no work on the problem of welding in the 1920s. What it did was at the request of the Sales Department, which wanted to market thin aluminum sheet for washing-machine tanks. The high-water mark for welding research in that period came in 1928, when $4,000 of a $600,000 budget was allocated to research in welding applications, mainly for aluminum furniture and the seams of aluminum boats, both products sold to the navy. The TDB also worked on welding at about the same time, but only as an afterthought, "as opportunity permits."[81]

The Technical Department program of the 1920s clearly reflected the limits of Alcoa's strategic vision at the time when it came to serving markets like the auto market. Though it had stretched to include both sides of the hybrid business, metalmaking and metalworking, its markets were defined strictly in terms of intermediate products. It was still up to the end-product producers to perform any applications research necessary to adapt aluminum for their own production processes.

ISSUES OF INTEGRATION

When the Technical Department was formed in 1919, Frary was a newcomer. He had respectable credentials, but others in Alcoa's technical community – especially Jeffries and Blough – had more experience with the company and much more credibility with its management. A decade later, Frary would emerge as the leader of Alcoa's entire R&D organization, the others having moved to new phases in their careers. All the evidence suggests that this was a natural progression on the part of the parties involved. Frary's career advanced within the Technical Department and its successor organizations; the others chose advancement outside. At the same time, Frary's success was based in part on his ability to incorporate their different technical visions into a composite vision, a technical platform strong enough for the entire company.

Vague references to problems of personnel are the only clues that remain to the stresses of integration that must have beset the unifying Technical Department in its early years. It would have been odd for one organization to have been created out of several forerunners without some discord. Lynite Laboratories, which had already achieved fame in the metals world on its own account, may have been a heavy meal for the infant Research Bureau to digest. There is, however, no evidence that Frary and Jeffries ever clashed. Jeffries was personable, dynamic, and unusually skillful at communicating in terms nonscientists could appreciate, and he was well known to Alcoa's top management. He and Frary seem to have developed an effective working relationship, and publications were later to come out under their joint authorship. Having already devoted 10 years of his career to building and running a laboratory, Jeffries may have welcomed someone else to shoulder the responsibility, leaving him the chance to do the research work that he was eager to do. When that work was finished, he sought more interesting problems in the larger organizational context of General Electric, where he eventually became a vice-president.[82]

The relationship between the Research Bureau and the TDB, sister organizations jammed into cramped shared quarters and competing for common resources, may have been slightly more difficult at first. Earl Blough, as former chief chemist and metallurgist, had reason to regard Frary as something of an upstart. Yet the two men probably were well suited to their respective parts of the Technical Department. Frary was far less inclined to be a bridge figure between research and operations than was Blough. After the Blough proposal of 1923 and the compromise that came out of it, there remains no evidence of ill-feeling on either side. Again, these were complementary personalities. Blough could get along in the plants, he could play a role in the American Chemical Society, and he could propose to direct academic-style studies. He saw no inevitable conflict between his preferred work and the demands of operations. Frary was happy in a narrower range of activities. He had joined Alcoa to escape contact with plant operations, and he devoted much of his institution-building effort to shielding his research staff from plant intrusion.

From the mid-1920s on, Frary displayed the style that would characterize his 30-year period of leadership. He was able to accommodate and give consideration to a technical vision broader than his own. His personal values were those of the consummate scientist, not the corporate manager. Unlike Blough or Jeffries, who both became vice-presidents, though neither at Alcoa, Frary cared for professional standing more than organizational standing or the politics that could accompany it. For Frary himself, personal satisfaction was tied to original work, and his ambitions were more likely fulfilled by the professional honors he achieved. Having no particular interest in advancement within the corporate hierarchy, he did not compete with those who wished to advance. He did not receive promotion outside R&D, and his disregard for this type of reward made him somewhat impervious to the criticisms of nontechnical managers who complained about his program. His authority within the company derived, first, from the thoroughness and the quality of the work that his organization performed and, second, from its economic value to the company in an era when there were big problems to be solved.

It was characteristic of Frary to see to it that the aluminum knowledge base was constructed as others would erect an edifice, careful brick by careful brick. Once in place, the structure might be used for all manner of purposes. Though he was not one to enjoy hobnobbing at plants, Frary dealt effectively with Alcoa's top management on terms they cared about. He became a master at conveying in his reports the sense that he had mobilized the forces of scientific inquiry to deal, once and for all, with even the smallest of the myriad problems of aluminum production. He was not shy about laying claim to the definitive, and he justified expenditure on fundamental work partly on this basis. Regarding the fundamental work on alloy systems, he commented that it would be published "in such a form that the work will be recognized as authoritative and need never be repeated by others." He calmly justified throwing large sums of money at a promising new process, and he was equally calm about announcing the arrival at a dead end, looking at it as a necessary experimental step completed before moving on, rather than as a costly failure.[83]

These characteristics of the Frary style made him a somewhat controversial figure with nontechnical managers. Although the technical organizations quickly achieved harmony in the early 1920s, friction occurred between the Technical Department as a whole and the operating divisions. In the late 1930s, the building of the R&D organization two decades earlier was remembered as a period of considerable discord between the technical and the nontechnical parts of the company. Frary's request that all new development projects mounted at the works laboratories be reported to the central laboratory, for instance, was taken as an infringement on the autonomy of the works laboratories. Charles Moritz, who had earlier accepted Hall's more intrusive behavior with aplomb, complained that Frary's reporting requirement would stifle all the initiative among his staff and work against "high grade men who take an interest in their work and wish to improve process operations."[84]

Frary also had difficulty educating senior management to accept the conditions that were necessary to support a fruitful science-based program, and from time to time he had to fight battles, or at least stand firm, on matters of policy or principle. It was especially hard to convince A. V. Davis of the value and necessity of allowing two-way flow of information between Alcoa and the rest of the scientific and professional community. That had long been a sore point with Davis. He made acerbic comments to Hall, for instance, when Joseph Richards returned from a trip to France at Alcoa's expense and addressed a meeting of the Chemical Society about what he had seen of the Serpek process in the French company that originated it.[85]

Frary insisted that researchers would soon lose access to outside information if they could not participate in conferences and publish papers, and he argued that no "good" scientist would work for a company that did not provide such opportunities. Early in Frary's tenure, the issue arose when Zay Jeffries submitted to Hoopes for routine approval a paper he had agreed to present to an automotive industry conference in Detroit in 1920. A. V. Davis vetoed the entire presentation on grounds that although no material was cited that was not already in the public domain, associating the ideas with Alcoa would signal competitors of Alcoa's intentions. Hoopes and Frary agreed between them that this was not an area where Davis could be allowed to prevail, and in this case he did not. No matter how legitimate Davis's concerns about competition, they argued, the need to allow for publication was central to the ability to build and keep an effective industrial research organization.[86]

Alcoa's senior management also showed a tendency to intervene in the technical program during the immediate postwar period in ways that sometimes verged on nuisance. Davis and Hunt both were capable of going outside channels to redeploy people or to insist on investigation of some new alternative process. The general feeling in the Technical Department was that this was just as disruptive as demands made by the operating units, demands they argued should be avoided by locating the Research Bureau apart from individual plants. In one sense, though, the effect of interference by Davis and Hunt may have been healthy – there was no question during this era that R&D mattered at the highest levels of the company.[87]

INTERNALIZATION

Alcoa's construction of an integrated R&D organization to complete the integration of its production system did not set it apart from its corporate peers in the period around World War I. Few substantial science-based companies of the time chose to do otherwise, and most had the same main objectives in mind: control, response to competitive threat, and the search for technical opportunity. Indeed, it is difficult to imagine how Alcoa could have built a successful aluminum business in the 1920s without some form of coordinated technical effort: The needs of science-based mass production were too compelling, advances in science were creating too many opportunities, and although the company was charged repeatedly with monopoly behavior, it had too many perceived competitors on its horizon to risk the uncharted seas of science-based enterprise without this form of navigational aid.

But if the internalization of R&D was an unremarkable business choice at the time, Alcoa's way of doing it was worthy of note. One historian of the period has recorded that although the conversion to mass production was virtually the American thing to do between 1900 and 1920, metalmaking and metalworking had the hardest time achieving it. Although modern factory management was first fully worked out in metals industries, mass production took longer to achieve in these industries than in the mechanical or refining industries because the materials were so hard to process and more difficult to work. Alcoa's conversion, involving a hybrid system of refining, metal production, and metalworking, each stage with its own particular complement of scientific knowledge, was exceptionally difficult.[88]

Moreover, the job was done well, so well that when Walter Rosenhain, the vocal opponent of industrialization of R&D in England, visited the Cleveland Castings Department of the Alcoa Research Bureau in 1923, he was moved to recant publicly his views opposing in-house industrial R&D. Perhaps the greatest authority on metallurgical research establishments of his time, Rosenhain had visited research laboratories and factories throughout Europe and the United States, and he was renowned for his disapproval of most research activity that did not go on under the roof of his own laboratory.[89] Yet, on his return to England he wrote the following:

At [Alcoa's] Cleveland laboratory and at the works of the Aluminum Company of America, particularly, there was ample evidence of the far-reaching application of scientific methods, not only in the industrial processes, but in regard to actual research. . . . While it may perhaps be fairly claimed that a large amount of the fundamental and pioneer work of metallurgical research, particularly in regard to aluminum alloys, has been done in England, there can be no doubt that the results of that work have been, and are being, more fully exploited in America under highly competent scientific guidance.[90]

Had Frary and his recruits been asked for their opinion on industrialization of science as they prepared to begin work at Alcoa at the end of the war, they doubtless would have demonstrated the same bias as Rosenhain. Their fondest wish was to achieve the seclusion they saw necessary for good original research. Yet the decade during which they had to wait to realize that objective was a fruitful one. As Blough made clear in his 1923 proposal for metallurgical research, the direct personal experience of operations was immensely productive of fundamental questions. It set up a creative tension that could be achieved in no other way.

Understandably, the wish for a well-equipped laboratory at a neutral location, or at least at a decent remove from the fumes of smelting, remained a high-priority objective for the Technical Department leadership. Its achievement in the next era of equipoise allowed the R&D organization to capitalize on the creative tension between fundamental research and applications by creating a satellite structure for advanced development. But in the 1920s, what Hoopes, Blough, Jeffries, and Frary had been trying to build was not a facility but a balanced R&D community, capable of generating useful knowledge and applying it to industry, and in that, as Rosenhain's assessment clearly shows, they were succeeding.

None of the other companies that competed in Alcoa's markets, whether international aluminum companies, domestic foundries, or suppliers of sheet and other fabricated products, was as integrated as Alcoa, and therefore none attempted to master the whole complicated spectrum of technical activities. It was a daunting task, not uniformly successful, but the fact of technical integration was what gave the company the ultimate advantage as an industrial innovator. It was this advantage that was displayed in Alcoa's most important project of its first international era: the project to supply high-strength aluminum for the U.S Navy's airship *Shenandoah*.

4

The Shenandoah

ZR-1 [the *Shenandoah*] flew over New Kensington a few days ago en
route to St. Louis. It was a beautiful sight and I cannot help but
feel that this ship made a wonderful impression on its trip. You
may also know that it was no small amount of personal satisfaction
to see the ship actually flying, and knowing that we, ourselves, had
put so much work upon it. I think that the Navy department is to
be congratulated on their work.[1]

For U.S. aviation, the flight of the navy's first aluminum airship
was the visible sign of a new era, the precursor of the all-metal
airplane. The substitution of light metal for wood in the construction of airships, pioneered by the German Zeppelin, would
transfer in the next decade to lighter, faster, greater-load-
bearing airplanes like the Boeing 247 and the DC-1. For Alcoa,
the event signified two important achievements: the opening of
an important and visible market and the cementing of an enduring relationship with a vital customer, the U.S. Navy. None of
this would have been possible without the integrated in-house
Technical Department that had been built in the 1920s.

It was not surprising that the naval contract for a U.S. version
of Duralumin, the German airship alloy, brought Arthur
Vining Davis to rethink his plans concerning the nature and
structure of Alcoa's in-house R&D. The navy was technically
Alcoa's most demanding customer, and though the attempt to
duplicate and improve on Duralumin and to fabricate the aluminum sheet and components from the strong alloy that resulted,
Alcoa's 17S, was not the only reason for organizing a sizable
corporate R&D capability, it was a most compelling occasion.
The airship project in its various stages was to continue for
more than a decade, playing such an important role in the
building phase of Alcoa's Technical Department that it left a
permanent stamp on aluminum R&D.[2]

The *Shenandoah*, ZR-1. (Smithsonian Institution, Photograph No. 89-16696.)

THE ZEPPELIN PROBLEM

Alcoa's agreement to supply the metal for the first phase of a U.S. dirigible program started as a high-level commitment by the company to become involved in the effort to solve what A. V. Davis called the U.S. military's "Zeppelin problem." Zeppelin warfare had its heaviest impact in Europe in the years before the United States entered the war. German Zeppelin raids made a vivid impression on the U.S. military establishment. The ultimate value of this astounding weapon was as yet unclear, but it looked as though it might be risky to ignore it. Before attempting to build a rigid airship of its own, the navy tried to buy one from the United Kingdom. Overseas armaments purchases were common, and Vickers Ltd. was willing to build an airship in the United States. Vickers was an integrated weapons builder supplying submarines and airships to the Royal Navy. It also had a controlling interest in the U.S submarine builder, the Electric Boat Company, in Groton, Connecticut, where an American airship could conceivably be constructed. The British Admiralty vetoed the sale, ensuring by that futile attempt to keep control of a new technology that it would transfer even more quickly. Writing much after the fact, Commander Jerome Hunsaker, U.S.N., noted that Vickers might well not have been able to deliver on such a project:

At this time Vickers was building rigid airships for the Admiralty in England, and claimed to be in a position to build one in the United States if the veto of the Admiralty could be overcome. The Bureau of C&R [Construction and Repair] was in negotiation with Vickers on this matter for some time, but it became clear later that Vickers was still experimenting and not really in possession of sound knowledge and experience.[3]

Commander Jerome Hunsaker, U.S. Navy. (Courtesy of the MIT Museum.)

The airships built by Vickers for the Admiralty were not successful and were never used by the Grand Fleet. Nevertheless, in 1916 Vickers was in possession of important knowledge and know-how concerning Duralumin and its use in airship design and construction. It was soon to abandon that knowledge in an economy move after the war in precisely the way Zay Jeffries had warned could happen to the Aluminum Castings Company (ACC).[4]

The desire to acquire airship technology led the U.S. Army and U.S. Navy to take the unusual step of joining forces in a common development project. A joint Army-Navy Airship Board was formed in October 1916 to build for the United States an airship of its own. Design and construction were handled by the U.S. Navy Construction and Repair Department because the navy was judged to have the most immediate need for airships for reconnaissance purposes, but expenses were borne jointly. At the end of the war, the airship work picked up steam. The navy needed this project to show those who advocated a separate air service, similar to the newly formed British Air Ministry, that an advanced airborne capability could be achieved in the United States without creating an independent third branch of the military.[5]

In July 1916 the navy's chief constructor, Admiral D. W. Taylor, approached A. V. Davis to ask Alcoa's cooperation in producing the strongest possible aluminum alloy for building a U.S. version of an airship. Although Admiral Taylor may not have understood it at the time, he was asking the company to take on a development project quite beyond the scope of its usual efforts. Alcoa's management pledged complete cooperation. Although the aviation market was tiny at the time, the potential market in shipbuilding could be large if the navy, heretofore resistant to Alcoa's every promotional gesture, could be converted to the use of aluminum.

To build the airship Admiral Taylor had in mind called for

Admiral D. W. Taylor.
(Smithsonian Institution,
Photograph No. 89-
16697.)

development of a number of fronts. He wanted an alloy as strong as the metal the Germans were using in their airship (composition then unknown to the U.S. producer), and he wanted production methods developed for extrusion, rolling, stamping, and fabricating appropriate components. The initial phase of the project would thus involve developing the new alloy in the laboratory and rolling and fabricating it in existing Alcoa production facilities, which thus far had been the standard approach to producing new products.

To meet the navy's requirement, the company assembled a team headed by Edward K. Davis, A. V. Davis's nephew. It comprised representatives from Sales (J. H. Finney in Washington), Production (A. Vail in Massena), and Engineering (E. Blough and C. Nagel from the Laboratories Department). To Earl Blough, then chief chemist and head of the Laboratories Department, the airship project was a turning point for Alcoa and certainly for his department. This was the first time in his memory that the company had tried to do research about what it would produce, rather than how it would produce it.[6]

It was important to develop a suitable material speedily, for airship design was just as much of an experimental process as was devising the new metal, and the designers awaited material specifications. As Admiral Taylor pointed out, the designers could do very little without knowing the properties of the material they would be using.[7]

Alcoa had previously tried, with no success, to produce alloys approaching the rumored strength, comparable to that of mild steel, of German Duralumin. As early as 1912, reports from Alcoa's agent in London, E. C. Darling, warned of the strong new aluminum alloy that Germany's Durener Metallwerke was producing under the Wilm patent. Blough and others in the Laboratories Department were frankly skeptical of the stories they heard of Duralumin's strength, for their attempts to roll experimental alloys containing the ingredients Duralumin was said to have ended in utter failure. Duralumin's mysterious strength was known to involve heat treating, for that much Wilm had published, but the correct temperature and the length of subsequent quenching were unknowns. Heat-treating techniques were familiar in the steel industry, but Wilm's empirical work was the first to show that heat treatment could have important hardening effects in nonferrous metals as well.

Alcoa's chief problem was that its knowledge of Wilm's achievements was confined to published writings and to rumor. Vickers had purchased the rights to Wilm's patent for both Britain and the United States and had given the U.S. rights to the Electric Boat Company.[8]

Alcoa's first response to the navy's challenge in 1916 was to start heat-treating and testing its strongest existing alloys, 6S and 15S, which contained zinc as the fortifying element. Previous analysis of an odd assortment of Zeppelin fragments had led experts to think that the important element in the strong alloys was zinc. By October 1916, Alcoa had its part of the program well under way. Working on the assumption that the structural members of the airship would be made of strong aluminum rod and bar stock, and mindful of the long lead times needed to acquire custom equipment, they ordered an expensive new mill to make 10-inch rod.[9]

New evidence then changed the project's orientation entirely. Commander Jerome Hunsaker, who taught the first course in aeronautical engineering at the Massachusetts Institute of Technology (MIT), sent Alcoa some fragments of girders that had recently been salvaged from a German Zeppelin downed in France. He sent similar fragments to the NBS, which had been working with the Duralumin problem systematically for some time. He asked if these two centers of aluminum expertise could explain the extraordinary hardness of these particular samples. The apparent availability of materials like these, lightweight yet strong, obviously had profound implications for the principles of aircraft design currently based on hardwood.[10]

Hunsaker's request led to a complete reorientation of both the navy's design and Alcoa's plans for production. Further pursuit of the aluminum-zinc alloys now seemed certain to be a blind alley; the aluminum-zinc fragments analyzed earlier probably had come from nonstructural parts of the airship, such as motor casings. The new fragments contained aluminum, copper, magnesium, and manganese. The presence of small amounts of these elements in some samples had earlier been discounted as insignificant because analysts had completely misunderstood the nature of alloy chemistry and the important role that could be played even by traces of certain elements. Moreover, the new fragments sent by Hunsaker, which were clearly from girders, showed that the structural members of this particular Zeppelin, and probably others like it, were made not of rod and bar but of parts stamped out of sheet metal.[11]

These findings changed the conceptual basis of the proposed airship design. Plans to use the new rod mill were scrapped as both the joint Army-Navy Airship Board and Alcoa returned to the drawing board. A new design and entirely new materials had to be considered. What this might entail was made clearer when the U.S. entry into the war began to give Alcoa new access to secret German information.

THE SPOILS OF WAR

When the United States and Germany went to war in April 1917, Alcoa became the beneficiary of several types of technical information, from both the Allies and the enemy, including the exact details of the Wilm Duralumin patents and a great deal of technical know-how concerning the way to produce and fabricate high-strength aluminum. Had the company not been involved in a development project with the navy at the time, its technical benefits from the war would have been far less than they were. As it was, navy construction and repair personnel, including Alcoa personnel serving in the military, took advantage of the unusual freedom of information at the time to learn all they could from other aluminum producers overseas, by fair means or, when necessary, by subterfuge.

Soon after the United States formally declared war, Alcoa obtained from the U.S. Alien Property Office a license to use the Wilm Duralumin patents in their entirety, just as the ACC did to use the patents in castings. These patents had been confiscated as alien property from the Electric Boat Company for the war's duration. Although it was then a simple matter to confirm the precise chemical composition of the Wilm alloy, it was still difficult, given the state of Wilm's documentation, to determine the amounts of heat treating and age hardening that were needed. But Alcoa technical personnel in 1917 no longer had to rely solely on trial-and-error methods. Through collaboration with George Burgess, NBS chief metallurgist, they now had access to Paul Merica's work at the NBS, illuminating hitherto unknown relationships between chemical composition and physical properties, and revealing the way alloy chemistry worked. With this added knowledge, Alcoa produced its alloy 17S, known mysteriously as "the airship metal." It appears that the Alcoa team at that time was unaware of the knowledge that Lynite Laboratories was also gaining in its research, despite the fact that the ACC was partially owned by Alcoa.

Mere possession of the knowledge of the chemical composition of the alloy was not enough, especially for wrought alloys, which then had to be rolled into sheet. Conrad ("Dutch") Nagel, then Blough's metallurgical assistant, later wrote that the patent was about as instructive in teaching one how to produce Duralumin as the most rudimentary cake recipe is for a cake. Blough's technical staff lacked an understanding of the fundamentals of heat treating and had to rely on trial-and-error methods to reproduce the strength of the alloy. Nagel said later that

I did practically all the work alone. . . . I weighed the charges, handled the remelting; when the melt seemed ready I called on plant labor to assist me in getting the crucible to the mold, and then I poured the ingot. . . . When I thought the ingot was properly cooked, I wheeled it to the Hot Mill, where it would be rolled, under the tolerant smiles of the hot roller. As often as not, the ingot broke so badly that I had to sweep the crumbs off the Hot Mill table with a broom, which in those days was considered a necessary piece of equipment when hot rolling 17S.[12]

Persistent empirical work of this laborious kind eventually produced results. Alcoa had already made, in November 1916, its own laboratory version of Duralumin. Using preliminary girder designs prepared by Hunsaker, this strong alloy was fabricated into test pieces to be shipped off to the NBS for comparison with its German counterpart. Tests showed that the girders were not as strong as the German girders, but that was believed to be the fault not of the metal but of Hunsaker's girder design. Hunsaker, by then head of airship work at the navy's Construction and Repair Department, declared the alloy problem as such to be solved. His approval gave Alcoa every reason to expect to get the larger order when it was issued. In May 1917 the NBS confirmed that the alloy met or exceeded the performance standards it was intended to match, exhibiting tensile strength of 50,000 pounds per square inch.[13]

For Alcoa, developing 17S was an important achievement, but 17S was not an ideal solution. Use of the German patent was legitimate while the war was on, but it would be open to

The flat sheet from which aluminum girders were fabricated was first rolled
on mills such as these in Alcoa's New Kensington plant, shown here in 1912.
Two men worked at each machine manhandling the sheet back and forth
through the rollers. Problems with achieving the desired levels of smoothness
and flatness, and the difficulties of metal contamination, were hard to avoid in
this environment.

challenge when the war was over, if not by the Germans then
certainly by the Electric Boat Company.[14] As Hunsaker testified
years later, the "airship metal" that Alcoa and the navy were
using was, effectively, stolen technology, and Alcoa would be in
a much more secure position were it to develop strong alloys
that were not identical in composition to Duralumin.[15]

A more immediate challenge to Alcoa's technical prowess lay
ahead, however. Having produced the hard alloy in the laboratory, means had to be found to roll it into wide sheet and fabricate channels and other forms from it. Stiffer and springier than
conventional aluminum, it proved very difficult to work, requiring different approaches to rolling and new designs for stamping dies. Months of further experimentation were needed to roll
the material to the desired flatness and smoothness. After that,
the question became how to achieve uniformity of rolling so that
all parts of a coil would be the same thickness.[16]

Alcoa's first attempt to produce 17S in quantity was in response to an order placed by the French government for several

tons of hard-alloy sheet, called Alcometal for promotional purposes. Problems with the order showed that the process was nowhere near commercial standard. The decision to produce the
material not at the headquarters plant in New Kensington,
where the laboratories were located, but at the rolling mill in
New York meant that the know-how gained in New Kensington
had to be transferred there. Earl Blough thus spent much of late
1917 at the Massena works. The material produced for the
French order displayed a dismaying assortment of defects: slivers, blisters, and buckles. Fortunately for the company's international reputation, if not for its finances, the war ended before it
could be delivered, and the French cancelled the order.[17]

While the Alcoa technical staff struggled to work out reliable
production processes, navy personnel learned as much as they
could from European plants before the curtain of secrecy was
drawn once more. A technical mission from the Bureau of Construction and Repair visited Germany, paying special attention
to the German state aluminum works at Staaken. Members of the
bureau also arranged to have themselves assigned to the Allied
peace missions so that they could engage in what amounted to
industrial espionage. Blough accompanied Commander Hunsaker, posing as his assistant, on visits to aluminum plants in England and France while the navy expressed interest in purchasing airships abroad. Little information was gleaned in answer to
direct questions, for the methods of producing hard-alloy sheet
were closely guarded trade secrets. Nevertheless, useful things
were observed, including the designs of the multiple rolling mills
at the Vickers plant in Bedford and the stretching tables used at
Staaken to achieve flatness.[18]

Navy airship designers also benefited from war booty. With
some difficulty they obtained a complete set of drawings of the
German Zeppelin L-49 from the British. Adapting those drawings as fast as possible for their own design purposes, they then
passed them to Alcoa without changing the metric measurements into the feet-and-inch measurements normally used by
Alcoa floor supervisors. Several months' delay ensued while
Alcoa's engineers revised all the measurements, only to discover
that there were grave inconsistencies between drawings. Work
could finally proceed only when a member of the navy's Construction and Repair Department came to sort them all out.[19]

This interior view of the *Shenandoah* shows its complex structure of high-strength aluminum girders assembled from channels cut from Duralumin or alloy 17S sheet. (Smithsonian Institution, Photograph No. 89-16695.)

PROTOTYPE AND PRODUCTION PHASE

The plan was to build the airship in stages, drawing on techniques of work organization that were developed for mass production of airplanes during wartime. Finished structural components for the airframe were to be shipped from Alcoa to be joined into subassemblies at the Naval Aircraft Factory, Philadelphia yard, and the subassemblies in turn were to be shipped to Lakehurst, New Jersey, for final assembly. Such "mass-production" methods were said to be much advanced over European methods, which involved careful individual fitting of each airship and therefore continuity of assembly from individual components to final airship.[20]

When the airship project entered its second phase, Alcoa embarked on a new and frustrating stage of its relationship with the navy that showed up not only the company's technical inadequacies but also the navy's cumbersome bureaucracy. The procurement process was taking such a long time that the navy

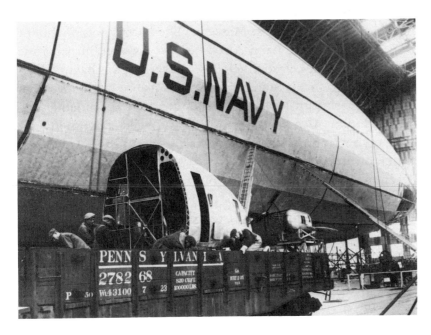

The final assembly stage of the airship's construction took place in Lakehurst, New Jersey. Subassemblies, such as the one being transported into place by railroad car in this photograph, were produced at the Naval Aircraft Factory, Philadelphia Yard, and then shipped to Lakehurst. (Smithsonian Institution, Photograph No. 78-8036.)

asked Alcoa to undertake experimental rolling work on making 17S sheet and fabricating components in advance of the formal requisition. Alcoa agreed to work without contract to accommodate the navy, but soon regretted it. The beginnings of the new prototype production phase were so fraught with conflict and difficulty that the navy threatened to give the business to competitors, while Alcoa questioned that the business was worth having.[21]

In fact, neither party was prepared to engage in developmental work effectively. Alcoa was doing its engineering in New Kensington and its production in Niagara. The bureaucratic delays endemic to the navy's Bureau of Construction and Repair, a problem that had been overcome during the war because officers had been willing to take extraordinary personal measures to cut through the red tape, became painfully evident in peacetime. Communication became more difficult, and it took a long time to make decisions.[22]

Problems arose in the prototype phase as soon as the naval

Aircraft Factory in Philadelphia began to deal directly with Alcoa's production staff at Massena. The factory was impatient for a quick response from Alcoa because its own bureaucratic procedures had taken so much time. Yet Alcoa was having difficulty reaching steady-state production because of the problem of working with unstable designs and small, experimental-size lots. Each time Alcoa tried to fabricate a particular component, new engineering changes came through, and the whole trial-and-error production process had to begin again. The work was extremely disruptive to regular output at Massena.

Massena also had a serious problem with naval inspection criteria and procedures. For every lot produced, Alcoa had to test five samples, and the NBS had to test five on behalf of the navy. Edward K. Davis wrote to H. E. Spalding in Alcoa's Washington office in 1918 that the navy's inspection criteria were "too rigid and more severe than circumstances warrant." It had taken 175,000 pounds of sheet, he claimed, to get 27,835 pounds past the inspectors. It became increasingly clear that Alcoa's shop-floor personnel at Massena, who were not highly skilled craftsmen, lacked both the tolerance and the understanding to do developmental work.[23]

J. H. Finney, working in Washington in early 1919 as Alcoa's sales representative, discovered that Alcoa was in danger of losing part or all of the airship metal business to competitors. The delays in the first phase of the program, and Alcoa's obvious difficulty in turning out good material at Massena, had prompted navy observers to consider other options. This was true even though their own bureaucratic procedures had contributed to the delays.

The navy had several other candidates for dirigible procurement. The Bausch Machine Tool Company of Worcester, Massachusetts, for instance, which was connected with Vickers, was offering to supply Duralumin-type components at a competitive price. Bausch was, in fact, a major supplier of Duralumin through the 1920s, and there was strong evidence that its quality was far superior to that of the alloy produced by Alcoa. It would continue to sell more Duralumin than Alcoa until 1927.[24]

Navy personnel had also formed a far more favorable opinion of Alcoa's overseas competitors' production capabilities than of Alcoa's own, and some favored having several different suppliers rather than single-sourcing. The French and the Germans, they noted, took more care with the process, and they seemed to have higher-caliber people working in their plants. Although the navy would prefer to use domestically produced materials, Alcoa realized it would have to make some changes to get the contract.

Alcoa's management came close to letting the airship contract go at that point, but its Sales Department was convinced that the airship would lead to a growing commercial business. There were indications that the automakers would take on airship construction after the prototype stage was completed. "The matter will have to come to a show-down," wrote Finney, "either we must demonstrate that we can supply 17S in sufficient quantities and of a grade at least equal to duralumin, or the order for the considerable quantity required for the Navy program will have to be placed abroad."[25]

A NEW STRUCTURE FOR LEARNING

Alcoa had already committed itself to setting up a separate centralized laboratory, but the difficulties of trying to coordinate by committee its separate production and laboratory departments on the 17S program pushed it toward more radical structural reorganization. Blough later commented as follows:

Such development as we made technically and such production as we made during the war showed us our most glaring needs. These needs were twofold; first, a very much increased technical staff with the best equipment available and a fabricating mill specially designed for the production of strong alloys. Both of these established and in addition a separate research department; separate in the sense that the pure research was separate from the technical department. With the establishment of these facilities in or about 1920, the progress in the production of the materials for airplane production was rapid both as to technical improvements and as to quantity production.[26]

The record does not show whether or not assurances from Alcoa influenced the contract award directly, but in December 1919 the preliminary contract for supplying most of the aluminum for the first naval airship, designated ZR-1, went to Alcoa. Contract 49491 was for prototype production, awarding Alcoa perhaps 95 percent of all the aluminum to be used. This amounted to about 60,000 pounds of aluminum finished parts at $1.045 per pound finished price, a total of $60,984. Bausch had submitted a sketchy bid for $0.91 per pound for strips only, and it was given a small contract for the program. Alcoa's advantage over any other domestic source was that it was willing to supply the whole contract. It had equipped itself with a 10,000-ton press and with rolling equipment able to roll 40-foot coils, a capability no one else offered to match, in part because it required working with unusually large ingots.[27]

The navy retained the element of competition by procuring other versions of airships abroad. After attempting to get one of the German Zeppelins, the navy bought an airship designated R-38 (U.S. ZR-2) from Britain, as well as a ZR-3 (called the *Los Angeles*) designed and built by the German Zeppelin Company in connection with reparations payments.[28]

Once the contract had been settled, development work on hard alloys was consolidated in New Kensington under the TDB, with assistance from the Research Bureau. Earl Blough, then head of the TDB, was assisted by Conrad Nagel, who served as project manager for the airship program. In mid-1919 the experimental rolling mill was set up under the TDB, and as soon as it could be arranged it was equipped with modern laboratory facilities. Within a year, a full-scale rolling facility was also installed at Arnold, with its own heat-treating facilities and specially designed rolling equipment, next door to the New Kensington plant. By 1922 the Arnold facility was turning out high-strength alloy at the rate of 25,000 tons of sheet per year. The struggle was by no means over when the whole 17S operation was shifted to New Kensington, however. Two more years of frustrating effort followed. Alcoa had, first of all, to break in its new equipment (which Blough described to Finney as "the neck of the bottle") and then achieve high-quality production.[29]

The location in New Kensington allowed top management to keep a close watch on what was going on with the 17S project. When yields plummeted and nothing was getting past inspection, Roy Hunt, then president, intervened personally to involve the Research Bureau. Blough was away in Europe, checking out overseas production processes, and Nagel, Blough's deputy, was trying to handle the yield crisis by himself. Frary and Hoopes were in Badin working on the Hoopes refining process. Without consulting either Hoopes or Frary, who were responsible for the research program, Hunt asked Jeffries, who was still in charge at the Lynite Laboratories, to come in and troubleshoot for the project. Jeffries was told to report to Frary, who learned of the arrangement from Nagel. "I do not want to have [Frary] or you think that I am 'butting in' unduly in this situation," Hunt wrote to Nagel, "but naturally we would like to have all of our people get the benefit of the advice of the Engineers associated with our Company."[30]

As the correspondence suggested, Hunt was sensitive to the diplomatic problem he was creating by violating the commitment made to Frary not to require the Research Bureau to be involved in anything that could be considered routine production problems. Bringing Jeffries in to look at the whole program was a vital step, however. First, it acknowledged the need to take a look at the problem from the perspective of research and development combined, and, second, it provided an opportunity to apply to the airship problem the knowledge Jeffries had gained on casting Duralumin at ACC during the war. The Research Bureau and Jeffries remained involved after Lynite was dissolved, and the project became the responsibility not just of the TDB, but of the entire Technical Department working in concert. The absorption of some Lynite people into the TDB also allowed the project to benefit from their earlier efforts to develop metallurgical standards and controls for the casting operations.

Yields remained a terrible problem for two years after the Technical Department was put in sole charge of the project. The navy complained that this was holding up construction. Blough laid the blame on Alcoa's Sales Department, which he said had agreed to tolerances an order of magnitude more restrictive than Alcoa had ever before met. Without consulting the technical people to see if it could be done, they had also negotiated unrealistic conditions of delivery. The navy had not been warned, for instance, that producing metal in a developmental plant was different from pushing metal out the door under wartime conditions. Extreme care had to be taken by highly skilled people, and such skilled people would not work at night. Each time material was rejected for whatever reason, rework and new production lengthened the delivery time considerably. Navy constructors made matters worse by referring to the contract as "a simple job," never acknowledging that they were asking for an unconventional size of an experimental material.[31]

President Roy A. Hunt.

SHARING THE RISK

By May 1921 the two parties had worked out a modus vivendi, with the navy relaxing some of its more rigid requirements. Nagel's steady barrage of letters to the navy's inspector of hull material had resulted in agreement that the latter's office would accept shorter lengths and rerolled sheets. The navy's complaint that it had been held up 14 months in getting the material it needed had to be seen in the light of its own mishandling of its control procedures.[32]

The navy's inspection process certainly was a major part of the difficulty. In September 1921 the naval inspector stationed in New Kensington had rejected 80 percent of the plant's entire weekly output. Then it was discovered that several months' worth of output had been unnecessarily scrapped because of a "white mark condition" that a higher authority had agreed to accept. It was a relief to many when, in September 1921, the Bureau of Construction and Repair itself finally organized a special-project operation, the Bureau of Aeronautics, to handle airships and other aircraft construction.[33]

Alcoa and the navy ultimately agreed to share the costs of experimentation. Alcoa reported, in a request for supplementary compensation, that some 53,000 pounds of aluminum intended for the airship program had been lost in producing the 60,000 pounds contracted for – 11,000 pounds in experimental work, 12,000 pounds rejected for rolling defects identified in-house, nearly 19,000 pounds lost in fabricated parts that either had not met specification or had been rendered obsolete by engineering changes, and more than 10,000 pounds for defects alleged by the inspector.[34]

A breakthrough came in December 1922, when the NBS, which was doing the navy's testing, declared that Alcoa's output was then consistently exceeding the German standard both in strength and in uniformity. Even after organizing the project under the Technical Department and applying Alcoa's collected knowledge from all sources, it had taken three years to achieve output that consistently met specifications.[35]

Small wonder, then, that the sight of the *Shenandoah* cruising majestically over New Kensington in the autumn of 1923 was an event for universal celebration at Alcoa. After a painful learning process, the successful completion of ZR-1 and the promise of further airships to be made of the same 17S, now a familiar product, were hard-won achievements.

The airship prototype project completed, Alcoa's technical organization was able to pursue a more balanced research program. Edgar Dix, who had initially gone from the Lynite Laboratories into the TDB, transferred to the Research Bureau, where he began the line of investigation that led to the development of Alclad sheet in 1927. This work on the problem of corrosion of strong alloys was, of course, prompted most immediately by the airship contract. The Alclad version of 17S, not available for the *Shenandoah*, would be specified for further airship projects.

CORROSION SCARE

For two years the *Shenandoah* was a project with which the company was happy to have its name associated. Alcoa was able to monitor the airship's performance and test such things as the appearance of corrosion as the airship was subjected to regular flying conditions. During its first extended cruise, the *Shenandoah* made an 8,000-mile trip across the continent and back through all kinds of weather. The navy was paying close attention to the airworthiness of the design, for several airships, including the R-38 purchased from Britain, had crashed in flight or broken up in bad weather on the ground. The *Shenandoah* did not share these problems until it had flown for two years – but then came disaster.[36]

On September 4, 1925, newspapers all across the country reported an incident that was potentially devastating news for Alcoa. The *New York Times* headline read "*Shenandoah* Wrecked in Ohio Storm; Breaks in Three and Falls 7000 Feet; 14 Dead, Including Commander, 2 Hurt." Earl Blough was already on his way to Caldwell, Ohio, accompanied by "Dutch" Nagel, when the story broke. The speed of Blough's response reflected more than one reason for urgency. The need to beat souvenir hunters in salvaging the wreckage was tied to the need to find out as quickly as possible whether or not metal failure had had anything to do with the accident. The potential harm the wreck might do to Alcoa's promising new business supplying aluminum for aircraft was immense. In fact, should any blame attach to aluminum at all, more than the aircraft business might be affected.

Captain Zachary Lansdowne, the senior officer commanding the *Shenandoah*, was one of the men who died in the airship's crash in 1925. He is shown here with a model of the Shenandoah (Smithsonian Institution, Photograph No. 89-16694.)

During the more than two years of inquiry that followed the catastrophe, Alcoa's Technical Department served as the company's first line of defense. It was a very different organization from the one that had first become involved with airships when it tried to address the navy's Duralumin problem in 1916. By the mid-1920s, the department was on a par with any other institution in the country in its ability to handle questions relating to aluminum technology.

Earl Blough's first reports from the scene of the accident were reassuring. Having made a visual inspection of as much of the tangled wreckage as he could, Blough concluded that all the breaks had been clean, and there was no sign at all of the dread corrosion. Alcoa received a contract to salvage the metal, with the intention of reusing what was, after all, a very expensive material in later airships. This arrangement had the added benefit of giving Alcoa ready access, for testing purposes, to everything that had escaped the looters.[37]

Crowds gathered at the site in Caldwell County, Ohio, where the rear section of the airship came down 3 September 1925, next to a cornfield. Of the 11 officers and 31 men aboard, 14 were killed and 2 injured. Because looters and souvenir hunters carried away important pieces of evidence, it was difficult to conduct a thorough investigation and salvage operation. (Smithsonian Institution, Photograph No. A43301-B.)

The naval inquiry that took place before the end of the year laid blame for the disaster on errors of human judgment, both in operating the vehicle at a time of equinoctial storms and for modifying safety valves in order to conserve scarce and expensive helium. At the time, practically no attention was paid to the role of the material. But further testing by the NBS, and continuing advances in metallographic analysis using x-ray technology, caused the matter of the *Shenandoah* to be taken up again. Each time, Alcoa's Technical Department, well equipped and in possession of relevant data, was prepared to defend the company's interests.[38]

In 1925 the NBS claimed that an elaborate set of tests based on new techniques had revealed that intercrystalline corrosion had occurred under the varnish that had been used on the *Shenandoah* to prevent corrosion. Picked up by the *Engineering News Record,* this claim was interpreted to mean that corrosion in frame parts had been an unacknowledged factor in the *Shenandoah* crash.[39]

Richard Templin, formerly at NBS, organized Alcoa's re-

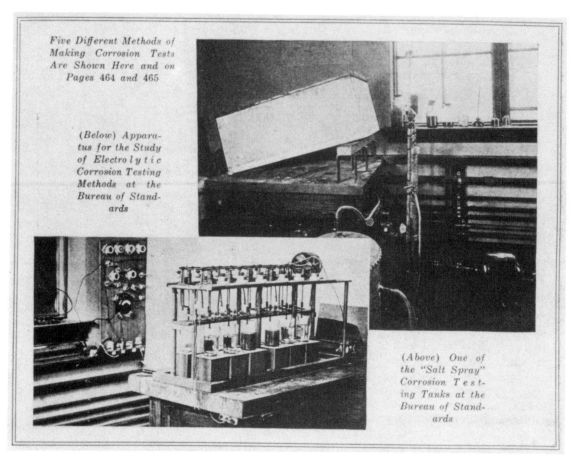

Five Different Methods of Making Corrosion Tests Are Shown Here and on Pages 464 and 465

(Below) Apparatus for the Study of Electrolytic Corrosion Testing Methods at the Bureau of Standards

(Above) One of the "Salt Spray" Corrosion Testing Tanks at the Bureau of Standards

Advanced equipment and methods for testing corrosion of aluminum and other metals were developed in the early 1920s at the National Bureau of Standards. Equipment such as this was also used at Alcoa's laboratories. (From *Iron Age*, 20 August 1925, pp. 461.)

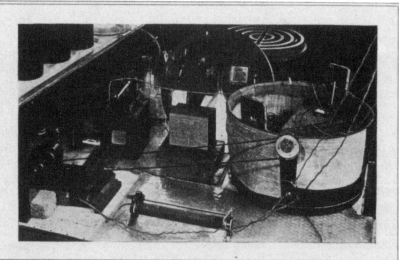

Continuous Immersion Corrosion Test Apparatus at the Bureau of Standards. Specimens are placed in various solutions in the bottles inside the tub. The temperature is thermostatically controlled. In the photograph the test is being run without aeration, which may be provided for

Alternate Immersion and Interrupted Immersion Corrosion Testing Apparatus at the Bureau of Standards. Specimens, suspended on glass hooks, are automatically dipped into and pulled out of a solution, or dipped in, pulled out and given time to dry before the next dip

sponse to these charges. In the process of gathering data and interpretations on this issue, he developed a sophisticated set of test equipment and procedures that made Alcoa's testing department a leading facility among light-metals establishments. Eventually, the NBS conceded that its case had been based on faulty testing procedures and did not stand up. When another expert metallurgist, Professor George Clark of MIT's Applied Chemistry Laboratory, was quoted in the *Herald Tribune* as supporting the idea that faulty metal was the cause of the *Shenandoah*'s demise, Clark wrote to apologize to Alcoa's management, saying that he had been misquoted. The new methods he was using to detect intercrystalline corrosion had indeed revealed evidence of the problem in *Shenandoah* fragments he had tested, but he did not mean to imply that these problems had contributed to the crash. Clearly, by the late 1920s, Alcoa's reputation for reliable testing was beyond dispute.[40]

While Alcoa was defending itself against adverse publicity, aluminum was becoming firmly entrenched in the aviation industry. The year 1927 was something of a turning point for aviation, and certainly for the metal airplane. Charles Lindbergh's plane, *Spirit of St. Louis*, used in his flight across the Atlantic, had an aluminum skin and a Liberty engine made of Alcoa aluminum castings. In the same year, the army set up Wright Field at Dayton, Ohio, as a home for the U.S. Army Air Corps program.

The *Spirit of St. Louis*, the aluminum-sheathed plane that Charles Lindbergh flew across the Atlantic in 1927, gave a large boost to the metal airplane business in the United States. (Smithsonian Institution, Photograph No. 71-1091.)

Major McDill of Wright Field was not prepared to commit to all-aluminum training vehicles without assurance that they could be trusted, no matter how much experience the navy had gained with them. But he was prepared to rely on Alcoa's data to support aluminum trainers. By that time, Templin's operation could make available "test and use data" that could be directly linked to engineering design and performance of aircraft based on scientific principle, not just experience.[41]

Also in 1927, the *New York Times* had a favorable story to report. At a ceremony to dedicate a memorial tablet made of metal from the wrecked *Shenandoah* airship at Lakehurst, New Jersey, Rear Admiral William A. Moffett announced funding for the next airship program. Alcoa would use the metal it had salvaged from the wrecked airship, he said, as part of the metal it would supply for construction of two larger dirigibles, which were to constitute a monument to the men lost in the *Shenandoah* disaster.[42]

Sadly, Moffett himself would perish in the crash of one of these flying ships only five years later, but by that time the concept of the all-aluminum aircraft was no longer hostage to the fortunes of any airship. From 1927 on, Alcoa became firmly established as the major supplier to the aviation industry, working directly with the many companies like Curtiss, Boeing, and Douglas that were designing all-metal aircraft. In the customer relationships established, Alcoa contributed not only the materials knowledge but also much of the expertise in designing aluminum structures. Most of the credit for this ability to supply the new industry, with know-how as well as material, belonged to Alcoa's central R&D organization.

The structure that integrated R&D as a major functional presence was certainly Alcoa's critical strength in the eyes of one knowledgeable independent observer. When cross-examined in Alcoa's antitrust case in 1940, Jerome Hunsaker testified that the outstanding advantage of dealing with Alcoa had been its character as an integrated producer with its own R&D, supplying the metal and working it under the same corporate roof. Whatever its doubts at the time, looking back he felt that the navy would have faced an impossible task had it tried to coordinate a supplier of innovative metal and an independent fabricator struggling to come up with new processes. Asked to give his opinion of Alcoa's R&D contribution, he replied:

The useful contribution is the making available to the aircraft industry of this country, strong aluminum alloy in many gauges and forms of uniform quality, which availability became the basis of the metal airplane industry and caused the revolution from stick and wire construction to all-metal construction.[43]

Alcoa's experience with 17S was an example of what could be accomplished when the state of technology permitted it and both the national climate for R&D and the context provided by the company were favorable. The prewar strides in metallurgical knowledge combined with the application of control techniques made possible advances in alloy formulation and metalworking that would have been inconceivable through trial and error alone. The cooperative efforts of many different research-performing institutions, private and public, before, during, and after World War I had contributed to these advances and to the rapid spread of knowledge about them.

Unlike Vickers, which had forfeited all of the know-how it had gained from acquiring and using Duralumin technology, Alcoa was able to build on the knowledge it acquired. That was possible because of the pooling of knowledge and know-how about the core technology accumulated through many different application experiences in different parts of the company, and the ability then to apply the pooled knowledge through the efforts of the Technical Department. The other aspect of the airship experience that was critical was the participation of a customer with interests in high performance and with a willingness, however reluctant, to share some of the risks and some of the costs. That was something that Vickers, for instance, did not have in the postwar era.[44]

During the period of research in equipoise after 1928, Alcoa's knowledge base would be extended from 17S to embrace other high-strength alloys, and the new understanding of the behavior of aluminum structures would serve as a platform for a huge business in aluminum for structural uses, from airplanes and railroad cars in the 1930s to high-rise buildings in the 1950s and beyond.

PART III

Splendid monopoly, 1928–1945

5

Aluminum research in equipoise

In October 1929, President Hoover used the occasion of the Golden Jubilee for the incandescent lamp to broadcast a plea for more industrial laboratories and more industrial support for research. Surpassing the importance of Edison's invention of the light bulb, he said, was the invention of modern methods of industrial research, using the team approach to solve problems. The days of the woodshed genius were past. It was the day of the well-equipped special research laboratory. Hoover spoke at what would turn out to be the pinnacle of fortune for industrial research before World War II. His terms of service, first as secretary of commerce and then as president, with his strong emphasis on associational action and government support for private cooperation, rather than government control, helped to ensure that industrial research, particularly research done in cooperation with other research-performing institutions, was seen as public-spirited activity. The public mood would soon reject both that technocratic vision and its presidential advocate.[1]

Even as Hoover spoke, Alcoa was completing work on its own new central research laboratory located on a bluff high above the Allegheny River, with the New Kensington works in the valley below it. Long overdue, as Edwin Fickes acknowledged in his memoir, it was to be the showcase for what had become a well-established research community and the hub of activity for an extensive network of branch laboratories. Outside observers remarked that it was a sign that the company recognized at last the contribution research had made to its commercial success. In fact, it was a more significant symbol: It meant that research was on the way to becoming a big part of Alcoa's strategy.[2]

The period from 1928 to 1951 was a golden age for Alcoa

183

Corporate Facts

Leadership: A. V. Davis, chairman of the board
Roy A. Hunt, president
Edwin S. Fickes, vice-president
George R. Gibbons, vice-president and secretary
W. P. King, vice-president
Winthrop C. Nielson, vice-president
Robert W. Withers, vice-president and treasurer

No. of Employees: 23,049

Primary production: 210.5 million pounds

Locations: ☐ Bauxite, AR; Moengo, Suriname;
Georgetown, British Guiana
○ East St. Louis, IL; Baltimore, MD; Arvida, Quebec
△ Niagara Falls, Massena, NY; Shawinigan Falls,
Quebec; Alcoa, TN; Badin, NC; Arvida, Quebec
■ New Kensington, PA; Massena, NY; Toronto, ONT;
Edgewater, NJ; Fairfield, CN; Buffalo, NY;
Oakland, CA; Garwood, NJ; Cleveland, OH;
Detroit, MI
● New Kensington, PA; Cleveland, OH; Badin, NC;
Buffalo, Massena, NY; East St. Louis, IL
▲ Pittsburgh, PA

Laboratory Facts

Leadership: Francis C. Frary, director of research
Herman E. Bakken, assistant director
Junius D. Edwards, assistant director

No. of Employees: 139

Expenditures $711,000

Figure 5.1. Corporate and laboratory facts, 1928.

Research, though those involved at the time would have been surprised to hear it described as such. The times were not, on the surface, easy ones. Yet the research organization, restructured and renamed the Aluminum Research Laboratories in 1928, maintained its essential stability and balance through stock market crash, depression, war, and extended antitrust litigation.

A ROLLERCOASTER CLIMATE FOR R&D

On the eve of the period of extraordinary business turbulence that was to characterize the 1930s and 1940s, national condi-

Figure 5.2. Corporate locations, 1928.

Herbert Hoover.

tions for research had never been better. Industrial research had come of age in the late 1920s. There were 1,500 research laboratories in industry, roughly four times the number at the start of the decade. It was estimated that $10 million and 3,000 workers were involved in pure science in the United States, and $200 million and 30,000 workers in applied science. Bell Telephone Laboratories alone spent $19 million and employed 6,000 people.[3]

Certainly it was a time of heightened research activity throughout the chemical and metallurgical industries. The close partnership between chemical engineering at the Massachusetts Institute of Technology (MIT) and numerous important research-performing companies was one outstanding example of the kind of cooperative relationship that had developed between many companies and universities. The head of DuPont's Chemical Laboratory echoed prevailing sentiment among business leaders:

Only an organization that is willing and anxious to further its research program with the best brains and equipment that can be obtained can hope to survive in the modern competition between whole industries for the control of markets.[4]

The chemical and metallurgical industries were estimated to be spending more than 2 percent of their asset base annually on research. Alcoa tracked closely what was going on in the allied chemical industries and kept in close touch with the professional associations that had grown rapidly in the interwar period. Lacking other research-performing companies in its immediate industry (i.e., other primary aluminum producers), it defined its technical community to include most of the electrochemical concerns. The company had more than 150 researchers at its central laboratory who were in touch with this community, and its own storehouse of usable knowledge was brimming with identified opportunities.[5]

For many companies, the depression years 1931–4 forced severe curtailment of R&D activities, and development was cut back drastically at Alcoa as well. But research at Alcoa enjoyed uncommon central support, not only because it had proved its financial worth to top management but also because its substantial research contributions leading to new products of national value provided one of the main arguments Alcoa used against

The entrance to Aluminum Research Laboratories, as it was called until the 1950s, when its name changed to Alcoa Research Laboratories. The ornate aluminum doors, windows, and spandrels emphasized the building's symbolic significance, making research the cornerstone of Alcoa's strategy during the 1930s and 1940s.

those who charged that its effective monopoly of primary aluminum was against the economic interests of the nation. The antitrust investigations that had dogged Alcoa's corporate footsteps during the 1920s continued through the 1930s. They would culminate in a lengthy and widely publicized legal battle that would only pause, as it turned out, during World War II. The initial verdict in 1941 – a clear declaration of Alcoa's innocence of all monopoly charges – would be reversed on appeal in 1945.[6]

In one sense, the war would be a relatively stable period for Alcoa Research, a time when its services, like those of other major laboratories in the country, would be willingly directed toward supporting Allied war aims. The objectives would be to support the production of large supplies of aluminum, to develop new high-performance materials, and to support major government programs. Unfortunately, this last policy would end in a bitter postwar conflict between Alcoa and the government over the rights to the technology developed. Its outcome would usher in a completely new conception of the role of R&D at the company.

FORMATION OF ALUMINUM RESEARCH LABORATORIES

A massive upheaval occurred in the company in 1928, when Alcoa split off its international operations to form a separate Canadian company, Aluminium Limited, headed by Edward K. Davis. The company's most experienced R&D manager, Earl Blough, joined Davis at the new company to head its R&D organization, later becoming a vice-president. Those changes prompted a complete restructuring of Alcoa's research establishment along lines consistent with Francis Frary's personal technical vision, which focused on the need to create appropriate conditions for nonroutine research. Frary had not been alone in calling for fundamental research, of course, but now he, alone, was left to select which areas the program would emphasize and in what order.

In the new Alcoa technical organization, R&D took on a complicated and diverse structure, designed to accommodate a diversity of technical needs. Research was centralized, while applied research and development were distributed among satellite locations, some controlled by Research and some by Operations and Sales. The reasoning behind the new organization was reminiscent of that behind the Lynite Laboratories – central Research was buffered as much as possible from the short-term needs of Operations and Sales. It absorbed outright the East St. Louis laboratory, formerly controlled by the Aluminum Ore Company. This laboratory, along with other satellite laboratories at Massena, Badin, Buffalo, and Cleveland, assumed responsibility for "special problems" in process development. The operating divisions had their own development arms in some cases, and in others they had technical advisors who, with satellite research laboratories close at hand, could sponsor process-improvement activities of their own. Operations had no reason to feel it had to control central Research.

The new structure was based on a more pronounced division of labor than had formerly existed between center and branch. If the center created a new alloy, the branch put it to use, designing the product and the process to produce it. Various alloy innovations illustrated this flow of technology very well. If the Aluminum Research Laboratories (ARL, also referred to as "the Laboratories") in New Kensington worked on the chemical and physical characteristics of a particular class of alloys, metallurgists at Massena would work on casting it into ingot and trying out its rolling characteristics. Laboratory researchers might work on finding just the right composition for an aluminum bearing, while development engineers worked at the same time on improvements to the design and on production of existing aluminum products, such as auto engines, pistons, and transmission housings. Within Alcoa's Cleveland works, the former Aluminum Castings Company, this division of labor also applied. But Cleveland contained all phases of R&D at one location and thus remained a much more self-sufficient community, as did East St. Louis. As the central laboratory at New Kensington became more specialized, the self-contained character of Cleveland and East St. Louis stood out as alternative models of the way R&D could be organized.

The TDB, having served its original purpose at the center and having lost Blough, was dismantled. Its more research-oriented parts were absorbed into ARL, while metallurgical control, with its band of technical supervisors, was placed under the control of Operations and dispersed throughout the operating locations "where it belonged," according to Frary. The TDB's Pyrometric and Specifications Sections also shifted to Operations, which thus acquired the means of controlling both instrumentation and data collection.[7]

Metallurgists, who were bound to view the move to the plants

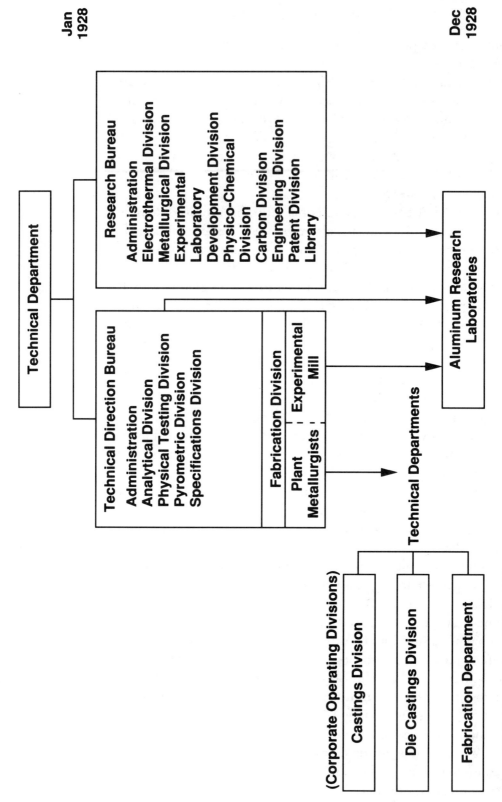

Figure 5.3. Reorganization of R&D, 1928.

in 1928 as a form of exile, lamented their reduced contact with the center. The dismantling of the TDB was a sign of its success in readying the plants to take technical responsibility: The original, centralized structure of the TDB had reflected technical deficiencies at the operating sites. Nevertheless, the metallurgists saw themselves as a government in exile and agitated to return to what they saw as their rightful place at the center. They wanted to refocus the spotlight on the fundamental study in metalworking that had been advocated in Blough's 1923 manifesto.[8]

The reorganization left Research in a preeminent position at the center. It answered directly to the chief engineer of the company, subject to the inactive review of the Research Committee, a small group of corporate executives who had a stake in technical issues: the chief engineer, the general superintendent, the vice-president in charge of fabricating plants, and the head of sales development. For the first time, Research was housed in a building that reflected its importance. Frary and his staff would now be rewarded for their patience, in part because substandard laboratory facilities had become an embarrassment to the company in an era when industrial research was practically equated with patriotic duty in the country at large. A. V. Davis, on one of his infrequent trips to New Kensington, had at last pronounced the old research quarters in the plant "a slop hole of a laboratory" and allocated $50 million to build a new one.[9]

At a time when the strategy of the company was to extend the uses of aluminum for structural applications of all kinds, the chance to build a new laboratory was an opportunity that could be exploited to the fullest. Not only could the new building design incorporate the latest ideas of what a modern chemical research laboratory should be, but it could serve as a showcase for aluminum structures. The new laboratory, referred to as Building 29, for the year it was erected, opened in January 1930. On a 14-acre tract high above the Allegheny Valley, it was well away from the smoke that hung around the New Kensington plant below it. Externally, the building's architectural style was classic, but the interior was modern, in tune with the latest thinking about the construction of functional research facilities.

The building was described in *Iron Age* as a "laboratory of dignity and beauty." Its splendid ornamental aluminum front

When the Aluminum Research Laboratories was built, New Kensington had become a thickly populated industrial city, with smoke from numerous coal-fired furnaces hanging in the valley around the works. ARL was located on the hill in the clearing above and to the right of the large center smokestack shown here. It had the advantage of close proximity to the plant for communications purposes; but its remoteness in style and location helped to shield it from day-to-day operating problems.

doors and classic pillars gave it a look of massive solidity that belied the traditional lightweight aluminum image. The philosophy behind the laboratory design was to use the native metal in every conceivable way, pioneering uses both structural and ornamental and setting a precedent for successful building experimentation, a policy that would continue with the Alcoa Building in Pittsburgh in the early 1950s. Junius Edwards, assistant director of research and Frary's right-hand man, wrote that

the laboratories, therefore, are not only a tribute to the versatility of aluminum and its alloys, when used for construction and for laboratory furnishings, but represent many innovations in design and equipment. From the ornamental aluminum entrance to the artistic grille work on the pent-house, outside and inside, aluminum is proving itself in these laboratories.[10]

Aluminum was everywhere, visible and invisible – from the elevator with hammered doors to the floors with aluminum strips in the terrazzo, the window castings, piping, ornamentation, furniture (especially innovative laboratory benches), railings, and paint. Many of the features – paint, floors, aluminum radiators, and piping – required preliminary research to determine the reaction of the aluminum to surrounding materials, and all would provide a chance for close daily follow-up.[11]

Junius Edwards.

The expense of the new laboratory building was a consequence not only of the custom work required for the special fittings but also of the high cost of state-of-the-art laboratory equipment. At the end of World War I, research in aluminum had been largely a form of chemical research, and laboratory equipment was mainly the equipment needed for analysis. One especially active decade had changed that. Metallurgical researchers of the 1930s had to combine the skills of electrochemists with those of physical metallurgists, and much that they did was carried out on a large scale and at high temperature. They needed not only special spectrographs, microscopes, and x-ray equipment but also furnaces fitted with precise controls and measuring devices. "In a measure this need for extensive equipment is common to all modern research," wrote Henry Gillett, of the Battelle Memorial Institute. "The days of surface prospecting and shallow mining for facts are pretty much past; we are in the days of deep mining, and deep mining is expensive."[12]

To Alcoa researchers who had long struggled with makeshift and cumbersome equipment, the whole research enterprise was transformed by their new quarters. For the first time it was self-contained and self-sufficient. It was no longer necessary to persuade the plant to do a special research melt and then wait for it to be scheduled, to take hours to rig up a temporary piece of apparatus only to tear it down again after one experiment, or to make do with approximate measurements. Old-timers' experience of having to invent all the research equipment before an experiment could be done began to fade into the dimly remembered past.[13]

The courtyard of the new building was specially designed to rig all configurations of test equipment and to accommodate medium-term experiments such as testing activated alumina for its adsorptive qualities, which were useful for filtering industrial wastes and later in air conditioning. The laboratory had its own melting, casting, and rolling equipment, including several electrical furnaces, on the ground floor. Smaller furnaces had

The front façade of the Aluminum Research Laboratories at the time of its dedication in 1930. The architect for the building was the well-known Henry Hornbostel.

Inside ARL as well as outside, aluminum was put to every possible use for ornamentation and for furnishings. The stairways inside ARL had aluminum risers and aluminum bannisters. The ARL library (next plate) had aluminum railings and aluminum furniture.

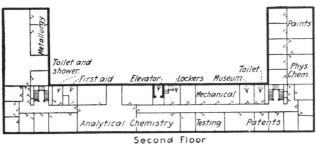

Second Floor

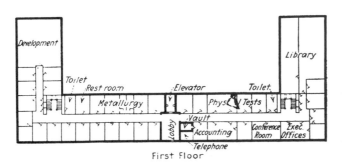

First Floor

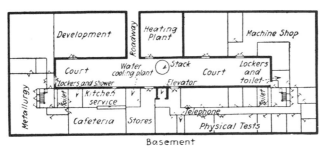

Basement

The state of the art in research-laboratory design and equipment changed rapidly in the 1920s. ARL benefited from that development and attracted much attention in professional circles for being one of the most advanced laboratories of its time. This floor plan and the pictures of the mechanical laboratory (next plate) appeared in *Iron Age* in January 1930.

195

Some Details of New Research Laboratory at New Kensington, Pa.

Extensive use was made of cast and wrought aluminun in the construction. Much of the exterior trim is cast aluminum—cornice, coping, belt courses, spandrel panels, mullions, doorframes (Fig. 1). Part of this metal is coated with vitreous enamel in colors, part is polished, part natural sandcast finish. A large amount of interior piping (some of it visible in Fig. 2, metallurgical laboratory, with furnaces and sheet rolls) is drawn aluminum and alloy. Pipes and ducts are made accessible throughout the building by being carried up in chases at outside columns (Fig. 2). The building houses a staff of about 150.

The lower four views are in the mechanical laboratory. Fig. 3 shows part of a battery of endurance-testing machines, one of the largest groups in existence. A 40,000-lb. vertical Amsler machine (Fig. 4) will take tension and compression specimens up to 10 ft. long; a 300,000-lb. machine is yet to be installed. Torsion testing (Fig. 5) and other work are fully provided for. There are many facilities for special testing, as exemplified by Fig. 6, showing a box girder of aluminum alloy under flexure test; hold-down bolts restrain the ends, and a lifting jack at midspan applies load.

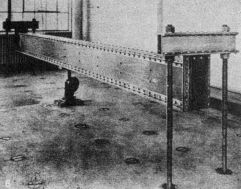

196

The physical chemistry laboratory (above) and the analytical chemistry laboratory (below) were both located on the second floor of the new building.

Determination of Oxygen and Hydrogen in Metals by the Vacuum Fusion Method. The sample is placed in a gas-free graphite crucible in the bottom of the silica tube at the left. The system is evacuated by the pump at the right. By means of the high-frequency induction furnace about the bottom of the silica tube the sample is melted. The gases are caught in suitable absorbents in tubes in the train on the desk. The tubes are then detached and weighed

The state of research equipment at any given time determines not only how much can be known but also whether or not analyses can be performed quickly and conveniently enough to solve problems when they arise. The pictures here and on the following pages taken at the National Bureau of Standards in Washington, show state-of-the-art equipment development for metallographic analysis in the 1920s.

Four Endurance-Testing Machines Used in the Engineering Mechanics Section of the Bureau of Standards for Testing Thin Sheet Metal. These have been used in an extensive study of the fatigue-resisting properties of duralumin for aircraft, and are specially designed to produce definite and measurable stresses in the specimens. Stress is measured with an optical lever system

198

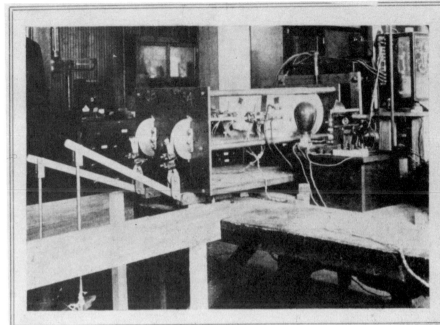

Two of the Eight "Flow Test" Units for Study of the Properties of Metals at High Temperatures. The specimens are mounted within the electric furnaces, whose temperature is regulated by controller at extreme right. The weights at the extreme lower left impose stress on the specimens through the lever system. A window in side of furnace (hidden by the electric light) can be opened and the elongation of the specimen measured by the traversing telescope

Quenching Media Are Studied in the Tin Can at Left, which Rests on a Pedestal, Rotatable for Stirring. Over the can is an electric furnace that can be opened at top and bottom. A steel specimen (shown at A, over the furnace) has a tiny thermocouple inserted into it and held tightly in contact with it. The thermocouple holder makes a watertight connection with the specimen, which is heated to the desired temperature in the furnace and then dropped into the quenching bath. The way the specimen cools is recorded by the thermocouple, in circuit with a tungsten "string" in the field of the strong electromagnet

Apparatus for Accelerated Simulated Atmospheric Exposure Corrosion Test at the Bureau of Standards. Specimens are supported in slots in the rings on the corner of the table, which are then put inside the double tub on the left. CO_2 and SO_2 in regulated amounts are passed in, and water in the bottom of the lower tub supplies water vapor. The extra upper tub shown at the right can be put on instead of the one shown in place, and water spray directed on the specimens to simulate rain. The temperature is thermostatically controlled

Part of the Equipment of the Metallographic Laboratory at the Bureau of Standards

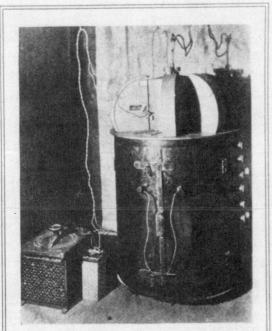

The X-Ray Spectograph Used at the Bureau of Standards in the Study of the Crystal Structure of Metals. The X-ray tube is inside the case. X-rays pass through windows in the upper part of the case, impinge on specimens in the quadrant-shaped "cassettes," and are reflected from the specimen to photographic films stretched over the curve of the quadrant. According to the arrangement of the atoms in the crystals, the X-rays are reflected at various angles and make lines on the film. From the spacing of these lines, the crystal structure may be deduced. The cassette at the left is rigged up for running a test on a heated specimen

Draw Bench at the Bureau of Standards

special controls designed for metallographic investigations, and the metallurgical laboratories had Zeiss microscopes and equipment to do photomicrographs with magnifications ranging from ×5 to ×16,000, which raised the study of the structure of metals to a new level.

New equipment made it possible to test both the metallurgical and mechanical properties and the strength of fabricated forms and structures. A 300,000-pound Amsler and hydraulic testing machine, a three-ton aluminum-alloy crane, and equipment for testing at temperatures as low as −112°C and as high as +1,200°C rounded out a state-of-the-art facility. The new testing apparatus was intended not only to support research but also to monitor the accuracy of tests done in the plants, to be sure that standards there were maintained.

The state of research equipment, which for so long had been a factor limiting the transformation of physical metallurgy into a science, was improving rapidly. That, in turn, raised the level of work that could be done and reduced the researcher time and the cost required to do it. ARL was the first industrial research organization to undertake routine x-ray examination of castings, using equipment installed in the Cleveland laboratory in 1927. In 1933 it built a new type of direct tension–compression fatigue machine for structural work; in 1935 it began using a photoelectric microphotometer in combination with a quartz spectrograph to analyze metal compositions; two years later it worked out a method of quantitative spectroanalysis that could be used in routine pot-room checks, reducing costs by eliminating more time-consuming chemical analysis. By 1940 the electron microscope began to have an impact on research, making possible study of the submicroscopic structure of aluminum alloys.

Equipped as well as or better than the best university laboratories of the day, the new establishment was also intentionally academic in tone. Research personnel were grouped in divisions according to disciplines: Metallurgical, Physical Testing, Analytical Chemistry, Physical Chemistry, and Chemical Development. Division heads met biweekly to discuss their priorities and their progress. Although still within walking distance of the plant, the new laboratory provided "a touch of seclusion for the scientist."[14] The organization of its interior space reflected the governing concept of research methodology. It was not designed for the teamwork characteristic of a development laboratory or of the fabled Edison invention factory, where one trained researcher might supervise many technicians or mechanics. Rather, it was set up according to "the unit system," designed to meet the needs of the individual researcher. Separate desks and innovative aluminum laboratory benches, each equipped with its own apparatus, awaited each member of the technical staff. For the first time there was room for an extensive library, containing 75,000 catalogued items and managed by a professional staff.

This change toward a more academic atmosphere at ARL in New Kensington could take place because its satellite laboratories had taken over the more immediate aspects of development work. Problems generated within the operating departments were to be solved at the branch-laboratory level, with supporting research from the center when necessary. Occasional collaborative programs between New Kensington and branch laboratories involved regular correspondence and trips back and forth between the personnel involved, but quite often they pursued largely independent, though coordinated, programs. All the division heads met monthly with Frary in New Kensington to coordinate activities, to share findings, and to plan the future program. Having spent the previous 10 years moving from one research site to another, Frary was now able to sit still and let the periphery come to the center.[15]

Frary encouraged his researchers to identify closely with their engineering and scientific professions, to attend professional conferences and society meetings, to write papers, and generally to keep in close touch with things going on in the outside scientific community. That not only kept open information channels to the outside world but also provided an objective yardstick by which the quality of research work could be measured and the worth of its contribution evaluated.

In time, the new specialized research structure and the housing of central research in a location set apart from normal operations would create barriers between Research and Operations, but that was not immediately evident. Researchers who, in their introductory assignments, had established close contact with particular operations only gradually lost touch with them. But those who joined ARL from the mid-1930s onward observed that the rest of the company hardly seemed to exist.

Francis Frary (second from left) meets with his immediate staff of research directors, Junius Edwards (left), Edgar Dix (standing), Herman Bakken, and Richard Templin. Dix is displaying a sample of the Alclad material that prevented corrosion in metal aircraft. To achieve Dix's revolutionary product, a method was developed to roll a protective layer of pure aluminum onto the surface of a high-strength alloy, making it highly resistant to corrosion.

By contrast, the outside world was an ever-present constituency to ARL researchers. As the applications for aluminum expanded and its product range increased, it took on more and more the status of a technical material, able to be tailored to specific applications because of the level of information available about it. This worked to Alcoa's advantage as sole primary supplier. Every improvement in industry knowledge was likely to result in added volume for some part of Alcoa's business.

The output of ARL's fundamental work was disseminated in a variety of forms: reports, technical papers, and books. Researchers were encouraged to work on such publications and received credit for them. In 1930, a two-volume work called *The Aluminum Industry,* by Edwards, Frary, and Jeffries, and published at Alcoa's expense, joined the ranks of important metallurgical texts. Its two volumes, *Aluminum and Its Production* and *Aluminum Products and Their Fabrication,* contained chapters by many of Alcoa's leading researchers, most written and edited on their own time. Between 1929 and 1939 *The Structural Handbook*, authored jointly by members of the Physical Testing Division and containing extensive information on the properties and design characteristics of alloy columns, beams, and girders, was issued and revised repeatedly in an effort to give the company a source of engineering information comparable to the handbook that was used by steel salesmen. Reports were also submitted to and published by the ASTM, the ASME, the NBS, and the Bureau of Aeronautics.[16]

THE RESPONSE TO THE DEPRESSION

The new laboratory building had barely opened its doors before the company faced a business downturn that made the difficulties after World War I seem trivial by comparison. Alcoa struggled to keep its substantial research budget intact as its position deteriorated, with the general economy, at the end of 1929. To an anxious confidential inquiry from President Hoover, who was trying to use White House influence to restore confidence and economic order, Frary responded optimistically that the company would still spend between $750,000 and $1 million on research, both fundamental and developmental. Soon Alcoa, too, would be forced to reassess its position.[17]

The entire national economy was plunged into an abyss of disillusionment and despair beginning in January 1931. By August 1932, industrial production had fallen 35 percent and unemployment had increased by 5 million workers. In New Kensington, as in other industrial districts around Pittsburgh, the signs of a mismatch between industrial supply and demand were everywhere apparent.[18]

During the four to five alarming years of ever-deepening economic distress, many companies that had only recently celebrated their progressiveness by opening new laboratories cut their research budgets drastically. Three hundred laboratories closed down altogether. The cuts in these most visible areas of corporate overhead were primarily economy measures, but they also reflected a public backlash against technology. Numerous articles and editorials argued that the technologists, never a mainstream group in popular eyes, had pushed their discoveries far beyond the point of social benefit. Scientific management and technological discovery harnessed to corporate ends

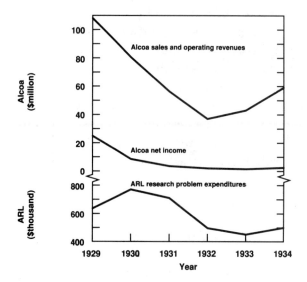

Figure 5.4. Alcoa research spending during the depresssion compared with revenue and net income. Sources: ARL annual reports, ALA; Smith, *From Monopoly to Competition*, Table B-2.

were seen to have conspired to cause an orgy of overproduction that saturated markets and threw people out of work.[19]

In these circumstances, Alcoa hewed to a less drastic course than many of its industrial neighbors. Its response to its own slackened demand was to maintain its metal price and to stockpile metal, financing the inventory by borrowing where necessary. It maintained a reduced but steady level of output, laying off some of its work force, but avoiding shutting down operations altogether. By keeping a stable work force, it was prepared to resume full-scale operations at the first sign that the economy was improving.[20]

Other than maintaining a state of preparedness in manufacturing, the company's strategy in the face of the cataclysm was to continue to develop promising new markets wherever possible, focusing especially on structural applications. ARL's specific contributions to this strategy were to seek better solutions to the corrosion problem, to tailor new high-strength alloys for each new structural use, and to work with leading-edge customers in each market in support of prototype applications.

As economic conditions grew steadily worse, layoffs occurred in ARL as in other parts of the company. The ARL's salary list was cut by 37 people during 1931, which "together with salary cuts and other economies" reduced the annual outlay for research by 25 percent. Money stretched farther in deflationary times, and cuts were absorbed in extraordinary items such as the consolidation of research operations, wherever possible. After the obvious belt-tightening measures had all been taken without cutting parts of the program, some of the more expensive developmental sites were trimmed. The experimental mill in New Kensington was shut down in 1931; the electrothermal pilot plant at Badin, which had proved the feasibility of the Hall dry process, ceased operations; the Buffalo branch laboratory, formerly part of the American Magnesium Company, closed in stages; and there was tight control of capital charges for new equipment. Some R&D functions that had previously been charged to overhead – such as the Jobbing Shop, which was set up to work with new applications in 1933 – were put on a self-supporting basis.[21]

The financial stringency of the times reinforced a frugal tendency in Frary's leadership that was to become one of the chief hallmarks of his style. Researchers' expenses were meticulously controlled during this period. Resources were always available to support travel for academic and professional meetings, but Frary treated other kinds of travel or entertainment at company expense as unnecessary junketing. Research personnel were not encouraged to take marketing people to lunch or to make trips to Alcoa plants, and those policies would continue long after the time of stringency had passed. Such policies reflected Frary's deeply ingrained personal priorities where research was concerned. External contacts with the scientific community were legitimate aspects of the researcher's work; contacts with markets were left to be made indirectly, through internal company channels.[22]

The most enduring adjustment to the economic depression turned out to be the way that was chosen to refocus the research program. What might have been a mutilation of the program, if cuts had been made across the board, turned out to be a constructive process. The chief mechanism employed to administer cuts and consolidations was a new committee system set up under the direct supervision of Alcoa president Roy Hunt and substantially dominated by the research organization.

To coordinate R&D and allocate decreasing resources among a proliferating group of technical activities, Alcoa chose to activate and extend the previously dormant Research Committee. It took on a two-committee structure in which an executive committee, called the General Committee, approved a line-item, problem-oriented research budget put together and justified by a "subcommittee," the Technical Committee. These two committees were constituted to give a voice in technical matters to the major corporate functions – top management, engineering, metal production, metal fabrication, and sales – but the largest representation and the chairs of both committees were given to Research. For many years the Technical Committee had only four members, three representing R&D and one from Sales, but ultimately it would embrace every organization within the company that needed funding for nonroutine technical projects. By 1934 each ARL division, as well as each technical department participating in "forward-looking activity" within Sales and Operations, submitted its annual budget to the Technical Committee and made monthly statements to show how actual costs compared with projections.[23]

Although the committee structure was created to control expenses, it quickly became a vital and effective organ for communication between the technical and nontechnical communities inside Alcoa. For 20 years the dominant voice on both committees was Research, principally because the General Committee secretary and the Technical Committee chairman were the same man, Herman Bakken, assistant director of research. Bakken became a master at communicating both horizontally and vertically, educating the nontechnical functions of Alcoa to the realities and value of R&D, educating senior management about ways of tapping R&D effectively, and educating R&D staff members to the needs and realities of other departments. He was able, by astute persuasion, careful selection of all subcommittee members, control of the agenda, and access to Alcoa president Hunt, to insulate nonroutine programs from destructive budgetary fluctuation and from other forms of interference. During Bakken's time, Research rarely had to curtail a program because of pressure from Operations or Sales. In effect, the old internal and external technical roles played by Hall

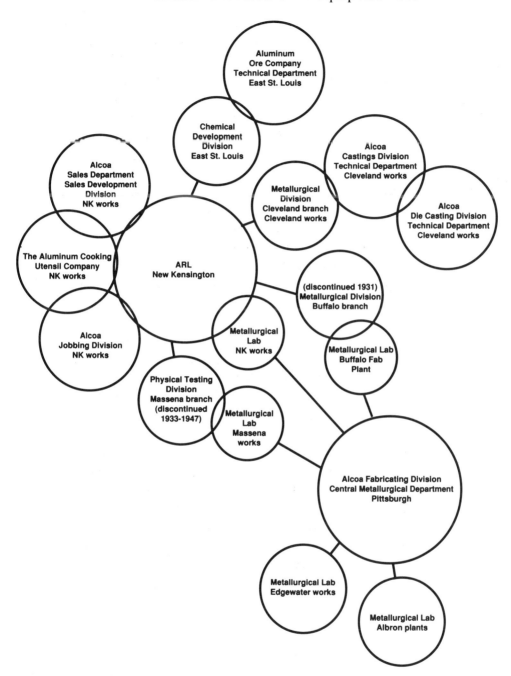

Figure 5.5. The R&D system in the 1930s: programs and budgets coordinated by the Technical Committee.

Herman Bakken.

and Hunt, and later by Hoopes and Fickes, were revived: Bakken was the voice of R&D to the rest of the company, while Frary was the voice of R&D to the outside world.[24]

Once in place, the Technical Committee's potential to serve as a two-way conduit – not only by approving research proposals but also by identifying researchable problems – was apparent. In 1931, when the need for immediate new business was most urgent, a questionnaire sent out through the good offices of the Sales representative to the Technical Committee elicited a flurry of responses resulting in new assignments to R&D staff. Projects were set up to color aluminum windows, to undertake the development of uniform finish on structural sheet, and to develop an alloy that would retain its bright surface and be readily cleaned. In some cases, all that was required for progress to be made was that an article be written for the *Alcoa Digest* summarizing what was already known within the research organization but had not been adequately disseminated to salesmen. Junius Edwards wrote on the use of aluminum in rotors, A. O. Chesley covered aluminum in radiators, and H. V. Churchill dealt with etching aluminum. Sometimes research projects were proposed, at least a quarter of which involved new alloys.[25]

When funds were scarce and jobs were affected, the Technical Committee's task was not easy, and its deliberations frequently degenerated into bitter wrangling. Bakken often had to remind his colleagues of the need to present a united front to the Research Executive Committee because so many of its members were anxious to cut technical spending. One topic that seldom failed to provoke acrimonious discussions between Research and Sales representatives on the Technical Committee was the manner in which a problem raised outside of Research should be addressed by research personnel. Did a systematic study always have to be conducted, or was it sometimes better simply to find an expedient? When embarrassing problems arose, such as the corrosion of foil supplied to Frigidaire Corporation for the lining of its refrigerators, the Sales Department was impatient to solve them as quickly as possible. Yet researchers considered such problems their concern only when they opened broader areas of inquiry. Bakken recognized such areas of disagreement as creative opportunities for communication. Because he insisted that the different viewpoints be aired, instead of simply compromised away, he did much to improve the level of interdepartmental understanding.[26]

By 1934 the company was pulling out of its economic trough, and the most insistent immediate problems had been addressed. The expanded Technical Committee was drawn into wider areas of activity, and the issues it considered became increasingly policy-oriented: standardization, sales service, the decision which alloy should be used for which application, and commercialization of new products. As the new product-oriented research program that it sponsored began to bear fruit in the late 1930s, the most important role of the Technical Committee would become planning for major new markets. By that time, it was recognized that the Technical Committee had developed an institutionalized way to look at the broader needs of the whole company and to take the longer view. Under its guidance, Alcoa achieved a good balance between fundamentals and applications, and the research program proved to be extremely prolific.[27]

RESEARCH IN DEPRESSED TIMES

A well-balanced research program is never easy to develop, least of all during economically difficult times. One man's balance is likely to be another's shocking extravagance. In the early years of the depression, the executives on the General Committee virtually eliminated new fundamental work, but even then they had the foresight to support continuation of work already under way:

The Committee recognizes that fundamental information will have a far reaching practical effect on the Company's net earnings and has recommended that such problems be continued. Illustrative of such a problem is the investigation, Gases in Metals. It is believed that the solution of this problem will be of great practical importance in connection with the elimination of blisters and slivers in sheet production.[28]

Fundamental research was something Frary would have been inclined to pursue anyway, especially because it had been pushed by others as well, but it was particularly well-suited to depressed times, once the initial emergency had passed. It was, after all, relatively inexpensive, requiring only the salary of the researcher, no travel, and very little extra equipment expense. Frary was the first to suggest that in the emergency, priority should go to research that would immediately support the ongoing business. He wrote to Jeffries that "in the present state of business it is essential that we concentrate as much as possible of our energy upon lines of research which are likely to be productive of immediate benefits to the Company by either decreased cost or increased sales." But after such opportunities were exhausted, records show that fundamental research accounted for 20 percent of the entire R&D budget – and it was an influential 20 percent.[29]

George Gibbons.

Some Alcoa executives believed that ARL had no business doing any kind of fundamental research. To men like George R. Gibbons, vice-president of the Sales Department, the very existence of the new laboratory was a sign that Alcoa was being sidetracked into excessive scientific work, more appropriate to universities. Any research labelled "fundamental and general" in the ARL budget had to be protected from Gibbons. Two of his querulous letters to Frary in 1931 clearly show the kinds of prejudices that existed. Gibbons complained that Research was not fulfilling its task of making "profits for the stockholders." He cited both chewing-gum wrappers and aluminum bronze powder as examples of Alcoa products that did not compete effectively: The gum wrapper paper did not adhere properly to the foil, and the aluminum bronze powder was not as bright as that supplied by other vendors. These shortcomings should be corrected, Gibbons said, by cooperation between Sales and the Laboratories.

Frary replied patiently to the first letter that he was all in favor of cooperation; it was indeed the responsibility of Research "broadly to earn money for the stockholders." But Gibbons's implication that Research spent its time "on what magazine writers extol as 'pure research'" was certainly untrue, he argued. If Gibbons were to read Frary's annual report, he would see that items classed under the heading "General and Fundamental Research" were no more than

a careful study of the scientific facts and principles which lie at the basis of our business and which we need to know accurately for the purpose of understanding the manufacturing phenomena and the complaints and difficulties which are continuously brought to us by the Sales and Operating Departments.[30]

In any case, Frary pointed out, under the new technical structure the foil mill had its own technical advisor whose business it was to field such problems. Gibbons's second letter made it clear that Frary's reply had fallen on deaf ears, but Frary simply ignored it. That he was able to ignore such jibes demonstrated his autonomy. He had both the responsibility and the authority to determine the best research program on behalf of the company as a whole.

The three most important technical areas in which ARL generated and published basic data stemming from long-term systematic work were alloy composition and properties, corrosion, and structures. Fundamental research on aluminum-based alloy systems, which was begun in mid-1926 in the *Shenandoah* aftermath, intensified in the 1930s with an extensive program of metallography to identify alloy constituents, using first a regular microscope and later x-ray equipment and the electron microscope. It had also been decided in 1926 that the level of understanding of corrosion was so low as to prevent the formulation of standard methods of corrosion testing. Researchers had begun collecting many samples of different aluminum alloys to be tested on a long-term basis under different climates and conditions. In 1931, fundamental studies began on the mechanism of corrosion itself, and work was undertaken to determine the effects of different fabrication methods.[31]

In the area of structural research, systematic laboratory testing was done using the Amsler machine to test the design and properties of aluminum structural members. Load, stress, impact, and fatigue were the critical factors. Extra-laboratory testing was conducted on the Smithfield Street bridge across the Monongahela River in Pittsburgh, which Alcoa had rebuilt using aluminum, and at other large engineering works owned by the firm.

Cooperative work with customers on structural projects greatly expanded in the wake of the successful work with the airship alloy and the growth of more sophisticated customers to cooperate along these lines. Airframe companies, for instance, hired highly skilled technical people, and both the Pennsylvania Railroad and the Pullman Company employed engineers who were extremely able, though often reluctant to adopt new materials. Alcoa employees in the Sales Development and Research Laboratories might spend months at a time on assignment at a customer's site. Ernest Hartmann, a structural engineer and future director of the Laboratories, spent eight months with the Pullman Company on analysis and redesign of one of its prototype aluminum cars after it had been in an accident.[32]

Several new classes of alloys, more workable than 17S, resulted from the combination of fundamental alloy work and cooperative work with manufacturers. Alloy 27S was developed in 1933 for use on the Smithfield Street bridge; 53S was developed the same year for beer-barrel sheet when the repeal of Prohibition made that a promising new market; and alloy 11S was produced for use in screw-machine work. Collaboration with United Airlines and with bus manufacturers in the mid-1930s helped to speed production of the new high-strength alloys 51S and 24S. The speed of alloy development depended in part on the ability to collect good performance data, a process that was greatly accelerated under wartime conditions. By the end of World War II, the company had produced 25 new alloys, most through close work with airplane manufacturers such as Hamilton Standard, Douglas, and Boeing.

The areas of research that had received the most attention during the 1920s, refining and smelting, were scaled back in the 1930s. Research effort in the area of smelting tended to concentrate on furnace linings and on achieving greater purity in the carbon anodes, both for the Soderberg continuous electrode and for individual prebaked carbons. Once the Bayer process had been made to work satisfactorily, its further improvement was left to chemical engineering, while the East St. Louis laboratory, now entirely under ARL, concentrated on developing and producing chemical by-products. In the mid-1930s it embarked on a new project to modify the Bayer process to handle nonstandard bauxites. Projects of this sort would have been viewed as needlessly speculative if the Aluminum Ore Company had been paying for the laboratory.

Under Frary, relationships among the branch laboratories, the ARL, and local plants were carefully structured and maintained to uphold the interests of the whole company over those of individual locations. Each was based on a clear division of labor, mutual respect, and constant vigilance on Frary's part. The difficulties of maintaining such relationships had been foreseen by Fickes and Hoopes years before, when they had fought for a neutral location for the corporate laboratory. Now that a central, autonomous laboratory had been created, Frary took great pains to preserve its sta-

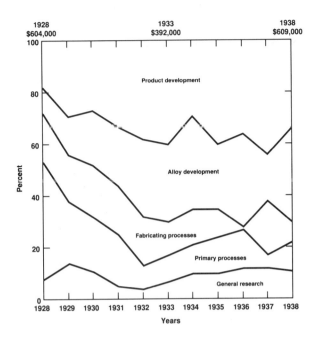

Figure 5.6. ARL program emphasis, 1928–38. Program categories as percentages of total expenditures. Source: Research Bureau annual reports, ALA.

tus, even in matters as seemingly trivial as the titles used in correspondence.

In 1936, this point came up explicitly when G. H. Wagner, head of the East St. Louis branch laboratory, after years of using no title on his correspondence, began signing his letters written on Aluminum Ore Company stationery "Director, Aluminum Ore Company Research Laboratories," with no reference to the Aluminum Company of America. When queried, he told Frary that this was to bring his correspondence "in harmony with the practice at East St. Louis," where others who were his local equivalents in rank signed as "Chief Engineer" or "Chief Chemist." "Of course, I realize," he wrote, "that inside the Company the set-up in connection with research is considerably different, but this is probably of no consequence in connection with outside companies."[33]

The lengthy exchange of letters that ensued among Frary, Wagner, Alcoa's executive vice-president Fickes, and East St. Louis works manager Charles Fox showed that it was of great consequence. Frary insisted that nothing be done to suggest that the branch laboratory belonged to the subsidiary. He admonished Wagner to make sure that his dealings with the out-

Charles Fox.

side world were clearly understood as representing the corporate laboratory, pointing out that this was of mutual benefit. The fundamental work funded by Alcoa had to be credited as such in the professional communities, not attributed to the Aluminum Ore Company. But equally, the East St. Louis laboratory's findings would have more credibility in the outside world because of ARL's reputation for independence and high research standards.[34]

Reminding Wagner that it was the company's deliberate policy not to establish separate research organizations in its different subsidiary companies, "but rather to tie the whole research group into one central organization," Frary proposed that all Wagner's letters be signed using some form of the title "Chief–Aluminum Ore Company Division, ALUMINUM RESEARCH LABORATORIES."[35] The gratifying response to this suggestion from Charles Fox got to the heart of the issue:

... I believe that the Aluminum Research Laboratories has established a name for itself as an impartial research institute not strictly subservient in its findings to the Aluminum Company of America. I presume it is this feature of the Aluminum Research Laboratories that Dr. Frary wants to preserve. I think that is well worth preserving, and if that feature of the Aluminum Research Laboratories is to be preserved, then I do not see any better way to do it than by the subscript suggested by Dr. Frary.[36]

More than 10 years of careful cooperative work had paid off. What could only be read as a resounding vote of confidence in the corporate research organization came from a man who was known for his independent cast of mind and for his resistance to anything that smacked of arbitrary exercise of control from corporate headquarters.

Frary needed the independence he had so patiently earned to keep his companywide R&D program synchronized with trends in the national climate for R&D. In the latter part of the decade, the research program Frary had pursued in the early 1930s came under severe criticism, especially from those who had wanted greater investment in the metalworking area. Yet this was retrospective criticism. To have launched a high-profile program on metalworking fundamentals in the early 1930s would have incurred unacceptable levels of capital investment in research equipment, and it would surely have defied the tenor of the times.

In 1934, influential scientists, led by Karl Compton of MIT, launched a major public-opinion campaign to suggest that the problem with science and industry in the 1920s had been "a misuse of science by industry." Technology had been created to rationalize and eliminate jobs rather than to create new businesses. It should be the job of science, Compton wrote in the *New York Times,* to "find ways of using the fruits of overproduction to create new industries." Critics of Compton's stamp were particularly harsh toward companies that dominated their industries. They charged that by getting out of the business of industrial research after the war, the federal government had permitted dominant companies to control the evolution of their respective industrial technologies in their narrow interests, while keeping smaller competitors from engaging profitably in research. Alcoa was certainly the dominant, indeed the only, research-performing company in its industry, but guided by Frary's research philosophy, its program could not be fairly accused of misuse of science. Both its fundamental research and its applied research were heavily directed toward creating new businesses, both for itself and for its customers.[37]

THE 1937 TECHNICAL SHOW

Nationally, the promotional efforts of the scientific community, led by Compton and by AT&T's Jewett, had the desired effect. They argued that there was a necessary role for scientific research in business, one that was different from its role in universities, namely, to create the basis for new businesses. Their argument was widely accepted in the business community, and by 1938 more than 50 companies featured research accomplishments in their annual reports. Westinghouse, for example, which had long concentrated almost entirely on applied work, set up a program to fund fundamental research. Each year, 10 two-year Westinghouse Research Fellowships were awarded, with annual stipends of $2,400, to support members of their technical staff to work on problems of their own choosing.[38]

It was in this era of renewed interest in industrial science that Alcoa's Technical Committee, in 1937, held a day-long technical show for 50 senior Alcoa managers from all over the company. The objective was to educate Aloca's nontechnical management to recent research achievements and their significance for the company. This reflected the concern of Bakken and others over the lack of technical awareness that they perceived among Alcoa executives at that time. In the current labor climate, many Alcoa managers regarded it as impolitic to express much interest in technological developments. Though that was understandable, it was a cause for worry for Bakken:

During the past year or so I have been preaching the desirability of the responsible people in our Company becoming more and more technically-minded and when I say technically-minded I refer to chemical developments, metallurgical developments and mechanical developments and even electrical developments. The present labor and commercial situation is not conducive to become technical-minded unless some artificial or pre-planned scheme is arranged to achieve this objective.

At the risk of being thought to be pro-German, Bakken declared that two trips abroad had left him "indelibly impressed" with the fact that German "commercial men, managers, executives, are exceedingly well informed technically."[39]

The technical show replaced the usual smaller, and more austere, annual budget-review meeting with the Research Executive Committee. To make the review of the technical program interesting, exhibits were added to the usual reports. Bakken confided in Hunt that he thought the resistance of "commercial people" to becoming better informed was due in part "to the fact that the average man looks upon technical matters as something that is weird and difficult of comprehension." He hoped that the technical show would help to break down this barrier. To increase its chances of success, he coached presenters as to the topics they should cover, provided displays and visual aids, and managed the program so that the less interesting speakers took as little time as possible. Roy Hunt heightened the interest by requiring all attendees to send him a written response at the end of the presentation. The show was held at the Aluminum Clubhouse in New Kensington in December 1937. Representatives of all parts of the technical community gave half-hour presentations on the year's developments, closely timed by Bakken, who had equipped himself with a clock and a gong.[40]

Twenty-five exhibits encompassed the range of activities under the purview of the Technical Committee, offering a good summary of the developments that the Alcoa R&D community regarded as its most important collective achievements since the

Alcoa executives at the time of the 1937 Technical Show. Seated, left to right, are: Senior Vice President George R. Gibbons, Senior Vice President Edwin S. Fickes, Board Chairman Arthur Vining Davis, President Roy A. Hunt, Vice President Charles B. Fox. Standing, left to right, are: Vice President George J. Stanley, Vice President Paul J. Urquhart, Vice President Irving W. Wilson, Senior Vice President Robert E. Withers, Vice President Safford K. Colby. (From Charles C. Carr, *Alcoa: An American Enterprise* [New York: Rinehart, 1952], p. 220.)

completion of the new laboratory building. Even advertising, which was included in the corporate R&D budget as a developmental activity, had a display comparing early promotional literature and ad copy to the offerings of 1937. Samples of new applications included beer barrels and oil drums, skis and ice-cube trays, refrigerator condensers, parts for air brakes, and a variety of products with anodic "Alumilite" finishes: venetian blinds, rayon bobbins, zippers, and tin and chromium-plated pistons. For the most part, though, the emphasis was on process improvements and developments that cut costs or raised the quality of familiar products such as cooking utensils, aluminum powder, paint, and foil. Primary processes were covered in an exhibit titled "Ore Product and Reduction Development," which displayed important new by-products of the refining process, synthetic cryolite developed at ARL's East St. Louis branch, and improved electrodes and pot linings. The newest and most significant fabricating innovation, the direct-chill ingot-casting process, was featured in two displays: "Metallurgical Developments" and "Remelting and Casting." Eight other units demonstrated a host of smaller-scale improvements in all of the fabricating processes: rolling, drawing, extrusion, die casting, hot and cold pressing, and forging. The exhibits documented progress in increasing the corrosion resistance of high-strength alloys, in establishing design criteria for structural uses of aluminum, and in improving joining processes, three areas critical to expanding applications. Finally, the show provided graphic documentation of the contributions of the R&D organizations to Alcoa's hegemony in aluminum technology in a chart showing the growth in the number of patents granted for both processes and products.

Reactions were overwhelmingly positive. The show, wrote one advertising executive, was the first in Alcoa's history to "display a graphic, physical, tangible group of results of what has been done, what is being done, and what is hoped to be accomplished in the not-too-distant future." He added:

The examples shown in the exhibit sell the visitor on the many interesting problems which are connected with the manufacture and exploitation of our products much more effectively than could any number of technical articles or papers. Visitors are urged to examine the objects carefully. The signs, instead of reading, "Please do not touch," as they do in so many exhibits, convey instructions of an entirely different nature. "Lift it," one sign commands. "Bend it," says another. "Pick it up," advises a third.[41]

The show was an important exercise in internal public relations – a necessary element for the smooth functioning of R&D, something that had been conspicuous by its absence. This was not an area of concern to Frary. Yet his researchers, in particular, who were accustomed to gauge their useful output by external criteria – patents received, papers and reports written, customer problems solved – were gratified at the warm response of the internal constituency. Gibbons suggested to Hunt that an exhibit based on the show should be a permanent feature at the ARL, offsetting the "rather uninspiring reaction" carried away by the many visitors taken through the Laboratories each year. "We have a fine showcase in our Laboratory, but it is only a sort of half-baked situation unless we can show the products that we produce in that Laboratory."[42]

The need for improved internal communications was evident in the shock expressed by key executives at the progress that had been achieved on critical research fronts. One Sales executive noted that, after hearing Edgar Dix's presentation on alloy development, he could now approach prospective customers with claims for aluminum's "corrosion resistance," rather than rely on negative, defensive strategies. Other nagging problems that had been solved or radically diminished through research included the control of streaking of products with anodized Alumilite finishes and control of ingot quality through better understanding of metal structure.[43]

M. E. Noyes, a sales engineer specializing in electrical conductor wire, recorded an exhibit that impressed him:

The matter of natural grain structure of original metal aroused my interest more than any other single feature of this exhibit. Apparently it has been demonstrated that original grain structure controls or at least influences grain structure of the metal in any subsequent product regardless of the number of times that the metal may have been remelted or reworked. The question immediately arises as to the possible improvement in physical properties . . . which may result from proper control of original metal.

Noyes added that he had been "haunted" by a worsening trend in the fatigue properties of transmission cables over the course of several years, and he wondered if there might have been some underlying change in the ingot from which this product was made. As a result of what he learned at the show, he arranged for the Technical Committee to help him organize a small project to study this problem.[44]

Clearly, the technical show was a turning point, much like the watershed in 1923 when Blough issued his manifesto calling for fundamental research in metallurgy, only this time the direction indicated was toward more effective applications. The show itself evoked two very different kinds of responses, positive at the accomplishments of an integrated in-house R&D program, but cautionary in that new and different needs had replaced the old ones. On the positive side, there was open recognition of how much had been accomplished during the previous decade to knit together the disparate parts of the company into a technical whole, with a common technical vision. On the negative side, however, there was the prospect of greatly increased demand because of the new threat of war in Europe, and there was the sense that a better information flow would be needed between technical groups and Operations if new technologies were to be implemented.

For those who remembered the difficulties of the previous generation, the receptivity expressed by men in operating divisions to the coordinated technical effort and cooperative spirit represented by many of the presentations was heartening. Thomas D. Jolly, vice-president of operations, could remember a time when such company unity would have been unthinkable.

When the Technical Direction Department and the Research Division were first established cooperation was practically negative. The old time operating men resented instruction given by "school boys" and when these new men visited the works to observe operations they were referred to as "snoopers". The operating men were afraid that credit for improvements would be appropriated by others and for this reason were not only reluctant to give information but in some cases actually made misleading statements. The irreconcilable operators are no longer with us and the technicians have mellowed somewhat as they have grown older. Opposition has disappeared and the various divisions are now cooperative instead of competitive. Without this development of cooperative spirit the display at the Club House could not have been nearly so extensive.[45]

Younger men in the plants asked for more chance to understand and identify with the technical vision of the company at large. R. S. Stokes wrote from the Mobile works: "As an outlander engaged in alumina problems, my visits among the metal-minded men of New Kensington have always seemed like those of a visitor from another planet." Entering into the spirit of the occasion, he suggested that his plant's location in a region of "salt air, highest rainfall in the United States, frequent fogs, and relatively high annual average temperature" would make it a good place for an outside testing site for new alloys and finishes. From the Fairfield works, Wiser Brown wrote: "It seems to me that in the Operating Department, at least, we become so engrossed with our own particular problems and phase of the Company's business that we are apt to lose sight of the broader Company picture." He wanted the information in the exhibits about advances at other plants, and the valuable interchange they provoked, to be made permanently available in some way, if only by having a few men in each plant "with more education, so to speak," of the kind provided by the technical show. R. T. Whitzel of the Massena works suggested a permanent travelling exhibit to keep people abreast of technical progress throughout the corporation.[46]

TARGET OF ANTITRUST

The sense of common technical purpose and of possibility generated by the research program was heightened by the realization that the integrated structure that made it possible was in serious jeopardy. In 1937 the New Deal Justice Department filed charges in U.S. District Court claiming that Alcoa had purposefully monopolized both alumina and aluminum-ingot production in the United States and that it had come to dominate in the production of certain fabricated products, such as high-strength alloy sheet, through unfair business practices. Government lawyers argued that Alcoa should be broken up, either vertically or horizontally, into several competing aluminum companies. Testimony began in the spring of 1938 and lasted until October 1941.

Attendees at the 1937 technical show, well aware of the threat to Alcoa's hard-earned unity, saw that as one of the show's most obvious messages. If only the judges who might try the case brought by the Justice Department could see the show themselves, suggested C. C. Carr, the need for integration would be clear. "They would get at first hand a real understanding of the necessity and importance of integrated technical research in a business so young and highly competitive with other materials."[47]

The potential loss of monopoly held at least as many uncertainties for Research as for other parts of Alcoa. Research owed its position as a central plank in Alcoa's business strategy in the interwar period in part to the company's status as America's long primary producer. S. K. Colby claimed in 1930 that the monopoly was "a knife that cuts both ways." Alcoa's unique position had necessitated technical self-reliance, but the technical mastery that resulted was arguably more important to the company than its pioneering experience or its control of sources of bauxite. Whether or not the company's management

Francis Frary with Safford Colby, to whom he reported after Edmund Fickes retired.

actually believed that argument, they certainly felt that its unique position had allowed Alcoa to make the most out of the investment in R&D. It was not at all clear that research results would be nearly as appropriate if other domestic primary producers were to enter the industry.[48]

The suit brought by the Justice Department, and the protracted trial that ensued, reinforced the company's own interpretation of its history and of its rationale for research. The importance of Alcoa's integrated R&D, for the nation and for the rest of the industry, was a key element in its defense against the charge of monopoly. A. V. Davis made this point repeatedly in his six-week-long testimony in the summer of 1939. When asked to speculate on the probable effects of dividing the corporation into several competing companies, he commented as follows:

There is perhaps no element in the growth and success of the Aluminum Company of America and the consequent benefit to the public in the way of reduced costs and improvement in product that could equal the research laboratory, and it would be impossible to duplicate that in a dissolution. The research laboratory is of vital importance, for instance, to the United States Government. The progress in airplanes and other military affairs has been made largely . . . as a result of the work of large and highly educated and highly skillful research laboratory workers and in the same way the improvement of the product and the improvement of the raw material and semi-finished materials, and so on, would be very much hampered and retarded unless one big laboratory is on the job.[49]

"Dutch" Nagel, another star witness, testified for 12 days between December 1939 and February 1940. He asserted that Alcoa's greatest competitive resource was human:

It takes years for men to acquire the knowledge and experience necessary to be really useful. . . . There is no source of highly trained men experienced in aluminum. The universities do not specialize particularly in aluminum. They turn out scientists but what is required in the aluminum industry in research and development of its products is also knowledge regarding aluminum. That can be acquired only by experience in the industry.[50]

Nagel developed in detail the role and significance of a centralized research organization, recalling as examples the solution of early problems with the composition of 17S, the elimination of blisters in sheet, and the gradual improvement in the quality of metal coming out of Hall-Héroult pots. Nagel also described how the Technical Committee functioned to pull it all together. He alluded to a new "Working Aluminum Program" as an example of a heavy investment in research that would be justifiable only because of the broad impact it would have across the many different fabricating units of the company.[51]

Judge Francis Caffey concluded the four-year legal action with a decision exonerating Alcoa on all counts. The Justice Department, he ruled, had failed to prove that there was an illegal monopoly, that allegations of conspiracy were justified, or that there had been restrictive practices. He found "no warrant in fact or in law" to split Alcoa up into four competing companies, as had been suggested. But he closed by saying that he fully expected the government to appeal, and as he predicted, the Justice Department quickly appealed his decision, placing Alcoa once again under the threat of dissolution. By this time with war threatening, Alcoa was no longer the sole producer of primary aluminum. In May 1941, Reynolds Metals Company had opened alumina and reduction plants, built with loans from the Reconstruction Finance Corporation. The war in Europe focused all eyes on high-volume production.[52]

WARTIME R&D

The technical show had raised the issue of process improvement and its connection to expanded output in no uncertain terms. I. W. ("Chief") Wilson, Alcoa's vice-president of operations, expressed great enthusiasm over recent advances in fundamental understanding of the structure and behavior of aluminum alloys. "Above all," he wrote to Hunt, "we need to know how certain of the alloys can best be worked in order to obtain maximum physical properties, improved appearance or surface finish, and minimum cost of fabrication. To my mind this clearly indicates the importance of the general research problem on this fundamental study of working of aluminum and its alloys."[53]

At the technical show, Bakken had alerted top management to the need for a Working Aluminum Program and the large capital expenditure in research equipment such a program would require. Nothing less than a major new initiative in applications was required to spread the benefits of research to all

Alcoa operations. Though the company was selling more than half its output as finished or semifinished products, relatively little work had been done on the metalworking processes by which they were produced. In this, Bakken said, the Laboratories had committed a "sin of omission,"

in that they [Research] have not been active enough studying working of aluminum problems and have therefore not given the help they might have to our Engineering and Operating Departments – We have a strong Metallurgical Department – We have over the past 10–15 years led the world in Alloy Development – We hope we can continue to do so. I submit however that it does not do us much good to have splendid alloys if we cannot work them or if in working them costs are too high for normal profit. Right today the selection of a new aircraft alloy hinges on whether we can economically work certain compositions. It is to be hoped that this meeting will see fit to provide suitable facilities so that we may go at this general problem in main fashion and make up for the time that I at least feel has in part been lost.[54]

To those in the laboratory, the show clearly demonstrated how little of their valuable work had penetrated to levels of the corporation where it could be applied. In a letter to Frary, Richard Templin, ARL's chief of physical testing, lamented that too little work had been done on production problems and that the knowledge they had was not being used to educate plant workmen and foremen on how to produce higher-quality metal with less scrap loss. "I think that many of us should blush for shame," he wrote, "and wonder why full advantage has not been taken of information and changes in fabricating practice," which could be "made rather quickly."[55]

The notion that metalworking should be elevated as a research priority was not new, but in 1937 its urgency was visible to all. Bakken's trips to Germany provided ample warning that Europe was once again stepping up production for war and that Alcoa would face the need to increase output many times over. Ironically, just as it took more than five years to address the change in technical direction after the need for it was recognized in 1923, the new Working Aluminum initiative was delayed for the war's duration. Management lost no time in appropriating the necessary capital investments – $150,000 for a large tensile testing machine, a 3-million-pound hydraulic press, and an addition to one of the ARL buildings to house the new equipment – all add-

The "Templin tester" was a huge precision testing and metalworking machine designed to improve ARL's physical testing capabilities and to experiment with methods of extrusion and forging in support of the "Working Aluminum" program. The largest piece of equipment in the Laboratories in the 1940s, its installation was delayed until after World War II.

ing up to more than one-fourth of the ARL's typical annual expenditures at the time. Nevertheless, before the equipment could arrive, the R&D organization was swept into a thousand wartime activities.

In 1938, Alcoa had been sitting comfortably on a 2.5-year aluminum reserve based on its current markets, but strong signals coming from aircraft producers and through Washington contacts confirmed the need to expand in anticipation of future demand. As a result, the company began a building program that ultimately consumed five years and $300 million and increased Alcoa's annual productive capacity from 293 to 828 million pounds of aluminum. In 1941, Alcoa began a separate building program under contract to the Defense Plant Corporation. This involved designing, building, and operating eight reduction plants, two big alumina plants, four special refineries for low-grade bauxite, and nine giant fabricating works. In the nation as a whole, productive capacity in aluminum expanded by 600 percent during the war, compared with 10 percent for steel and 50 percent for copper.[56]

All of that expansion greatly strained the resources of the central research organization. Like many other industrial organizations, ARL lost many of its younger staff members to the draft, and women first entered ARL in significant numbers as technicians during that time. On the home front, many researchers were called upon to help design and then operate the new plants, so that, to a great extent, the actual conduct of research was left to senior personnel. Alcoa's senior researchers, identifying closely with their professional peers in the scientific fraternity, threw themselves into the war effort. For several years they completely disrupted their regular activities, and their work was donated to the government by the company.[57]

Frary and his lieutenants served on various advisory boards to the armed services, in particular on project groups of the War Metallurgy Committee, of which Zay Jeffries was a member. Herman Bakken was a research supervisor for projects on magnesium production; Harry Churchill worked on establishing standards for spectrographic analysis; Junius Edwards served on a committee studying the chromic acid anodizing process; and Frary worked with the various committees of the alumina group, which sponsored work on extracting alumina from clay and supported Alcoa in the development of its "combination process" for low-grade bauxite ore. Frary also consulted to the Chemical Warfare Service, the National Inventors Council, and the Office of Scientific Research and Development. He was also a member of the Non-Ferrous Metallurgical Advisory Board of the Ordnance Department. Alcoa researchers contributed as consultants to two atomic bomb programs: the Manhattan Project, on problems of corrosion and joining,

Table 5.1. *Defense Plant Corporation plants, number of personnel, 1941–6*

Plant	1941	1942	1943	1944	1945	1946
Refining						
Baton Rouge, LA	0	244	1,758	806	92	1
East St. Louis, IL	0	2	85	81	21	10
Hurricane Creek, AK	15	740	1,537	1,303	734	0
Mobile, AL	0	0	81	55	28	15
Smelting						
Burlington, NJ	0	100	856	465	69	0
Jones Mills, AK	12	1,097	1,404	1,113	721	13
Los Angeles, CA	9	800	1,006	669	82	15
Mead,WA	16	742	1,039	1,070	724	1
Queens, NY	0	194	1,373	716	34	0
Riverbank, CA	0	57	521	339	41	0
St. Lawrence, NY	13	919	978	30	10	0
Troutdale, OR	18	746	826	715	455	1
Fabrication						
Canonsburg, PA	0	47	657	941	425	48
Chicago, IL	0	86	1,233	1,931	1,304	76
Cressona, PA	0	61	1,914	1,634	20	8
Glassmere, PA	0	0	0	67	55	0
Kansas City, MO	0	44	1,013	1,779	913	0
Monroe, MI	0	0	369	637	503	13
Newark, OH	0	59	990	1,104	872	76
New Castle, PA	0	135	778	988	614	51
Phoenix, AR	0	62	1,526	1,860	1,736	41
St. Paul, MN	0	1	35	1	0	0
Trentwood, WA	0	170	1,649	2,275	1,752	17
Headquarters						
Pittsburgh office	33	69	123	87	45	13
Total	116	6,375	21,751	20,666	11,270	399

studied at the metallurgical laboratory of the University of Chicago, and Project Y in Santa Fe, New Mexico.[58]

At the same time, the laboratories continued to act as a central technical resource for the greatly expanded production facilities. Since 1928, Harry Churchill, chief of the Analytical Chemistry Division, had been working on adapting the quartz spectroscope for use in plants. Spectrographic laboratories were installed experimentally at the Massena and Vancouver reduction plants, and subsequently they were added to every

Alcoa smelter and built into all of the reduction plants constructed for the Defense Plant Corporation. Throughout the war, his son, Raynor Churchill, assistant chief of ARL's Analytical Chemistry Division, travelled around the country with a representative of ARL, the company that made the spectroscopes, maintaining the sensitive instruments and advising plant metallurgists on how to use them.[59]

Frary strenuously resisted the efforts of outsiders to take away his few senior researchers on a full-time basis for any special projects. He was successful because ARL was itself conducting research of great significance to the war effort, particularly in the area of aeronautics, where huge increases in government funding created demands for rapid advances. The Cleveland Research Division focused its efforts on improvement of alloys and foundry techniques for producing airplane-engine cylinder heads, landing gear, and other parts, while metallurgists at New Kensington worked on extrusion of high-strength alloys, which had become a bottleneck in the production of various airplane parts.[60]

ARL's Engineering Design Division devoted its attention almost exclusively to working closely with aircraft designers and builders, meeting regularly with them to keep abreast of evolving materials needs and publishing some 37 reports on aluminum properties and design specifications for aircraft. In alloy development, the big push was first to provide data that would open the way for acceptance of a new high-strength temper for the standard aluminum-copper aircraft alloys, referred to as "super Duralumins," and subsequently to develop a new generation of alloys based on the combination of aluminum, zinc, and magnesium. These new materials, including alloys 76S and 75S, saw wartime service primarily in large forged propellers, but after the war they became the standard aircraft metals for all applications.[61]

The effect of the war on Alcoa R&D was to push its capability rapidly in the direction that had been considered so important before the war: toward a much greater ability to frame important applications problems and to apply existing knowledge in solving them. Most of Alcoa's R&D personnel were heavily exposed to "customers," both internal and external, in the form of Alcoa plants and weapons manufacturers. Yet, because of Frary's success in insisting on the urgent wartime need for their

This reversing hot mill at the defense plant in Trentwood, Washington, was designed and built by an equipment company, United Engineering and Foundry Company, and Alcoa working together. Large-scale equipment such as this became necessary to roll what was, for that time, ingot of very large size. The oil-based lubricant used and the semimanual nature of the equipment severely limited what could be done with this generation of equipment.

services within the company, both in research and in operations positions in the plants, they had relatively little exposure to the other key external constituency, the scientific community at large. Other R&D-performing companies such as General Elec-

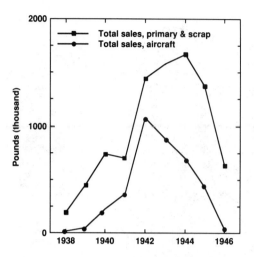

Figure 5.7. Alcoa's World War II production. Source: "Industrial Classification of Sales (Summary)," AA, env. 296.

tric, RCA, and DuPont, many of whose researchers were on loan to the big cooperative projects such as radar or radio, gained far more from the wartime experience along this dimension. Lack of such national scientific exposure contributed to Alcoa's turning inward in the postwar period.

THE POSTWAR AGENDA

Defense-related research continued throughout the war, but by 1943 much of the pressure on production was relieved, mainly by virtue of the massive buildup of the preceding five years. In 1943, primary production peaked at almost 2 billion pounds, with another 500 million pounds produced from scrap. At the same time, U.S. fabricating capacity was so great that 271 million pounds of aluminum were imported from Canada to be made into finished products for the Allies. Aluminum was the first basic war material to be removed from priority control, and cutbacks began at the most costly smelting operations as early as December 1943.[62]

To most of Alcoa's leaders, the basic outlines of the postwar period seemed clear well before the war's end, and the relief that came late in 1943 allowed them to turn their attention to planning for the future. The prevailing forecast for the postwar period, both inside and outside the company, was that increased

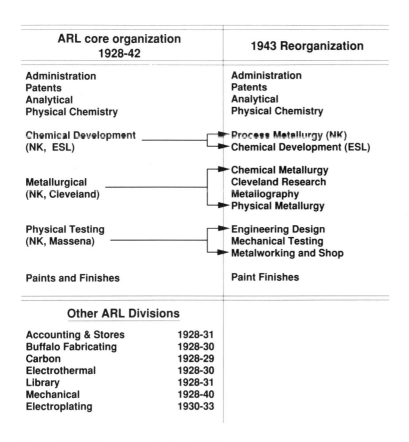

ARL core organization 1928-42	1943 Reorganization
Administration Patents Analytical Physical Chemistry	Administration Patents Analytical Physical Chemistry
Chemical Development (NK, ESL)	Process Metallurgy (NK) Chemical Development (ESL)
Metallurgical (NK, Cleveland)	Chemical Metallurgy Cleveland Research Metallography Physical Metallurgy
Physical Testing (NK, Massena)	Engineering Design Mechanical Testing Metalworking and Shop
Paints and Finishes	Paint Finishes

Other ARL Divisions

Accounting & Stores	1928-31
Buffalo Fabricating	1928-30
Carbon	1928-29
Electrothermal	1928-30
Library	1928-31
Mechanical	1928-40
Electroplating	1930-33

Figure 5.8. ARL reorganization, 1943.

capacity, competition, and the huge surplus of aluminum that had accumulated would combine to cause an explosion of light-metal usage once the economy was demobilized.[63]

R&D would have a crucial role to play in adapting aluminum to nonmilitary uses, and ARL would be under the gun to develop new applications as rapidly as possible. The old, loose, discipline-oriented structure of the Laboratories had already proved itself both too cumbersome and too science-oriented to serve such a purpose well. A major reorganization in 1943 addressed the need to commercialize new technologies by splitting three large, diverse divisions into nine more streamlined and tightly focused ones. Planning for the postwar period focused attention on problem areas, highlighting enabling technologies that would have to be developed to bring good applications to market. For example, in a letter directed to the Technical Committee in March 1944, Gibbons complained strongly about the failure to develop good joining techniques, a problem that had dragged on unsolved for decades and that now would keep aluminum out of important high-volume markets such as ship-building. "The one great need and lack in the application of aluminum in a big way in many fields," wrote Gibbons, "is the inability to weld it without destroying the physical properties of the welded section."[64]

For its part, the Technical Committee was anxious to return to the agenda set aside because of the war, now made even more urgent by the prospect of a postwar boom. In 1938, 200 million pounds of aluminum to be fabricated into products had posed a challenge to quality control and productivity in the plants. Alcoa faced the prospect of emerging from the war with capacity to produce 750 million pounds in sheet metal alone, not including castings, forgings, and extrusions. The pressure on fabricating plants would be intense, and the Working Aluminum Program conceived before the war would be more important than ever. The capital investments in research equipment and facilities, already in place, and the R&D reorganization, currently under way, had to be accompanied by a major effort in implementation on the operations side. The huge expansion in number of plants, the scarcity of trained technical personnel to staff them, and the expected pressures for output all suggested a mammoth program to be executed.

In addition to the reorganization of research, there was an expansion of development activities in other parts of the technical community. In 1944 the metallurgical departments of the fabricating divisions were unified and given corporate-division status under "Dutch" Nagel. The new Metallurgical Division had responsibility for research conducted in the plants. Shortly after the war, Engineering established its own more permanent "laboratory" at the Cleveland works to develop new fabricating equipment, largely in response to innovations coming out of ARL. This laboratory came into being when the chief electrical engineer, Donald Bohn, set to work to design and build an induction heating furnace, which was needed to complete the manufacture of forged airplane propellers. Sales Development, which had its origins in the tradition of "missionary selling," also expanded at that time. There, too, "Dutch" Nagel had played an important role by educating customers in the aircraft industry in ways to avoid corrosion by proper construction tech-

Conrad ("Dutch") Nagel.

The Cleveland plant, which played a particularly active role in the war effort, was the home of two of the development divisions that became important to Alcoa after World War II: the Sales Development Division and the Equipment Development Division. Cleveland also handled much of the direct contact with that vital new customer, the U.S. Air Force.

niques. After 1940, Sales Development added product development to its function of technical assistance to customers, establishing a separate facility at the Cleveland works to produce prototype castings and forgings to customers' specifications.[65]

With such an array of technical needs and programs requiring attention, the familiar structure and modus operandi of the Technical Committee began to seem inadequate, at least to some members of the committee. In January 1944, Bakken drew up a proposal for expanding the committee and its responsibilities. He suggested that it be enlarged and given new powers. The committee would no longer be the "fact-finding" and "recommending" group established in 1933, but would have authority to "initiate and assist in the formulation" of R&D programs and to prepare the budgets for them, to coordinate and "expedite" work in the various technical organizations and to "avoid unnecessary duplication of effort," to assist and supervise bringing innovations into use, "i.e., new alloys, new products, new equipment," and to continue to serve the General Committee by recommending "company action" on important matters.[66]

What Bakken proposed amounted to a radical departure, suggesting the sense of urgency that imbued the postwar agenda. Such a radical departure had its negative implications. For the various R&D groups, it suggested project initiation, even imposition, from above. For Operations, it threatened the undermining of local initiative for process improvement. But in 1944 Bakken was a man in a hurry, and he feared leaving the needed major improvement to incremental efforts on the part of those already under pressure. While taking "some degree of satisfaction" in the completed budgets for 1944, Bakken wrote confidentially to Hunt, he also felt strongly that there were "many elements" still missing:

I am not at all satisfied as yet that we have in our research and development dockets enough effort directed toward Process improvement and Product development. The growth of this kind of effort proceeds slowly and in no small measure depends upon needed facilities as well as personnel to properly conduct it. . . . I think we are all thoroughly convinced that lower cost and more efficient processes, as well as entirely new products, must be developed to permit us to move the metal tonnage that we shall want to move.[67]

The undertaking he envisioned would require a large corporate investment, not only in facilities and funding but also in personnel. Fundamental research, alloy development, and the work on primary processes – the program of the 1930s – had required a staff composed primarily of chemists and metallurgists. To carry out a large-scale program on downstream production and applications, the Laboratories would have to add a full complement of engineers and technicians.

A successful effort would also involve all of the units of the corporation over which the Technical Committee had budgetary control, including a number of development organizations that had started before the war and had become nearly as big as ARL: the Equipment Development Division under Engineering; the satellite R&D departments under Metallurgy, functioning within the operating divisions; the Jobbing Division; and the Sales Development Division. In 1944 the combined budgets for the technical departments of the Fabrication and Castings Divisions came close to equalling that of the Laboratories. This fact, Bakken said, reflected a determination to ensure that Operations remained "development-minded" as it grew larger. In addition, he fully expected to see the mechanical development budget of the Engineering Division grow rapidly in the coming years, for "we need more mechanical developments to go hand in hand with our chemical and metallurgical developments."

Bakken was not proposing that ARL give up its central role in the company's R&D effort. "Development activity by the Operating group must be kept orderly," he cautioned; duplication of effort and competition with ARL were to be avoided. In fact, central coordination would be more important than ever, and fundamental research would be required in greater amounts than before. There would be a role for scientific research in the corporation – not just in breaking through to new technologies, but, equally, in raising the level of existing ones. Certain problems on the research docket, such as "Miscellaneous Physical and Chemical Investigations," "Working Aluminum," and "Improvements in Metallurgical Practice," could be seen, Bakken told Hunt, "as prospecting problems out of which we will get the practical leads that we shall need for the broad task of Process improvement and Product development." While some might argue that such research was "too academic and not practical enough," in fact, Bakken said, "one cannot be practical without first having information and experience upon which to formulate a practical outline of development."

In December 1944, a high-level group of managers, representative of all the corporate departments, met in Pittsburgh to discuss some of the issues Bakken had raised. The memorandum they produced, entitled "Manufacturing Development (or Process or Methods Development)," documented their struggle to promote "long-range, broad-gauge" innovation that required effective cooperation among many different operational and managerial units.[68]

Over and over they considered the problem of keeping the operating side of the company "development-minded." If R&D were to expand, these leaders perceived a potential problem in the plants' becoming divorced from R&D, viewing it as solely the responsibility of the Laboratories. Seeking to avoid this, the group explicitly rejected a "top-down" approach to innovation. Instead, they believed the "ideal method" would be "to encourage an overall coordinated effort in manufacturing developments by individuals in all departments and plants through improved functioning of the present organization." In order to achieve that improved functioning, they proposed to address five specific problem areas: shortages of personnel throughout the corporation; the increasing specialization of company engineers and their activities; the frequent lack of coordination of the various corporate departments (Engineering, Metallurgical, Operations, Research, Sales) in many development projects; insufficient budgeting and planning of projects; and the problem of conflict between individuals, caused either by overlapping duties or by clashing personalities. Solving these problems would "stimulate initiative in manufacturing developments from the 'bottom up'."

Though they were dubious about increasing the Technical Committee's authority in the tops-down way Bakken thought was necessary, they ended up using the committee for want of a better solution. To ensure that individual initiative would continue to be fostered within the company and that the operating divisions would remain development-minded, the Technical Committee was charged not to control, but rather to encourage, to coordinate, and to support. All these warnings notwithstanding, the new Technical Committee, partly out of necessity, took on a much more activist role. It did disavow any direct participation in the actual carrying out of R&D projects, a task that rested solely with the "department or division involved." Yet it promised to be active in other ways, taking on the reponsibility to "correlate and keep active" programs dependent on more than one group, as most of them were, to organize subcommittees to oversee "specialized matters," and to press for commercialization of R&D results – "new alloys, new products, new techniques, new processes, new equipment."

Having issued a moderate statement expressing these sentiments, the Technical Committee set about deciding how to accomplish its objectives. Committee membership had been enlarged from 7 to 10. The new group included five original members: R. V. Davies (Sales), A. B. Wilber (Jobbing Division), C. E. Burch (special member from Accounting), Nagle, and Bakken. Its five new members were Frank Magee (vice-president for production), R. B. Derr (alumina, cryolite, and chemical products), L. Litchfield (ore materials), B. C. McFadden (mechanical engineering), and G. M. Rollason (die casting). Bakken, Nagel, and Magee played leading roles in determining policies and proce-

dures. What emerged, the concerns of management notwithstanding, was a committee that sought to play a far more active
role than its predecessor in promoting and guiding R&D efforts
throughout the corporation, along lines similar to those proposed by Bakken early in 1944.[69]

LOSS OF MONOPOLY

In March 1945, in a decision that made legal history, Judge
Learned Hand, presiding over a special three-judge panel of
the Circuit Court of Appeals, created by Congress, handed
down a judgment against Alcoa that completely and irrevocably
reversed Judge Caffey's earlier ruling. Finding that it was not
necessary to intend to monopolize in order to violate the provi-
sions of the Sherman Antitrust Act, Judge Hand ruled that
Alcoa's overwhelming dominance of the primary side of the
aluminum industry constituted a de facto monopoly. Sixty percent of the market for primary aluminum would not constitute
monopoly, he wrote, but the line had been crossed somewhere
between 60 percent and the 90 percent that Alcoa controlled in
1938. Nevertheless, he acknowledged, industry conditions had

Judge Learned Hand.

changed since 1937, when the government had filed its original
suit. By 1945, Alcoa had a competitor in primary production:
Reynolds Metals. The further disposition of the government-
owned aluminum facilities that Alcoa had leased and operated
during the war would determine whether or not a monopoly
still existed in the postwar era. "Dissolution is not a penalty, but
a remedy," Judge Hand noted in his opinion. "If the industry
will not need it for its protection, it will be a disservice to break
up an aggregation which has for so long demonstrated its efficiency." Until the disposition of the defense plants was negotiated, therefore, Alcoa would operate once again under the
threat, but not the certainty, of dissolution.[70]

No part of the company had more cause to be outraged and
offended at this treatment by what was seen as a hostile and
ungrateful government than Alcoa's research organization, and
none was likely to be more profoundly affected by dissolution.

FROM COOPERATION TO COMPETITION

The round of negotiations that turned primary production of
aluminum into a full-fledged oligopoly in the United States

commenced in the summer of 1945. Alcoa's management, represented by Chairman Arthur Vining Davis, President Irving W. "Chief" Wilson, and General Counsel Leon Hickman, expected some consideration from the government, having contributed mightily to the war effort. The war agencies, especially the War Production Board, acknowledged "great respect for Alcoa's efficiency and good will" during the war, and Alcoa took pride in its war record. The company's leaders entered the negotiations hoping to be permitted to lease or buy some of the 20 government-owned defense plants the company had built and operated during World War II. But when the talks ended in 1948, Alcoa had been forced to relinquish all but one of the defense plants to new competitors and to relinquish its patent rights for key alloys as well as process patents that were critical to the profitable operation of the plants, without royalty or substantial compensation.[71]

Given the terms of the agreement that had made Alcoa the chief operator of the aluminum defense plants, such an outcome was totally unexpected. A 50-page document personally executed in August 1941 by A. V. Davis and the head of the Reconstruction Finance Corporation (RFC), Jesse Jones, had spelled out the agreement between Alcoa and the RFC, which had supplied the capital to build the plants. It seemed to many to anticipate eventual Alcoa takeover of at least some of the plants. Continuity in employment was a major postwar objective for a Democratic administration that had needed a war to get the country back on its feet, and Alcoa's continued operation of the plants seemed the most likely way to ensure continuity.[72]

But another important postwar objective for the Roosevelt and Truman administrations was to increase competition. This implied the undermining of large industrial monopolies, not just in aluminum, but in industry after industry in which virtual monopolies had been tolerated or, in some cases, actively fostered by earlier administrations. Within the government, opinion was divided whether the national interest would best be served by breaking up Alcoa, the course advocated by New Dealers in the Justice Department, or by simply building up its domestic competition, the course advocated by many interests in states where Alcoa-operated defense plants had provided many new jobs. The compromise between different government points of view reached by W. Stuart Symington, head of the War Assets Administration, was to force Alcoa to assist in creating its own competition, that is to say, an aluminum industry with several companies able to compete effectively. Accordingly, Symington auctioned off all the defense aluminum plants, which accounted for over 30 percent of the industry's entire capacity, to new competitors. By 1950, Richard S. Reynolds, the tobacco-fortune heir who had formed Reynolds Metals, and Henry J. Kaiser, who had entered the aluminum industry from steel, had bought or leased all but one of the plants that Alcoa had previously built and run, using Alcoa's own most recent technology. The result was a U.S. aluminum industry consisting of three major, fully integrated producers: Reynolds Metals, Kaiser Permanente, and Alcoa. The three would compete in the marketplace, and they would also compete in technology, for both Reynolds and Kaiser set up their own in-house corporate laboratories, staffing them at least in part with former Alcoa personnel.[73]

By the end of the immediate postwar era, Alcoa R&D faced profound changes in virtually every aspect of its institutional life: the R&D climate, the company context, and the research program. For R&D, the age of voluntary association between public and private institutions was fading away in the face of an activist, and potentially controlling, government. Instead of a large degree of technical cooperation between research-performing institutions and between customers and suppliers, the national trend was toward greater competition for the expanding government funding and for the limited supply of scientifically trained manpower. R&D was still a major part of Alcoa's company strategy, but the strategy was changing toward concentration on heavy output, with research emphasizing applications to support it.

When a research enterprise such as ARL became part of a commercial enterprise, an alternating pattern seemed to be the natural order of things: an intense period of applications generating an acknowledged need for fundamental research, and then an intense period of fundamental work generating compelling opportunities for commercial applications. To match the new applications-oriented program of the postwar era, not only the structure of R&D but also its entire relationship to the rest of the company would change. As a result, Alcoa R&D would turn away from active professional involvement in the broader scientific community. Another prominent feature of the change in focus would be a much more elaborate and active committee system, with subcommittees and task forces, charged not only to plan for innovation, but to see it carried out.

These were not changes that were welcomed, or even accepted, by any part of Aloca's management at first. The 1930s R&D structure, with its diversity, its room for multiple initiatives, and its cooperative relations between satellites and center, had produced a few outstandingly successful projects in its period of equipoise. Nowhere was the value of "development-mindedness" in operations, coupled with the fundamental knowledge base to sustain it, more evident than in the technical breakthroughs that led to the key patents at issue between Alcoa and the government in the post–World War II period.

6

Patents become pawns

Patent policy was a matter of dispute between the federal government and big business after World War II. Whereas after World War II the government had released back to their owners the patents that it had collected for defense reasons, after World War II it laid claim to all patents on work conducted either wholly or in part within government projects or dependent on government funding. Policymakers heeded the counsel of scientists, in particular, who urged that companies be prevented from taking control of entire areas of developing technology. This argument aroused deep concern among corporate managers that government intervention would wipe out their valuable proprietary rights in technologies. Those fears fueled corporate opposition to the National Science Foundation when it was proposed in 1942, and in the postwar years such concerns caused a number of companies, including Alcoa, to shy away from accepting government funding for R&D.[1]

In the negotiations between Alcoa and the government after World War II, the ultimate sticking point was the government's demand that Alcoa make available to its new competitors, on a royalty-free basis, several of its most recent patents. During the war, patented processes that were needed to operate the government-owned defense plants had been used free of charge under the terms of the agreement. Alcoa believed that this provision terminated when it ceased to operate the plants. But the federal government, intent on enforcing more open competition in technology, insisted that the patents were part of the defense plants' facilities. This was considered to be especially true in those cases where a plant was the site at which a patented process or product had first been brought to full commercialization. To those unfamiliar with science-based development, or interested in achieving a greater social good, this was construed to mean that the government had financed, and therefore had rights to, the technology.[2]

THE PATENTS AT ISSUE

Alcoa's most formidable competitive advantage after the war was not its modern facilities, which could be replaced, but the technical know-how to build and operate them. Traditionally, Alcoa had not patented its process technologies. Judge Caffey noted in his 1941 ruling that Alcoa controlled no patents necessary to the successful operation of competing aluminum companies. Alcoa's chairman, A. V. Davis, confirmed Caffey's judgment in a statement made at the joint congressional hearings in October 1937, noting that "the manufacturing processes involved are unpatented and well-known."[3]

In fact, by the end of World War II the company had applied for and had been granted a number of key patents. The most important of these covered the "combination process" for recovery of alumina from low-grade ores, the direct-chill casting process, which made possible the casting of large, high-strength alloy ingots, and the composition of two important new aircraft alloys, 75S and 76S. These patents gave Alcoa a significant economic advantage over any competitors, as both Richard Reynolds and Henry J. Kaiser, then the most likely candidates to take over the defense plants, were quick to point out.

Government confiscation of the patents would not solve the problem, as Alcoa's cooperation was indispensable if the plants were to be operated by anyone else – just how indispensable became increasingly apparent as the government sought buyers for its plants. However, A. V. Davis claimed that the patents were legally the assets of Alcoa stockholders and adamantly refused to make Alcoa know-how available to any other producers who might step forward to run the plants.[4]

To ARL, the government's assumption of rights to Alcoa technology was even more a slap in the face than it was for the company at large. To those involved with R&D, the turning over of these patents, covering some of their most significant innovations, amounted to the confiscation of company assets. The patents under dispute were highly symbolic, involving a history of Alcoa R&D stretching back over decades. In effect, what was being asked was that the fruits of very long streams of cooperative research and experimentation be given away, royalty-free, to companies that had gone through none of the work and made none of the investment, to enable them to compete against Alcoa.[5]

The technologies that these key patents represented had been initiated and developed in branch locations, with the active support of ARL. They were the results of years of concentrated work, including systematic fundamental research on a set of general problems. Their implementation had involved a great deal of interaction between the different arms of Alcoa's diversified technical community: Metallurgy, Engineering, and Research. Their surrender, painfully strung out over a period of years, marked the end of an era for Alcoa's technical community and for the company's policy toward R&D.

ROUND ONE: THE COMBINATION PATENT

The first patent that attracted government attention covered a process for the recovery of alumina from lower-grade domestic ores at economically feasible prices. This was the combination process, so called because it combined a lime-soda sintering process with the customary Bayer refining process, making possible the extraction of a greater proportion of alumina from high-silica ores. Associated patents covered continuous digestion and the use of starch as a settling and filtering aid.[6]

Alcoa had recognized the need for such a process when German convoys threatened U.S. sea-lanes during the early years of World War II, disrupting the supply of Caribbean bauxite. Fortunately, the East St. Louis division of ARL, located at Alcoa's Aluminum Ore Company subsidiary, already had the technology for such a process on the shelf. The combination process was commercialized quickly and used at the defense plants throughout the war. It was patented by Alcoa in 1945.

After the war, the free availability of the combination patent became a necessary prerequisite to the government's new competitive arrangements in the aluminum industry, for the technology it covered had been built into the Hurricane Creek refinery that Reynolds proposed to purchase. Because high-quality domestic bauxite was projected to be in short supply, inability to operate that large facility would have left the new competitors

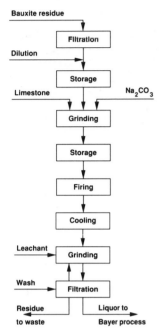

Figure 6.1. Lime-soda sinter process. Source: L.K. Hudson, C. Misra, and K. Wefers, "Aluminum Oxide," *Ullmann's Encyclopedia*, vol. A1, p. 584.

still dependent on Alcoa for alumina. Moreover, the patent gave Alcoa an overall cost advantage of $10–12 per $40 ton of alumina over any other producer.[7]

The research behind the combination patent originated in efforts at Alcoa's East St. Louis operations over a period of 30 years to make the Bayer process more cost-effective. The use of the lime-soda sinter process derived first from the hybrid approach to refining alumina that the Aluminum Ore Company had used during its gradual transition to the full Bayer process between 1909 and 1913. Although Charles Martin Hall had complained of the diseconomies of the hybrid approach and had been critical of the Aluminum Ore Company for not copying the process used by overseas competitors, the effort to develop a process in-house, before Bayer was adopted, proved in the long run to have been effort well spent. It had given the company a knowledge base solidly grounded in experimentation that laid the foundation for a much broader approach to refining problems than would otherwise have been possible. The base was expanded and enriched during the 1920s by the program of fundamental research initiated by Frary as part of his concerted effort to understand and better control Alcoa's primary processes.

Work directly related to the combination process as such began in 1924, when the East St. Louis laboratory started to experiment with digestion of various types of bauxite. Recalling part of Hall's original attraction to alumina – that, in theory, every clay bank was a mine of aluminum – Alcoa researchers tried to find ways to broaden the spectrum of usable raw materials. For the next few years the laboratory "prosecuted this word vigorously" using European monohydrate bauxites. In the same period, the effort to commercialize Hall's so-called dry process for producing alumina supported a related stream of research on furnace extraction, or sintering, including the operation of a pilot plant at Badin. In 1928, the Hall dry process was installed at a new refinery at Arvida, Canada, spun off to Aluminium, Ltd. the same year. But given the ample supply of high-grade bauxite from Alcoa's overseas holdings, the standard Bayer process was still the most cost-effective technology for the Aluminum Ore Company. With the coming of the 1929 depression, this research program ended.[8]

Alcoa resurrected combination-process research and took it

to a new plant-scale pilot phase in the late 1930s. Initially, neither government money nor government initiative entered into the project. The company was sitting on large amounts of useless high-silica bauxite in Arkansas, and ARL was able to offer the prospect of recovering as much as 90 percent of the alumina that bauxite contained. The government became involved when, soon after the United States entered World War II, the Alumina Group of the War Metallurgy Committee, of which Francis Frary was a member, addressed the problem of finding methods for recovering alumina from domestic materials. Anticipating the need to double aluminum production in the very near future, the U.S. Bureau of Mines proposed a costly, brute-force approach to process huge amounts of high-silica bauxite using flotation methods that would recover only 25–30 percent of the alumina. The War Metallurgy Committee decided instead to fund several different industrial approaches to recovering alumina from clays in an attempt to find lower-cost alternatives.

At that time, Alcoa's small-scale pilot plant using the lime-soda sintering process was the only project that had already demonstrated feasibility for any material other than high-grade bauxite. Because Alcoa had already put five years of work into the new process, the War Metallurgy Committee considered this project eligible for support even though it did not use clays as such. After further trials, Alcoa's process was selected by the Light Metals Section of the War Production Board, headed by Zay Jeffries, and Defense Plant Corporation sintering plants were installed at government expense at the four alumina refineries operated by the Aluminum Ore Company, including East St. Louis and the new Hurricane Creek plant.[9]

The advantages of the combination process at the time were indisputable, though later discoveries of plentiful high-grade bauxite made this technology unimportant in the long run. The Bayer process recovered only 70 to 85 percent of the alumina contained in the ore, whereas, according to one postwar assessment, the combination process recovered 95 percent, regardless of grade of ore used. In addition, 60 to 65 percent of the soda charged to the Bayer process could be recovered, thus decreasing lime and soda requirements. The result for Alcoa was cheaper alumina from high-silica bauxite than the company could produce at East St. Louis from regular bauxite.[10]

Here, red mud out of the Bayer process is mixed with lime and water in large tanks to release alumina and soda from the silica.

By contrast, none of the other projects funded by the government met their goals of producing usable alumina from raw materials other than high-grade bauxite. Alcoa's prior investment in R&D had given it a significant edge in this effort, for none of the other companies had such a head start in their research. Even more important, none had a deep base of knowledge and know-how comparable to that which Alcoa had assembled in ARL's long-term program conducted at East St. Louis.[11]

IMPLICATIONS FOR R&D POLICY

In the end, Alcoa was unable to prevail in its fight with the government, and in February 1946 Alcoa officials reluctantly agreed to turn over the combination patent as part of the Hurricane Creek facility. Stuart Symington, key administrator of the War Surplus Property Board, made it clear that he would lease Hurricane Creek to Reynolds without Alcoa's consent and would indemnify Reynolds for its costs in a patent suit if necessary. Alcoa could have chosen to sue Reynolds over the use of its patent, but with the threat of antitrust litigation still hanging over the company, it could not risk the unfavorable public image of obstructing a speedy return to business. Moreover, there was still reason to hope that some of the plants not yet disposed of might go to Alcoa if it cooperated on the combination patent and related patents necessary to operate Hurricane Creek.[12]

Stuart Symington.

The one stipulation Alcoa insisted on was that Reynolds give back, free of charge, any subsequent improvements it made to the technology. Eventually this "grant-back" provision was disallowed on the grounds that it set a precedent unacceptable to the government, which maintained its right to the patents without any form of compensation. In these deliberations, as in the larger ideological disagreement about proprietary technology, the government did not view the combination patent as the by-product of a long-term investment in the knowledge base or as an intermediate step toward full understanding of the refining process. It was merely an asset changing hands.[13]

A. V. Davis retired from the bargaining table in disgust before the settlement was reached, conceding successive pullbacks by telephone rather than in person. To him, the taking of the combination patent was the moral equivalent of grand larceny. Not only did it mean Alcoa's loss of its cost advantage, but it was a breach of what Davis viewed as Alcoa's most impenetrable line of defense, its patent control and its know-how.[14] In order not to let the government win all the points in the public-opinion debate, however, Alcoa's press release announcing the agreement was accompanied by a letter from Davis to Symington that ended with the following paragraph:

Except for the public considerations which you have presented to us so effectively, we could not consider a royalty-free license under such a valuable asset. However, we are glad to accede to these considerations and, if by so doing we have contributed in any substantial way to the solution of the complex problems of surplus property disposal confronting the Congress, the Surplus Property Administration and other governmental agencies, we are well repaid.[15]

Francis Frary about the time of his Perkin Medal lecture.

Several months before Alcoa made this concession to the government, Francis Frary, in his 1945 Perkin Medal lecture, drew on ARL's work with both the Bayer process and the combination process to describe the nature of industrial research. As a consequence of its wartime program, he said, Alcoa had gained a deeper understanding of the principles of the Bayer process and, as he was quick to point out, an expanded sense of how much more there was still to be learned. As a result of the intensive wartime work, the Bayer process could now be explained in scientific terms as

the possibility of obtaining a relatively stable supersaturated solution of alumina in caustic soda, containing about twice the equilibrium concentration, and of subsequently precipitating out the excess alumina as hydrate by seeding and gradual crystallization (extending over several days).[16]

At the end of the war, the fact that there was still much to be learned about the behavior of the Bayer process underscored one of the tenets of Frary's belief in fundamental research. Frary viewed the combination process as one branch in the mainstream of work leading to complete understanding of the chemistry of alumina refining. No one yet knew why the decomposition of the solution in the presence of the "seed" hydrate should be so gradual and so incomplete. For Frary and ARL it had not been the prospect of an individual breakthrough but the challenge of the unknown – the gradualness, the incompleteness, and the nature of the alumina crystals that resulted in such costly problems in refining and smelting – that had warranted the attention of ARL researchers for over 25 years and that would continue to repay further study.

Frary's perspective offered a telling corrective to a postwar world that viewed large scientific "breakthroughs" as the principal justification for investment in R&D. The combination process, he noted, involved no more than sintering the red-mud by-product of the Bayer process with limestone and soda, leaching out the sodium aluminate formed in the sintering, and returning it to the Bayer process to be recovered as alumina: "Simple enough, but made practical only by years of intensive study of the chemistry of aluminates and silicates." It was the long years of patient, fundamental research, far more than the crash program of the late 1930s, that enabled Alcoa to commercialize the combination process when it was needed. The same kind of work was required, Frary suggested, if further advances were to be made in the area of refining:

Other available raw materials for the extraction of alumina are tempting because of their greater abundance and wider distribution. From years of work on them we have come to the conclusion that the solution of the problem of economically utilizing them requires a more painstaking and complete investigation of the simple chemistry of alumina compounds, rather than some brilliant revolutionary theory or reaction. Complexity in simplicity still balks us and beckons us on.[17]

At the peak of his prestige, Frary was a powerful advocate for his viewpoint. Yet the outcome of the first round of the battle between Alcoa and the government raised troubling issues about the future of fundamental or general research. Frary had devised and justified his R&D program at least partly on the assumption that knowledge was a strong defense against competition. ARL's ability to develop the combination process so quickly that it looked like innovation on demand seemed to demonstrate the validity of this assumption. But if others could appropriate the assets derived from research, with no investment in the knowledge base, questions were likely to be raised by some in Alcoa about the economic justification for future long-term research programs.

ROUND TWO: DIRECT-CHILL INGOT CASTING

Negotiations over disposal of the government-owned defense plants and over the remaining patents at issue carried well into the postwar period. As the government's intentions became increasingly clear to Alcoa officials, the company hung on to its patents for alloy composition, casting, and metalworking, which, though not indispensable to the operation of the aluminum fabricating plants, still gave the company some economic advantage. Reconciled to having to replace the defense plants with plants of

The conventional method of ingot casting before the direct-chill casting method was invented severely limited the size of ingot that could be made.

its own, Alcoa moved quickly to build a new integrated works at Davenport, Iowa, incorporating the most modern technologies in its arsenal. One that promised to make Alcoa especially competitive was the direct-chill (DC) ingot-casting technique, covered by patents granted in 1942. Again the government wanted free use, for the technique was essential to the production of high-strength airplane alloys, 75S in particular. For that matter, the patent that covered the 75S alloy was also at issue.[18]

Prior to development of the DC process, ingot casting had been done in permanent, cast-iron tilt molds that were expensive to make and maintain and that severely limited the size of ingot that could be cast. Conventional-process ingot or slab, as the ingot was called when it was intended for further working, came in sizes no larger than $4\frac{3}{4} \times 12 \times 20$ inches, just over 100 pounds in weight. The DC process provided a revolutionary alternative to tilt molds. Instead of cooling the hot metal by dipping a solid mold in oil or cool water, the DC process sprayed water, or another cool liquid, directly on the hot metal as it emerged out of a bottomless mold. Not only did this allow a greater variety of sizes of ingots to be made using the same apparatus, but because of the more rapid cooling it greatly improved the quality of the ingot's internal structure, thus allowing much larger ingots to be cast.

Forerunner of all forms of continuous casting for aluminum, the DC process was invented in 1930 by William T. Ennor, metallurgist at Alcoa's Massena works. Developed by Ennor in close cooperation with the Massena plant engineers and in consultation with ARL in New Kensington, the DC process was introduced into operation in 1934. This speedy implementation of a radically new process exemplified the interdisciplinary cooperation that Alcoa's balanced technical community achieved before, and during, World War II.[19]

Both the Massena works and Cleveland works, where research related to the DC process was performed, provided good environments for this kind of experimentation in the 1930s. They had strong improvement-minded managers and good working relationships among their own internal technical departments. Moreover, plant metallurgists like Ennor, only recently transplanted from the Technical Direction Bureau in New Kensington, still had well-established connections with central Research.[20]

The driving force behind all casting development was the need for ingots of ever larger sizes to serve the new structural markets that were opening up in the 1930s. The prospect of much higher volumes of sheet-metal sales to the emerging aircraft industry, in particular, made the limitations on ingot size an onerous constraint. Over the years, increases in ingot sizes and mill sizes had gone hand in hand. In 1929, Alcoa had built a large new rolling mill at Massena, and it needed large ingots to produce large coils of aluminum to be drawn into electrical transmission wire. As ingot sizes increased, however, their quality tended to decrease. This was costly in terms of both wasted raw materials and excess labor charges, because it required the extra effort of a process called "scalping," which involved paring rough surfaces off the metal after the ingot was broken down, before it was rolled into sheet.[21]

Alcoa's metallurgical organization at the time, under pressure to develop better casting methods, was conducting systematic studies of ingot pouring in the fabricating plants. Theodore D. Stay, who was in charge of alloy development at the Cleve-

The Massena works and laboratory were where much of the work on the direct-chill ingot-casting method was done.

land branch of ARL, was also working on the problem, focusing on methods of pouring aluminum alloys for castings and forgings. He studied the breakdown of large ingot in steel-plant blooming mills for ideas applicable to aluminum fabrication and began experimenting with wide horizontal molds, called "bathtub" molds. Stay was sent to Massena to test the bathtub molds, assisted there by a newly hired Rensselaer Ph.D. Walter Dean.[22]

The bathtub mold proved unsatisfactory, as the internal structure of the metal varied too much from top to bottom. Stay and Dean then tried vertical water-dipped molds, 12 by 12 inches. These were introduced into operation in early 1930, but the straight water-dipped approach soon proved to be a dead end. The 12-by-12-inch conventional ingots did not cool rapidly enough at the center, and their uneven porosity produced poor-quality sheet. It was at that point that William Ennor began to take the lead in developing a new casting technique. Ennor, a chemical engineer of an inventive cast of mind, had joined Alcoa after graduation from the University of Wisconsin. He was hired into the Technical Direction Bureau in 1924, several years before all metallurgists were dispersed to the plants, and at Massena he served first as technical supervisor and later as chief metallurgist. It was "Dutch" Nagel, then head of the metallurgical department of Alcoa's fabricating division, who granted Ennor permission to experiment with his idea for a different approach to casting.[23]

Ennor's first experiments were directed at testing the feasibility of a new mold, and with it a new cooling technique. His idea was to release the bottom of a well-lubricated standard mold after the metal inside had solidified just enough to form an outer shell. As the ingot emerged, it was to be doused, dipped, or sprayed directly to speed solidification of the metal inside the shell. Initially this approach failed because the ingot did not slip through the mold as easily as Ennor had expected, and the solid outer shell tended to tear. He had overestimated the amount the metal would shrink during solidification. His first attempts on the small cylindrical ingots used to produce wire thus ended in failure.

William T. Ennor.

With the help of the reference librarians at ARL, Ennor retreated to the patent literature, looking for evidence of similar approaches to casting. He discovered that others had envisioned an expanding or bottomless mold, but that his concept of combining the use of such a mold with the application of liquid coolant directly onto the metal, in order to increase the rate of solidification and thereby refine the internal structure of the ingot, was original.

A further set of experiments followed that proved the effects of the DC aspect of Ennor's process. One face of an otherwise conventionally molded and well-insulated ingot was opened and sprayed directly with coolant. Microscopic examination of the ingot thus produced plainly showed that the quality of the metal on the side that had been sprayed was significantly better than that on the other sides. These experiments demonstrated, in Ennor's words, "the extremely rapid freezing that could be obtained by applying cooling water directly to the metal." If it could be made to work, the new process clearly had attractive implications, not only in the reduction of cost for casting in different-size molds but also in the potential improvement in ingot quality.[24]

Ennor next worked with Massena engineers to design new molding equipment. Again the patent literature was helpful, showing what had worked and what had failed in experiments with different kinds of molds. By 1933, he was conducting experiments almost continuously, varying head sizes, rates of speed of lowering the ingot, temperatures, and types of coolants. The 1933 testing program, though wholly empirical, was sufficiently systematic and comprehensive to serve as the basis

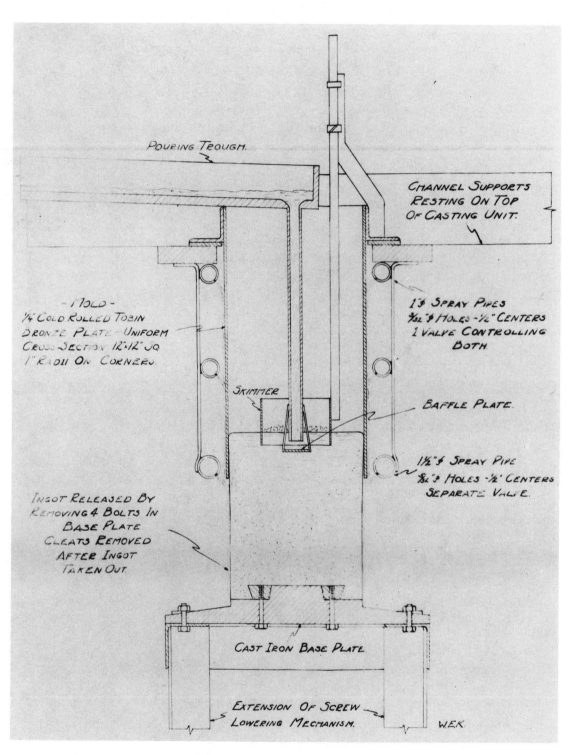

Sketch of the apparatus used for casting DC ingots around 1934. (From Metallurgical Report #34-C-1, Massena, 1934, entitled "Progress Report – Ingot Development, Directly Chilled 12″ × 12″ Ingot," by Ennor, King, and Heath, ATC report #42592.)

for much later development. The complete technique was successfully demonstrated in February 1934, when

12″ × 12″ directly-chilled ingots were first cast using the 20″ × 20″ water-dipped ingot platform as the lowering mechanism. After preliminary difficulties with surface tearing had been eliminated by the use of wax and later grease as a mold coating, results were so promising that a separate experimental unit was built and put into use in December, 1934.[25]

This performance convinced Alcoa's Fabrication Division that DC ingot casting was ready for wider use. During 1935, both the New Kensington works and the works at Alcoa, Tennessee, where John Hood was chief metallurgist, installed their own DC ingot-casting equipment. The speed with which use of the equipment spread showed how desperately the works needed larger-size, better-quality ingots. It soon became clear, however, that the equipment was far from perfect. A whole new set of problems arose when the technique was used to cast the high-strength alloy ingots that airplane producers were demanding in increasing quantities. Hood reported from Tennessee that there had been no trouble with the casting of the softer alloys, high in aluminum, such as 2S, but the more brittle aircraft alloys, such as 17S and 24S, were vulnerable to stress fractures during cooling.[26] But by 1935, the staff at the Massena works was no longer capable of addressing the problems that were arising with the new process. Ennor became seriously ill in the fall of 1934, and though his colleagues attempted to correct what were described as "the serious problems of splitting and fractures" in DC ingots, they lacked the expertise to find an adequate solution. In that situation, they turned for help to Alcoa's central research laboratory. At that point, such support could not be taken for granted.

In the mid-1920s Frary deliberately shielded the ARL from urgent requests from the works for assistance in problem-solving. Alcoa researchers were expected to do careful, thorough, systematic, and often theoretical work, unhurried by deadlines. They were accustomed to choosing projects on the basis of research merit rather than on their immediate importance to the plants. Since moving into the new laboratory building, Frary had insisted on such policies on the grounds that they were necessary to ensure uninterrupted conduct of the research program. But they were also, in many ways, quite practical. Although ARL had the most advanced analytical equipment of the day, running serious tests was still time-consuming and labor-intensive. Most of these urgent problems were more effectively, or at least more quickly, solved by trial and error, based on plant know-how.

Nevertheless, in the summer of 1935 the Physical Testing Division of ARL came to the aid of the Massena project. The resulting collaborative effort between researchers and plant metallurgists demonstrated just how difficult it was to create an effective working relationship between two groups of people whose technical priorities were different and who lacked experience in working together. The project aimed at solving the DC ingot-splitting problem lasted for more than a year. Both sides received a valuable education, and the direct confrontation between the empirical and theoretical methods paved the way for the especially harmonious partnership between ARL and the works that lasted until after the war.

Richard Templin, head of the Physical Testing Division, assigned one of his bright young researchers, R. G. Sturm, to look into the problem at Massena in the summer of 1935. Sturm reported back to Templin that the problem was a heat-transfer problem that would be amenable to theoretical solution if he could get enough accurate and consistent data.

The problem has appealed to the writer as a problem in heat transfer or temperature gradients which should be subject to analysis. . . . The application of the laws governing the flow of heat together with a definite knowledge of boundary conditions should lead to an analytical determination of temperature gradients and to the factors which control them.[27]

Ennor had been plotting temperature curves at Massena, based on readings obtained by implanting thermocouples in cooling ingots, but Sturm rejected those data as having been gathered with insufficiently rigorous standards. Templin and Sturm proposed to run tests with their own superior instrumentation at ARL on aluminum stock of a different size, available at the New Kensington works. Ennor was convinced that Sturm was underestimating the complexity of the cooling problem because of lack of awareness of the many different factors in the plant that could affect it.[28]

Meanwhile, plant metallurgists, unable to wait on theoretical solutions, kept experimenting with different cooling approaches, such as reducing the cooling gradient (thus decreasing the quality) or using different nozzles to atomize the spray. Nevertheless, despite their differences in approach and in sense of priority, Nagel urged the Physical Testing Division to remain involved. He wrote to Templin:

I hope you and Mr. Sturm will continue to keep in touch with the D.C. ingot project, not only in our Massena problems but also those at Alcoa and Arnold because we are by no means out of the wood.[29]

Dependence on the ARL for research support was frustrating to works personnel working on the DC ingot project: Turn-around time was slow, and the analysis also seemed to leave out important aspects in the interest of achieving precision and rigor. Returning to his job in early 1936 after his illness, Ennor was distressed at the lack of progress in the preceding months. Sturm's most recent report, using cooling data, drew a set of conclusions completely opposite to those derived from work conducted elsewhere in the Laboratories, using actual stress data. The metallurgists wanted to be receptive to new approaches and very much wanted ARL's continued support, but Ennor worried that ARL was not treating the problem with the urgency it deserved.[30]

To speed the work along, Ennor proposed that Massena buy the appropriate testing equipment – strain gauges costing about $175 each – so that the plant could gather its own set of stress measurements from production-size ingots. Concerned that testing of that kind done at plant locations might get out of hand, Templin vigorously opposed that request, arguing that data produced under less than ideal conditions could be very misleading.[31]

Finally, a conference at New Kensington produced a compromise approach that satisfied all sides. There were informative exchanges on the technicalities of temperature curves and the issues related to testing, such as where it should be done, and by whom. According to Sturm's report, the conferees discussed selection of a representative ingot and arrived at "a common understanding of the methods of analysis and their applicability." He also noted that he had arrived at "a clearer understanding of the practical side of the problem." Ennor agreed to an extensive data-gathering exercise to record variables such as rate of casting, temperature and quantity of water used in chilling, temperature of the metal entering the mold, and composition of the metal.[32]

Cleveland, too, became more intensively involved with the DC process at that stage. Stay contributed observations from data gathered at the ARL Cleveland laboratory concerning the effects of using different alloying elements and the relationship between grain size and ingot cracking. Louis Kempf committed his entire group to the task of developing mold coatings for the DC process. Though the separate streams of experimentation and research would not converge until after the war, much of the work done at Cleveland on fundamentals related to casting different types of alloys would ultimately have direct bearing on DC casting problems. In the postwar era, the Cleveland works led the way in casting large ingots using DC methods.

Despite its vexing problems, DC casting quickly became the dominant method in all of Alcoa's fabricating plants. Late in 1936, the New Kensington works reported not only substantial savings from reduced scrap and scalping but also the last-minute avoidance of a lawsuit threatened by Boeing that had seemed "a near certainty." The plant had tried unsuccessfully six times to produce a big Boeing order using conventional tilt molds, but had managed to ship the order, which had been on the books for a year, only after it tried the new casting method. By the end of 1937, DC ingots accounted for half of Alcoa's production of rolling ingots. During the war, all high-strength alloys were cast using the DC method, even though many of them still showed tendencies to crack.[33]

The exciting news of Ennor's new casting process was first announced to a wider Alcoa audience at a 1937 meeting of metallurgists in Pittsburgh. Ennor was undeniably, Nagel said, "Daddy" of the DC ingot. Nagel described DC as follows: "of all the many operations in our fabricating plants . . . both metallurgically and mechanically . . . one of the most inspiring as representing technical development." DC casting was also the highlight of the 1937 technical show. In his letter of comment on the program, Francis Frary went out of his way to recognize the efforts of Nagel's metallurgical staff, suggesting that much more could be accomplished if the plants had more people like them, provided they had time to do more than routine work.

Experimental mold used in a test of DC coolants. (From Metallurgical Department report, Newark, Ohio, works, by William T. Ennor, "Ingot Development – D.C. Coolants," 15 October 1945).

Clearly, the significance of Ennor's achievement was not lost on the broader technical community.[34]

At the same time, however, ARL's collaboration in the project seemed to open the way for greater involvement of Research in developing fabricating technology. With the exception of the Physical Testing Disivions, ARL had had little to do with the DC program as such in the early and middle 1930s. But in 1937 the

Direct-chill casting remains the standard casting technology in use in the metals industry. It made possible the casting of multiton aluminum ingot without which postwar aircraft designs would not have been possible.

Laboratories installed a small, experimental DC unit at New Kensington. That was the beginning of a trend toward active laboratory participation in plant-scale development that was to transform the research mission after the war. In the short run, bringing the DC process into the Laboratories was a key factor in the rapid commercialization of a new class of aircraft alloys – the third patented technology to which the government laid claim.

JET-AGE ALLOYS

Like the combination process and DC ingot casting, the aircraft alloys in dispute between Alcoa and the government in 1945 represented a substantial investment in R&D and long years of research. In the mid-1930s, alloy development moved into high gear with a program focused on producing higher-strength metals than those currently used, the aluminum-copper-magnesium compositions that had evolved out of Duralumin. During the war, Alcoa's sales engineers worked closely with aircraft manufacturers on the design principles employing these "super Duralumins" – alloys 24S and 14S – that were the mainstays of the nation's air fleet. But at the same time, researchers were doing the empirical work that resulted in alloys 76S and 75S, the aluminum-zinc-magnesium-copper compositions that were to provide the material for jet aircraft in the postwar era.

For more than a decade the ternary system combining zinc and magnesium with aluminum had been known to yield a product with especially high tensile strength. It was also susceptible to stress-corrosion cracking (SCC), a complex, interactive phenomenon related to internal stresses "locked up" within the metal during production and fabrication. SCC could result in catastrophic metal failure even in relatively mild corrosive conditions. This was a problem that absolutely had to be solved before the new alloys could be commercialized.[35]

Alloy researchers under Edgar Dix had been studying SCC since 1930, and in 1940 Dix advanced a theory that was believed to explain the mechanisms behind it. In the same year, a prototype airplane wing from the first version of Al-Zn-Mg-Cu sheet developed serious SCC after only a few months in storage. Ultimately, Joseph Nock, working with small DC ingots cast on the premises at ARL, solved the problem empirically, demonstrating that small amounts of chromium added to the Al-Zn-Mg-Cu composition yielded resistance to SCC that had long been sought.[36]

That breakthrough led rapidly to commercialization of the forging alloy 76S and the sheet-metal alloy 75S introduced and patented in 1942 and 1943, respectively. So urgent was the wartime demand for higher-strength sheet that airplane manufacturers incorporated 75S into provisional designs almost im-

This picture of a monocoque fuselage, common to most aircraft from the 1930s onward, shows why larger ingots were needed to fabricate the large structural members of airplane bodies. (From C. F. Nagel, Jr., and F. C. Pyne, "Aluminum Alloys Up to Date," *Aviation*, July 1934, p. 213.)

mediately, circumventing the customary lengthy introduction process. Within months it was used as the upper skin and stringers on the wings of the new B-29 Super Fortress bomber, reducing its weight by 180 kilograms.[37]

Yet, successful though it was as a product, 75S had one al-

This picture of stress-corrosion cracking on an experimental wing section illustrates the 24th Edward de Mille Campbell Memorial Lecture, "Aluminum-Zinc-Magnesium Alloys," presented by E. H. Dix, 19 October 1949. (From *Transactions of the American Society of Metals*, vol. 42, 1950, pp. 1057–127.)

most insuperable drawback for Alcoa plants: It was exceedingly difficult to cast without cracking. This problem was exacerbated by the pressure to introduce the new alloys so quickly and by wartime conditions in the plants. Toward the end of the war, cracking became a problem with all high-strength alloys because greater amounts of scrap aluminum had to be used in production. For five years after the new alloys were introduced, the leading plants struggled unsuccessfully to cast large 75S ingots using the new DC method. They were unable to achieve ingots larger than 12 × 12 inches.[38]

Quite apart from the patent dispute, the continuing DC ingot program and the postwar struggle to cast 75S posed a central dilemma for Alcoa's research establishment. On the one hand, these key process and product innovations demonstrated beyond doubt the value of investment in fundamental and long-term research. Development of the DC process and of the new generation of alloys, and the growing understanding of corrosion phenomena, had drawn heavily on the store of in-house knowledge and know-how that Alcoa had accumulated over the years. At the same time, the size, the complexity, and the dynamic quality of programs like the DC ingot program posed difficulties for ARL in 1945, as they challenged the very characteristics that sustained long-term research. Other postwar conditions would make it necessary for ARL to change the way it operated, but the DC program was perhaps the single most visible sign that this would be unavoidable.[39]

To some extent, the magnitude of this dilemma was obscured by wartime conditions. For most technical personnel, the war was a broadening experience that heightened their awareness of the need for greater attention to applications. For example, Ennor, like many others, was transferred to Operations to fill the huge managerial gap created by the defense plants. His personal drive to continue systematic research on DC casting did not abate when he became plant manager at Newark, Ohio. If anything, the new post simply gave him more ideas and a broader perspective on the problems.

Conversely, Ennor brought to his new position the outlook and experience of the research metallurgist, and he was quick to initiate the kind of interaction that had proved so useful in the original DC ingot project. In 1945, he directed a series of systematic tests on different DC coolants. The information obtained in these tests was immediately passed along to Massena through E. M. Kipp of ARL, who linked it to fundamental work carried out at the laboratories some years before "with respect to the relative coolant capacities of various mineral oils and their corresponding water in oil emulsions." Kipp also offered to do supplementary fundamental work on oils and emulsions at the higher temperatures now needed. Indeed, it seemed as though the Laboratories had fundamental information pertaining to almost any problem that arose if a way could be found to tap it. This role as central storehouse and clearinghouse for relevant information would become ever more important for ARL as applications projects multiplied and the network of plants became increasingly complicated.[40]

Ennor pushed constantly for more and better support from

Research, prompted by problems his Newark plant was having in rolling 24S. It was not that Research was neglecting its job, but rather that conditions were changing. The problems that were arising at the end of the war were big ones, and the technology was changing quickly. Ennor saw the need for a multifaceted research approach at the Laboratories, not just the unrelated efforts of individual researchers. In August 1945 he wrote directly to Theodore Bossert, Nagel's successor as chief metallurgist of the Fabrication Division, to propose an interdisciplinary research program, using all the latest equipment available, to address the 24S difficulty and others like it. It would include testing by Templin's organization, analysis by physical metallurgy, and x-ray studies of casting cross sections, as suggested in a recent article by a maker of x-ray equipment.[41]

Bossert supported Ennor's proposal and raised the matter with the appropriate parties at ARL right away. But it was not to be done overnight. To mount a team effort of the sort Ennor suggested would be a radical departure for the Laboratories of the 1940s, geared as it was to the individual specialist. Moreover, keeping up with developments at the growing number of plants, which were all pursuing their own improvements, was a mounting logistical challenge. In the end, it was Ennor who coordinated further extensions of ARL's involvement in development of what came to be called "semicontinuous casting." He was better equipped than most ARL personnel to handle the kind of large-scale project management that development of fully continuous casting would require. In 1947 he was invited to become assistant director of ARL, to run a fundamental study related to DC casting. Ennor visited ARL to work with Dix, Nock, and others in Physical Metallurgy, and then stayed on to coordinate applications throughout the plants that did ingot casting.[42]

In the immediate postwar era, the works continued to take the lead in improving methods of DC casting and experimenting with processes to filter and degas the molten metal as it was poured. But two factors combined to curtail plant experimentation after the war: the shortage of technical expertise in the postwar works and the continuing drive for increases in output that made experimentation disruptive. Massena and Cleveland continued to contribute to the evolution of ingot casting, but the impetus for further improvement shifted to the central laboratories.

What was not adequately appreciated in the postwar company was how important the satellite structure that had produced these key technologies had been to their speedy application and development. While postwar innovation was proceeding at a rapid pace, the fate of the several patented products and processes around which much of it revolved remained undecided. By the time the patent controversy was finally settled, the R&D structure that had produced the technologies the patents represented had undergone profound change.

THE BATTLE ENDS

In 1947, Alcoa filed to have its monopoly suit concluded, and the Justice Department countered with yet another request that Alcoa be broken up. Neither petition was granted, and the court decided to take the issue of dissolution under advisement for a period of five more years. By that time, however, conditions in the industry were not what had been expected before the end of the war. For one thing, there was more than enough aluminum business to go around – so much, in fact, that independent fabricators claimed they could not get adequate supplies of metal. Moreover, while the Justice Department continued to argue for Alcoa's breakup, the Defense Department was increasingly concerned about the ability of Alcoa and its competitors to supply the defense-related materials it needed. The War Assets Administration (WAA) accordingly moved for compromise. In defiance of the Justice Department's wishes, the WAA offered Alcoa the chance to buy, for $5 million, the new Massena plant, which was deteriorating after several years of having been shut down. In return, Alcoa was asked to make concessions on the rest of the patents in dispute and to close its old Massena plant.

This deal satisfied all parties, save the Justice Department, and in November 1948 the agreement was announced. Under its terms, all patents in question were available either free of charge or at a nominal royalty to all U.S. aluminum producers. This arrangement included all alloy patents, the DC process, and a number of other patents in the fabricating field. WAA agreed to make a one-time payment of $115,000 for a license for all Alcoa's machine patents used in the government-built plants that the company had operated during the war. It was also agreed that future process patents would be available, royalty-free, to all companies in the industry.[43]

This decision marked a decisive turning point in Alcoa's R&D history, and oral tradition identifies the end of Alcoa's monopoly as a watershed for Research. No longer able to appropriate the results of its efforts, the company began to consider R&D in a different light: still very much a strategic asset, but one that had to be guarded much more carefully than before. Alcoa thus came out of World War II drawing different conclusions as a company about R&D than many other leading-edge companies. DuPont, for instance, committed itself to doing more fundamental research in-house, as a way of "contributing our fair share to the world's storehouse of basic knowledge," on the grounds that it was no longer possible to rely on basic science from foreign universities. But Alcoa, having shouldered the burden of scientific inquiry for aluminum before the war, and feeling robbed of its fruits both in modern plants and in patents, was less inclined to build the knowledge base.[44]

ALCOA ADJUSTS TO ITS NEW ROLE

Competition and growth brought about a striking transformation in Alcoa in the immediate aftermath of the war. Although it was less evident in the research facilities, feeling ran high against Kaiser and Reynolds. A sense that those who left to work for the new competitors had betrayed Alcoa poisoned the competitive climate for decades.

In Alcoa Research, by contrast, far less appeared to have changed, and the essential continuity seemed to be preserved. Budgets continued on a steady upward trend. In the context of the extremely favorable postwar market for light metals, funding for research was not a problem. Programs mapped out in the late 1930s went ahead as planned. Francis Frary remained director, and the organization retained its same basic shape into the early 1950s.

But for research policy at all levels, the patent dispute brought about a profound transformation, the effects of which became evident only gradually. Over time, Alcoa Research became much more sensitive to the implications of the new competitive climate. Although research departments at Kaiser and Reynolds were slow in developing, the role of R&D in the industry was quickly recognized as having changed. Before the war, new knowledge was bound to benefit either Alcoa or its customers. Afterward, new knowledge could be critical to the competitive ability of other parties.[45]

Ironically, neither the government's rationale for its position on the patent issue nor Alcoa's reaction to the loss of its patents conveyed a complete picture of how R&D at Alcoa had accomplished what it did, or of what it had contributed to the company and to the society at large. Both parties to the dispute treated the patent issue as though research could be wholly embodied in a measurable asset that could be bought, sold, and traded. Neither seems to have anticipated what might be lost to the company, or to the country, when Alcoa, and other companies that were the major research performers in their industries, no longer willingly augmented the common knowledge base.

Alcoa's previous self-interested willingness to share information about aluminum technology did not end, but it was reduced and confined more carefully to limited subjects. Alcoa management reacted by deemphasizing patent activity and relying on secrecy to protect both intellectual property and know-how. This policy took away the incentive of patent-seeking for Alcoa researchers and made a substantial difference in the careers of technical personnel hired after the war.

Not surprisingly in the changed circumstances, direct contact with the government was treated with greater caution than before. This attitude closed a channel for professional contact that became increasingly important nationally in the postwar era. Direct government funding policies for industrial R&D, through defense agencies and through the National Science Foundation, made these networks standard avenues of professional interchange and peer review just as Alcoa was pulling away from them.

Likewise, the attitude toward fundamental research at Alcoa gradually changed. It was still regarded as valuable and necessary, but the old ability to build the general aluminum knowledge base well in advance, according to the dictates and rhythms of the work itself, and without concern for immediate need, became a thing of the past. A shortage of technical talent and an urgent need for transfer of existing knowledge made this shift almost inevitable. In the process, the equipoise of R&D

in the 1930s, that fragile state of balance between the long term and the short term, the applied and the general, began slowly to break down. At the same time, Alcoa, like many other companies, misread R&D successes of the wartime era and began to take for granted technology's ability to deliver on cue. This "blockbuster" expectation was shared by many companies that invested large sums of money in research after the war, for few of their managers had knowledge or experience of the way technology had contributed to success.

PART IV

The era of oligopoly, 1945–1968

7

New directions in R&D

As they entered the postwar world, Alcoans responded to the government's move to break up Alcoa's aluminum monopoly with anger, but not dismay. They had what turned out to be well-placed confidence in the technological capability they had built during the previous monopoly era. Aluminum was, as their new competitor David Reynolds pointed out, a "battle-tested metal." As in many U.S. industries after World War II, the challenge was to recast for civilian markets what had been developed for military uses. In the space of the next decade Alcoa did just that.[1]

Alcoa's corporate strategy was two-pronged: It would build on its technological lead to develop products for latent, high-volume markets for which steel, having barely expanded output during the war, would not be in a position to compete, and it would replace the modern plants it had been forced to give away to competitors with even more modern plants of its own. The idea was to make everything possible from aluminum, an objective that would involve fervent "missionary selling" on the part of Alcoa Sales. At the same time, high priority would be given to both product and process research. Top management in this era intended to achieve such scale and volume that Alcoa would become more like a metals company, albeit a leading-edge company, and less like a chemicals company in style and in spirit. This change in company character implied an even greater change in the character of research, which was also affected by a radical transformation in the climate for R&D.

RESEARCH: THE BILLION-DOLLAR BUSINESS

At the close of World War II, the national climate for industrial R&D was greatly altered from what it had been in the heyday of

275

Corporate Facts

Leadership: A. V. Davis, chairman of the board
Roy A. Hunt, president
George R. Gibbons, senior vice-president
Robert E. Withers, senior vice-president
Milton M. Anderson, Safford K. Colby,
Thomas D. Jolly, George J. Stanley, P. J. Urquhart,
Irving W. Wilson, vice-presidents

No. of Employees: 59,223

Primary production: 823 million pounds

Locations: □ Bauxite, AR; Moengo, Suriname
○ East St. Louis, IL; Mobile, ALA
▽ Rosiclare, IL
△ Alcoa, TN; Badin, NC; Niagara Falls, Massena, NY;
Vancouver, WA
■ Alcoa, TN; Bridgeport, Fairfield, CN; Buffalo, NY;
Cleveland,OH; Detroit, MI; Edgewater,
Garwood, NJ; Lafayette, IN; Massena, NY;
New Kensington, PA
● New Kensington, PA; Cleveland, OH;
East St. Louis, IL
▲ Pittsburgh, PA

Laboratory Facts

Leadership: Francis C. Frary, director of research
Herman E. Bakken, assistant director
Edgar H. Dix, Jr., Junius D. Edwards,
Richard L. Templin, assistant directors

No. of Employees: 383

Expenditures: $1,794,000

Figure 7.1. Corporate and laboratory facts, 1945.

ARL. Federal government funding of research in industry did not fall off in peacetime, as it had after World War I, but continued on a path of exponential growth. Expenditures by the Defense Department alone rose from $26 million in 1940 to $6.8 billion in 1966. Channeled primarily through the military services and through defense-related agencies such as the Atomic Energy Commission, these funds fostered the creation of many new research laboratories, public and private, and promoted competition among them. One government objective, though a lesser one, was to break what it viewed as the stranglehold that large, individual, science-based companies had on the nation's

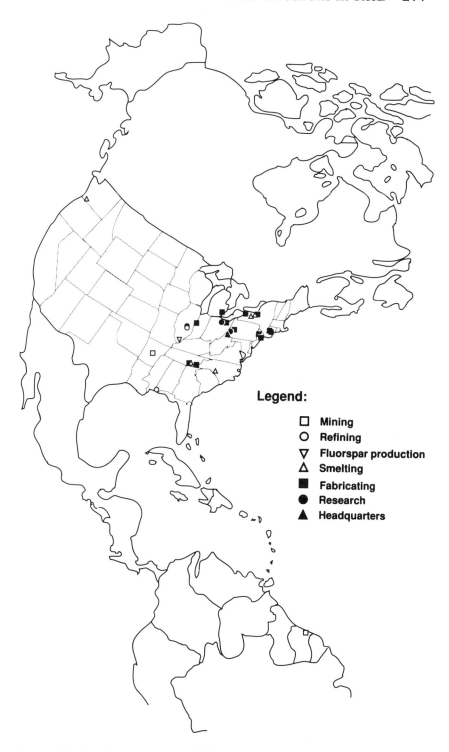

Figure 7.2. Corporate locations, 1945.

future.[2] A more important reason for the new government activism in R&D was the view that the United States had too long relied on fundamental work done by other, mostly European, countries and needed, as a matter of security, to produce its own science. Federal funding encouraged research competition among government, industrial, and academic laboratories, breaking down the traditional division of labor wherein basic research was the responsibility of the universities, and the problem of applications belonged to industry. Competition was heavy for trained research personnel. Research scientists and engineers enjoyed high salaries and great prestige, as the nation looked to them for the scientific breakthroughs and the blockbuster innovations that would give it undisputed world leadership in technology.[3]

Like the views of many of the older science-based companies in industrial chemicals and metals, Alcoa's view of research as a competitive weapon mirrored these national trends in some ways, but was different in others. In the debate over science policy, which raged during the years 1945–50, large business concerns that had strong research programs before the war tended to oppose an activist government role in coordinating and funding science in industry. Alcoa's recent losses of proprietary technology made it very suspicious of government intentions. So great was the government's injection of funds into industrial research that no company could be entirely unaffected, but Alcoa participated in the boom largely in indirect ways, by accepting a few large pieces of capital equipment directly from the government and by accepting contracts with airframe companies that were, in turn, funded by government money. This had the advantage of keeping government hands off its technology, but the price was Alcoa's gradual isolation from some of the main currents of scientific development, which increasingly flowed from government funding networks.

As Alcoa's long list of publications relating to fundamental developments in the 1930s and 1940s attested, the company had created a base for technical self-sufficiency before the war. Now the internal consensus at ARL was that Alcoa was sitting on a great store of knowledge awaiting application. This gave aluminum an advantage in comparison with the newer physics-based fields such as electronics, aeronautics, and nuclear energy, where much basic research and advanced development

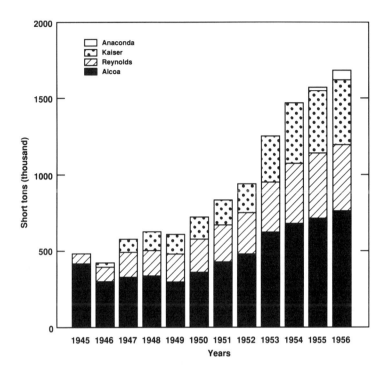

Figure 7.3. Primary aluminum production, monopoly to oligopoly. Source: "United States Primary Aluminum Production, 1934–1974," AA, env. H-1825.

remained to be done. It was in those fields that the government was concentrating the largest amounts of R&D funding.[4]

MISSION FOR TECHNOLOGY

In 1955, *Fortune* magazine declared Alcoa's adjustment to competition to have been a "splendid retreat." Though its share of the primary aluminum market had dropped from more than 90 percent to 40 percent, its sales had grown fourfold over prewar levels, and its current annual profits were at least 23 percent higher than in any previous year. *Fortune* attributed this phenomenal performance largely to an aggressive capital expansion program, backed up by research, and a strengthened centralized management. The program of capital spending on which the company embarked after the war demonstrated, *Fortune* said, "a superb sense of timing and decision," for although Alcoa executives during the war had worried about how to move the huge tonnages of metal pouring out of

Aerial view of the Davenport plant under construction in December 1947.

its plants, they had also anticipated the potential for a rapid expansion of aluminum usage.[5]

In the 1920s, a lack of money for dedicated research facilities and the unwillingness of Alcoa's operating sites to cooperate in technical integration had forced the Research staff to venture into Operations. The field assignments during that earlier period of emphasis on applications had provided unwelcome but valuable exposure to the realities of the Alcoa works. This time, the factory came to the laboratory, where massive new capital equipment was installed to allow research into pressing large-scale process problems. Staff changes reinforced this industrialization of research. The fast growth of the Laboratories made it unnecessary to slough off any old disciplines, but new hires came primarily from among the engineering and mechanical specialties.[6]

In 1946, construction began on a huge new sheet-and-plate mill in Davenport, Iowa, a plant that incorporated Alcoa's most advanced fabricating technology and displayed the most up-to-date applications, particularly in electrical wiring. Further expansions at Davenport, and at the rod, wire, and cable plant in Vancouver, Washington, were announced in 1949. The following year Alcoa opened a new smelter in Point Comfort, Texas, utilizing natural gas as fuel – a technology made possible by

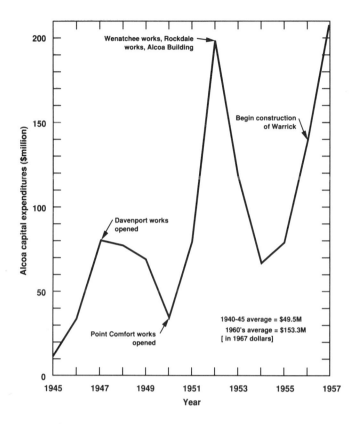

Figure 7.4. Alcoa capital expenditures, 1945–57. Source: Smith, *From Monopoly to Competition*, Table B-2.

specialized diesel engines developed by Alcoa during the war for one of the Defense Plant Corporation facilities that had been sold to Reynolds. The military mobilization that began in 1950 in response to the situation in Korea prompted both Reynolds and Kaiser to expand their smelting facilities, and Alcoa kept pace, opening two new smelters in 1952. The first smelter, in Wenatchee, Washington, was dependent on a further modification of the Bayer process enabling Alcoa to utilize northwestern laterite ore as a source for alumina. The second, located in Rockdale, Texas, was a "top-secret" facility, using low-grade lignite to generate steam-powered electricity, another new technology developed by Alcoa's researchers and engineers. In 1955 there still was no end in sight to Alcoa's expansion. Money already appropriated for future buildings would bring its total postwar capital expenditures to a whopping $1 billion.[7]

Twenty million dollars of the capital program went to construct the Alcoa Building on Mellon Square in Pittsburgh, completed in 1952. Like the earlier New Kensington laboratory, it was a showcase for aluminum in every conceivable application and a symbol of the many accomplishments of the research organization. "With the exception of the steel of the frame, some gypsum for plaster, and a little wood, wool, and leather in the furnishings," *Fortune* noted, "it is almost impossible to name a part of Alcoa's building that isn't forged, rolled, pressed, extruded, or otherwise made of aluminum." This included much of the furniture and most of the artwork as well.[8]

The gray Alumilite finish of the Alcoa Building's outer skin represented one of the more highly visible contributions of research to new applications. In 1954 the company erected an office building in Cincinnati with the first colored aluminum exterior, displaying blue, gold, and silver. According to Frary, colored coatings were born by accident, when R. B. Mason spilled red ink on a sample of oxide-coated sheet, but behind this fortuitous discovery lay extensive work on electrochemical finishes, including much fundamental study, going back more than three decades.[9]

By 1955 there were more than 300 aluminum-skinned buildings either finished or under construction.[10] These impressive architectural applications represented the culmination of an effort to penetrate the market for construction materials, such as aluminum siding, roofing sheet, windows, nails, fixtures (doors, screens, sills, blinds), and piping for heating and ventilation ducts. Altogether, the building and construction market had become Alcoa's leading customer, consuming almost one-fifth of its total output in 1946, as compared with only 8 percent before the war. Shortages and higher prices of other materials helped to open the door for such applications.[11]

The rapidity and ease of the changeover to aluminum, so unlike the tortuous substitutions of earlier eras, were largely attributable to the wealth of information accumulated by ARL on the properties and working characteristics of aluminum. Alcoa and other producers aggressively disseminated this information to manufacturers. One production-shop worker was quoted in *Iron Age* as summing up "the entire fabricating and manufacturing story concerning substitution" quite simply:

If you are going to use aluminum to the best advantage, just forget that you spent 20 years in the steel sheet shop, put yourself in the

The Alcoa Building.

Alcoa's efforts to gain a larger share of the construction market for aluminum extended to building all-aluminum demonstration houses such as this Valley Development Aluminum House in Davenport.

hands of the aluminum engineers and answer all their questions in full, do exactly what they say and everything will turn out fine.[12]

In its inner workings, the Alcoa Building demonstrated other important new applications, such as electrical wiring, made possible by improved soldering techniques developed by ARL in 1946. One of the biggest challenges for ARL in applying aluminum in the Alcoa Building was to prevent corrosion in the heating system. That was accomplished by using specially treated water and maintaining careful control over the pH balance. Alcoa did not recommend aluminum to others for this particular application, but based on the results of extensive testing for corrosion, it did recommend its use in containers for a wide variety of chemicals and petroleum products.[13]

CENTRALIZATION

The new corporate headquarters was more than a showcase. Like the New Kensington laboratory in 1929, it signified a transition to greater centralization, this time not just in R&D but in all aspects of the company's management. It also marked "a kind of watershed between the old Alcoa and the new and modern corpo-

ration," for the first executives to inhabit it were a new generation of corporate leaders. A. V. Davis remained as chairman of
the board until 1957, when the period of threatened dissolution
finally officially came to an end, but the great vice-presidents of
the monopoly era – Safford K. Colby and George Gibbons –
died in office in 1949, and Roy Hunt stepped down as president
in 1951, succeeded by Irving W. Wilson. "Chief" Wilson had
joined Alcoa in 1911 and had worked his way up through Engineering and Operations. He had long been Davis's right-hand
man as vice-president for operations.[14]

I. W. ("Chief") Wilson.

Wilson's style of management was more flexible and open
than that of the old guard, and he was able to draw the reins of
power more tightly from the center without giving offense. The
opening of the Alcoa Building in 1952 brought together some
1,000 corporate managers and staff members who had previously been spread around Pittsburgh in eight separate offices.
Wilson created a number of new top executive positions into
which he moved the upcoming generation of corporate leaders,
including Frank Magee, who became executive vice-president,
and Minton M. Anderson, vice-president for personnel and
industrial relations. Another new appointee was Frederick J.
"Fritz" Close, manager of market development, who was in
charge of new products.[15]

SETUP FOR APPLICATIONS

At the Laboratories, too, a change in leadership signaled Wilson's intention to bring the diverse and highly independent
divisions of the corporation into line. Francis Frary retired as
director of ARL on December 31, 1951, the last of his generation to step down. His successor was Kent R. Van Horn, who
had been an assistant director and head of the Cleveland research division. Van Horn was a native of Cleveland and a
graduate of Case Institute, where his father had been a faculty
colleague of Zay Jeffries. At Jeffries's suggestion, he attended
graduate school at Yale, because it had the most modern program, based on the "new metallurgy," derived from x-ray analysis. When Van Horn completed his doctorate in 1929, he talked
to Jeffries about employment and was encouraged to apply at
Alcoa's Cleveland research laboratory. Van Horn was thrilled
by this suggestion, as he later recalled:

Kent R. Van Horn.

I had read about Hall and his formation of the aluminum company and what they had done [and] my ambition all through Yale was to get a job from Alcoa and do research on metallurgy, on aluminum. . . . I was all set to work for Alcoa before they even heard of me.[16]

At the Cleveland laboratory, Van Horn conducted fundamental research on alloys, using its well-equipped x-ray laboratory. He published widely, particularly in the area of x-ray methodology. He became actively involved in the American Society of Metals, the leading professional society for metallurgists, and established a national reputation in 1944 and 1945 as its vice-president and then president.

In 1950, Van Horn was promoted to associate director, over the heads of several more senior research "chiefs," and brought to New Kensington as Frary's heir apparent. Of all the possible candidates, at age 45 he was the youngest man of sufficient stature for the post. Bakken, at age 58, had been associate director since 1942 and had proved himself to be an effective manager, but he lacked a Ph.D. and had little standing outside Alcoa. Edwards and Templin were both in poor health. Edgar Dix, also age 58, had a national reputation in alloy development and metallography as a result of his extensive publications, but he lacked scientific credentials and had little management experience. The choice of the new director could not have been easy – to facilitate the change, Frary was retained past the normal retirement age, a decision that ran very much against Alcoa's policy. Van Horn's reputation as a strong manager, demonstrated at the Cleveland laboratory, added greatly to his appeal in Pittsburgh at a time when ARL was required to play a leadership role in large-scale applications of technology.[17]

Van Horn moved quickly to establish a style of leadership that contrasted vividly with Frary's somewhat aloof, academic manner. On his arrival, for instance, he arranged an individual get-acquainted dinner with each ARL researcher. He sought to lead the Laboratories by setting good policies and personally seeing that they were carried out. Comfortable with Alcoa's top management in a way that Frary could never have been, Van Horn was well chosen to help draw ARL into the closing circle of centralized policy-making and control.[18]

To some extent, the managerial policies that Van Horn instituted were necessitated simply by the rapid expansion of the

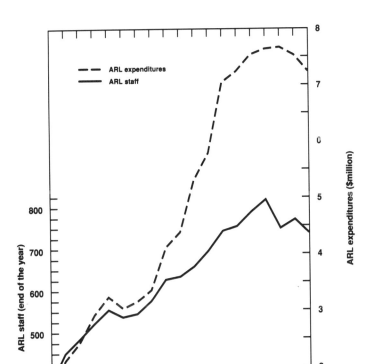

Figure 7.5. ARL program expenditures and staff, 1945–63. Sources: ARL annual reports, ALA; Alcoa Research Laboratories History, vol. 2-B, Alcoa Plant Histories.

Laboratories. The whole operation had become more diverse and more complicated to manage than in Frary's era. Drawing heavily on the advice of M. M. Anderson, the new vice-president of personnel, Van Horn established a pay scale for the first time, making research salaries less arbitrary and bringing them in line with what other laboratories were paying. At a time when professional management was becoming more important, Van Horn took more interest in people's career paths and generally strove to impose a degree of order and stability on the working lives of his research staff that Frary had never deemed necessary.

The growth in program and personnel made space a perennial problem at New Kensington. In 1944 the Cleveland laboratory had been moved into new quarters outfitted with the latest equipment, including separate x-ray and x-ray diffraction laboratories and a high-frequency electric furnace for work on alloy compositions. The Alumina and Chemicals Division at East St. Louis had entered new quarters in 1949. At New Kensington, steps were taken to ease the crush for space as soon as possible after the war, with a second building in 1944, made out of surplus metal, and a third in 1951. Floors were strengthened and power plants upgraded, but the change in the nature of the program was so dramatic that the look of the New Kensington laboratory was always a bit incongruous, as though someone had chosen to rent a college lecture hall to use as a factory. Van Horn was constantly concerned about the crowded conditions.[19]

In 1955, ARL acquired 50 acres of steep hillside running down to its existing 14-acre property. Plans proceeded for an elaborate, stepped structure to be built on this site, but the request for authorization went no farther than the desk of Executive Vice-President Frank Magee. Magee vetoed the proposal – not because it was too large, but because it failed to take into account the longer-term needs of the research organization. He pressed the Laboratories to look for an entirely new location without the limitations imposed by the hilly New Kensington terrain. An economic downturn, however, strung out the building of the new facility for more than 10 years. No one would actually inhabit the new "campus," located near New Kensington in rural Upper Burrell, Pennsylvania, until 1965. Meanwhile, problems of space and facilities at New Kensington were addressed in a piecemeal fashion, involving the kind of renovations and rentals characteristic of all "temporary" arrangements.[20]

It was not, therefore, as the possessor of elaborate new laboratories that, in 1956, the American Institute of Management (AIM) featured Alcoa in its yearly *Manual of Excellent Managements*. Instead, it praised the company's investment in R&D, the largest of any metals firm relative to its gross income, and the management of its laboratories: "Its research climate is one of the very best to be found anywhere. Here lies the principal explanation of the great progress made by both the aluminum industry and Alcoa," the AIM noted. Alcoa had met its competition by reducing production costs while maintaining the quality of its products, and it had led the industry in developing new applications. The institute claimed, with the usual hyperbole, that "no other company has made a greater economic contribution to the American people." Effective teamwork among Re-

These two huge forging presses located at the Cleveland works, a 50,000-ton Mesta and a 35,000-ton United, were used to make the large forgings for the postwar generation of aircraft, beginning with the B-52s. They represent the increase in scale that Alcoa's business underwent after the war.

This aerial view of ARL shows how the research facility was outgrowing its original site when it reached the level of 500 to 700 people in the 1950s. The second and third buildings, erected in 1944 and 1951, were needed to accommodate the huge change in the scale of research that Alcoa experienced in the 1950s, when it added production-scale equipment.

search, Production, and Sales was the reason for this stellar performance.[21]

Alcoa's R&D organization had earned the praise. The year 1956 was the company's best ever, with corporate earnings at an all-time high. Investment in fundamental research over the years was paying rich dividends, as ARL and the development organizations moved effectively to implement the postwar agenda.

NEW RESEARCH MISSION

Faced with pressing needs for vastly increased output in the late 1940s and early 1950s, even such a staunch advocate of the long view as "Chief" Wilson was less interested in continuing general research into metal structure than in applying what was already known. He wanted to curb the natural tendency of researchers to hoard their results too long, and he wanted to ensure that in the postwar period they would be sensitive to Alcoa's need for new products. Alloy developers, he noted, for example, should stop focusing on high-technology aircraft alloys and work on more practical compositions that could utilize scrap metal, because it could be purchased cheaply and worked easily by Alcoa's customers.[22]

Wilson need not have worried. If there was opposition to the full-scale drive for applications in any part of the Alcoa R&D organization after the war, it was muted. The potent combination of top-management attention, new leadership, major capital investment, and a group of timely retirements yielded mass conversion to a new way of thinking about the appropriate mission for R&D.

Van Horn's clear mandate in the new era of competition was to build ARL's relationships with internal customers and to serve their needs, uniting the different disciplines and the different development groups in a common cause. Gone were the days when Bakken had to make an impassioned plea to top management to get an expensive piece of machinery for ARL. Currently, in most instances, experiments could be made on large-scale equipment right on the premises. With a free hand in hiring, Van Horn was able to change the character of the research staff by bringing in new people whose training and creativity lay in applied research and who were thus disposed to tackle production problems. As Templin, Edwards, and others with the "Bureau of Standards" background retired, they were replaced with individuals of a new stamp, willing to cross disciplinary boundaries and to work with others to solve problems. Thus, gradually and with little apparent conflict, Van Horn was able to reshape both the organization and its program to achieve the kind of process improvements and product developments that Wilson and his lieutenants desired.[23]

The impact of the changing focus of the research program was dramatic, but not painful. In a period of retrenchment or even stability in budgets, such a radical reorientation would have been disruptive at best. But the postwar boom allowed the ARL to take off in new directions without abruptly abandoning its traditional commitments. In 1944, research classified as "Product Problems," mainly alloy development, accounted for 43 percent of the Laboratories' expenditures, while "Process Problems" took up 32 percent. By 1949 the situation was reversed, with only 37 percent devoted to products and 49 percent to process research. Much of the money spent by ARL on process problems in this period went to large-scale, high-cost projects on primary processes. This included new work on the Bayer process and on the use of lignite as fuel, supporting development of the smelting plants at Wenatchee and Rockdale. It also included a revival of smelting research, an area that had been virtually dormant since the late 1920s. Here the effect of the loss of monopoly was pronounced, as the sudden emergence of strong domestic competitors in primary production made Alcoa feel vulnerable in its basic technology.[24]

In 1945, ARL designed and built an experimental potline at its New Kensington laboratory, and the following year it took up serious research in the smelting field, starting more or less where it had left off almost 20 years before. The Process Metallurgy Division attacked the problems of operating efficiency and productivity with a program of experimentation based on plant experience, while the Physical Chemistry Division conducted fundamental research into operating conditions, primarily bath composition.

Recognizing the difficulty of experimentation in working reduction plants, in 1946 the management authorized construction of a new building at the Alcoa works in Tennessee to house a large experimental potline, later known as "Potline B." To guide the "forward-looking" program of the Reduction Division, including the program for Potline B, the Technical Committee created a small, high-level subcommittee, the Aluminum and Carbon Committee, which included "Dutch" Nagel, V. C. Doerschuk, head of the Reduction Division, and Francis Frary, among others.[25] Research on the conventional Hall-Héroult process at Potline B focused primarily on improving current efficiency and pot productivity by increasing pot size and controlling operating conditions more closely. Doing parallel work with its own smaller-scale potline, ARL contributed information that helped to guide efforts toward improved control. Fundamental studies of bath composition led to some exciting early results in the laboratory pots, including a reduction in power consumption of 2.5 kilowatt-hours per pound through addition of lithium fluoride to the bath.[26]

As in the 1920s, ARL was quick to look into any new process that seemed to be a lower-cost alternative to the Hall-Héroult cell. In 1948 it seriously examined two promising methods of purifying aluminum by "distillation," from alloys produced electrothermally. For several years thereafter, between 35 and 45 percent of expenditures for smelting research went to investigations of various electrothermal processes, primarily direct re-

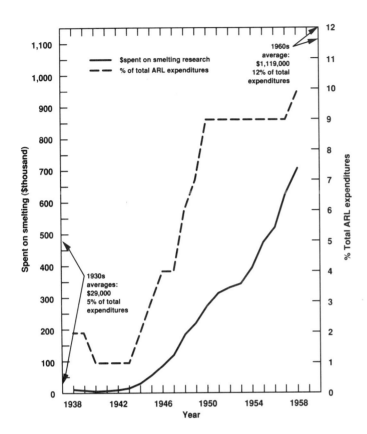

Figure 7.6. Revival of smelting research, 1938–58. Depicted in 5-year moving averages. Sources: ARL annual reports (1938–51), ALA; Alcoa Technical Committee, technical budget and program (1952–58), AA-Boyers.

duction and the oxycarbide process, which the company later patented. Clearly, the desire for a major breakthrough that would put Alcoa ahead of the pack made the Laboratories keen to embrace new processes.

Pushing the smelting program forward aggressively in both laboratory and plant-scale facilities was expensive. The experimental potline at ARL required the addition of many new people, and researchers in this field spent much of their time travelling between New Kensington and Tennessee. The program was extremely important to Alcoa's top management. In 1950, a year in which overall expenditures at the Laboratories were cut back because of a drop in corporate earnings, money spent on smelting almost doubled. In the next decade it would hold constant at an average of 9 percent of the ARL budget. By 1953, the annual bill for smelting R&D throughout the company had risen above $1 million.[27]

The work on refining and smelting had results of obvious and visible competitive value. But in any one year, 40 to 50 percent of ARL expenditures for process innovation went into problems such as "Working Aluminum," "Improvements in Metallurgical Practice," "Oils and Lubricants," "Paint and Lacquer Finishes," and "Castings, Process Development," all research projects that were aimed at making progress on a broad front through small-scale innovations. Casting, forging, and extrusion received special attention because they had long been neglected in favor of work on the rolling of high-strength alloy sheet, and between 1945 and 1960 ARL mounted literally hundreds of projects in these areas. The large number of small, interrelated projects that went forward in this way could be categorized under five headings: fire-fighting, problem-solving, systematic data analysis, systematic experimentation, and fundamental work. These projects had enormous cumulative value, and all involved real plant problems identified by operations personnel.[28]

Much of the work to be done in fabricating plants could be called fire-fighting: getting a piece of equipment to work correctly, finding the cause of an explosion, or launching an all-out assault on a problem, such as the defects in extruded products called "die lines" (the unwanted lines left in the metal where two halves of a die met). These random events, for the most part, could be fed into other, more systematic research studies if research-trained people worked on them. Other projects involved gathering and analyzing production data that existed in plant records or were developed through experimentation. Examples of this type of work included correlating extrusion temperatures to the properties of extruded products and correlating die temperature to the amount of force required to shape the metal by die forging. These analyses provided a much-needed factual basis for operational control. Systematic experimental projects tightly focused on specific aspects of existing technology included the development of a process for spraying Alclad coatings on extruded products, the substitution of synthetic material for sand in casting molds, and the development of improved core binders (substances to hold the material in shape during casting).

Where needed, ARL still initiated studies of fundamental

principles. For instance, a project begun in 1954 used radioactive tracers to track and analyze the flow of metal during extrusion, with the goal of increasing extrusion speeds and improving the quality of products. In general, however, it was the development organizations that assumed responsibility for the broad, synthetic technical vision guiding the company's pursuit of its postwar, postmonopoly agenda. Research played a supporting role as the repository of expertise on specific technologies, but not the author of grand designs.

CENTRALIZED TECHNOLOGY

A severe shortage of qualified technical personnel, which continued after the war, though somewhat less severely, made it necessary for the Metallurgical Division to shift to the Laboratories its responsibility for methods and standards in handling analytical equipment. In that way it was possible to spread the available expertise rather thinly around the corporation. The centralizing impulse picked up momentum of its own, however, as researchers whose mission it was to improve on analytical methods and standards became impatient with plant metallurgists who did not adhere strictly to the guidelines laid out for them. Edgar Dix complained to the Technical Committee, for example, that staff in the plant metallographic laboratories were not following the guidelines for interpretation of their analyses because they viewed the guidelines as "only advisory." Though Dix allowed that metallography remained "more an art than a science," he wanted the same authority in his area as Nagel had given to researchers in chemical and physical testing, that is to say, the authority to go into the plant laboratories for routine inspection and supervision.[29]

An impetus to keep central control in ARL also came from the push of rapidly evolving testing technology, such as occurred when the spectroscope was replaced by the quantometer for rapid metal analysis shortly after World War II. The quantometer evolved rapidly over the next decade and a half, incorporating electronic computation and digital printout. In general, there was an explosion of new technology applicable in the area of analysis and inspection, as infrared light, high-frequency sound waves (ultrasound), and radioactive tracers became available. The Laboratories adapted these for use in

Alcoa's plants and in most cases maintained supervisory control over their operation.[30]

A further justification for central control over new technologies was the perceived need for secrecy. As the company struggled to hold its own against the aggressive marketing efforts of Reynolds and Kaiser, manufacturing innovations became increasingly important as competitive weapons. Both the Laboratories and the plants were constantly losing trained personnel to competitors, and limiting the circulation of technical information was one way to minimize the damage inflicted by these departures.[31]

Another reason for ARL to strive for control over technology was the competition it faced internally from other technical organizations. The 1937 technical show had helped to engender within the company a high degree of technical unanimity, a common purpose, and a common vision of what was needed. But pressures created by rapid expansion, both during and after the war, and by competition, had fostered development activities throughout the company that threatened the common purpose and tended to fragment the technical vision.

In the early 1950s, the independent development groups under the corporate Sales, Engineering, and Metallurgical Divisions were all led by strong managers with legitimate claims to a voice in R&D policy-making. All these groups had come of age during the war and currently were competing with ARL on several fronts: for authority in a particular area of expertise, or for power in the committee system, or for control over the research agenda, and, eventually, in every instance, for R&D funds.

Having taken up responsibility for the broad range of Alcoa's technical problems, Van Horn abandoned the position of independent arbiter staked out by Frary and placed himself in the middle of this simmering political situation. At Cleveland, research was a cooperative endeavor, and his experience there with plant personnel and strong development organizations made him receptive to their claims. He became committed to forging a smoothly functioning R&D organization and eliminating the competition and tension that previously had made cooperation difficult. The way in which Van Horn approached these issues and his striking success in resolving them to his satisfaction ensured that the change in direction in the immediate postwar, postmonopoly years would be lasting.

GROWTH OF DEVELOPMENT

Alcoa's development organizations became increasingly powerful as a result of the new mission to apply existing knowledge and know-how to marketable products. From the mid-1940s to the mid-1960s, Engineering, Sales, and Metallurgy were "development-minded" and equipped with their own laboratories. As chief metallurgist and a key member of the Technical Committee, of which he became chairman in 1950, "Dutch" Nagel became the principal architect of the production–research axis on which the company's technical agenda turned for roughly 20 years. The breadth of his influence increased after 1945, when Metallurgy established a reduction department of its own. When Potline B was created in 1948, it was Nagel who had oversight of its budgets and program.[32]

Nagel was intent on stabilizing and optimizing Alcoa's existing processes, a goal that militated against major product innovation at the plant level. While he welcomed ARL's initiative to establish control over testing and analytical laboratories, he complained about the disruptions of introducing new alloys, suggesting that researchers seemed to care more about advancing aluminum technology than about maintaining quality and profitability in the plants. As chief metallurgist, Nagel could be a powerful ally of the research engineers when their objectives matched his, but he was a forceful opponent when they did not.[33]

Another strong central organization with a claim to authority in the technical community was the corporate Engineering Division. Engineering and ARL worked closely together on many projects, as in building the showcase structures at the Davenport works and the Alcoa Building, which drew on Laboratories personnel for "fire-fighting" support. ARL and Engineering Division personnel jointly built and operated a test room for the aluminum ceiling and heating panels proposed for the Alcoa Building. As the steel frame of the building was going up, they worked together to solve the problem of hanging the exterior aluminum panels so that they would not shift and creak with

Elbert Howarth.

temperature changes. In another project, Elbert Howarth of ARL and Don Bohn, chief electrical engineer, worked together to devise a means of controlling vibration in the large radial engines installed at the Point Comfort works. When it came to cooperative work in a context other than such special projects, however, competition sometimes arose between corporate engineers in the Engineering Division and research engineers at ARL.[34]

In 1944, Engineering formally established a development budget to cover work such as building and wiring the experimental reduction line at Potline B. This Engineering Division development budget hovered around a modest 4 percent of total R&D spending into the 1960s. In 1960, Engineering Division management gave its laboratory at Cleveland more visibility and a greater role in the company at large by designating it the Alcoa Equipment Development Division (AEDD). It then expanded rapidly, and its budget doubled, surpassing $1 million in less than a decade.[35]

The Development units under the Sales Division also flourished in this period. The Jobbing Division, created in the early 1930s, and the "technical department" of the Aluminum Cooking Utensil Company were unified in the late 1940s and renamed the Alcoa Process Development Laboratory (APDL). Located at the New Kensington works, APDL focused largely on joining and finishes. From 1954, it operated a packaging laboratory that became increasingly important as Alcoa focused its efforts to develop new markets on consumer products rather than industrial and architectural applications. From the late 1950s onward, the process engineers of APDL, with their closer customer contact, could claim a significant role in setting the research agenda.[36]

Sales Development also began to take initiative in mounting projects, and it established facilities at New Kensington to fabricate prototypes of its own new product ideas. A number of successes confirmed the effectiveness of product engineering and made Sales Development a strong competitor for R&D funds within the Technical Committee system. Cans featuring the easy-open end, commercialized by several major can companies, provided Alcoa's first big success in the beverage-can market. Another was a composite aluminum-foil-and-fiber container for frozen citrus juice that Alcoa sold to Minute Maid in

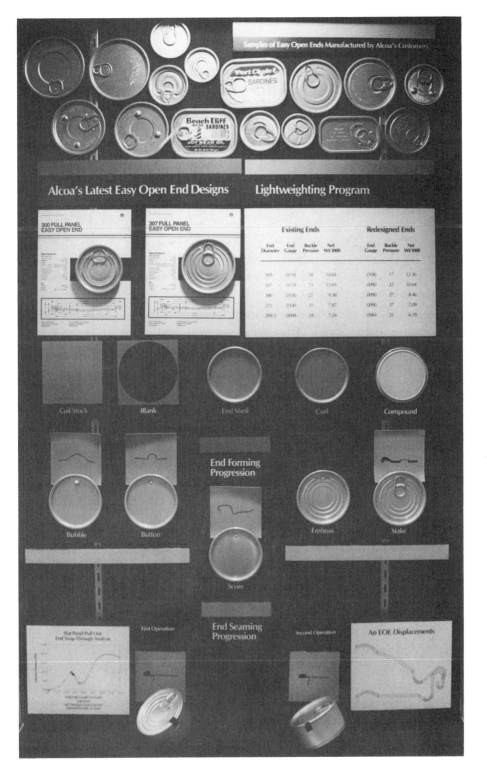

Some of the many versions of the easy-open end, which provided entrée for Alcoa and its competitors to develop a huge new business in can sheet.

1959. Between 1957 and 1958 alone, difficult years economically for Alcoa, the expenditures of this division leapt from $286,000 to $1.4 million to support pioneering work that eventually led to a greatly expanded market for aluminum sheet to make cans. After five years of continuing growth, Sales Development was split into two divisions: Application Engineering (the original technical consulting function) and the Alcoa Product Development Division (APDD). Both of these became significant players in Alcoa's technical community.[37]

Yet another actor on the stage was the Commercial Research Division, established in 1953. As Alcoa's product focus shifted to consumer applications, and as the art of selling developed into more sophisticated marketing, this group carried more and more weight. Its reports came to the Laboratories as highly confidential information to be circulated to only a few people in positions of authority. Some were very tightly focused, such as "Aluminum Foil Potato Chip Bags" (1953), "Large Press Aluminum Extrusions" (1956), and "Survey of Residential Window Purchasing Practices" (1963). Others that were much more far-reaching included "World Consumption of Aluminum" (1959), "The Market for Aluminum Mill Products in Mexico" (1960), and "Selected Defense Industry Applications for Heat-treatable Alloy Plate, 1963–1967" (1962). The trend was toward research-based "marketing plans," either annual or longer-range, that would predict technological opportunities and spell out R&D objectives.[38]

It was the task of the Technical Committee to coordinate the activities of all of these groups and mesh them with the activities of ARL. As development programs and budgets expanded and became more complex in the postwar years, so did the committee system. In 1945 there were five standing subcommittees; by 1950 there were 10 subcommittees.[39] One or more members of the Technical Committee, and representatives of each part of the company that would be involved in or affected by innovations in a given area, sat on each subcommittee. The rapid expansion of this system drew many individuals into the process of planning R&D; it also transformed its basic character from that of a leadership team into the classic form of a bureaucracy. Van Horn clearly saw the potential of the committee system for pulling together R&D into the sort of integrated system that had worked on a smaller scale at Cleveland. When he became

Table 7.1. *ARL and the Development Division's share of R&D expenditures (%)*

Unit	1951	'52	'53	'54	'55	'56	'57	'58	'59	'60	'61	'62	'63	'64	'65	'66	'67	'68	'69	'70	'71
ARL	54	56	54	57	56	55	55	51	51	53	53	52	50	53	54	56	55	60	59	59	57
Metallurgical Division	13	13	18	16	15	15	15	12	11	10	11	11	9	9	6	5	6	6	7	6	5
Potline B	11	12	11	11	15	15	13	11	11	11	6	7	11	8	7	9	8	8	8	8	13
Alcoa Product Development Division	4	3	4	4	3	3	3	3	3	3	5	6	6	6	8	8	8	7	8	8	8
Refining Division	5	5	3	2	2	2	2	1	2	2	2	2	2	2	2	1	1	1	1	1	1
Engineering Division	7	4	3	3	4	3	2	4	4	5	2	3	2	1	1	1	1				
Sales Development	3	3	3	3	3	2	2	10	10	7	7	8	7	3							
R&D Administration								0	1	0	0	1	0	1	3	1	3	1	1	1	2
Sales Department										3	0	2	2	2	2	1	1	1	1	0	0
Alcoa Equipment Development Division									3	4	4	5	6	7	7	8	9	8	7	7	
Alcoa Product Development Division													2	6	6	5	5	6	7	5	
Miscellaneous & subsidiaries	3	4	4	4	3	6	6	8	6	6	7	5	7	8	4	5	4	2	2	3	2
Total expenditure ($ million)	6	6	8	8	9	11	13	14	15	16	15	14	14	14	14	16	18	19	21	22	26

director of research, he made the committee system his power base.

EVOLUTION OF THE COMMITTEE SYSTEM

In November 1949, Herman Bakken sent a memo to the division chiefs of ARL, congratulating them on completion of the 1950 budgets and program. In that 19th year that he had presided over the budget-making process, Bakken expressed pride in the "meaty" research agenda they had proposed: "We appear to have overcome the disturbance brought on by the war and I think it is definitely shown that we are back on the research job in a creditable manner." He approved of the "realistic ring" of the research program:

I thought I saw in the statement of our problems unmistakable evidence that our people are profiting by the contacts many of them have with our various Technical Subcommittees and individuals from other divisions of the company. I found no instance where the contemplated work might be characterized as impractical or visionary and yet there was plenty [of] evidence that considerable thinking had been put forth in the formulation of the program.[40]

Bakken's reassignment to the Aluminum Ore Company in 1950, as vice-president and general manager, disrupted the programmatic continuity that had prevailed during his long tenure as chairman of the Technical Committee and had contributed to the satisfactory state of research that he perceived in 1949. When he left ARL, the committee came under the domination of Metallurgy and "Dutch" Nagel. The tight, stable, and essentially research-dominated group became more diffuse, less stable, and more activist in orientation. Soon it was enlarged to include all the company's technical interests and made to report directly to "Chief" Wilson. In another important change, part of its membership began to rotate annually, increasing the exposure and opportunities for communication at the expense of some of the continuity.

In a confidential letter to Frary describing the changes that were to be made when he stepped down from the chair of the Technical Committee, Bakken related that new people would be selected to serve on the subcommittees, to bring them more in step with the times. On the Subcommittee on Finishes, for example, the number of representatives from ARL would be reduced from four to two, and the chairman, Assistant Director of Research Junius D. Edwards, would be replaced by someone "much closer to the customer demand and needs than our people in Research." The purpose of these changes was to redirect the focus of the committee away from research, toward "commercial development and exploitation of finishes."[41]

At the same time, a high-level Research Policy Committee was formed to bring ARL more in line with other divisions of the company. As long as Frary remained director, Research retained much of its independence. But well before his departure, pressures were mounting to make its systems and procedures more like those of other technical functions. The planning and budgeting process was one area where the implications of this change were most apparent.[42]

In 1949 the Technical Committee expanded the format of its annual budget presentation to include a detailed description of the progress during 1949 as well as the proposed work for 1950, taking over from Frary the role of presenting R&D to the company's management.[43] In the process, the ARL problem numbering system, in use since 1919, gave way to a new set of project categories, which facilitated the Technical Committee's understanding of the process of setting and maintaining priorities within a broad and complex program. This was an essential step if the committee was to accomplish its objectives of minimizing duplication of effort and ensuring that each division would work on pressing problems and not waste time and money on "fruitless projects."[44]

As desirable as these goals were, Frary nevertheless warned of dangers in carrying them out. In the past, he had presented an annual budget that reported expenditures for specific problems only in his end-of-the-year summary. In this view, the new annual Technical Committee "Technical Budgets and Programs," which would show both what was budgeted for each category of work and what was actually spent, portended a significant loss of independence for the Laboratories:

In comparing the amount budgeted for a given problem with the amount spent, it should be remembered that the emphasis on the different problems often changes during the year, and men have to be taken off work on one problem to push the work on another

Table 7.2. *Changes in research expenditure categories, 1951*

ARL problem categories, 1950

    I. General
- Analytical methods
- Mechanical testing methods
- Metallographic methods
- Radiographic methods
- Contingent research

   II. Process problems
- Surface-treatment processes for Al and Mg
- Paint and lacquer finishes
- New Alumina processes
- Fluorspar and cryolite processes
- Bauxite and Bayer-process problems
- Working aluminum
- Reduction problems
- Improvements in metallurgical practice
- Oils and lubricants
- Melting problems
- Joining processes
- Develop equipment to produce and fabricate Al and Mg products
- Production processes for alloying materials
- Refining and reclamation processes
- Castings, process development

 III. Product problems
- Miscellaneous physical-chemical investigations
- Chemical and corrosion properties of aluminum and alloys
- Aluminum paint
- Mechanical properties of Al and Mg alloys
- Design of Al and Mg structures
- Alloy and product development
- Chemical-products development
- Electrical conductor problems
- Aluminum milk-bottle hoods
- Services of outside laboratories and technical organizations

  IV. Service work
- Magnesium investigations
- Patent work
- Requested work for Alcoa divisions (7 problems)
- Requested work for Alcoa subsidiaries (5 problems)
- Equipment built for capital account ARL and for sale

Table 7.2. *(cont.)*

R&D budget categories, 1951
    I.   Ores and mineral raw materials
             Bauxite
             Other aluminous ores
             Fluorspar
             Other minerals

    II. Alumina, cryolite, and aluminum fluoride process investigations
             Bayer-process improvements
             New alumina processes
             Cryolite and aluminum fluoride process improvements

    III. Chemical-products development
             Chemical aluminas for sale to others
             Chemical fluorides for sale to others

    IV. Power development
             Internal-combustion engines

    V.   Aluminum reduction
             Electrodes
             Pot design and operation improvements
             Fume control
             Thermal processes

    VI. Metal-melting and ingot-casting investigations
             Improvements in melting practices
             Improvements in ingot-casting practices
             Metal-reclamation project

    VII. Aluminum products: alloy, process, product, and equipment development
             Anodes
             Sheet and plate
             Extruded products
             Tube and pipe fittings
             Wire, rod and bar
             Rolled structural shapes
             Cable
             Cable accessories
             Foil
             Albron, paste and powder
             Collapsible tubes and thin-wall containers
             Impact extrusions
             Rivets and nails
             Screw-Machine products
             Forgings

Table 7.2. *(cont.)*

Sand castings
Permanent-mold castings
Plaster-process castings
Die castings
Customer's ingot
Jobbing Division products
Aluminum Cooking Utensil Company products
Aluminum Seal Company products
New products

VIII.   Magnesium development investigations

IX.   Sales Development expenditures (allocated to products under VIII)

X.   Development expenditures of a general nature
  Joining investigations
  Finishing investigations
  Aluminum-wrought-alloy development
  Aluminum-casting-alloy development
  Develop methods for determining characteristics of aluminum
  Oils and lubricants
  Aluminum Packaging Laboratories
  Contingent research
  Services of outside laboratories and technical organizations
  Development of metallurgical practices and processes at ARL
  Product development for Alcoa customers
  Development expenditures not otherwise provided for

which has become more important. The problem budget is therefore only a rough guide to the relative importance of the various problems, as they appeared toward the end of the previous year, while the general expenditure budget is our best estimate of the amount required to operate the Laboratories.[45]

To some it might seem a trivial matter, but by removing the crucial allowance for uncertainty in longer-term and exploratory work, such a system could, over time, drive a research program into shorter-term, more predictable work. Such R&D would meet its targets and reliably deliver what could be foreseen, but that style of resource allocation would foreclose the

unforeseeable, the serendipitous, and probably the most fundamental innovations.

The first sign of what would eventually take place throughout the committee system was the formation of a subcommittee
on alloys. More powerful than other subcommittees at the time,
it was given responsibility and authority not only to approve
new alloys but also to follow through on the steps leading to
their commercialization. This was a wide-ranging set of powers
that was to presage a more activist role for all subcommittees as
time passed. Edgar Dix, longtime alloy researcher and assistant
director of research until 1958, was made chairman of the Subcommittee on Alloy Development, but he took grave exception
to its new directive style. He resisted the idea that his committee
should play a "policing" role over experimentation in the
plants, arguing that it would stifle initiative, and he was angered
by the suggestion that researchers at ARL should not work on a
new alloy composition unless the committee had previously established the need for a new material.[46]

Dix might object strenuously to the idea of subcommittees
telling Operations and Research what to do, but that was exactly
what Van Horn had in mind. The new director of research was
indefatigable in his promotion of the subcommittees, attending
a large proportion of their meetings himself. At Van Horn's
urging, three new subcommittees were created during the
1950s. By the mid-1960s, the system would encompass 24 separate entities, including the various task forces and problem
groups established as subgroups of the subcommittees.[47]

Unlike Frary in this, as in other respects, Van Horn treated
the committee structure as his preferred vehicle for exercising
influence within the corporation. He served on the Technical
Committee from 1950 until his retirement in 1970, and he was
its chairman from 1963 until 1970. Having done so much to
foster its development over 20 years, he came to see himself as
something of a father to the committee system.[48] He was largely
responsible for pushing through the transformation in which
subcommittees, and the task forces that worked for them on
specific problems, assumed a leading role in shaping and managing R&D, relegating the Technical Committee to general
oversight and approval. That was just the kind of direction by
committee that "Chief" Wilson and his contemporaries had
sought to avoid in 1944, but it was so much in line with other

trends inside the company in the postwar period that, even without Van Horn, some such change probably would have taken place.

In 1956 the name Aluminum Research Laboratories was changed to Alcoa Research Laboratories. The new name gave belated recognition to the altered relationship between the company and the Laboratories. In a world in which more than one primary aluminum company conducted in-house R&D, research had become a proprietary commodity. The name change inaugurated a serious search for a new campuslike laboratory site in the vicinity of New Kensington, and the idea of a consolidated R&D facility was suggested early in 1957. This concept flowed smoothly out of the centralizing trend of Van Horn's directorship, with its emphasis on the integration of R&D through the subcommittee system. Yet it was by no means clear at that stage what the reporting relationships of the various development organizations would be within the consolidated entity, nor was it clear that they would move intact to the new location.[49]

Had the economic conditions of the early 1950s continued while the technical center was being planned, the pendulum might well have swung back to the kind of centralized but independent research organization that Frary had established – the kind symbolized by the old ARL building on its hillside site. Van Horn, who initially drove the system toward integration of R&D, later came to feel a need to reinvigorate fundamental work and to reassert research priorities. He might well have engineered such a pendulum swing. That possibility was abruptly foreclosed, however, by the crisis that descended on Alcoa and the aluminum industry in the middle of 1957.

CRISIS AND CONSOLIDATION

The fifth straight year of rising revenues and profits, 1956 was the best year Alcoa had ever had. Heavy postwar demand had been augmented by the military buildup for the Korean War, and stockpiling agreements with the government absorbed excess output generated by new smelting facilities brought on-line in 1950 and 1952. Shortly into the new year, a $54 million expansion was completed at the Davenport works, doubling its capacity. Still under construction were a new alumina works and expanded smelting facilities at Point Comfort, Texas, another smelting expansion at Wenatchee, Washington, and a huge new reduction works at Warrick, Indiana. Alcoa, like other aluminum producers, was extremely optimistic about continuing expansion of its markets.[50]

A national recession beginning in 1957, however, suddenly put aluminum into oversupply. Alcoa's competitors had expanded even more rapidly: Total domestic production of aluminum had increased by a factor of 10 since 1939, and in 1957 Reynolds, Kaiser, and Anaconda controlled 55 percent of that capacity. In March 1958, a sudden drop in the price of primary ingot, the first price reduction since 1946, burst the bubble of growth and profitability that had enveloped the industry since the war. Alcoa's profits continued to fall until 1961 and rose only slowly after that. By 1965, profits were still 36 percent below the high of 1956.[51]

The crisis struck at a moment of transition for Alcoa. In 1957 the antitrust case was closed for good, the lurking fear of dismemberment laid to rest, and A. V. Davis was finally able to retire. "Chief" Wilson moved up as chairman, and Frank Magee became president just as the recession was gaining momentum. Magee was forced to cut back on primary production both in 1957 and in 1958. When the new alumina plant at Point Comfort came on-line in 1958, the Aluminum Ore Company works at East St. Louis closed for good. The following year, construction of the Warrick smelter was stopped. It later started again, but then only on one of its proposed five potlines. Before Alcoa emerged from the five-year "profit meat grinder," weeds would grow up through the concrete floors of the empty potrooms, and rust would accumulate on the huge machinery that was to mine nearby coal deposits intended to power the Warrick works.[52]

Frank Magee.

Magee's major thrust to counteract the crisis was toward controlling costs and improving production processes in order to compete more effectively in new and existing markets for fabricated products. To that end he greatly accelerated the process of centralization begun under Wilson by appointing three executive vice-presidents. The new "geography" of top management, Magee explained, woud help to "expedite important policy decisions in all phases of the business." Similarly, he looked to stronger, more centralized management of R&D to expedite the process of innovation, and for this he relied on the committee system. "Time is our greatest problem," Magee declared:

We all realize that R & D implies time-consuming activities, but it must be streamlined. What we are presently attempting – and what the committee can accomplish – is to get from starting point to objective as quickly as possible.[53]

Magee's impatience with R&D struck a chord that was to be heard in executive offices and boardrooms across the country, as inflated and unrealistic expectations for R&D came home to roost. Companies and government agencies alike, having invested large amounts of money, expected to get exactly what they believed they were paying for, and what the scientific community had led them to believe could be had – innovation on demand. Much of value was emerging as a result of these investments, but it was seldom as predictable, as timely, or as economical as in their carefully laid plans.

Government spending for R&D, which had expanded so quickly and for so long, levelled off for a short time in the mid-1950s, and at that time there might well have been a major national assessment of the benefits from those expenditures. But such an assessment was put off for a decade when the Soviet satellite *Sputnik* was launched in 1957. Government funding for weapons research and space-related activities resumed its upward trend, not to level off again until 1966, and the conditions of inflated research costs and shortages of scientifically trained manpower returned. Midcourse corrections that might have changed the national climate for research were aborted. The effect on companies like Alcoa was to make connections to that national scientific community even less accessible, less relevant, and less affordable than before. The Alcoa technical community withdrew further into itself and looked to opportunities that were perceived as involving less risk.[54]

One effect of the crisis was to push Alcoa to diversify into real-estate development and to expand into international markets where it had not been since 1928. Magee established an international division in 1958 and entered into partnership with the Furukawa Electric Company to operate a fabricating plant in Japan. During the following year Alcoa competed furiously, though unsuccessfully, with Reynolds for control of British Aluminium, Ltd. Soon after, it formed a partnership with

Imperial Chemical Industries to operate fabricating plants and a secondary smelter in Wales, and within a few years it became involved in other joint ventures in Mexico and Venezuela. In the same period, Alcoa undertook development of new primary facilities in Paranam, Suriname, and joined several Australian companies in a $100 million project to mine bauxite and produce aluminum there as well, all in anticipation of rapid growth in the worldwide market.[55]

These moves were similar to those of other U.S. companies in the late 1950s. Faced with tough competitive situations in the home market, they chose to expand overseas, where existing technologies could be extended over larger markets, and to diversify their operations. Neither move appeared to have an immediate effect on R&D. Yet in providing opportunities that were alternatives to those generated by investment in technology, diversification and international expansion challenged a number of well-established corporate R&D organizations to reassert their claims to a special place in their companies' strategies.[56]

The aluminum crisis and Magee's response to it brought to a rapid culmination the process of centralization that had begun in 1950. "Dutch" Nagel retired in January 1957. His successor as chairman of the Technical Committee, for only a short time until his retirement, was G. D. Welty, manager of engineering sales. Welty took a fresh look at the organization and procedures of the committee system and initiated planning for a consolidated technical center.[57]

The top-management group in the committee structure, the Research Policy Committee, had set up a planning mechanism for the new R&D facility, but otherwise had taken no direct part in shaping a technical vision, or in communicating a strategic direction to the technical community. It had delegated those tasks entirely to the Technical Committee. Welty prodded top management to become more fully involved in R&D. "You support it – generously," he wrote to Magee, "but you do not really know much about what goes on there."[58]

Welty proposed that the chairman of the Research Policy Committee should also be the chairman of the Technical Committee and that the latter should be reconstituted to include all of the subcommittee chairmen. In his opinion, it was the subcommittees that held "the real vitality" and the subcommittee chairmen who embodied "the real strength" of the committee system:

It is in the deliberations of [the subcommittees], composed of carefully selected representatives from Sales, Engineering, Research and Operating, where decisions are reached which determine the direction Research is to take. The Director of Research has the responsibility for carrying out work which they indicate should be undertaken. I offer for consideration the thought that these Technical Committee Subcommittees might, in a similar manner, provide guidance to Process Development through a Director of Development.[59]

Welty's recommendation that there should be coequal directors of Research and Development reporting to the Technical Committee touched off a political crisis for Van Horn that ran parallel to the crisis that the corporation as a whole was passing through. In a stroke it completely redefined the relationship between ARL and the committee system, sweeping away the long tradition of independence for Research. Van Horn had fostered the rise of the subcommittees, and now, ironically, he was to be reduced to the role of executor of subcommittee plans. He fended off the proposal for a director of development but could not block the empowerment of the subcommittees.[60]

As corporate earnings continued to fall during 1958, Magee looked for ways to tighten his grip on production costs and quality and to ensure that Alcoa was getting full return on its large investment in R&D. Many of Welty's ideas about how to mold the subcommittees to make them more forceful were adopted. The Research Policy Committee became a committee of vice-presidents, renamed the Technical Policy Committee.[61] The Technical Committee became the Research and Development Committee, reorganized to include the subcommittee chairmen. The positions of both chairman and secretary of the R&D Committee were made full-time positions and constituted a new management function with oversight of R&D. To assume these key positions, Magee tapped his chief and assistant chief metallurgists, Theodore W. Bossert and John H. Alden. These choices signified both the power of the Metallurgical Division and Magee's preoccupation with production-oriented R&D. Within a year of that appointment, Bossert was named vice-president for R&D.[62]

Magee paid lip service to research, especially to fundamental research, but he treated it as an expenditure of resources rather than as a source of opportunity. That was one of the places where obvious economies could be made, and he was determined to tighten control over spending in that area. In 1959 he explained to an interviewer for *Modern Metals* that while research had to have the support of top management to remain independent, "nevertheless we must be realistic and make sure that we get the most for each research dollar, and in the shortest possible time." He pointed to Bossert and the committee system as the means by which he hoped to achieve that end. Early the following year, Magee took the next logical, though sensitive, step and brought Van Horn formally under the control of the new vice-president for R&D.[63]

Theodore Bossert.

In fact, the change was a formality, for Bossert and Alden had already taken into their office control of R&D budgets and programs. To the subcommittee chairmen they gave the authority and responsibility to "start, assign priority, rigorously prosecute and finish . . . projects coming under their respective jurisdiction." Budget making was to be conducted according to "ground rules" established by the Technical Policy Committee, dictating the total amount that could be spent. Once the subcommittees had determined the priorities of projects under their control and had assigned tasks to the various Research or Development organizations, the chairman of the R&D Committee would write to each division and department head, Van Horn included, to inform each of his operating budget for the coming year.[64]

As Alcoa's fortunes moved toward a nadir in 1961, so did those of Van Horn and ARL. The deepening crisis brought the first layoffs in Research since the 1930s. Taking place on a day that would forever be remembered as Black Friday at the Alcoa Laboratories, the layoffs came completely without warning and had a devastating and prolonged effect on morale.

R&D COMPETITION

While he suffered reversals at the corporate level, Van Horn had been trying to revitalize a laboratory he saw in need of major change. In June 1958, anticipating the September retirement of Edgar Dix as assistant director of ARL, Van Horn had proposed a reorganization of the Laboratories, the first since

Van Horn and his first R&D management team standing on the steps of ARL. Front row left to right: Philip Stroup, Edgar Dix, Kent Van Horn, William Ennor, and Ernest Hartmann; Back row: Vivian MacDonald, Orlo Proctor, George T. Reynolds, and M. W. Daugherty.

1943. Several new divisions had been added in the postwar period – Lubricants in 1947, Electrical Engineering in 1948, and Foil and Packaging in 1957 – but no attempt had been made to address organizational issues arising from rapid growth and the changing research mission.

"In some areas," Van Horn told the Technical Policy Committee, ARL's divisions had developed "more according to the capabilities of certain division chiefs than to functions or responsibilities." The retirements of Frank Keller and Robert I. Wray, longtime leaders in research metallography and development of paints and finishes, respectively, opened the way to reorganization of their divisions and to Van Horn's more institutionalized bureaucratic approach. Metallography became a service group for ARL as a whole, while its research group moved into Physical Metallurgy. A new Finishes Division was formed by combining sections of Metallography and Process Metallurgy with Paint Finishes.[65]

In other instances, the rapid growth during the postwar pe-

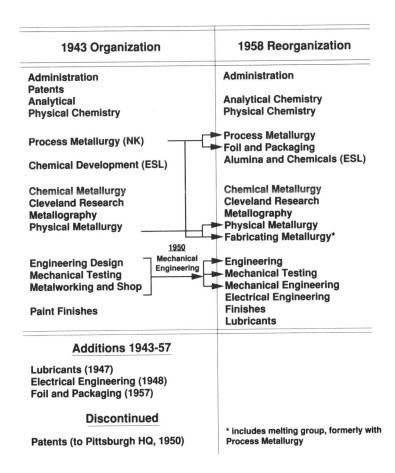

1943 Organization	1958 Reorganization
Administration Patents Analytical Physical Chemistry	Administration Analytical Chemistry Physical Chemistry
Process Metallurgy (NK) Chemical Development (ESL)	Process Metallurgy Foil and Packaging Alumina and Chemicals (ESL)
Chemical Metallurgy Cleveland Research Metallography Physical Metallurgy	Chemical Metallurgy Cleveland Research Metallography Physical Metallurgy Fabricating Metallurgy*
Engineering Design Mechanical Testing Metalworking and Shop Paint Finishes	1950 Mechanical Engineering Engineering Mechanical Testing Mechanical Engineering Electrical Engineering Finishes Lubricants

Additions 1943-57	
Lubricants (1947) Electrical Engineering (1948) Foil and Packaging (1957)	
Discontinued	
Patents (to Pittsburgh HQ, 1950)	* includes melting group, formerly with Process Metallurgy

Figure 7.7. ARL organization changes, 1943–58.

riod had made units so large that division chiefs were consumed with administrative matters and unable to devote sufficient attention to the substance of the work being carried out in their fields. The Physical Metallurgy Division, for instance, posed a serious problem. "Frankly," Van Horn confided, "we are not satisfied with the progress in fundamental physical metallurgy at ARL in recent years." He proposed to split this division into two parts. Fabricating Metallurgy would work on the metallurgical aspects of process development in forging, rolling, forming, heat treatment and aging, and "alloy development of a very practical or short-range nature." It would also include a group working on melting and ingot casting, transferred from Process Metallurgy. The remaining staff in Physical Metallurgy would then be free to focus on long-range alloy development and on fundamental research related to alloys and alloy behavior. To revitalize Physical Metallurgy at New Kensington, Van Horn imported a number of key researchers from the Cleveland laboratory, including Harold Hunsicker, long involved with alloy development, who was to lead the reorganized division. Bringing these key researchers to New Kensington and consolidating there the research effort in physical metallurgy stimulated work in certain areas, such as advanced ingot-casting methods.

The former chief of Physical Metallurgy at New Kensington, William Fink, was promoted to the new position of scientific advisor, where his role was to sponsor activities in support of fundamental research in all the divisions. Except for work on smelting and corrosion, Van Horn acknowledged, fundamentals had received "inadequate attention . . . in recent years."

We find that communication of new ARL developments among scientists below the status of division chief is weak. Fink would arrange seminars, in various research areas, of the appropriate fundamental scientists of all divisions to discuss new theories, mechanisms and investigational tools. He would also spend more time at technical meetings around the country and in universities following and applying in ARL the work in fundamental or basic chemistry, metallurgy, engineering, etc.[66]

Since Van Horn had been director of ARL, the percentage of the Laboratories' budget devoted to basic research had fallen from about 25 percent to between 10 and 15 percent. That trend ran counter to developments outside Alcoa, where, during the same period, an upsurge of fundamental research in metallurgy had resulted in a number of important new theories. Whereas in 1940 there had been only a handful of useful books in metallurgy – all standard reference works that conveyed no more than general principles – by 1958 there was a host of specialized studies, including textbook material on the physical metallurgy of aluminum alloys. This research had both deepened the knowledge base in metals science and broadened the discipline, through application of knowledge of nonmetallic substances, to the point that the field should properly have been called "materials science." Van Horn was properly concerned at the level of fundamental research in Alcoa in 1958.[67]

However, there were problems in effecting a renaissance that he did not address. As had been amply evident in previous episodes of program development, changing a program implied changing the staff as well as the structure. People who had been selected not for their research orientation or for their effective contact with the scientific community but rather for their ability to integrate successfully with Development and to respond effectively to internal customers could hardly be expected to produce the results that Van Horn was seeking. There was considerably less room for maneuver than there had been at the beginning of his career as director, when a major change of course was facilitated by the fact that the company was growing and budgets were expanding. Currently, radical economies were the order of the day.

During the depression of the 1930s, Frary had economized on the most expensive parts of the program, that is, on development, and had pushed ahead aggressively on fundamentals. He was able to do so because his independent judgment and technical vision were understood as a protection for the future, and because Alcoa's monopoly made it possible to assume that all benefits of the investment in R&D would be captured sooner or later. From the late 1950s on, the situation was quite different. Development was in the driver's seat, and no voices in the dwindling Research community were prepared to articulate an independent technical vision. Moreover, Van Horn placed little importance on finding a different type of technical personnel to support the change he wanted. Although he set Fink up as liaison to the scientific community, he left in place all of the policies of the postwar era that insulated the Laboratories from the outside and worked against effective fundamental research.

To some extent, the environment that had spawned innovations like the combination process and direct-chill ingot casting had begun to disappear well before Frary retired. Conditions at Alcoa's plants in the 1950s and 1960s, which continued to prevail – labor conflict, the shortage of technical personnel, and the heavy emphasis on increasing productivity – made it unthinkable that bench-scale work could be transferred directly into the plants.[68] With the physical space at New Kensington increasingly crowded with large machinery to support plant-scale activity, and with a much smaller proportion of ARL researchers committed to bench-scale, academic-style research, it was hard to convince young, research-oriented graduates to start their careers at

Alcoa. In any case, university researchers were hearing virtually nothing about Alcoa's technical achievements.[69]

Alcoa's concern for secrecy, which had intensified in response to the new competition, mounted steadily in the postwar period. That further inhibited both the capacity and inclination for path-breaking work among its research staff. In the 1950s, even Frary began to caution technical personnel against discussing work in progress in papers or presentations. Such occasions, he suggested, should be used primarily to "point out Alcoa's pioneering development." Within a decade, that view of conference participation had been enshrined in formal policy.[70]

The internally focused, closed-door research policy Alcoa adopted was not shared by the newer entrants to the industry, Reynolds and Kaiser. Both started significant research efforts, but they tended to specialize in certain kinds of research activity, rather than cover the board the way Alcoa did, and they shared their technical results through the Aluminum Association. Alcoa's Technical Policy Committee, not wishing to give out the results of Alcoa's far larger R&D investment, and assuming their company to be well ahead of the others, laid down firm guidelines limiting participation in projects sponsored by the Aluminum Association. The company's policy could not have been clearer: "Alcoa's hard won information should be carefully guarded." This stance made it difficult for the association's Research and Development Committee to function and brought down a fair amount of criticism on Alcoa's representatives. Bossert, as vice-president for R&D, suggested to corporate management that Alcoa's "ultimate interest" could be served by a "somewhat less rigid" attitude toward collaboration with the Aluminum Association. But the desire to maintain secrecy was overriding.[71] In 1960, the R&D Committee developed a restrictive program of closing "leakage loopholes" and warned ominously about the dangers lurking at professional-society conferences.

Instances are known where recording devices have been used at panel discussions at technical society meetings, thus recording statements that have been thought to be verbal. In fact, anyone entering into discussions at technical society meetings, trade shows and the like, must weigh carefully whether his discussions accrue to Alcoa's benefit, or whether they may give away assets he has no right to divulge.[72]

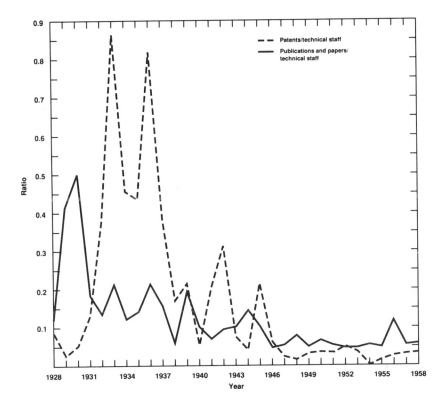

Figure 7.8. Trends in ARL patents and publications, 1928–58. Sources: Alcoa Laboratories Information Department; Alcoa Patent Department.

Meanwhile, larger forces at work in the company and the aluminum industry conspired to foreclose Van Horn's attempt to rebalance ARL's program and strengthen the fundamental research elements in it. Reports in the late 1950s that Alcoa maintained "the largest research organization with the biggest budget of any basic materials producer" and that it continued to do the lion's share of R&D in aluminum, even as its share in sales was dwindling, were greeted with more alarm than pride in senior management circles. "Fundamental research is important," said Frank Magee, "but we must also keep our eye on the end-use field." This dictum signed the death warrant for most fundamental research projects at a time when a small but coherent program, well connected to outside sources of materials research, could have made a large difference.[73]

The plans for a consolidated R&D center were closely tied to all these issues of technical politics. In 1957, Alcoa acquired 2,300 acres in Upper Burrell township, near New Kensington, and began serious consideration of the shape the new facility would take. By 1960 it was decided that the center would bring together on one site all the scattered, separate R&D organizations and would be named the Alcoa Technical Center. The architects and the corporate planning committee presented an initial proposal for 14 major buildings, including 6 for ARL alone. Scientists and engineers were to be brought together in a "campuslike" setting that would promote cooperation and interchange but at the same time provide the space necessary to accommodate all the facilities required for them to work effectively. Next to human intellect and ingenuity, the planners stated, the most valuable element in R&D was time:

> The sense of urgency is felt throughout the activities of the Center and every facility and convenience is justified if it will accelerate the progress from the idea to the end production. Delays and loss of momentum due to antiquated methods of providing tools, equipment and materials to the scientists and engineers, or inflexibility in their housing, are inexcusable in a technical center, particularly one concerned with the fast-moving technology, and the ever-broadening applications of the aluminum industry.[74]

Consolidation was viewed as key to cutting the "time element." The choice of the name Alcoa Technical Center over alternatives that included the words "research" and "development" signified Alcoa's intention to "do away with" this "outmoded dichotomy." The layout of the buildings must be such, the architects declared, as to promote integration into "a *single* closely-woven pattern of increasing diversification."[75]

During most of 1961, the planners struggled hard against the company's "critical cash position," and the following year Alcoa requested the architects to redesign the center to bring the 10-year projected cost down from $74 million to $51 million. It was then that key decisions were made about which organization would be the first to move to the new location, and how large and well equipped the first building would be. Conditions at ARL in New Kensington were so cramped at that time that there were desks in the halls, and some divisions had to move out entirely, either to rented space in the vicinity or into vacant areas of the New Kensington works. Yet conditions for the Alcoa Process Development Laboratory (APDL), also located in the works, were equally as bad or worse, described by Van Horn as a "hellhole." So it was agreed, much to the dismay of many in Research, that the first building at the technical center would be for APDL.[76]

Van Horn supported that decision in large part because APDL received so many visits from Alcoa's customers. Many of the areas in which it specialized – joining, finishes, and especially packaging – were viewed as critical to the recovery and future growth of the company's sales. His support for Sales Development was also a fortuitous political move, however, for it allied him with the rising group in management led by John D. Harper and Frederick ("Fritz") Close.

NEW MARKET STRATEGY

Harper and Close were the team selected to propel Alcoa out of the slump it had been in since 1958. Harper experienced a "meteoric rise" during the crisis years, from production manager to president of Alcoa. Considerably younger than either Wilson or Magee at the time of their appointments, he was viewed as a "freewheeling spirit" and a "breath of fresh air" at corporate headquarters:

John Harper.

According to Alcoa people, John Harper is the first Alcoa executive since the war to grasp the totality of the company: He is as much concerned with marketing as with production, as much concerned with sales as with research, and, perhaps, most important, as much concerned with stiffening Alcoa's competitive sinew as he is with maintaining its historic position as the undisputed leader of the U.S. aluminum industry.[77]

Harper's mission in 1963 was to turn the company around. Magee had been unable to do that, and Alcoa's recovery from the 1957–8 recession had been slower than that of any of its competitors; its share of the market fell in the decade after 1956 from 45 to 35 percent in primary ingot and from 38 to 33 percent in fabricated products. Harper's strategy for bringing Alcoa out of this trough had several major components, each of which had significant implications for Research: He planned to renew the traditional emphasis on aerospace alloys, to capture new, high-volume markets through low-cost mass production of rigid container sheet, and to develop a new smelting process that would achieve a major breakthrough in lowering primary production costs. In short, Harper intended to use R&D not mainly as a source of cost-cutting innovations, as Magee had done, but rather as the source of strategic opportunity.[78]

"Fritz" Close, executive vice-president for sales and marketing and the leading advocate of aggressive product development, shared this view of R&D as a generator of opportunity. He had advanced in management largely by virtue of his pioneering campaign in the 1940s to promote architectural applications of aluminum, and he was not afraid to voice his view that many of Alcoa's troubles in the crisis years were due to the fact that the company lagged behind its competitors in moving into new market areas. In 1962, Close fought fiercely against cutbacks in spending for the proposed APDL building, arguing that Alcoa would lose out in rigid containers and fall behind in joining if APDL was held back in its work. Not a technical person by training, Close was an R&D booster, and under Harper he became the executive to whom the vice-president for R&D reported.[79]

Harper and Close looked to Alcoa's technical community to make the new program a reality, and some of the innovations they sought required radical, not incremental, changes. Their strategy dictated that Marketing as well as Production would set the R&D agenda, and it placed a premium on effective cooperation between ARL and the development organizations, not on their competition. Harper looked to Van Horn to see that the challenges were met and the cooperation achieved. Thus, as the tide of the crisis turned, so did the course of Van Horn's career. On Bossert's retirement in 1962, he was appointed vice-president for R&D.

Harper was open to changes in corporate organization that would improve the chances for R&D to take a more forward-looking role. In November 1963 he announced yet another major reorganization of the committee system. The Technical Policy Committee was disbanded and the R&D Committee reconstituted, its membership reduced to nine high-level executives representing Research, the development organizations, and the corporate Engineering, Production, and Marketing Divisions. The most significant change, however, was to reduce the committee to an advisory role, assigning ultimate responsibility for the R&D program to one individual: Van Horn. Harper announced that as vice-president and chairman of the R&D Committee, Van Horn was to "assume complete accountability for Alcoa's R&D effort and for all technical matters in these fields." From that moment until his retirement in 1970, Van Horn directed, from his office in Pittsburgh, the entire subcommittee system and, through it, ARL and all of the development organizations. He reported only to "Fritz" Close, executive vice-president for marketing and chairman of the board of directors from 1965 to 1970.[80]

Van Horn's ascendancy gave Research a visible presence in the ranks of top management that it had never before enjoyed, but it did not restore the independence Research had had under Frary. Van Horn's style was to serve top management by implementing its directives, not by offering an independent technical vision. His choice as director of ARL, Ernest Hartmann, had little interest in formulating policy outside his own specialty, which was engineering. Though active in professional societies, he had little experience of contact with the scientific community and no means of building such contact. Van Horn himself continued to direct most of the Laboratories' activities through Hartmann, speaking to him daily by telephone.[81]

Within three months of his appointment to chair the R&D Committee, Van Horn implemented Welty's idea of appointing a coequal director of development. His choice for the position was Robert N. Wagner, Alcoa's chief electrical engineer. Wagner's internal influence with development organizations was strong, and his appointment was critical to the successful consolidation of Research and Development.

A perfect embodiment of the top-down approach that Alcoa's leaders had disavowed in 1944, the new system meant that the entire R&D function would be essentially a technical extension of top management. There could be no possibility of creative tension. This was the ultimate version of technology harnessed to corporate ends; it remained to be seen whether or not it would produce innovation on demand.

Robert Wagner.

Execution of the program had clearly become a subcommittee job. Harper charged each subcommittee chairman with "complete accountability for establishing priorities, the assignment of projects to a laboratory or plant, and the coordination, promotion and general direction of programs," as well as with responsibility for their implementation. R&D managers might sit on, and even chair, subcommittees, but the real initiative in setting the agenda was in the hands of Marketing and Production:

Priorities on new product development projects will be set by Sales Department representatives on subcommittees or in the R&D committee, and priorities on process development projects will be set by Operating Department representatives. Necessary adjustment of priority between committees will be set by Dr. Van Horn with the advice and help of the R&D committee.[82]

The major driver of the research program, as Alcoa emerged at last out of the recession, with Harper firmly at the helm, was the development of the proposed reduction facility at Warrick, Indiana – where construction had been suspended since 1960 – into an integrated smelting and fabricating plant dedicated to high-volume production of rigid container sheet. In a bold move to preempt the market for thin-sheet packaging, Harper and Close elected to put in place the most advanced process technologies possible, including continuous horizontal casting and high-speed rolling.[83]

These technologies could not simply be borrowed from steel, nor were they in use by other U.S. aluminum companies. They had to be developed – and quickly – once the decision to go forward with the new sheet mill was made. As described in Chapter 8, that accelerated program involved the combined efforts of all technical departments. It called for casting specialists at the Laboratories and in the plants to develop a continuous, horizontal, direct-chill casting process superior in speed and in quality of casting to anything that had previously been developed in the industry. It also required researchers in alloy development to come up with improved materials, while specialists in lubricants and rolling developed the high-speed rolling technologies necessary to produce at competitive prices the rigid container sheet and end stock that were to be sold to can companies for aluminum ends and all-aluminum cans.

NEW RESEARCH DIRECTIONS

With the Warrick program moving forward, Harper and Close sought to stimulate the research organization to produce further technically-based opportunities in fairly short order. In this context, the R&D Committee initiated a program to sponsor work outside of the subcommittee system under a regular budget category, "Directed Fundamental Research" (DFR). Approved projects were to be given a priority "as high as any assigned by the subcommittees," and the subcommittees were specifically told that they could not push this work aside in favor of high-priority applied research. By 1965 the proportion of research expenditures devoted to fundamentals had slumped to 9 percent. The DFR program constituted an acknowledgment of the need to work around the subcommittee system to promote technologies that might be considered too risky or threatening to existing processes or both.[84]

The Marketing, Production, and Development managers who dominated the R&D Committee at that time accepted the dictum that "fundamental research is important" and were willing to support it, within limits. But they were impatient for results, and they were skeptical of ARL's ability to deliver. The new program, suggested committee member E. M. Strauss, could go in one of two directions: It could foster research that would provide a basis for "new technology, new systems or new products not presently conceived," or it could support work on "definable problem areas" that would remove known obstacles to further exploitation of existing technologies, such as further study of the mechanism of corrosion and stress-corrosion cracking in high-strength alloys. Projects proposed by researchers probably would be of the latter sort, because technicians naturally wanted to solve the problems confronting them. But to be truly valuable, Strauss argued, this program should support the more radical type of basic research. Otherwise the committee risked confining itself "to simply establishing more knowledge about the things we know today."[85]

As Strauss predicted, the work proposed and accepted under the DFR program was invariably focused on well-defined problem areas. Producing no exciting breakthroughs, the DFR program was to struggle on into the 1970s, only to be swept away by a new wave of cost reductions. No one in the R&D Committee advanced Frary's argument that radical departures were generated by sustained efforts to understand existing technologies, and corporate managers tended to blame the disappointing results of the projects sponsored under DFR on the researchers. Only in instances where it was truly protected from the subcom-

Ernest Hartmann.

mittees did fundamental research produce significant results, as, for example, in alloy development, which was supported by government contracts, and in smelting, which was blanketed by secrecy and lavishly funded as a high-priority project.[86]

Though the members of the R&D Committee shared the rather unrealistic expectation, which was all too common in American management circles at the time, that long-term results could be achieved in short-term ways, they were right about the limitations of ARL in the mid-1960s. The customers with whom researchers were in contact were mainly price-minded, not performance-minded. At the same time, having closed most of the doors to the scientific community at large, Alcoa had ensured that the people who remained inside ARL were not people committed to cutting-edge research in new materials. Such people usually left the corporation or found less frustrating positions outside Research. Circumscribed in their contacts with the outside scientific community and even, to some extent, in their access to the work of others at ARL, researchers became dependent on published literature and, increasingly, on information channeled through other corporate divisions to find out what was going on in the outside world.[87]

LEADER BECOMES FOLLOWER

In 1960 the R&D Committee decreed that all subcommittee programs should pass through Commercial Research before they moved on for approval. Within the committee, infrequent discussions of long-range planning revolved around measures such as this, intended to provide the means of tapping into forecasts made routinely in marketing groups, and "the importance of guidance from Sales was emphasized again and again." Van Horn, too, largely conceded responsibility for planning to Sales. He simply passed along to Hartmann the year's long-range marketing plans, prepared by Industry Sales, having underlined all of the references to research and ARL, so that the Laboratories could plan an agenda accordingly.[88]

Van Horn had long accepted guidance from outside the Laboratories, and his removal to Pittsburgh turned the guidance into outright direction. Much of his personal energy and technical interest in that period, from 1963 to 1970, were poured into editing a three-volume series of technical books on aluminum, written by ARL personnel and eventually published by the American Society of Metals in 1967. Although most of that work was done on weekends, it was a consuming project, and a large proportion of Van Horn's correspondence with the Laboratories concerned editorial problems rather than issues related to current research.[89]

Van Horn's style as a benevolent autocrat meant that those he promoted to work with him were not people of independent views. Hence, his successors as director were even less inclined than he to take the lead in forging an independent technical program or vision. Neither Ernest Hartmann, Van Horn's gentle and self-effacing successor, nor James Newsome, next in line after Hartmann, was one to buck the established trend.

The logic of the situation in which Alcoa found itself in the late 1960s was that Research could play a strong supporting role to Development, if Development could be the source of opportunity and initiative. That formula could work exceedingly well for certain kinds of innovative activity and in some cases could even result in radical market outcomes, such as high-volume production of rigid container sheet. It was less successful in other areas, especially those in which Alcoa's research base had become too depleted to provide guidance and support. The problem for those investing money in R&D was to know the difference.

By the late 1960s the Alcoa technical community was stuck between the proverbial rock and the hard place. Its position was similar to that in many "mature" companies of the era. On one hand, pressure was mounting from marketing strategists for innovations that would catapult Alcoa into new high-volume markets. The stock market increasingly rewarded the company that proved capable of blockbuster technical achievements. But the R&D organizations at Alcoa were enmeshed in a system that made them dependent for direction on the very people who called on them for new ideas.

Under the guidance of the subcommittees, the researchers were capable of implementing and greatly improving existing technologies, and they were capable of leaping ahead into uncharted territory in process technologies, such as continuous horizontal casting or high-speed rolling, as long as the research base was already there to support it. They were also capable of taking up a competitive idea and drawing on their incomparable base of know-how to improve on it. There were significant innovations in ingot casting and improvements in ACSR during the 1950s and 1960s, and important equipment developments took place, such as continuous-casting machinery and Stockbridge dampers for cable. Similarly, ARL took up a German innovation, sintered aluminum powder, and rapidly improved on it to achieve great success in powder metallurgy production of high-performance aircraft alloys.[90]

But only in rare instances could the kinds of innovations the technical community was able to produce catch the imagination of managers whose careers had advanced under the rising star of Marketing. In professional management circles, marketing was viewed as the distinctively American contribution to management and one of the surest signs of sophisticated management capability. In that context, Alcoa's technical community seemed comparatively stodgy and unproductive. The problem was compounded by the growing disjuncture between expectations for R&D and the reality of what it could actually produce. All suggestions that any part of the technical community might be called on to offer a legitimate vision for the company's future were simply rejected. "Today, the market dictates the product," wrote one executive, "and the R&D groups are one critical step removed from feeling the necessary pulse."[91]

The market did dictate the product in more ways than one, but it was rarely Alcoa that took the dictation first. In the 1960s, Reynolds, in particular, showed itself capable of leading the way, with a number of important product innovations. In the area of primary process technologies – more threatening to Alcoa because of its lingering self-image as, first of all, a primary producer – it was not the domestic competitors who were the technical challengers, but international companies such as Alcan and Pechiney. No longer much of a pioneer, as Close often observed, Alcoa, with its rare combination of depth and breadth, nevertheless proved to be quite good at turning a few of the key innovations first produced by others into winners. As Chapter 8 shows, several of Alcoa's most important R&D programs in the 1960s and 1970s demonstrated this capability for creative "followership."

In August 1968, John Harper announced a major corporate reorganization, a change that was also in step with leading managerial practice around the country. The Operations and Sales

Divisions were restructured to create two profit centers. One, for mill products, incorporated existing Fabricating and Sales organizations; the other, for primary products, took in Raw Materials, Refining, and Smelting and added a newly developed marketing group. Profit centers with strong data-collection and data-analysis capabilities made it possible for costs to be watched more closely and matched more carefully with revenues at the level of the business than previously. Intended to encourage more focused management, the reorganization had the unintended consequence of making it virtually impossible for Alcoa's R&D community to change, either in image or substance, the pattern of technical followership into which it had fallen. In fact, the Alcoa R&D organization, when forced to justify its program in terms of the new profit centers, experienced greater pressure for productivity and cost justification, with less differentiation from other kinds of corporate operations, than ever before.[92]

8

Aiming for steel: top-down innovation

John Harper's mission to bring Alcoa out of its long slump began to show results toward the end of the 1960s. To sustain the recovery into what was widely expected to be a period of cutthroat competition, each new profit center was endowed with at least one major R&D program. Harper's strategy of capturing high-volume markets by replacing steel involved focusing research and development on these few key programs.[1]

Publicly, Harper stated that in addition to emphasizing aerospace alloys, where the company had long been the recognized leader, Alcoa would enter a new battlefield: rigid container sheet (RCS), where steel had held sway because of its low production costs. This involved important process innovations in both casting and rolling. The other massive R&D project Harper did not announce was a breakthrough in primary aluminum smelting being developed, under tight security, at a new Smelting Process Development Laboratory. This was the aluminum chloride process, later known as the Alcoa Smelting Process (ASP). In 1968, both of these major R&D projects were making the transition from technically feasible prototype to commercial use.

Though the new R&D initiatives were top-down projects, in the sense that they had been dictated and sponsored by the highest levels of management, individually they were managed differently. In the case of RCS and the casting and rolling innovations that supported it, the subcommittee system worked as it was intended, pulling together and coordinating a complex, fragmented, and internally competitive technical community and producing the web of interlocking improvements that were necessary to give Alcoa solid leadership in RCS. ASP, by contrast, all but circumvented the system, the project being known only to a small group of managers and technical people directly involved with it. Together, the two approaches highlighted the strengths and the weaknesses of Alcoa's postwar method of organizing R&D.

AIMING FOR STEEL

Competition with steel had long been regarded throughout the industry as the way out of aluminum's chronic market instability, but new aluminum process technologies were needed to make it possible. Primary production using the Bayer and Hall-Héroult processes was extremely costly in energy use, and fabrication nowhere near equalled the efficiencies of high-volume steel production. Even the largest aluminum plants in the early 1960s were still laid out in the lower-volume, job-shop mode, fine for custom-produced airplane alloy, or one-of-a-kind orders for large buildings, but not appropriate for high-volume sheet. To enter markets like the RCS market, which was steel's most vulnerable market economically, Alcoa would have to pursue a program of major innovations to achieve economies at several points in the process.[2]

The new Warrick plant, the first to be dedicated to one high-volume aluminum product, offered Alcoa the chance to leapfrog its competitors in processes where it had fallen behind. In some areas that would be done by following the example steel had already set, even adapting steel's production equipment and methods, for steel had achieved rolling speeds, and consequently productivity levels in fabrication, far ahead of those in the aluminum industry. The first of the programs intended to give Alcoa a new economic profile, ASP, had its beginnings well before the Warrick plant was conceived, in exploratory smelting research begun in the 1950s at ARL and Potline B.

FROM BENCH TO PROTOTYPE

After a postwar decade of intensive improvements in the Hall-Héroult process in pursuit of ever greater economies of scale, the conventional smelting process seemed to be approaching its practical limit, if not its theoretical limit. Looking back from a 20-year vantage point, Allen Russell, who had been the top research officer in charge of the new smelting process for many years, summed up the main limitations of the Hall-Héroult cell this way:

... the commercial technology for smelting aluminum from Bayer-purified alumina was far from perfect. It was relatively energy inefficient, required a large number of expensive individual cells, demanded an extensive environmental control system and required pure alumina feedstock, pure carbon anodes and uninterrupted power.[3]

Russell described some of the specific deficiencies: current efficiency in the middle 80 percent range; a cell configuration that required almost annual relining and therefore necessitated an open design; power usage of 7.5 kilowatt-hours per pound of aluminum produced; labor intensity at every stage.

The view of the Hall-Héroult process as essentially a "spent" technology was colored by the awareness that exciting exploratory activity was going on in the international scientific community around a number of alternatives to Hall-Héroult. One of the most active programs was at Alcan, which had worked on direct reduction in great secrecy all through the 1950s and entered a pilot-plant phase in 1960.[4] Hall-Héroult process researchers at Alcoa, who knew that some of their most important knowledge had never been applied to the existing process, still wanted to keep working on it. Current Hall-Héroult pots had been designed for ease of operation rather than for optimum economy. But the smelting division was reluctant to use precious capital for more Hall-Héroult smelters when so many radical alternatives were being pursued.

A program of exploratory research into alternative smelting methods had been going on at ARL for some time. The company had kept track of fundamental patents that were being issued in Europe and had purchased licensing rights to those that it considered potentially threatening in the smelting area. No conclusions had been reached as to the best alternative to pursue on technical grounds.

Work on the alternative that was ultimately chosen for development, the aluminum chloride electrolytic cell, had started in 1951, when experiments had been done on several candidate competitors to the Hall-Héroult process. Members of the Aluminum and Carbon Subcommittee were attracted to this alternative because it would eliminate the use of fluoride, the fumes of which posed such an environmental hazard that, every year, substantial R&D funding was dedicated to the fume problem. But a new electrothermal process, the oxycarbide process, took precedence until 1955, when tests showed it to be uncompetitive.[5] In 1956, work resumed on aluminum chloride electrolysis, with good results. The aluminum chloride process offered a number of advantages, in addition to freedom from fluoride fumes, most of them derived from the fact that it had an inert, nonconsumable anode. Its closed-cell design operated at lower temperatures with higher current efficiency (the percentage of the electricity passing through the cell that is actually used to produce aluminum) and lower consumption of power than the existing open cell.

A clear disadvantage of the aluminum chloride cell, however, was that it required an additional step between refining and smelting – a chemical reactor that would convert alumina to aluminum chloride, which could then be fed to the cell. ARL developed the concepts for this reactor in 1957. The extra step was recognized as a drawback, but it was partially mitigated by the potential for offsetting revenues from licensing and from the sale of aluminum chloride. These advantages did not influence the original selection of the aluminum chloride cell, but when economic analysis of the process sharpened in later years, they would become important factors.[6]

From 1957 to 1960 ARL made good progress, solving a number of critical problems with the closed-cell system. In 1960 it operated a 4,000-ampere cell for 20 days, producing 920 pounds of aluminum. But the aluminum chloride cell was still only part of a wide-ranging program that explored a variety of alternative processes and also sought improvements to the Hall-Héroult process, through fundamental study of bath composition and through experimentation to find an inert, nonconsumable anode material. This same territory had been visited many times in the course of Alcoa's R&D history, so that another look was not necessarily noteworthy. In fact, toward the end of the year, ARL lost interest in the aluminum chloride cell, judging its future prospects to be "barely competitive with the Hall process." By September, in the press of other work, the Laboratories put aside the aluminum chloride process. Had that not been the project that had been pushed the furthest toward embodiment when the need for tangible results arose, it most likely would have remained on the shelf.[7]

However, at the September 1960 meeting of the Smelting Subcommittee (formerly the Aluminum and Carbon Subcommittee), John Harper strongly opposed ARL's decision to drop work on the aluminum chloride process on the grounds that Alcoa might want a procedure that did not rely on fluorides. The subcommittee therefore instructed ARL to move forward with the aluminum chloride cell, aiming for a pilot plant at Potline B by 1962, and funding the work by "rearranging and curtailing" other projects as necessary, even if other work had to be assigned a lower priority as a consequence. That was two years earlier than researchers believed feasible, but management's message was clear: It wanted results, and it wanted them quickly.[8]

In an earlier era, such arbitrary dictation of technical choices would have been highly unlikely, but by 1960 the shift toward corporate management's involvement in planning research, begun after Frary's retirement, had gone beyond the point at which ARL could control its own program. In any technological arena regarded as critical to Alcoa's strategic position, Frank Magee and the other company leaders considered it management's prerogative to set priorities for R&D. In various ways they put pressure on the subcommittees to control expenditures and to emphasize "projects of major importance that promise to produce dividends in a reasonably short time." Harper saw this as just such a case.[9]

Innovation in smelting was considered such a high priority that even amid the widespread budget-cutting that took place in the downturn of 1957–61, smelting projects were spared. In 1959 the top-level R&D Committee began an intensive study of systems to ensure secrecy at ARL and Potline B. In that frame of mind, management was unwilling to let go of a process that had attractive characteristics just because of ARL's technical reservations. The Laboratories management was not being asked for its independent judgment; rather, it was expected to deliver on commitments made at the top.[10]

Able to offer no conclusive arguments against the choice on technical grounds, ARL spent the next year, and $255,000, designing a pilot plant around which to make some economic estimates. At the same time, Harper sent a young planning-staff analyst, Krome George, to work out the numbers on the aluminum chloride process. George's calculations indicated that the new alternative could achieve no more than a standoff against current Hall-Héroult technology in operating costs (set at 15.4 cents per pound of aluminum produced by the aluminum chloride process, with reactor), but they indicated a $10 million advantage for aluminum chloride in capital costs, measured at the level of a new 60,000-ton-per-year smelter. Krome George's analysis appeared to validate Harper's decision to override ARL's technology-based judgment.[11]

Quite capable of reading the handwriting on the wall, ARL's smelting researchers came up with an estimate after a year of design that was much more encouraging than it had been previously. In a larger aluminum chloride smelting plant, they reasoned, operating costs could be reduced to 9.84 cents per pound. For the first time since 1924, the Laboratories set out to pursue, to pilot-plant scale, a single competitor to the Hall-Héroult process.[12]

ASP: TOP-DOWN CHOICE

The first truly international symposium on the extractive metallurgy of aluminum held in the United States took place in the spring of 1962 in New York City at the annual meeting of the American Institute of Mining and Metallurgical Engineers (AIME). For Alcoa researchers, who were then only rarely permitted to consort with other industrial scientists, the occasion provided a heady dose of intellectual stimulation laced with alarm. In the previous year, several major international competitors had staked claims to a range of alternative smelting processes by announcing major pilot activities: Olin-Matheson Chemical Corporation, with a new acid process for producing aluminum from clay and shale; Pechiney, with an electrothermal process similar to the oxycarbide process that Alcoa had recently developed but abandoned; Alcan, with monochloride purification of directly reduced aluminous ores; British Aluminium and Kaiser, with refractory hard-metal cathodes in Hall-Héroult cells; Reynolds, with direct reduction, followed by centrifugal purification. Not since the days of the combination-process patent had so much attention been paid to the possibility of finding new ways to alter the economics of producing primary metal.[13]

Alcoa's management greeted the reports on the New York conference with evident displeasure. At the May 1962 meeting of the Smelting Subcommittee, G. T. Holmes, its chairman, noted the following:

Progress reported on aluminum smelting at New York, and very likely the latest developments were not disclosed, indicates that [Alcoa] is not ahead of the competition. Management is critical of this fact since total spending in Potline B, both operational and fixed capital, has now reached a substantial sum.[14]

The committee had to accept the conclusion that Alcoa was lagging. Moreover, if the reported findings of competitors were valid, the research team in process metallurgy appeared to have been making some questionable technical choices. Sharp inquiries from top management had already drawn defensive responses from both ARL and the Smelting Subcommittee charged with oversight of Potline B.

The assistant director of ARL and chief of process metallurgy, P. T. Stroup, having read the Pechiney patents, conceded that ARL's recent dismissal of the electrothermal process may have been premature, but he cited the excuse of inadequate research facilities. Alcoa's failure to push its own oxycarbide process to the same conclusion, he explained, was due to the ARL's inability, because of lack of a large enough transformer, to process at sufficiently high temperatures. His explanatory memo to John Harper had gone the rounds at Pittsburgh headquarters and returned adorned by a severe note from Frank Magee: "If this were *considered desirable* I would hope such a limitation would not have stood in the way of such an important technical development."[15]

Philip Stroup.

Smelting Subcommittee members placed some of the blame for Alcoa's position on the company's research policies, recording in their minutes that Alcoa's "policy of noncollaboration with competitors makes development more difficult and magnifies the need; and Potline B has provided satisfactory designs for presently proposed potline installations." In other words, both the research team and Potline B had been proceeding within the confines of postmonopoly policy and in the spirit of the R&D philosophy mandated by Harper and Magee for the preceding few years. Nevertheless, the committee chairman, G. T. Holmes, noted that the inescapable message of Alcoa's position was that more attention would have to be given to long-range planning.[16]

The disquieting disclosures by competitors riveted top management's attention on the prospect of cutting off further exploratory research and forcing immediate selection of one radical alternative to Hall-Héroult. Beginning in 1962, the highly secretive project that would later become known as ASP would not cease to have both the benefits and the disadvantages of this high-level visibility. Total commitment was demanded, and ARL offered little resistance to the radical reorientation of the smelting research program pushed by Alcoa's top management. In 1962, pressure mounted to scrap all research on the Hall-Héroult cell planned for the next year, including the search for a nonconsumable anode for the Hall-Héroult cell, in order to provide the maximum funds and manpower for continuing work on aluminum chloride. By 1964, a year in which spending for all smelting research rose to 13 percent of the total ARL budget, only one man in the Process Metallurgy Division was left working on Hall-Héroult problems, largely to provide consulting to the plants. The Physical Chemistry Division did not reduce its counterpart work on the Hall-Héroult process quite as drastically, but the shift was still dramatic.[17]

The absence of dissent or even comment from the senior Laboratories management was testimony to the change Alcoa's research organization had undergone under Kent Van Horn's leadership. The complete diversion of funds from current process improvement was a marked departure from earlier R&D program planning. Francis Frary had pursued a more balanced policy, unwilling to abandon improvement for current processes even when pushing for promising alternatives. The wisdom of the sudden tilt toward aluminum chloride did not go completely unchallenged, however, especially as the concurrent search for improved electrode materials for the Hall-Héroult process had already turned up a likely prospect, titanium diboride, that was eventually to produce dramatically more efficient Hall-Héroult-type cells. In October 1961, at a meeting of the Smelting Subcommittee in which Harper began to apply heavy pressure for moving aluminum chloride rapidly out of the Laboratories to Potline B, Noel Jarrett of the Process Metallurgy Division stated his objections quite plainly:

Noel Jarrett.

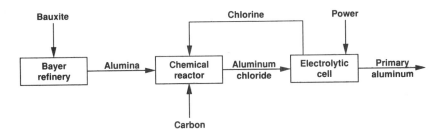

Figure 8.1. Alcoa Smelting Process. Source: Alcoa Laboratories.

It seems unreasonable that the chloride cell can take our present process apart into two separate stages, introduce a third chemical step, and come out cheaper. Perhaps we need to take an entirely new look at Hall cell design and come up with a cell with the advantages of the chloride cell.[18]

Jarrett wanted to undertake bench-scale work aimed at such a design, but though he continued to act as a gadfly on the subject of Hall-Héroult process improvement, his time, like that of everyone else in the division, was completely consumed by work on aluminum chloride. Harper's goals for the new process were clearly stated. They went beyond simple achievement of improved, even radically improved, power efficiency to include the following:

1. Better working conditions;
2. Fewer environmental problems – hence the appeal of the enclosed cell;
3. Lower unit energy consumption;
4. Freedom from fluoride dependence;
5. Lower capital and operating costs, most likely to be achieved by larger capacity units.[19]

The underlying philosophy was to maximize total return on investment, with special emphasis on reducing capital investment, and to save on construction costs and labor. The existing Hall-Héroult process provided the yardstick against which the performance of the new process would be measured, in capital investment and operating costs per pound. As long as no further work was done on Hall-Héroult, this remained a static target. Progress on the project was measured by repeated exercises in economic analysis, a process that participants found useful at the design stage as a way of identifying elements that required more attention. Few, if any, questions were raised as to how reliable the numbers proposed could possibly be when the workings of one process at full scale were extremely well understood, but the second was still wholly untested.

HALL-HÉROULT PROCESS REDUX

With ARL's research capacity completely consumed by the work on aluminum chloride, basic work on Hall-Héroult technology, such as it was, could go forward only outside the Laboratories, principally at Potline B. During the next seven years, from 1961 to 1968, Hall-Héroult research pushed ahead in fits and starts, constrained by the talent available, and frequently interrupted by demands for stepped-up support for the plants. G. T. Holmes, secretary and later chairman of the Smelting Subcommittee, shouldered the responsibility for keeping Hall-Héroult work alive. Holmes argued a variation on the old Frary theme: that work on the existing technology could not safely be abandoned until aluminum chloride smelting was a "demonstrated success." With what proved to be remarkably accurate foresight, he commented to Philip Stroup:

While we enthusiastically push the aluminum chloride cell and its companion reactor to commercial realization, there is at least one potential change in the Hall-Bayer process that might place it again in the most economical position. That would be the development of an inert, non-consumed anode lasting for say, one year. This would eliminate the reactor which is a necessary but expensive part of the aluminum [chloride reactor] process and yet allow us to apply our new concept of compartmentalized cell design to the Hall Cell. Our development work on the aluminum chloride cell in this case would not be wasted but give us a lead in learning the construction and operating characteristics of this cell design.

Pointing out that Jarrett was right in saying that "if we don't look for it we'll never find it," Holmes suggested that his subcommittee should arrange to equip a laboratory for work on high-pressure, high-temperature chemistry "to look for us."[20]

ARL was torn between responding to Holmes's subcommittee and keeping its strategic focus. Overburdened already, and with clear signals from ARL management regarding where his priorities lay, Stroup replied to Holmes that the search for the inert anode had been proceeding on a hit-or-miss basis for a long time and would have to continue to be a long-term program, not a "crash program."[21]

Holmes kept on promoting interest in new cell designs for the Hall-Héroult process, aiming at the same goals that Harper had outlined for a replacement for the Hall-Héroult process, noting that "basically what is needed is a major change that can produce at much lower [kilowatt-hours per pound] with less labor and investment." His proposal involved "the largest pre-baked block we can now bake" as anode, lasting up to 10 times longer than current models, and sealed to avoid oxidation. The subcommittee, in fact, voted in 1963 to increase its budget to support both aluminum chloride and the new Hall-Héroult cell, but, in reality, bench-scale work for radical Hall-Héroult improvements had to be done at ARL, and ARL had neither room nor time for it.[22]

Nevertheless, the subcommittee's continued quest for improvement of the Hall-Héroult cell kept ARL personnel thinking about the Hall-Héroult process even when they were not working on it. Although only one half-time researcher, Warren Haupin, spent time on conventional smelting in 1964, his work produced some promising developments in inert anode materials for the Hall-Héroult cell. As Allen Russell observed, "the only fundamental merit in the aluminum chloride process is the inert anode," and an "inert Hall anode would probably give Hall a solid lead commercially."[23]

Warren Haupin.

ENVIRONMENTAL CONCERNS

The Smelting Subcommittee had other demands on its development resources in the mid-1960s that pushed improvements in the smelting process in different directions. A noteworthy environmental lawsuit against the Harvey Aluminum Company diverted the subcommittee's attention to applications at the works between 1965 and 1967. The court ruled that, based on a comparison with a Reynolds plant, Harvey was not meeting the standard of best practice by making use of the currently known pollution-control techniques. Alcoa could be similarly vulnerable if, having developed appropriate technology at its experimental potline, it failed to implement that technology. The Smelting Subcommittee's Task Force on Potline B, which had focused on technical improvement, was reconstituted as the

Task Force on Potrooms, with a mandate to implement the technologies developed at Potline B, especially those for control of fluoride emission.[24]

The sudden shift to implementation in the plants placed heavy demands on available technical expertise. Efforts to improve plant practice often foundered during the mid-1960s because of the difficulties of overcoming plant apathy and resistance. Plant personnel did not feel themselves to be responsible for R&D, especially as they were expected to do it "as add-ons to the regular plant assignments." It was especially hard to get support from plant shops and maintenance personnel, who had neither a specific charge nor time off from day-to-day tasks to do the work.[25] "Chief" Wilson's prewar fear that Operations would lose all sense of responsibility for process improvement had, in fact, come to pass. At the research end, the lopsided response of diverting *all* money to applications was questioned, because it mortgaged the future of the Hall-Héroult process. Even unlimited money would not overcome the scarcity of skilled technical people available, both at Potline B and in the plants. The situation, in fact, worsened when, in 1969, Potline B was eliminated altogether in favor of work on the aluminum chloride cell.[26]

Meanwhile, a foreign competitor's new plant in the United States seemed to call into question the "total return on investment" philosophy behind the aluminum chloride process. Claims in 1966 that the Intalco plant in Washington state, partially owned by Pechiney, was producing aluminum at the most efficient rate ever (6.0–6.3 kilowatt-hours per pound) prompted Holmes and others to revisit the idea of the energy-efficient pot. Specifications for a new Alcoa experimental pot were drawn up, based on what was known of the Intalco pot. Tests of this new pot concept showed, however, that measured against the broader criteria of capital investment, including construction, and labor costs, and in the context of Alcoa's relatively good energy position, the Intalco pot could not compete against the big, high-current-efficiency pots Alcoa was already running.[27]

ASP TECHNOLOGY TRANSFER

The aluminum chloride development, meanwhile, was managed like the come-from-behind effort it was. Not only was

ARL under heavy pressure to pour on as much manpower as the project could absorb, but time pressure dictated that the development effort proceed as much in parallel with the research effort as possible. Experienced plant engineers, therefore, joined the project much earlier in the cycle than usual, in order to bring themselves up to speed. The idea was to reach each next stage of the always complicated phase-up process with as little loss of continuity as possible. That was expensive; it was also disruptive to good research. The presence of highly competent plant engineers at such an early stage, with their natural intolerance for the ambiguities of research, was a mixed blessing. The popular tools of project management, such as "critical-path analysis," were used in planning the project, though some questioned their applicability in a project in which so much of the technology was still unproven. The many data-gathering exercises took their toll on the research side of the project, at times threatening to interfere with the direction of the research.[28]

Under pressure to cut corners and compress timetables wherever possible, planners deliberately ignored past experience and took calculated risks, choosing, where necessary, to fix problems later rather than hold up all interrelated phases of the project in its earlier stages. Advancing a counterintuitive proposition that was never borne out, Holmes wrote to the chief engineer, Benjamin Sloane, that "we can get around this time cost by taking larger risks money-wise." The idea was to compress the scale-up process into a very short period: The aluminum chloride process was to reach full-scale commercial production and surpass the Hall-Héroult process in efficiency and cost-effectiveness in less than one-tenth of the 75 years it had taken to bring the Hall-Héroult process to its current state. Each successive increment took nine months to run in, and the plan was to try to do the scale-up in as few steps as possible.[29]

Although the original intent was to build two large units, one at ARL and one at Potline B, ARL's severe space limitations in the 1960s made that impossible. With no room at the Laboratories for the 45,000-ampere pot, the only one constructed was at Potline B, renamed the Smelting Process Development Laboratory (SPDL) in 1969. The distance that researchers had to travel from New Kensington to SPDL, in Alcoa, Tennessee, undercut effective research involvement in the project. For all practical purposes, contrary to intentions, that constituted the handoff point from research to development. The extra travel time for the researchers precluded the kind of interactive relationship that had been planned for that stage.

Another constraint on the project was the cloak of secrecy that made it increasingly difficult to tap sources of expertise outside the group of people actually assigned to the project. By the mid-1960s, only a small group of people received aluminum chloride reports before subcommittee meetings, and eventually such reports ceased to be circulated at all. Instead, at the meetings they were handed to the core members who needed to have them, and collected afterward.[30]

Secrecy was considered increasingly important as it became clear that what was being learned through work on the aluminum chloride process could have breakthrough implications for the Hall-Héroult process as well. For example, Warren Haupin constructed a see-through cell that allowed researchers to study problems such as current efficiency and cathode cracking from new perspectives. Another breakthrough came with the concept of a compartmentalized cell, and a third was the bipolar cell, invented while the smaller, scale-up monopolar cells were being constructed. Without telling the rest of the Smelting Subcommittee, the smaller Task Force on Potrooms decided to skip several intermediate stages in bipolar-cell development and to link a large bipolar cell to the reactor. Perhaps predictably, the first version of this large-scale cell aborted, but a redesigned successor achieved greater success.[31]

Every change that had to be made in the process in response to such new discoveries about design brought the researchers under intense pressure, owing partly to the expense of holding up construction at the pilot site. Their struggles to cope with a sludge problem in the reactor, for example, brought the prototype effort at SPDL almost to a halt. Naturally, researchers were very uneasy with the "crash" program and the inflexible conditions it imposed on them.[32]

THE CRITICAL REVIEW

In October 1968, six years into the project, a review meeting convened to consider previous experience with the aluminum chloride process. The meeting's objective was to decide the timing for proceeding to the prototype phase, which would involve building a plant-scale facility. The prototype was to function almost entirely under the aegis of SPDL, where, for financial and security reasons, Potline B was to be phased out. Management pressure to push ahead was relentless. Even though the discussion that took place covered a long list of unresolved problems and many acknowledged risks, it soon became clear that the choice to continue to the next stage was no choice at all.[33]

Senior ARL members of the project, Philip Stroup and Allen Russell, opposed moving to plant scale at that time. Pointing to the difficulty of modifying the plant once it moved into prototype, they asked for at least a year's delay to resolve problems at bench scale. But the advocates of speed argued that the problems had mostly been with earlier designs, that the current SPDL improved version had been moving briskly, and that a delay for further research at bench scale would hurt the momentum of the development phases.

Allen Russell.

Even strong advocates had to admit that economic comparisons between the aluminum chloride process and the Hall-Héroult process, as of 1968, were at best ambiguous. In terms of current operating efficiency, aluminum chloride electrolysis required fewer kilowatt-hours per pound (4.16 versus 6.7), but the conventional process was greatly superior in terms of the life of pot linings (1,200 versus 540 days) and was better in terms of alumina utilization (90 versus 70 percent). The capital costs of the aluminum chloride process were currently judged to give it "at worst" a standoff with Hall-Héroult, and operating costs were said to be no more than 1 cent per pound less, though others argued that 0.6 cent would be more accurate.[34]

Kent Van Horn sided with the advocates of fast scale-up. He pushed the management imperative, saying that "the Company's management continues to be impatient with the pace of this project and a delay will not be well received." The ensuing "vigorous debate," which revolved largely around "the economics of delay," ended in compromise. Stroup and Russell gained a six-month reprieve, while the prototype team received approval for an immediate request for authorization for engineering costs. The authorization for full-scale work was withheld pending "reasonably satisfactory demonstration of 1) raw materials utilization and 2) ten compartment cell performance."[35]

Thus, over the grave objections of the researchers on the project, the review meeting approved the prototype with only a minor delay. It was a precursor of many meetings to come. Through a decade of further effort and investment, the aluminum chloride process passed through various checkpoints and, renamed the Alcoa Smelting Process (ASP), was handed on to the prototype phase at the Anderson County works in Texas. Each time, the 1968 meeting was replayed in one form or another: A long list of problems or unresolved issues was raised, and a decision was made to go ahead, and fix them later. The arguments about whether or not to go forward at each point stayed within the R&D hierarchy, and there is no evidence that the top corporate managers pushing ASP had a clear picture of the cumulative technical risks that were being taken as the project proceeded.

IMPROVED HALL-HÉROULT PROCESS

Although a few real technical miracles were achieved under the ASP program, certain realities were never faced. Chief among these was the fact that the Hall-Héroult process had become a moving target. Ironically, ASP, with all its advantages – visibility to top management, ample resources, a sense of high priority and urgency – created an ideal set of conditions for work on the Hall-Héroult process to proceed behind the scenes, especially after the transfer of ASP to SPDL in 1968.

Traditionally, efforts to improve the Hall-Héroult process had focused on increasing current efficiency and on making the cells easier to operate, thereby reducing manpower. But, strongly motivated by the performance that ASP had achieved, ARL personnel set radical new objectives for Hall-Héroult. They could take all the time they liked, with no crash-program pressure, and through the work on the aluminum chloride process they had accumulated a great deal of knowledge about electrolytic cells that they could apply to the Hall-Héroult process. In 1969, for instance, based on experience with the prototype ASP cell, they proposed to work at achieving greater energy efficiency in Hall-Héroult cells by decreasing the distance between the anode and cathode. They also planned to improve bath circulation along the lines of the design for the aluminum chloride cell. The Smelting Subcommittee gave its support for these changes, recognizing that radically improving the old process could be far less risky than introducing a new one.[36]

By the time they were drawn into another round of heavy support for ASP in the 1970s, the Laboratories team dealing with the improved Hall-Héroult process had sufficient technological momentum that it was able to keep up a steady stream of developments at bench scale. By 1972 it had designed a new, energy-efficient Hall-Héroult-type cell and was in the process of introducing the promising new electrode material titanium diboride. The following year its laboratory-scale cell operated at 4.2 kilowatt-hours per pound, with 92 percent current efficiency, compared with the best previous Hall-Héroult performance of 6.4 kilowatt-hours per pound at 95 percent current efficiency. The economics implied by these figures were not far from the ultimate goals for ASP.[37]

What made life eternally difficult for the developers of ASP were the unanticipated systems problems it encountered when it went into pilot operation. Chief among these were the continuing troubles of the chemical reactor. Ironically, Alcan abandoned its touted monochloride purification process – which had contributed so much to the competitive atmosphere in which ASP was born – because it, too, encountered insurmountable problems with a complex chemical reactor. Both companies had outstripped the knowledge base in their own industry, and neither had gained access to knowledge outside their industry that might have helped. Eventually Alcoa did seek help from outside sources, but not until it had devoted large sums to making do without it.[38]

The story of ASP in its early, and probably determinative, phases, prior to 1972, involved more than the choice of a process without due respect to technical limitations; it was a telling example of trying to manage a research-based project using brute-force techniques. G. T. Holmes later voiced the frustrations he shared with the few who had been closely involved with ASP over the years:

During the thirteen years I have been associated with the Alcoa Smelting Process, I have been hoping for some instances of serendipity to relieve the heavy slogging through increasingly complicated technical problems to evermore expensive solutions. I am still looking, and I am sure so are you and your staffs.[39]

Nevertheless, the crash program continued into the early 1980s, allowing no room for serendipity. In fact, all of the benefits of serendipity in smelting research appeared in the Hall-Héroult process column. Writing to suggest major modifications to the 15-year-old Hall-Héroult pot design to match technology currently available in the marketplace, G. T. Holmes commented to Charles Parry:

> It's heresy to say this, but as one of the many creators of the Alcoa Smelting Process, perhaps I can take the liberty, "Proceeding to this further scale up of the Hall Process will also provide improved alternates to the current Hall pots if we need to build more capacity before the new process is ready."[40]

NEW PROCESSES FOR WARRICK

Alcoa researchers were alarmed to learn, toward the end of 1961, that Reynolds Aluminum had set its strategic sights on dislodging tinplate and galvanized-steel sheet from the container market. Still reeling from the shock of the Laboratories' first postwar staff reductions, they were deeply frustrated by the company's apparent business-as-usual attitude regarding the development of low-cost, mass-production processes.[41]

In January 1962, the news that yet another subcommittee task force had been formed to oversee rolling research inspired James Dowd, assistant chief of the Lubrication Division at ARL, to write a lengthy and outspoken confidential letter to Kent Van Horn. Dowd warned that Alcoa would inevitably respond with a piecemeal effort if this strategic opportunity were left to the subcommittee system. It was well within Alcoa's grasp to compete for the same vast markets as Reynolds, he argued, but that would require a reconceptualization of the whole fabrication process as a first step toward implementing the several individual technologies that ARL would have to develop and transfer to Operations. If Alcoa did not attempt to lead the industry with a coordinated effort, Dowd warned, it faced a future in which "we will be continually scrambling to keep our head above water." He called on Van Horn to formulate a new technical vision and to sell it through the Technical Committee to top management, pushing Alcoa into a pioneering strategy in fabrication.[42]

In the corporation at large, Dowd continued, "there does not appear to be any one person or group who is considering the whole problem, tying all the pieces together, and pointing out

James Dowd.

the areas in which additional R&D is required. . . . Consequently our program is somewhat haphazard with numerous gaps to it." Likewise, he characterized the ARL as being in a wholly reactive mode. It "confined our activities to specific aspects of the problem referred to us by the plants or Pittsburgh or else to specific aspects which can be conveniently assigned to individual divisions." Dowd's letter did not confine his criticisms to the subcommittee system:

Another area in which research has, I feel, been deficient is that we have not become sufficiently involved in the plant problems associated with sheet fabrication. We have isolated ourselves and hence frequently have only a superficial awareness of the problems. . . . Close personal contact with the plants and the plant personnel is required to properly assess this and similar problems, to properly solve them, and to properly sell the solutions to the plant people.

Dowd recommended what amounted to a project-management approach to achieving real mass production of aluminum. ARL should "select a person or task force to coordinate all of the research aspects of the over-all problem," with at least one person taking it on as his sole responsibility.

Many senior research people shared the opinion that the blame for R&D's failure to take a broad strategic perspective rested on the fragmented nature of the company's technical program. Neither the subcommittee system, which had the responsibility for shaping the research program, nor ARL as an institution exercised the initiative to pull things together. Both parties were "victims of our system." Dowd's ARL superiors supported his call for a bold new approach and urged Van Horn to ignore "time-honored boundaries" and address the problem from casting to selling.[43]

Nothing came of this plea for formulation of a broad technical vision for fabrication until Harper and Close assumed the leadership in 1963. The decision then, to go forward with the new Warrick plant for thin sheet, energized and focused a companywide program. Events accelerated in 1964 when the steel industry broke with its long-standing industry tradition of uniform pricing to announce special pricing for containers. In a memo headed "The Steel Industry," Close advanced some of the arguments Dowd had raised earlier. Aluminum needed to make greater efforts to find volume markets, but to compete with steel, aluminum processes would have to equal the man-minutes per unit that steel had achieved.[44]

Once Harper and Close accepted the challenge of making Warrick an integrated smelter and fabricating plant dedicated to mass production of rigid container sheet, they committed Alcoa to accepting significant technical risk. Warrick not only would be equipped with the highest-speed cold-rolling equipment then available, made possible by new water-based lubricants that ARL had been developing for some time, but also would be designed for continuous operation at every step of the process. The goal of a fully continuous plant would be especially difficult to achieve because the company was determined to act quickly, to secure as large a share as possible of the market for aluminum sheet used to make cans. ARL, Engineering, and Warrick operations were thus placed under tremendous pressure to advance on all fronts rapidly and simultaneously, and other parts of the company, such as the Davenport plant, were called on to assist the effort.[45]

HORIZONTAL DIRECT-CHILL CASTING

In the casting arena, the mandate for selecting the process to be used at Warrick was given to Marvin Gantz, head of Alcoa's Smelting Division. He challenged ARL to adapt horizontal casting, previously used only for small-scale ingots, for large-cross-section ingots of the kind cast vertically at Davenport. Horizontal direct-chill (HDC) casting of large ingots was one of the most ambitious technologies to be adopted at the Warrick plant. It was first considered for implementation at Warrick when it was discovered that the subsoil at the site would not allow for the exceedingly deep pit needed to do DC casting in the usual vertical position. The compelling reason to adopt HDC, however, was that it made possible continuous casting. Emerging from the mold in the horizontal direction, ingots could be sawed across and removed without starting and stopping the process. That not only allowed for more productive use of equipment but also eliminated much of the scrap that was produced in discontinuous methods.[46]

Continuous casting was already in limited use in the steel industry, but it was decided that Alcoa's priorities were different from those of steel manufacturers, and therefore new methods had to be developed in-house. For steel, speed and output were the prime considerations. But a major cost in the conventional forms of aluminum-ingot casting was in melt losses, that is to say, in scrap generated throughout the system that had to be remelted. In 1964 that factor accounted for half the total ingot cost at Davenport, which translated into 21 percent of the cost of a finished pound of can stock. A continuous process would solve that problem to a great degree.[47]

The goal set for casting by Gantz, for Research and Operations alike, was to achieve an automatic ingot plant. The concept of a fully automated continuous-casting operation posed a number of challenges: It required highly reliable equipment and solutions for problems pertaining to mold design, life, and changes. When Gantz extracted from ARL's Kenneth Brondyke a commitment to develop large-scale HDC for Warrick, it was not clear that such a thing was technically feasible in the time available. Brondyke, who admittedly was not a casting expert, somewhat incautiously accepted the goal on behalf of the researchers. The researchers in the Ingot Casting Division, headed by Robert Spear, were doubtful at first that it could be done. Previous work on continuous casting had been conducted on a small scale at Massena, but applying that to large-cross-section ingot was a different matter altogether.[48]

Like the ASP project, the development of HDC was a crash program. During 1963 the casting research team worked in two shifts to prove the technical feasibility of the process on a bench-scale unit installed at ARL. Time was short, because demand for can stock was increasing rapidly, and it was imperative to reach full-scale output at Warrick as quickly as possible. However, the HDC program had some advantages over the ASP program. It had no systems problems of the magnitude involved in the aluminum chloride reactor, and the process was closer to realization at bench scale. Exploratory research had been conducted some time previously, and researchers were able to confirm technical feasibility before the project moved to the next stages.[49]

Kenneth Brondyke.

CASTING ANTECEDENTS

The HDC program had several streams of in-house work on casting research to draw on, in addition to the DC work itself:

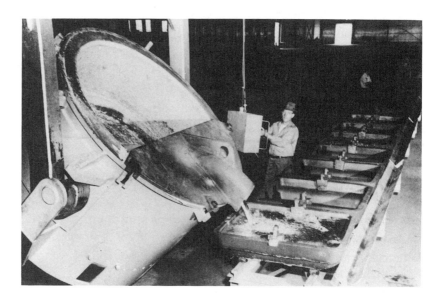

A caster at Alcoa's Warrick works pours the first 700-pound ingot in the method used prior to the development of horizontal direct-chill casting at Warrick.

Small-scale continuous work, small-scale HDC, fundamental work on solidification, and the program for casting large ingots all contributed useful information. In the early 1950s, a three-way "shoot-out" to achieve large-ingot casting pitted casting groups at Massena, Cleveland, and Alcoa, Tennessee, against each other. Eventually, the Cleveland approach prevailed, but all three efforts provided insights that contributed to the new project. However, that combination of various aspects of earlier techniques for continuous casting, horizontal casting, and large-ingot casting led to the reappearance of problems that had been considered solved earlier, such as tearing or lack of flatness in the ingot.[50]

As soon as the basic feasibility of HDC for large ingots was demonstrated, in November 1963, Engineering was given the go-ahead to lay out the Warrick plant's casting area. The research unit still had difficulty achieving the necessary flatness, but it assumed that the flatness and other remaining problems would shortly be resolved, and it supported the go-ahead decision. Working out the necessary methods would have been difficult had it not been decided in 1964 to invest more than a million dollars in capital costs, and $25,000 in monthly operat-

An experimental casting unit at the Arnold plant.

ing costs, in a plant-scale HDC unit capable of casting ingot over 10 feet in width at the old Arnold plant adjacent to the New Kensington works. That unit, the first working prototype HDC caster, was operated by a research team under the technical leadership of Joseph Nock and the administrative leadership of Kenneth Brondyke.[51]

The team quickly found that the scale of their experimental equipment posed difficult research problems. For instance, huge amounts of metal were required for each casting trial. Fortunately, the Arnold plant had two 50,000-pound furnaces that could be fired up to produce the necessary experimental heats, as well as a loading dock and transportation linkages that allowed for heavy trial ingots to be trucked away. The combination of technical problems in achieving uniform solidification and mechanical problems associated with materials handling meant that there had to be unusually close cooperation on this project between scientifically oriented research engineers and problem-solving engineers. The Arnold facility made it possible for different HDC approaches to be investigated on an experimental basis before installation in the plants.[52]

Once the prototype process had been worked out at Arnold, the new casting method was tested in continuous production in

Production version of a horizontal direct-chill casting unit.

a Davenport pilot unit, where plant engineering skills and experience were particularly strong, and where the metal produced could be used. The transfer from Davenport to Warrick was accomplished by a special HDC sheet-ingot task force that disbanded as soon as the transfer was complete. That phase of the project involved close interaction between the plant team working on the process and the research team still working with the prototype facility at Arnold. The program had advantages over other transfers attempted at the time, for R. E. Dieffenbach, chief metallurgist at Davenport, had formerly been at ARL's Cleveland laboratory, was well known to some of the key researchers, and was able to go to Warrick frequently to lend his expertise.[53]

By July 1965, some of the major tearing problems had been eliminated, or at least explained, and satisfactory ingot was being cast. Then it was a matter of working with the process to get it up to desired speed. In early 1966 the HDC research team could report a rapid scale-up and impressive accomplishments. In 1965, output of metal at Warrick had risen from 35 million pounds in March, with 61 percent recovery, to a December output of 37 million pounds, with 89 percent recovery. The average length of a single run had also increased from 30 hours to over 50 hours. Moreover, results from casting remelt ingot showed vastly superior quality over the best remelt ingot available previously. To sustain these improvements, efforts were made to rotate plant metallurgists through tours of duty at ARL to bring them up to date and to expose their research counterparts to more of the reality of plant life.[54]

As HDC applications began mushrooming throughout the company, with new, smaller HDC casting units being installed at many plant locations, ARL faced a new dilemma. Each application exposed new problems that raised enticing possibilities for further research. Researchers were torn between achieving more complete application of existing knowledge and wanting to direct their efforts toward gaining new knowledge, which obviously could yield important and rewarding results. For example, it was apparent that new fundamental work, especially mathematical modelling of different casting processes, would support fully automated casting. It would also be useful to investigate the variables associated with heat transfer and ingot solidification.[55]

Yet the claims of the plants that needed support could not be ignored. Faced with the prospect of operating increasingly sophisticated technologies, plants complained that they were not getting the help they needed from the center, and the tempo of their complaints increased as the decade wore on. The potential offered by improvements in casting was there for all to see, but Operations did not have enough well-trained experts to realize it on their own. That problem would increase as Operations became more productivity-conscious.

NEW ROLLING TECHNOLOGIES

At the same time that HDC casting was being developed and installed at Warrick, the combined efforts of alloy-development, lubricant, and rolling-research specialists were producing the high-speed rolling technologies that were essential to make the rigid container sheet to be sold to can companies for aluminum-can ends and bodies. However, lacking a special pilot site for fabrication technologies similar to Smelting's Potline B or Ingot Casting's Arnold facility, ARL had no prescribed pathway in the early 1960s by which to transfer its individual fabrication innovations when they were ready for implementation in the plants.

The first new fabrication technology ready for transfer was a water-based lubricant system, intended to replace conventional mineral oil lubricants in cold-rolling mills. ARL's Lubricants Division completed this technology at bench scale in 1961. Coupled with forms of computer control already under study in the Alcoa Equipment Development Division (AEDD), water-based lubricants were expected to enable aluminum-rolling equipment to reach levels of output comparable to those achieved in the high-speed rolling of steel.[56]

The difficulties that arose when the system was ready for plant trial vividly demonstrated the obstacles to executing significant process change through a subcommittee system dominated by metallurgists. ARL expected water-based lubricants to be the first of a series of process innovations in the plants, only some of which would come from Research. A new generation of high-speed rolling equipment would be introduced that in turn would allow for applications of further research work in computer-control theory applied to rolling technology. However, early attempts to get Metallurgy and Engineering to cooperate in implementing this new generation of rolling technologies ran into a stone wall.

The major thrust of the central Metallurgical Division under Nagel and his successor Bossert had been to stabilize fabricating processes and emphasize quality assurance, at least in part by discouraging new alloy introductions and major process changes. Engineering was in charge of rolling equipment, and its development arm, AEDD, handled new-equipment design and procurement. With this divided organizational responsibility, it was unclear who should spearhead implementation of major new improvements to fabrication technology – who should adapt the technology for different plant conditions, work out new practices, and train operators and maintenance people. Engineering took the view that when plants were not yet using to the fullest extent what they already knew how to do, further innovation was a waste of resources. Each plant had its own jealously guarded "black book" of rolling practice based on experience, and all were resistant to major changes.[57]

It took two years before Walter Dean, assistant director of ARL, was able to get a subcommittee formed for sheet, plate, and foil. Meanwhile, as director of ARL's Lubricants Division, James Dowd was named to coordinate the transfer of water-based lubricants. His first task, before spending several years at Alcoa, Tennessee, and then Davenport, was to sell the program to all of the subcommittees, task forces, and development groups whose cooperation was needed. That involved persuading them to include it in their planning, to try for major gains rather than modest ones, and also not to "fragment the problem as usual."[58]

The factor that finally held sway over Alcoa's early-1960s inertia was the growing demand for rigid container sheet that threatened to outstrip Alcoa's ability to supply it. Spurred on by "Fritz" Close, in February 1963 Alcoa announced publicly that it intended to spend heavily for high-speed rolling equipment at Warrick. The timely appointment of Robert Wagner, former chief electrical engineer, as the first director of development smoothed the way for creation of the necessary level of cooperation between the different development departments. Aided by the chief metallurgist, John Hood, Close launched a light-gauge-sheet expansion program.[59]

With rolling, as with casting, the plan for transferring new technologies was to start them at the existing rolling mills at Davenport and Alcoa, Tennessee, and then equip the new Warrick plant with the best, proven technology. Task forces made up of Operations and R&D people from both rolling mills took on the task of transferring the technology. By 1964 the team at Davenport achieved the first high-speed, multistand, precision cold rolling of light-gauge sheet, having introduced a new alloy, 5082, for highly strain-hardened, thin-sheet products. The project was sensitive, for in the labor climate of the 1960s automatic controls were viewed as a threat to operators, and as the engineers had feared at the outset, the plants frowned on taking on projects that could cause disruption of their output. Experience with the new rolling technologies, however, gradually changed plant attitudes.

Both Davenport and Alcoa realized large benefits almost immediately from the new lubricant program. Davenport reported aggregate savings of over $500 million, with increased rolling capacity of 36 million pounds in its first two years, for an increase of $830,000 in the plant's gross margin. Alcoa, Tennessee, which had the new lubricant system on its single 44-inch mill, also reported good results. Compared with the results for conventional mineral-oil lubricants, there were also reductions in downtime and almost complete elimination of delays for cooling the mill.[60]

Five-stand, four-high continuous rolling mill at Davenport works. The crane has just removed a coil of rolled metal and is transporting it to storage. Each change of coil on these continuous mills produces a large amount of scrap, as the mill settings have to be adjusted manually at the beginning of each new roll.

Despite Warrick management's declared preference for its own homegrown people and its tendency to view Alcoa Technical Center personnel as outsiders, by September 1965 Dowd reported that several production lines had been installed and were being debugged. They had produced good sheet at maximum speeds, though they were having trouble with the electrical controls. That was not surprising given the complexity of the new control systems and the lack of familiarity with such controls among maintenance personnel.[61]

Dowd's experience at Warrick reinforced his view that for the next few years, rolling research had to increase, and it convinced him that much of it would have to be done in the plants. Research objectives would be to improve flatness and surface quality.[62] As in casting, ARL personnel in Fabrication Metallurgy were working on turning the art of rolling into a science, developing mathematical models for both hot and cold rolling, and defining "as quantitatively as possible" the factors that inter-

fered with good production. Only with good mathematical models was it possible to have a sound basis for modifying practice
and for designing further new equipment. Their aim was eventually to produce the "bible" on aluminum rolling. A systematic
approach based on accurate data would allow them to "leap
ahead instead of creep forward."[63]

Rolling researchers needed to convince both Engineering
and the plants that turning rolling into a science was worthwhile. In 1965, meetings were held to acquaint engineering
personnel with rolling theory and to explain how certain types
of common rolling problems could be addressed by applying
theory. Engineers who only a few years earlier had taught ARL
how the plant mills were programmed found these presentations useful. It was agreed to hold a seminar later that year
aimed especially at younger plant management, "many of
whom have had little or no opportunity to study or discuss mill
design, rolling theory, lubrication, automation and other rolling problems."[64]

At the same time, the researchers involved in doing the rolling studies were handicapped by lack of sufficient access to the
plants and lack of pilot facilities. The move to the Alcoa Technical Center was delaying valuable work and would continue to
do so for more than two years. ARL rolling studies remained at
a standstill while equipment to go into the new R&D facility was
being designed.[65]

THE CAN ITSELF

Rigid container sheet (RCS) was a product innovation made
possible by numerous interlinked product and process innovations, including new alloys and new tempers, new lubricants,
new coatings, and, eventually, much more scientific control of
rolling mills. It also required changes in production methods
and organizational practice. Can sheet was used for several different products: at first, tab stock and end stock supplied for
easy-open ends used on both tinplate and composite aluminum-
and-fiber cans, and later, body stock supplied to can makers for
the all-aluminum can that gradually took over the beverage-
container market after 1970. In all, RCS involved several new
alloys and tempers, including aluminum-magnesium for end
stock and aluminum-manganese for body stock. In each case,

metal had to be supplied in much greater volumes than had previously been needed in the aluminum business, and that made production of the product especially demanding.

The sales effort for the new thin sheet exhibited the same disjointedness and fragmentation that characterized the fabrication program. Once thin sheet was offered on the market, sales personnel took over from ARL the role of prime mover in the development of can sheet. That caused disarray at ARL as the priorities of the marketplace suddenly began to vie with developmental priorities. Alcoa was still in the process of developing the appropriate combination of high-strength alloy and temper to go with the water-based lubricant system when sales personnel complained that their customers were asking for thin-sheet products that they were not yet able to supply. Because Alcoa's initial sales strategy for can sheet was to supply whatever its major customers wanted, sales priorities were not Alcoa's to control. That fact led to a type of reactive development program that was especially hard to coordinate.[66]

Alcoa had been criticized in the past for integrating forward and undercutting the companies that purchased its metal. Its strategy for RCS was not to compete with Alcoa customers by producing and selling finished cans, but rather to sell them thin-gauge sheet, along with all necessary technical support for whatever can design they wished to adopt. In that way they hoped to encourage the major can companies, especially American Can and Continental Can, and a few of the larger or more innovative breweries that made their own cans, such as Adolph Coors in Colorado, to adopt aluminum for their containers. Different Alcoa development organizations were working with different major customers on new container concepts. It was a tremendous drain on Alcoa's development capabilities, but the market dictated such an effort.

The key assumption behind the strategy was that the can companies were making a simple economic decision. Once the price of aluminum was reduced to within a few cents per pound of the tinplate conventionally used for cans, can makers were expected to adopt aluminum quickly, because of its superior qualities. Compared with tinplate, aluminum featured superior workability and lighter weight for lower freight costs. It would not corrode, it would provide longer shelf life for canned products, and it would be more compatible with printed graphics.

Aluminum containers could be made using several different processes. For many applications the easiest approach was to adapt the standard three-piece can for aluminum by using a specially cemented seam. That choice also had the virtue of versatility, for can makers could switch back relatively easily to tin. The decision from which there could be no retreat for the can manufacturers was the conversion from the three-piece can to the two-piece can. Two-piece designs used one of three processes: impact extrusion; drawn or double drawn; drawn and ironed. The seamless two-piece design was desirable for beverage cans because of the difficulty of joining aluminum at the seam. For beer cans it was essential, because beer was pasteurized, and cans had to withstand high temperatures and pressures.[67]

The container market of the early 1960s, in fact, offered a confusing array of different materials, processes, and styles. Tinplate, aluminum, glass, and plastic were all possible alternatives, and the prospect of continuing volatility in materials prices made can companies reluctant to lock themselves into a single choice. In the face of such market turbulence, can makers and breweries proved to be a conservative and wily lot. The big can companies were in no hurry to make a large commitment to expensive retooling. Anticipating major expenditures in new equipment, training, and methods, they chose to wait and see, forcing their suppliers to take the technical risks and absorb the costs of change. That strategy served them well. Even the steel industry showed signs that it might respond vigorously to the threat to its market by developing thinner forms of tinplate and new forms of tin-free steel for containers.[68]

CONTAINER BACKGROUND

Alcoa had a sales program for RCS as early as 1960. In 1961 it informed important customers that it would supply can ends for citrus cans, and it developed a joint program with Minute Maid to supply easy-open ends for juice cans. In the early 1960s, ARL was involved only when it was asked to provide specific pieces of technical support through development organizations. In 1962, when a trade publication described Reynolds's can-making initiatives, the Alcoa technical community decided to investigate competitive initiatives for itself. APDL personnel were sent out to buy a tuna fish can at the local store, and what they found showed that they had some catching up to do. But APDL soon ran into trouble when it experimented with making impact-extruded cans for tuna fish and other canned meats, because it knew too little about the food companies' business. It quickly abandoned the attempt to make cans itself and switched to investigating cements, soldering methods, adhesives for can seams, and other aspects of aluminum-can shelf life.[69]

Reynolds, by contrast, had taken a tightly focused approach to containers early in the game. In 1960 it set up its own can-making research center in Richmond, Virginia, to develop technologies and design new products. After investigating and developing through the prototype stage several different approaches to aluminum can making – impact-extruded, drawn, drawn and ironed – it focused on the drawn-and-ironed (D&I) can, using a lightweight alloy, and proceeded to put together its own complete can-making operation. Not waiting for customers to make up their minds to invest in new capital equipment, Reynolds produced several of its own closures, and a tall soft-drink can. In 1965 it introduced its new D&I can. Setting up can-making plants adjacent to several large breweries, it went into the business of making beer cans, capturing between 20 and 30 percent of the Anheuser-Busch can requirements. The rest of that giant brewery's cans, about 1 billion per year, still came from American Can and Continental Can, the former providing a conventional three-piece can with cemented seam, the latter making a two-piece can that was impact-extruded and ironed.[70]

Reynolds made a highly visible pioneering move that earned it, and the aluminum can, much attention, and its achievement was honored by a 1968 award from the Packaging Institute. Yet the Reynolds activity was slow to make an impression on Alcoa, which continued to view the steel industry, not Reynolds, as the competitor to beat in the container market. As a consequence, Alcoa remained for some time in a quandary, placing equal emphasis on the product and the process innovations involved, with neither driving the other.

Until 1964, RCS fell under two subcommittees: the Subcommittee on Sheet, Plate, and Foil and the Subcommittee on Packaging. There was no task force to focus on its development, whose coordination depended on informal networks run by interested engineers. Cliff Sands, in Rigid Container Sales, for instance, circulated correspondence to a "Rigid Container Responsibility List," and Philip Althen, of Package Engineering, maintained his own "Can Sheet Responsibility List." As a result, there was a tremendous amount of overlapping work, often with the two subcommittees following the same development project, each asking for different things from it.

Perhaps predictably, some things fell through the cracks. In 1962–4, for example, each development organization had its own scenario for the direction that can sales would take, at least partly because the customer projections that were shaping Alcoa's outlook were all different. Sales was forecasting that major customers would be using aluminum in a conventional three-piece can with seams, and drawn cans would become important only at some future date. APDL, on the other hand, was working with lapped seams and, after 1963, with D&I cans as well. At the same time, AEDD was producing equipment to make cans by impact extrusion. Work continued on this process for several years, even after it was clear that D&I cans, introduced by Reynolds, would take over the marketplace, because American Can wanted to stick with impact extrusion. Meanwhile, a strong business had developed selling end stock and tab stock to can makers who did not compete with major customers, and processes for producing that stock using water-base lubricants were perfected at Alcoa, Tennessee.[71]

Accustomed to viewing its strong technical support for customers as one of its chief competitive advantages, Alcoa faced a serious problem with RCS: how to satisfy demand from many different customers, all pursuing different processes, while ensuring that Alcoa would eventually recover its investment in technical assistance. When Continental Can contacted John Harper to say that it had established a new R&D organization, that created another classic dilemma. How much information about its secret formulations for lubricants, alloys, and the like could Alcoa safely share with one of its largest customers without giving away its know-how to competitors?[72]

NADIR OF THE CAN-SHEET PROGRAM

The organization that ultimately emerged within Alcoa as the leader in development of the all-aluminum can was APDL. Under Howard Dunn's leadership in the early 1960s it expanded as quickly as its cramped circumstances in the old New Kensington plant complex would permit. It created several different easy-open ends of its own to sell to can makers; with Minute Maid it developed a composite orange-juice can using foil-coated fiberboard with a strip-off top that did not require a can opener, and it designed new lightweight beer kegs with special linings and coatings and new aluminum spout mechanisms. It was "Fritz" Close's insistence that APDL's work was of the highest importance that earned it priority in the move into the Alcoa Technical Center ahead of other organizations. Yet APDL's impending move into new quarters delayed coordinated activity for some time.

Under Close's influence, the informal interest groups in Sales and Engineering that had been tracking RCS products and processes were reconstituted as formal task forces: the RCS Task Force, under the Subcommittee on Sheet, Plate, and Foil, and the Task Force on Rigid Containers, under the Subcommittee on Packaging. Put together to mount a coordinated assault on the market, the new task forces soon found that Alcoa's RCS program had serious problems that needed to be addressed in a coordinated way.[73]

The first RCS product innovation that Alcoa pushed especially for cans was a high-strength temper for RCS alloys, called H-19. With H-19 sheet on the verge of high-volume production in 1966, Alcoa considered itself in a "strong and unique" competitive position in the can market. Though Reynolds and Kaiser would certainly have the sheet before long, Alcoa planned to maintain its advantage through the use of superior coatings, which it was producing at its Richmond, Indiana, plant.[74]

At the April meeting of the R&D Committee, called to review the Alcoa effort on H-19 sheet, all progress reported was reassuring. If, as looked likely, the Reynolds D&I can appealed to many customers, Alcoa was ready with what it believed to be a superior product to use in that process. APDL was working on the drawing characteristics of various alloys in the H-19 temper, and ARL's Physical Metallurgy, Finishes, and Lubricants Divisions were all engaged in cooperative work to evaluate alloy, temper, surface treatment, coating, and lubrication effects on drawability. The key advantage for Alcoa was that it had deep know-how in all of these areas. Secure in its sense of preparedness, Alcoa pushed for the largest possible sales of H-19 sheet, to gain overall market acceptance for H-19 quickly and to get the jump on steel.

But the scale-up volume production brought out numerous latent difficulties. When H-19 sheet reached the market in quantity, complaints rolled in from customers. Alcoa's product had problems with flatness, finish, the effect of its lubricants on the ability to clean the end product, increases in scrap owing to the need for scalping, and the undesirable phenomenon called "earring" (turning up at the edge). Matters did not improve when Alcan launched a highly visible and focused crash program on flatness. If customer complaints were to be believed, the thin sheet that customers were receiving from Alcoa's plants was of poorer quality, on some dimensions, than was sheet from all other competitors. Although its competitors were also having problems, Alcoa's own comparative tests confirmed the gloomy finding that Alcoa's problems were worse.[75]

Although some scale-up difficulty could be expected, the chief problem was that the plants lacked the expertise they needed to support their new technologies. Dowd, at Warrick, requested consideration for an "aggressive high-priority program" at ARL to address the multitude of difficulties that were plaguing the new high-speed rolling mills and also the water-based lubricant installations at Davenport and Alcoa, Tennessee. In many instances, solutions depended on an understanding of fundamental principles, such as those of emulsion chemistry, and that kind of expertise was available only at ARL. One response to the problem was to set up a task force on water-based lubricants to do coordinated troubleshooting.

Eventually, customer complaints pushed Alcoa into additional organizational steps to remedy the confusion that Alcoa's multiple programs, projects, and task forces had created in the minds of customers and Alcoa personnel alike. At a meeting of the RCS Task Force, one APDL engineer complained of "too much overall confusion, both internal and with the customer." Alcoa needed to establish firm limits on the specifications for material it would supply and stop trying to do everything for everyone. Reluctantly the company recognized the advantage Reynolds had gained by settling early on one approach to the all-aluminum can. Alcoa still had several such approaches competing with each other for resources and research support. At the risk of offending some customers, it, too, would have to narrow down to a single concept.[76]

LEAPFROGGING WITH THE B-24

Rumors that steel companies were planning to enter the competition to produce D&I cans provided whatever further motivation was necessary for Alcoa to change its approach to the container market entirely. The choice was made to follow Reynolds's lead and support the D&I can under the leadership of APDL. APDL, previously hamstrung by inadequate quarters, had just settled in at the Alcoa Technical Center. It now had ample space to set up a new experimental can line using D&I technology, which it had already been investigating. Although behind, Alcoa had several exploitable advantages. Reynolds had concentrated on can production, but Alcoa had developed deeper experience with lighter gauges, with the H-19 temper, and with the methods of rolling it.[77]

In 1967 the APDL Packaging Division developed a design for a lightweight can called the B-24 that capitalized on the weight advantage conferred by the high-strength H-19 temper in a way that its competitors could not imitate. The design called for the can to be domed after coating, and a special bottom design gave it extra strength to resist crushing even when a significantly lighter-gauge metal was used. The B-24 can gave all the previously separate lines of development a common objective. The new can took advantage of the best that had been learned in many areas: water-based lubricants, the H-19 temper, tailor-made alloys such as alloy 5182, coatings, cleaners, finishes, and numerous other small but important interlocking developments that together added up to a deep base of usable knowledge.[78]

In order to concentrate on speedy development of the D&I technology, APDL and AEDD arranged to concentrate their efforts largely on customers' development problems. AEDD discontinued its impact-extrusion program. ARL absorbed work APDL had traditionally handled, including counselling Sales concerning the nature of different coatings, lubricants, and specifications. ARL continued in its support role, doing backup testing and evaluation for both development divisions. In that way, as other overburdened development departments passed along their extra work, ARL's program gradually took on more of the short-term support function and less of the "forward-looking" concern that had been its traditional mission. The result was a significant hiatus in longer-term work, exacerbated by crowded conditions and the prolonged delay in getting into new quarters.[79]

Alcoa's new focus on clearing up the quality problems incurred in its rush to market made can makers more receptive to the H-19 temper, but for two years strenuous efforts failed to convince them to adopt the whole Alcoa can concept with its several radical components. Its quantum advantage in weight – 28.6 pounds per thousand versus the next best, 34 pounds per thousand – was not enough by itself to sell cautious can makers, many of whom had already had some difficulties in getting process technologies supplied by Alcoa's pioneering competitors to work. Without the can makers' wholesale commitment, which would involve reequipping themselves with special-purpose equipment, Alcoa remained vulnerable to the danger of can makers switching to substitute suppliers, especially steel. Even though it had completely sold its entire RCS production in 1967 and expected to be selling at capacity until 1970–1, when production expansion was planned, Alcoa was in the uncomfortable position of being heavily dependent on two large customers: American Can and Continental Can.[80]

Once again, in June 1968, "Fritz" Close forced the issue. A visit to Anheuser-Busch, whom Close had been cultivating for some time, revealed that Reynolds was test marketing a lightweight can weighing less than 30 pounds per thousand. Alcoa Sales concluded that only by setting up a full-scale can-making operation, complete with graphics and finishing – in other words, only by bearing the entire cost of process development – could major can producers be persuaded to switch to the B-24 profile. As part of a presentation by Industry Sales to management, citing the need for additional rolling-mill capacity, it was proposed that R&D funds be allocated to purchase commercial equipment for a full-scale can line. At an expenditure of half a million dollars stretching over two years, that represented a significant chunk out of an already eroded R&D budget.[81]

"Fritz" Close.

The matter caused a showdown between Sales and R&D, which Sales won easily. When in July 1968 J. J. Solomon at APDL questioned a directive from Sales to produce several thousand cans for Anheuser-Busch's Tampa brewery to test

run in August, he learned that "Fritz" Close, chairman of the
board, had personally promised August Busch III several thousand complete aluminum cans. To make Busch wait for any of
its thousands of cans would be, Cliff Sands wrote to Solomon, a
"major faux pas on our part." In any case, he noted, if the
Development Division was really ready, as it said it was, to produce cans, then it should be no problem to produce several
thousand of them.[82] In a statement of policy for his salesmen in
the field, Sands noted that

Alcoa is not in the can business nor do they intend to enter the can
business either directly or through encouragement to packers of
any kind. However, Alcoa has conceived a concept of a drawn and
ironed can which can be produced as economically and possibly
more economically than any other commercial container on the market today. Since this concept has many radical innovations, it is necessary for us to design, develop, and sometimes build equipment in
conjunction with certain other types of commercial equipment to
produce a can layout that will, in part, be installed at our Alcoa
Technical Center, Process Development Laboratories. It is our intent to recommend this line and its specified equipment to commercial can makers, captive can manufacturers, and those companies
who recently have entered the container market although they are
not directly in the beer and beverage areas but intend to enter
them.[83]

While Alcoa continued to avoid competing directly with its customers, it served notice on the foot-dragging container industry
that it would not shrink from encouraging and giving technical
assistance to new entrants.

Kent Van Horn, then in the twilight of his career, went on
record as opposing the diversion of funds from R&D to the
commercial production of cans. He saw it as an unsettling inten-
sification of an already disturbing trend. The RCS tasks that
should legitimately be covered by R&D funds and R&D manpower, principally metalworking R&D, such as ironing, had, in
his opinion, already been substantially completed. There was
still need for more work on the quality of sheet reaching customers, especially flatness, where Alcoa's product was known to be
lagging behind those of Alcan and Reynolds. But funding a can
line to produce thousands of cans for testing was beyond the
scope of R&D as he saw it. That would require R&D personnel
to be trained for production work, and it would reduce still

further an already depleted long-term research budget ear-marked for fundamental work. Van Horn's opposition was over-ridden two years in a row, for although Alcoa was then ahead in overall sales of can sheet, it was in danger of losing the RCS battle in the long haul. The Pittsburgh Sales Department reported that of the three main contenders in the American market supplying the new body sheet, as opposed to can sheet for all applications, Alcoa was still last.[84]

After a year of examining the unfinished prototype B-24 cans, all major customers remained admiring but skeptical. Continental Can had been having difficulty using H-19 sheet in its own can lines since May. "Alcoa was finally asked to help solve some of their problems and a modification in our fabricating practice has been most helpful, noted one report on a customer call." Anheuser-Busch, which had been purchasing all-aluminum cans from Reynolds, had committed $50,000 to line and equipment modifications in order to give Alcoa's lightweight can a try, but they expected to have commercial-quality cans to evaluate. Different variations of the same story came from most customers. They wanted not just a few cans but thousands of finished cans for process testing and market research.[85]

To the immense frustration of the R&D community, neither Sales nor anyone else addressed its central concern: the limited supply of R&D talent available at ARL and APDL to work on future problems as well as current ones. Van Horn summed up the problem this way:

In conclusion, it is the commercial decision that the line as now proposed is necessary to pursue the market and that it is the best way for Alcoa to spend R/D time and money to accomplish this goal. The biggest loss is in the dilution of R/D manpower in non-R/D work in order to answer a commercial need.[86]

Van Horn was poorly armed so late in his career to defend that point of view. It was simply not his style to fight the decisions of top management. R&D was promised more money, but received no relief from the problem of having to divert its scarce expertise. Management was more than willing to open its purse for anything associated with what appeared so sure a winner, but the destructive collateral effects on research capability were neither questioned nor understood. To Sales, the need was of emergency proportions, and again Sales prevailed, be-

The Alcoa Process Development Laboratory set up an experimental version of a can-filling line as soon as the new Building A could be inhabited.

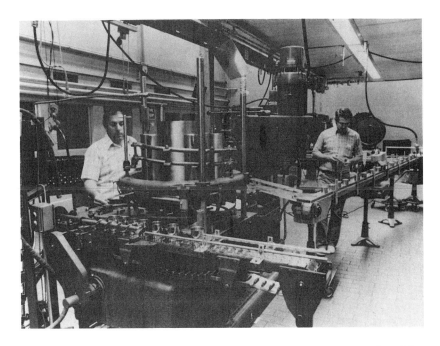

A much-expanded can line complete with conveyor, decorator, and washing apparatus was installed in Building A in the early 1970s.

cause the expense was so easily justified. By its own calculations, the additional projected sales of the B-24 can, though only 16 to 17 percent of the market, would mean $100 million in sales for Alcoa by 1975. It seemed commercial folly to omit any step that might ensure a bigger slice of such a market.[87]

The requests for appropriations were approved, and the can line was expanded to include equipment for washing, handling, and decorating. Ironically, completion was delayed for a year because of a holdup in delivering the washing equipment. By 1971 the B-24 line was declared "operational." Apparently the ancillary equipment that had raised so much controversy had not been crucial after all. Alcoa's sales shot up, and thanks in part to the B-24 effort, Alcoa body-sheet sales rose to near parity with Reynolds. In one year, 1971, projections for future sales doubled, to nearly $200 million by 1975.[88]

RCS, Alcoa's come-from-behind success, became the company's most important single product for the next 20 years, the mainstay of the business. Calculated according to the new method of judging R&D investments, the projected return was impressive. Money invested in R&D directed at body stock between 1967 and 1974 added up to $2.25 million, in support of sales that were projected at $306 million between 1971 and 1976. In the popular new calculus of the business world of the 1960s, that was a "return on research" of better than 100 to 1. Not calculated was the opportunity cost of spending the money on a can-washing line that never became operational, rather than on the fundamental research needed to carry forward into the next generation of automated rolling.[89]

THE DECLINE OF RESEARCH

The equipping of Warrick, and the RCS program into which it led, resembled the urgent programs of World War II. The ability to produce, under pressure, a product that could outshine all of the other competitive entries was heavily dependent on a decade-long effort by both Research and Development. Although Reynolds had been first to establish the aluminum-can concept, it was Alcoa's significant cumulative expertise – reflected in the product itself and in the myriad individual collateral improvements – that made it possible for aluminum to hold and dominate the beverage-can market. By the 1980s, over 90 percent of this entire market was using aluminum. For its part, Alcoa had taken significant risk at a critical time, and although the course of the project had not been smooth, the company had achieved a commanding technical position. Moreover, payoffs for its intensive effort would be evident in other areas besides the all-important RCS product. It was commitment to continuous operation at Warrick that, in turn, laid the groundwork for the economic recycling technologies of the succeeding era.

This time, however, Alcoa's overall course diverged from earlier experience in one crucial way. In the decade after World War II, Alcoa's R&D organizations had followed up on the fundamental questions that the intensive period of wartime applications had generated, even as it restructured itself for more effective applications. It was, in fact, that fundamental work that prepared the company for its successful HDC ingot-casting program, as well as for the new technologies in high-speed rolling. With RCS, however, the company paid a higher price. The phaseout of longer-term research turned out to be not just a temporary episode but a continuing trend.

In fact, Research and Development became so closely inter-twined that in the next era they were indistinguishable. R&D received credit for its role in assisting customers, but there was little awareness that it had also provided the technologies – such as the lubricant chemistry that had resulted in a whole new area of study – that had given the company its competitive advantage. In some circles, R&D was seen not as the contributor of the indispensable, enabling technologies but as the organization that held out against the last phase of the RCS campaign. As one exasperated researcher wrote to Walter Dean concerning another large research-based program, in the several years it usually took for a research development to "reach important production stature," people in Operations tended to forget that the innovation was a "research contribution." He added plaintively, "I would be interested in learning whether you can visualize any method for capitalizing on this information in order to demonstrate the value of research efforts."[90]

A revealing message from a Sales Department executive to members of his own organization showed how the nature of R&D was misperceived by the rest of the company. Salesmen should sell "the one area where Alcoa excels beyond all of our competition," he urged, "i.e., R&D in basic research, equipment development, process development, or applications engineering." Alcoa should not accept technical contributions as a "responsibility," he said, but publicize them, pointing out that "you get more than a pound of aluminum" from Alcoa. The notion that Alcoa still had such a balanced R&D program in the late 1960s was a misconception. Not only was little being done to replenish the fundamental R&D that had been exhausted in application, but few R&D personnel remained who had an independent view of what would constitute a balanced program.[91]

BIG-TICKET PROJECTS

Both ASP and RCS, and the difficulties they posed for Alcoa Research, pointed to trends that were typical in many professionally managed companies in the 1960s and 1970s. That trend intensified at Alcoa as it took on its new, high-volume identity. In the new era of competition with steel, the importance of the long-term, the fundamental, and the risky was all but forgotten. Where volume markets were prized above all, the small often could be mistaken for the trivial. R&D learned to tie its program elements to big-ticket projects. "Fritz" Close's instructions to Howard Dunn as to the kinds of projects that merited research attention illustrated this point. As Dunn noted,

> Mr. Close continuously emphasizes the need for Alcoa to be forward looking in areas which will absorb large tonnages of aluminum. The aluminum easy-open end is a good past example. I would like to put together for him a portfolio indicating some of our current projects in this area, which we can report on from time to time, and which we can add to as appropriate.[92]

The limitations of the top-down approach to managing innovation practiced by most large companies at that time could be seen in the choices of major innovations made by Alcoa when it went after steel. Top managers could not focus on everything. Their reasons for backing particular opportunities were heavily influenced by competitive maneuvering and economic need. If they lacked experience with R&D, or with operations improvement, in their early careers, they were all too likely to disregard, often completely, the independent technical view that could distinguish between feasible opportunities and those that were not. At a time when the financial community was enforcing a new standard of management conformity across American big business, it was a rare manager in a capital-intensive business who could ignore the prevailing view that R&D managers were prima donnas who could never let go of their pet ideas, people who had to be challenged and prodded to perform.[93]

In fact, Alcoa R&D managers in the 1960s were cast from a different mold than was the stereotypical researcher. They were more process-oriented, less theoretical, and less in touch with the broader scientific community than either their predecessors or many of their contemporaries. Some of them, especially the ones who came out of the Cleveland laboratory, were interdisciplinary in their work patterns. They shared neither the excesses nor some of the strengths of their flashier R&D counterparts in "high-tech" industries like electronics or aeronautics.[94]

In some cases, a challenge from above to "do the impossible" could be met with alacrity. In the case of several technologies that were commercialized during the 1960s, for which the knowledge base and the infrastructure were in place to support them, a top-management challenge to move quickly to produce major improvements was ideal. In the case of HDC casting, the groundwork, in all respects, had been done. Fundamental work on solidification provided the necessary metallurgical knowledge. The Cleveland background provided scientists and engineers with the experience of cross-disciplinary teamwork. Speedy prototyping was possible because of the investment in the experimental Arnold facility, and effective technology transfer to Davenport could take advantage of the engineering networks in place. Because no previous technology had to be supplanted at Warrick, there was no existing technical community to block HDC's installation.

But neither RCS nor ASP had as complete a set of positive ingredients as had HDC casting: a sufficient knowledge base, a broad-gauged and balanced applications team, a pilot facility located near Research, continuity supporting the technology transfer process, and a receptive "customer." RCS involved a difficult coordination task, with its competing approaches and competing customers. It lacked a previous knowledge base in rolling theory, and it had to establish a new pattern for technology transfer without the aid of either a good experimental site or a clear set of organizational responsibilities. "Fritz" Close was essential to RCS, not only to add urgency and visibility but also to cut through and override the complications produced by the customers and committee channels. Had he not retired, Close might also have guided RCS through a complete cycle, in the sense that he might have appreciated the need for greater future investment in fundamental rolling technology. But it was Harper who stayed on, and Harper was much more attuned to prevailing management doctrines. He clearly subscribed to the blockbuster mentality that obsessed so many postwar managers in dealing with their R&D organizations. The success of RCS only reinforced that expectation. Moreover, Harper had a personal stake in ASP, having insisted on its selection at the start.

ASP had many of the necessary ingredients for success: an experimental site, an interdisciplinary team, and good channels for transfer. But in two respects it was the least well endowed, and those turned out to be crippling. It lacked a sufficient fundamental base of knowledge, and it lacked willing interaction with a customer. Harper's top-down intervention was more of a hindrance than a help, for by running interference with the ultimate user, he forced large-scale investment to outrun technical achievement. The record does not show whether Harper refused to listen to the independent technical assessments of ASP that might have allowed him to change course earlier or whether he had simply created a climate that shut off all independent assessments before they reached him.

The next stages for both ASP and RCS exposed the weaknesses in the knowledge base that began to be apparent during the 1960s. In previous projects, such weaknesses were addressed by redirecting a significant portion of the R&D program back to fundamentals. This time, a different avenue was taken, and outside sources were consulted. The ASP program, for instance, brought in Lummus Engineering to help it solve the chemical-reactor problem. By the mid-1970s, the control problems raised by high-speed rolling would drive Alcoa to find control theorists from abroad. Those specialist consultants, whose expertise had been developed for steel, opened a new chapter in the control of high-speed mills. Those borrowings from leading-edge steel technology were the good side of aiming for steel. But it also was apparent to some R&D performers that steel, in other ways, was an unfortunate competitor to use as a point of reference.

PART V

International competition, 1968–1983

9

Beyond the research base

For Alcoa's R&D organization, the period of the 1970s and early 1980s was one of gradual reform and rebuilding. It was a time when the technical leadership and later the company at large had to rediscover its dependence on science and technology as an essential feature of its existence. Only when that dependence was reaffirmed could the necessary structural changes take place to rebuild an organization capable of supplying and implementing a coherent technical vision for a new era. In the meantime, the Laboratories and the company drifted, buffeted by external events and unable to come up with a match between strategy and technical capability.

Within the technical community, two contradictory reform objectives competed for attention in the early 1970s: productivity and creativity. Weighing heavily in the balance between them was Alcoa's deteriorating profit margin. Hindsight suggests that Alcoa, like many other companies at the time, was going through a self-imposed aging process, having largely cut itself off from its traditional sources of technological renewal. It required more than a decade to reconnect with them.

INDUSTRIAL R&D DEFROCKED

The disenchantment in the nation at large with R&D, and especially with Research, which had begun in the mid-1960s, intensified in the early 1970s. A growing antagonism between government and industry seemed to be taking an especially high toll on research. Federal funding for R&D performed in industry continued to decrease, with funding for basic research going more to universities, and research funding in general becoming more mission-directed, emphasizing a few big projects. The

379

Corporate Facts

Leadership: Frederick J. Close, chairman of the board
John D. Harper, president and CEO
W. H. Krome George, executive vice-president for finance
John S. Harrison, executive vice-president for mill products
John M. Mitchell, executive vice-president for primary products,
allied products, and international

No. of Employees: 46,532

Primary production: 2188 million pounds

Laboratory Facts

Leadership: Kent R. Van Horn, vice-president for R&D
James W. Newsome, director of research
Robert H. Brown, Walter A. Dean,
Elbert S. Howarth, Philip T. Stroup, assistant directors
J. Howard Dunn, director of development
W. W. Binger, manager of Alcoa Process
Development Laboratories
Robert G. Hampel, manager of Alcoa Equipment
Development Laboratories
Rodney L. LaBarge, manager of Alcoa Product
Development Laboratories

Expenditures $11.2 million, ARL
$18.8 million, total R&D

Figure 9.1. Corporate and laboratory facts, 1968.

antagonism between government and industry stemmed from a regulatory environment that, coupled with a rising consumer movement, caused companies to divert significant portions of their research budgets to performing environment-related and product-safety-related work. An increase in energy-related research, following quickly on the heels of the 1973 oil embargo, further intensified the diversion of research funds away from normal channels. Subsequently, as interest rates increased rapidly, real levels of R&D spending headed into a deep trough.[1]

Another trend that worked against R&D was the move toward diversification in an attempt to counter economic cyclicality. With the growing popularity of analytical tools in professional management, risk came to be calculated in quantifiable terms, and the uncertainties of technical risk, compared with other forms of investment, seemed increasingly unacceptable to professional managers. Companies everywhere sought formulas for R&D productivity. Many technology-based companies sought

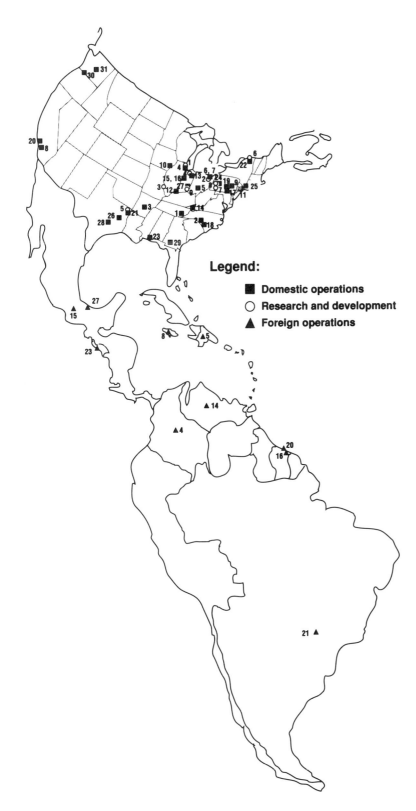

Legend:

■ Domestic operations
○ Research and development
▲ Foreign operations

Figure 9.2. Corporate locations, 1968.

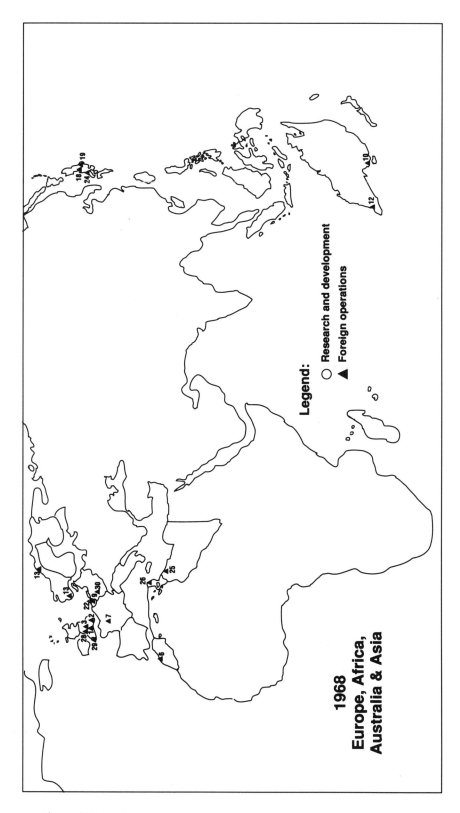

Figure 9.2. *(cont.)*

382

Domestic operations:

1 Alcoa, Tennessee
Tennessee Operations
Primary aluminum, fabricating ingot, remelt
ingot, plate, sheet, painted sheet, impact
slugs, foil, Alcoa Wrap products, powder and
pigments, welded tube

2 Badin, North Carolina
Primary aluminum, fabricating ingot,
remelt ingot

3 Benton, Arkansas
Arkansas Operations
Bauxite, alumina and alumina chemicals

4 Chicago, Illinois
Alcoa Castings Company
Die castings

5 Chillicothe, Ohio
Wear-Ever Aluminum, Inc.
Cooking utensils

6 Cleveland, Ohio
Fabricating ingot, remelt ingot, castings
(premium-engineered), forgings
(hammer and press), magnesium and
titanium forgings

7 Cleveland, Ohio
Alcoa Castings Company
Aluminum and magnesium castings
(permanent-mold)

8 Corona, California
(under construction)
Premium-engineered castings

9 Cressona, Pennsylvania
Fabricating ingot, estrusions

10 Davenport, Iowa
Fabricating ingot, plate, sheet,
painted sheet, foil

11 Edison, New Jersey
Alcoa Castngs Company
Die and permanent-mold castings

12 Evansville, Indiana
Warrick Operations
Primary aluminum, fabricating ingot, remelt
ingot, sheet

13 Fort Wayne, Indiana
Rea Magnet Wire Company, Inc.
Insulated aluminum and copper magnet wire,
ceramic-insulated and resistance wire,
aluminum magnet strip

14 Franklin, North Carolina
Natahala Power and Light Company
Owns and operates hydroelectric power
plants and an electric utility system
in North Carolina

15 Lafayette, Indiana
Fabricating ingot, extrusions, tube

16 Lafayette, Indiana
Rea Magnet Wire Company, Inc.
Insulated aluminum and copper magnet wire

17 Lancaster, Pennsylvania
Closures, electrical conductor accessories.
fasteners, nails, rivets, screw machine products

Domestic operations (Cont.):

18 Laurinburg, North Carolina
Rea Magnet Wire Company, Inc.
Insulated aluminum and copper magnet wire

19 Lebanon, Pennsylvania
Foil, light-gauge coiled sheet, formed containers

20 Los Angeles, California
Vernon Works
Fabricating ingot, castings (sand, plaster-process,
permanemt-mold, premium-engineered), inpact
and forging stock, extrusions, forgings, rivets
tooling plate, tube

21 Marshall, Texas
(under construction)
Alcoa Conductor Products Co.
Electrical conductor

22 Massena, New York
Primary aluminum, fabricating ingot, remelt ingot,
bloom, bar, impact slugs, rod wire, electrical
conductor and accessories

23 Mobile, Alabama
Alumina, hydrated alumina

24 New Kensington, Pennsylvania
Food service utensils, manufactured products
(special fabrications, catalog items, impact
extrusions), powder and pigments

25 New York, New York
Alcoa Steamship Co., Inc.
Transports alumina and bauxite from the
Caribbean area to the United States and Europe
and offers a variety of cargo services in
other areas

26 Point Comfort, Texas
Oil and gas, alumina, hydrated alumina, aluminum
fluoride, cryolite, caustic soda, chlorine, primary
aluminum, fabricating ingot, remelt ingot

27 Richmond, Indiana
Closures, machinery for applying closures

28 Rockdale, Texas
Primary aluminum, fabricating ingot, remelt
ingot, powder rod

29 Tifton, Georgia
Tifton Aluminum Company, Inc.
Extrusions

30 Vancouver, Washington
Primary aluminum, fabricating ingot, remelt
ingot, extrusions, rod, wire, electrical conductor

31 Wenatchee, Washington
Primary aluminum, fabricating ingot, remelt ingot

⭘ Research & development

1 Chicago, Illinois
Alcoa Castings Company

2 Cleveland, Ohio
Castings and Forgings Division,
Alcoa Research Laboratories

3 East St. Louis, Illinois
Alumina and Chemicals Division,
Alcoa Research Laboratories

Figure 9.2. *(cont.)*

383

○ Research & development (Cont.)

4 Fort Wayne, Indiana
Rea Magnet Wire Company, Inc.

5 Marshall, Texas
(under construction)
Insulated Conductor Division,
Alcoa Research Laboratories

6 Massena, New York
Electrical Engineering Division,
Alcoa Research Laboratories

7 Merwin, Pennsylvania
(Pittsburgh post office address)
Alcoa Technical Center
Alcoa Equipment Development Division;
Alcoa Process Development Laboratories;
Fabricating Metallurgy Division,
Alcoa Research Laboratories

8 New Kensington, Pennsylvania
Alcoa Research Laboratories;
Alcoa Product Development Division

9 Richmond, Indiana
Closures Section, Alcoa Product
Development Division

▲ Foreign operations

1 Aylesbury, England
International Alloys Limited
Secondary remelt and fabricating
(extrusion) ingot

2 Barking, England
Impalco Foils Limited
Foil, formed containers

3 Birmingham, England
International Alloys Limited
Secondary remelt ingot and alloys

4 Bogotá, Colombia
Capco Limitada
Closures

5 Cabo Rojo, Dominican Rep.
Alcoa Exploration Company
Bauxite

6 Casablanca, Morocco
Moroccan Aluminium Company
Architectural products

7 Châteauroux, France
Alcoa, France S.A.R.L.
Extrusions

8 Clarendon Parish, Jamaica
Alcoa Minerals of Jamaica, Inc.
Bauxite

9 Druten, the Netherlands
Lips Aluiminnum N.V.
Sheet, extrusions, tube, manufactured products

10 Geelong, Australia
Alcoa of Austrralia Limited-Point Henry Works
Primary aluminum, remelt and fabricating ingot,
extrusions, tube, rod, bar, plate, sheet, foil

▲ Foreign operations (Cont.)

11 Jarrahdale, Australia
Western Aluminium No Liability
Bauxite

12 Kwinana, Australia
Western Aluminium No Liability
Alumina

13 Lista, Norway
Elektrokemisk Aluminium A/S & Co.
(under construction)
Primary aluminum

14 Mariara, Venezuela
Corporación Venezolana de Aluminio
C. A.-Covenal
Extrusions, tube

15 Mexico City, Mexico
Alcomex, S.A.
Extrusions, tube
Tapas y Envases, S.A. de C.V. Closures

16 Moengo, Suriname
Suriname Aluminum Company
Bauxite

17 Mosjøen, Norway
Mosjøen Aluminiumverk, Elektrokemisk
Aluminium A/S & Company
Primary aluminum, remelt and fabricating ingot

18 Nikko, Japan
Furukawa Aluminum Co., Ltd.
Sheet, plate, rod, wire, forgings

19 Oyama, Japan
Furukawa Aluminum Co., Ltd.
Extrusions, tube, rod, bar, castings (die,
permanent-mold)

20 Paranam, Suriname
Suriname Aluminum Company
Bauxite, alumina, promary aluminum, remelt
and fabricating ingot

21 Poços De Caldas, Brazil
Companhia Mineira de Aluminio-Alcominas
(under construction)
Bauxite, alumina, primary aluminum,
fabricating ingot

22 Rotterdam, the Netherlands
Alcoa (Nederland) N.V.
Tasbular alumina

23 San Salvador, El Salvador
Alcoa do Centro América, S.A.
Extrusions

24 Shiga, Japan
Furukawa Aluminum Co., Ltd.
Extrusions

25 Tripole, Libya
Aluminum Company of Libya Limited
Architectural products

26 Tunis, Tunisia
Industries Maghrébines de L'Aluminium (IMAL)
Architectural products

Figure 9.2. *(cont.)*

△ **Foreign operations (Cont.)**

27   Veracruz, Mexico
Aluminio, S.A. de C.V.
Primary aluminum, remelt and fabricating ingot

28   Warwick, England
Warwick Production Company Limited
Engineered and jobbing products

29   Waunarlwydd, Wales
Inperial Aluminium Company (Wales) Limited
Extrusions, plate, sheet, tube rod, bar

30   Worms am Rhein, West Germany
Wicander & Co., K. G.
Closures

Figure 9.2. *(cont.)*

solutions through acquisitions. Focusing on markets as the organizing principle, rather than on shared technologies and know-
how, some companies diversified into wholly unrelated technologies. Others diversified into completely nontechnical enterprises
because those seemed far less risky than hard-to-quantify new
technologies, and easier to predict for the benefit of financial
markets that based their judgments on fiscal measures. The effects of all these trends were not uniform across industries or
across companies within industries, but they were rarely, if ever,
positive for individual R&D laboratories.[2]

INTERNATIONALIZATION OF ALUMINUM

The shift toward a new, highly competitive international period
for aluminum, begun in the late 1950s, was changing the industry, eroding the national oligopoly. In the late 1960s the big three
U.S. producers found themselves facing increasing competition,
on their own turf as well as abroad, from a large number of new
foreign and domestic entrants. Both Swiss Aluminium Ltd. and
the French firm Pechiney set up integrated enterprises in the
United States and made names for themselves in leading-edge
aluminum technologies. Worldwide, Pechiney was involved in
primary production in five nations, and Swiss Aluminium in
eight. Alcan, an international player since before World War II,
was a shareholder in aluminum smelters in eight countries outside North America at that time.[3]

Established metals companies of all kinds were diversifying
into aluminum, countering aluminum's invasion of other mar-

kets. Steel and copper – National Steel, Anaconda, and Revere Copper and Brass – ventured into smelting, a move that John Harper interpreted as a resounding endorsement of aluminum's future prospects. National Steel, he said, "undoubtedly wishes to participate in the projected growth of our industry."[4] Harper's optimism was based on the assumption that having finally broken through to mass markets in the United States, aluminum had become, like steel, a "big industry." His strategy was to develop high-volume markets internationally "by playing the same marketing techniques all over the world." For Alcoa, the days of missionary selling were over.[5]

R&D competition accompanied competition in markets. Alcoa still took pride in having the largest metals laboratory outside the Soviet Union, and in the United States in the late 1960s it was still popularly regarded as the leader in comprehensive technology. However, just as Alcoa's share of U.S. primary production had shrunk to one-third of the total, as against 25 percent for Reynolds and 20 percent for Kaiser, its share of U.S. aluminum R&D was also only one-third. Moreover, the company freely conceded that in some areas its claims to leadership were based less on recent scientific achievement than on applications expertise – on know-how, not know-why. After coming from behind with RCS, it was confident of its ability to commercialize new technologies faster than other companies. Behind the scenes, on the primary end, Alcoa was staking its future on a research breakthrough, its revolutionary smelting process. The assumption was that with ASP, Alcoa could retake any lead it might have forgone.[6]

In the 1970s, Alcoa reasserted its leadership over domestic R&D competitors, but by that time, Reynolds and Kaiser were no longer the only, or even the major, competitors in R&D. In reaction against the costly failure of its alternative smelting process, Alcan had decentralized its R&D and was investing heavily in improved technology for producing high-quality sheet. In Europe, France's Pechiney was the enterprise to be watched. Bolstered by French public policy to invest in technological progressiveness through government laboratories, Pechiney reasserted its early scientific excellence. In 1966 it opened a new research center at Voreppe, housing several hundred technical staff, devoted to metallurgy and product development. Pechiney led in improvements to the Hall-Héroult process. Its energy-efficient pot technology, first seen in the United States

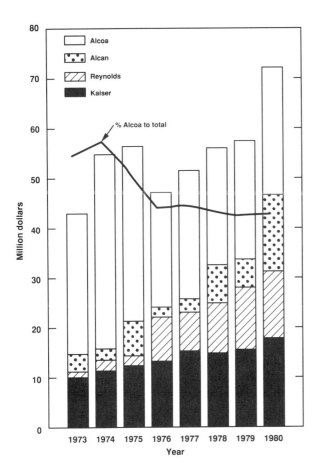

Figure 9.3. Comparative R&D spending, aluminum oligopoly, 1973–80. Source: R&D Committee records, AA-Boyers.

at its Intalco plant in Washington state, proved to be visionary after the energy crisis erupted in the early 1970s. By the mid-1980s, over half of the world's reduction plants were utilizing Pechiney technology.[7]

The 1970s also brought advances in computer process controls that, because they were applicable to many different research methods and production processes, opened whole new areas for aluminum competition and introduced new players. Many of the computer controls developed for steel could be modified for other metals as well. Work of that kind was going on in university laboratories, in the research centers of major computer companies, and in government R&D centers in Europe, Japan, and the Soviet Union.[8]

John Harper's optimism about Alcoa's ability to outshine its rivals in an expanding market became frayed at the edges when two successive decreases in aluminum prices, in 1970 and 1972, were followed by unprecedented cost increases. In 1973, the first of many worldwide economic shocks occurred, heralding the end of the postwar dominance of the U.S. economy. That shock was the energy crisis that resulted from the oil embargo imposed by the Organization of Petroleum Exporting Countries (OPEC), and it was soon followed by a temporary levy on bauxite imposed by the International Bauxite Association. The costs of purchasing energy and raw materials for aluminum production doubled between 1973 and 1976. The unsettled economic environment, and the financial consequences that resulted, contributed to the kind of sudden change in expectations for Alcoa R&D that historically had been reserved for wars and depressions.[9]

Having achieved a coup with RCS by the early 1970s, Alcoa's management was intent on finding further high-tonnage applications for aluminum. When no equally promising opportunities came immediately to the fore, they blamed the R&D organization for the company's inability to produce breakthroughs on demand, although experience suggested that responsibility might more sensibly be shared. Operations was resisting new technology rather than fostering it, and there was little support for R&D investment unless near-term payback was virtually guaranteed. The notion that high-tonnage applications might emerge from small, experimental businesses drawing on leading-edge research was rejected out of hand.[10]

As it settled into its expensive new home in the countryside near New Kensington, Alcoa's technical community was painfully aware of its own shortcomings in company eyes. Yet the vicissitudes of the industrial climate and the national climate in the 1970s, and the corporate strategy designed to respond to them, worked strongly against the kinds of changes that would enable R&D to set its house in order.

ALCOA TECHNICAL CENTER

The relocation of R&D at Alcoa Technical Center (ATC) took place more than a decade after it had originally been planned. The move extended over a period of eight years and, like the

Aerial photograph of the 2,300-acre Alcoa Technical Center grounds taken in 1965 when Building A, the Alcoa Process Development Laboratories, had just been completed (from pamphlet entitled "Alcoa Technical Center: Phase 1: Alcoa Process Development Laboratories"). From this angle it is possible to see the interior courtyard around which the APDL administrative offices are grouped. Numbers refer to further phases of construction to be carried out over the next decade.

formation of the original laboratories in the 1920s, required enormous amounts of managerial effort. Yet physical consolidation was the easiest part. It would take another five years to form an integrated whole out of the diverse collection of R&D communities that Alcoa had accumulated since World War II. Part of the difficulty was that the move occurred in stages. The development divisions became stronger competitors for R&D funding after moving into their new facilities in Building A, in 1965, and Building B, in 1968. They were well entrenched by the time Research arrived.[11]

Kent Van Horn's career drew to a close as his vision of ATC was fully realized. One of his last acts as vice-president was to send Assistant Director Walter Dean to close down the venerable Cleveland Research Division. Its research personnel who had not already moved to ARL at New Kensington then did so, joining either Fabricating Metallurgy or the alloy-development group within Physical Metallurgy. When these divisions later moved to ATC, other parts of the old ARL remained behind, including the Process Metallurgy Division, headed by Noel Jarrett, kept under wraps because of its ASP work, and the R&D administrative offices, waiting for their space in Building D to be completed. East St. Louis, the last satellite laboratory to close, would not move to ATC until after 1976.[12]

Research moved into its strikingly beautiful Building C at ATC in 1972. Situated on a rural rise dominating the approach to the center, Van Horn's dream laboratory, with its dark gray

Interior view of Building C housing the Chemical and Metallurgical Divisions of Alcoa Research Laboratories. This photograph shows one of the 10-foot-wide service corridors that run the entire length of each floor. Service corridors contain all the utilities and serve as passageways for material delivery, in addition to permitting movement from one laboratory to another.

aluminum exterior, presented a stark but lovely contrast to the rolling countryside that surrounded it. It was the interior space, though, that was Van Horn's "pride and joy":

In the center of the building is where we have all the services. There's a big space and then we put a lab on each side of the center well; and if you wanted AC/DC, water, gas, you just went to the corridor and it was all exposed, not in the floor. That's the way to build a lab. In New Kensington all the services were in the pipe chases – it was an old lab. And in Cleveland I built a lab and it's all the way around – on the outside of the building. . . . But you had to go to the floor to get the connections. In New Kensington on the floor all the time some valve was leaking. This [new lab] is something! Everything is all color coded, different services and pipes. You just go from these inside labs to the center well. That's the design . . . my pride and joy! It cost like hell, too.[13]

If Building C was Van Horn's architectural monument, the achievement of a consolidated R&D organization, renamed

Alcoa Laboratories in 1973, was his legacy. Though the "primary purpose" of the reorganization was said to be for better execution of R&D projects and more effective long-range planning, Howard Dunn, vice-president for R&D and newly appointed director of the Laboratories, and Eric Walker, vice-president for science and technology, presented it as the logical culmination of long-term trends. "It has been fairly obvious that there is no clear distinction between Research on the one hand and Development on the other. Combining the previous departments eliminates this anomaly." The reorganization did not change governance, which continued to function with the same director, associate directors, and assistant directors it had when it was a dedicated research facility.[14] (See Fig. 9.4)

The new ATC was a very different place in outlook and spirit, as well as in physical appearance, from the serenely dignified ARL it replaced. When it had moved into its new facility at New Kensington in 1930, Research had been completely sure of its role within the corporation. The physical separation of the Laboratories had complemented that role. In contrast, the feeling at ATC was one of isolation. To the consolidated R&D organization – Alcoa Laboratories – formed in 1973, physical separation was a barrier in the effort to define for itself a role that the company was prepared to understand and accept.

The isolation of R&D was rooted in the period before the final consolidation. It had been fostered by Alcoa's policy of secrecy, which currently was being carried to greater lengths than ever before because of fear of new competitors. In 1968, John D. Harper distributed a memorandum throughout the corporation exhorting Alcoans to be careful to protect their proprietary technology against both outright and subtle inquiries. The diversifying steel companies, he warned, were in an industry in which there was free exchange of information, and they would consider it proper to take advantage of information developed by Alcoa R&D in order to enter the new industry:

At virtually every operation we have some technique or piece of equipment developed by Alcoans which provides a competitive advantage for Alcoa and thus a more secure future for us all. But the advantages are ours only so long as the technical capacity we develop is known and used only by Alcoa. Keeping this advantage is a job for all of us – a job that grows more important (and more difficult!) every day as the competition grows stronger.[15]

R&D Organization, September 1972

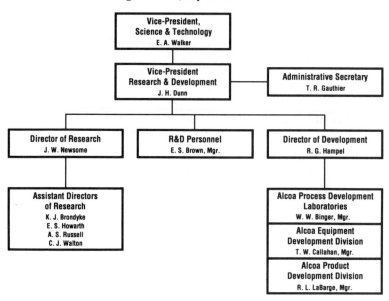

Figure 9.4. Creation of Alcoa Laboratories, 1973.

Conflict with organized labor during that period also contributed to the feeling of deep mistrust in the increasingly hostile Alcoa plant environment. Alcoa's important proprietary technology was in the form of unpatented trade secrets and therefore was vulnerable at the plant-floor level. Personnel turnover, which was high in some locations, might lead to damaging leaks to competitors who were not above hiring away operating staff to get information. In extreme cases, such as that involving lubricants, the Laboratories shared technical information about formulations only on a "need-to-know" basis.[16]

ATTEMPTED REFORM

In the disoriented period when the move to ATC was taking place, R&D leaders sponsored a program of intensive self-examination designed to address some of the problems that seemed to beset the technical community. A range of topics was put up for discussion, including how to foster creativity, how better to transfer new technology from R&D to Production, and how to set priorities. Yet the main thrust of the reform that ensued was not to create a better enviornment for R&D but to

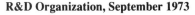

R&D Organization, September 1973

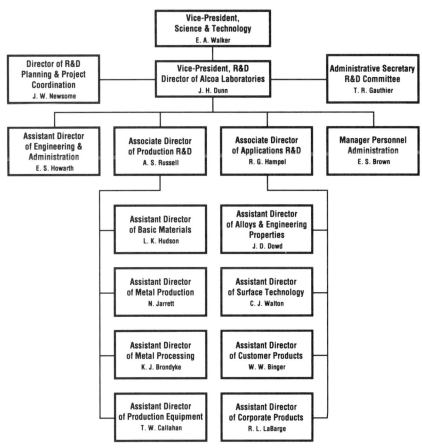

Figure 9.4 (continued)

remove many of the distinctions that made R&D different from the rest of the company. Its principal outcome was a control system that tied the technical program, hand and foot, to the operating divisions.[17]

The new Project Evaluation System, devised with a great amount of effort over two years by leading members of the Laboratories staff, was linked with a measure allocating R&D costs to two profit centers: Primary Products and Mill Products. That replaced the old system that had divided projects into categories of product and process and carried them as a corporate expense. The new system strengthened R&D's focus on projects that could be quantified, further discouraging not only long-term work but also work that held other forms of uncertainty – new

Aerial view of the Alcoa Technical Center, taken about 1976, showing building A (left), B (top right), C (right middle), D (upper center), and E (behind building D).

Building A, completed in 1964, housed three divisions: Joining and Metalworking, Packaging, and Finishes. Laboratory areas were designed to accommodate a wide range of full-scale process equipment, including the full-scale can line. The building itself used new architectural applications of aluminum both inside and outside.

Building B housed the Alcoa Equipment Development Division and the Fabricating Metallurgy Division of Alcoa Research Laboratories. It was completed in 1968.

Building C, the new home of the Chemical and Metallurgical Divisions of Alcoa Research Laboratories, was completed in 1971. It later housed research into new high-strength materials. A unique aluminum-casting process was used to produce the dark gray exterior finish.

Completed in 1975, Building D contained the ATC administrative offices, the library and information center, and the cafeteria.

Building E housed the Engineering Design and Mechanical Testing Divisions of Alcoa Laboratories, along with the Engineering Department and Receiving, Shipping, and Stores.

materials, for example, or systems where only extensive experimentation could reveal the possible costs and benefits. All R&D
efforts that were not devoted to supporting current operations,
the largest component, were focused on objectives that purported to guarantee high-tonnage outcomes, such as the aluminum car.[18]

For the R&D managers, the internal reform brought their
organization into line both with the prevailing mood of the
corporation at large and with practices in R&D management
that were becoming popular in corporations throughout the
country. An important enabling device was computer data processing, which had reached the point where it could become a
powerful information-gathering tool. Faced with the prospect
of coordinating literally hundreds of small projects generated
by subcommittees and task forces, Alcoa R&D managers welcomed the computer with open arms and were in the vanguard
in applying it to their work.

The creation of profit centers, and the fascination with the
electronic data storage and analysis that had brought them into
being, had a powerful impact throughout the company. *Business Week* noted of Alcoa that "the very existence of the profit
centers has generated a new aggressiveness on the part of their
managers, who are painfully conscious of the earnings they
generate these days."[19]

For engineering-oriented technical staff, who were in the
vast majority, the new measurement system was an appealing
chance to add greater precision at the cost of some additional
paperwork. For those who were still performing research, as
in the alloy-development program, it conjured up a stultifying
picture. The two opposing views of the direction that laboratory management was taking surfaced when groups studying
organizational structure and creativity questioned the wholesale commitment to detailed project-control systems. A vivid
and depressing picture of occupational life for the researcher
emerged from their recommendations concerning "organizational barriers to creativity":[20]

A. Provide relief from continuous bonfire existence, continual goad-
ing by innumerable coordinators and expediters, frequent subcommittee status reports – to permit pursuing more forward-looking
R&D.

B. Reexamine subcommittee structure and responsibilities to minimize cross-referencing and necessity for duplication in reporting on
subcommittee-originated and subcommittee-prosecuted projects.

C. Establish policy whereby a certain percentage of engineer or scientist time can be made available for unrelated independent research.

D. Changes in Alcoa patent policy and practices to stimulate more
creative productivity.

E. Changes in Alcoa publication policy to provide creativity motivation via improved professional recognition.

Harold Hunsicker.

Harold Hunsicker, leader of the group discussing creativity,
added his personal coda of other items that would contribute to
a more creative climate. He suggested awards for creativity, a
scientific-technical ladder, and more appreciation and recognition on the part of R&D management of the demands and
contributions of the creative process. Critical environmental
conditions, he said, included

the honest desire for and commitment to creativity on the part of
management; faith in opportunity for progress – great horizons to
be crossed; tolerance for dissent, for nonconformity and for mistakes; firm, continuing objectives – know what they're shooting for;
flexibility for action and follow-through; recognitions and rewards –
recognition by peers.

The need to mention such ideals was eloquent testimony to the
contrast between Alcoa's R&D community of the Frary era and
the ATC of a generation later.[21]

For a while, it seemed that major parts of the agenda for
change sketched out by Hunsicker's group might gradually be
implemented. Top management was seeking evidence of creative thinking on the part of the R&D community, and Howard
Dunn and James Newsome continued the discussion groups into
a second round, adding follow-up projects where original
groups had identified problems. A dual-ladder system involving
parallel technical and administrative career paths was adopted,
along lines similar to those followed at other R&D laboratories.
In a time when administration had been assuming an ever higher
profile, the scientific option needed to be strengthened to convince people that staying on the scientific ladder was not a dead
end.[22]

R&D LEADERSHIP AFTER VAN HORN

Some of the impetus for reform at ATC came from John Harper, who was taking steps to stimulate more innovative thinking in the company at large. In the late 1960s he launched a junior-executive discussion group, called the "Future Planning Committee," to encourage creative thinking about the relationship between the company's technical program and its long-term strategy. Led by newly elected Alcoa chairman, "Fritz" Close, that committee represented an unusual effort to bring men at the board-of-directors level into contact with middle-level management attitudes and decisions. Future Planning Committee sessions tended to reveal the self-doubt and confusion as to ultimate purpose among Alcoa's technical leadership. In one discussion of long-range strategy and opportunities, James Newsome, spokesman for the Laboratories, pleaded for guidance from Marketing and Operations, "so we can concentrate our attention on those areas which offer real profit potential."[23]

James Newsome.

This sense of not knowing what the rest of the corporation expected of them was common at ATC. The high rank accorded to "Project Determination, Evaluation, and Justification" on the list of objectives R&D managers intended to pursue in 1969 underscored their insecurity. "Technical Planning must always be in accords with 'Corporate Objectives,' " wrote Howard Dunn to Kent Van Horn in 1969. "If one doesn't know his 'Corporate Objectives' and can't find out – write one's own. Question: What are Alcoa's Corporate Objectives?" It was not a rhetorical question. At one point, the chairman of the Project Evaluation Task Force suggested that his group adopt DuPont's statement of R&D philosophy, as they were unable to find one at Alcoa.[24]

The problem in achieving a coherent R&D mission was two-fold. The people Kent Van Horn had chosen to work for him were not encouraged to think independently, and no immediate successors remained in place long enough to forge their own programs. After the longevity enjoyed by both Frary and Van Horn, the top post at Alcoa Laboratories changed several times in rapid succession. Rather than selecting, in the early 1970s, someone young enough to offer an extended period of leadership, Alcoa allowed a generation of R&D managers to climb the ladder to the top of a very graduated hierarchy and, one after

J. Howard Dunn.

another, to retire. Some held the title of vice-president, and some did not, but none left his own mark on the organization, its program, or its relations with corporate headquarters. That pattern also reflected practices in the rest of the company, where turnover in all positions was becoming common. At Alcoa, as at many U.S. companies in the 1960s and 1970s, rapid advancement was prized as the main sign of achievement.

Howard Dunn succeeded Van Horn as vice-president of R&D and chairman of the R&D Committee. In that post he presided over the final consolidation at ATC in 1973 and served as Alcoa Laboratories' first director for a year before his retirement in 1974. He had come out of APDL, which he headed from 1959 to 1967, before becoming director of development.

Dunn's promotion coincided with the unusual hiring of an outsider, Eric A. Walker, to fill the new position of vice-president of science and technology and chief scientist. Walker was a former president of Pennsylvania State University, a long-time consultant to Alcoa, and a friend of "Fritz" Close, a loyal Penn State alumnus. After earning a Harvard doctorate in electrical engineering, he had taught and headed departments at several universities, but aside from consulting, he had no significant industrial experience. Walker's coming elevated the status of the scientific viewpoint within the corporation's circles to a level equal to or above that enjoyed by the engineering or development viewpoint. He reported directly to the chairman and attended meetings of the board of directors to discuss the R&D program. Within a year he became a member of the board of directors.[25]

Although he was Alcoa Laboratories' most visible representative in the 1970s, Walker was as much a critic as a champion of the technical community. As the first outsider to be admitted into the inner circle of top-management, he ruffled more than a few feathers in other parts of the company hierarchy. During the five years in which he served, he promoted two causes: greater funding for leading-edge research, and opening up Alcoa R&D to the technical community outside the company. Unfortunately, most of what he did to promote fundamental R&D, by influencing or circumventing the subcommittee system, was visible but rootless, and disappeared as soon as he retired. The opening to the larger context, on the other hand, was an enduring contribution to Alcoa Laboratories.

THE BIG THAW

When Eric Walker joined Alcoa, "Fritz" Close dubbed his friend "vice-president of the future." That private joke expressed their shared wish to promote diversification through research into wholly new product areas and ultimately, perhaps, even abandonment of primary aluminum production. Close was retiring as Walker arrived at Alcoa, but the new vice-president had the full support of John Harper. Introduced as someone hired to consult with "our scientific and technological divisions," Walker's brief was to help reorganize and reform the Research organization. Upon arrival he joined the Patent Committee, chaired by Howard Dunn, and shortly thereafter was charged with responsibility for creating a program for marketing Alcoa's proprietary technology. Those appointments signaled Harper's intention that Walker should have a hand in shaping broad R&D policy.[26]

Eric Walker.

Appraising the Alcoa R&D culture with the critical eye of one who had been hired to change things, Walker found ATC to be so inward-turning that it was almost hermetically sealed against new ideas. It seemed completely preoccupied with company business and its own ATC business. The overwhelming emphasis of the technical program was on short-range problems, a consequence of a research agenda fragmented by many contending interests and of an R&D leadership that had no taste for resisting the tendency to spread the company's technical resources thinly over a vast range of problems. The possibility of research into materials other than aluminum had received no attention, Walker found, and little effort had been put into research of any kind that could not be fully commercialized in one form or another within a few years.

With Harper's blessing, Walker devoted his main attention to reversing the trend toward short-term work. Walker urged Alcoa Laboratories to take on once again the responsibility for being the visionary element in the company, arguing that Alcoa's strategy should include "keeping abreast of new concepts originating or being advanced in the Universities (and other agencies, including government or industry)." Dunn, Newsome, and the director of development, Robert Hampel, were all asked to help form a long-range R&D planning committee outside the existing committee system. Its scope would cover organization, scientific spheres of interest, budget, and physical requirements. Walker noted that "the plan, of course, should be coordinated with the Company's plan for increase in sales, but should also explore new areas which might be profitable to Alcoa."[27]

Newsome and his assistant directors agreed to solicit from the Laboratories division chiefs lists of projects in all the broad categories of aluminum technology where it was agreed that Alcoa should "maintain or establish leadership." They would also look for projects leading to greater diversification. "These programs would, of course, not be subjected to project evaluation," Newsome recorded. Research personnel were urged to come forward with all ideas, including "half-baked ideas," for technology Alcoa might develop in the next decade. They were also urged to suggest ways to enhance the Laboratories' image in the corporation.[28]

The reforms already in progress at the Laboratories could be construed as impediments to the new direction Walker sought. He pointed especially to the way in which the recently popularized management systems might be working against research. "There was the message," reported Newsome to Dunn, "that we are probably trying to go too far with Project Evaluation in Research." Walker also questioned the balance of the program, saying that the $250,000 currently allocated to Directed Fundamental Research (DFR) was not enough:

State-of-the-art Research might be a more appropriate title and funds in this area might be increased to several million dollars. I think that [the state of the art] must include forward-looking research which opens new frontiers for Alcoa.[29]

Newsome admitted that the new views warranted "serious consideration," but Walker's bold approach to the issue made the research managers nervous. They were accustomed to concealing DFR in other categories, and they feared that once visible in the aggregate, such projects would be vulnerable to drastic cuts. "Hopefully the costs would not be assigned as R/D directly, to specific profit centers, but would be considered separately, perhaps as a distributive corporate expense," Walker noted. In fact, corporate money allocated to DFR increased substantially during Walker's tenure. He circumvented the problem of cost allocation by increasing the size of the budgetary pie, rather than by cutting the pieces into different sizes. In that way he avoided taking on Sales and the subcommittee system, both dominated by the mental straitjacket – Walker called it the "sales mentality" – of looking for payout in two years.[30]

Although he criticized the subcommittee system and its effect on the R&D agenda, Walker did not challenge it directly. The system had been enlarged and extended far beyond its original technical aims and was well regarded within the company as an all-purpose coordinating mechanism. By 1969, a network of 100 subcommittees governed Alcoa's affairs, each with its own set of "subcommittees" and its own task forces. Committee meetings served important company purposes: They provided a chance to gain exposure at a companywide level, a chance to make contacts, and a chance for rising stars to gain visibility outside their own organizations. The problem was that with the encompassing of a broader agenda, the system had lost the ability to differentiate between R&D and more immediate kinds of problems. All decisions were made on similar, somewhat political, grounds, and little time was devoted to longer-term matters.[31]

In an attempt to join the system rather than beat it, Walker convinced Harper to form a new R&D Policy Committee superimposed on the subcommittee system, with four "subcommittees" of its own, each charged to push for longer-term projects. Three of these were structured around profit centers – Mill Products, Primary Products, and Subsidiaries and Affiliates – and were assigned to oversee existing subcommittees in related areas of technology. Their role, exercised at the end of the budgetary process, was mainly one of approval. The fourth, which Walker chaired, was the Corporate R&D Committee. It commanded a sizable budget and oversaw committees that Walker considered to be of critical importance to Alcoa's long-term prospects, including Alloy Development, Environmental Control, Finishes, Joining, and New Materials for Fabrication. In addition, the Corporate R&D Committee had a number of special "review and budgeting" assignments that permitted it to initiate projects on its own. A clear distinction was made between the accountability of this committee and those of the other three. While the latter were charged with responsibility for "formulating an R&D program to assure the continued profitability and growth of each production and marketing category," Corporate R&D was to formulate "a program to support the overall R&D effort and to keep abreast of the state-of-the-art [and] a program to support the Company's objectives for growth and diversification into new areas." Clearly Walker had carved a niche for himself within the subcommittee system.[32] (See Appendix B, p. 536.)

For several years, Walker convinced his senior management colleagues to address his priorities by raising the total amount invested in R&D rather than by the more difficult route of shifting money out of the subcommittees' budgets. Between 1970 and 1975, R&D expenditures rose from $24 million to $42 million, a substantial increase, even allowing for inflation, which was running at an all-time high of over 10 percent at the time. Most of the increase went to the Laboratories through the Corporate R&D Committee, while normal development budgets allocated to support work took corresponding cuts. Funding of corporate R&D exceeded $1 million each year.[33] (See Figure 9.7, p. 413.)

Corporate R&D funded new ventures outside the scope of the existing subcommittees, such as exploratory R&D, state-of-the-art research, fundamental work on "mechanisms or processes" not related to any specific commercial effort, and "items of unusually long range, broad scope or significantly beyond known parameters." For 1973, the Laboratories put together a budget for $1.4 million in projects to be funded under these guidelines, the largest chunk of it, about one-fourth, to go to Physical Metallurgy and Chemical Metallurgy for fundamental work related to high-strength alloys. Some of the other projects dealt with aluminum of extremely high purity, superalloys, and superconductivity, and there were "unassigned" funds for exploratory research and new problems that might come up during the year. Walker's high-level promotion of R&D and the money he was able to channel into long-range and fundamental research provided a potent shot in the arm for the Laboratories.[34]

SALE OF TECHNOLOGY

The opening of the R&D community to the outside world that took place on multiple fronts during the years Walker was there included cooperative work with outsiders, better contact with universities, and increased government contracting. Yet by far the greatest opening, with the most dramatic effects, came through the purchase and sale of technology. The news that Alcoa would change its long-standing policy and sell technology reached the Laboratories in July 1970, when it learned that the Anaconda Company, in the midst of a large-scale program to integrate and expand the aluminum segment of its diversified primary-metals business, planned to build a new smelting plant, with Alcoa as engineer-constructor. "This milestone in Alcoa's history," Harper announced, is "a reminder that our technical capability can pay off in many ways."[35]

In a sense, the decision to sell technology to a competitor was simply an acknowledgment of reality: If Alcoa did not build Anaconda's smelter, someone else would. Technology sale was a sign of the times – capital was expensive, and R&D was out of favor, and so many companies in the early 1970s were looking to turn their internally produced technologies into technical assets. Alcoa was in good company, including Dow, DuPont, General Electric, and Reynolds, to name only a few.[36] The new policy could also be seen as one of many steps toward the company's stated goal of diversification. With that in mind, Harper took pains to make clear to the technical community that it should not be viewed as a change in the company's attitude toward safeguarding its ongoing R&D:

You should realize that our sale of this know-how in no way alters our emphasis on developing proprietary processes or our policy of preserving confidential information. We are selling a well-defined package of know-how, and its sale does not mean any change in our concerted drive to develop new and improved processes. In fact, what we are selling to Anaconda is valuable precisely because it is proprietary, and our opportunity to market this know-how package to others will depend upon its remaining so.[37]

Internally, the decision to patent and sell technology was viewed as a victory for R&D, the first time it had prevailed against Sales in over a decade. Sales executives had long opposed sharing any process technology that would allow others to improve the quality of their products, even if they paid for the information through a licensing agreement. Quality, they argued, was Alcoa's strongest suit. As one Sales executive noted, "no royalty, whether it be $\frac{1}{2}$ cents per pound or 2 cents/lb. would really make up for the loss of the competitive advantage we have and hope to enlarge upon." In step with that attitude, official patent policy was basically defensive, tending, as R&D

leaders pointed out, to depress creativity rather than to foster it. "I really think our attitude should be one of aggressiveness," Director of Development J. H. Dunn argued. "There is not much incentive to our people in getting patents from a defensive standpoint, even though at times this might be the logical reason to do so."[38]

Ever since its creation in 1963, Alcoa's Patent Committee had been the battleground for these conflicting points of view. By the late 1960s, Alcoa lagged well behind Kaiser, and particularly behind Reynolds, in the number of patents it was obtaining each year. Armed with that fact, Dunn, as a member of the Patent Committee, undertook a reevaluation of Alcoa's invention-record system, which was supposed to enable and encourage scientists and engineers to put forward their work for possible patenting. Looking over the file of invention records, Dunn concluded that the ideas generally were of high caliber, but were few in number. "Assuming most of our people *must* have had some good ideas," Dunn asked, "why didn't they file Invention Records?" A questionnaire circulated throughout the company revealed that managers did not assume responsibility for implementing the invention-record system, that many people were uninformed of its existence, and that many of those who did know of it were skeptical of its significance. "No action is taken on IR and later a patent on [the] same idea is issued to Kaiser or Reynolds," complained one respondent. Another wrote that "when we turn down trying to get a patent on two IR's from one good man, we can be sure we won't get any more from him."[39]

Dunn's report prompted the Patent Committee to undertake the writing of a manual on patent policy and the invention-record system whose stated purpose was to stimulate creative activity. A further incentive to obtain patents was a new technical awards program, the first awards program at Alcoa connected with R&D. Award recipients received plaques at the annual meeting, which included both laboratory and plant personnel.

Eric Walker's appointment to the Patent Committee, and the decision to sell technology, put patent policy in a completely different light. With Walker and Dunn collaborating, word soon filtered down to Newsome and to Robert Hampel, Dunn's successor as director of development, that suggestions for technology to patent and sell would be welcome. Dunn requested lists of "salable know-how" from each R&D division, and Walker ob-

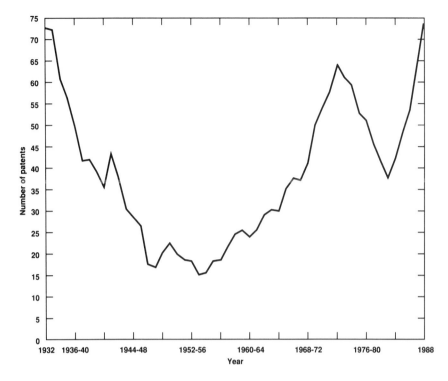

Figure 9.5. Trends in Alcoa patents, 1932–88, five-year averages. Source: Alcoa Patent Department.

tained from John Harper a formal charge "to review our overall patent policy in view of present-day conditions."[40]

Acknowledging that it would constitute a change from existing policy, Harper supported the notion of patenting aggressively, because he saw it as a source of potential revenue. "The alternative," he noted, "has been the loss of know-how by one of several means but with [no] compensation to us." Accordingly, every innovation was to be reviewed with the idea that "it should be blanketed with patent applications unless there is some overriding reason to delay obtaining this protection." Such a policy would protect Alcoa's "lead time" to make use of the innovation in its own plants before licensing it to others and would gain it a competitive advantage in marketing. The virtue of that approach was that if enough patents were issued around any technology, it would be difficult to determine which were the important ones.[41]

Ideas for "salable know-how" began to bubble up at a rapid rate as word of the new initiative spread through the technical community during the winter of 1970–1. From Process Metallurgy, Noel Jarrett proposed many ideas in various stages of development: Hall-Héroult process innovations; three processes for metal purification, including an alternative to the Hoopes three-layer cell; four processes for reclamation of usable metal from scrap and pot skimmings; and five pieces of equipment classified as useful for "general chemical engineering." J. W. Clark, of the Engineering Design Division, suggested selling its expertise in structural design and testing, theoretical and experimental stress analysis, computer programming and mathematical services, and ballistic testing and armor development. The development divisions had more ideas.[42]

So enthusiastic was the response that in February 1971, a small task force, chaired by Eric Walker, was appointed to define a procedure for the sale of know-how. A questionnaire sent out to 350 Alcoans soon generated an inventory of more than a thousand salable items, and a team from the Laboratories met to organize and evaluate that list in July. Only then did serious objections to selling technology begin to surface from cautious Alcoa executives. Those included the quite legitimate points that Alcoa knew how to market aluminum profitably, but not technical services, and that the marketing effort would cost too much. The idea, after all, was to make money with little new investment. There was also the fear that the program would artificially sustain segments of the corporation that "internal requirements" dictated should be cut back.[43]

The new policy on patenting and sale of know-how, hammered out the following year, incorporated a number of significant victories for the marketing side of the debate on patent policy, leaving room for continuation of unpatented protection in the old style and providing for executive review "in cases of major impact on Company profits or potential liability."[44] With Walker pushing hard on technology sale, a Technical Marketing Division (TMD) was formed, with Roger Sharp as manager. The case for aggressive patenting and sale of technology was secured by the success of the new division, especially in the face of declining profits from aluminum sales. In 1975, when after-tax income was a scant $64.8 million, the $7.3 million from sale of technology was very welcome. In 1980 the Patent Committee disbanded, its oversight deemed unnecessary in an area where the issues were no longer in dispute.[45]

The salable technology and expertise that flowed from Alcoa's technical community after 1971 gave visible proof of the degree to which it had been stifled in the preceding years by the heavy burden of secrecy imposed on it. On the plus side, the opening of the doors to the outside world permitted Alcoa to test, for the first time in decades, its revered assumption of technical superiority. That was a chastening experience in some areas. On the negative side, the release of pent-up frustration on the part of an organization that felt unappreciated, coupled with a sense that everyone was doing it, prompted a lack of caution concerning future competitive costs. Before long, the availability of so much previously secret aluminum technology would narrow the gap between the leading producers and new entrants to the industry. That, in turn, would increase Alcoa's need to implement a new generation of process technology. One of the chief places where Alcoa planned to spurt ahead was with its new smelting technology, and, accordingly, it allowed much old Hall-Héroult process technology to go, hoping that that would lead its competitors to commit so much capital to Hall-Héroult that they would be unable to switch.

OPENING AVENUES OUTSIDE

In line with the new policy on technologies, the aluminum chloride cell was "blanketed with patents" in preparation for its public emergence as ASP in January 1973, while plans progressed for a pilot plant in Anderson County, Texas. Yet even as the project moved forward, there was growing fear that unsolved problems in the production of aluminum chloride would doom the new facility to commercial failure. To give it maximum attention, a special committee was formed, including Harper's heir apparent, Krome George, Walker, and others. Its charge was to develop an alternative to the proposed chemical reactor for the production of aluminum chloride. Walker's stamp was on these proceedings, for they quickly moved toward calling in an outside firm, Lummus Engineering, to help design an improved chemical plant.[46]

A few years earlier, such an admission of need for outside technical help would have been unthinkable. In 1974, however, the company formally acknowledged that there were many areas in which it was not the technical leader and could

Robert Hampel.

no longer be self-sufficient. It was willing to purchase as well as sell technology. Roger Sharp's TMD, having established the contacts and skills required in such transactions, was given that responsibility.[47]

Walker's hand was also evident in the appointment of Robert Hampel, then director of development, as director of technical development, reporting to Walker. Hampel's role in this newly created post was not only to take over responsibility from Howard Dunn for the subcommittee system but also to coordinate the company's efforts to transfer technology both inside the firm and to the market. He was also asked to implement a project approach to R&D management by setting up multidisciplinary, task-specific project teams and by organizing and staffing "joint venture activities and cooperative programs of a major nature with outside companies and universities."[48]

Acceptance of government funding for research was another significant change in policy that Walker influenced in the early 1970s. Burned by the outcome of the postwar patent dispute, Alcoa had remained largely aloof during the boom in contract research of the 1950s and 1960s, and only under Harper's leadership did it begin to relax its aversion to taking government money. The first small proposals for government funding were made in 1959, and from then until 1963 its government awards totaled a little over $1 million, about half going to ARL for research. The level of government-funded R&D then increased slowly, never exceeding $1 million in any one year.[49]

The only areas to seek government funding were those involved in alloy development, materials testing, and design and construction of specific pieces of military equipment. It was pointless to try to maintain complete secrecy in those areas, because the military services and the industries serving them had a policy against buying materials from only one source. Though Alcoa viewed alloy development as one of its strongest areas of technical leadership, there was no advantage in proprietary technology and no reason other than tradition that R&D in that area should forgo support from the federal government.

As a leader of the postwar big-science community, Eric Walker knew that contract research was an important avenue of communication between the Laboratories and the external R&D community. As with the restrictive patent policy, the chief disadvantage of Alcoa's insularity lay in the negative effects it had on research personnel, foreclosing contacts between Alcoa scientists and the contract-research network, which had become a far more important factor in the scientific professions after World War II. In August 1971, Walker presented to the R&D Committee, as a fait accompli, a policy statement on government contracts that called for increasing the level of participation "to the point that about 10 percent of our total R&D efforts at any one time might be employed in that direction." Walker presented that to the R&D Committee, and especially to its chairman, Howard Dunn, primarily on its financial merits:

We can regard the [government] research as being desirable if we can get the government to pay for some work which we might do anyway or because the early involvement in a Research and Development project will give us an inside track on a future production contract.[50]

To increase the level of government funding, Walker took several measures to promote increased interaction between Alcoa scientists and their counterparts in government laboratories. As in the past, formal relationships would continue to be managed by the company's Government Market Development Office in Washington. In addition, Walker proposed appointing a government-contracts coordinator to work at ATC overseeing proposal writing and making sure that "all the boiler plate has been added." The impetus for research still had to come from the scientists themselves, who would shape the technical content of proposals and conduct or direct the work. "Personal meetings between government scientists and Alcoa scientists will often be desirable," he stressed, "and these can be arranged directly." Though no commitments should be made under such circumstances, Walker clearly envisioned the kind of open dialogue that had long been suppressed as a matter of policy.[51]

Though Alcoa saw a benefit in accepting government funding for selected parts of its R&D program because of the excitement that the leading-edge work offered to researchers, the company still avoided sharing any of its processes through those channels. That became an issue in the late 1970s, when the defense agencies began to place greater emphasis on technology transfer among its contractors. For the most part, the company continued to refuse work under any contracts specify-

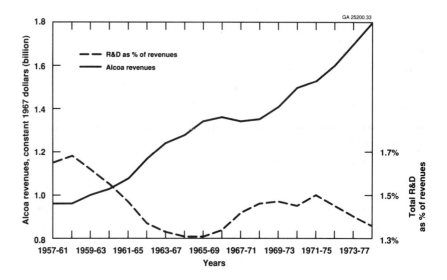

Figure 9.6. Trends in R&D spending, 1957–78, five-year averages. Sources: "Relation of Technical Budget Expenditures to Consolidated Net Revenues and Operating Margins," AA-Boyers; Smith, *From Monopoly to Competition*, Table B-2; R. E. Spear, "Population and Budget History," 15 December 1987, ALA; Consumer Price Index from *Statistical Abstract*.

ing that resulting technology had to be made available to all producers under royalty-free licenses.[52]

John Harper and Eric Walker retired at the same time, in 1975. The transition occurred just as the company's revenues took the first precipitous drop on the economic roller-coaster ride that would usher in the 1980s. The days of fat budgets and acknowledgment of fundamental R&D came to an abrupt end as Alcoa entered its most extreme period of top-management dictation to R&D. Harper's successor, Krome George, was a finance-minded executive who had never been comfortable with the changes Walker had tried to make. Because Walker had worked through top management and around the system, rather than by changing either the people in the R&D organization or its fundamental relations with the rest of the corporation, his most obvious policies were easy to reverse. Moreover, his highlighting of fundamental research, by putting it in visible budget categories, made it much easier to eliminate than ever before. Under the conditions of the mid-1970s, when sudden changes in the economic environment certainly seemed to justify emergency measures, the corporation rejected the new per-

W. H. Krome George.

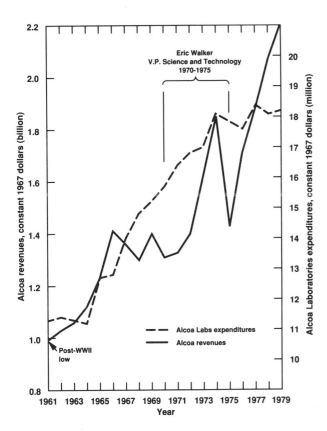

Figure 9.7. Alcoa Laboratories expenditures, 1961–79. Sources: Smith, *From Monopoly to Competition*, Table B-2; Spear, "Population and Budget History," 15 December 1987, ALA; Consumer Price Index from *Statistical Abstract*.

spectives Walker had tried to introduce as the unsuitable ideas of an outsider.

R&D UNDER SIEGE

Krome George left no doubt about the revolution he proposed to effect in R&D. He quickly abolished Walker's superstructure of high-level subcommittees, directed the R&D Policy Committee to meet jointly with the Executive Operating Committee, and moved toward giving the operating divisions authority to establish R&D priorities, review programs, and determine budget allocations. Most companies had only recently instituted high-level R&D committees to relate R&D to company strategy. But for Alcoa, where such linkages had been in existence in some form since the depression of the 1930s, it could be argued that the idea was about to be taken to logical, dysfunctional, extremes.[53]

R&D was the only part of the company that, so far, had not made sacrifices in a time of general belt-tightening; while the rest of the corporation had been cut back, its expenditures had increased significantly during Walker's vice-presidency. George halted the growth in R&D budgets, and he set his own new priorities for R&D based on factors that he identified as critical. They included external conditions (environmental restrictions, the continuing energy crisis, and the rising cost of bauxite), the economic climate that held down prices, the difficulty of raising capital, and the need to reduce "supervisory costs" in R&D as elsewhere in the corporation. All of these factors, George said, dictated a single guiding principle, which he spelled out as no new product or market, just improved process and efficiency. At the level of corporate strategy, George's philosophy mandated commitment to primary production. That led, within a few years, to increased investment overseas, with new smelting capacity in Australia and a major new joint venture in aluminum refining and smelting in Brazil. In its own way, that policy of costly overseas expansion in developing areas would prove to be as much a straitjacket for Research as direct budget cuts.[54]

The philosophy George espoused was by no means unique to Alcoa. Faced with expensive costs of capital and other significant trends in the national climate for R&D, companies that were acknowledged leaders in industrial R&D, such as DuPont and Dow, were drawing in their horns. They cited uncertainties about government policy that might affect them (such as government regulation and energy policy), the consumer movement, and increasing pressures from company managements to demonstrate why their companies needed short-term payoffs from R&D. Acknowledging that his policy spelled continuing reductions in spending for research, George suggested that no real damage would result, provided the appropriate steps were taken "to assure the utmost performance by our R&D personnel." He added:

It will not be an easy task to redirect our R&D efforts as this memorandum describes, preserve the Company's long-standing technological leadership, continue emphasis on creativity and maintain an environment in which technological advancement can continue to flourish. It can and must be done.[55]

The task of following through on that somewhat improbable scenario fell to R&D managers Robert Hampel and Allen Russell, who became vice-presidents when Howard Dunn retired in September 1974. Russell, who had been a leader in the development of the Alcoa Smelting Process, became head of Alcoa Laboratories, while Hampel continued as head of technical development. Both men reported to William C. Woodward, assistant to the president, and a stranger to R&D.

Hampel began his new job in 1976 by once again revamping the subcommittee system. He issued a call to the newly appointed committee members to take their responsibilities seriously and to abandon any provincial attitudes they might be tempted to bring to their work. Following George's guidelines, Hampel turned over the annual budget-making process to the R&D Policy Committee and urged that the subcommittees confine their activities to a high-level planning function, matching the level of R&D request to the level of strategic need. The key change was that subcommittees no longer simply allocated funding; they dictated the program as well. The job of executing the plans was given to the task forces.[56]

Although that system apparently left managers at the Laboratories with only the task of "interleaving" the projects that had been approved and prioritized into a program of R&D, their role was not necessarily passive. With one-third representation in the subcommittee system, and with the secretaries to the subcommittees invariably coming from their own organization, R&D leaders were still in a good position to propose projects for the subcommittees to consider, and they had the opportunity to shape their deliberations. Moreover, by reformulating project-description forms, called "D-sheets," to cover funding for a two-year period, Hampel hoped to "obtain a longer horizon" at that stage of the process and at the same time gain greater control at the top. He also initiated a program of "continuous budgeting" under which, initially, 95 percent of the yearly budget was allocated in the fall in the traditional process, and the rest at quarterly intervals throughout the year. Gradually the system moved toward more uniform allocations. The idea was to permit greater flexibility and "to foster new project submission throughout the year." Still, the overriding objectives of all these measures were to make the operating side of the corporation take ownership of the budget-making process and to render it transparent to the scrutiny of top management.[57]

BUSINESS UNITS AND R&D

Beginning in 1978, Hampel moved to implement George's directives more fully by restructuring the categories of R&D to permit allocation to the business units. Hampel's conception of the "emerging business units concept" was that business units should take ownership of the subcommittees that served them and assume responsibility for planning for all of their own technical needs. He modified the budget allocations to give them complete control:

Each Business Unit and each Subcommittee should now be ready to accept the responsibility for developing its ability to be responsive to changing conditions 10 or 15 years in the future and therefore the accountability for its own long-range R&D.[58]

Hampel's reform was partially successful, but his hopes of encouraging the business units to take a long-range view proved overly optimistic. The new budgeting format certainly allowed them to enforce their views more effectively on the process of R&D planning, but they accepted the prevailing attitude in many market areas that aluminum had matured to the point where money spent on new-product development and new-market penetration would be money down the drain. As one business-unit executive noted, "cash flow and return on investment is the name of the game."[59]

Looking back on that period, some Laboratories leaders later wondered why they had not exercised the authority they had at the time. As custodians of technology, they certainly had considerable power over technical choices, had they chosen to exercise it. Some subcommittees invited R&D initiatives, asking the Laboratories leaders what they thought the program should be. But the technical community at the time apparently was overawed in the face of the new techniques for economic evaluation and business planning and was not prepared to play a leadership role.[60]

The Project Evaluation System, combined with the reformed

subcommittee system, enforced a bias toward short-term thinking in the research community. Only projects that could be planned, justified, budgeted, and timed with a fair degree of certainty could be successful in the new planning structure. That virtually ruled out the kinds of uncertain projects that might lead to major new growth markets. R&D managers in 1978 warned program planners about "frequent criticisms" concerning R&D staff, who, they said, were seen as more interested in working on problems than solving them, not dealing with realistic schedules, creating unnecessary projects to sustain their existence, and not dealing with the real cost of R&D.[61]

Hampel's device for sustaining the more delicate aspects of the R&D program was to keep some broad programs – alloy development, energy, environmental control, finishes, joining, and product standards – under a separate, Corporate R&D Committee, which had three task forces on long-range technical policy: Processes, New Ventures, and Fundamentals. But by the time he retired in 1980, Hampel was discouraged about that aspect of what he had tried to accomplish. "The Committee has not produced the results I envisioned," he wrote, and "as I have mentioned from time to time, it is difficult to find Officers, and others of stature, who have interest in, let alone affirmative convictions about, the scope and direction of this Committee."[62]

Efforts to draw forth long-range R&D by tinkering with the subcommittee system continued into the 1980s, with few significant results. Long-term work in some areas was pursued in spite of the subcommittee system, supported by government funding or by top-management commitment, but rarely by the business units. Only after 1981, when a severe downturn in the industry undermined the validity of the key assumptions on which the strategy of the late 1970s had been based, did business units recognize the need for serious technical work of a longer-term nature.

In 1982 the Operating Committee abolished the R&D Policy Committee, declaring its intention "to focus increased attention on technology and its importance to the Company's activities in the future." Corporate managers who were sympathetic to long-range work understood that it needed to be shielded from contact with the Operating Committee. Marvin Gantz, chairman of the Subcommittee for Corporate R&D, warned its members that they would have to carry the ball, nurturing a few fundamental and long-range projects.[63]

By that time, the R&D community had relinquished much of its role in, and therefore its potential influence on, the subcommittees. In an era of overwhelming emphasis on productivity, managers at the Laboratories viewed the investment in manpower required to play an active part in the subcommittee system as too costly. At the same time, however, they had begun to work *outside* the system to establish a program through which they could eventually develop the means to take their own systematic look into the future. In 1975, Robert Spear, assistant director in charge of ingot casting, was introduced to the subject of technology planning at an executive education seminar. Shortly thereafter, he persuaded Allen Russell to let him set up a two-man team for technology planning and forecasting, composed of Norman Cochran and Charles Yohn, who soon began to involve laboratory directors in producing 10-year forecasts for their technologies. Over time, the mode of systematic long-range thinking they introduced took root at the Laboratories, and the organization gained the ability to relate its program to the strategic concerns of the firm.[64]

Robert Spear.

Collateral efforts began at Alcoa headquarters. In 1979, President William B. Renner decided to add to the task forces of the Committee for Corporate R&D Projects a new group called the Major Projects Search Team. "Many of you will recall," said Renner, "that we have tried several times to develop new ideas from our people and to date very little has resulted. I suspect this might be because the efforts have not had the endorsement or dedication of management." By that time, aided by its new planning perspective, Alcoa Laboratories was ready to begin promoting its own work by identifying different aspects of it with strategic-thrust areas. The next step, which took a few more years, was to begin to "cast a forward shadow," identifying technologies as yet unfamiliar to the rest of the company that would, or could, have a major impact on Alcoa's future business.[65]

THE R&D PROGRAM IN THE SEVENTIES

Four kinds of activities accounted for most of the R&D program in the late 1970s. ASP, or chemical work related to ASP,

Recycling facility at the Warrick plant in Indiana.

continued to dominate the longer-term efforts. Externally related work having to do with environmental programs and energy technologies accounted for a second component. Environmental projects made a steadily increasing claim on the Laboratories' budget; a subcommittee on environmental control was
created in 1971, and from 1975 onward it was one of the largest
items under the budget category of corporate R&D. Aside from
recycling, the bulk of this money was directed toward pollution
control at Alcoa's plants. A substantial chunk was also spent on
developing processes to recover soda and usable solids from

red-mud lakes, a project directed by Allen Russell when he became vice-president for science and technology in 1978.[66]

Alloy researchers had little inside funding, but they found support through government funding. Once they had finished with the advanced casting projects, casting researchers applied their knowledge of solidification to the reverse problems of melting raised by recycling. The fabrication researchers whose work pertained to mill products found the slimmest pickings and felt the most completely excluded. They worked on projects to apply rolling theory to mill control, pursued improvements in the aluminum food can, and continued to try to attract auto-company interest in the aluminum car. But as one of their research directors later observed, for them, the period from 1975 to 1982 was a "seven year hibernation."[67]

Allen Russell's leadership as director of Alcoa Laboratories was devoted mainly to furthering the ASP project, for which he had long been an effective advocate. Russell had no personal research agenda in other areas, and he never tried to become an independent voice in management circles. On the other hand, in a way that Van Horn, for instance, would never have done, Russell allowed a strong cadre of second-level R&D managers to develop around him. Those individuals quietly developed their skills in managing technology, managing contacts with the outside world, and generally making it possible for the Laboratories to be a more effective technology resource for the company at large. When Russell moved to Pittsburgh as vice-president, his successor as Laboratories director, Kenneth Brondyke, continued that policy of allowing strong group leadership. The managers in question – Robert LaBarge, Wayne Binger, Robert Spear, James Dowd, and Noel Jarrett – provided the nucleus for the second Laboratories reform that took place in the early 1980s. Part of the impetus for that reform came from the central management. But another source was the reaction to having gone through a period when so much of the Laboratories' total program was focused on smelting technology.[68]

In 1976, Russell outlined the Laboratories' program for the coming year for the new Strategic Planning Committee. About 25 percent of the budget was allocated to ASP and Hall-Héroult process research, and close to 60 percent was earmarked for work supporting well-established markets, such as containers, flat-rolled products, and automotive products. The research objectives within these market categories were heavily focused on cost reduction and product support. Russell acknowledged to the strategic planners that the developments sought were almost entirely incremental in nature. But, he argued, their effects would be cumulative and would contribute to continuing cost reductions.[69]

Asked to speculate for top management about Alcoa's possible future high-growth markets, Russell suggested railroad cars, solar energy, and strong aluminum wire. Privately he acknowledged that the emphasis in the program was not going down well in some circles at the Laboratories. As he noted to Fred Fetterolf,

> you are correct that many of our R&D people look on our program as too short range. Since I think the program overall is about right this year, I have to share with you any resulting criticism. I do not sense this as a major source of unhappiness at the Tech Center. Most people work diligently on the approved programs.[70]

That the program was short-range in emphasis, and likely to continue so, was evident in Hampel's response to a University of Pennsylvania survey conducted in 1977. After consultation with top management, Hampel projected a 2 percent allocation to "basic research" through 1980. Projects expected to last longer than five years were on the decline, from 15 percent in 1967 to 10 percent and falling in 1977. The same trend held for wholly new products or processes: A decade earlier 25 percent of the R&D budget would have been so aimed, and in 1977 the figure was 15 percent. In 1980 it would be 10 percent. With the new system in place, Hampel hoped to reduce "risky" projects to zero by 1980. In answer to the question "What factors do you regard as important in causing the decline in basic longer term and more risky R&D?" Hampel listed maturity of the aluminum market, limitation of basic supply, lesser need to create demand, and increased interest in cash-flow optimization.[71]

Once again Alcoa was in good company. R&D-performing institutions throughout the United States at that time were emphasizing improvement of existing products and processes in the belief that the return on such investments would be considerably more secure than the return on innovative projects. Criticizing unfavorable government policies toward industrial R&D, one thoughtful article in a major R&D journal cited five "causative factors" as determinants of more cautious U.S. industrial policies toward research: top-management control of the R&D function; past innovations leading to current development emphasis; erosion of corporate profitability; government support, regulation, and intervention; and energy problems.[72]

Although all of the foregoing factors influenced R&D decisions at Alcoa, the overriding factor in determining R&D budgets and program was undoubtedly the opportunity cost of ASP. The Anderson County pilot plant in Palestine, Texas, opened in 1976, two and one-half years and millions of dollars after ground was first broken. In the meantime, ASP continued to labor under the burden of unsolved technical problems involving the chemical train and pollution control. Those required continuing heavy R&D expenses. In addition, there were underlying economic problems. Despite its elegance and efficiency, the aluminum chloride cell still depended both on the Bayer process and on its expensive chemical reactor to obtain aluminum chloride for electrolysis. A separate R&D program was therefore set up to develop a completely new process to make aluminum chloride by chlorination of clay.[73]

What made the ASP project so attractive in the mid-1970s, despite its continued difficulties, was the continuing high cost of energy following the OPEC price increases. As the money poured into ASP from all directions, it came increasingly to be seen as "the most important project ever undertaken by Alcoa." With one such large investment in "forward-looking" R&D, no others seemed either affordable or necessary to maintain Alcoa's public image as a technical leader. While the effect of that attitude on other areas of research was devastating, within the field of primary processes ASP brought a windfall of unanticipated benefits.[74]

Krome George once recounted a story of a visit to Alcan's Arvida smelter during the 1960s, when the competition among aluminum producers to develop an alternative to the Hall-Héroult process was at its height. He was chatting with the plant manager, "a good old traditional Hall process guy," and pointed to the building where, he knew, they were working on their direct-reduction process, recently announced as a major breakthrough. George asked the plant manager, "Joe, what's that big tower over there?" Joe answered, "Oh, we call that the shrine." "Why do you call it the shrine?" George returned. Joe replied, "Cause that's where the miracle is going to happen." "Sarcastic as hell!" George noted.[75]

A decade later, that joke might have described the attitude that ASP evoked in some of Alcoa's own "good old traditional Hall process guys." Nevertheless, the alternative-process work helped to stimulate highly creative responses among Hall-process researchers. Although support for work on the Hall-Héroult process was always cut first when budgets were slashed, whenever there was time and money, Noel Jarrett and others in Process Metallurgy worked furiously to apply all they had learned from ASP to other processes. In the mid-1970s that work had strong management backing because of its potential value as salable technology. By 1975, Technology Marketing had firmly established that Alcoa could no longer compete in the smelting area with 15-year-old pot designs. That determination quickly opened the way to a new investment in developing more efficient, environmentally sound Hall-Héroult technology, and budget allocations at the Laboratories for that purpose soon began to rival those for ASP.[76]

Smelting researchers pointed out that a whole range of primary processes could flow from the fundamental work that had been carried on under ASP. One of these, they noted, was a direct-reduction process for making aluminum-silicon alloy, which could then be used in the Hoopes refining process to produce commercial-grade aluminum. They anticipated that a purification process producing pure aluminum from alloys could be perfected to supplant the Hall-Héroult process. The strategic implications of that idea went well beyond the highest hopes for ASP. In the short run there would be a ready market for the aluminum-silicon alloy. "Concurrently we could be working on electrolytic purification schemes that could lead Alcoa to have a non-electrolytic process (or at least have greatly reduced the use of electric power in the smelting of aluminum) after we have sold our competitors the Alcoa Smelting Process.[77]

In 1979, continued technical problems with the pilot plant in Anderson County, Texas, in particular difficulties with the slurry reactor in the chemical plant, made it necessary to delay the next planned scale-up toward full-scale production. The production work force was cut back, and the Anderson County works became an R&D facility dedicated to resolving the remaining technical problems with ASP in conjunction with the smelting researchers at the Technical Center. C. Fred Fetterolf, operations manager for mill products, took over coordination of the ASP project and reorganized the ASP Subcommittee to support him. Fetterolf was committed to resolving all the remaining uncertainties and putting the plant back on schedule for full-scale production by 1987. Over many objections that too rapid a scale-up was risky in the absence of complete understanding, he pushed hard for aggressive timetables and for holding the line on budgeted development costs.

Two years of work on parallel approaches to the chemical reactor – the slurry system and a high-temperature fluidized bed – eventually produced an ASP system that would work. But as analyses by outside consultants (Resource Planning Associates) and by inside evaluators showed, ASP's previous economic advantages over the Hall-Héroult process, still rapidly improving in efficiency and in environmental control, had dwindled to a draw. Moreover, by 1981 Alcoa was suffering severe capital constraints that made the required immediate investment in the intermediate chemical-plant stages very unattractive.

In 1982 the combination of an abundant and increasing aluminum scrap supply and growing aluminum capacity abroad called into question the wisdom of adding further smelting capacity in the foreseeable future. Anaconda, which had been interested in sharing in ASP development, wanted to know why it made sense to spend so much money on a break-even proposition. Though Alcoa declared its intention to continue ASP research work in the Laboratories, delay in scaling up from the 42-inch version to the 8-foot version of the reactor effectively put an end to further ASP development.[78]

CASTING BECOMES RECYCLING

Meanwhile, dividends were flowing from the work that had been done on HDC casting. As the possessor of the only casting laboratory large enough to do research on full-size ingot, Alcoa had a unique advantage in the industry well into the 1970s. Indeed, for a time it was the only company to have the capability to cast large-size 7075 ingot, a major requirement of the aircraft producers. At the same time, the fundamental work that had been done on solidification made it possible for a small new effort to begin on recycling, for solidification and melting were two sides of the same basic coin. Work on a continuous, high-speed melting process to match the continuous-casting process already in operation at Warrick began in 1969. The key problem to be solved was to turn cans back into cans. Competitors like Reynolds were using aluminum scrap for die casting, but obtaining "pure" metal was a much more difficult matter.[79]

Funded at first largely by external grants, the recycling program demonstrated an important lesson in technology management. In the late 1960s, expansion of the recycling program beyond the obligatory accommodation of scrap from the immediate system was viewed only in terms of its public-relations appeal. Those who believed that Alcoa's future was staked on its primary smelting business were naturally skeptical of an aggressive recycling program intended to reuse the maximum amount of aluminum as an environmental measure. To them, it was little more than a consumer nuisance. But having become oriented toward thinking more broadly about technology forecasting and the possible convergences of social and technical trends, the Laboratories casting group envisioned a scenario in which recycled aluminum could account for a major segment of "raw-materials" supply.[80]

Recycling was barely tolerated within much of the Alcoa community from 1978 to 1982, but because of that it had the advantage of proceeding at its own unhurried pace. When, in 1982, the company faced the radical realization that market conditions would no longer justify further investment in smelters, recycled aluminum offered an economical and publicly popular way of increasing capacity and market penetration. The program was also one of the first credible signs that the Laboratories might be able once again to offer its own independent technical vision.

THE EXPANDING RESEARCH ENVIRONMENT

One of the more controversial consequences of Alcoa's policies of the 1960s and 1970s was the decision to buy, rather than make, some of the major new process technologies that went into plant modernization. For example, what proved to be a highly successful adoption of a noninteractive control system for automating rolling mills was at first viewed as a judgment and a threat against those engaged in fabrication R&D at the Laboratories. Later, it came to exemplify the way in which creative borrowing could increase R&D productivity without sacrificing technical leadership. During a decade of collaboration with Broner, an English consulting firm, Alcoa acquired not only an important technology but also the core of a new body of knowledge that the Laboratories could appropriate and extend without hiring permanent new technical staff.

Central Engineering turned to the outside consultants in 1978, after they had worked with the English steel industry developing model-based computer software to control cold-rolling mills. The Broner system was designed to eliminate factors that made it difficult to operate rolling mills in a completely automatic mode. It was also intended to standardize rolling-mill setups and reduce setup downtime, a problem that was particularly costly for mills that produced a wide variety of products. The Laboratories put together an interdisciplinary team, combining its own laboratory staff and plant engineers, to work with these consultants on adapting the computer models for one Warrick cold mill. That done, the team then moved from plant to plant extending the technology both to hot-rolling mills and to mills for cold-rolled products other than can sheet. Not only were the new controls highly successful in reducing scrap and increasing quality, but the knowledge gained about advanced rolling models formed the basis for a computer simulation of the rolling process that made possible a continuing fundamental program on rolling technology at the Laboratories.[81]

Like the work with Lummus Engineering on the chemical-reactor phase of ASP, the Broner collaboration served to open up the R&D community to new approaches and new bodies of knowledge and to demonstrate alternatives to the simple make-or-buy option of the earlier era. If Alcoa Laboratories was no longer able to cover all the technical bases, it could still serve as the main channel by which the company could acquire leading-edge technology. Moreover, if the technology it borrowed could be had on an exclusive basis, as in the Broner case, it could become as much of a competitive advantage as completely proprietary work. The realization of that fact did much to dispel

The cold-rolling mill installed in Building B of the Alcoa Technical Center in the early 1970s was brought up from the New Kensington plant when it was closed down. Adapted for computer control, it allowed Alcoa researchers for the first time to try out their computer-control research at their own facility, the way smelting and casting researchers had been able to do at the ARL and Arnold facilities.

the "not invented here" response that plagued many U.S. R&D establishments in the 1970s.

The work with the noninteractive control system generated useful technologies and fostered skills in more effective technology transfer between Research and Operations. The Laboratories' positive response to that and to other instances of technology borrowing contrasted with the response of Alcoa's central Engineering Department, which was becoming less effective in the transfer of technology into the plants. In the late 1970s, Engineering, as an organization, concentrated on earning payoffs for its old skills by selling plants to outside buyers. Traditionally, Engineering had taken responsibility for transferring equipment developed by the engineering development organization, AEDD. In the late 1970s it adopted a strategy of buying turnkey innovations (ready to use with little adaptation) from outside suppliers. The result was that its own skill base was becoming obsolete, especially its mastery of computer technologies. In the early 1980s, much of the Engineering organization was broken up and dispersed to the plants, leaving a void that the Laboratories were challenged to fill.

Building on the good experiences with Lummus and Broner, the corporate policy supporting purchase as well as sale of technologies opened the way to a few cooperative ventures. One of those was a program with Delft University, in the Netherlands, to develop an aluminum-laminate composite, dubbed ARALL. One of the very few new-product developments before 1983, ARALL later became the basis for a more extended program on high-strength materials.[82]

Other forms of outside contact picked up more slowly in the late 1970s. The pursuit of government contracts did not reach the 10 percent target level for funding that had been set by Eric Walker. Successful contract research depended on building relationships between researchers at Alcoa and technical personnel within the government, and that was a slow process. Encouragement from above and the establishment of a full-time contracts coordinator at ATC had an immediate but temporary impact: The amount of contract work rose sharply in 1977–8, but fell back again thereafter. Moreover, the range of such work expanded relatively little outside the long-established pattern of alloy development, corrosion testing, and structural-design work for military systems.[83]

Nevertheless, Alcoa's widening contract network gave researchers a chance both to benchmark their own work and to establish closer contacts with the external scientific community. And soon it began to produce unexpected opportunities. Late in 1980, J. W. Evancho, recently appointed manager of technical development under Hampel, received an article noting the development of superplastic aluminum alloys by Rockwell International. It contained a scribbled note: "This is the type of work Alcoa should be doing." Evancho discovered, on investigating the matter, that researchers in Alloy Technology had repeatedly been turned down when they had proposed work on superplasticity to the Committee for Corporate R&D. Familiar with the technology through contract work to produce materials for Rockwell's development program, they had ideas of their own they wanted to try. "The bright side of the matter," Evancho noted, "is that our people have not given up and continue to pursue their ideas by whatever means may be available."[84]

Table 9.1. *Million-dollar R&D accomplishments, top ten, 1976–80*

Description	Rank	1981 value (millions)
Reduce fines in smelting-grade alumina	1	$57
6009 and 6010 auto-body-sheet alloys	2	$35
Tight-gauge sheet expansion, Tennessee	3	$30
Alloy change for painted trailer sheet	4	$26
Axial-flow pump for continuous scrap melting	5	$26
Determine sulfur dioxide distribution in Rockdale lignite	6	$21
B-52 reformed beer and beverage end	7	$18
Redesign B-53 can bottom to reduce gauge	8	$18
Chrysler R-car one-piece bumper	9	$12
Computer aids to mine planning	10	$ 8

That experience validated the argument for government work, for the state of preparedness Evancho saw in alloy researchers had a lot to do with their familiarity, through government contacts, with the materials field. In alloy development, researchers with government backing had been able to do work that no subcommittee would have funded. A team working on splat quenching – a method for rapid solidification of molten alloys – for instance, turned to the U.S. Air Force in 1979 when that work was abandoned by Alcoa in favor of strip-casting techniques that were nearer to commercialization. In 1981, when the corporation once again became interested in splat quenching, the work was still alive because of a three-year, government-funded program and was ready to move ahead rapidly. Likewise, the Naval Air Systems Command supported fundamental research in new-alloy development, sustaining Alcoa's program during the years in which the mature-market mentality would otherwise have shut it down. Thanks to that support, Alcoa Laboratories was already on the way to developing a new generation of high-strength aircraft alloys when that became an important objective.[85]

To be sure, creative accomplishments were not limited to work outside the purview of subcommittee funding, as they might have been in companies with little interaction between product and process work. Alcoa researchers were always aware of the

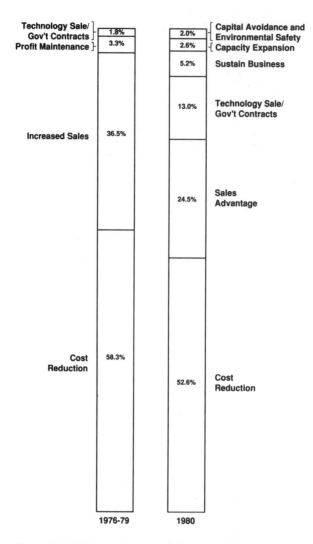

Figure 9.8. R&D major accomplishments by category (categories redefined in 1980). Source: C. P. Yohn, "Five-Year Summary and Assessment of R&D Major Accomplishment Evaluations," 14 August 1981, ALA.

enticing project possibilities that could arise in even the most mundane problem-solving circumstances. In 1981, Charles P. Yohn, a statistician and technical planner whose job it was to calculate such measures, compiled a list of 25 "million-dollar accomplishments" made by R&D in 1980, all in alloy development or process improvement and control, and most of which had been sponsored through the subcommittee system. On his top-10 list for 1976 to 1980, he presented innovations with "present value" between $11 million and $57 million. Yet these were low-risk projects, the value of which was due primarily to their larger scale, prompting technical managers to remark that research had come to mean high-difficulty engineering. In the early 1980s, the company, which had come to look on ATC mainly as a short-order, technical-service organization with side interests in alloys, quality control, and ASP, wanted more from its technical community. That led corporate management to examine the R&D organization and its program more closely and, for the first time in many years, in a new light.[86]

R&D TURNAROUND

The turnaround for R&D began in 1981, when Fred Fetterolf, head of operations for mill products, did an eight-month stint as vice-president for science and technology, a post that then included oversight of Alcoa Laboratories. Fetterolf was en route to the vice-presidency for mill products and later, in 1983, the presidency of the corporation. His short tenure in science and technology framed a period of serious examination of the problems that seemed to beset Alcoa Laboratories. Early in 1981 he visited the research facilities of other companies, including Minnesota Mining and Manufacturing and General Electric, to examine and discuss alternative structures and policies for R&D. During the same period, Alcoa's board of directors devoted a series of meetings to similar issues.[87]

C. F. Fetterolf.

Other developments at the top of the company signaled revived interest in planning for technology. In January 1982, a new office was added in Pittsburgh for technology planning, with G. Keith Turnbull, formerly from the Laboratories and later a member of the corporate planning staff, as director, Charles Yohn as manager, and C. Norman Cochran as technology forecaster. The new arrangement placed both technology planning and the Laboratories directly under Marvin E. Gantz, Jr., vice-chairman of the corporation. The placement of the Office of Technology Planning at corporate headquarters, reporting directly to Gantz, was significant. Turnbull had been an advocate for risk-taking and excellence in technology at a time when that position was unpopular. Both Cochran and Yohn came from Alcoa Laboratories, where they had been working since 1980 on a long-range technical plan for ATC. Together these men began to challenge Alcoa's senior executives to consider its technical strategy as part of broader company strategy. Within the Committee for Corporate R&D, Yohn's ideas and the statistics he compiled to support them began to receive serious attention and were passed along to the Operating Committee and the board of directors.

Yohn argued strongly in favor of shifting the R&D "portfolio" away from heavy investment in process technologies, such as ASP, that promised a relatively low return for the money spent and toward others, such as recycling, that promised a higher return. The main emphasis, however, should be on new applications and new products. Yohn summarized his criteria for R&D in the 1980s as the following: minimal effort on capital-intensive technologies; process-improvement R&D focused on cost reduction, with minimum capital; increased work on product differentiation; increased support for new products and applications; provision of seed money for pioneering work on revolutionary technology. In short, he suggested no less than complete reversal of the policies of the 1970s.[88]

Also seeping into top-level discussions was the information, gained largely through Technology Marketing, that Alcoa was losing out by keeping its technical activities so secret and its technical community so isolated from the world outside. Early in 1981, Krome George and others on the Technical Policy Committee heard, and after lengthy discussion concurred with, the arguments of Robert F. Slagle:

Alcoa's percentage contribution to the total R&D effort of the Industry has dropped considerably since the 1960s. There is a significant increase in R&D effort by companies other than Alcoa to advance the state-of-the-art of aluminum technology. . . . The net result is [that] Alcoa may be falling behind.[89]

The committee agreed to remedy the situation by accelerating the kinds of activities the Laboratories had started to encourage, including fostering cooperative work with university researchers, expanding relationships with outside consultants, and moderating policies that restricted professional activities. It was also agreed to seek closer working relationships with customers to develop new technologies, modelled on the relationship with Ford in a program to sell auto-body sheet and that with Boeing to develop aircraft alloy. For the first time, Alcoa's leaders acknowledged the possibility that its determination to keep its technology all to itself may have cost the company as much as its competitors.

LABORATORIES REFORM AGAIN

Faced with this new set of expectations and opportunities, Alcoa's R&D management, led by a reluctant Kenneth Brondyke, took steps in 1981 and 1982 to reorient as quickly as possible. Never an easy task, that reorientation was made more difficult and painful by the fact that the aluminum business was once again in a severe downturn in the early 1980s. In 1982, Alcoa Laboratories was required to reduce its staff by 10 percent in compliance with a companywide program, called an overhead value analysis (OVA), conducted with the help of the McKinsey consulting firm. Bringing the first major layoffs in R&D since Black Friday in 1962, the OVA added an air of crisis to that period of change at ATC.[90]

The reorganization of Alcoa Laboratories swept away the structure of associate and assistant directors that had been in place since the creation of ARL in 1928. In the late 1970s, that structure had collapsed, so that a single associate director had supervised the assistant directors of all the technical divisions. The cumulative effect of that change, along with all those that had preceded it, had been to burden the assistant laboratory directors with immense amounts of paperwork. All of them, when asked, admitted to having to spend more than three-quarters of their time on people issues, rather than technical issues, leaving a gap in technical direction at the highest levels. A major objective in 1981, therefore, was to create a structure that would rectify that imbalance at all lower levels, promote a new technical seriousness, and foster development of a new generation of technology-oriented leaders.[91]

In May, Alcoa Laboratories was reorganized into seven major sectors. The process-oriented sectors, Refining R&D, Smelting R&D, Fabrication R&D, and Casting R&D, were headed by technical directors. In the other sectors, Primary, Mill Products, and Corporate, the holder of the top position was given a new title: operations director. The creation of these positions was a step toward achieving greater breadth and the balance desired in R&D management. The first operations directors, Peter Bridenbaugh, T. W. Callahan, and Charles Fletcher, were brought into

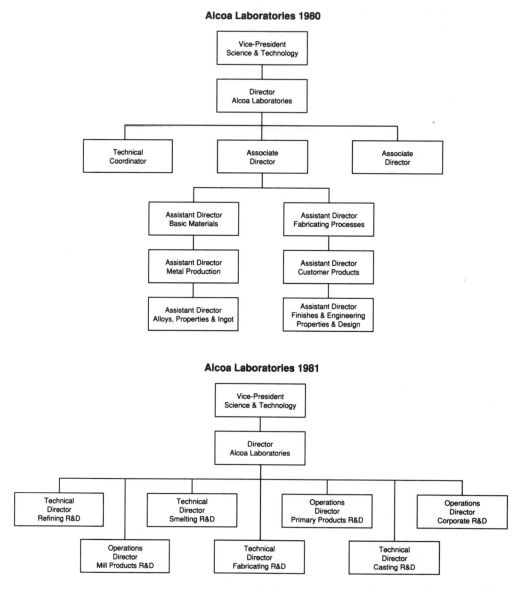

Alcoa Laboratories 1980

Alcoa Laboratories 1981

Figure 9.9. Alcoa Laboratories reorganization, 1981.

the Laboratories from other parts of the corporation. Experienced in high-level operations management, they were charged with handling major administrative matters, especially interfaces with the business units. They had been personally involved in numerous episodes of technology transfer, and they offered the prospect of smoother linkages with the most important operating units. Their taking over these functions gave the senior technical directors the chance to concentrate on planning programs and providing intellectual leadership in their technical areas.[92]

NEW MISSION, NEW LEADERSHIP

From the perspective of the Laboratories in the early 1980s, it was the opening up of the corporation in so many ways during the previous decade that spurred top management to reconsider the role of technology at Alcoa. But for Krome George, it was economic realities that brought about the final conversion. In Alcoa's annual report for 1982, titled *Responses to a Changing World,* the retiring chairman explained his position largely in terms of the uncontrolled expansion of worldwide smelting capacity and the initiation of aluminum as a trading commodity on the London Metal Exchange. That had brought on, George said, the phenomenon of "partial 'uncoupling' of the production of ingot and its further fabrication." Alcoa's strategic response would be "relatively simple," he added:[93]

We will not build new primary capacity simply to sell metal into the open commodity market, with its increasing risks of volatility and uneconomic pricing. On the contrary, we intend to develop our smelting capacity as we are convinced of its lasting competitive advantage, and where it fits with our long-range objectives of further fabrication and participation in the key growth economies of the world.

Linked to this would be a renewed effort to develop new applications and new markets for aluminum, following in the footsteps of Alcoa's "aluminum pioneers," whose efforts had led to successful replacement of "wood in building products, tinplate in beverage cans, copper in electrical conductors, and zinc, steel, and cast iron in vehicles and appliances."

Krome George attributed the sobering outlook for Alcoa's major products to the mature-market philosophy its leadership had adopted. George's successor, Charles W. Parry, who had helped to forge and later to rethink the policies of the 1970s, echoed the commitment to the reversal of policy in a speech entitled "New Directions in Aluminum Research," given to the Light Metals Group of the Metallurgical Society of AIME. In a reference to ASP, Parry noted that Alcoa had shut down the Anderson County works to resume development of the chemical train, which was still "less satisfactory than the cells." The company had not abandoned its hopes for achieving a breakthrough with aluminum chloride electrolysis, but it had backed down from push-

Charles Parry.

ing it through to the exclusion of other long-range projects. It had begun to bring a better balance into its R&D program. Parry went on to sketch out a policy of investment in a broad spectrum of more risky, long-term R&D founded on a new set of attitudes toward the technical community:

> We must overcome the existing mindset that requires all decisions to be clearly related to earnings per share . . . we should have the strength to fund [high-risk R&D] and keep on funding it . . . we need to strengthen existing relationships between industry and academia, and where there are no relationships we need to develop them . . . we need to learn to be more comfortable with dreamers . . . even those whose ideas are sometimes outrageous to financially oriented business minds.[94]

Parry could have added that the new mission for Alcoa Laboratories required a rapid change in its own collective mind-set. It had become an organization accustomed to focusing on belt-tightening, one that conceived its contribution to company welfare mainly in terms of performing its service function on the lowest budget possible. Now Alcoa Laboratories was challenged to develop a new sense of itself as Alcoa's investment in the future, a generator of new opportunities, and a place that could attract the kind of research personnel needed to support this new identity. Moreover, the transformation would have to take place under less than ideal circumstances. A whole new research staff was needed in certain areas, but at the same time, the Laboratories had to continue to assist the plants in their efforts to keep their existing processes competitive. Having just experienced the trauma of OVA, further layoffs were not an option, but neither would it be possible to effect change wholly through incremental hiring, as Van Horn had done in the post–World War II era.

To carry out this complicated mission, Alcoa's top management intervened to change the Laboratories' senior management team, removing those most closely associated with the old mission of primary smelting and operations support, but leaving the rest of the team intact. Kenneth Brondyke, who had been Allen Russell's chosen successor and was therefore identified with the old mission, was succeeded by Peter Bridenbaugh, then operations director for mill products R&D. Bridenbaugh combined long experience with technology transfer inside Alcoa with a Ph.D. in metallurgy from MIT. The MIT credentials gave him access to the national materials-research community.

Bridenbaugh began his new assignment with several important advantages. He was supported by the strong group of technical directors who had spent the previous several years thinking through the 10-year outlook for each of their areas of aluminum technology. He had the mandate of top management to strengthen new-materials capability and to add entire new programs where appropriate. And he was given the budget to support those changes. However, had the previous opening up of the Laboratories not paved the way for the program shift, such a transformation would not have been possible. Fortunately, some of the more progressive members of the postwar generation among the Laboratories research staff and its technical leadership were around long enough before they retired to help ease the transition.

NEW DIRECTIONS

During the decade of the 1970s, Alcoa had followed two clear policies toward R&D: It had thoroughly implemented both the latest tools and the practices that were regarded as good R&D management, and it had balanced its program. Within that context it could still claim, throughout the decade, more progressive R&D than its domestic competitors in the metals industry and considerably more progress in process modernization. But by the early 1980s it was clear that those policies, emphasizing short-term goals, accountability, and cost control, reinforced by the national climate of growing disenchantment with R&D, added up to a prescription for technical maturity. Pursuit of the strategy that management was proposing would require that Alcoa break out of that mold, and, in effect, return to an older corporate identity – that of an R&D leader and technology pioneer.[95]

The technical vision that the Laboratories offered in support of the post-1983 strategy called for winding down the primary smelting research, continued emphasis on recycling, heavy focus on new high-strength aluminum alloys, and collateral initiatives in new materials – ceramics and composites. That radical change in program emphasis would be possible only by taking maximum advantage of outside sources such as collaborative programs with universities, outside consultants,

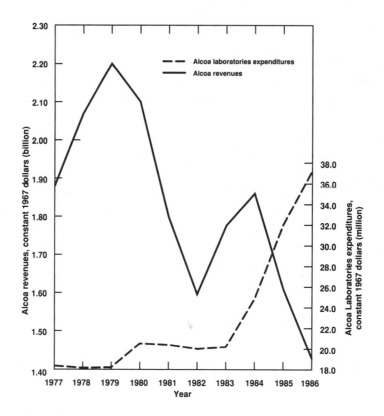

Figure 9.10. Alcoa R&D spending, 1977–86. Sources: Smith, *From Monopoly to Competition,* Table B-2; Spear, "Population and Budget History," 15 December 1987, ALA; *Statistical Abstract.*

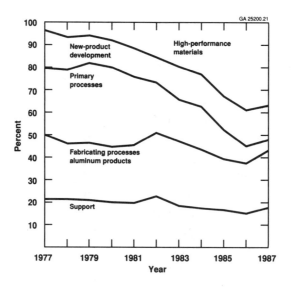

Figure 9.11. Alcoa Laboratories program emphasis, 1977–87. Program categories as percentages of total expenditures. Source: R. E. Spear, "Budget Summary, 1976–1978," 15 July 1988, ALA.

government sponsorship, and joint technical ventures with leading-edge customers and suppliers. The program for high-strength materials, already under way by 1983, combined all of these approaches.

Most of Alcoa's research organization had shut itself off from the technical mainstream for so long that it would take a while to reestablish contact. The alloy research program, however, had kept a small but vital foothold that allowed it to stay connected. It was that small program that formed the basis for one of Alcoa's best future opportunities, one that would be crucial to its continued presence in a key market. Within the program for high-strength materials, the development of aluminum-lithium alloy was the furthest along and offered the best hope that, at least for the short run, aluminum could hold its own in the next generation of structural materials adopted for aircraft. The appeal of that program was the chance once again to work collaboratively with the government and with a leading-edge customer. That experience made it clear to what extent aluminum, as a material, had reached a historic crossroad.

10

The challenge of composites

In March 1976, *Iron Age* reported that the National Aeronautics and Space Administration (NASA), interested in transferring technologies developed for the space program to commercial uses, had begun to implement a 10-year, $110 million program to develop composites, particularly graphite-epoxy composites, as structural materials for aircraft. According to Richard Heldenfels, director of structures at NASA's Langley Research Center, a major turning point was at hand:

It's similar to the transition that took place in the Thirties when aluminum replaced the airframes made from fabric, wires and steel tubes. I believe that composites will account for 50 to 60 percent of the aircraft structure by the turn of the century.[1]

Many Alcoans dismissed such chilling predictions as overstated, but in fact, driven by the impact of the oil crisis on its fuel costs, the aerospace community was seriously beginning to "think composites." A radical reduction in fuel consumption was called for, and reduction in the overall weight of aircraft structures was one obvious way to achieve that. Within the space of a few years, the entire aluminum industry was galvanized by the very real threat of nonmetallic substitute materials.

Several leading international aluminum producers developed aluminum-lithium (Al-Li) alloys as the best stopgap protection against replacement by composites. By 1982, Alcoa would be in the forefront of this Al-Li development. With the full and active support of top management, marketing, and production, the corporation would be heavily committed in both resources and reputation to a project, conducted in partnership with Boeing Aircraft Company, that was viewed by many as the most innovative R&D program the company had undertaken in recent memory. In those thrilling days the long years of work that led up to Al-Li alloys would be all but forgotten. Yet they were the essential foundation for all that followed.

THE CONTINUING PROBLEM OF STRESS-CORROSION CRACKING

The development of the World War II generation of alloys 75S and 76S had depended on a practical solution to the problem of stress-corrosion cracking (SCC). In 1950, Edgar Dix declared in a lecture that the problem had been solved with 75S:

> In over seven years of commercial use of products of this alloy, no important incident of stress-corrosion cracking has occurred in service, and only a few minor cases suspected to be the result of stress-corrosion cracking have been reported.[2]

At the time Dix spoke, the sheet alloy 75S, renamed 7075 under the system of classification introduced by the Aluminum Association in 1954, was fast becoming the predominant aircraft material of the postwar era. But the rapid evolution of aircraft design soon brought the problem of SCC back into focus.

The basic construction for aircraft through World War II was the "sheet-and-stringer" design, involving an outer skin of thin sheet or plate riveted to a riblike framework. Postwar designs, however, like Boeing's B-52 bomber and General Dynamics' F-111 fighter, relied on thick materials for massive structural parts, such as landing gear and wing supports, or for unitary skin sections and large structural members machined from thick plate or extrusions. Alcoa and the aeronautical industry soon discovered that a number of standard alloys, including 7075 in its highest-strength temper, T6, did not exhibit the same combination of desirable properties in thick sections as they did in thin materials. SCC reemerged as a critical problem. Subsequently, other characteristics, not previously considered important, came to be defined as key performance criteria. One of these was resistance to "fatigue," or failure caused by the stress and strain of continual motion; another was fracture toughness. Highly dependent on alloy microstructure, these new problems severely challenged alloy developers, highlighting the incompleteness of their understanding of the phenomenon of precipitation hardening, which gave high-strength aluminum alloys their distinctive properties.[3]

Standard sheet-and-stringer construction used for aircraft before World War II.

Through the 1950s, funding for basic research at Alcoa was cut back in alloy development, as in other areas, so that the effort to address these problems had to follow other avenues of investigation. In 1952 the Subcommittee on Metalworking set up an unusual fact-finding mission, assigning two metallurgists from the Cleveland laboratory and the central metallurgical

Fuselage section of B-52 aircraft being hoisted into position at Boeing aircraft assembly plant. (Smithsonian photo no. 89-16692)

A B-52 aircraft in flight. (Smithsonian photo no. 89-16693)

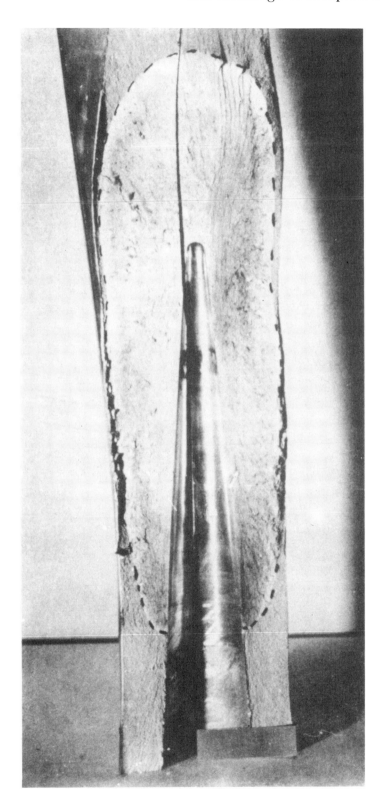

This photograph shows a stress-corrosion fracture of a forged propellor made of Alcoa 7076. The fracture resulted from stresses caused by rapid quenching. (From the 24th Edward de Mille Campbell Memorial Lecture, "Aluminun-Zinc-Magnesium Alloys," presented by E. H. Dix, Jr., October 19, 1949, *Transactions of the American Society of Metals*, vol. 42, 1950, pp. 1057–127.)

department to gather information from all the plants and laboratories working with aircraft materials to suggest explanations for the behavior and properties of high-strength alloys in thick sections. The project yielded no immediate solution to the problem of SCC, but it did bring to light a number of ways that alloy properties could be improved by changes in plant practices and pointed the way to a promising future research agenda when support for it could be found.[4]

For the short term, Alcoa dealt with the problem of SCC through an informational campaign aimed at helping aeronautical engineers and airframe manufacturers use existing materials in ways that would minimize the possibility of failure. It was known that the "overaged" temper designated T73 conferred excellent resistance to SCC, but at a sacrifice in strength. With aircraft designers continually pushing toward faster planes and larger payloads, Alcoa assumed that the weight penalty associated with a reduction in the strength of structural alloys would be unacceptable to its customers and sought other solutions.[5]

In 1954 the company had an unfortunate experience with outside alloy research when it commercialized an alloy developed in Germany that was reported to have good resistance to SCC in laboratory corrosion tests, but in service proved to be much worse than the alloys it had replaced. That unhappy episode opened the way for Alcoa's commercial introduction, in 1961, of its own T73 temper for 7075 products in thick sections. That innovation virtually eliminated the threat of SCC and at the same time created an intense demand for a new alloy that would have the same resistance to SCC without the attendant loss in strength. Alcoa began to experience this commercial imperative just as other revitalizing forces were taking hold in the alloy development program.[6]

FUNDAMENTAL RESEARCH IN ALLOY DEVELOPMENT

One purpose of the Laboratories' reorganization in 1958 had been to stimulate fundamental research in all divisions, but especially, as Van Horn pointed out, in Physical Metallurgy, the division responsible for alloy development. To revitalize that program, Van Horn selected Harold Hunsicker, from Cleveland, to be division chief. Because of the company's financial crisis, culminating in the Black Friday layoffs at the Laboratories in 1961, the

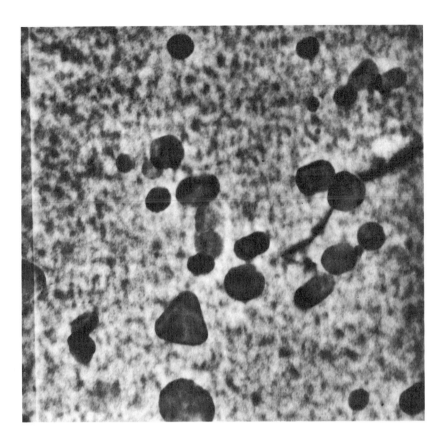

The advent of the electron microscope changed what researchers could hope to understand about the physical and chemical properties of alloys and the relationships among them. This transmission electron micrograph (×193,000) is of a 7075-T4 alloy aged 25 years at room temperature.

reinvigoration of research in physical metallurgy got off to a slow start. But the effort picked up in 1962, aided by new equipment and advanced research techniques. In the early 1960s, Alcoa metallographers adopted an electrochemical method, developed in Cambridge, England, for making thin-foil specimens, to be examined by electron microscope. That technology opened a new window on alloy microstructure through which many aspects of precipitation hardening could be observed for the first time. In alloy development, the mainstream channels had always been defined by practitioners rather than by scientists, and explanations for alloy behavior typically lagged practical developments. Only after some 40 years of research, assisted by the advent of x-ray microscopy and, later, transmission electron mi-

croscopy, had scientists fully understood the mechanism of precipitation hardening that gave Wilm's Duralumin its unusual
strength as a result of heat treatment. Even then, the process was
clearly defined only for aluminum-copper compositions, and the
behavior of aluminum-zinc-magnesium-copper alloys, such as
7075, remained something of a mystery.[7]

In the 1960s, with its new research technology, ARL moved to
the forefront of alloy research. The company's restrictive publication policy kept Alcoa from playing a leadership role in the
scientific community, but the fundamental knowledge gained
paid off handsomely in its alloy development programs, just as it
did in ingot casting.[8] Technology leadership in high-strength
alloys was part of the corporate strategy enunciated by John D.
Harper when he assumed the presidency in 1962. The Laboratories was able to give Harper what he wanted by the end of the
decade with the development of a number of important new
alloys, in particular alloy 7050, which solved the problem of SCC
in thick sections, and the high-fracture-toughness alloy 7475.
Both these alloys were unusual and highly significant in the degree to which their development was dependent on and guided
by an understanding of the relationships among composition,
heat treatment, and final properties.[9]

In the late 1960s the aerospace industry was rocked by
crashes of a number of the U.S. Air Force's F-111 fighter
planes. The prolonged investigation that ensued had tremendous impact not just on aerospace designers but on the entire
materials industry. It showed the cause of the crashes to be
failure of a steel part in which a microscopic crack, under the
stress of flight, grew rapidly to catastrophic proportions. As a
result, fracture toughness – the ability to resist such rapid crack
growth – was established as a critical property for all structural
aircraft materials. A whole new discipline, fracture mechanics,
grew up within materials science, as "toughness" was further
defined and analyzed, and testing procedures and standards
were devised.

All of the emphasis in the aircraft industry on fracture
toughness – like the widespread concern over SCC and, indeed, like the furor over corrosion in the days of the *Shenandoah*
and the navy's "flying boats" – had a profound impact on the
stream of alloy research that had flowed more or less without
interruption at Alcoa since the discovery of Duralumin. More-

over, because alloys of other metals, notably stainless steel, nickel, and magnesium, were heat-treatable like aluminum, research on phenomena such as fracture toughness was pursued on a broad front, cutting across industrial categories. As a result, researchers in alloy development remained connected to the mainstream of materials science to a greater degree than did Alcoa people in other fields.[10]

Alloy developers were also connected to the outside through government contract work, and the program benefited greatly from its strong customers, especially the U.S. Navy and Air Force. The project that produced alloy 7050 was funded largely by the U.S. Naval Air Systems Command (NAVAIR). This project established a relationship with NAVAIR reminiscent of the relationship between Alcoa and the Navy formed around the *Shenandoah* project during and after World War I. Richard Schmidt, head of the materials and processes branch and director of the 7050 project on the navy's side, was so enthusiastic about alloy 7050 that he took the initiative for speeding its widespread adoption in naval weapons and airframe parts and encouraged private airframe manufacturers to do the same.[11]

ORIGINS OF ALUMINUM-LITHIUM

As the 7050 project drew to a close, Schmidt questioned his contacts at the Laboratories about potential new alloys for development under contract. Hunsicker suggested the aluminum-lithium system as a likely candidate, and Schmidt made known the navy's willingness to consider a proposal for work in this area. Drawing on work done at Alcoa in the 1950s and on foreign, primarily Soviet, sources, James Staley and Joseph Evancho put together a proposal to investigate aluminum-magnesium-lithium (Al-Mg-Li) alloys. Their project was accepted for 12 months of funding beginning early in 1973. The main thrust of this first contract program was simply to produce and evaluate Al-Mg-Li alloys. One of the reasons that attracted NAVAIR to the program was that Soviet researchers were known to be working on it.[12]

Alcoa had commercialized an aluminum-lithium alloy, 2020, as early as 1957, using a 1945 patent under which Alcoa's I. M. LeBaron had patented a heat-treatment process for an Al-Cu alloy containing 1 percent lithium. That material had clearly demonstrated both the great potential advantages and the liabilities of lithium as an alloying element. Alloy 2020 in the high-strength temper, T6, was equal in strength to the strongest Al-Zn-Mg-Cu alloy, 7075-T6, with elastic modulus (stiffness) 8 percent higher, and density (mass per unit volume) 3 percent lower. It was the stiffness property that Alcoa researchers were particularly interested in pursuing because it created the potential for using thinner and hence lighter-weight sheet on aircraft. Alloy 2020's primary application was in parts of the wings and tail of the U.S. Navy's RA-5C Vigilante aircraft, and the experience with that plane proved that early aluminum-lithium alloy to have high resistance to fatigue, corrosion, and SCC.[13]

Alloy 2020 was plagued, however, by excessively low fracture toughness. Alcoa's technical publications always alluded to that deficiency and cautioned that special care must be taken in design and fabrication of alloy 2020 parts. In addition, because of its extreme reactivity to other elements, the presence of lithium posed severe production problems. In order to produce sound ingots, the plants had to melt and cast aluminum-lithium in an inert atmosphere, so that the lithium would not absorb excessive hydrogen or form an oxide coating on the metal surface. That meant segregating furnaces and casting equipment and rigorously following special procedures to keep the lithium from coming into contact with the outside atmosphere. In 1974, alloy 2020 was withdrawn from production, partly because its low fracture toughness greatly limited its marketability, but also because it was extremely unpopular in the plants. The bad production experience with that alloy lingered on in the minds of senior technical personnel at Alcoa, including Norm Nielson, who was later to become chief metallurgist.[14]

Meanwhile, the same kinds of problems were inhibiting the first NAVAIR contract on Al-Mg-Li alloy development. The choice of that alloy system had been dictated largely by the claims of Soviet metallurgists for their alloy, 01420, containing between 4 and 7 percent magnesium, and 1.5 to 2.6 percent lithium. The Soviets, led by I. N. Fridlyander, had been working on Al-Li alloys since the early 1960s. They were familiar with LeBaron's patent and had developed the alloy VAD23, roughly equivalent to alloy 2020, in 1963. Alcoa metallurgists were familiar with Fridlyander's published work, and part of their intent in pursuing the Al-Mg-Li system was to test the

Soviet results independently, using familiar procedures and standards of measurement.[15]

Research done for the first NAVAIR contract verified that the Al-Mg-Li alloy system produced the same attractive high ratio of stiffness to density as alloy 2020, but that it was beset with equal, or worse, problems of fabrication. In addition, the fracture toughness of the Al-Mg-Li alloys was well below the acceptable standard. Evancho, the principal investigator, reported that in one set of tests the alloys fractured so quickly that "the recording system could not follow the event." Nevertheless, the promise of superior properties remained. Evancho proposed that the work be extended through 1974 to investigate compositions containing cadmium and beryllium, drawing on Alcoa's experience with alloy 2020 and on Japanese and British work with Al-Cu and Al-Li alloys.[16]

Although that early work on Al-Li systems produced no breakthrough, it laid the foundation for progress, largely by providing fractured Al-Mg-Li material for micrographic examination. The work with Al-Mg-Li alloys, and with alloy 2020, brought to light a common problem – high levels of hydrogen gas – that was suggested as a possible source of low fracture toughness. In the fall of 1974, Edward Balmuth, a metallurgist at the Naval Air Development Center, assumed primary technical responsibility on the navy side for Al-Li alloy development. With Balmuth's encouragement and assurance of financial support, Evancho formulated a proposal for research. The investigation of the causes of low fracture toughness would be pursued on two fronts. "Structural examinations," the study of alloy microstructure, dependent on advanced research technology, would continue. But, Evancho said, the analytical tools for detection of the atomic compound of lithium and hydrogen were "not readily available." He therefore proposed "an empirical approach" to determine whether or not hydrogen was the cause of low fracture toughness. He wanted to address the problem of fracture toughness in lithium-bearing alloys generally, using both Al-Mg-Li and 2020-type compositions as subjects of study.[17]

The extended contract covering Al-Mg-Li alloys continued into 1975, and the work on fracture toughness proposed by Evancho was funded by NAVAIR for the following year. During the course of 1976, however, Evancho moved off the project to study auto-body sheet, and primary responsibility for the fracture-toughness project shifted to Thomas H. Sanders, Jr., who had recently come to Alcoa with a Ph.D. in metallurgy from the Georgia Institute of Technology. Sanders made rapid progress through systematic study of fracture behavior in Al-Mg-Li, Al-Cu-Li, and binary Al-Li alloys. Within a year he had eliminated Al-Mg-Li compositions from consideration, and by vacuum-casting to better control impurities he had successfully produced a binary Al-Li alloy with high stiffness and acceptable fracture toughness. Moreover, Sanders was convinced he was close to a truly high-performance Al-Cu-Li alloy, equal to alloy 2020 in every respect, but with improved fracture toughness. He sought and obtained an extension of the NAVAIR contract to work toward a clearer explanation of the fracture behavior of those alloys.[18]

Sander's results were so exciting that Balmuth proposed a new Alcoa project to his NAVAIR superiors, one to develop the manufacturing technology that would be necessary to scale-up whatever alloy composition Sanders eventually developed.[19] Alcoa was not nearly as enthusiastic as NAVAIR about the prospect of moving the project from conceptual understanding to technical feasibility. That was getting into the area of process technology that Alcoa traditionally had chosen not to open to government funding. Moreover, the production experience with alloy 2020 was still fresh in everyone's memory. The prevailing attitude in the Subcommittee on Alloy Development was that although Alcoa would carry on research in that area with government funding, it did not intend to commercialize an Al-Li alloy, regardless of the navy's desire to do so. Gregory Barthold, who managed Alcoa's Washington contracting office, confided to Staley that Sanders's promising results would create "the problem of selling the scaleup of his work to Alcoa management."[20]

In January 1977, Staley circulated the shocking statement of NASA's Richard Heldenfels on the imminent takeover of aircraft structures by composites. In his cover letter, Staley expressed a sense of frustration with Alcoa's corporate position on aerospace alloys in general. He believed that Alcoa's market forecasters were completely ignoring the potential threat of new materials to Alcoa's aircraft-industry sales. Alcoa funding for programs to develop improved aluminum alloys had been drastically reduced, in part because it was assumed that new alloys would at best simply replace the old; they would not add

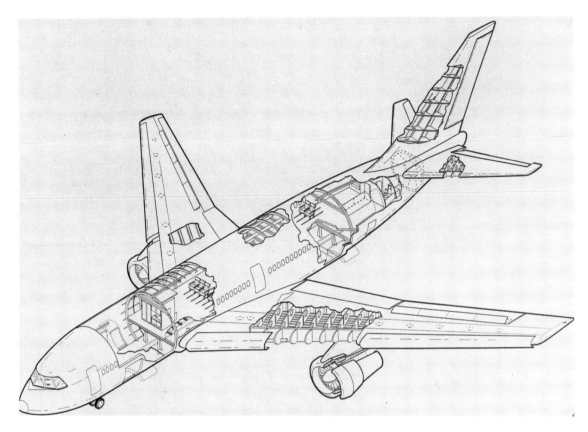

to the overall volume of sales. No consideration seemed to be given to the possible drastic reduction, or complete loss, of the market.

The argument against corporate spending at that time was strengthened by the expectation that the Department of Defense would underwrite further research into aerospace alloys, and Alcoa was moving into full swing with its program to secure financing of a substantial portion of its R&D effort through government funding. But, Staley argued,

continued reliance on the federal government to fund programs to upgrade aluminum aircraft alloys will be insufficient to prevent the transition from aluminum to composite structure for aircraft. To counter this threat, I believe that prompt action is needed to prevent or forestall the replacement of aluminum by composites. In my opinion, "we can't wait for tomorrow."[21]

Alcoa and NAVAIR were approaching confrontation over continued support for Al-Li development, their policies being

This drawing of a generic aircraft shows where experts in the early 1980s were predicting that composites would replace aluminum in commercial aircraft by the 1990s. In addition to composite skin replacing aluminum alloy sheet to reduce the weight of certain parts, it was expected that composites would be used to make the kind of structural members shown in the cutaway sections of the aircraft. Predictions ranged as high as 90 percent of the aircraft, by weight, being replaced by composite materials.

at cross purposes. A new emphasis within the Department of Defense to avoid sole-source procurement situations put pressure on agencies such as NAVAIR to foster more competition in R&D. In addition, the navy began to insist that future contracts be written on a cost-sharing basis, rather than on a fixed-fee-plus-expenses basis. That type of contract would require a complete reversal of Alcoa's long-standing position on Al-Li alloy development at precisely the time when R&D was struggling under the cloud of "mature-market thinking" and competing, with difficulty, for funds within the business units. During a temporary suspension of NAVAIR funding pending negotiations, Alcoa supplied funds to tide the project over, but not because of a change of attitude. "We still feel," wrote the head of Aerospace Marketing to Staley, that "the great majority of this R&D expense must be borne by others as the uncertainties and time to pay back just don't provide commercial justification at this time."[22]

In October, Reynolds Metals, having been encouraged by NAVAIR's Balmuth to get into the work, was awarded a contract for research to improve the fracture toughness of Al-Li alloys. Balmuth's initiative to "shop" Alcoa's original work to other companies infuriated Alcoa Laboratories management, although it was well within NAVAIR's rights. A separate Alcoa proposal to carry out development of ingot-casting technology – the second half of Sanders's original program – was shelved. After six years of pioneering work in Al-Li alloy development, the partnership between Alcoa and NAVAIR seemed on the verge of dissolution. Indeed, despite the promise of Sanders's work, it looked as though Alcoa might well back away completely from that area of alloy technology.[23]

OUTSIDE ACTIVITIES

Outside Alcoa, in the broader materials-research community, the momentum for Al-Li alloy development was building rapidly. Soviet researchers continued to report enthusiastically on alloy 04120, which was believed to be already sufficiently advanced for flight testing. Although there was no indication that the Soviets had solved, or even addressed, the problem of low fracture toughness, presumably they had solved many of the manufacturing difficulties associated with Al-Li materials. Metallurgists in Japan, France, West Germany, and Great Britain were also all working in the field.[24]

In the United States, development proceeded on a widening front. As researchers in both corporate and university laboratories turned their attention to Al-Li alloys, the work done at Alcoa provided an important part of the shared knowledge base in the field. Metallurgists at Kaiser, Reynolds, and government research agencies, as well as both military and civilian aircraft designers, were kept abreast of Alcoa's findings. Though Alcoa's Editorial Committee expressed discomfort with publication of information on alloys the company had no intention of producing commercially, the navy could not be prevented from circulating the results of research for which it had paid.[25]

In a related development in 1978, Alcoa became committed to a broader involvement with the emerging field of high-strength materials as a subcontractor to Lockheed Missiles and Space Company in a large-scale program in powder metallurgy to develop Al-Mg-Li alloys, funded by the Air Force Materials Laboratory and the Defense Advanced Research Products Agency (DARPA). Although the role of the Laboratories was primarily to supply materials for analysis, the personnel involved worked together and published some of their results jointly with metallurgists at Lockheed.[26]

Alcoa's relative indifference to the Al-Li program helped to spread the work around. In mid-1979, Balmuth left NAVAIR for the General Dynamics Materials Research Laboratory in Fort Worth, Texas. At roughly the same time, Sanders left Alcoa for the Fracture and Fatigue Research Laboratory at the Georgia Institute of Technology. There he continued to pursue and publish research on Al-Li and, with a colleague, Edgar A. Starke, Jr., organized the First International Al-Li Conference, which took place in Georgia in May 1980.[27]

The widespread ferment among researchers in materials science attracted the attention of aircraft designers, who could readily envision broad application of an improved Al-Li alloy, if one could be developed. Government funding policies fostered that interest. Lockheed had a strong foothold in the field because of its contract work on Al-Mg-Li alloys, and other companies, such as McDonnell Douglas, began to express interest in bidding with Alcoa for government contracts on Al-Li. In 1979 the Naval Ordnance Laboratory, with NAVAIR funding, produced extrusions of a variety of Al-Li compositions and sent them to a number of major companies, among them Northrop, Lockheed, McDonnell Douglas, Rockwell, General Dynamics, and LTV, for evaluation. All were aware of the great potential of these alloys, as well as their nagging problems.[28]

PARTNER IN COMMERCIALIZATION

Alcoa's strongest commercial customer at the time was Boeing, which was working on applying new materials to its commercial aircraft. In the late 1970s, Alcoa Laboratories collaborated with Boeing to produce two new materials tailored for Boeing's use in its 757 and 767 aircraft, then under design. Based on that good experience, the two companies formed, in mid-1979, a joint task force to identify and plan R&D projects of mutual interest. Al-Li alloy development was given high priority in the agenda of that group. Boeing's interest at that time was primarily in Al-Mg-Li alloys, but its enthusiasm for *any* Al-Li material was clear. Alcoa pointed out that Al-Mg-Li alloys would present even greater manufacturing problems than alloy 2020 and other Al-Cu-Li compositions, but Boeing pursued its agenda independently, negotiating with Alcoa Laboratories through Sales for the purchase of Al-Mg-Li compositions for test purposes.[29]

In 1980, Alcoa was still funding R&D for Al-Li at a very low level and with the greatest reluctance.[30] When alloy researchers tried to get more internal funding in order to keep from sharing ingot-casting know-how with the government, they were rebuffed. J. P. Lyle, head of alloy development, recorded the subcommittee's reasoning at the time as follows:

Alcoa would have a strong competitive advantage in its superior facilities and experienced personnel. These factors would offset the loss of control over basic knowhow, and Alcoa would get paid for doing R&D it would have to do anyway.[31]

Part of the reasoning, even on the part of higher Laboratories management, had to do with continued skepticism as to the technical feasibility of Al-Li alloys. Though much interest had been generated, researchers had yet to demonstrate that they could solve the critical bench-scale problem of low fracture toughness, described by Robert Spear, division head, as "a killer."[32]

The improving technical prospects for Al-Li alloy development gave the program an internal momentum that carried it along despite corporate misgivings. Sanders's two years of work at Alcoa had provided critical information about the microstructural characteristics associated with low fracture toughness. His findings pointed to three likely explanations for this weakness: the behavior of Al-Li combinations during precipitation, related in some way to grain size and structure; the presence of "tramp" elements, such as sodium, potassium, sulfur, and hydrogen; and high hydrogen content. During 1979 the work was taken up at ATC by A. K. Vasudevan. Using old samples of alloy 2020 plate, Vasudevan was able to achieve a 30 percent improvement in fracture toughness by thermomechanical treatment (TMT), a program of heat treatment with hot and cold rolling that made the alloy more fine-grained and resistant to fracture.[33]

The clincher came when Vasudevan was able to produce castings of some experimental compositions, using a salt-flux cover, that held promise for solution of the production problems. In May 1980, Staley created a "road map" for Al-Li development that predicted solution of the fracture-toughness problem by the end of 1981, and an alloy for flight testing as early as 1986.[34]

As technical feasibility began to seem more assured, pressure mounted from both interested military agencies and Boeing. Alcoa's Seattle sales agent forwarded an article from *Boeing News* that detailed a $26 million development program funded by NASA and aimed at application of graphite-epoxy composites to the latest airframe designs. The new materials, the article stated, would save as much as 1,250 pounds in the new 767 plane, and a proportionate amount in the smaller 757. "I think," he wrote, "we should encourage Jim Staley to hurry up with the lithium alloys." Eventually, word penetrated to the highest levels of the company. When Marvin Gantz visited Boeing, the issue of the Al-Li program was raised directly, prompted, although he did not know it, by requests from senior Alcoa Laboratories personnel who, unable to penetrate upward through the subcommittee structure, had resorted to approaching top management through a third party. They were successful.[35]

In the final weeks of 1980, Alcoa Laboratories achieved the

turnaround it had been seeking. Alloy Technology and Ingot
Casting made their case at a special meeting of the Subcommittee on Alloy Development, and the committee approved the
formation of an Al-Li project team to push commercialization
of Al-Li. They also agreed to fund the critical ingot-casting
element internally, committing to produce and evaluate only
four Al-Li-Cu compositions under government contract. Moreover, the committee supported an accelerated program in
which alloy development and development of ingot-casting technology would proceed simultaneously, shortening the time
frame for achieving materials suitable for customer evaluation
to four years. Acceptance of the higher-risk, higher-priced parallel path signaled the importance that would be placed on Al-
Li alloy development and betokened acceptance of the Laboratories' claim that the chances of success were very good.[36]

ALUMINUM-LITHIUM COMMERCIALIZATION, YEAR 1

In view of the highly interactive nature of the work, a cross-
disciplinary team was needed. Its members included Staley, as
project manager, John Jacoby from Ingot Casting, Thomas
Scott from the Fabricating Technology Division, and A. K.
Vasudevan and Warren Hunt from the Alloy Technology Division. The Al-Li project was one of the first to have a full-
fledged project-management structure within the Laboratories.
Within a year, its leadership moved out of the hands of alloy
specialists to people who could take more of a systems perspective because of their more varied experience. It was also recognized that continuity was sufficiently important to the project to
make it a full-time responsibility of one person.[37]

Project objectives were both technical and operational: to develop production practices to control impurities, such as hydrogen, sodium, and potassium, and to determine the composition
and heat treatment able to produce the microstructure necessary for acceptable fracture toughness. Although those goals
were considered highly achievable, there remained the more
difficult issue whether or not the tight controls that would be
necessary to produce Al-Li alloys would ever be possible under
plant conditions. Staley wondered if they could convince the
plant personnel to accept Al-Li alloys.[38] The problem of scale-
up loomed large in the work of the project team in the next few

years, made considerably more difficult by the erosion of technical expertise at individual plants during the 1970s.

In the month following Staley's initial memo, meetings were held to establish the goals and priorities of the team's efforts. Critical input, based on their knowledge of what would be "marketable," came from the two most interested commercial customers, Lockheed and Boeing, and from aerospace experts in Technical Marketing. The group defined three property goals: highest strength plus corrosion resistance; moderate strength with highest durability and "damage tolerance," that is to say, resistance to failure from fracture, fatigue, and SCC; and moderate strength plus suitability for "minimum practical thickness applications," such as thin sheet for aircraft structures. The objective was to match the best existing alloys in each of these categories with Al-Li alloys having lower density and/or higher elastic modulus. It was decided that the first two goals could be met by improvements to alloy 2020, while the third would most likely require development of a new composition with lithium content higher than that of 2020. Ongoing work by Vasudevan had demonstrated improvements in strength with a 3 percent Al-Li-X composition. It was therefore decided that fundamental work to determine what the third element of this third alloy should be would continue as background to more rapid development of the high-strength and high-damage-tolerance alloys.[39]

After six months it was decided to focus on an Al-Li system with copper as the third element. Experimental compositions were chosen with 1.5 percent, 2 percent, and 3 percent lithium, with varying levels of copper, and with minor additions of elements known to improve properties in other alloys, such as magnesium, silicon, manganese, and zirconium. Because the difficulty of casting ingots was roughly proportionate to the level of lithium, the 1.5 percent and 2 percent alloys could be developed quickly, while work on the 3 percent lithium composition would have to proceed more slowly.[40]

PRODUCTION HAZARDS

The handling of molten Al-Li compositions remained the most difficult aspect of the project. Central to the accelerated development program was installation of a 20,000-pound-capacity melting furnace, necessary to cast plant-size ingots at ATC. By

July 1981 it was clear that all of 1982 would be required for developing pilot-scale melting and casting procedures. Plant-scale development would have to be deferred until 1983.[41]

Throughout the first year, Ingot Casting continued to have difficulty producing sound ingots at bench scale. The problem was the need for constant containment of the molten lithium, not only to control impurities but also as a safety precaution. Solid lithium in water would fizz, burn, and finally explode, and molten lithium would explode on contact with water.[42]

Because any molten aluminum alloy could explode on contact with water, control of that hazard through the use of coating substances had been a large part of casting development since the advent of direct-chill technology in the 1930s. By the summer of 1981, the Laboratories had an ongoing experimental program to study the causes of violent molten-aluminum–water reactions and to improve on existing methods of prevention. In late September, after 100 successful tests of standard alloys using a new coating system, a trial of a 3 percent lithium alloy produced a severe explosion. That event convinced the team that no coating material then known would work on such an alloy. Alcoa alerted the Aluminum Association and took steps to notify researchers abroad of the potential hazards involved in working with Al-Li alloys.[43]

Following this explosion, all experimental casting of Al-Li alloys ceased, and a search began for an alternative ingot-casting process. It was finally decided that ATC should install, for laboratory purposes, an adaptation of an existing casting process involving a cooling system in which water came into contact only with the outside of the ingot mold. That reduced the risk of water contact, but did not eliminate it entirely, because accidental "bleedout" of molten metal was always a possibility. Because of slower cooling, the properties of the resulting ingot were somewhat inferior to those achieved with standard DC casting.[44]

After a year-long struggle to perfect the adopted casting process, Ingot Casting produced an entirely different casting system, one that used a substitute medium for cooling. The problem with this solution was that the best alternative fluids were flammable. All of the testing of molten metal in water was conducted in an outdoor concrete explosion bunker. That precaution proved to be fully warranted when a later explosion pro-

pelled scrap from the test unit out an open side of the bunker with enough force to sever a five-inch-diameter tree 200 feet away. Experimentation with various nonwater coolants was also carried out in the test bunker until one was selected in July 1982. The bunker continued in use even after that, as safety controls and fire-fighting procedures were worked out. Again, all of those precautions were shown to be prudent when a major fire occurred in April 1983, during debugging of the new casting system.[45]

A full-scale aluminum-lithium casting pit allows researchers not only to develop ingot-casting technologies for this highly sensitive alloy but also to develop process innovations that can in turn make possible future product modifications.

Indeed, the reputation of Al-Li alloys was so bad that throughout Alcoa no one ever questioned the wisdom of taking every precaution possible, or of broadly publicizing the hazards involved within the technical community. Early in the project, the ingot-casting team consulted people in the plants that had produced alloy 2020 prior to 1974, in order to anticipate known problems and dangers.[46] Between January and April 1983, a "risk-assessment" team representing Ingot Casting, Facilities Engineering, Safety and Industrial Hygiene, and an outside consultant, Design Sciences, Inc., conducted a fault-tree analysis that pointed to improvements that could be made to the new plant-scale casting operation to make it safer.[47]

PROJECT IN HIGH GEAR

By 1981 there had emerged a widespread consensus in the aerospace industry that graphite-epoxy composites could largely displace aluminum in aircraft structures within two decades. Coming at roughly the same time as the realization that money was not going to be made again in smelting, that message brought Alcoa top management sharply to attention. The "threat of composites" was a powerful motivator. Alcoa budgeted $1 million for continued development of Al-Li in 1982, and the Laboratories no longer had to argue the case for investment in alloy technology. Instead, its directors were pressed to give assurances that the Al-Li project and, to a lesser degree, the development of high-strength powder-metallurgy alloys, had been given "most urgent" status.[48] Up to that time, application of powder metallurgy to high-strength alloy production had received higher priority at the Laboratories because it attracted higher levels of outside funding. Al-Li, however, was regarded as easier to achieve, as it involved the more familiar ingot-metallurgy production techniques. It was therefore the best candidate for a transitional product to more exotic high-strength materials.

Opportunity, as well as necessity, brought about the rapid development of Al-Li alloys from lab to production scale, giving Alcoa its competitive edge in that technology. In January 1982, Walter Cebulak succeeded James Staley as Al-Li project director. Cebulak had the breadth of experience that was required for management of a greatly enlarged program. In his first statement on the project's status for Chairman Krome George, Cebulak noted that Al-Li would enable Alcoa to stave off the immediate threat of composites. Moreover, he pointed out, Alcoa's solutions to the fracture-toughness problem and its development of safe and reliable manufacturing processes would give the company a competitive advantage, even though it could never hope to be a single-source supplier.[49]

Time was crucial, for Alcoa Laboratories was aiming for the "very narrow time window" during which Boeing's commercial aircraft division would evaluate materials for its newest 7X7 aircraft. It was also proposing to conduct its program using some fairly unconventional methods, arguing that Alcoa would have to accelerate the pace of its Al-Li program and share evaluation of its alloys with its development partner while they were still in early stages. As Cebulak wrote to Brondyke in February 1982,

our airframe customers . . . have indicated very strong willingness to share in early evaluation and in the risk that they will evaluate some materials that will not be commercially viable, in order to step up the pace of material availability to them. The benefit to Alcoa for stepping up this pace is undercutting the inroads that composites are making to our markets, at the earliest possible time. The customer benefits by getting something new that offers him a performance advantage in airplanes earlier than he is going to have it if we continue our normal approach, in generating a very high assurance of product performance with less customer interaction.[50]

Within two months of that proposal Alcoa concluded an agreement with Boeing to cooperate in rapid development of Al-Li alloys. Aside from the recent experience the two companies had in working together, that was a natural partnership for a number of reasons. Boeing had long been willing to invest heavily in new materials, and its 757 aircraft, for instance, introduced two new alloys, a high-strength titanium alloy and a powder-metallurgy aluminum alloy, 7090. Boeing had been quick to develop and utilize composites, but it had also been investigating and analyzing Al-Li alloys on its own for several years.

The agreement with Boeing, concluded in late March 1982, had as a clear technical goal the selection of Al-Li ingot-metallurgy compositions "suitable to both parties for production and airframe hardware commitment" by the end of 1983. Until that date, both companies were bound to secrecy regarding the candidate compositions. Afterward, Boeing would be free to seek multiple sources for the new alloys, and Alcoa would be free to market them to other customers. The existence of the agreement was not kept secret, though it was not broadly advertised.[51]

Acceptance of Boeing's timetable implied a big financial commitment by Alcoa. There was no doubt, however, that Al-Li development would benefit from information generated by Boeing's prior, and ongoing, R&D and from the aggressive participation of the Boeing Metal Technology (BMT) organization in the testing and evaluation of candidate alloys. It was also assumed that the cooperative program would give Alcoa's alloys a competitive advantage with that major airframe customer.[52]

As the project ran its course over the next few years, Alcoa benefited in other ways as well. While manufacturing technology, especially ingot casting, was carefully excluded from the sphere of shared information, development in that area was driven strongly by Boeing's need to move quickly to evaluation of full-scale materials. By the conclusion of the project, Alcoa was well ahead of its competitors in casting large Al-Li ingots. Similarly, the pressure to move quickly through the necessary steps of alloy development – solving the problem of fracture toughness, optimizing the composition to secure all of the desired properties, and verifying every decision with thorough testing – demanded an aggressive approach, integrating fundamental research directly into the experimental process. The enthusiasm for such an approach, generated by the successes with alloys 7050 and 7475, could be tested and tempered by experience with the less familiar, and more intractable, Al-Li system.

In March 1982, Warren Hunt outlined the program designed to solve the fracture-toughness problem. The new laboratory casting unit, which was not continuous, but used a fixed-length mold, would produce lab-scale (4 × 8 × 30 inches) ingots of 15 different compositions, representing, collectively, all of the prior work done on Al-Li-X systems, both inside and outside Alcoa. Fundamental work to establish the relationship between microstructure and properties in these alloys, it was argued, would test existing theories about the causes of low fracture toughness and, it was hoped, point to the most promising compositions. The ultimate objective, Hunt stated, was to move as quickly as possible to pilot-scale (16 × 30 inches) continuous-cast ingot, so that the results of the fundamental work could be verified and scale-up problems uncovered at an early stage. To accomplish that in the time given required significant shortcuts in the traditional alloy development process. Evaluation of experimental alloys would be limited to a few "critical tests" of performance, along with examination of microstructure, and selection would be guided both by theory and by observation. As Hunt wrote,

alloy selection for fundamental work in areas such as corrosion and fatigue will be based on the understanding of the mechanisms involved as a function of composition and processing rather than only on evaluating the most promising alloys from the first iteration. This will allow development of a basis for future results as well as a time savings of approximately four months. The latter will be valuable as an "early warning" of potential problems in these areas which will allow them to be addressed at an earlier point in the program.[53]

Although the first set of alloys was not cast until December, a leading candidate emerged quickly, even before the full analysis of the first set was complete. It was a composition of roughly 3 percent copper and 2 percent lithium (Al-3Cu-2Li) that satisfied two of the three property goals, highest strength and highest damage tolerance, with a 7 percent reduction in density. In November 1982, Cebulak suggested that this basic composition was a strong candidate for commercialization, to be explored more fully, and it could well serve as "a benchmark against which other alloys can be compared."[54]

The decision by Boeing to delay development of its 7X7 plane and to focus instead on the shorter-term goal of direct substitution of Al-Li alloys in its existing models, the 747 in particular, was critical for the pace of the Al-Li project. Early in 1983, Ralph Sawtell took over the leadership of the project from Cebulak, who became head of Alloy Technology. In April, Sawtell reported Boeing's change of emphasis and outlined the various ways in which it would affect the timing of development of alloy and casting technology. Boeing immediately began to press for rapid completion of the second iteration of candidate compositions, which Alcoa Laboratories was able to accomplish by mid-July only by manning double shifts on the lab-scale casting unit and by calling forth extraordinary efforts from every division to produce rolled and extruded materials suitable for testing by Boeing.[55]

In addition, Boeing's decision to aim for application in existing models meant that production-scale ingots would be needed at an early date. Construction of a pilot-scale unit of the newly designed casting equipment, capable of producing 10,000-pound ingots, had a proposed start-up date some time in the second quarter of 1983. Because of Boeing's change of mind, plans for a unit to cast 20,000-pound ingot had to be made immediately in order to meet production schedules to supply materials for the 747. Similarly, the plants, particularly Davenport, had to prepare quickly to fabricate test materials, and later full-scale parts, for Boeing. Project engineers, both at the Laboratories and at Davenport, struggled to meet those objectives on schedule without sacrificing the opportunity to learn from early experience with the new alloys. At ATC, a computerized data bank was established to save vital information obtained during production of test materials for subsequent analysis. At Davenport, an Al-Li project team was set up to "maximize our learning experiences while supplying urgently needed samples of Al-Li products to Boeing for testing."[56]

The new emphasis on short-term application of Al-Li alloys in existing aircraft designs complicated the task of alloy development, as the new materials had to match the old rather precisely in order to permit direct substitution. The substitution program presented a "somewhat different technical challenge" from simply optimizing Al-Li compositions, because some of their most valuable properties, low density and high modulus of elasticity (stiffness), might have to be traded off to achieve a better fit. Acceptance of the revised objective for the project therefore made close cooperation between Alcoa Laboratories and Boeing an absolute necessity. In some instances, BMT said, reengineering of parts to fit Al-Li alloys might be possible. In others, acceptable trade-offs in properties would have to be determined.[57] In many ways, the project was a valuable learning experience for Alcoa. Closer exposure to customer design considerations revealed, for instance, that the new aircraft designs required low density to be maximized even over stiffness. Understanding that, alloy researchers were able to modify their research goals for the future. They had gained a new way of seeing things.

As they worked on the new set of problems during the course of 1983, additional complications arose. Following a meeting with Boeing, Alcoa's marketing manager for Al-Li alloys, Del Naser, found that in gauge-for-gauge substitutions, *typical* properties could become as important as *minimum* properties. Naser noted:

When an original wing design is tested to destruction, it generally fails at some margin above the calculated design ultimate load. This can be 5 to 15%. The FAA attributes some of this over achievement to the actual material properties being nearer or at typical, rather than at minimum values. The manufacturer is then allowed to take advantage of the extra strength in uprating gross take-off weight . . . and in most aircraft models, this generally happens.[58]

By the end of 1983, as Alcoa Laboratories was just succeeding in casting 10,000-pound ingots of its most promising alloy compositions, the whole issue of typical versus minimum properties threatened to become "a real bag of worms." However, the possibility for direct substitution had come to be seen as a major selling point for Alcoa's Al-Li alloys, an "unprecedented" opportunity for rapid penetration of the aerospace materials market. Naser predicted that within two years of their introduction, annual sales would leap from 5 to 30 million pounds.[59]

Alcoa applied for a patent on the new casting process in November 1983 and 11 months later broke ground at ATC for a dedicated Al-Li ingot-casting facility capable of producing 20,000-pound ingots up to a capacity of 2 million pounds per year, "sufficient to support several major airplane programs, at least in their initial stages." During the same time period, alloy MB80 was registered with the Aluminum Association as X2090. In order to speed up the process of evaluation, Alcoa reestablished its relationship with NAVAIR, signing a contract under which sample products would be sent to 30 airframe manufacturers and government laboratories and submitted to identical tests, with the results being compiled and analyzed jointly by Alcoa and the navy. Subsequently, the experimental designation was removed from alloy 2090, and Alcoa registered three additional alloys, which became the 8XXX (Al-Li-Cu-Mg) series.

Alloy 2090, with 2.2 percent lithium, met the goal of highest strength with reduced density, making it comparable to 7075-T6. The three 8XXX alloys, containing between 2.4 percent and 2.6 percent lithium, included a high-strength alloy with highest damage tolerance, a moderate-strength alloy that was highly corrosion- and SCC-resistant, and a low-strength, minimum-density alloy. In short, the obstacle of low fracture toughness was surmounted, and all the property goals established for the project achieved. As so many times before, those practical goals were achieved without a complete understanding of the microstructural phenomena responsible for the success. In the wake of the Al-Li project, however, research in this area became an open and cooperative effort in which Alcoa metallurgists, Vasudevan in particular, worked and published with university researchers funded by the company and by the government.[60]

That new openness reflected Alcoa's changed attitudes toward outside contacts. It also acknowledged the reality that leading-edge research in that field was going on throughout the industry and that Alcoa's competitors were fast making inroads in its dominant position.

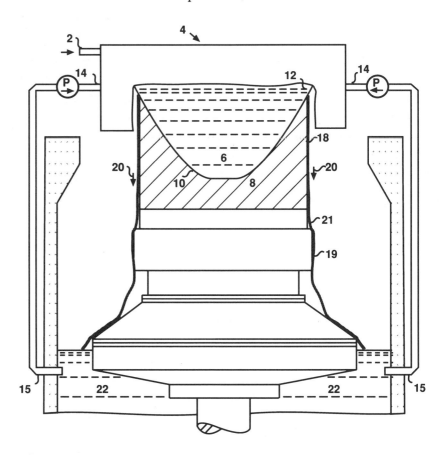

Figure 10.1. DC casting process for Al-Li alloys. Molten metal at about 1,320°F is passed in a line (2) through a direct-chill casting device (4) to the interior (6) of the ingot (8). The interior (6) includes a molten pool having a solidus line (10) that forms initially as a solid shell (12) at a solidus temperature on the order of about 1,100°F. Coolant at a temperature substantially below 1,100°F (about 120°F is preferred for safety considerations) is passed in a line (14) to the casting device (4), which is adapted to place the coolant in thermal contact, such as including but not limited to heat transfer through a mold surface (not shown), such that molten metal (6) is continuously cast as shell (12). The starting block (19) initially is placed directly under or inside the casting device (as shown), permitting the continuous-casting process. The shell (12) grows in thickness while the ingot (8) is cooled by direct chill. Source: John E. Jacoby, Ho Yu, and Robert A. Ramser, U.S. Patent No. 4,610,295 (9 September 1986), summarized in "Patent Spotlight: Direct-Chill Casting of Aluminum Alloys," *Light Metal Age* (April 1987):34–7.

INTERNATIONAL COMPETITION IN ALUMINUM-LITHIUM

Alcoa Laboratories had not previously been challenged by competitors in alloy development, as in other fields. Indeed, in the United States, Alcoa held the patents for 90 percent of all the

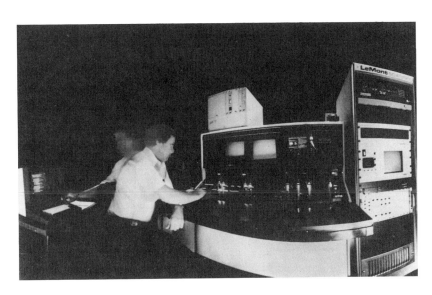

An analytical transmission electron microscope provides scanning transmission electron microscopy and x-ray analysis capabilities to determine chemical compositions of very small volumes of material. This allows scientists to understand the precise makeup of grain boundaries, precipitates, and constituents in any material examined. (From "The Material Difference," Alcoa Laboratories publication.)

alloys in common use. For Al-Li, however, there were several strong outside contestants. At first, the Soviet metallurgist Fridlyander led the field, more or less alone. His Al-Mg-Li alloy 01420 posed a challenge, in part because so little was known or understood about it, or about Al-Li alloys generally. Only in 1981, after extensive research and evaluation, was Alcoa able to eliminate Al-Mg-Li compositions from serious contention for full-scale development.

British Aluminium became the next serious contender in the Al-Li race, mounting an extensive research program strongly supported by government funding. Early in 1981, Staley evaluated the status of Al-Li development at British Aluminium, which he judged to be no further along than at Alcoa. He perceived British Aluminium to be hindered by a lack of fabrication facilities for R&D, as they were casting lab-scale ingots but had not made either fracture-toughness or fatigue tests on their candidate alloys. "British Aluminium's approach to alloy development," Staley wrote, "is to send a lab-fabricated product to their customers, ask them to evaluate it and tell BA how it's deficient, and then begin again."[61]

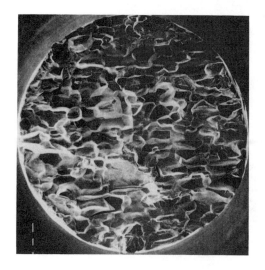

Electron micrographs of aluminum-lithium
alloys illustrate how computer-enhanced research tools reveal in minute detail the
properties of materials produced under different conditions. Above: A ⅛-inch-
diameter tensile bar (×30) made of Al-3Li.
It has been peak aged and subjected to hy-
drostatic testing. Right: Two merged photomicrographs (×100 and ×500) of porosity
in a 2090 ingot cast in 75 percent argon
atmosphere. Below: Fatigue-crack growth
in a 2020 ingot (Al-5Cu-1Li) that has been
subjected to an overload (×300).

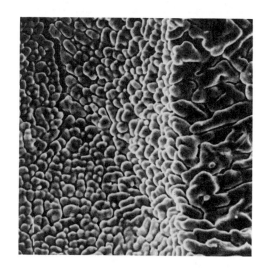

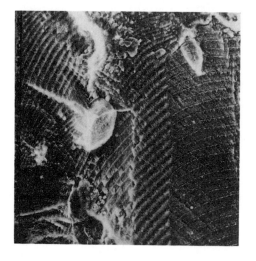

Although such an approach seemed inefficient to Alcoa's researchers, long accustomed to self-sufficient R&D programs, it had its virtues, such as the sharing of learning and risk with potential customers, as the Laboratories' experience with Boeing was to show. Moreover, in contrast to Alcoa's careful, "low-profile" stance, which was accentuated by the close, secrecy-bound agreement with Boeing, British Aluminium's high-profile program helped to create for it an aura of technical leadership. Its candidate alloys circulated widely in the aerospace industry two years before Alcoa publicly announced the existence of its alloys. During that period, various Alcoa customers, both military and commercial, at times felt angry at being excluded from a program of such obvious significance, and at times were suspicious that Alcoa Laboratories was finding the problems related to Al-Li development insurmountable. In the opinion of many observers, British Aluminium had the competitive edge in that area, especially when in November 1982 it began to advertise its Al-Li alloy, which was patented by the Royal Aircraft Establishment of the British Ministry of Defence.[62] So much impact did that have that in 1983 Alcoa decided to abandon its low-profile stance and announce the existence of its own alloys, using the trade name Alithalite.[63]

British Aluminium's work became more threatening when it merged with Alcan International in 1983. Alcan's European operations had the manufacturing capability, especially in sheet and plate, both critical to aircraft construction, to commercialize Al-Li alloys. Even more critical to the R&D competition was the bringing together of two advanced research facilities in Britain, with a mandate to lead the new company into new areas of technology. In one British journal, Geoffrey Scamans, a senior scientist at the laboratory in Banbury, England, was quoted to the effect that Alcan's top management was "thrusting money into our hands to allow us to go in exactly the directions we want." Al-Li alloy development was a major beneficiary of that corporate policy.[64]

Less well publicized, but absolutely critical, was the fact that the creation of British Alcan Aluminium (BAA) brought together British Aluminium's alloy composition and Alcan's Al-Li casting technology. Early in 1982, Alcoa had proposed a cooperative casting-safety program to both British Aluminium and Alcan, but only the latter had been interested in participating. Because Alcoa Laboratories seemed close to a solution at that time, the offer was withdrawn. However, Alcan continued to work independently and arrived at its own solution. In November 1982, when British Aluminium announced its Al-Li alloy, no mention was made of casting-safety problems, and sheet and plate fabricated from lab-scale ingots of 400 kilograms (880 pounds) were offered for evaluation. Four months later, after the Alcan purchase, BAA publicity on Al-Li alloys took a quite different stance on the issue of ingot casting:

The biggest problem had been how to use the direct chill method to cast ingots. Aluminium-lithium is highly explosive in contact with water and as water comes within two inches of the molten alloy that presents a difficulty. . . . [BAA] is now producing 200 kg ingots from an experimental casting process and expects to be able to turn out 2 tonne ingots by late next year.[65]

The creation of BAA presented Alcoa Laboratories with a formidable competitor. Late in 1983, at a U.S. Air Force–sponsored symposium of engineers and researchers from both aircraft and aluminum companies, Al-Li alloys were hailed as a major breakthrough, and BAA was seen as the leader in developing them. The more open and apparently more advanced British technology seemed to promise early selection of their Al-Li materials for evolving aircraft designs.[66] In 1986, BAA's alloy became the first to fly, on the McDonnell Douglas F15 Eagle fighter and the British Aerospace fighter, named, rather oddly, Experimental Aircraft Programme. By that time, too, Pechiney was offering an Al-Li alloy, and Reynolds and Kaiser had advertised Reyalite and Kallite. Nevertheless, Alcoa could take considerable comfort in the lead afforded by its heavy investment in full-scale casting technology. Alcoa was not viewed as the pioneer in Al-Li development, but once again its long experience in interactive programs of commercialization would stand it in good stead.

THE IMPORTANCE OF ALUMINUM-LITHIUM

The Al-Li project accentuated the degree to which aluminum science, like the industry as a whole, had regained the international scope it had had in the years before 1928. Aluminum R&D was strongly affected by the new trends that were influencing the entire industrial-research climate in the early 1980s, involving cooperative relationships between companies and with other research-performing institutions. The wealth of new, complex arrangements of all kinds signified a period of technological search and regrouping.

Boeing's willingness to share the risks of Al-Li alloy development contrasted sharply with the attitude of can makers toward the development of RCS, which had forced Alcoa to absorb virtually all the risks of innovation. A major aircraft redesign was an infrequent event, but Boeing's tendency to compete on performance made it proactive with regard to new materials when it did redesign. The comparison between Boeing and the can makers underscores the significance of working with different kinds of customers. During the 1960s, Alcoa had committed itself primarily to high-volume aluminum users, and there was a long-term cost to concentrating on such customers, who were not motivated to keep current with rapidly changing technologies. A large part of that cost was the toll exacted by the perception that Alcoa's technology was mature.

Speaking with the short memory of a postwar generation, one Seattle sales executive wrote of the Al-Li project that "Alcoa has never worked harder on a program nor more closely with a customer." But another vital element of the program was the small-budget bench-scale and fundamental work that had been carried on throughout the 1970s in alloy development, primarily with government funding, which drew on even longer streams of research in alloys and casting. Publicity statements in the 1980s touted the heavy investment and innovative management approach that brought the new alloys to production scale in a fraction of the usual number of years. These statements ignored both the prior spadework and the company's previous reluctance to invest in Al-Li at all. In fact, it could be said of Al-Li that the critical element in Alcoa's performance was less the heavy commitment made under time pressure than the dependence on the Laboratories' accumulated knowledge, organizational experience, and capabilities – fragile factors that having nearly stalled in the 1970s, had to be jump-started in the 1980s.

Epilogue: Aluminum enters Indian summer

Between 1986 and 1988, Alcoa Laboratories celebrated the combined centenaries of the Hall-Héroult process and the founding of Alcoa with a series of eight international scientific symposia. Those events brought together many of the world's leading authorities from industrial, academic, and government circles to share information on electrochemistry, ceramics, solidification, physical metallurgy, polymer science, deformation mechanics, structural materials, and sensors. Alcoa's ability to attract researchers of international stature to those conferences was a measure of how far the Laboratories had come in opening to the outside world and reestablishing its standing in the worldwide technical community. It also reflected the route the Laboratories had taken to generate new opportunities for Alcoa across a broad spectrum of materials technologies and to move forward in fundamental understanding of all the materials that might affect Alcoa's business. Behind the more obvious celebratory reason for the symposia lay the belief that the sharing of information would shorten the time required to commercialize new technologies. Less evident to the scientific community at large than was Alcoa's enhanced standing, but perhaps more important to Alcoa, was the profound change that the relationship between the Laboratories and the rest of the company had undergone in the 1980s.

ALCOA IN THE EIGHTIES

The company itself had assumed quite a different character since 1983. In that year Alcoa had accelerated an ongoing reorganization of its administrative structure, decentralizing its operations and reducing the size of corporate staffs at the Alcoa

475

Building G of the Alcoa Technical Center houses the Composite Manufacturing Technology Center. Here knowledge about engineered materials generated in Alcoa Laboratories is applied to produce new products by interdisciplinary teams made up of product and process engineering specialists and scientists with expertise in many different high-strength materials.

Building in Pittsburgh by transferring their responsibilities to the divisions and business units. Then, in 1986, the corporation was organized into five market-oriented business groups: Materials Science, Aerospace and Industrial Products, Packaging Systems, Primary Products, and International (which was later dispersed among the other four divisions). As a result of such changes, Alcoa had taken on a more technologically oriented profile. It had acquired or had started developing businesses in composite materials, ceramics, separations, and polymer packaging systems.

Alcoa Laboratories was intimately involved in many of these businesses. Taking a page out of its own history of more than half a century earlier, it had even erected a composite manufacturing facility capable of producing full-scale, prototype products on the grounds of Alcoa Technical Center.

It was Charles Parry who, as Alcoa's chairman, had fostered the strategy featuring a pronounced shift toward new materials.[1] Ironically, fears that he might have carried his program too far too fast led Alcoa's board of directors to replace him in 1987 with the first outside chairman in the company's history. The new chairman, Paul O'Neill, inherited a company with a much broader set of technical options than had been available to his predecessor. He also faced an economic outlook for aluminum that had completely reversed itself in the previous five years. Whereas in 1983 the price of aluminum had dropped to less than 50 cents per pound, by 1988 it had reached more than $1 per pound. Sales in the industry were at healthier levels than they had been for years. Profits and stock price also soared. O'Neill faced the classic dilemma of all industries dependent on established technologies. After passing through a period that had seemed to augur almost certain decline, aluminum had entered what scholar David Landes has called an "Indian summer," a period of time in which a mature technology facing eventual obsolescence shows strength and resilience in fighting off replacement technologies. There was no way of foretelling how long such a period might last, whether only a few years or decades, but meanwhile Alcoa had constructed for itself a technical platform that could support moves in several different strategic directions.[2]

CULTURAL CHANGE AT THE LABORATORIES

From 1983 to 1988, Alcoa Laboratories underwent changes as profound as the changes that had taken place during and after World War II, when it had moved from bench-scale research to the heavy-equipment era of the Working Aluminum Program. Not since the postwar attempt to aluminize the world had new-product research been considered such an essential plank in the research platform. Building on the foundation laid in the previous era of technology planning, Alcoa Laboratories redefined its mission and rebalanced its program toward the creation of new opportunities in materials technology. It was the stated objective of its new leadership to make Alcoa Laboratories a "World Class" scientific and engineering organization.

The aim was to change the culture of the Laboratories as quickly as possible, to make it a place that would be pursuing technological excellence in all aspects of its program. Because of the recent layoffs and their impact on morale, it was not possible to achieve that change by simply changing staff. Cultural change was achieved in other ways, through hiring, through use of outside consultants, through encouragement of advanced degrees, and through increased contacts with outside sources of technology. To create an environment productive for research, the four-track system was continued, performance reviews were carefully linked to clearly stated laboratory objectives, and risk-taking was encouraged.[3] By 1985 the technical staff had increased in size from 900 to 1,100, and many more technical-staff members had enrolled in further advanced-degree programs. In 1986 the percentage of technical staff with advanced degrees had risen from 44 to 60 percent, and the objective was to increase that to 75 percent by 1990. To eliminate dysfunctional organizational barriers, previously separate laboratory divisions reached out to become more closely involved with each other and with customer divisions as well. Project-management and team approaches already begun also received increased emphasis.[4]

Cultural change was above all a matter of a new style of leadership. The Laboratories' new director, Peter Bridenbaugh, seized every opportunity to communicate the nature and significance of the changes taking place. His message was threefold: Monolithic aluminum had settled into maturity; the company's traditional view of itself as first and foremost a primary aluminum producer was passé; the future lay with engineered materials (meaning specially tailored alloys and composites of one kind or another) and beyond intermediate products with components and systems. He warned that if aluminum did not join the world of versatile materials capable of being engineered to diverse specifications, it could easily find itself replaced by these kinds of materials. The need for change was seen as a positive development for the Laboratories. There was excitement in the opportunities available and in the renewed commitment of the company at large to its product technology. For the first time in years Alcoa Laboratories was being encouraged not only to find new-product opportunities and wider business opportunities but also to replenish its stock of fundamental knowledge.[5]

Alcoa's renewed commitment to strategic use of technology manifested itself in a variety of ways. Bridenbaugh was promoted to vice-president, a position that had been withheld from his predecessor as a signal that Alcoa Laboratories itself was in disfavor. The R&D budget, which had decreased in 1983, increased sharply in 1984 despite the dramatic fall in aluminum prices. The new level of expenditure was sustained for the next five years, so that after a decade of conservatism and general stringency, Alcoa Laboratories was able to strike out in new directions. The substantial allocation of funds to R&D supported the acquisition of a new generation of experimental equipment, advanced information technology, in-process testing, and various forms of experimental mills and pilot plants located at the Laboratories.

Carrying out the new strategy of diversification through technology, in the middle 1980s Alcoa purchased a collection of high-technology companies, most of them small and related to materials technologies that Alcoa Laboratories was interested in pursuing. Meanwhile, Alcoa's leadership arranged international joint ventures with a few key players in leading markets or in technologies complementary to Alcoa's – Fujikura in Japan, and Metal Box in England. In order to participate in the new world of custom-tailored materials, Alcoa needed to become more closely acquainted with its diverse markets and with the way different materials could serve market needs. Bridenbaugh stressed that historically it had been the materials suppliers' responsibility to build the knowledge base about the fundamental physical nature of their materials and their use characteristics. Although that undeniably involved a major investment in time and effort, those suppliers that were capable of providing comprehensive user information along with the materials themselves would be able to command premium prices and customer loyalty even in a market in which primary aluminum producers had proliferated.

The philosophy of adding value to the product led to a new systems approach to product categories. In packaging, for instance, the new approach went far beyond the introductory phase of the can-sheet business in the 1960s and 1970s, when Reynolds and Alcoa had both erected demonstration facilities for can production. Armed with novel concepts in food-can technology jointly developed with Metal Box, Alcoa aimed to forestall the inroads plastics companies were attempting to make in the container-sheet business by offering aluminum containers specially coated for each food product. In addition, it supplied the production equipment to produce the materials and the technical expertise to install and use it.[6]

The all-aluminum-car concept was similarly revised from the simple substitution of aluminum auto-body sheet for heavier steel of the mid-1970s to the Aluminum Intensive Vehicle program, a "materials systems" approach that used different mate-

The display of food cans shown here indicates the way that business for aluminum food cans has developed from small precoated cans used principally for meat and fish products to larger electrocoated cans for liquids and water-packed foods that require special can coatings and structural designs that resist crushing or denting.

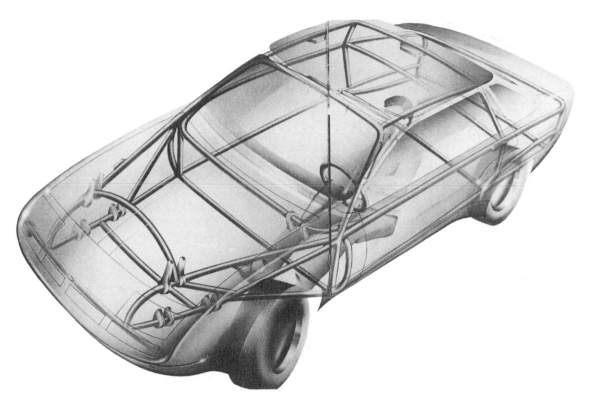

rials in a space frame concept offering weight reduction and reduced manufacturing costs.[7]

In another significant "systems" project, Alcoa promoted a new laminated material called ARALL Laminates that it had developed with Delft University. The new material was made of layered aramid fiber and aluminum sheet to provide "fatigue critical" components for aerospace applications. In 1987 the ARALL laminate project, which was wholly supported by the Aerospace and Industrial Product Business Unit, achieved corporate-venture status as managed by Alcoa's Sheet and Plate Division based in Davenport, Indiana. Expected to develop into a $50 – 100 million business, its interim production combined efforts of several Alcoa locations, including the Laboratories' new Composites Manufacturing Technology Division and the Davenport works.[8]

A symbolic but important sign that Alcoa intended to reclaim its domestic birthright to leadership in technology was its new technical-awards program. In addition to an expanded awards program internal to the Laboratories, the corporation launched

The "Aluminum Intensive Vehicle" program is based on a space-frame design concept that maximizes the use of aluminum not only by displacing heavier materials but also by drastically reducing the number of parts and changing their nature to reduce or eliminate retooling costs. If the engineering and production problems can be overcome, the unitized automobile body of the 1980s made up of over 400 separate parts will be supplanted by a space frame using as few as 75 parts.

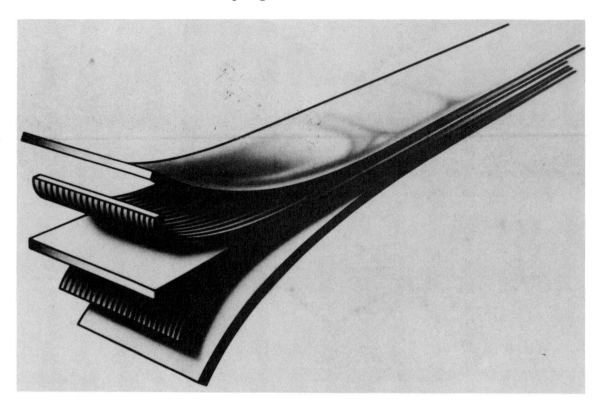

Highly engineered components made from composite materials like this ARALL Laminate, a polymer-reinforced aluminum laminate, combine the best characteristics of two or more materials. To make products out of such materials will require entirely new production methods. Alcoa scientists predict that they will be able to make specialized sheet products by casting products to small gauges and then building up structures by laminations.

a high-profile set of corporate awards for contributions in technology.[9] Beginning in 1984, each year individual contributors and research teams were honored, the individuals with the Francis C. Frary Award for Career Accomplishment or the Chairman's Award for Significant Technical Accomplishment, and the teams with the A. V. Davis Award for Project Achievement. After so many years when patents had been a bone of contention, the company pursued an aggressive patenting policy, serving notice that it would prosecute competitors who infringed its patents without taking a license from Alcoa.[10]

Between 1983 and 1986, Alcoa's R&D program moved away from its traditional concentration on the primary aluminum processes, smelting and refining, toward much heavier emphasis on value-added aluminum products and advanced manufacturing-process developments. New-product and new-process programs jumped from 4 percent of the 1980 budget of $79 million to 17 percent of the 1986 budget of $125 million. The process-automation category went from zero in 1980 to 4.5 percent in 1986. Smelting and chemicals research, including alumina research, declined to approximately 5 percent of the 1988 budget from more than 40 percent of the 1983 budget.

COMPANY RESPONSE

The changes at the Laboratories reverberated through other parts of Alcoa. The effects of the R&D reforms were felt the more intensely because they occurred just at a time when the entire company was deep into organizational restructuring. From the Operations point of view, Alcoa Laboratories was redefining its program and deemphasizing its support for day-to-day operations and for aluminum-related research at a time when Operations felt its need the most. Central Engineering – a powerful force in the organization that had been accustomed to exercising almost absolute control over choices of technology for the operating sites – had just been dispersed to the divisions, and the responsibility for transferring technology was left undefined. Operating locations were assigned responsibility for selecting, acquiring, and implementing their own process technologies. Although for some that was a daunting prospect, others found it long overdue and pushed to extend their control over matters technological to R&D as well.

Opinion in the company varied widely as to the appropriateness of the strategic shift toward new materials. The traditionally strong aerospace business that supplied aircraft sheet, for example, was opposed to pushing materials substitution in aircraft too aggressively. Group Vice-President Vincent Scorsone advocated a measured approach to composites that allowed for preservation of the capital assets already invested in producing aluminum products. "If the Labs wants to understand our business strategy," he explained,

they need to fully appreciate our dedication to protecting the current manufacturing asset base and to the concept of fundamental process understanding as vital to production differentiation. These fundamentals link me closely to the role of aluminum in Alcoa's future. We can hold composites off by aggressive lightweighting of aluminum alloys. Al-Li is proof of that. I also believe we'll be in the aluminum business for some time to come. That's not to say, however, that we're adverse to the R&D folks developing laminates or composites. I would like to be able to fabricate them in our current facilities though.[11]

These "pin grid array" electronics packages are the first products from Alcoa's subsidiary, Alcoa InterCon-X (AIX). These multilayer ceramic packages incorporate many of the materials and technologies that Alcoa Laboratories has been working on in the late 1980s. The alumina-based ceramic package used to connect a computer chip with its host computer also contains metals and polymers. The success of Alcoa's ceramics business will depend in part on the ability of Alcoa researchers to learn how all the different materials behave in interaction with each other.

Other parts of the company wanted to control their own R&D programs completely. The new ceramics business, for example, proposed to go outside for its research.

While the responses of the rest of the company toward the changes at the Laboratories caused some dissension, they also confirmed that the cultural change toward a more thoroughgoing emphasis on technology was gradually taking hold throughout the company. In the early 1980s, when sales were down and the price of aluminum was at a very low level, there was a natural reluctance on the part of Operations to endorse a major reallocation of money to R&D. When the market turned around and revenues rose, the situation soon moved to a pressured outlook for Operations that, judging from tradition, would be just as likely to divert attention away from technology. But efforts taking place at corporate headquarters, led by the Technology Planning staff, were creating an increased technological awareness among senior managers that was also permeating the operating divisions. Keith Turnbull, vice-president for technology planning, and his associates worked to convince all the operating divisions that their processes were reaching the point of diminishing returns and to acquaint them with what was going on internationally in their industry and in other industries. Through these efforts, and by means of their own increasing contacts with the outside, Alcoa's operating divisions confronted directly the long-range implications of the competitive state of aluminum process technology. The Japanese were applying statistical process-control techniques and adopting new computer technologies and were achieving productivity levels unheard of at Alcoa. Strategically as important was the realization that the use of flexible, advanced manufacturing techniques was also an essential complement to the successful development of engineered-materials businesses. That realization created common ground between Research and Operations the way the need for a Working Aluminum Program had created common ground in the 1940s.[12] In that context, the knowledge that Alcoa Laboratories was spearheading a drive to lead the company into replacement technologies helped to spur existing operations to improve their processes. Renewed interest in technology as a competitive weapon led the operating divisions to make fresh demands on the Laboratories and to push for more allocation of R&D resources to Operations. Keith Turnbull observed that a change had taken place in the way Operations and the Laboratories were relating to each other:

Traditionally, new technologies have radiated from the Labs to our operating locations. With advanced manufacturing, however, the pull comes from the manufacturing floor. Plant managers have to decide – and have decided – the approach they want to take to implement advanced manufacturing. But they cannot do it alone. They will depend on a wealth of expertise at the Labs to help them meet their objectives.[13]

In response to these demands the Laboratories continued to adjust the balance of its R&D program. In 1986, in a noticeable shift from the broadening efforts of only a few years earlier, Bridenbaugh acknowledged a necessity to allocate more corporate R&D budgetary support to advanced manufacturing for plants. The Laboratories' horizon foreshortened in other areas as it backed away from its original pursuit of broad-front opportunities in new materials that might be realized in the longer term but would take heroic efforts to achieve. Instead, it focused on niche markets for new materials that would be likely to break even soon after introduction. Without curtailing sustained efforts, it also shifted some resources toward new businesses selected for their more immediate promise for success.

REFOCUSING ALCOA'S STRATEGY

By the time Paul O'Neill took office in 1987, the company's strategic options had both broadened and come more sharply into focus. The business media were quick to detect in Paul O'Neill's appointment a major change in direction for Alcoa.[14] O'Neill, like senior executives in manufacturing companies across the United States in the last half of the 1980s, placed heavy emphasis on the continued health of the core technology and expressed misgivings about pursuing breakthrough technologies. But in the Alcoa of the late 1980s, it was a mistake to interpret these changes in philosophy as anything resembling a reversion to the past. Even two years of stepped-up fundamental research had uncovered major opportunities in aluminum that would have made a wholesale shift to new materials seem premature. In short, the strategic refocusing was already taking place. Moreover, Alcoa, unlike many U.S. manufacturing companies, had been developing for some time the capabilities to support rapid process modernization. After several years of reorganization, and with the benefit of its investment in outside learning, Alcoa had more opportunities than it could reasonably support. The corporation's task, presented with the Laboratories' more fully developed vision of the technical possibilities, was to make the strategic choices among them.

In the spring of 1988, Alcoa's president, Fred Fetterolf, presented the redirection of the Laboratories' mission as a positive sign that the company had successfully integrated its corporate strategy with its technology strategy:

About a year ago, we stepped back and realized that while the Labs was driving a host of new technologies, the corporation simply could not afford to support any more ventures than those already identified. As a result, our emphasis is now on supporting our core business and developing the new businesses we already have in place. This is a shift from the broader charter under which the Labs had been operating. The Labs' challenges are now to: narrow its focus; help prove that we can make money in the new businesses we have selected; and improve upon our existing aluminum-related businesses. This is going to require more interaction between the Labs and our plants and businesses.[15]

By 1988 the Laboratories budget as such had levelled off, and more of its funding was once again being channeled through the business units, a group by then expanded to include start-up businesses such as ceramics and separations. The level of the Laboratories' budget, unchanged for the following year, had been pegged at a figure that top management believed to be sustainable regardless of future ups and downs in the basic business. To ensure that Laboratories technology was in fact being implemented, Bridenbaugh was assigned to take broader responsibility, to be "chief technologist" for the entire company, with oversight of all R&D taking place throughout the corporation.

Alcoa had reached the end of the first aluminum century with more opportunities than anyone had envisioned several years earlier. Having narrowed down to a few strategic options, it considered itself in a position to pursue coherent strategies ranging all the way from the lunge into electronic ceramics that had been initiated during the Parry years to a substantial reemphasis on the more traditional, but still challenging, aluminum R&D programs. That technology, once thought to be mature, showed some signs of revival. Although new research technologies such as computer modelling could not alter the fundamental constraints of aluminum technology, they did make it far easier to realize substantial returns from investment in incremental process changes such as significant reductions in rolling-mill downtime or new approaches to forging. No longer facing the stark prospect of either abandoning a core technology or facing immanent business decline, the company appeared to have the luxury of shifting gradually into new businesses as they developed. As can happen with technologies that are challenged by advanced substitutes, earlier reports of the death or saturation of worldwide aluminum markets had been greatly exaggerated. Aluminum appeared to be entering a prolonged Indian summer as opportunities in packaging, transportation, building, and construction opened up on an international scale.

Although the original intent of the sudden increase in R&D investment at the Laboratories – the desire for large diversification opportunities – was no longer viewed as an urgent necessity, it would be a mistake to forget the role that the search for those opportunities had played in creating the Indian summer. By 1988 the Laboratories had entered into the more broad-based engagement with the rest of the company that it had sought since the early 1970s. The most significant change was that some parts of the company had once again begun to apply a suction to its R&D organization, to look for a partnership with the Laboratories that would leave neither control of, nor responsibility for, technology simply to that specialist function. That was a note that Paul O'Neill sounded when discussing R&D at Alcoa:

I have a problem with the concept of a separate and separated R&D activity. I think separatism defeats what we are trying to do and what we need to accomplish. What we need to accomplish necessitates scientists and engineers and technologists being part of a working team – not a separate group of people who *provide* solutions, but people who work with other people to *create* solutions. That's why I resist the idea of research and development as a separatist notion, because to me that's antithetical to the needs of our enterprise.[16]

Alcoa's operations were not only taking ownership of the need for continuous improvement in the quality sense but also were beginning to accept the notion that it was up to them to invest their own energy and resources in experimentation. That left the Laboratories with a qualitatively different kind of support role than the one it had deemphasized five years earlier. Whether or not the Laboratories would be able to pursue the kind of balanced agenda that had characterized its most productive periods in earlier eras remained to be seen.

Meanwhile, the extent to which technological renewal seemed to be taking hold throughout Alcoa was demonstrated in the R&D awards for the centennial year of 1988. In a telling symbol of the rebalancing of activity, for the first time the A. V. Davis Award went to a technology developed primarily outside the

Laboratories, by teams from Lebanon, Pennsylvania, and from Brazil.

Though the strategic choices that had been made in terms of curtailing further new-business work were less farsighted than some members of the technical community, remembering the heady days of the early 1980s, might have preferred, two important aspects of the new directions of the 1980s remained in place. First, fundamental research aimed at continuing to build the knowledge base remained at a steady 20–25 percent of the overall Laboratories budget, and the expectation that the R&D community would maintain an independent view remained intact. As Paul O'Neill put it, it was important to have "a culture where knowledgeable dissent is an accepted norm."[17] Peter Bridenbaugh echoed those sentiments from the R&D perspective:

As the guardians of the long-term view for our company it is still incumbent upon the Labs to pursue high-risk technologies and to continue to raise critical issues concerning Alcoa's future threats and opportunities. We said we were going to reinvigorate fundamental research, and that effort, already established, continues unabated.[18]

To ensure that aluminum's prosperity did not undercut Alcoa's ability to commercialize its new technologies, Alcoa Laboratories would focus its attention on keeping the company's technological options open.

Conclusion

The practice of history does not license us to predict what will happen to Alcoa, or to R&D at Alcoa, in the future. The purpose of this study is not to emphasize or point to the need for any particular historical outcome, for outcomes are tentative matters indeed. But this look at a century of R&D in the shifting climate of national and international events, and in the particular context of one company, does permit some conclusions about the nature of R&D as an industrial activity. These conclusions revolve around the three themes noted in the introduction: the peculiar challenges of process innovation, the effect of organizational maturity on technology, and the importance of technical vision for the prospects of company renewal.

THE DISTINCTIVE NATURE OF PROCESS R&D

In the increasingly competitive international environment for industry in the 1980s, the role of process R&D has become a subject of intense interest. Many view the evidence of current U.S. deficiencies in manufacturing capability as unprecedented in the American experience. But Alcoa's rude awakening to its competitive shortcomings in the international arena just before World War I reminds us that the decade of the 1980s is not the first time that leading American companies have lost business because of deficiencies in their manufacturing processes. Part of what makes the continuing business of modernization so difficult lies with the extraordinary difficulties of managing process R&D.[1]

To the outside world, Alcoa R&D has been better known for its strong position in aluminum-alloy research than for its process research. Fully two-thirds of all the alloys registered with

491

the Aluminum Association have been developed by Alcoa. The company's effort to "aluminize the world" after World War II led to a generation of new-product developments that extended the range of aluminum products to a degree unimaginable before the war. Moreover, since the early days of Alcoa's R&D organization, there has always been some research that has not involved developing either new products or new processes. Rather, it has involved understanding the fundamentals of aluminum as a material, or it has involved gathering information on aluminum in use. Examples of the former would be the comprehensive program on phase diagrams of different aluminum alloys conducted under Frary in the 1930s and 1940s, or the important study of the physical characteristics of aluminum using x-ray or spectrographic techniques. This line of research still continues at Alcoa, employing powerful computers to model and simulate with ever greater accuracy and detail the relationships among alloy composition, microstructure, thermo-mechanical processing, and performance. Vital research programs of long standing include efforts to understand the phenomena of corrosion and, later, stress-corrosion cracking.

Nevertheless, much of Alcoa's R&D program over time has been inextricably linked to process innovation – finding new ways to make or do things – or process improvement – discovering or adapting better ways to make the same thing. Some process R&D has been of a fundamental nature, being focused on the principles that underlie generic process types, such as refining, smelting, casting, extruding, forging, or rolling; much more has been applied – that is, solving process-specific technical problems. Major process R&D programs at Alcoa, such as the ones that developed the combination process, the direct-chill ingot-casting process, water-based lubricants, the Alcoa Smelting Process, and the inert anode for electrolytic cells, incorporated important breakthroughs. They also benefited from the cumulative impact of countless incremental changes. Other important process changes were entirely incremental in nature, such as the gradual increases in the efficiency of the Hall-Héroult smelting cell achieved through better control of electrolytic-bath composition, the improved design and purity of carbon anodes, and the improvement in ingot quality through development of technology to degas and filter molten metal.

Manufacturing-process R&D in a capital-intensive industry like aluminum poses awkward organizational dilemmas, and it is a voracious consumer of specialized capital equipment. The common R&D procedure for most new processes consists of several stages of scale-up from bench scale, through one or more pilots at less-than-production volumes, to production scale. Sooner or later it is necessary either to try out new processes inside the plant environment (usually with costly disruption to regular production) or to install full-scale production equipment in a laboratory or quasi-laboratory setting. Neither approach is ideal for all parties, and both are enormously expensive either in capital cost or in opportunity cost associated with equipment downtime. Through the years, Alcoa has invested immense amounts of money in setting up and operating what in product programs are termed "test beds," and in process industries are called "pilot facilities" – areas where products or processes can be put through their paces before they are turned over for salable production.

The experimental mill used to develop Duralumin in the 1920s was only the first of many large-scale operations devoted to investment in ongoing process improvement. Today, advanced modelling and simulation techniques make it possible to conduct within the computer itself many of the experiments formerly possible only by using actual physical equipment. Still, the huge complexities of the manufacturing floor make the experimental use of production equipment essential to the ultimate implementation of process change. Some of Alcoa's experimental facilities, like Potline B, were located at or near plant operations, while others were part of the huge amount of capital equipment that turned Alcoa's postwar R&D campus into something resembling a production site. Alcoa Laboratories today houses full-scale equipment for the fabrication of aluminum beverage containers and easy-open ends, along with commercial-scale production facilities for aluminum-lithium alloys and prototype parts made from laminate and composite materials. Over the years, the Laboratories' experimental facilities have played a critical role in innovation, allowing the works to try out improvements to their existing processes and to test alternatives without disrupting operations, and also serving as important training areas for researchers and nonresearchers alike. In the rush to bring the Warrick plant on line in the 1960s, Alcoa was able to make much more rapid progress in ingot casting than in rolling, largely because the ingot-casting team had its Arnold laboratory, while researchers in rolling waited in limbo to move to ATC.

Another distinctive characteristic of process R&D is its interdisciplinary nature. Whereas certain types of product R&D can be conducted wholly within the bounds of one discipline, that is rarely the case for process R&D. All but the most rudimentary process changes usually involve multiple scientific disciplines and a number of craft or experience-based skills as well. Programs such as those to develop rigid container sheet or aluminum-lithium alloys, which might be considered product programs, actually involved numerous interlocking developments on the process side. Each required a complex mixture of science and engineering disciplines, as well as several operations specialties. Neither could have been successful if any part of Alcoa's highly integrated technical community had been unable to do its part.

This characteristic has significant implications for R&D management. First, as we have seen, these complex projects require management at two levels – at the level that governs individual developments, but also at the level that facilitates the critical interactions between them. Second, as Alcoa's experience shows, once a successful process innovation has been achieved, it becomes difficult to dislodge, because changes to any part of the system imply changes in many parts.

Alcoa's early strategy of integrating its operations to include all stages of the aluminum manufacturing process imposed on the company a tremendous burden – the need to master and keep advancing at a steady pace all parts of the integrated system. While integration provided key economic and strategic advantages for Alcoa, it also required constant managerial attention. President Irving W. ("Chief") Wilson was the most vocal advocate for, but certainly not Alcoa's only believer in, the philosophy of seeking constant technological improvements at the operating sites. The dangers of forgetting that philosophy were amply demonstrated in the era after World War II, when intense pressures for ever greater output, an increasing economic need for cost savings in a newly competitive environment, and a growing animosity between labor unions and managers caused many works to eliminate their on-site R&D programs. When in the 1970s, for cost-cutting and marketing reasons, most of the company's R&D expertise was concentrated at Alcoa Technical Center, Operations ceased to consider process improvement or modernization to be its responsibility.[2]

One of the reasons they left the responsibility for process improvement to others was the growing cost of research equipment. Another was the increased skill levels and degrees of specialization associated with doing R&D work. When Earl Blough and "Dutch" Nagel first tried to produce Duralumin before World War I, a researcher could be a jack-of-all-trades. But by the time DC ingot casting was under development, in the mid-1930s, it was already clear that orthodox research techniques were moving beyond the training or experience of most plant-level engineers. The choice facing all companies when that happened was to increase the skill levels of the plant engineering force or concentrate the research work in the central location where a few highly trained people could handle most of the more demanding technical work for the company.[3]

These current problems should not mislead us into thinking that it has ever been easy to manage process R&D. The characteristics we have just cited are inherent features of the activity. It has always been necessary to coordinate many different kinds of work with widely varying rhythms, to achieve communication between specialists who talk different scientific and managerial languages, and to resolve the natural disagreements in values and philosophy between craftsmen and scientists. The latter relationship, in particular, can be a powerful source either of dysfunctional conflict or of creativity. Shop-floor personnel who have the vested interest of hands-on experience with existing technology can challenge researchers to break out of linear thinking and come to new insights, or they can refuse to cooperate and keep the process functioning forever as an aging art. In enlightened situations it has been the role of R&D management to get craftsmen and engineers to complement each other, rather than obstruct each other. At Alcoa, such a situation existed most notably at the Cleveland works, where Research, Engineering, Sales Development, and Operations had a highly interactive and generally harmonious relationship. It was that arrangement that served as Kent Van Horn's ideal when he came to take over the R&D organization in New Kensington.

As we have seen, Alcoa put tremendous emphasis on process improvement and larger-scale process innovation in the period after World War II. The Working Aluminum Program, initiated in the late 1930s but carried forward after 1945, the large-scale ingot program, the revival of smelting research in the 1950s that evolved into the immense effort on the Alcoa Smelting Process of the 1960s and 1970s, the Warrick plant with its aggressive, linked modernizations in ingot casting, rolling, and recycling – these and many other programs made Alcoa an outstanding example of a U.S. company dedicated to innovation in process technology. But after World War II, changing conditions for research in Alcoa, as in many American companies, definitely conspired to make process R&D much more difficult to conduct effectively.

Chief among these conditions was the enormous growth in volume output and in the scale of manufacturing equipment. Other factors undercutting widely applicable process R&D at Alcoa were the withdrawal of experimental capability from the operating sites, the concentration of the R&D budget in ASP research, and the consolidation of all R&D at the Alcoa Technical Center. In the interests of organizational efficiency, ready access to necessary operating information was curtailed, marketing interests became dominant, and it became harder to differentiate research from development. Less obvious problems were the cutback in investment on fundamental research that left rolling (unlike casting, for instance) without an adequate knowledge base to draw on when it needed to modernize. As we have seen, companywide policies protecting know-how also had their effect, for inhibitions on the free flow of information between companies made it hard to gain access to external technology to compensate for gaps in the internal knowledge base. In a company that for decades took for granted its own technical self-sufficiency, the hardest adjustment was learning how to "borrow" again from outside sources of scientific expertise. Experiences such as the Broner mill-control program demonstrated that a different orientation and different skills were needed to acquire technology from the outside and adapt it, as compared with generating it internally.

Equally severe, though less visible, pressures working against effective process innovation at Alcoa were developments in society at large that affected all U.S. companies. When, in the postwar era, the federal government pumped funding into industrial R&D, it focused primarily on fundamental and product-related R&D. Because Alcoa was hardly disposed to court direct government funding in the aftermath of the monopoly judgment, the government's R&D funding policy appeared irrelevant. Nevertheless, the company could not avoid being affected by conditions within the national research community at large. The research-performing universities, currently funded as never before, attached highest priority and highest professional status to those areas in which the bulk of federal funding was concentrated: electronics and aeronautics. Demand for Ph.D. physicists, and to a lesser extent Ph.D. chemists, soared, as did their prestige, while regard for those in the more traditional fields such as mechanical engineering and metallurgy slumped. From the 1960s on, anything associated with the manufacturing floor was considered by the professions to be of low status, an attitude that gradually pervaded much of American society.[4]

Beginning in the late 1970s, Alcoa was in the vanguard of companies seeking to reverse those trends. Well before the decline in process technology came to be viewed as a national dilemma, Alcoa's laboratories and its corporate technical staffs began to address the problem internally. But efforts to change the prospects for effective process innovation at Alcoa, as in all established American companies, had to overcome powerful organizational realities.

LIMITATIONS OF BUREAUCRACY

There is much to be said about the larger costs and benefits of institutionalizing R&D. Studies have shown that in the United States before World War II, companies in science-based industries that invested steadily in R&D were more stable and more successful than companies that did not.[5] Scholars have attributed the success of the modern corporate structure in the scientific epoch to hierarchical control of all its means of production and distribution. Among these they include the ability to coordinate through control of technical information, to monitor and evaluate production processes, and to allocate resources among different opportunities. In-house R&D has been credited with giving the modern company the ability not only to integrate important technical information across functions but also to improve its processes and to create new market opportunities.[6]

Even though the historical evidence is strong that integration of R&D, and its control by the managerial hierarchy, gave the companies that invested in it a significant competitive advantage in the first half of the twentieth century, it nevertheless begs certain questions. Was the advantage sustainable? What are the limitations of integration for R&D? Did the conditions that made that performance possible continue to hold true in the second half of the century? Did they apply to the same types of R&D as before?[7]

Measuring Alcoa's pattern of R&D evolution against the stages at Bayer provides us with some tentative answers. Alcoa's organizational evolution took longer, and its institutions were more resilient than those at Bayer. With a more complicated (because more fully integrated) set of processes to master, and with a large market that it dominated Alcoa took more than 50 years to reach the fifth stage of routinization of innovation.[8] It was only in the late 1950s that Alcoa's R&D organization became less responsive to its strategic needs. And although its fully developed R&D control structure, in the form of an increasingly baroque subcommittee system, was cumbersome, Alcoa still was able to enter a vast new market for rigid container sheet 40 years after the opening of the monumental Aluminum Research Laboratories.

Nevertheless, Alcoa's experience of the 1970s, like that of many other large R&D-performing companies, suggests that the effectiveness of hierarchy and control over R&D had definite limitations. Allowed to proceed to its logical extremes, the institutionalization of R&D eventually undercut its value to the company. Cutting Alcoa's research staff off from each other, and from the outside world, stanched the flow of the technical knowledge and information that would allow the Laboratories to form an independent assessment of the state of technological opportunity. Setting up individual corporate organizations in metallurgy and engineering, each with separate power bases, eventually blocked the smooth flow of technology to the plant floor. Creating an elaborate hierarchy of development laboratories, and then controlling the research process as though it were the same activity as development, isolated the research function and reduced the flow of market and process information that Research needed to define the company's most important long-term problems. Quantitative management techniques, such as discounted cash flow, net present value, and project evaluation, misapplied to research-based projects, killed off the uncertain but promising in favor of the certain and unexciting. When Alcoa's R&D organization became a repository of static information – a body of knowledge cut off from regeneration through research – rather than a clearinghouse for dynamic information, either internally generated or available from outside sources, it could no longer perform the mission for which it was created.

In R&D, as in other activities, only strong leadership can offset or reverse the effects of hierarchical rigor mortis. Alcoa had its share of strong leaders, both inside and outside R&D, and they help to account for the resilience of its institutions. In Zay Jeffries, Francis Frary, and Kent Van Horn the company had three effective prototypes of R&D leadership. Jeffries and Frary both had the ability to create and convey a technical vision without losing sight of the need to balance the fundamental and the immediately useful. Van Horn was exceptionally able at working with the rest of the company. He used his considerable charisma to foster the company's most effective hierarchical mechanism in the subcommittee system, a device that served as an extremely important integrating mechanism in the efforts to achieve process innovation after World War II. But Van Horn also pushed the subcommittee system too far, and he sacrificed the Laboratories' necessary autonomy. By the time he recognized that his system was helping to undermine the next phase of investment in fundamental R&D, it was too late for him to change. His successors had neither the organizational clout nor the time in office to remedy the problem.

Alcoa's experience also illustrates that some of the influences leading to technological maturity are beyond the control of any one company, embedded as they are in the industrial culture. It was more than mere coincidence that Alcoa found itself with rigid and unresponsive R&D at much the same time that many other companies were discovering the same problem. In many cases, the core technologies, though not identical, derived from the same electrochemical base and were at similar stages of evolution.

Moreover, quite apart from the technologies involved, what all these companies had at the time were similar organizational characteristics and professional managerial philosophies. Alcoa's subcommittee system, for instance, had a close counterpart in the well-known "Objectives, Strategies, and Tactics" planning system that was for so long the hallmark of R&D at Texas Instruments and that was adopted in modified form by many other companies.[9] The move to divisional structures in many firms, substituting internal incentive, control, and resource-allocation devices for direct feedback from the market, clearly had a negative effect on the ability of those companies to allocate resources to longer-term and uncertain projects. That was especially true when the projects were not large and were not directly sponsored by top management. At Alcoa, which remained functionally organized for longer than most major corporations that produced diverse products for different markets, the transition into a multidivisional structure had some bad side effects on ongoing R&D arrangements. It was the movement toward allocating R&D costs to profit centers, begun in the mid-1970s, that signaled the end to such important experimental assets as the Arnold casting unit and Potline B.

Other important determinants of maturity for Alcoa, as for similar companies, were the state of the technology in its major industry and the condition of the national R&D infrastructure. Nowhere was that more evident than in the change in Alcoa management's attitude toward R&D during World War II. Prior to the war, Alcoa might have liked to emulate the mass-production metal producers in the steel industry, but markets would not permit it. Instead, it identified with the high-technology companies of the day, its electrical-company customers and, later, the aircraft and engine companies. The nature of its competitive horizons changed drastically at about the time it shifted to competing with steel in the 1960s. When the target competitors were steel companies, and the leading-edge customers were the ultracautious can companies, it was easy for Alcoa to regard itself as an unusually progressive metals company investing in R&D well above industry norms. For a company that was still pursuing dynamic objectives, steel-industry norms made very misleading benchmarks.

Meanwhile, in the country at large, the channels of technical information that had been important to companies like Alcoa before World War II became less useful sources of dynamic influence afterward. As we have seen for companies in the process industries, universities no longer played a positive role. Instead, they accorded negative status to manufacturing and to the engineering fields associated with it. Students were taught to believe that the highest form of scientific achievement was in theoretical research of a highly specialized nature. The engineering directorate of the National Science Foundation funded almost exclusively science-based engineering projects. Few engineering schools remained closely tied to industry. Interdisciplinary study of the kind required by process work was not encouraged.

Alcoa's R&D of the 1970s lost contact not only with the strategic mainstream of its own company but also with the professional scientific community that might have been able to expand its vision of what was possible. When Alcoa evolved into the fifth, routinized, stage of R&D development, much of its program, save for the highly secretive ASP, involved unquestioning obedience to the dictates of Marketing and short-term technical support for Operations. Marketing scorned its old missionary philosophy, and R&D lacked both the incentives and the credibility to offer persuasive alternatives to industry norms. The Laboratories were in no position to render the kind of independent assessment of the state of advancing materials technology that could provide the corporation with a coherent long-term technical vision for the company.

TECHNICAL VISION AND RENEWAL

Once the situation was recognized, it took more than a decade to reverse. Even if the company had chosen to start a new R&D effort from scratch and to set up wholly new laboratories separate from Alcoa Technical Center and devoted entirely to new materials, it still would have taken much time. As Frary discovered in the 1920s, R&D institution building in established companies is a lengthy process. Moreover, a laboratory devoted to replacement technologies is the least popular of institutions in an existing business, no matter where it is housed.

This is, in essence, the "Indian summer of obsolescence." It is the reluctance of existing producers to accept renewing innovation and timely self-obsolescence, not the failure of the producers of new technologies to transfer it, that leads to institutional rigidity. Often that phenomenon is mistaken for technological maturity. The tendency many companies have to blame R&D organizations for failure to transfer their developments puts the onus on the wrong party.

Of course, R&D must have the latitude to look beyond the confines of its own industry. When R&D becomes institutionalized, it can easily become imprisoned in current markets and lose the capacity for an independent technical vision. Innovation, even large-scale process innovation, carried out in service to a technologically static market can lead to costly mistakes. A good example of this is the Three Mile Island nuclear power plant, which adopted what were considered state-of-the-art computer controls. Identifying too closely with prevailing technology in the fossil-fuels industry, it did not seek the best controls technology available for nuclear plants, even though such controls had long been used in the nuclear navy. Alcoa's ASP program had a similar problem. It relied too long on the state of knowledge inside the aluminum industry before calling in Lummus Engineering and gaining access to process technology better understood in the chemical industry.

Access to an independent vision does not have to lead to strategic mayhem. The strategic choice may be to serve existing markets with existing products, but processes developed outside an industry may make it possible to serve those existing markets in a radically improved way. It is the role of R&D to make that possible.

Alcoa's R&D organization laid the groundwork for renewal in the late 1960s with a self-study. It took until the late 1970s before it could be said to have gained effective access to the external technology that was vital to continued modernization of aluminum production. In the early 1980s it made strenuous attempts to improve the technical information flow from the outside world, both nationally and internationally. In addition to major changes in hiring and program, management arranged multiple technical alliances to share and acquire technology. By the mid-1980s, Alcoa Laboratories had once again plugged in to the broader international scientific community, and its staff was actively involved with some of the latest developments in materials technology. Only then was it able to generate a portfolio of technological opportunities and to offer an independent judgment on the state of relevant materials technology.[10] Meanwhile, with the decentralization of the company at large and the dispersal of its central engineering organization, Alcoa's plants worked on improving their environments for technical change. Operations took more responsibility for pushing the company's technology. That ensured that Alcoa would preserve its strategic option to remain a leading aluminum company.

Revitalizing the Laboratories alone would not have sufficed for renewal. In the first half of the 1980s, management appeared to be relying on that approach without involving the rest of the company. But the sudden increase in laboratory budgets, and the sharp change in R&D's program agenda, put the rest of the company on the defensive. In the long run it was recognized that an assessment of advancing technology not tied to company structure, capabilities, or directions would have been useless. No matter how well conceived, the technical vision generated by the Laboratories could not provide a strategy for the company – only a feasible synthesis of possibilities. It was management, not the Laboratories, that had to make the ultimate choice, accepting some possibilities, rejecting others. When Alcoa's new leadership made its own assessment, it did not elect to pursue all of the opportunities the Laboratories had outlined. But the ability to disagree, the creative tension between the two, was perhaps the surest sign that renewal could occur. R&D was contributing while neither dictating the technical agenda nor dominating the company's strategy.

Alcoa's renewal experience, even though we do not know its outcome, suggests a view of the way R&D serves industrial purposes that is different from the traditional impression. For R&D, neither complete subservience nor complete independence is a reasonable alternative. The attempt to control the technical effort and focus researchers on more timely and useful objectives can deprive a company not only of access to the latest technology but also of the separate perspective corporate R&D was established to develop. The appropriate task of managing R&D is not to achieve either complete harmony between the Laboratories and the corporation as a whole or unity with the scientific community at large; rather, it is to maintain constant tension between the two. A creative tension must also be preserved within the R&D program, between the operating need and the new opportunity, between the immediate and the long-term, between the fundamental and the applied. Managing R&D is finding the elusive balance point on these several different axes.

The technical vision that is the corporate laboratory's mission emerges at the balance point. The opportunities it offers cannot be so obvious that the company will readily embrace them, nor so farfetched that it will dismiss them out of hand. Francis Frary, whose sense of balance was acute, once remarked of the combination process that "complexity in simplicity still balks us and beckons us on." Only the laboratory that can serve that sort of vision can ultimately live up to its true purpose.

Note on sources

Alcoa maintains three major repositories of corporate records, from which we drew most of the documentary sources for this book. These are the corporate archives at Aluminum Company of America headquarters, Pittsburgh, Pennsylvania (Alcoa Archives); the Alcoa Records Storage Center, in Boyers, Pennsylvania; and Alcoa Laboratories Archives, at Alcoa Technical Center, Alcoa Center, Pennsylvania. We have also used a few external document collections as well as the periodical literature of the last 100 years pertaining to the aluminum business and to metallurgical research and practice. In addition to documents, we have drawn upon interviews of Alcoa personnel, conducted by members of The Winthrop Group, Inc., between 1983 and 1988, in connection with several history projects related to the company's centennial.

ALCOA DOCUMENTS

One beneficial result of the monumental antitrust litigation against Alcoa, which began in 1937 and was not finally resolved until 1958, was that the company undertook to write and document its history in minute detail in order to demonstrate how the business had been built and maintained against all competition. Because of that, there exist a number of valuable manuscript histories in the company's archives, including the voluminous "Histories of the Manufacturing Properties of the Aluminum Company of America, Affiliated Companies, and Defense Corporation Plants." These "Alcoa Plant Histories" typically contain anecdotal material on the early years of the plants, describe technical and product innovations, and record essential facts about buildings, personnel, and production. They were written originally in the 1930s but were updated annually until 1961. Among them, the three-volume history of Alcoa Research Laboratories was, of course, invaluable for the present study. Of the other plant histories, the history of Massena works was particularly useful because it includes the "Early History of Aluminum Extrusion," describing William Hoopes's efforts to produce strong conductor wire, leading up to the development of aluminum cable steel-reinforced (ACSR).

Another essential source, bound with the Alcoa Plant Histories, is Edwin S. Fickes's "History of the Growth and Development of the Aluminum Company of America." As Alcoa's first chief engineer, Fickes was well positioned to perceive and comment on the technical affairs of the company in the critical period from 1900 to the early 1920s, when the need for a central research organization was recognized and addressed. Essential details on Alcoa's early efforts to produce high-strength alloys are provided by Earl Blough's memo to Roy Hunt (23 June 1953), "Development of Strong Alloys by Alcoa," and by his "Statement Presented to Ford Motor Company, Ford Archives" (30 April 1957). John W. Hood's "History of Alcoa Aluminum in Aircraft, Alcoa Contributions Toward Aluminum Alloy Development" (1971) carries this story further, pulling together a number of sources, including correspondence and testimony regarding the navy contract covering production of high-strength sheet for the *Shenandoah*. Both Blough, Alcoa's first chief chemist, and Hood, chief metallurgist in the early 1960s, were personally involved in the developments they described, but also went to some lengths to document the facts they presented.

Another key manuscript is the "History of Research and Development, Aluminum Company of America," a year-by-year summary of all experimental work conducted by the company from 1888 to 1961, compiled originally by Francis C. Frary in 1937 and then updated by Frary and others annually until 1961. This document, along with Frary's annual reports and financial statements for 1919–1950, laid the foundation for our analysis of the long-term trends in the R&D program during the three decades of his directorship. For a more personal, "insider" view of the history from Frary's perspective, we were fortunate to have the transcript of a speech he gave in 1963, surely to an Alcoa audience, titled "History of Early Aluminum Research."

Among the archival materials there are also several important bodies of correspondence that have helped us both to verify and to flesh out the story described in the manuscript histories. Both the Alcoa Archives and Alcoa Laboratories Archives contain essential collections of letters to and from Charles Martin Hall. It is largely from these that we have drawn our interpretation of Hall's role in the technical affairs of the corporation. Similarly, Fickes's all-important role is illuminated by his correspondence, and all the affairs of the company are reflected to some degree in the correspondence of Arthur Vining Davis. Another important group of letters comprises those exchanged between Earl Blough and Roy Hunt in the 1950s on the subject of alloy development, of which the memo cited earlier is one. Conrad F. ("Dutch") Nagel, Jr., also participated in this exchange, contributing valuable details and substantiating the historical record with excerpts from original laboratory reports and correspondence.

The most important body of correspondence for our purposes has been that preserved on microfilm at Alcoa Laboratories Archives, encompassing a major part of all the routine correspondence, both intramural and extramural, of Alcoa Laboratories personnel from 1919 to the present day. The only records systematically excluded from the archives are those of the personnel department, which would have allowed us to document in detail the trends in hiring, promotion, and compensation of the research staff. Beyond this, there are certainly random memos and letters that have, over the years, fallen through the cracks of this theoretically comprehensive archival system. However, it is supplemented by a large collection of correspondence, minutes, and reports of the Technical Committee and various subcommittees, maintained in the records storage system in Boyers, Pennsylvania. Overall, administrative policy and the process of decision making for R&D are extremely well documented.

Alcoa Laboratories maintains a complete collection of laboratory reports, which in certain cases have been essential to our understanding of technical developments. We have also relied heavily on the company's technical publications. Principal among these are Junius D. Edwards, Francis C. Frary, and Zay Jeffries, editors, *The Aluminum Industry*, 2 vols. (1930), and Kent R. Van Horn, editor, *Aluminum*, 3 vols. (1967). In addition, we have drawn on a number of technical pamphlets and on many articles published by Alcoa researchers over the years that are cited individually in footnotes.

The history of nonferrous metallurgy, especially in the modern era, is a too thinly covered subject. Except for the invaluable work of scholar Cyril Stanley Smith, relatively little work has been done by historians on nonferrous metallurgy as an industrial activity. Fortunately, a few research scientists at international aluminum companies have taken a side interest in history and have published articles on particular technologies in conjunction with their scientific papers. Alcoa researchers have been among the leading contributors to this genre. Their efforts and those of their counterparts at the major aluminum companies in North America and Europe brought forth a fascinating centennial volume of picture essays and accompanying papers: Warren S. Peterson and Ronald E. Miller, *Hall-Héroult Centennial: First Century of Aluminum Process Technology, 1886–1986* (1986).

A search of the secondary literature to be found in trade journals and scientific periodicals in the United States and Great Britain yielded a rich mixture of contemporary articles and historical reviews that was indispensable in piecing together the early history of the evolution of metallurgical science prior to World War II. Articles covering the emergent industry are to be found in the *Journal of the Franklin Institute, American Manufacturer, Scientific American,* and *Iron Age.* For intensive coverage of light-metals research and research laboratories, *Iron Age* (vol. 104–122) and the *Chemical Engineering News* and *Industrial and Engineering Chemistry* (vol. 15–25) prove to be particularly informative. Early articles by Robert Archer and Zay Jeffries (*Iron Age,* vol. 115), by Walter Burgess (*Journal of the Franklin Institute,* 1916) and by Paul Merica of the National Bureau of Standards before World War I (*Chemical and Metallurgical Engineering,* vol. 19, no. 3–8), a four-part series of articles by Henry Gillett devoted to research at the National Bureau of Standards (NBS) metals laboratory in the 1920s (*Iron Age,* vol. 115–122), and key review articles by Gillett after he left NBS to join Battelle Institute (*Industrial and Engineering Chemistry,* vol. 22) allow one to piece together an overview of the state of metallurgical research when nonferrous metallurgy was first becoming a science during the 1920s and 1930s. Pictures of laboratories and laboratory equipment contained in these articles are especially instructive. In England, the *Engineer, Engineering, Metallurgia,* and the *Journal of the Institute of Metals* throughout the period 1900–1930 are especially rich in coverage of nonferrous research reports, aluminum products, and production processes. Especially informative are the articles and historical reviews by Sir Walter Rosenhain in the *Journal of the Institute of Metals* (1919) and in *Engineering* (vol. 112).

Other important external sources about Alcoa prior to World War II can be found in books and documents that deal with the implications of Alcoa's monopoly of primary aluminum production. Donald Wallace's *Market Control in the Aluminum Industry* (1937) is a multifaceted look at the evolution of the worldwide aluminum industry and its technology during the period in which Alcoa dominated the U.S. industry. *Fortune* called Alcoa "the most investigated company in America," and hearings conducted on the many occasions Alcoa was investigated provide another source of information. In particular, the voluminous testimony from the two landmark antimonopoly cases provide unparalleled data, especially the transcripts of testimony by A. V. Davis, "Dutch" Nagel, and Jerome Clarke Hunsaker of MIT. For more specific references to all of these items, consult the notes related to the era in question.

INTERVIEWS

Finally, our understanding of both administrative and technical aspects of the history of R&D at Alcoa has been enriched by our discussions with company personnel. The transcripts of these interviews are now part of Alcoa's permanent archives. The list below indicates those interviews that we have drawn on directly in writing this book.

Interviewee	Title at time of interview	Interview date
Peter Bridenbaugh	Director of Operations, Alcoa Laboratories	May 1983
	Director of Alcoa Laboratories and Vice President – Research and Development	January 1984 & March 1985

Walter A. Dean	Former Assistant Director of Research	March 1985
J. Howard Dunn	Vice President, Research and Development	August 1987
Charles Fletcher	Operations Director, Alcoa Laboratories	May 1983 & January 1984
Edward B. Foote	Former Alcoa patent attorney	June 1985
W. H. Krome George	Former Chairman and CEO	August 1983
John Hatch	Former Quality Assurance and Chief Metallurgist, Ingot and Powder	January 1985
Robert Hampel	Former Vice President, Technical Development	March 1985
Elbert Howarth	Former Associate Director, Alcoa Laboratories	January 1985 & August 1987
Harold Hunsicker	Former Technical Manager, Alloy Technology Division, Alcoa Laboratories	January 1985
Noel Jarrett	Technical Director, Chemical Engineering R&D	January 1985
Joseph Laemmle	Senior Technical Supervisor, Fabricating Technology Divisions, Alcoa Laboratories	April 1984
Allen S. Russell	Former Vice President and Chief Scientist	January 1985
Keith Turnbull	Vice President, Technology Planning	July 1983 & November 1984
Robert E. Spear	Former Technical Director, Castings R&D, Alcoa Laboratories	June 1988
James D. Dowd and Robert E. Spear	Former Technical Director, Advanced Manufacturing R&D, Alcoa Laboratories	June 1988
James T. Staley	Technical Manager, Alloy Technology Division, Alcoa Laboratories	April 1984
Philip Stroup	Former Assistant Director of Research	August 1985
Kent R. Van Horn	Former Vice President, Research and Development	June 1984
Eric A. Walker	Former Director and Vice President, Science and Technology	March 1985

Appendix A: Alcoa timeline of technical achievements

Primary processes	Fabricating processes	New products	Alloy development
1886 C. M. Hall discovers electrolytic smelting process			
1889 Hall's patent granted		1889 Cooking utensils	1890 Electrical conductor grade alloy developed
		1891 Elevator enclosures & grilles	1892 Special alloy for horseshoes
	1892 First rolled sheet & plate produced at New Kensington		
1893 Developed use of hydroelectric power for smelting – the first industrial user of Niagara Falls power		1894 Parts for bicycle frames	
		1895 Electrical bus bars	
		1897 Electrical conductor wire for telephones	

511

Primary processes	Fabricating processes	New products	Alloy development
1902 Alumina plant built at East St. Louis	1904 First extruded shape produced at Massena	1899 Conductor wire for cross-country transmission	1906 Hard (Al-Mg) alloy 3S for cooking utensils, pipe, other uses
	1905 First foil rolled at New Kensington	1901 Sheet for automobiles	
	1906 First cast-aluminum auto engine parts commercially produced	1903 Airplane parts for Wright brothers' first plane	
1909 Begin use of Bayer process at East St. Louis	1912 First permanent mold casting of aluminum	1909 Aluminum Cable Steel Reinforced (ACSR)	1910 Alloy 112 (Al-Cu) for foundry use
	1916 First production of high-strength Al-Cu alloy 175 (Duralumin)	1910 First chemical product – alumina for abrasives	
		1912 Cast-aluminum pistons for auto engines	

1918 Forged auto engines and connecting rods, and cast crankcases, cylinder blocks, and cylinder heads

1920 Modified silicon alloys

1920 First production of refined high-purity Al by Hoopes process; first water-dipped ingots

1921 High-strength heat-treatable casting alloy 19S; high-strength forging alloys 25S and 51S

1921 Determination of effects of impurities on conductivity of electrical conductor wire

1921 Determination of electrical conductivity of molten cryolite bath, effects of impurities

1922 Electrical conductor wire with guaranteed consistent conductivity

1923 First structural parts of high-strength aluminum – in railroad cars

1923 Developed anodized coating that can be colored with dyes

1923 Hall dry-process alumina

1926 Alclad: corrosion-resistant form of high-strength alloy sheet, with bonded pure-aluminum surface layer

1926 Aluminum furniture

Primary processes	Fabricating processes	New products	Alloy development
1927 Soderberg-electrode reduction cells introduced at Alcoa works	1927 First industrial x-ray unit for inspection of castings and welds, at Cleveland works; water-cooled ingots up to 1,000 lb		1927 Corrosion testing methods for high-strength alloys developed
1928 Siphon tapping of smelting cells	1928 2,500-lb water-cooled ingot for forging stock and structural shapes	1928 First anodized (Alumilite) cast spandrels for large buildings; rowboats; residential shingles	1928 High-strength Al-Cu forging alloy – one of the "super Duralumins" of World War II
1930 Developed dry process for manufacture of aluminum fluoride	1929 First successful arc welding of aluminum	1930 Improved activated alumina with high absorptive efficiency; aluminum-foil insulation	1903 Low-coefficient-of-expansion alloy 4032 for forged pistons; discovered stress-corrosion cracking in alloys
1931 Discovered high fluorine emissions at ore-preparation plant in Bauxite – correlated to discoloration of children's teeth	1930 Developed fluxing process to remove gas from molten metal to reduce blisters in sheet	1931 Ready-mixed aluminum paint	1931 High-strength Al-Cu alloy 2024: a "super Duralumin"
	1931 Developed production of aluminum-coated steel shapes		
	1932 Templin automatic electrical extensiometer to record yield strength and tensile strength simultaneously		

1933 Manufacture of bright aluminum sheet by strip rolling

1934 Counter-current regenerative digestion process for bauxite

1933 First aluminum bridge deck on Smithfield Street Bridge in Pittsburgh; first aluminum brewery tanks and beer barrels

1934 Al-Mg alloy 5052: a strong, non-heat-treatable alloy for sheet and plate

1934 Etched aluminum lithography sheet

1935 Al-Mg-Si alloy 6061: the least expensive, most versatile heat-treatable alloy

1935 Direct-chill ingot-casting process; process for hollow extrusion using porthole die

1935 Forged hollow aircraft propellers; composite aluminum-steel armor plates

1937 Improved process for making cryolite – the Heiser process

1937 Alumilite sheet for protective and decorative coatings; zinc-clad aluminum sheet for soldering applications

1938 Routine spectrographic analysis of aluminum introduced at New Kensington works

1939 Forged cylinder heads for air-cooled aircraft engines

1939 Introduced use of starch in Bayer process to improve settling and filtration

1939 First hot-line strip rolling of high-strength alloy sheet – the basis for later development of continuous sheet rolling

Primary processes	Fabricating processes	New products	Alloy development
1940 Continuous precipitation in Bayer process – improved product and increased process capacity			1940 High-strength Al-Zn casting alloy 7076; discovery of use of chromium addition to prevent stress-corrosion cracking in Al-Zn alloys
		1941 Tabular alumina grinding balls	
1942 Commerical use of Alcoa combination process for refining low-grade bauxite ore; developed use of natural gas to generate power for aluminum reduction			
	1943 New, low-cost rolling lubricant	1943 Stepped extrusions for aircraft structures	1943 Al-Zn sheet and plate alloy 7075 – the standard for aircraft production after World War II; began use of electron microscope to study submicroscopic structures of alloys
	1944 First production use of inert-gas tungsten arc welding for "canning" uranium slugs; low-temperature lubricated extrusion process	1944 First aluminum bridge span for Grasse River bridge (Massena, NY)	

1945 Process for making wide extrusions by flattening

1946 Improved wire-drawing lubricants; ultrasonic inspection of wrought alloy products

1947 Ultrasonic inspection of aluminum ingots; emission photoelectric polychromator (quantimeter) co-developed for chemical analysis control in the aluminum industry

1948 Commercialized inert-gas arc welding

1949 Permeable-plaster-mold casting process; die-casting process for highly stressed auto structural parts

1946 First use of closed smelting cell, permitting collection and neutralization of fumes

1947 Power crust breakers for smelting cells; began use of large-scale prototype cells for smelting research at Alcoa works (Potline B)

1945 Aluminum farm roofing; structural shapes with sprayed-on Alclad coating for corrosion resistance

1947 Expanded ACSR conductor for high-voltage transmission lines; premium-strength castings

1949 Patterned aluminum sheet for wall facings

1949 Forged bearings for aircraft

1950 Structural aluminum parts for steamship superstructure; aluminum tubing with both internal and external cladding for corrosion resistance

1947 Al-Zn alloy 7277 for hot-driven rivets

1950 Al-Mg alloy 5357 for bright finishing

Primary processes	Fabricating processes	New products	Alloy development
	1951 First forgings on 15,000-ton press		1951 Al-Zn alloy 7178 for aircraft – higher strength than 7075; Al-Mg alloy 5254 for welded pressure vessels
1952 First large-scale use of solid fuel (lignite) to generate power for aluminum smelters		1952 Calcium aluminate cement for high-temperature use in cast refractories	1952 Al-Si casting alloy F132 – became the standard material for automotive pistons
	1953 Continuous degassing process for molten metal		
	1954 2.5-ton ingots produced for U.S. Air Force "Heavy Press" program	1954 Alcoa "Structural Colors"	1954 Al-Cu alloy 2219, the first readily weldable high-strength heat-treatable alloy
	1955 Commercial use of new process for continuous filtering of molten aluminum using tabular alumina bed	1955 All-aluminum out-door phone booths	
1956 First use of coal to power aluminum smelters; commercial use of controlled-atmosphere tunnel kiln for baking carbon anodes	1956 Solid-state degassing process for improving quality of aluminum forgings		

1957 Commercial use of continuous filtering and degassing process for molten metal

1957 Aluminum "sandwich" building panels with a core of formed plastic insulation

1957 High-strength Al-Li alloy X2020

1958 First continuous heat-treating furnace for high-strength aluminum sheet

1958 Aluminum sheet with baked alkyd enamel finish; spangle sheet and multicolored extrusions and impacts

1959 High temperature digestion process for monohydrated bauxites

1959 Ultrasonic welding of aluminum; automatic continuous aluminum-slug casting unit

1959 Ballistic armor plate; structural components for missiles and space vehicles (Titan and Saturn); aluminum swimming pools

1960 Fluidized-bed fume-recovery process

1960 Hazelett continuous-slab casting implemented at Alcoa works

1960 Aluminum auto radiators; composite juice container with foil-fiber body and aluminum ends; pull-tab opener for aluminum can ends

1960 Al-Mg alloy 6262, a free-machining high-strength alloy for screw-machine products

1961 Freeze-purification process for producing super-pure aluminum

1961 Plastic-coated aluminum sheet; Teflon-coated aluminum frying pans

1961 Commercialized the T73 temper for alloy 7075 to minimize stress-corrosion cracking

Primary processes	Fabricating processes	New products	Alloy development
		1962 Ultra-thin foil for "echo" satellite balloon experiments; expandable aluminum support beams for reinforced-concrete construction work	1962 Al-Mg alloy 5053, the first high-strength bright-finishing alloy
1963 Automated alumina feeders for smelting cells	1963 Began production of sheet ingot by horizontal DC casting process; high-speed multistand cold rolling of precision light-gauge H19-temper sheet	1963 Aluminum-sheathed coaxial cable; preassembled cable in pipe (PCP) for electrical distribution systems; all-aluminum easy-open ends for beer and soft-drink containers	1963 High-strength H-19 temper for rigid container sheet; Al-Mg alloy 5082 for highly strain-hardened thin-sheet products
1964 First computer-controlled potline	1964 High-speed batch-anodizing process; production of powder-metallurgy-forged pistons	1964 Extrusions with full range of architectural finishes; air-expanded 500,000-V ACSR; premium engineered castings for aircraft pylons	
1965 System for x-ray analysis of bauxite	1965 Produced 7-ton coil of rigid container sheet (RCS); developed computer control of hot-reversing mill and hot-strip mill; cleaning and conversion coating processes for surface preparation of RCS	1965 Flavor-lok closures for beverages; anodic finishes for aluminum in gold and black; smooth-wall formed-foil containers	1965 T76 temper for resistance to exfoliation corrosion in high-strength Al-Zn alloy 7178

1966 Process for producing large, thin-walled castings for aerospace applications

1966 Air-formed foil containers; stericap closure for pharmaceuticals; completely disposable infant-formula package; highway-median barrier system

1967 Multiple-draw process for producing formed containers; high-speed mill for producing welded radiator tube; produced large, continuous-cast, self-palletizing ingot with improved metallurgical qualities

1967 New two-piece design for lightweight beverage can; porcelain enameling sheet for producing colored cookware

1967 Al-Mg alloy 5182, stronger and with improved forming and fabricating qualities for RCS

1968 Operation of first commercial die-casting equipment using ACURAD process

1968 High-purity alumina for electronic, mechanical, and nuclear ceramics; aluminum-plastic tear-off (APTO) closure for wide-mouth jars and cans

1968 Alloy CK70 for making drawn containers from cooled sheet in H19 temper

Primary processes	Fabricating processes	New products	Alloy development
1969 Alcoa 398 process for eliminating fluoride pollutants from aluminum smelting processes; commercialization of a new process to produce aluminum fluoride and cryolite	1969 Alcoa 384 process for continuous casting of textured architectural plate; commercial feasibility of aluminum powder metallurgy; production of 20-in.-thick horizontal-DC-cast ingot	1969 New low-cost calcined alumina for commercial ceramic processes; covered, insulated conductor wire; ALUMIFRAME extruded-aluminum construction system for home construction	1969 High-strength Al-Zn alloy 7475 with high fracture toughness
	1970 Continuous heat treatment of 84-in.-wide sheet; production of premium castings with unusually high strength and close tolerances	1970 Polyvinylchloride (PVC) – Alcoa's entry into manufacture of plastic compounds	1970 New combination of Mn-Mg alloy CH14 with H-19 temper to produce a lower-cost material for rigid container sheet; new powder-metallurgy alloys
	1971 Fume-free processes for removing impurities from molten metal; Alcoa 531 process for laminating polypropylene films to can and end stock; world's fastest multistand cold-rolling mill for rigid container sheet; 220-in. rolling mill with Alcoa-developed		1971 High-strength Al-Zn alloy 7050; new alloys for high-luster automotive sheet

1972 Improved alloys for conductor wire, auto body sheet, air-conditioner tube

1973 Al-Zn alloy 7046 for maximum weight reduction in auto bumpers

1974 New Al-Mg alloy for rigid container sheet requiring less magnesium

1972 Two-piece "child-proof" safety closure; Steri-twist tamper-proof closure to prevent contamination of pharmaceuticals; Hiluster automotive trim

1973 Alcoa B48 tabless easy-open end for beer and beverage cans

1974 High-efficiency XL-174 lubricant for the metalworking phases of drawn-and-ironed can production; the Proper Application Tester – a device for checking the integrity of packages for carbonated beverages

computer controls; manufacturing processes for Alcoa Featherlite all-aluminum cans

1972 Produced the largest isothermal forging ever – the bulkhead for McDonnell Douglas F-15 fighter aircraft

1973 Developed capability to cast up to 26-in.-thick ingot

1974 New manufacturing and testing technology for production of Alclad air-conditioner tubing

1973 Alcoa smelting process announced – a new electrolyte process for aluminum reduction

1974 Pilot operation of a process to recover alumina from anorthosite or any alumina-silica compound; Alcoa 446 process to remove harmful emissions from carbon-baking furnace exhaust; flash calcining process using less energy than conventional alumina calcining kilns

Primary processes	Fabricating processes	New products	Alloy development
	1975 Alcoa 503 process for improved recovery of aluminum from remelt scrap; dry powder lubricant for aluminum forging that creates no fire or smoke; Interactive Graphics Die Design program for computer-assisted design of extrusion dies; multitemperature cooling system to increase output and improve quality of foil production		1975 Announced development of a superconductor alloy approaching the theoretical limit of electrical conductor efficiency
	1976 Computer controls to improve thermal efficiency and reduce fuel consumption of preheat, reheat, and annealing furnaces; improved equipment for producing fine aluminum powder, with reduced metal loss through dust emissions	1976 Two-piece deep-drawn aluminum food can; B-57 ultralight beer and beverage can; B-76 slide tab end for beer and beverage cans	1976 New alloys for auto body sheet with improved strength and manufacturing characteristics

1977 Alcoa 697 process for low-current-density aluminum smelting

1978 Began operation of world's largest and most versatile alumina and chemicals pilot plant at Alcoa Technical Center; significant design improvements in carbon-anode baking furnace to increase production and reduce energy consumption

1979 Pilot reactor for production of aluminum-silicon alloy through direct (carbothermic) reduction; developed standard techniques for routine sampling and analysis of fluoride emissions from aluminum smelters

1977 Improved energy-efficient scrap-melting systems for cans

1978 Alcoa 685 process for energy-efficient, phosphate-free cleaning of rigid container sheet; achieved high-speed casting of auto body sheet alloys through improvements in HDC casting process

1979 Alcoa 622 process for in-line purification of molten metal

1979 Alcoa Vertical Axis Wind Turbine System in experimental phase; improved finishes for forged automotive wheels

1977 Improved alloys for auto bumpers and trim

Primary processes	Fabricating processes	New products	Alloy development
1980 Alcoa of Australia completes the third potline at Point Henry and breaks ground for second smelter at Portland. Development continues on the Alcoa Smelting Process (ASP) at Anderson County, Texas; the cells exceed expectations; the chemical plant that provides the aluminum chloride to the cells requires further R&D. Patented Alcoa 729 process commercialized; carbonated coolant for ingot casting effective in conjunction with electromagnetic casting.		1980 "Lightweighting" of beverage cans; 24 12-oz cans made from 1 lb of aluminum; supplied first production-size sheet of SPF-quality alloy 7475 for forming evaluation	1980 Research on aluminum-lithium alloys renewed; wrought P/M alloys 7090 and 7091 are registered

1981 Electromagnetic casting (EMC) investigated at ATC

1982 ASP pilot plant idled due to lack of cost-effective way to make aluminum chloride feedstock. Point Comfort gas-fueled smelter closes permanently. R&D on carbothermal reduction of aluminous materials discontinued. Aluminothermic reduction first employed commercially to produce magnesium at Addy, WA (NWA).

1981 Atomized-powder plant at Rockdale begins production; installation of model-based noninteractive gauge and tension control on Warrick cold mill and Tennessee 80-in. hot continuous mill

1982 New aluminum powder plant at Pocos De Caldas begins operation

1981 Electro-Coat process helps make aluminum food can competitive; Metal Box joins Alcoa to improve process. Aluminum Intensive Vehicle (AIV) research begins; aluminum structural parts could cut total weight by 29%.

1982 Vernon (CA) produces first commercial powdered-metal aerospace forgings; R&D began in 1978. Development of Vertical Axis Wind Turbine abandoned by Alcoa.

1981 Design and construction of special facilities for melting and casting Al-Li alloys undertaken; Alcoa warns other companies of the dangers of mixing molten Al-Li with water

Primary processes	Fabricating processes	New products	Alloy development
1983 Alcoa's first electromagnetic casting (EMC) unit began producing ingots at Tennessee Operations	1983 Upgrading of hot lines at Tennessee and Warrick is part of $370 million modernization. Computer-integrated manufacturing (CIM) put into place at Warrick Operations.	1983 Research expands in advanced ceramic powders and parts; $4 billion markets in U.S. Vidalia (LA) chemical plant opens to make desiccants and absorbents for petrochemical industry.	1983 Aluminum-lithium ingots cast, evaluated at Alcoa Laboratories. Al-Mg-Si alloy developed originally for auto bumpers proves itself as alloy 6013-T4, with exceptional forming capabilities for aerospace applications.

Source: "Technical Highlights Relating to the History of A.C.O.A., 1886–1979," ALA. The timeline for the years 1980 to 1983 was prepared by William B. Frank, Alcoa Laboratories Information Department.

Appendix B: Evolution of the committee system and corporate organization for R&D

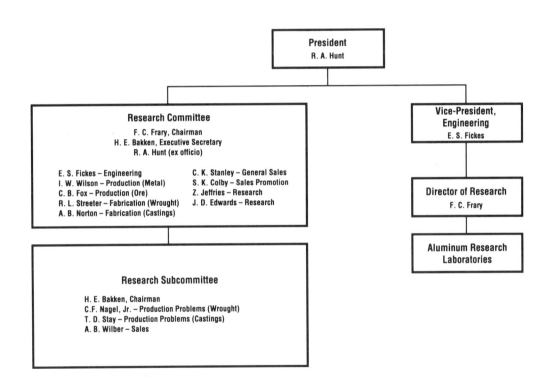

President
R. A. Hunt

Research Committee

F. C. Frary, Chairman
H. E. Bakken, Executive Secretary
R. A. Hunt (ex officio)

E. S. Fickes – Engineering
I. W. Wilson – Production (Metal)
C. B. Fox – Production (Ore)
R. L. Streeter – Fabrication (Wrought)
A. B. Norton – Fabrication (Castings)

C. K. Stanley – General Sales
S. K. Colby – Sales Promotion
Z. Jeffries – Research
J. D. Edwards – Research

Research Subcommittee

H. E. Bakken, Chairman
C.F. Nagel, Jr. – Production Problems (Wrought)
T. D. Stay – Production Problems (Castings)
A. B. Wilber – Sales

Vice-President,
Engineering
E. S. Fickes

Director of Research
F. C. Frary

Aluminum Research
Laboratories

1931

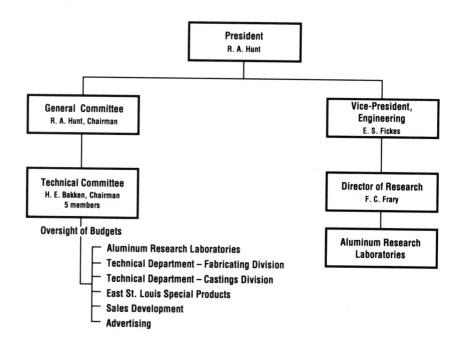

1933

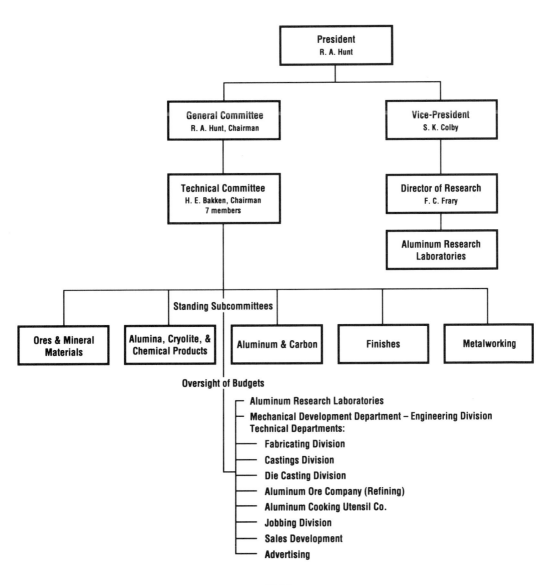

1944

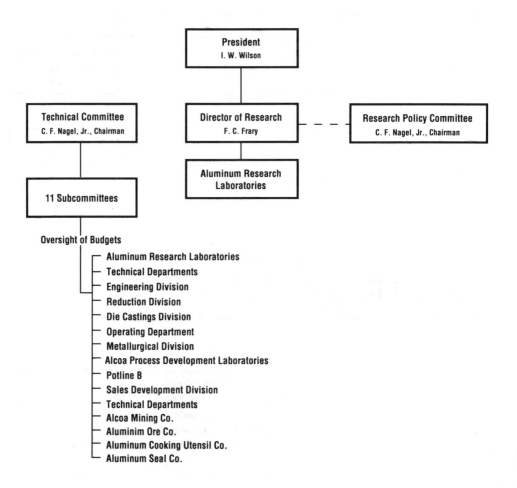

President
I. W. Wilson

Technical Committee
C. F. Nagel, Jr., Chairman

Director of Research
F. C. Frary

Research Policy Committee
C. F. Nagel, Jr., Chairman

Aluminum Research Laboratories

11 Subcommittees

Oversight of Budgets

- Aluminum Research Laboratories
- Technical Departments
- Engineering Division
- Reduction Division
- Die Castings Division
- Operating Department
- Metallurgical Division
- Alcoa Process Development Laboratories
- Potline B
- Sales Development Division
- Technical Departments
- Alcoa Mining Co.
- Aluminim Ore Co.
- Aluminum Cooking Utensil Co.
- Aluminum Seal Co.

1951

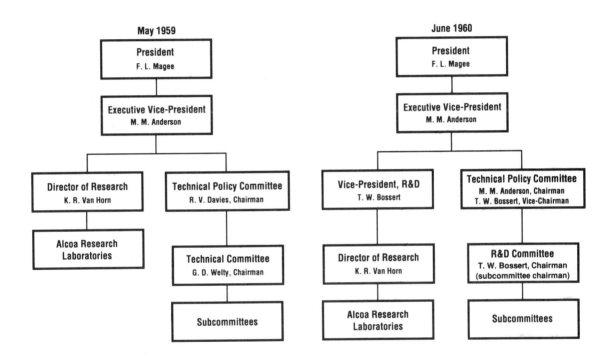

1959-1960

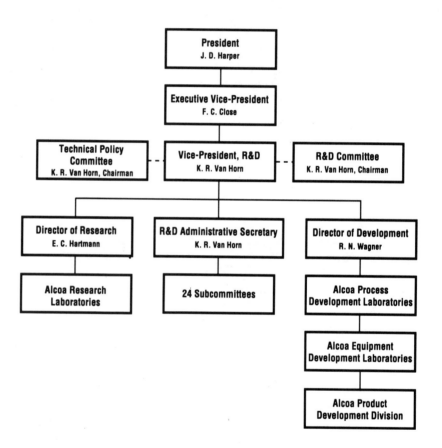

May 1963

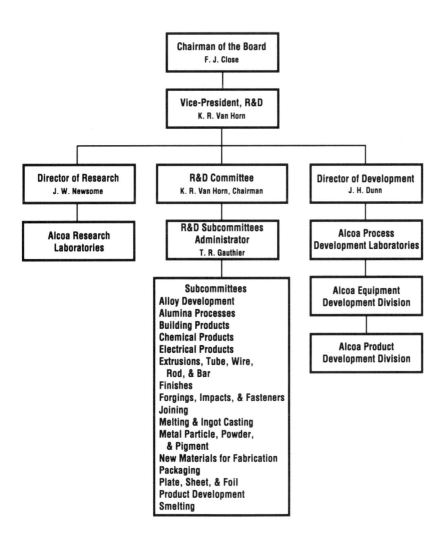

Chairman of the Board
F. J. Close

Vice-President, R&D
K. R. Van Horn

Director of Research
J. W. Newsome

R&D Committee
K. R. Van Horn, Chairman

Director of Development
J. H. Dunn

Alcoa Research
Laboratories

R&D Subcommittees
Administrator
T. R. Gauthier

Alcoa Process
Development Laboratories

Subcommittees
Alloy Development
Alumina Processes
Building Products
Chemical Products
Electrical Products
Extrusions, Tube, Wire,
  Rod, & Bar
Finishes
Forgings, Impacts, & Fasteners
Joining
Melting & Ingot Casting
Metal Particle, Powder,
  & Pigment
New Materials for Fabrication
Packaging
Plate, Sheet, & Foil
Product Development
Smelting

Alcoa Equipment
Development Division

Alcoa Product
Development Division

1968

Chairman of the Board & CEO
J. D. Harper

Vice-President Science & Technology
E. A. Walker

Vice-President, R&D
J. H. Dunn

Director of Research
J. W. Newsome

Alcoa Research Laboratories

Director of Development
R. G. Hampel

Alcoa Process Development Laboratories

Alcoa Equipment Development Division

Alcoa Product Development Division

R&D Policy Committee
W. H. K. George, Chairman

Mill Products R&D Committee

Primary Products R&D Committee

Corporate R&D Committee

Subsidiaries & Affiliates R&D Committee

Administrative Secretary R&D Committee
T. R. Gauthier

Mill Products Subcommittees (5)

Primary Products R&D Subcommittees (5)

Corporate R&D Subcommittees (7)

Subsidiaries & Affiliates R&D Subcommittees (5)

1972

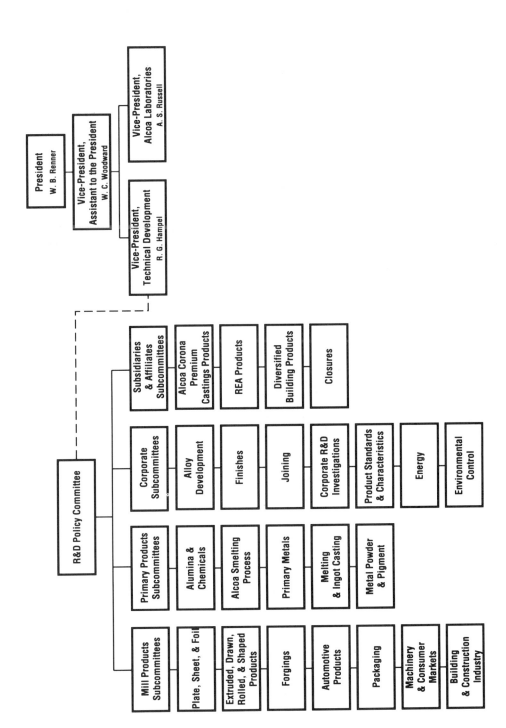

President
W. B. Renner

**Vice-President,
Assistant to the President**
W. C. Woodward

**Vice-President,
Alcoa Laboratories**
A. S. Russell

**Vice-President,
Technical Development**
R. G. Hampel

R&D Policy Committee

**Mill Products
Subcommittees**

Plate, Sheet, & Foil

Extruded, Drawn,
Rolled, & Shaped
Products

Forgings

Automotive
Products

Packaging

Machinery
& Consumer
Markets

Building
& Construction
Industry

**Primary Products
Subcommittees**

Alumina &
Chemicals

Alcoa Smelting
Process

Primary Metals

Melting
& Ingot Casting

Metal Powder
& Pigment

Corporate Subcommittees

Alloy
Development

Finishes

Joining

Corporate R&D
Investigations

Product Standards
& Characteristics

Energy

Environmental
Control

**Subsidiaries
& Affiliates
Subcommittees**

Alcoa Corona
Premium
Castings Products

REA Products

Diversified
Building Products

Closures

1976

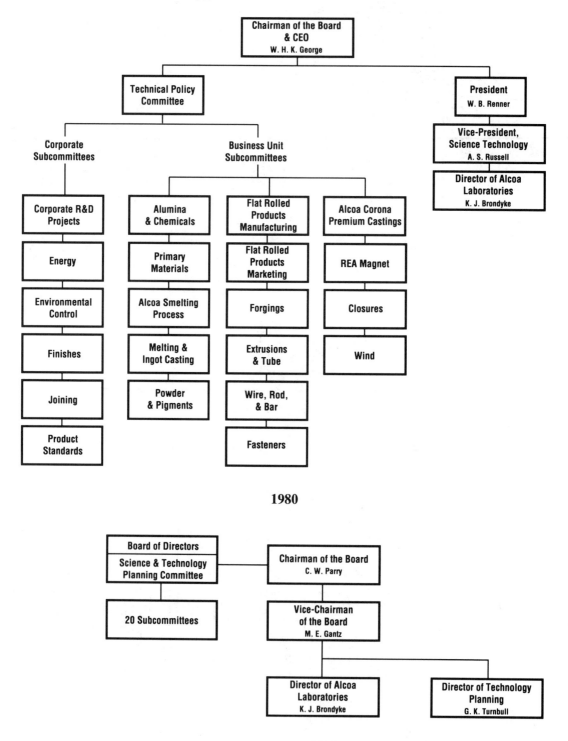

1980

1983

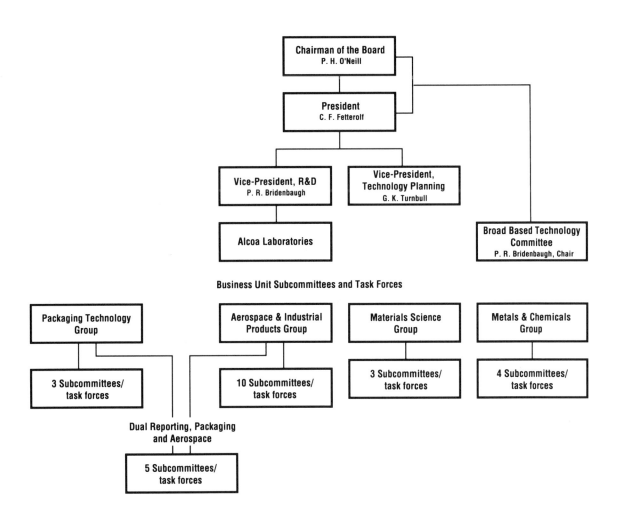

1988

Appendix C: Alcoa classic research papers

A "classic" paper is defined by the Institute for Scientific Information by its frequency of citation in the literature of its field. The number of citations required for designation as a classic paper varies widely from sub-field to sub-field. This list indicates the most frequently cited Alcoa research papers.

Citations
to 1988

31   H. V. Churchill, "Occurrence of Fluorides in Some Waters of the United States," *Industrial Engineering Chemistry*, 23(1931):996–8.

48   E. H. Dix, "Acceleration of the Rate of Corrosion by High Constant Stresses," *AIME Transactions*, 137(1940):11–40.

89   J. R. Churchill, "Techniques of Quantitative Spectrographic Analysis," *Industrial Engineering Chemistry*, 16(1944):653–70.

74   W. A. Anderson et al., "Recrystallization of Aluminum in Terms of the Rate of Nucleation and the Rate of Growth," *AIME Transactions*, 161(1945):140–72.

56   J. D. Edwards et al., "Electrical Conductivity and Density of Molten Cryolite with Additives," *Journal of the Electrochemical Society*, 100(1953):508–12.

176   F. Keller et al., "Structural Features of Oxide Coatings on Aluminum," *Journal of the Electrochemical Society*, 100(1953):411–19.

190   A. S. Russell, "Alumina Properties," Alcoa Technical Report #10 (1953); revised by A. S. Russell et al. (1956); revised by J.

541

W. Newsome et al. (1960); revised by K. Wefers and G. M. Bell, as "Oxides and Hydroxides of Aluminum," Alcoa Technical Paper #19 (1972); revised by K. Wefers and C. Mishra (1987).

60   C. N. Cochran and L. M. Foster, "Vapor Pressure of Gallium, Stability of Gallium Suboxide Vapor, and Equilibria of Some Reactions Producing Gallium Suboxide Vapor," *Journal of the Electrochemical Society,* 109(1962):144–8.

137   K. R. Van Horn, ed., *Aluminum,* 2 vols. (Metals Park, OH: American Society for Metals, 1967).

64   W. H. Gitzen, ed., *Alumina as a Ceramic Material* (American Ceramic Society, 1970).

29   A. K. Vasudevan et al., "Contribution of Na-segregation to Fracture Behavior of Al–11.4 atomic %–Lithium Alloys," in *Aluminum-Lithium Alloys II,* Proceedings of the Second International Aluminum-Lithium Conference, Metallurgical Society of AIME (1984), pp. 181–99.

This list was compiled by Nick Kotow, Alcoa Laboratories Information Department, from *Science Citation Index,* 1955–1964, 1965–1969, 1970–1974, and from *Scisearch* online database, 1974–1989, published by the Institute for Scientific Information.

Appendix D: Alcoa technical awards

1984

Francis C. Frary Award – Warren Haupin, for contributions to smelting research.

Arthur Vining Davis Award – The team that developed water-based lubricants for Alcoa's cold rolling process:

Arvid W. Anderson
Philip P. Appleby
George H. Blake
John T. Bunting
Richard T. Campbell
Robert P. Carter
Anthony J. De Ardo
James D. Dowd
Harold S. Evans
Charles P. Fletcher
Paul E. Griswold
Robert E. Heffner
Ralph H. Heller

Carl L. Jones
Ronald J. Kegarise
Norman W. Nielsen
Sid A. Paradee
Albert A. Perrier
Russell W. Plummer
Richard E. Ray
David L. Schaffer
Warren L. Stritter
G. Alfred Teasley
Fred R. Thomas
William A. Thomas
Leon J. Ulczycki

1985

Francis C. Frary Award – Robert Spear, for contributions to casting and ingot technology.

Arthur Vining Davis Award – The project team that developed a fluoride emission control and recovery system:

William R. Allen
Sam T. Banakes
J. F. Clark

C. Norman Cochran
Robert L. Coffman
James W. Colpitts

Clayton C. Cook
John W. Dyer
William M. Fish
W. B. Frank
Joseph E. Gibb
Rudolph L. Guilloud
Jerry R. Haaland
Walter W. Hill
Herman J. Hittner
G. Thomas Holmes
B. Robin Hood
Stanley C. Jacobs
Noel Jarrett
Charles L. Jordan
Lester L. Knapp

Ralph Lawson
R. Franklin Lyerly
George E. Moretz
Walter O. Ogle, Jr.
Edward J. Seger
Andrew J. Sevic
William C. Sleppy
Bernard M. Starner
Richard C. Studley
G. Ross Swany
George H. Traylor
Nathaniel Wells
Warren W. Wentzel
W. V. M. Williams

1986

Francis C. Frary Award – James Dowd, for contributions in rolling, lubricants, process design, welding, cost reduction, heat treatment, and automation.

Arthur Vining Davis Award – The team that developed closed-loop recycling:

Gary G. Blagg
Lee Blayden
Ken Bowman
James R. Bowser
Virgil P. Butrum
Gerald E. Carkin
Jeffrey B. Gorss
Joseph R. Herrick
Robert B. Hubbard
Michael J. Kinosz
Richard Labar
James McIntee

Ronald E. Miller
Robert J. Ormesher
Larry W. Palmer
Charles E. Parker
H. Gray Reavis, Jr.
Elwin E. Rooy
Adam Sartschev
William R. Sharkins
Robert E. Spear
G. Keith Turnbull
Jan Van Linden
Chester L. Zuber

The Chairman's Award – Noel Jarrett, for work in primary metals on the Alcoa Smelting Process, metal purification techniques, and enhancing environmental processes of aluminum smelting.

1987

Francis C. Frary Award – Rolf Rolles, for contributions in the development of diverse new products and processes.

Arthur Vining Davis Award – The team that developed and implemented a noninteractive control system for aluminum rolling mills:

Thomas Allen	Jim Lacey
Jim Banks	Larry Lalli
William Beck	David Nolen
William Bennon	Mark Puda
Alfred Breaux	James Sanders
Ronald Bredenkamp	Donna Schneider
Gerard Ceurvorst	Larry Shell
Walter Crawford	Jack Sloane
Mike Clifford	Larry Spies
Jim Dowd	Fred Stewart
Rick Ebert	Paul Talda
Garry Ernsberger	William Tillie
Robert Fanning	Marion Waltz
Matt Finn	Keith Wetzel
Billy Jaggers	Ann Whitty
David Knapp	Woody Woodburn

The Chairman's Award – John Jacoby, for contributions in casting large aluminum-lithium ingots, and James Ralphe, for achievements in alumina production.

1988

Francis C. Frary Award – James Staley, for contributions in alloy development and quality control techniques.

Arthur Vining Davis Award – The team that developed and commercialized a generation of aerospace and defense alloys:

Bruce E. Anderson	Robert H. Brown
William A. Anderson	Stanley J. Cieslak
Lee E. Aughinbaugh	Walter D. Coker
Daniel C. Boley	Robert E. Davies
Charles E. Brooks	James L. Eriksson
Melvin H. Brown	Edmund C. Franz

Robert L. Garrett
Luther Greenhill
Ray M. Hart
John E. Hatch
Harold Y. Hunsicker
John E. Jacoby
R. Steve James
Ronald J. Kegarise
Franklin L. King
Paul W. Kroger
Sootae Lee
Bernard W. Lifka
John Liu
Paul L. Mehr
Larry N. Mueller
Norman W. Nielsen
Glenn E. Nordmark
Christopher R. Owen

Robert C. Pahl
Basil M. Ponchel
Chester S. Recko
Raymond T. Richter
Ralph R. Sawtell
Richard Schmidt
Sylvester Scott
Eugene D. Seaton
Samuel L. Shelby
Dell F. Skluzak
Arvid H. Sorenson
Donald O. Sprowls
Edwin H. Spuhler
James T. Staley
Richard J. Stokwisz
James D. Walsh
Robert W. Westerlund

The Chairman's Award – William Dunlap, for contributions in precision forgings; Daniel Hugh, for contributions to rolling systems; and Ambrose Rust, for contributions to the Hall Smelting Cell.

1989

Francis C. Frary Award – Joseph Laemmle, for contributions to lubricant technologies.

Arthur Vining Davis Award – The team at Lebanon Works that improved continuous caster technology; and the team at Alcoa Aluminio S.A. that developed a commercial process for producing high alpha alumina chemicals in an Alcoa fluid flash calciner:

Nestor Andrade
Larry L. Bishop
Ricardo Carvalho
Ronald Chabal
Terrance Clever
Kenneth H. Daullary
Thomas W. Ebright

Jose Roberio Farias
Paulo Silas Ferreira
Donald D. Finkel
Michael R. Garrison
Amarildo Goncalves
William E. Harris
Dennis P. Heagy

William H. Hoffman

Jack Kastner

James Kosh, Jr.

James T. Longenecker

Larry G. McKinney

Leonard T. Miller

Alan Pearson

Hilary J. Picard

James G. Riegle

Joao Carlos Da Silva

David R. Smith

Earl E. Smith

Edwin W. Smith

Harold K. Stoner

Frank P. Swigon

Richard B. Tallarico

Janie L. Waybright

Richard E. Wenrich

The Chairman's Award – Thomas Drumwright, for contributions to Non-Destructive Evaluation; James Knepp, for contributions to lubrication technologies applied to rolling; Jan Van Linden, Sr., for technology for recycling used beverage containers; and Robert Westerlund, for modifying heat treating operations at Davenport to produce a number of alloys.

Notes

INTRODUCTION

1 Louis Galambos, "Technology, Political Economy, and Professionaliza-
tion: Central Themes of the Organizational Synthesis," *Business History
Review*, 57(Winter 1983):471–93. For more on the major organizational
innovations, see Alfred D. Chandler, Jr., *The Visible Hand: The Managerial
Revolution in American Business* (Cambridge, MA: Harvard University
Press, 1977), Chandler, *Strategy and Structure: Chapters in the History of the
Industrial Enterprise* (Cambridge, MA: MIT Press, 1962), and Chandler
and Herman Daems (eds.), *Managerial Hierarchies: Comparative Perspectives
on the Rise of the Modern Industrial Enterprise* (Cambridge, MA: Harvard
University Press, 1977). Daems, in his essay "The Rise of the Modern
Industrial Enterprise," says that "the picture is now complete: the modern hierarchical firm evolved to coordinate the flow of goods, to monitor
the units, and to allocate resources to them; it carried out all these functions by means of hierarchical management structure." One of the ways
in which this structure improved and stabilized the profits of the modern
firm was through "careful planning and scheduling of the work of the
industrial laboratory, in order to make it operate efficiently and effectively." It "had to be hierarchical," he maintains, "because market scheduling would have left too much room for opportunistic behavior and strategic maneuvering" (*Managerial Hierarchies*, pp. 203–22). For the role of
institutionalized R&D, see David Landes, *The Unbound Prometheus: Technological Change and Industrial Development in Western Europe from 1750 to the
Present* (Cambridge University Press, 1968), p. 482.

2 David F. Noble, in *America by Design: Science, Technology, and the Rise of
Corporate Capitalism* (Oxford University Press, 1979), p. 4, defines modern
science-based industry as "industrial enterprise in which ongoing scientific investigation and the systematic application of scientific knowledge
to the process of commodity production have become routine parts of the
operation." According to Noble, only two industries "grew out of the soil
of scientific rather than traditional craft knowledge," the chemical and
the electrical. These, in turn, revolutionized others. Most metals, along
with the extractive, petroleum, rubber, and automotive industries, were
affected by what Noble terms "the scientific revolution." See also Landes,
The Unbound Prometheus, p. 325, and Martha Moore Trescott, *The Rise of
the Electrochemicals Industry, 1880–1910: Studies in the American Technological Environment* (Westport, CT: Greenwood Press, 1981), pp. 12–15.

3 Accounts of this emergence can be found in Thomas P. Hughes, *Networks*

549

of Power: Electrification in Western Society, 1880–1930 (Baltimore: Johns Hopkins University Press, 1983), David Hounshell and John K. Smith, *Science and Corporate Strategy: DuPont R&D, 1902–1980* (Cambridge University Press, 1988), George D. Smith, *From Monopoly to Competition: The Transformations of Alcoa, 1888–1986* (Cambridge University Press, 1988), Reese V. Jenkins, *Images and Enterprise: Technology and the American Photographic Industry, 1839 to 1925* (Baltimore: Johns Hopkins University Press, 1975), and Trescott, *Rise of the Electrochemicals Industry*. See also Nathan Rosenberg, "Technological Interdependence in the American Economy," *Technology and Culture*, 20(January 1979):44–5. Rosenberg observes that the vital role of the electrochemicals industry in spurring change in other industries was relatively invisible, comparable to the role of transitors in recent years.

4   See, in particular, David A. Hounshell, *From the American System to Mass Production, 1800–1932: The Development of Manufacturing Technology in the United States* (Baltimore: Johns Hopkins University Press, 1982). The same revolution was taking place in Europe, especially Germany. See Robert Locke, *The End of the Practical Man: Entrepreneurship and Higher Education in Germany, France and Great Britain, 1880–1914* (Greenwich, CT: JAI Press, 1984).

5   See Leonard S. Reich, *The Making of Industrial Research: Science and Business at GE and Bell, 1876–1926* (Cambridge University Press, 1985).

6   Nathan Rosenberg, "The Commercial Exploitation of Science by American Industry," in Robert Hayes, Kim Clark, and Chris Lorenz (eds.), *The Uneasy Alliance* (Boston: Harvard Business School Press, 1985), pp. 19–51, points out that while the major innovations in steel production were based on science that had long been known, larger-volume production created a need for process improvements that involved scientific testing and analysis and much more exact control procedures than ever before. Thus, there were increasingly greater returns to investment in science in that industry, as in others. See also Geoffrey Tweedale, *Sheffield Steel and America: A Century of Commercial and Technological Interdependence, 1830–1930* (Cambridge University Press, 1987), pp. 33–5. The competition between the craft ethos and the scientific ethos had been a recurrent theme in the application of science to industrial purposes throughout the industrializing world. See also Locke, *The End of the Practical Man*, and Michael J. Piore and Charles F. Sabel, *The Second Industrial Divide: Possibilities for Posterity* (New York: Basic Books, 1984), chapters 6 and 9. For the views of early twentieth-century observers, see W. R. Barclay, "The Relationship between the Laboratory and the Workshop," *Journal of the Institute of Metals*, 21(1919):291–6, and Fred Lantsberry, "The Scope of the Works Laboratory," *Journal of the Institute of Metals*, 21(1919):301–8. Another major limitation on the transformation of metallurgy into a science had to do with the state of applicable research technology. As Zay Jeffries pointed out in his review of metallurgical progress in 1926, metallurgical study progressed with the speed of effective observation. Instruments and methods for accurate and speedy physical testing were crucial to metallurgical advances. See Zay Jeffries, "Engineering and Science in the Metal Industry," *Mechanical Engineering*, 48(January 1926):8–16.

7   On the early struggle to create markets for aluminum, see Smith, *From Monopoly to Competition*, pp. 78–94. Smith quotes Alcoa's Arthur Vining

Davis: "While it was a great and wonderful thing to invent the process for making aluminum, it was a totally different and as it actually turned out an infinitely more difficult problem to make aluminum commercially, and a still greater problem to utilize the aluminum when made" (p. 77).

8 For an example of what could happen when research and industry were separate, so that little information flowed directly between them, see Margaret B. W. Graham, "R&D and Competition in England and the United States: The Case of the Aluminum Dirigible," *Business History Review,* 62(Summer 1988):261–85. Both Alfred Chandler and Nathan Rosenberg have pointed to the internalization of R&D as a distinguishing feature of corporate life in Germany and the United States, as compared with Great Britain. Evidently, need, and therefore potential returns to investment in science, was not the determining factor, for Britain had the largest markets of all for such science-based products as dyestuffs. If need was not the missing determinant, then capabilities and also the national climate for research and the context for research in companies were the critical factors. As Alfred Chandler has pointed out, even in the United States, not all large companies chose to incorporate R&D as a regular company activity. Many chose to rely exclusively on outside sources of technical information, such as the independent laboratories and the universities. See Alfred D. Chandler, Jr., *Scale and Scope: The Dynamics of Industrial Enterprise* (Cambridge, MA: Harvard University Press, 1990), p. 12.

9 See Georg Meyer-Thurow, "The Industrialization of Invention: A Case Study from the German Chemical Industry," *Isis,* 73(1982):363–81. Hughes, in *Networks of Power,* pp. 140–74, offers a related concept of phases in his discussion of technological momentum. Alfred Chandler, Jr., in "From Industrial Laboratories to Departments of Research and Development," in Hayes et al. (eds.), *The Uneasy Alliance,* pp. 53–7, proposes an alternative two-stage model for industrialization of research: Stage One is testing and control; Stage Two is development related to specific products and processes. See also Jonathan Hughes, *The Vital Few: The Entrepreneur and American Economic Progress* (Oxford University Press, 1986), pp. 3–6, who identifies five categories of economic development that can be sequential, but can also coexist in the same economy. These categories are similar to the ones we identified in the Bayer experience.

10 See, for instance, Paul R. Lawrence and Davis Dyer, *Renewing American Industry* (New York: Free Press, 1986), who looks at the renewal phenomenon on an industry-by-industry basis, William J. Abernathy, Kim B. Clark, and Alan M. Kantrow, *Industrial Renaissance* (New York: Basic Books, 1983), and David Halberstam, *The Reckoning* (New York: Morrow, 1988). Historian William Mass has commented that the Draper Company, which held the second highest number of patents of any company in the United States, after General Electric, in 1902, gave up its aggressive product R&D program in the 1920s when it developed a standard high-volume loom. When Draper was acquired by Rockwell in the 1960s it forfeited its technological lead among textile-machinery makers altogether. Oral comment following the paper entitled "Developing and Utilizing Technological Leadership: Vertical Integration, Industrial Research and Business Strategy at the Draper Company, 1816–1930," *Business and Economic History: Proceedings of the Business History Conference*

(April 1989). RCA, which until 1957 controlled a huge collection of "radio-related" (i.e., radio and television electronics) patents and operated the preeminent all-electronics laboratory in the United States in the 1950s, dissipated its commanding technological lead in consumer electronics in the 1960s. Its diversification into nonelectronically based consumer goods and services gradually undercut internal support for its electronics R&D program. See Margaret B. W. Graham, *RCA and the Videodisc: The Business of Research* (Cambridge University Press, 1986).

11 This interpretation was first made popular by J. A. Schumpeter, *Capitalism, Socialism, and Democracy*, 3rd ed. (New York: Harper & Row, 1942), p. 132, who declared that the takeover of innovation by corporate America had made invention and innovation an altogether predictable, even boring, activity. Meyer-Thurow, in "The Industrialization of Invention," pursues much the same line of argument for German industrial research. David S. Landes, in *The Unbound Prometheus*, followed the same interpretation, and David Noble's *America by Design* took the argument to its logical and ideological extremes. It is important to note that all of these interpretations are based on the relationship between science and industry prior to World War II.

12 George Wise, "Ionists in Industry: Physical Chemistry at General Electric, 1900–1915," *Isis*, 74(1983):7–21, refers to what went on in this early period of industrial research in the United States as "the collision between academic and industrial values." He points out that both the scientists and their scientific fields were unalterably changed by the relocation from university to company laboratory, but that the transformation was anything but smooth. W. Bernard Carlson summarizes the literature on this question thoroughly in his article "Academic Entrepreneurship and Engineering Education: Dugald C. Jackson and the MIT–GE Cooperative Engineering Course, 1907–1932," *Technology and Culture*, 29(January 1988):536–67. Other important summary pieces in the historiography of professionalization include Louis Galambos, "Technology, Political Economy, and Professionalization," George Wise, "A New Role for Professional Scientists in Industry: Industrial Research at General Electric, 1900–1916," *Technology and Culture*, 21(1980):408–29, and Peter Meiksins, "The 'Revolt of the Engineers' Reconsidered," *Technology and Culture*, 28(April 1988):219–46.

13 Margaret B. W. Graham, "Industrial Research in the Age of Big Science," in Richard S. Rosenbloom (ed.), *Research in Technological Innovation, Management and Policy*, vol. 2 (Greenwich, CT: JAI Press, 1985), pp. 47–79, and Daniel Kevles, *The Physicists* (New York: Knopf, 1977). See also Hounshell and Smith, *Science and Corporate Strategy*, pp. 336–55.

14 Graham, "Industrial Research in the Age of Big Science," W. Rupert Maclaurin, "The Organization of Research in the Radio Industry after the War," *Proceedings of the I.R.E.* (September 1945):567–70, and Arthur A. Bright, "War, Radar and the Radio Industry," *Harvard Business Review* (Winter 1947):255–72.

15 See Lester Thurow, "A Weakness in Process Technology," *Science* (December 1988). Alcoa has done far more than other large U.S. metals companies to keep its processes current, especially compared with the mainstream U.S. steel industry, which stands rightly accused of having failed to innovate technologically and organizationally. Summary accounts of

these failures can be found in Lawrence and Dyer, *Renewing American Industry,* and Michael L. Dertouzos, Richard K. Lester, Robert M. Solow, and the MIT Commission on Productivity, *Made in America: Regaining the Productive Edge* (Cambridge, MA: MIT Press, 1989).

TECHNICAL NOTE

1 Junius D. Edwards, "The Story of Aluminum," in Junius D. Edwards, Francis C. Frary, and Zay Jeffries (eds.), *The Aluminum Industry,* 2 vols., *Vol. 1: Aluminum and Its Production* (New York: McGraw-Hill, 1930), p. 124. The following description of the Bayer process is based on that source and on W. A. Anderson and W. E. Haupin, "Aluminum and Alloys," in *Encyclopedia of Chemical Technology,* 3rd ed., Vol. 2 (1978), pp. 140–4.

2 An overview of these is available in Anderson and Haupin, "Aluminum and Alloys," pp. 138, 142–4.

3 Nils Oeberg and Rudolf O. Friederich, "Outlook of the Bayer Process," in Warren S. Peterson and Ronald E. Miller (eds.), *Hall-Héroult Centennial: First Century of Aluminum Process Technology, 1886–1986* (The Metallurgical Society, Inc., 1986), pp. 144–53, and J. P. McGeer, "Environmental Control in Our Industry, An Overview," ibid., p. 169. That volume contains 10 excellent essays and an 84-page pictorial essay that, in itself, provides invaluable information on the development of aluminum process technology.

4 Anderson and Haupin, "Aluminum and Alloys," pp. 144-7.

5 Anderson and Haupin, "Aluminum and Alloys," pp. 132–43. That article also describes other, newer aluminum refining processes: zone refining and fractional crystallization.

6 N. E. Richards, "Evolution of Electrolytes for Hall-Héroult Cells," in Peterson and Miller (eds.), *Hall-Héroult Centennial,* pp. 114–19; Warren E. Haupin, "History of Electrochemical Energy Consumption in Hall-Héroult Cells," ibid., p. 110; J. P. McGeer, "Hall-Héroult: 100 Years of Process Evolution," *Journal of Metals,* 38(November 1986):31.

7 Junius D. Edwards, "Materials for the Reduction Process, Electrolyte and Carbon Electrodes," in Edwards et al. (eds.), *Aluminum and Its Production,* p. 291; McGeer, "100 Years of Process Evolution," p. 29.

8 McGeer, "100 Years of Process Evolution," pp. 27–8; D. Belitskus, "Carbon Electrodes in the Hall-Héroult Cell: A Century of Progress," in Peterson and Miller (eds.), *Hall-Héroult Centennial,* pp. 130–43.

9 Haupin, "History of Electrochemical Energy Consumption in Hall-Héroult Cells," pp. 106–13; McGeer, "100 Years of Process Evolution," pp. 27–8; B. J. Welch, "Gaining That Extra 2 Percent Current Efficiency," in Peterson and Miller (eds.), *Hall-Héroult Centennial,* pp. 120–9. The theoretical perfect efficiency for the process is established by Faraday's law; see Francis C. Frary and Junius D. Edwards, "The Production of Aluminum," in Edwards et al. (eds.), *Aluminum and Its Production,* p. 315.

10 Warren S. Peterson, "Cast Shop Technology and Reclamation: 100 Years of Progress," in Peterson and Miller (eds.), *Hall-Héroult Centennial,* pp. 155–6.

11 Peterson, "Cast Shop Technology and Reclamation," p. 156; E. H. Dix, Jr., "Melting Aluminum," in Edwards et al. (eds.), *Aluminum and Its Production*, pp. 273–89.

12 Anderson, "Cast Shop Technology and Reclamation," p. 160.

CHAPTER 1

1 Donald H. Wallace, *Market Control in the Aluminum Industry* (Cambridge, MA: Harvard University Press, 1937), app. B, p. 529; Alfred Cowles, *The True Story of Aluminum* (Chicago: Regnery, 1958), passim; Joseph W. Richards, *Aluminium: Its History, Occurrence, Properties, Metallurgy and Applications, Including Its Alloys*, 2nd ed. (Philadelphia: Baird, 1890), pp. 17–45.

2 So influential were the Cowleses in the American metallurgical establishment that a special issue of the *Scientific American* in 1890 gave columns of coverage to the Cowles aluminum smelting process and the Héroult process. It made no mention at all of Hall or the PRC, which by then dominated aluminum production. See *Scientific American*, Supplement 753 (7 June 1890):12024–5.

3 See Sanborn Insurance Company map series issued by the U.S. Library of Congress. Maps are available for both Pittsburgh and New Kensington, providing detailed drawings of many of the establishments in the vicinity of different PRC works. The actual PRC facilities themselves were not depicted, presumably because the insurance inspectors were denied access.

4 "Pure" aluminum referred to unalloyed aluminum. For many years it would not be possible even to approach chemical purity because of the impurity of inputs and the primitiveness of the process.

5 J. T. W. Echevarri, "Aluminium and Some of Its Uses," *Journal of the Institute of Metals*, 1(1909):125–43. By 1909, a listing of aluminum end products ran to dozens of items made out of wire, sheet, tubing, and castings.

6 World production of steel increased 30-fold in the last decades of the nineteenth century, the lion's share of the increase taking place in the United States, according to T. K. Derry and Trevor I. Williams, *A Short History of Technology* (Oxford University Press, 1960), p. 486. See Peter Temin, *Iron and Steel in Nineteenth-Century America* (Cambridge, MA: MIT Press, 1964), pp. 109–12, and Geoffrey Tweedale, *Sheffield Steel and America: A Century of Commercial and Technological Interdependence, 1830–1930* (Cambridge University Press, 1987), pp. 15–29, 188–9, for particulars about the Pittsburgh experience.

7 Walter Rosenhain, "What Industry Owes to Science," Parts I and II, *The Engineer*, 122(1 December 1916):478, (8 December 1916):505. To be sure, "scientific methods of research" and "the direct application of scientific principles" had contributed to both the Bessemer and the open-hearth processes. In the early 1880s in England, scientific methods were first being used to produce alloy steel when Robert Hadfield produced his manganese steel. The level of laboratory standards needed for alloy work was not achieved in the U.S. steel industry until well past the turn of the century. See Tweedale, *Sheffield Steel and America*, pp. 32–5. See also Zay Jeffries, "Engineering and Science in the Metal Industry," *Mechanical Engineering*, 48(January 1926):8–16.

8   See Echevarri, "Aluminium and Some of Its Uses," pp. 127–30.

9   Alfred E. Hunt refers to the praises that aluminum earned for its properties when produced electrochemically in Europe, especially by Société Anonyme de L'Aluminium, Merle and Co., and Pechiney & Co. The shift to electrochemical production in the United States produced aluminum that was more impure and of inferior quality, "to the serious retarding of the introduction of the metal in the arts." See Hunt, "Aluminum Manufacture in Europe," *Aluminum World*, 3(October 1896):3. Recently, Warren Peterson has explained why that was the case: Casting shops ran into the problem of "silicon pickup" by molten aluminum when it was melted for casting. That had not been a problem with the older processes, but plagued casting after the Hall-Héroult process became the sole provider of ingot. See Warren S. Peterson, "Cast Shop Technology and Reclamation: 100 Years of Progress," in Warren S. Peterson and Ronald E. Miller (eds.), *Hall-Héroult Centennial: First Century of Aluminum Process Technology, 1886–1986* (The Metallurgical Society, Inc., 1986), p. 155.

10 Wallace, *Market Control*, app. A, p. 525. Several recent authors have stressed the peculiarly interdependent nature of the electrochemical industry, and consequently the importance of the particular region in which an individual enterprise grew up. For example, Darwin H. Stapleton, "Early Industrial Research in Cleveland: Local Networks and National Connections," presented to the Economic History Association, April 1987, points to the role of the Brush laboratory when he argues persuasively the importance of studying economic history regionally. Robert Locke, *The End of the Practical Man: Entrepreneurship and Higher Education in Germany, France, and Great Britain, 1880–1940* (Greenwich, CT: JAI Press, 1984), discusses the regional characteristics of the European electrochemical industry in his appendix on electrochemistry, and Martha Moore Trescott, in *The Rise of the American Electrochemicals Industry, 1880–1910: Studies in the American Technological Environment* (Westport, CT: Greenwood Press, 1981), also emphasizes regional character. Pittsburgh has not typically been considered an electrochemical center, while Cleveland is noted for having been the first industrial center to make good without very close coal supplies. The PRC had to move its reduction operations away from Pittsburgh to Niagara when it wanted an adequate source of cheap electric power to support rapid expansion. See George D. Smith, *From Monopoly to Competition: The Transformations of Alcoa, 1888–1986* (Cambridge University Press, 1988), pp. 80–2.

11 Joseph Richards, "Address to the Electrochemical Society in 1903," quoted in Wallace, *Market Control*, app. A, p. 526.

12 Wallace, *Market Control*, app. B, pp. 528–31. In 1886 the Cowleses had been awarded two medals by the Franklin Society as leaders for their work with electric furnaces and refractory (high-melting-point) materials. For the most succinct account of the history of the effort to find an inexpensive means of producing aluminum, see J. W. Richards, "The Aluminium Problem," a lecture delivered at the Franklin Institute, January 12, 1891, in Carnegie Library, Pittsburgh, PA. A more detailed contemporary treatment is to be found in the three editions of *Aluminium*, published between 1887 and 1896, by the same author. See also F. C. Frary, "Re: *The True Story of Aluminum*, by Alfred Cowles," Alcoa Archives, Aluminum Company of America, Pittsburgh (hereafter cited as AA).

13 Clapp became a Pittsburgh notable, serving as the president of the board of the University of Pittsburgh and chairman of the board of the Carnegie Institute. See Chester G. Fisher, "From Carbon to Carbon: A History of the Pittsburgh Section of the American Chemical Society," pamphlet celebrating the Golden Anniversary of the American Chemical Society, 1903–1953 (Pittsburgh: ACS, 1953), p. 29, and "The Aluminum Company of America," *Fortune*, 10(September 1934):49.

14 Wallace, *Market Control*, app. B, pp. 528–31.

15 For a fuller account of the founding of Alcoa, see Smith, *From Monopoly to Competition*, pp. 19–35.

16 Hall's process was covered by U.S. Patent 400,766, April 2, 1889. Professor Seabury Mastick, lecturing on chemical patents at Columbia University in 1915, noted that the patent correspondence suggested some possible confusion on Hall's part as to what the original part of his invention really was: "It may be that at this point of time Hall himself did not appreciate that the process, regardless of the form of apparatus used, was the broad and valuable invention. The solution he found had just barely eluded many far more eminent scientists and inventors throughout the industrial world at the time." Quoted in Wallace, *Market Control*, app. B, p. 527. See also Harry N. Holmes, "A Great Pupil and a Great Discovery – Both Supported by a Great Teacher," *Science*, 83(21 February 1931):175–7. For a more detailed technical discussion of Hall's invention, see N. E. Richards, "Evolution of Electrolytes for Hall-Héroult Cells," D. Belitskus, "Carbon Electrodes in the Hall-Héroult Cell: A Century of Progress," and Warren E. Haupin, "History of Electrochemical Energy Consumption in Hall-Héroult Cells," all in Peterson and Miller (eds.), *Hall-Héroult Centennial*.

17 J. W. Richards, "The Aluminium Problem," p. 3.

18 Francis Frary, Alcoa's first formal research director, later privately dismissed Hall's discovery as "obvious." As no one had yet hit upon it in the United States, that judgment was not altogether fair to Hall, but it referred to the fact that, like many other highly successful inventors before him, Hall had recombined elements that others had already tried. Deville had tried electrolysis, but abandoned it because of the expense and difficulty of supplying enough electric current with batteries. Hall and others realized that with the invention of the dynamo in 1870, large amounts of electric current could be counted on to be available for industrial use. See Francis C. Frary, "History of Early Aluminum Research," transcript of a speech given in 1963, Alcoa Laboratories Archives, Alcoa Technical Center, Alcoa Center, PA (hereafter cited as ALA), pp. 8–9.

19 As quoted in N. E. Richards, "Evolution of Electrolytes for Hall-Héroult Cells," in Peterson and Miller (eds.), *Hall-Héroult Centennial*, p. 115, Héroult wrote: "The principle that I want to patent for the production of aluminum consists of decomposing alumina in solution in molten cryolite bath by means of electric contact with the carbon crucible which contains cryolite and on the other hand another agglomerated carbon electrode which is submerged in the bath. This composition produces the decomposition of alumina when applying current of weak potential. Oxygen moves to the anode and burns it. Aluminum is deposited on the sides of the crucible which makes the cathode and precipitates as droplets in the bottom."

20 A somewhat inaccurate summary of Hall's patent and the litigation that

followed occurs in Wallace, *Market Control*, app. B, pp. 527–37. For technical accuracy, see Smith, *From Monopoly to Competition*, pp. 35–40. Both the Wallace and Smith accounts relied on information from former Alcoa patent attorney Edward Foote. For a more general discussion of patents in that period, see David F. Noble, *America by Design: Science, Technology, and the Rise of Corporate Capitalism* (Oxford University Press, 1979), pp. 84–109.

21   The Cowleses first claimed that Hall had not recognized the sufficiency of the internal heat generated by the electrolysis because his patent application, and his configuration on the Cowles premises, had employed an external source of heat for the reduction pots. Hall could show that although the description of the apparatus in his patent applications had assumed external heat, he had anticipated the possibility of larger-scale pots with internal heat in his correspondence with his sister Julia: "In some respects this invention is going to be better than I anticipated; thus the resistance of the liquid is exceedingly low. Also it is evident from the experiments that the waste heat of electricity, which must be used anyway, will be nearly or quite enough to keep the solvent melted." Quoted in Junius D. Edwards, Francis C. Frary, and Zay Jeffries (eds.), *The Aluminum Industry*, 2 vols., *Vol. 1: Aluminum and Its Production* (New York: McGraw-Hill, 1930), p. 27.

22   Wallace, *Market Control*, app. B; Edwards et al. (eds.), *Aluminum and Its Production*, p. 30.

23   N. E. Richards, "Evolution of Electrolytes for Hall-Héroult Cells," in Peterson and Miller (eds.), *Hall-Héroult Centennial*, p. 115.

24   *Engineering*, the English journal of the Institute of Mining Engineers, 50(24 October 1890):480–2; *American Manufacturer and Iron World*, 47(10 October 1890):7–8.

25   Edwards et al. (eds.), *Aluminum and Its Production*, p. 30.

26   Joseph Richards, "Recent Advances in the Aluminium Industry," *Aluminum World*, 6(May 1900):149.

27   Alfred E. Hunt, "Measurement of Electric Energy," *Aluminum World*, 3(October 1896):3; "Aluminum Manufacture in Europe," ibid., 3(November 1896):23–4.

28   After an extensive tour of European aluminum sites in 1898, Richards reported that "in some respects British Aluminium (run by Mr. Restivo and his assistant Mr. Echevarri) is the model aluminium company in the world." They already owned their own bauxite supplies and made their own carbons. *Aluminum World*, 5(October 1898):6–8.

29   See Trescott, *The Rise of the American Electrochemicals Industry*, p. 47.

30   S. K. Colby, "Commercial History of Aluminum," in Edwards et al. (eds.), *The Aluminum Industry*, 2 vols., *Vol. 2: Aluminum Products and Their Fabrication* (New York: McGraw-Hill, 1930), p. 5.

31   Daniel Boorstin, *The Americans: The Democratic Experience* (New York: Random House, 1973), pp. 189–93, and Davis S. Landes, *The Unbound Prometheus: Technological Change and Industrial Development in Western Europe from 1750 to the Present* (Cambridge University Press, 1968), pp. 315–17, cover the lag in standard-setting between the United States and European countries. Slowest to achieve uniform standards was Great Britain.

32   See J. Towns Robinson, "Development of Aluminium Alloy Forgings and Stampings," *Metallurgia* (February 1945):182–3. In that article, Robin-

son, technical superintendent of England's High Duty Alloys, Ltd., a subdivision of Rolls-Royce, writes of the early difficulties in working light alloys: "The new technique and the equipment were modified step by step as practical experience in the working of the alloys was accumulated. The lower and far narrower range of temperature for the working of light alloys compared with steel presented many problems and uncertainties which seem trivial today, but which in those days meant all the difference between success and failure." Other problems included a lack of suitable furnaces for working and heat treatment. Electric furnaces designed for ferrous alloys were unsatisfactory owing to imperfect control at the lower temperature ranges required. Pyrometric control was essential, but the instrumentation was unsuitable. Even hammers, guides, and forging and stamping equipment all had to be modified.

33 Records of all of the experimental work conducted for the company from 1888 through 1960 are summarized, year by year, in "History of Research and Development, Aluminum Company of America," a typescript document compiled by Francis C. Frary for the years 1888–1937, and by Frary and others at Alcoa Laboratories for subsequent years (hereafter referred to as Frary et al., "History of Research and Development," with specific reference to the year or years in which work was conducted), manuscript, Historical Drawer, ALA.

34 *Aluminum World,* 4(November 1897):23.

35 *Aluminum World,* 2(March 1896):119.

36 Smith, *From Monopoly to Competition,* pp. 84–7.

37 "Richards' Hardened Aluminium," *Aluminum World,* 7(March 1901):116.

38 Handy and Regelsberger had been publishing their methods and results liberally, according to *Aluminum World,* 2(November 1895):21, and their knowledge of the subject seems to have been one of the main sources used by Richards in the third edition of his *Aluminium,* published in 1896.

39 "A New Treatise on Aluminum," *Aluminum World,* 3(June 1897):167.

40 Volume 1, Number 1, of *Aluminum World* was issued in October 1894. The periodical later branched into two journals: *Metals Industry* and *Bronze Journal.*

41 "Aluminum for the Defender," *Aluminum World,* 1(August 1895):205.

42 James C. McGuire, letter to the *New York World,* 8 August 1895.

43 "Aluminum for the Defender," *Aluminum World,* 1(July 1895):181. Robert J. Scott, one of the original PRC investors, was superintendent of the 33rd Street mill of Carnegie Steel.

44 Richmond Pearson Hobson, assistant naval constructor, U.S.N., "Notes on the Yacht 'Defender,' and the Use of Aluminum in Maritime Construction," *Aluminum World,* 4(October 1897):2–3, quotes a paper contributed to the U.S. Naval Institute, Annapolis.

45 George K. Burgess, chief, Metallurgy Division, Bureau of Standards, "Some Problems in Physical Metallurgy at the Bureau of Standards," *Journal of the Franklin Institute,* 182(July 1916):19–35.

46 In April 1895, for example, that column reported a study on impurities in commercial aluminum by H. Moissan. It identified the most common impurities (iron and silicon), their sources (electrodes and crucible), and the apparent effects on the mechanical properties of aluminum when worked in various ways. *Aluminum World,* 1(April 1895):124.

47 *Aluminum World,* 3(May 1897):145, 4(November 1897):25.

48 Frary et al., "History of Research and Development," 1888–91.

49 "Professor Joseph W. Richards," *Aluminum World*, 8(May 1902):156, quotes Richards's obituary in *Journal of the Franklin Institute.*

50 *Aluminum World*, 1(April 1895):131; R. D. Billinger, "America's Pioneer Press Agent for Aluminum," *Journal of Chemical Education* (June 1937):253. On the state of metallurgy, see Burgess, "Some Problems in Physical Metallurgy at the Bureau of Standards." See also a recent discussion by Geoffrey Tweedale about the comparative states of American and British metallurgy in the late nineteenth century: Tweedale, *Sheffield Steel and America*, pp. 33–5. Note that Professor Richards and others used the English spelling, "aluminium," until after the turn of the century, when American usage settled on "aluminum."

51 Trescott, *The Rise of the American Electrochemicals Industry*, gives a thorough account of early electrochemical enterprises that grew up in the Niagara Falls area. See also Thomas P. Hughes, *Networks of Power: Electrification in Western Society, 1880–1930* (Baltimore: Johns Hopkins University Press, 1983), pp. 139–41, Wallace, *Market Control*, app. A, pp. 520–2, and Joseph Richards, "The Electro-Chemical Industries at Niagara Falls," *Aluminum World*, 8(April 1902):131–2.

52 On the professional cultures of Niagara and Cleveland, see Trescott, *The Rise of the American Electrochemicals Industry*, pp. 135–53, and Noble, *America by Design*, pp. 36–9. See also "American Electro-Chemical Society," *Aluminum World*, 8(January 1902):77, and Wallace, *Market Control*, app. A, p. 526. These cultural distinctions may have contributed to the rivalry that existed in Alcoa between the Cleveland laboratory and the New Kensington laboratory.

53 Richards, "Electro-Chemical Industries at Niagara Falls," p. 132.

54 F. H. Allison, Jr., "The Metallurgy Department of C.I.T.: The First Thirty Years: 1903–1935," in Gerhard Derge (ed.), *Metallurgy at Carnegie: From Metallurgy and Mining to Metallurgical Engineering and Materials Science* (Pittsburgh: Carnegie-Mellon University, 1986), pp. 2–10. Thomas Hughes has identified the stages leading to establishment of a new industry as moving from individual inventor, to company investment in facilities and resources, to involvement with educational infrastructure, and to the ultimate creation of technical professions. He calls this movement "technological momentum." See Hughes, *Networks of Power*, pp. 14–15, and Hughes, *Elmer Sperry, Inventor and Engineer* (Baltimore: Johns Hopkins University Press, 1971), pp. 63–70.

55 In 1904, New Kensington had to take on calcining the alumina because the Massena works had complained of finding pieces of furnace lining in the material coming from East St. Louis. Pennsylvania Salt was one of the old-line chemical companies transformed by the electrochemical revolution. First situated in western Pennsylvania, it entered electrochemicals in 1890 and set up new operations in Michigan. At the time it supplied the PRC with alumina, it would still have used expensive old-style methods for manufacture. Trescott, *The Rise of the American Electrochemicals Industry*, pp. 95–6.

56 The companies that made up the Aluminum Castings Company were as follows: the former Allyne Brass Companies of Cleveland, Ohio, Michigan, and New York; the Syracuse Aluminum and Bronze Company; the Eclipse Foundry Company of Detroit; and the Alcoa Foundry located in

New Kensington. The consolidation took place in early 1909 and was formalized on August 13, 1909. The company faced a fast-growing demand for castings to feed the new automobile industry. Edwin S. Fickes, "History of the Growth and Development of the Aluminum Company of America. Vol. 17-B: Histories of the Manufacturing Properties of the Aluminum Company of America, Affiliated Companies, and Defense Corporation Plants," AA, p. 76.

57 Information about the building of the technical staff is found in Fickes, "History," pp. 109ff.

58 Fickes became a director and senior vice-president of Alcoa and a director of many other companies. He was also a director of the Metallurgical Advisory Board of the Carnegie Institute of Technology and a member of a wide variety of engineering and scientific associations, including the American Society of Civil Engineers, the American Institute of Mining and Metallurgical Engineers. He was a fellow of the American Geographical Society, and a member of the American Association for the Advancement of Science.

59 Earl Blough and Edwin Fickes both travelled extensively abroad in the periods just before and just after World War I. Fickes's first trip abroad on Alcoa business was to England in 1907, when he visited with Edward C. Darling, Ashbury's successor, who established a London sales office for the Northern Aluminum Company. See Fickes, "History," p. 64.

60 C. M. Hall to George Hall, 21 April 1904, in Hall Correspondence, Historical Drawer, ALA; Fickes, "History," p. 98. On Hall's role in the company after his move to Niagara Falls, see Smith, *From Monopoly to Competition*, pp. 122–5. Smith's interpretation reflects the discontent of the operating side of the company with any longer-term research activity, which they saw as useless and disruptive tinkering. From the technical perspective, Hall's research activities did not go far enough. Fundamental research into the properties of metals required more than a works laboratory and the efforts of one or two men if it was to have any chance of producing significant results.

61 In 1898, for instance, the *Journal of the Franklin Institute* reported on an article in *London Engineering* by Professor Roberts-Austen, chemist to the British Mint, and by a man named Becker, former manager of the Société Industrielle d'Aluminium, proposing use of calcined bauxite instead of alumina in smelting. Reported in *Aluminum World*, 3(December 1898):50. On the world at Alcoa, see Frary et al., "History of Research and Development," 1899–1900.

62 *Aluminum World*, 2(April 1896):137.

63 The modification was to charge the Bayer-process solution with sodium carbonate and lime rather than caustic soda to produce a cheaper caustic that was easier to filter. See Frary, "History of Early Aluminum Research," p. 4. Alcoa licensed the Bayer process in 1905. See Smith, *From Monopoly to Competition*, pp. 99–100.

64 "Process of Purifying Bauxite," *Aluminum World*, 7(July 1901):795, reported three patents granted to Charles Martin Hall for purifying bauxite and purified crystalline aluminum. See also Francis C. Frary, Junius D. Edwards, and Ralph B. Mason, "Electrothermal and Miscellaneous Furnace Processes for the Production of Alumina," in Edwards et al. (eds.), *Aluminum and Its Production*, pp. 236–40.

65   C. M. Hall to C. B. Fox, 3 August 1910, ALA.

66   American bauxites were higher in silica content than European bauxites, and silica caused serious losses of both soda and alumina, forming an insoluble compound of sodium aluminum silicate that was carried away in the red-mud residue. See Technical Appendix and Junius D. Edwards and Ralph B. Mason, "The Production of Alumina," in Edwards et al. (eds.), *Aluminum and Its Production,* p. 127. The adaption of the Bayer process to local conditions required major facilities enhancements, including a new powerhouse and boilers, along with new tanks and facilities for making caustic soda. C. M. Hall to A. V. Davis, E. S. Fickes, and C. B. Fox, August 1910, and E. S. Fickes to C. M. Hall, August 1910, ALA.

67   There were many other examples of entrepreneurs acquiring outside technologies during the same era, including Henry Ford, Andrew Carnegie, and Thomas A. Edison. See, for instance, David Halberstam, *The Reckoning* (New York: Morrow, 1986), pp. 73–4, who points out that Ford modeled his moving assembly line after the overhead trolley used by Chicago meat-packers. On the German advantage in chemical knowledge, see Locke, *The End of the Practical Man,* pp. 33–50, and Georg Meyer-Thurow, "The Industrialization of Invention: A Case Study from the German Chemical Industry," *Isis,* 73(1982):363–81.

68   Blough to Hunt, 28 June 1953, AA env. 486, Blough recalled that incident for Hunt by way of correcting a statement in Charles Carr's history of Alcoa that Blough had invented 3S in 1916. See Charles C. Carr, *Alcoa: An American Enterprise* (New York: Rinehart & Co., 1952), p. 137. Conrad Nagel later corroborated Blough's statement from company records of alloy development, citing especially Earl Blough to A. V. Davis, 23 January 1906, and William Hoopes to A. V. Davis, 7 February 1906. The correspondence showed that Davis was paying close personal attention to the problem at the time and that Blough was issuing regular reports on the progress in correcting the Eastman trouble. See C. F. Nagel, Jr., to R. A. Hunt, "Re: Early History of Duralumin," 18 November 1953, AA. See also J. T. Staley, "History of Wrought Aluminum Alloy Development," 7 February 1986, p. 3, ALA. Earl Blough, "Statement Presented to the Ford Motor Company," 30 April 1957, AA, more fully described the primitive state of Alcoa's prewar technical capabilities.

69   Colby, "Commercial History of Aluminum," p. 7.

70   This discussion draws on Noble, *America by Design,* chapter 7, "Science for Industry: The Organization of Industrial and University Research," pp. 110–66. See also Leonard S. Reich, *The Making of American Industrial Research: Science and Business at GE and Bell* (Cambridge University Press, 1985), George Wise, "A New Role for Professional Scientists in Industry: Industrial Research at General Electric, 1900–1916," *Technology and Culture,* 21(July 1980):408–29, and David Hounshell and John K. Smith, *Science and Corporate Strategy: DuPont R&D, 1902–1980* (Cambridge University Press, 1988).

71   Fickes, "History," pp. 79–80.

72   On Carnegie Steel, see Paul A. Tiffany, "Corporate Culture and Corporate Change: The Origins of Industrial Research at the United States Steel Corporation, 1901–1929," paper presented to the 29th annual meeting of the Society for the History of Technology, 25 October 1986, p. 5. In 1907, Carnegie Steel, U.S. Steel's largest subsidiary, even chose a

laboratory manager and appropriated $100,000 to start a central laboratory. The company backed out when the new director, having toured European research sites such as Robert Hadfield's research laboratory in Sheffield, requested greater funding to construct experimental furnaces and rolling mills. On General Electric, see George Wise, "Ionists in Industry: Physical Chemistry at General Electric, 1900–1918," *Isis*, 74(1983):7–21. Trescott, *The Rise of the American Electrochemicals Industry*, pp. 226–86, shows how limited were the numbers of graduates from the few programs in electrochemical disciplines before World War I.

CHAPTER 2

1   Edwin S. Fickes, "History of the Growth and Development of the Aluminum Company of America." Vol. 17-B: "Histories of the Manufacturing Properties of the Aluminum Company of America, Affiliated Companies, and Defense Corporation Plants" (hereafter cited as Alcoa Plant Histories), Alcoa Archives, Aluminum Company of America, Pittsburgh, PA (hereafter cited as AA), p. 9.

2   Major sources for the account of ACSR are H. L. Harper, "Early History of Aluminum Extrusion," in "Massena Works History, Vol. 9-B-1," Alcoa Plant Histories, AA, S[afford] K. Colby, "The Commercial History of Aluminum," in Junius D. Edwards, Francis C. Frary, and Zay Jeffries (eds.), *The Aluminum Industry*, 2 vols., *Vol. 2: Aluminum Products and Their Fabrication* (New York: McGraw-Hill, 1930), pp. 11–13, Theodore Varney and Junius D. Edwards, "Electrical Conductors of Aluminum," ibid., pp. 701–22, William H. Hoopes Correspondence, AA, env. 63, and "The Development of Aluminum and the Aluminum Industry" (1940), manuscript, Historical Drawer, Alcoa Laboratories Archives, Alcoa Technical Center, Alcoa Center, PA (hereafter cited as ALA), pp. 1–7. For the vagaries of the cookware market, see George D. Smith, *From Monopoly to Competition: The Transformations of Alcoa, 1888–1986* (Cambridge University Press, 1988), pp. 84–7. On the electrical industry, see Thomas P. Hughes, *Networks of Power: Electrification in Western Society, 1880–1930* (Baltimore: Johns Hopkins University Press, 1983), especially chapter 6, "Technological Momentum," pp. 140–74.

3   Hughes, *Networks of Power*, p. 162. The observations and analysis conducted there by Charles F. Scott and Robert Mershon led to important practical information in the form of tables about the losses to be expected at different voltages for different wire configurations.

4   Tests are reported by Varney and Edwards, "Electrical Conductors of Aluminum," pp. 701–2, and R. J. Anderson, *The Metallurgy of Aluminum and Aluminum Alloys* (New York, 1925), pp. 286–7, quoted in Donald H. Wallace, *Market Control in the Aluminum Industry* (Cambridge, MA: Harvard University Press, 1937), p. 14–17.

5   "The Development of Aluminum and the Aluminum Industry," p. 1. This wire measured from 0.203 inch to 0.293 inch in diameter.

6   Fickes, "History," pp. 9–10.

7   Wallace, *Market Control*, p. 15.

8   S. K. Colby, "Aluminum Company of America," *Industrial and Engineering Chemistry*, 23(November 1931):1318–20; Wallace, *Market Control*, p.

21. Aluminum wire had been made as early as the early 1890s, for Wallace reports that wire accounted for 0.5 percent of aluminum sales in 1893.

9   Fickes, "History," pp. 9–10.

10 C. M. Hall to A. V. Davis, 23 December 1889, Hall Correspondence, Historical Drawer, ALA.

11 Colby, "The Commercial History of Aluminum," p. 12; William Hoopes to Messrs. Bakewell and Byrnes, 15 January 1904, AA, env. 94.

12 According to "The Development of Aluminum and the Aluminum Industry," p. 2, each of these strands measured 0.221 inch in diameter. The quality problems are recounted in "Early History of Aluminum Extrusion."

13 Colby, "The Commercial History of Aluminum," p. 13.

14 Hoopes Correspondence, 1 January to 30 June 1910, AA, env. 63. Hoopes requested testimony from Californian and Hawaiian electric companies on aluminum-cable endurance and service: Hoopes Correspondence, 1 January to 30 June 1910, AA, env. 66. On comparative prices of metals, see Wallace, *Market Control*, Table 1, p. 17. Wallace gives 3.3 as the "indifference ratio" for aluminum to copper, that point at which customers had no preference for one metal over another for similar uses. The table shows that between 1900 and 1907 the price ratio of a pound of aluminum to a pound of copper fluctuated between a high of 2.84 in 1902 and a low of 1.88 in 1906. That fluctuation was caused by a rise in the cost of copper; the price of aluminum remained constant at 33 cents per pound.

15 C. M. Hall to A. V. Davis, 23 December 1899, in "Copies of Selected Correspondence from Alcoa Files at Niagara Works" (hereafter cited as Niagara Correspondence), Historical Drawer, ALA. Charles F. Scott was one of the leading Westinghouse engineers who did extensive invention and research into all phases of electrical transmission.

16 Fickes, "History," pp. 9–10; interview with Elbert Howarth, former associate director of Alcoa Laboratories, 10 January 1985, by Margaret B. W. Graham.

17 Hall to Davis, 6 August 1900, Niagara Correspondence, ALA. William Hoopes, U.S. Patent 673,364, 30 April 1901. See Francis C. Frary and Junius D. Edwards, "The Production of Aluminum," in Edwards et al. (eds.), *The Aluminum Industry*, 2 vols., *Vol. 1: Aluminum and Its Production*, (New York: McGraw-Hill, 1930), pp. 321–2.

18 Hoopes to A. V. Davis, 20 August 1902, AA, env. 63. There was extensive correspondence between Hoopes and Davis during August and September 1902, with Hoopes writing from John Martin and Company in San Francisco.

19 W. Hoopes to A. V. Davis, 15 August 1902 and 20 August 1902, AA, env. 63. In the latter, Hoopes enclosed a letter from Mr. Hine of John Martin and Company to Mr. Robert Doble concerning award of a wire contract for the Guanajuato Electric Power Company. Hine instructed Doble to cooperate fully with Hoopes and to let him see all figures and data.

20 W. Hoopes to A. V. Davis, 20 August 1902, AA, env. 63.

21 W. Hoopes to A. V. Davis, 9 September 1902, AA, env. 63.

22 "The Development of Aluminum and the Aluminum Industry," p. 1. On Alcoa's sales of wire, see Wallace, *Market Control*, Table 2, p. 21.

23   Correspondence between A. C. MacDougall and W. Hoopes, 3–6 March 1906, AA, env. 64.

24   W. Hoopes to A. C. MacDougall, 29 October 1909, AA, env. 64.

25   Fickes, "History," pp. 9–10.

26   Fickes, "History," p. 10.

27   "The Development of Aluminum and the Aluminum Industry," p. 2; Hoopes to Bakewell and Byrnes, 15 January 1904, AA; Harper, "Early History of Aluminum Extrusion."

28   William Hoopes to Norman Robertson, 20 October 1904, in Harper, "Early History of Aluminum Extrusion"; Hoopes to Robertson, 12 July 1906, and 13 November 1906, AA, env. 63.

29   Harper, "Early History of Aluminum Extrusion." See also letters from L. A. de Cazenove to Hoopes on proposed equipment for extrusion: 12 July to 10 December 1906, AA, env. 63. These contain estimates for the cost of producing 5,000 pounds per day of extruded wire at 0.78 cent per pound.

30   The patent of 1907 was shared with Norman Robertson and stipulated aluminum cable having a core of another metal.

31   For many years the company used "A.C.O.A.," not "Alcoa," as the abbreviated version of its name. However, for simplicity and consistency, we have chosen to use Alcoa exclusively for the period after 1907.

32   Wallace, *Market Control,* p. 16; Table 2, p. 21.

33   The many-page technical documents sent out to salesmen in circulars explained how to calculate the deflections of steel-reinforced aluminum cable. A revealing memo (William Hoopes to A. M. Nutt, 14 December 1911, AA, env. 65) admits of no very simple method for doing this. Further documents ("Re: Aluminum Cable Steel Reinforced," 23 May 1912, AA, env. 68) contains charts for calculating weights and strengths for different sizes of cable and their copper equivalences. Frank Magee, former CEO and chairman of the board of Alcoa, in an interview with George D. Smith, 18–19 January 1984, recalled how hard it was to overcome the skepticism of purchasing agents of electrical utilities and electric railways.

34   W. Hoopes to H. M. Hall, 6 February 1911, AA, env. 67.

35   H. M. Hall to W. Hoopes, 31 January 1911, AA, env. 67. The "drop of the beam" method was a technique for establishing the amount of strain a wire could withstand. It involved dropping a beam of a prescribed weight, attached to the wire to be tested, from increasing heights until the wire broke. On the problem of standards, see David F. Noble, *America by Design: Science, Technology, and the Rise of Corporate Capitalism* (Oxford University Press, 1979), pp. 69–83, and Hugh G. Aitken, *Scientific Management in Action: Taylorism at the Watertown Arsenal* (Princeton University Press, 1985), pp. 85–134. Aitken shows that Watertown Arsenal was, at the time, engaged in a tremendous effort to apply accuracy of measurement to all areas of industrial life.

36   A. M. Nutt to W. Hoopes, 25 January 1911, AA, env. 67.

37   W. Hoopes to H. M. Hall, 26 October 1909, AA, env. 64. See also Charles W. Cheape, *Family Firm to Modern Multinational: Norton Company, A New England Enterprise* (Cambridge, MA: Harvard University Press, 1985), for an example of a company selling abrasives, following much the same strategy at the same time.

38 D. B. Rushmore to W. Hoopes, 11 October 1907, AA, env. 63.

39 J. T. W. Echevarri, "Aluminium and Some of Its Uses," *Journal of the Institute of Metals,* 1(1909):125–43.

40 "Aluminum and the Emergency," *Fortune,* 23(May 1941):66–8.

41 Francis C. Frary, "History of Early Aluminum Research," transcript of a speech given in 1963, Historical Drawer, ALA.

CHAPTER 3

1 Edwin S. Fickes, "History of the Growth and Development of the Aluminum Company of America." Vol. 17-B: "Histories of the Manufacturing Properties of the Aluminum Company of America, Affiliated Companies, and Defense Corporation Plants" (hereafter cited as Alcoa Plant Histories), Alcoa Archives, Aluminum Company of America, Pittsburgh, PA (hereafter cited as AA), p. 79.

2 S. K. Colby, "The Commercial History of Aluminum," in Junius D. Edwards, Francis C. Frary, and Zay Jeffries (eds.), *The Aluminum Industry,* 2 vols., *Vol. 2: Aluminum Products and Their Fabrication* (New York: McGraw-Hill, 1930), p. 20.

3 Donald H. Wallace, *Market Control in the Aluminum Industry* (Cambridge, MA: Harvard University Press, 1937), p. 572, whose Table 39 ("Estimated Production and Foreign Trade in 1912 and 1913") shows that imports reached a level 50 percent as great as the level of domestic production.

4 Staffed initially with four researchers, the research program at NPL expanded to include the efforts of more than 30 researchers. See A. Kelly, "Walter Rosenhain and Materials Research at Teddington," *Philosophical Transactions of the Royal Society of London, Series A,* 282(1976):8. George L. Kelley, "Significant Progress in Research in Metals," *Annals of the American Academy of Political and Social Sciences,* 119(May 1928):24–31, recounts how early metallographic studies (studies of crystalline structure using the microscope) led to theories of metal hardening and in turn to high-strength alloys for various applications.

5 Wallace, *Market Control,* chapter 7. Francis Frary gives details of Wilm's discovery in "Aluminum – How and Why," *Civil Engineering,* 8(January 1938):19–22. The patent cluster included the following: a 1905 patent registered in Britain as 19282/05 by Conrad Claussen, chemistry Ph.D. from Berlin, for a process of improving aluminum alloys by heating and chilling; another patent, no. 26322/07, filed by Centralstelle für Wissenschaftliche Technische Forstellungen; and German patent No. 6485/10, filed by Wilm in 1909 for a process for improving alloys. For further details of developments in the German electrochemicals industry, see Wallace, *Market Control,* pp. 149–72, and Robert Locke, *The End of the Practical Man: Entrepreneurship and Higher Education in Germany, France, and Great Britain, 1880–1940* (Greenwich, CT: JAI Press, 1984), pp. 50–75.

6 Wallace, *Market Control,* p. 21, notes that several automobile producers were using over 1 million pounds of aluminum per year in that period. Aluminum could not penetrate any further into the automobile engine, however, until research had developed alloys suitable for making pistons and connecting rods, for example. An aluminum-copper alloy was used in the engine crankcase and water jackets of the Wright brothers' pioneer-

ing plane at Kitty Hawk, and by World War I airplane engines had many aluminum parts: George D. Smith, *From Monopoly to Competition: The Transformations of Alcoa, 1888–1986* (Cambridge University Press, 1988), pp. 128–9.

7   Fickes reported, on visiting Hall in 1911, that Hall had still not recovered from his operation of two years earlier: Fickes, "History," p. 98. However, in a letter to Fickes, 9 August 1910 (AA, env. 251), Hall made it clear that he had every intention of taking up where he had left off with the Bayer-process implementation.

8   Hall to Charles H. Moritz, 25 April 1913, and Moritz to Hall, 26 April 1913, AA, env. 190–B.

9   Hall wrote to Moritz from Florida that "the office people seem to have stopped sending me the daily reports of Massena, Shawinigan, and Tennessee. Please see that I get these promptly, either directly or through the Niagara Falls office." Hall to Moritz, 20 November 1914, AA, env. 190-C.

10 Hall wrote to Davis that Hoopes had rather dragged out the instrumentation question, and he later complained that Hoopes and Blough were not making their temperature measurements accurately enough. See Hall to Davis, 7 March 1913, and 29 September 1913, AA, env. 190-B. Hall responded to Hoopes's long account of work going on at East St. Louis on recovery of alumina and soda from red mud by saying that he had been in touch with Charles Fox about that for some time. See Hall to Hoopes, 14 July 1913, AA, env. 190-B. See also Hall to Moritz, 13 January 1913, and Hall to Hoopes, 29 January 1913, 30 January 1913, and 10 February 1913, AA, env. 190-B. Hall continued the stream of correspondence once he returned to Niagara in June 1913 and later in the year when he went to Pasadena for the winter: Hall letters to Davis, Hoopes, and Fox, June–December 1913, AA, env. 190-C.

11 Alfred D. Chandler, Jr., *The Visible Hand: The Managerial Revolution in American Business* (Cambridge, MA: Harvard University Press, 1977), pp. 266–7, describes how the introduction of improved flow in metalmaking enterprises, exemplified by Andrew Carnegie's pioneering efforts in that area, required "placing vigorous management controls over" the despots who had previously handled the activities on the shop floor.

12 Moritz to Hall, 25 February 1913, AA, env. 190-B.

13 A. V. Davis to Hall, 26 September 1913, and the reply, 29 September 1913, AA, env. 190-C. When Dr. Serpek visited the United States, Davis was careful to allow him to see the works at Niagara "as little as possible." See Hoopes to Hall, 20 June 1913, AA, env. 190-C. On Hall's conception of aluminum production, see Warren Haupin, "History of Electrical Energy Consumption in Hall-Héroult Cells," in Warren S. Peterson and Ronald E. Miller (eds.), *Hall-Héroult Centennial: First Century of Aluminum Process Technology, 1886–1986* (Metallurgical Society, Inc., 1986), pp. 106–13. The Serpek process involved furnace treatment of bauxite to produce aluminum nitride, which could be digested with the Bayer process, producing both alumina and a salable by-product: ammonia.

14 Darling to A. V. Davis, 1 November 1913, AA, env. 190-C. See also Darling to Davis, 7 November 1913, in C. M. Hall Correspondence, Alcoa Laboratory Archives, Alcoa Technical Center, Alcoa Center, PA (hereafter cited as ALA).

15 Moritz to Hoopes, 22 October 1909, in Fickes Correspondence, AA.

16 Correspondence between Moritz and C. M. Hall, beginning 13 May 1913, and continuing for the rest of the year, AA, env. 190-C. During that period, all senior executives were involved in troubleshooting the blister problem at Massena. They came to the conclusion that the problem was not in the pouring or rolling of ingots, but originated in the primary metal.

17 C. F. Nagel, Jr., speech to Alcoa metallurgists' conference, 4 June 1937, ALA.

18 Moritz to E. H. Acton of the Shawinigan works, captioned "EXPORT METAL SHIPMENTS," 13 March 1914, AA, env. 190-C. Also, John W. Hood, "History of Alcoa Aluminum in Aircraft: Alcoa Contributions Toward Aluminum Alloy and Structural Developments in Aircraft," manuscript, Historical Drawer, ALA, p. 84, notes that at that time there was regular sampling by the Remelting Departments at the New Kensington and Niagara works, which prepared alloys for ingot casting and subsequent fabrication, and that Blough had recently instituted a system of control that was working successfully at New Kensington, Massena, and Niagara, using standard laboratory records.

19 Moritz to Acton, 13 March 1914. Moritz attached letters from E. C. Darling and from the Birmingham Aluminum Casting Company to support his statements.

20 Fickes, "History," p. 65.

21 George K. Burgess, "Some Problems in Physical Metallurgy at the Bureau of Standards," *Journal of the Franklin Institute,* 182(July 1916):19. See also H. W. Gillett, "Metals Studied for Fifteen Years," *Iron Age,* 122(30 August 1928):509–72, for a review of NBS achievements in the first 15 years.

22 See Paul Merica, "Aluminum and Its Light Alloys, Parts I–V," *Chemical and Metallurgical Engineering,* 19(August–October 1918):135–640, passim; Merica, "Heat Treatment and the Constitution of Duralumin," *Scientific Papers of the United States Bureau of Standards,* 347(1919):225–40; *Bureau of Standards Bulletin,* 15(no. 271, 1919):450–60; *Transactions of the American Institute of Mining and Metallurgical Engineers,* 64(no. 41, 1920). These publications described advances in understanding the heat-treating and age-hardening phenomena in Duralumin made by Merica and his colleagues at the NBS and by Zay Jeffries and Robert S. Archer, coworkers at the Lynite Laboratory of the Aluminum Castings Company in Cleveland, which in 1920 became the Cleveland branch of Alcoa's Research Bureau. Occasional references show that Jeffries and Archer were in close touch with the researchers at NBS. See also Junius D. Edwards, "Fifty Years' Progress in Aluminum," *Industrial and Engineering Chemistry,* 18(September 1926):923; Archer and Jeffries, U.S. Patent 1,472,739 (October 1923).

23 Between 1908 and 1912, William Coolidge, on the General Electric research staff, led the way in metallurgical research in his effort to develop ductile tungsten for lamp filaments. With virtually no scientific knowledge base in metallurgy to draw on, Coolidge utilized his training in physics and chemistry at MIT to explain what he observed when experimenting with the physical properties of the metal. That work was widely recognized at the time as pioneering scientific research and received the Rumford Medal of the American Academy of Arts and Sciences in 1914. Leonard S. Reich, *The Making of Industrial Research: Science and Business at GE and Bell, 1876–1926* (Cambridge University Press, 1985), pp. 114–20.

24   W. Hoopes to C. H. Moritz, 29 May 1917, AA, env. 671. Even in 1917 it was not easy to find someone suitable, as Hoopes noted: "Getting a man for this job seems to be rather a difficult matter and it has become quite apparent that we shall have to take a man from someone else." Biographical material for Francis Frary comes from Junius D. Edwards, "The Medalist and His Work," in "The Presentation of the Acheson Medal of the Electrochemical Society, Inc. to Dr. Francis Cowles Frary, September 12, 1939," and James G. Vail, "The Personal Side of the Medalist," pamphlets, AA, env. 671, and from Webster N. Jones, "The Scientific Achievements of the Medalist," *Industrial and Engineering Chemistry*, 38(February 1946):127–8.

25   Moritz to Hoopes, 2 June 1917, AA, env. 671. On Frary's view of the opportunity presented him, see Edwards, "The Medalist and His Work," pp. 4–9. Reich, *The Making of Industrial Research*, pp. 249–57, points out that many companies used General Electric's laboratory as a model, beginning in about 1910. General Electric's Willis Whitney was something of a proselytizer on the subject, publishing articles describing and promoting his conceptions of industrial research.

26   Davis to Hoopes, 10 October 1917, Hoopes to Frary, 10 October 1917, Frary to Hoopes, 11 October 1917, Moritz to Hoopes, 24 October 1917, AA, env. 671. See also Frary to Davis (n.d., but presumably January 1918), and Davis to Frary, 15 January 1918, AA, env. 671, when Frary was a captain in the Ordnance Officers Reserve Corps at Edgewood Plant, Edgewood Arsenal.

27   U.S. Senate Subcommittee on War Mobilization, *The Government's Wartime Research and Development, 1940–1944*, 79th Congress, 1st Session, Subcommittee Report #5 to the Committee on Military Affairs of the U.S. Senate (March 1945). This report outlines the World War I experience and its aftermath, when the government withdrew from an activist role, citing that withdrawal as a major factor in its recommendations for a more activist government role at the end of World War II. See also Ellis W. Hawley, *The Great War and the Search for a Modern Order* (New York: St. Martin's Press, 1976), pp. 226–8. One example of the search for wartime substitutions resulting in applications of earlier research was United Lead Company's commercialization of Frary's high-strength lead alloys, including one called "Frary Metal." See Jones, "The Scientific Achievements of the Medalist," p. 127.

28   "Memo to Cleveland Laboratory File" (n.d., but obviously postwar, because it refers to the Laboratories' use during the "Reconstruction Period"). Lynite Laboratories reported to F. A. Parkhurst, who was responsible for introducing scientific management techniques throughout the company's foundries: Parkhurst to Jeffries, 23 February 1916, Cleveland Research File, ALA.

29   Jeffries received a D.Sc. from Harvard in 1918. When later asked by a Case colleague, Professor Van Horn, if his son should attend Harvard to do doctoral work in metallurgy, Jeffries recommended Yale instead, because it had adopted x-ray equipment in addition to microscopy. The son, Kent Van Horn, became Frary's successor as head of the Aluminum Research Laboratories: interview with Kent R. Van Horn, former vice-president for research and development, Aluminum Company of America, by Margaret B. W. Graham and George D. Smith, 4–5 June 1984. Biographical information on Zay Jeffries is from *The Dictionary of Scien-*

tific Biography, Vol. 7, pp. 92–3, and a personnel file dated 26 September 1936 in Historical Drawer, ALA.

30 This procedure was explained in Instruction 130 to plant managers, which directed that "every new and useful idea originating within this organization" was to be recorded on forms FAP 178 or 179, "regardless of whether they refer to products made, used or sold by this Company, or processes involved in the making of such products," memo, 27 June 1917, ALA. On the creation of a development department, see E. E. Allyne, "Change in Organization and Department Lineup," memo, 25 September 1917, Cleveland Research File, ALA. On the public image of Lynite Laboratories, see "Evolution of the Lynite Laboratories," *Iron Age,* 104(17 July 1919):149–54.

31 For references to Jeffries's and Archer's most important contributions to the understanding of heat treatment and age hardening, see note 22.

32 Zay Jeffries, memo, 31 March 1920, and R. E. Carpenter, "The Organization of Lynite Laboratories" (n.d., but about 1919), Cleveland Research File, ALA.

33 Jeffries to Allyne et al., "Metallurgical Outlook for Aluminum Manufacturers, Inc.," 5 January 1920, ALA.

34 Jeffries, "Metallurgical Outlook." A. V. Davis was one of the recipients of Jeffries's memo, and in the early 1920s he paraphrased that argument in correspondence to several Alcoa executives when he sought their support for a central R&D capability. See, for example, A. V. Davis to C. B. Fox, 10 February 1919, ALA.

35 The record does not show whether or not those laid off stayed in other parts of Alcoa. Of the 20 definitely kept on, it appears that only 5 remained in the Cleveland laboratory, while the rest were assigned elsewhere in the parent company technical organization. Francis C. Frary, "History of Early Aluminum Research," manuscript, transcript of a speech given in 1963, Historical Drawer, ALA, p. 11.

36 For example, Theodore Stay, who served as supervisor of Lynite Laboratories, sent Blough a sample of the forms they used in their technical work, which he called "the ounce of prevention rather than the pound of cure." T. D. Stay to E. Blough, 27 January 1919, ALA.

37 "Rosenhain Centenary Conference: The Contribution of Physical Metallurgy to Engineering Practice," *Philosophical Transactions of the Royal Society of London, Series A,* 282(1976):20–2. The phase diagrams and equilibrium diagrams developed at the NPL under Rosenhain's leadership defined the knowledge base for nonferrous metals, and the exacting research traditions he followed set a standard to be emulated. Rosenhain was particularly expert at demonstrating the critical relationship between science and practice. He often observed that if it had been possible to apply what the NPL knew by 1909 about alloy composition and working, Duralumin would have been an English discovery rather than a German. See also Walter Rosenhain, Sydney L. Archbutt, and D. Hanson, "Researches on Aluminium Alloys," summary of the 11th report to the Alloys Research Committee, *Engineering,* 112(28 October and 4 November, 1921):595–645.

38 The relationships between all these different cultures and the educational systems in different European countries in the nineteenth and early twentieth centuries are addressed by Robert Locke, *The End of the Practical Man.*

39   See Walter Rosenhain, "Science and Industry in Relation to Nonferrous Metals," *Journal of the Institute of Metals,* 21(1919):377–412, O. Nissen, "Aluminum Manufacturing Processes Used in Europe," *Chemical and Metallurgical Engineering,* 19(15 December 1918):804–15, and Fred Lantsberry, "The Scope of the Works Laboratory," *Journal of the Institute of Metals,* 21(1919):301–8.

40   Paul D. Merica, "The Trend of Research in the Nonferrous Industry," *Industrial and Engineering Chemistry,* 15(September 1923):895; Merica, the former NBS researcher, was at that time head of the research laboratory of International Nickel Company, and he later became its president. Ernest A. Smith, "The Development of Nonferrous Metallurgical Research," *The Metal Industry,* 16:327–31. For the NRC study, see Ruth Colds (ed.), *Industrial Research Establishments of the United States,* National Research Council bulletin No. 2 (Washington, D.C.: NRC, 1921). A useful survey of that era can be found in the final chapter of Reich, *The Making of Industrial Research,* pp. 239–57.

41   Fickes, "History," p. 205; Research Committee memo, 15 December 1918, ALA. The Research Committee met at the Hotel Belvedere in Baltimore "for the purpose of discussing, in an informal manner, some of the present problems and future work that would come under the jurisdiction of the Research Staff . . . and the adaptability of that work to applicants that were to be interviewed at the Edgewood Arsenal on the 16th."

42   Fickes, "History," p. 205. Five of the first six hired went to Massena to work on building an aluminum nitride furnace for the Serpek process. Another took up a fellowship at the Mellon Institute for the same project. Of the 22 additional salaried staff hired during the year, many went directly to Badin, North Carolina, to work with Hoopes on his aluminum refining process. One of the newcomers was Junius D. Edwards, a former Frary student at Minnesota who was hired away from the National Bureau of Standards in April 1919 and set to work on reduction-bath problems.

43   Frary, "History of Early Aluminum Research," pp. 7–8; A. V. Davis to C. B. Fox, 10 February 1919, quoted in Hood, "History of Alcoa Aluminum in Aircraft." Davis had gained a new perspective from sitting on the ACC Technical Committee. He wrote to Fox, at East St. Louis: "In a general way I might say that my idea of laboratory work is very much the same as that of auditing work." The central technical authority, he added, would not control, but would supervise; and the difference between the new research laboratory and the "regular" laboratory (soon to become the Technical Direction Bureau) was that the new one would be wholly devoted to nonroutine work.

44   A. V. Davis to Zay Jeffries, 22 November 1921, ALA.

45   Zay Jeffries to F. C. Frary, 30 December 1920; Research Committee minutes for 25 November 1921 and 22 December 1922, ALA. At both of these meetings the Research Committee discussed Davis's desire to push development of aluminum-silicon casting alloys, which he viewed as an alternative to Duralumin for many applications.

46   Fickes, "History," p. 206.

47   Frary, "History of Early Aluminum Research," p. 15; Fickes, "History," p. 206.

48   Fickes, "History," p. 205.

49 Hoopes and Frary to Davis, 15 February 1919, ALA.

50 Technical Direction Bureau annual report, 15 July 1919 to 1 March 1920, ALA.

51 Technical Direction Bureau annual report for 1923, ALA. On the hot-top mold work, see C. F. Nagel, Jr., to W. H. Hoopes, 20 August 1923, ALA.

52 R. L. Templin to F. C. Frary, "Report of Testing Division" for 1919 and 1921, ALA.

53 See Frary to Operating Committee, "Progress Report," 3 March 1919, ALA. Experienced metallurgists, in particular, proved very difficult to find and could command very high pay.

54 The first meeting between the research staffs of the ACC and Alcoa, attended also by Davis and Allyne, was held in Cleveland in February 1919. Hood, "History of Alcoa Aluminum in Aircraft," p. 159. The meeting at which research turf was divided occurred in April 1920 at Cleveland, with Jeffries, Frary, Blough, and Davis attending. See Jeffries to Frary, 30 December 1920, ALA. There was so much to be learned about "the properties, manufacture and heat treatment" of the new alloys 25S, 51S, and a series of casting alloys, Edmund Fickes wrote later, that it was not until 1925 that the company could put them on the market in considerable quantities. See Fickes, "History," p. 208.

55 Research Committee minutes, 22 December 1922, ALA. The scrap problem was especially serious when scrap metal began to come in from Europe, forming a large part of the 18 million tons that entered the market in 1920 and 1921.

56 The Technical Direction Committee was created in April 1923; its membership included Edwin Fickes, Charles Fox, Robert L. Streeter, Irving W. Wilson, Frary, and Hoopes. E. Blough to W. Hoopes, 14 April 1923, and C. F. Nagel, Jr., to Hoopes, 18 June 1923, ALA. On the workings of the committee, see J. O. Chesley to F. C. Frary, 30 December 1922, W. Hoopes to F. C. Frary, 9 January 1923, and Research Bureau annual report for 1919, ALA. The report notes that the Aircraft Committee on Aluminum had held several meetings but had accomplished nothing.

57 In 1918 the Research Committee had developed a list of seven "live" subjects for research, two having to do with product (shrinkage of aluminum ingots and tempering and heat-treating for alloys) and the rest concerning major inputs and primary processes (digestion of aluminum nitride; production of pure carbon from pitch; elimination of copper from carbon butts; production of flaky ore, anhydrous cryolite, and fluoride). Research Committee memo, 15 December 1918, ALA.

58 Moritz to Frary, 8 January 1919; Frary to Moritz, 15 January 1919, ALA. The other subjects of concern were as follows: a quick method of determining sodium content in the bath; an accurate method of analyzing the bath for fluorides; the relationship among bath composition, oxidation of aluminum, and specific gravity; the effect of anode–cathode distance on oxidation of aluminum; the effect of bath temperature on oxidation of aluminum; determination of decomposition voltage; the cracking temperature in the electrode baking process to get best results. By the end of the year the staff had grown to include 16 chemists and chemical engineers, 2 mechanical engineers, 1 electrical engineer, 1 metallurgical engineer, 1 librarian, 3 technical assistants, 1 library assistant, and 3 stenogra-

phers. The librarian, Mary Holton, was assisted by other professional librarians in organizing Alcoa's system. The location near Pittsburgh, with its good resources, also made it easier to provide a comprehensive service. Mary W. Holton to F. C. Frary, 14 June 1919, and Research Bureau annual report for 1919, ALA.

59 Research Bureau annual reports for 1919, 1920, and 1921, ALA.

60 Research Bureau annual reports for 1919 and 1920, ALA.

61 Plans for the organization and program of the early Technical Department are contained in memos from Hoopes and Frary to A. V. Davis in February 1919, and in Frary, "Progress Report to the Operating Committee," 3 March 1919, ALA.

62 Research Bureau annual report for 1924, ALA.

63 E. H. Dix, Jr., to F. C. Frary, 7 May 1925, ALA, reports on the work of the Metallurgical Division, noting that the most important work was Problem 86, which involved working out the elements of the various alloy systems, made possible by the availability of 99.99 percent pure aluminum from the Hoopes process.

64 The key paper published by Jeffries and Archer on precipitation hardening was "Slip Interference Theory of the Hardening of Metals," *Chemical and Metallurgical Engineering*, 24(1921):1057–67. For advances on other fronts, see Zay Jeffries, "Engineering and Science in the Metal Industry," *Mechanical Engineering*, 48(January 1926):8–16, and Paul D. Merica, "The Trend of Research in the Nonferrous Industry," *Industrial and Engineering Chemistry*, 15(September 1923):895–7.

65 Research Committee minutes, 22 December 1922, and Zay Jeffries to William Hoopes, "Re: Modified Silicon Alloy Situation," 25 June 1923, ALA. In the Research Committee meeting cited, Jeffries reported on a visit to Union Carbide and on their work on alloys with valuable electrothermal properties.

66 Arthur V. Davis to Edward K. Davis, 26 June 1923, ALA. On the application of aluminum to automobiles, see R. S. Archer, "Commercial Alloys in Aluminum," in Edwards et al. (eds.), *Aluminum Products and Their Fabrication*, pp. 213–14, and Archer and Zay Jeffries, "New Developments in Aluminum Alloys," *Iron Age*, 115(26 February 1925):666–8.

67 Jeffries to Hoopes, 25 June 1923, ALA.

68 Fickes, "History," p. 206; Frary, "History of Early Aluminum Research," p. 21.

69 G. H. Wagner, "Research at East St. Louis – A Brief History, 1923–1952," in Alcoa Plant Histories, Vol. 2-B, AA, p. B-140; Research Bureau annual reports for 1923–1927, ALA. The quotations are from the 1923 and 1925 reports.

70 Technical Direction Bureau, annual report for 1923, ALA.

71 Zay Jeffries to F. C. Frary, 30 December 1920, ALA.

72 The basic outline of the committee's decision took shape well before Blough's 1923 "manifesto." See Research Committee minutes, 25 November 1921 and 22 December 1922, ALA. In those years the impetus to expand the Research Bureau Metallurgical Division came largely from A. V. Davis's insistence that emphasis be placed on aluminum-silicon casting alloys, which he viewed as the best alternative to Duralumin-type alloys. If that had continued to be the main agenda item in 1923, the expansion of the Metallurgical Division undoubtedly would have occurred entirely in

Cleveland. The creation of a separate research group in New Kensington, equal in size to that in Cleveland (four researchers in each place), signaled that equal importance was to be placed on wrought alloys. Because Blough was a member of the Research Committee, where these issues were undoubtedly discussed more than once between 1921 and 1923, it seems likely that the final outcome was a compromise worked out among Blough, Frary, and other committee members. The Research Bureau obtained its rolling equipment in 1926.

73 Edward K. Davis to Earl Blough, 27 April 1925, ALA, E. H. Dix, Jr., to F. C. Frary, "Report on the New Kensington Section of the Metallurgical Division for 1924," ALA, shows that the earliest problem investigated was fundamental principles underlying grain growth of aluminum alloys, as demonstrated in the silicon-aluminum series.

74 Archer, "Commercial Alloys of Aluminum," pp. 213–15.

75 E. H. Dix, Jr., to Dr. Francis Frary, "Re: Origin of Alclad," 30 June 1927, ALA.

76 Frary, "History of Early Aluminum Research," pp. 14–15. J. B. Barnitt to E. S. Fickes, May 1925, ALA, called for new space for the Research Bureau Development Division because of the terrible overcrowding and unhealthful conditions caused by dust from work on bronze powder.

77 Frary paid tribute to Hoopes in both ceremonies in which he was honored with professional society medals, the Acheson Medal and the Perkin Medal. See Francis C. Frary, "Electrochemical Recollections," speech at presentation of the Edward Goodrich Acheson Medal of the Electrochemical Society, Inc., of New York, 12 September 1939, pamphlet, AA, env. 671, and Frary, "Adventures with Alumina," *Industrial and Engineering Chemistry*, 38(February 1946):129–31.

78 Frary, "History of Early Aluminum Research," p. 21. Of the Hall dry process, Frary said that "it paid for itself because before that time the East St. Louis alumina plant said, 'We have a perfect process; you can't improve it.' . . . As quickly as they saw that here was a process that looked as though it might displace East St. Louis, they thought maybe it would be worthwhile looking to see. And they found they could make a good many improvements which would reduce the cost."

79 Frary, "Future Development in the Light Metals," *Industrial and Engineering Chemistry*, 18(1926).

80 See Robert R. Updegraff, "Aluminum Tells Its Story," *The Magazine of Business* (August 1929):123–5, 168–70.

81 Frary, "History of Early Aluminum Research."

82 An example of Jeffries's persuasiveness is seen in A. V. Davis's correspondence with Charles B. Fox, in which he explained the need for a new central research laboratory, echoing a much more coherently presented philosophy of the function of research spelled out in Jeffries, "Metallurgical Outlook" (Davis to Fox, 10 February 1919, ALA). Jeffries's long and distinguished career lasted into the 1950s at General Electric, where he is still remembered as a revered figure. Interview with Lowell Steele, retired General Electric Laboratory employee, by Margaret B. W. Graham, 24 August 1988.

83 Research Bureau annual report for 1927, ALA.

84 Moritz to Frary, 26 May 1919, and Frary's reply, 28 May 1919, ALA. Other evidence of the friction can be found in the commentary on the

1937 technical show, when different works managers reminisced about the "bad old days" of the 1920s when they were at odds with the Technical Department. See Chapter 5, note 45.

85   A. V. Davis to Hall, 4 February 1913, AA, env. 19. Davis declared himself "very much upset." Not only would the French regard this as breach of confidence, but it would injure the interests of the Aluminum Company of America.

86   On developing publication policy in general, see F. C. Frary to W. H. Hoopes, 10 June 1920, and A. V. Davis to Zay Jeffries, 22 November 1921, ALA. See also Hoopes to Jeffries, with a copy to Frary, 22 November 1921, attached to a memo, Frary to A. P. Hall, 12 April 1949, AA.

87   Earl Blough remarked of Roy Hunt that there was no point putting off anything he asked, as he had a very effective tickler system and had a right to ask, Blough to Nagel, 22 September 1919, ALA.

88   See Chandler, *The Visible Hand,* pp. 258–9.

89   "Dr. Walter Rosenhain," *Obituaries of Fellows of the Royal Society,* 1(1932–5):353–9.

90   Walter Rosenhain, "Science and Industry in America, Aluminium and Light Alloys," *The Engineer,* 136(28 September 1923):330–1.

CHAPTER 4

1   E. Blough to J. H. Finney, 4 October 1923, Alcoa Laboratory Archives, Alcoa Technical Center, Alcoa Center, PA (hereafter cited as ALA).

2   Francis C. Frary, "History of Early Aluminum Research," transcript of a speech given in 1963, Historical Drawer, ALA, p. 7.

3   Quoted in John W. Hood, "History of Alcoa Aluminum in Aircraft: Alcoa Contributions Toward Aluminum Alloy Developments in Aircraft," manuscript (1971), ALA, p. 9.

4   Vickers held a license for the Duralumin patents, had a separate Duralumin Department, and was using Duralumin in the construction of a succession of airships. But, short of cash after the war, it closed down its Duralumin Department and sold off John Booths, the casting subsidiary that produced it, to the auto industry, forfeiting its accumulated know-how in the new technology in exactly the kind of short-sighted move Jeffries had warned ACC against in his "Metallurgical Prospectus." See Margaret B. W. Graham, "R&D and Competition in England and the United States: The Case of the Aluminum Dirigible," *Business History Review,* 62(Summer 1988):261–85.

5   Hood, "History of Alcoa Aluminum in Aircraft," pp. 30–5.

6   Earl Blough to Roy A. Hunt, "Development of Strong Alloys by Alcoa," 23 June 1953, and Blough, "Statement Presented to the Ford Motor Company, Ford Archives," 30 April 1957, Alcoa Archives, Aluminum Company of America, Pittsburgh, PA (hereafter cited as AA), env. 486.

7   D. W. Taylor to Aluminum Company of America, 23 August 1916, ALA.

8   Edwin S. Fickes, "History of the Growth and Development of the Aluminum Company of America." Vol. 17-B: "Histories of the Manufacturing Properties of the Aluminum Company of America, Affiliated Companies, and Defense Corporation Plants" (hereafter cited as Alcoa Plant Histories), AA, pp. 109–10; Blough, "Statement Presented to the Ford

Motor Company." Blough, in his statement, said that they tried to verify the heat treatment and the spontaneous aging that Wilm claimed to have developed, but the work went very slowly for lack of facilities and lack of trained staff. He also said they were aware only that Electric Boat Company had the German patent, not that it came via Vickers. The patent cluster included a 1905 patent registered in Britain as 19282/05 by Conrad Claussen, chemistry Ph.D. from Berlin, for a process of improving aluminum alloys by heating and chilling, and 26322/07 filed by Centralstelle für Wissenschaftliche Technische Forstellungen, and 6485/10 filed by Wilm (1909 in Germany) for a process for improving alloys.

9   Blough to J. H. Finney, 16 October 1916, ALA.

10   Hood, "History of Alcoa Aluminum in Aircraft," p. 10. Under the general direction of Dr. G. K. Burgess, head of metallurgy for the National Bureau of Standards, Paul Merica had directed a fruitful nonferrous-metals research program from 1914 to 1916. See Merica, "Heat Treatment and the Constitution of Duralumin," in *Scientific Papers of the United States Bureau of Standards,* Vol. 347 (Washington, D.C.: USBS, 1919).

11   Blough to Finney, 16 October 1916, ALA.

12   C. F. Nagel, Jr., speech to Alcoa metallurgists, New Kensington, 4 June 1937, ALA, pp. 7–8.

13   A. E. Vail, "Duralumin," 7 November 1916, and S. W. Stratton, "General Conclusions and Remarks," 22 January 1917, ALA.

14   J. H. Finney to General Sales Office, 8 September 1919, ALA. Finney called the "submarine Boat people" a serious threat because they claimed the sole right to distribute Duralumin in the United States and proposed to supply it from Britain. They threatened a suit versus all other suppliers. In the end, the navy contracted with Alcoa as an agent of the government and worked out a purchase of patent by the Chemical Foundation.

15   Testimony of Commander Jerome Clark Hunsaker, in *United States vs. Aluminum Company of America,* New York, 25 April 1940, quoted in Hood, "History of Alcoa Aluminum in Aircraft," p. 60: "We had in fact stolen it from the Germans."

16   Hood, "History of Alcoa Aluminum in Aircraft," pp. 55–6. Frary said that German producers of Wilm's alloy also had a difficult time producing it and persisted only because Count Zeppelin insisted on having it for dirigibles. See Francis C. Frary, "Aluminum – How and Why," *Civil Engineering,* 8(January 1938):19–22.

17   S. W. Stratton to Pierre Gillet, 18 April 1918, and Gillet to Blough, 11 October 1918, ALA. Stratton, of NBS, informed Gillet, who was chief inspector for the French high commission, that the sheets produced by Alcoa for the French did not meet specification because they had been used to train a new lot of men in heat treatment, presumably at Massena. See also Hood, "History of Alcoa Aluminum in Aircraft," p. 89, and Blough to H. M. Hall, 15 November 1917, ALA. Michelin had also been trying to buy Alcometal from Alcoa to make Breguet bombers, but could not get clearance from the U.S. government during the war. The French said that Alcoa's metal was superior in strength to Duralumin, though they had yet to learn how to fabricate it into the tubing they wanted. H. D. Sill to E. Blough, 26 October 1917, and reply, 30 October 1917, ALA.

18   Hood, "History of Alcoa Aluminum in Aircraft," pp. 137–42, 204, mentions several attempts by Alcoa personnel, in collaboration with navy

personnel, to gain process information from other Duralumin producers abroad. On the secrecy at Vickers, see Jerome Hunsaker to Earl Blough, 15 May 1920, ALA. See also the Vickers, Ltd., papers, Duralumin File, Cambridge University Library, Cambridge, England, and Graham, "The Case of the Aluminum Dirigible," p. 269.

19 Hood, "History of Alcoa Aluminum in Aircraft," p. 16. The basic design was therefore that of the German L-33, with modifications according to the L-49.

20 William F. Trimble, "The Naval Aircraft Factory, the American Aviation Industry, and Government Competition, 1919–1928," *Business History Review,* 60(Summer 1986):175–98.

21 D. W. Taylor to Aloca, 25 June 1917, ALA.

22 Hood, "History of Alcoa Aluminum in Aircraft," pp. 27ff.

23 Davis to Spalding, 16 October 1918, and reply, 19 October 1918, ALA. Spalding obviously feared that Alcoa would default on the contract. See also Frary, "History of Early Aluminum Research," in which Frary talks about the difficulties of providing acceptable materials for "the blimp."

24 Earl Blough remembered later that Mr. Stout, an early aircraft producer, "took a very strong position that the material we supplied was unsatisfactory in all respects" and "secured all of his requirements from a small company then in existence called the Bausch Machine Tool Company of Worcester, Mass." Bausch also testified against Alcoa during its later monopoly trial, arguing that had Alcoa not engaged in anticompetitive behavior, Bausch would have prevailed, owing to its superior quality. Blough, "Statement Presented to the Ford Motor Company," pp. 4–5. That argument was wrong, of course, because Bausch had not equipped itself to roll the wider sheet needed to make girders. Bausch's interest in Duralumin was a way to keep its work force employed in a cyclical downturn. See also George D. Smith, *From Monopoly to Competition: The Transformations of Alcoa, 1888–1986* (Cambridge University Press, 1988), pp. 171–3.

25 John H. Finney to Theodore Varney, 21 March 1919, ALA. Finney said it looked as though certain automobile interests would soon take up manufacture of that kind of machine in a commercial way. He also pleaded with A. V. Davis to make a decision to supply the navy on its terms, arguing that it would be better that the material be supplied from the United States rather than from Britain (Finney to Davis, 15 April 1919, ALA).

26 Blough, "Statement Presented to the Ford Motor Company," p. 4.

27 J. H. Finney to E. Blough, 1 December 1919, ALA.

28 Hunsaker noted that the navy designers received invaluable help from their former enemies in the design phase of ZR-1 (Hood, "History of Alcoa Aluminum in Aircraft, pp. 19–20).

29 Blough to J. H. Finney, 30 October 1919, ALA.

30 Hunt to Nagel, 16 September 1920, quoted in Hood, "History of Alcoa Aluminum in Aircraft," p. 134.

31 Blough to inspector of hull material, 9 February 1921, and Blough to Nagel, 9 February 1921, ALA. Blough complained that Finney paid more attention to his customers' interests than he did to Alcoa's: Blough to Finney, 26 March 1920, ALA. For his part, Finney passed along the navy's complaints, noting the "rather unpleasant" attitude that existed at

the Naval Aircraft Factory considering that particular contract. G. C. Westervelt to J. H. Finney, 18 November 1920, and Finney to E. K. Davis, 19 November 1920, ALA.

32   C. F. Nagel, Jr., to Blough, 9 May 1921, and G. C. Westervelt to A. V. Davis, 9 September 1921, ALA.

33   Hood, "History of Alcoa Aluminum in Aircraft," p. 85.

34   R. A. Hunt to Lt. J. A. Davis, 2 June 1922 (an 18-page letter entitled "Subject: Contract 49491 – Request for Reimbursement of Losses"), quoted in Hood, "History of Alcoa Aluminum in Aircraft," pp. 146–59.

35   J. H. Finney to E. Blough, 26 December 1922, ALA.

36   On the first flight, see Ralph H. Upson, "Metalclad Rigid Airship Development," *Journal of the Society of Automotive Engineers,* 7(February 1926):19.

37   E. Blough to A. V. Davis, 8 September 1925, "Re: Shenandoah Wreck," R. D. Weyerbacher to E. Blough, 30 October 1925, and E. Blough to F. J. Gauntlett, 28 September 1925, ALA.

38   *New York Times,* 12 December 1925; Hood, "History of Alcoa Aluminum in Aircraft," p. 189; R. D. Weyerbacher to E. Blough, 30 October 1925, ALA.

39   "Deterioration of Duralumin in the 'Shenandoah': Results of Bureau of Standards Tests Brought Out Before Court – Intercrystalline Corrosion Widespread," *Engineering News Record* (26 November 1925); E. Blough to J. O. Chesley, 8 December 1925, Blough to E. E. Free, 29 December 1925, and E. K. Davis to E. E. Free, 7 January 1926, ALA. The *Engineering News Record* printed an apology to Alcoa on 17 January 1925, but the controversy continued into 1926.

40   George L. Clark to A. V. Davis, 26 February 1927, ALA. On the claims of NBS, see R. V. Davies to E. Blough, 27 January 1927, and reply, 29 January 1927, ALA. Test results on USS *Shenandoah* showed that the material in the girders was "as good as the day it was put in." The report, Davies said, "for practical purposes nullifies many of the statements previously made by the Bureau of Standards in their earlier report."

41   McDill to Charles Templeton, 15 September 1928, ALA.

42   *New York Times,* 17 May 1927.

43   Hunsaker testimony in *U.S. vs. Aluminum Company of America,* 25 April 1940, quoted in Hood, "History of Alcoa Aluminum in Aircraft," p. 69.

44   Graham, "Case of the Aluminum Dirigible," pp. 272–84. See also R. P. T. Davenport-Hines, *Dudley Docker: The Life and Times of a Trade Warrior* (Cambridge University Press, 1986).

CHAPTER 5

1   Hoover's speech is quoted in H. W. Gillett, "Metallurgical Research from the Chemical Point of View," *Industrial and Engineering Chemistry,* 22(1930):233.

2   Edwin S. Fickes, "History of the Growth and Development of the Aluminum Company of America." Vol. 17-B: "Histories of the Manufacturing Properties of the Aluminum Company of America, Affiliated Companies, and Defense Corporation Plants" (hereafter cited as Alcoa Plant Histories), Alcoa Archives, Aluminum Company of America, Pittsburgh, PA (hereafter cited as AA), p. 279. For the outsider's view, see E. E.

Thum, "Laboratory of Dignity and Beauty," *Iron Age*, 126(17 July 1930):162–4.

3   H. W. Gillett, "Metallurgical Research," p. 232. Gillett estimated that the chemical and allied industries and the metallurgical industries were spending more on industrial research than was any other sector of the economy, at 2.4 percent and 2.1 percent of invested capital, respectively.

4   "A Million Dollar Research Laboratory," *Mining and Metallurgy*, 11(August 1930):400–1. See also John Servos, "The Industrial Relations of Science: Chemical Engineering at MIT, 1900–1939," *Isis*, 71(1980):531–49. DuPont was making significant commitments to fundamental research at the same time under the leadership of Charles Stine. Its new fundamental research laboratory, budgeted at $115,000, opened in 1929 and was immediately dubbed "Purity Hall" inside the DuPont technical community. As David A. Hounshell and John K. Smith point out in "The Radical Departure, Charles Stine's Fundamental Research Program," chapter 12 in *Science and Corporate Strategy: DuPont R&D, 1902–1980* (Cambridge University Press, 1988), pp. 223–48, fundamental research was a proselytizing movement in the 1910s amd 1920s, with Arthur D. Little and Eastman Kodak's C. E. K. Mees as two of its chief evangelists.

5   Francis C. Frary to I. W. Wilson, 5 June 1951, Alcoa Laboratories Archives, Alcoa Technical Center, Alcoa Center, PA, (hereafter cited as ALA), responding to Wilson's request to compare Alcoa's spending for research and the budgets of 11 companies cited in Joseph V. Sherman, "Chemical Research Serves as a Barometer of Future Growth Possibilities," *Barron's* (16 April 1951).

6   Twenty-one separate investigations or legal actions were directed against Alcoa between 1911 and 1941: 9 by the Department of Justice and 12 by the Federal Trade Commission. See George D. Smith, *From Monopoly to Competition: The Transformations of Alcoa, 1888–1986* (Cambridge University Press, 1988), pp. 60–1, and chapter 5, "Undoing the Monopoly," pp. 191–249.

7   Francis C. Frary, "History of Early Aluminum Research," transcript of a speech given in 1963, Historical Drawer, ALA, p. 14.

8   On the desire for greater contact with central R&D, see C. F. Nagel, Jr., speech to Alcoa metallurgists, New Kensington, 4 June 1937, ALA. Information on general conditions for metallurgists from interview with John Hatch, former director of quality assurance and chief metallurgist for ingot and powder, with Margaret B. W. Graham, 7 January 1985 (hereafter cited as Hatch Interview). Hatch joined the Metallurgical Department in New Kensington in 1940 under "Dutch" Nagel and Theodore Bossert, just at the time when the metallurgical part of the community was becoming most powerful.

9   Frary, "History of Early Aluminum Research," p. 15. In 1929, President Hoover anxiously surveyed industry for its intentions regarding continued support of R&D. Frary's response is in Frary to S. D. Kirkpatrick (editor of *Chemical and Metallurgical Engineering*), 2 December 1929, ALA.

10 Junius D. Edwards, "Heating, Piping and Ventilating in the Aluminum Research Laboratories," manuscript, AA, env. 335; Edwards, "Exemplary Adaptation of Aluminum to Construction," *Chemical and Metallurgical Engineering*, 37(July 1930):428–9. See also Thum, "Laboratory of Dignity and Beauty," p. 162.

11 Descriptions of the new ARL appeared in numerous articles in the trade press, including those cited in notes 3, 7, and 15. See also "Model Research Laboratory Dedicated by Aluminum Co. at New Kensington, Pa.," *Paint, Oil and Chemical Review* (5 June 1930):9, 26, and W. S. McArdle, "Aluminum Utility Exemplified in a Modern Research Laboratory," *Journal of Chemical Education,* 9(May 1932):834–9. For comparisons with other laboratories of the time, see H. W. Gillett, "Standards Bureau Metal Research," *Iron Age,* 116 (20 August 1925):461–5, 1513, and Gillett, "Active Metallurgical Research," *Iron Age,* 116 (22 August 1925):536–42.

12 H. W. Gillett, "Metallurgical Research," p. 233. On the equipment in the new laboratory and its expense, see Frary to Kirkpatrick, 2 December 1929, ALA. Another factor in the laboratory's expense was the expectation of moving to heavy-duty process development at the laboratory. The laboratory was supplied with electric power sufficient to run experimental smelting cells on site. As such it was the largest user on the West Penn Electric Company power line. Edwin Fickes is credited with having built the laboratory with a large chimney to alert the power company that Alcoa would generate its own power if it were charged unduly high rates for electricity. Interview with Ernest Hartmann, former director of research, Aluminum Company of America, by Margaret B. W. Graham, 29 November 1984 (hereafter cited as Hartmann Interview).

13 On the trials and challenges of early R&D, see Nagel, speech to Alcoa metallurgists.

14 Thum, "Laboratory of Dignity and Beauty," p. 163.

15 On relations between the Cleveland laboratory and New Kensington, see interview with Harold Y. Hunsicker, former technical advisor, Alloy Technology Division, Alcoa Laboratories, by Margaret B. W. Graham, 9 January 1985 (hereafter cited as Hunsicker Interview).

16 Francis C. Frary, et al., "History of Research and Development, Aluminum Company of America," manuscript, ALA (records all of the experimental work conducted for the company, year by year, from 1888 through 1960; hereafter cited as Frary et al., "History of Research and Development," with specific reference to the year or years in which work was conducted), 1926–39.

17 Frary to Kirkpatrick, 2 December 1929, ALA.

18 Ellis Hawley, *The Great War and the Search for a Modern Order* (New York: St. Martin's Press, 1979), chapter 11, "The Hoover Visions at Bay," pp. 192ff.

19 Caroll W. Pursell, "Government and Technology in the Great Depression," *Technology and Culture,* 20(1979):162–74. Hawley, *The Great War and the Search for a Modern Order,* pp. 159–60, observes that all intellectual elites in the 1920s and 1930s, especially scientists, became both isolated and fragmented, partly because they rejected beliefs that were still widely held by the mainstream public.

20 See testimony by Executive Vice-President George R. Gibbons to the naval inquiry board, 1934, in John W. Hood, "History of Alcoa Aluminum in Aircraft: Alcoa Contributions Toward Aluminum Alloy Developments in Aircraft," manuscript (1971), ALA, p. 135. That was a hostile inquiry and an embarrassing one in tone. However, Gibbons succeeded in undercutting the opposition, presenting convincing evidence that Alcoa was not making high profits, that it was providing many people with jobs, and that

it was doing socially beneficial things. In 1934, total Alcoa inventories were about 290 million pounds as a result of two years of stockpiling in 1932 and 1933, for which the company borrowed money so as not to curtail production. Gibbons testified further that the company spent $1–2 million on support of research, contributing among other things to the design of airplane propellers.

21 H. E. Bakken to ARL department heads, 2 December 1931, ALA; Aluminum Research Laboratories annual report for 1931, ALA.

22 Hunsicker Interview. Hunsicker said it practically took an act of Congress to get permission to visit anywhere west of the Mississippi.

23 On the creation of the committee system, see H. E. Bakken to A. B. Norton, 8 July 1931, ALA, which describes a meeting of all senior technical officers and executives of all departments concerned with technical matters, held on 7 July 1931, at corporate headquarters. The Research Executive Committee had 12 members, including Hunt ex officio, with four from Research, and Frary as chairman. The second committee, originally called the Research Subcommittee, was renamed the Technical Committee in 1933, when its purview was expanded to take in the Technical Departments of the Fabrication and Castings Divisions and Sales Department. Its four original members included Herman Bakken of ARL as chair, "Dutch" Nagel from the Technical Department of the Fabrication Division, Theodore D. Stay of the Technical Department of the Castings Division, and A. B. Wilber, representing the Sales Division. On the budgeting process, see "Technical Budgets and Programs" for the years after 1934 in ALA, and P. J. Urquhart to H. E. Bakken, 12 February 1934, ALA, in which Urquhart, a corporate controller, asks for comments on a newly developed reporting form that allows expenditures to be tracked against budget on a monthly basis.

24 See, for example, H. E. Bakken to R. A. Hunt, 21 May 1934, and reply, 22 May 1934, ALA.

25 See H. E. Bakken to C. F. Nagel, Jr., T. D. Stay, and A. B. Wilber, 13 July 1931, ALA, in which Bakken argues that alloy development should be the first topic of consideration. At that time it was getting over $30,000 of research money for the first half of the year and occupying 13 full-time men at New Kensington and Cleveland.

26 Bakken to T. D. Stay, 23 February 1933 and 31 May 1934, ALA. Controversy usually arose over who would foot the bill, as in the case of joint tests of overhead transmission wires between Research and the Vibration Committee, where the latter agreed to pay the cost of the test wire if the former would provide the necessary research observers to carry out the tests. Bakken noted that "after our usual amount of heavy argument, it was finally recommended that the Vibration Committee would enter a request for authorization for $1,500."

27 On standardization, see C. F. Nagel, Jr., to H. E. Bakken, 19 March 1934, ALA, where the throughput costs of producing too many different grades and tempers at the Arnold sheet mill and the desirability of reducing the number were discussed. Also, H. E. Bakken to Technical Committee, 31 December 1936, ALA, reported that Hunt had assigned to the committee the broad general problem of standardization as it related to alloys, processes, etc. On alloy application, see "Recommendation of Sub-Committee," 22 March 1933, ALA. On commercialization of new prod-

ucts, there are many memos documenting communication between the Technical Committee and Advertising and Sales on that subject.

28   "Report of the Research Sub-Committee on Problems of Aluminum Research Laboratories," 27 July 1931, ALA.

29   Frary to Jeffries, 11 June 1931, ALA. The controversy over the value of fundamental research was playing out at that period in the handful of laboratories where it was conducted. At DuPont, Charles Stine had argued that fundamental research was a far more sensible investment for a company to make than what he called "pioneering applied" research, which was limited by practical if long-term goals, because the former was bound to result in discovery of useful knowledge. But other DuPont technical managers were just as insistent that fundmantal work had to pay its own way. Hounshell and Smith, *Science and Corporate Strategy,* pp. 224, 237.

30   Gibbons to Frary, 18 June 1931 and 11 July 1931, and Frary's response, 19 June 1931, ALA.

31   E. H. Dix, Jr., "New Developments in High Strength Aluminum Alloy Products," *Transactions of the American Society for Metals,* 35(1946):130–55

32   Hartmann Interview.

33   G. H. Wagner to F. C. Frary, 15 December 1936, ALA.

34   Frary to Wagner, 28 December 1936, ALA.

35   Frary to Wagner, 28 December 1936, ALA.

36   C. B. Fox to E. H. Fickes, 26 December 1936, and Frary to Fickes, 21 December 1936, ALA.

37   See Karl Compton, letter to the *New York Times,* 24 February 1934. For similar criticisms, see A. Bright and J. Exter, "War, Radar and the Radar Industry," *Harvard Business Review* (Winter 1947):567–70.

38   Margaret B. W. Graham, "Industrial Research in the Age of Big Science," in Richard S. Rosenbloom (ed.), *Research on Technological Innovation, Management and Policy,* Vol. 2 (Greenwich, CT: JAI Press, 1985), pp. 47–79.

39   H. E. Bakken to G. M. Rollason, 8 November 1937, and Bakken to Roy A. Hunt, 26 November 1937, ALA.

40   Bakken to Hunt, 26 November 1937, ALA; "Seventh Meeting of the General Committee, Dec. 16th. 1937, Aluminum Club, Chairman's Copy of Program," ALA. A stand-up lunch was necessitated by the small size of the card room in the Aluminum Clubhouse.

41   Douglas B. Hobbs to Charles C. Carr, 20 December 1937, ALA.

42   G. R. Gibbons to R. A. Hunt, 21 December 1937, ALA.

43   George J. Stanley to George R. Gibbons, 19 December 1937, ALA.

44   M. E. Noyes to G. J. Stanley, 4 January 1938, ALA.

45   T. D. Jolly to Roy A. Hunt, 20 December 1937, ALA.

46   R. S. Stokes to C. B. Fox, 20 December 1937, Wiser Brown to Allen B. Norton, 20 December 1937, and R. T. Whitzel to R. R. Stevenson, 23 December 1937, ALA.

47   C. C. Carr to S. K. Colby, 26 December 1937, ALA.

48   "Probably no single factor has had more influence upon the commercial growth of the aluminum industry in the United States than the fact that there is but a single producer in America. This has been a knife that cuts both ways." S. K. Colby, "The Commercial History of Aluminum," in Junius D. Edwards, Francis C. Frary, and Zay Jeffries (eds.), *The Alumi-*

num Industry, 2 vols., *Vol. 2: Aluminum Products and Their Fabrication* (New York: McGraw-Hill, 1930), p. 19.

49   *United States of America vs. Aluminum Company of America, et al., Highlights and Summaries of Opening Statements and Testimony, June 1, 1938–August 3, 1939* (hereafter cited as *Summaries of Testimony*), vol. 3, p. 1553. Davis's testimony consumed a little over 3,000 stenographic pages.

50   *Summaries of Testimony,* vol. 4, pp. 2439–40.

51   *Summaries of Testimony,* vol. 4, pp. 2359–61, 2432–5, 2438.

52   Caffey is quoted in "Alcoa's Clean Bill," *Business Week* (18 October 1941):24. See also Harold Stein, *Disposal of the Aluminum Plants,* Inter-University Case Program, CPAC No. 6 (New York: Harcourt Brace & Co., 1952), pp. 317, 319.

53   I. W. Wilson to Roy A. Hunt, 21 December 1937, ALA.

54   H. E. Bakken, "Request for Authorization," 28 October 1938, ALA.

55   R. L. Templin to F. C. Frary, 22 December 1937, ALA. Frary's letter on the technical show (Francis C. Frary to S. K. Colby, 21 December 1937, ALA) was cooler in tone, but argued forcefully for the need to put more money into expanding and raising the level of qualifications of the fabricating-plant metallurgical staff under Nagel so that they could have greater freedom from routine control work to undertake significant development work. Holding up as an example the development of the direct-chill ingot-casting process (see Chapter 6) by William Ennor, a plant metallurgist at Massena, Frary wrote that the investment "would give us an excellent return, not only in financial savings, but in improvements in quality which will reduce customer irritation and complaints."

56   Frank L. Magee, "Aluminum Production," speech, 11 March 1948, Industrial College of the Armed Forces, publication No. L48-109, 1948, pp. 9–10.

57   See F. C. Frary to A. L. Hughes, 27 July 1943, ALA, in which Frary turned down Hughes's request for personnel to work at Santa Fe on Project Y.

58   Francis C. Frary to G. R. Gibbons, "Contributions of Aluminum Research Laboratories to the War Effort," 3 October 1944, ALA; "The Light Metals," *Business Week* (28 August 1943):46. For more on the way industrial research in general contributed to the war effort, see Graham, "Industrial Research in the Age of Big Science," Ronald Kline, "R&D: Organizing for War," *IEEE Spectrum* (November 1987):54–60, and U.S. Senate Subcommittee on War Mobilization, *The Government's Wartime Research and Development, 1940–1944,* prepared by the Bureau of Labor Statistics, 79th Congress, First Session Subcommittee Report No. 5 to the Committee on Military Affairs of the U.S. Senate, March 1945.

59   Frary, "History of Early Aluminum Research," pp. 32–3.

60   F. C. Frary to Hughes, 27 July 1943, ALA.

61   Frary, "Contributions of Aluminum Research Laboratories to the War Effort"; E. H. Dix, Jr., "Aluminum Alloys – 1940 to 1950," *Metal Progress,* 58(October 1950):484–9.

62   Magee, "Aluminum Production," pp. 10–11.

63   See Thomas E. Lloyd, "Alcoa, with Eye on Government, Girds for New Domestic and Future Canadian Competition," *Iron Age,* 158(March 1946):99, 124, 132, T. D. Jolly, "Aluminum Capacity Soon to be Seven Times Peacetime Peak," *Steel,* 111(30 November 1942):45–6, "Excess

Aluminum," *Business Week* (25 December 1943):34ff., W. L. Rice, "Competition Will Boost Use of Aluminum," *Iron Age,* 153(10 February 1944):140, and "Aluminum: Large Increase in Use Is Forecast," *Engineering and Mining Journal,* 145(February 1944):81

64   G. R. Gibbons to S. K. Colby, 24 March 1944, ALA.

65   Interview with Elbert Howarth, former assistant director, Alcoa Laboratories, 10 January 1985, by Margaret B. W. Graham (hereafter cited as Howarth Interview); interview with J. Howard Dunn, former vice-president for research and development, Aluminum Company of America, by Margaret B. W. Graham, 4 August 1987; C. F. Nagel, Jr., to Earl Blough, 28 March 1928, in Hood Manuscript, pp. 211–13. When Ernest Hartmann joined ARL's Engineering Design Division in 1929, he found that much of his work involved cooperation with the engineers of the Sales Department, as in helping the Pullman company apply aluminum in construction of railway cars (Hartmann Interview).

66   H. E. Bakken, "Outline of A.C.O.A. General Committee and Technical Committee System of Carrying Out Research and Development, Including Proposed Changes," 12 January 1944, ALA.

67   This quotation and the following three paragraphs are from H. E. Bakken to Roy A. Hunt, 17 February 1944, ALA.

68   This and the following two paragraphs are drawn from F. L. Magee, "Memorandum Re: Manufacturing Development (Or Process or Methods Development)," 27 December 1944, ALA.

69   Various memos describe the working out of the operational details: C. F. Nagel, Jr., to H. E. Bakken, 7 May 1945 and 28 September 1945, and F. L. Magee to H. E. Bakken, 2 October 1945, ALA. In his letter of 7 May 1945, Nagel proposed essentially the same procedures as had always been followed, suggesting that the concerns voiced by management over top-down R&D stemmed largely from ignorance of the committee's activities "as brought to light by the meeting that precipitated the current memorandum" – i.e., the December 1944 meeting on manufacturing development. Magee's memo of 2 October 1945 offered a list of Technical Committee functions, including initiating, budgeting, and assigning departmental responsibility for R&D projects.

70   Judge Hand's opinion in *United States of America vs. Aluminum Company of America, et al.,* quoted in Stein, *Disposal of the Aluminum Plants,* p. 319.

71   The War Production Board is quoted in Stein, *Disposal of the Aluminum Plants,* p. 324, and Frary to Gibbons, "Contributions of Aluminum Research Laboratories to the War Effort," which indicates that most of ARL's wartime work was done on a pro bono basis, the company absorbing even the travel expenses in most cases. The plants that Alcoa relinquished included the government's only two alumina plants, eight of the nine reduction plants, three of the eight extrusion plants, one of the two rod-and-bar plants, two sheet mills, and four forging plants. See *Iron Age,* 158(3 October 1946):98–9. Stein, *Disposal of the Aluminum Plants* gives a complete account of that transaction from the government's point of view. Harold Stein served as special advisor on surplus-property problems to Judge Vinson, director of war mobilization, and was thus present during many of the negotiating sessions. For a more recent account, drawing on internal Alcoa sources, see Smith, *From Monopoly to Competition,* pp. 233–42.

72 "Peace Treaty for Alcoa," *Business Week* (18 November 1948):23. Stein, *Disposal of the Aluminum Plants,* p. 250, said that most government officials assumed that the peculiar arrangement requested and received by Alcoa was designed to permit Alcoa to retain control into the postwar period. But the government lawyers involved, believing that government interests were not adequately preserved in the contracts, inserted cancellation clauses that were ultimately invoked. Alcoa also failed to secure purchase options on any of the plants, at the express order of President Roosevelt, on advice of the secretary of the interior, who believed that the new plants should be sold to other producers after the war.

73 Stein, *Disposal of the Aluminum Plants,* p. 321. Symington was a former president of Emerson Electric Company and a personal friend of President Truman. According to Stein, Symington relied most heavily on the guidance of the U.S. attorney general in his dealings with Alcoa. The attorney general was, in effect, applying the recent judgment in the aluminum case. The selling price of the property was said to be 30 cents on the dollar, an outrage from Alcoa's point of view, as the company would enjoy no discounts for the new facilities it erected in the postwar years. However, that was not out of line with the bargain-basement prices charged for war-surplus property in other industries, such as electronics assembly.

CHAPTER 6

1 Margaret B. W. Graham, "Industrial Research in the Age of Big Science," in Richard S. Rosenbloom (ed.), *Research on Technological Innovation, Management and Policy,* Vol. 2 (Greenwich, CT: JAI Press, 1985), pp. 47–97; A. Bright and J. Exter, "War, Radar, and the Radio Industry," *Harvard Business Review* (Winter 1947):255–72; W. R. Maclaurin "The Organization of Research in the Radio Industry after the War," *Proceedings of the I.R.E.,* 33(September 1945):567–70; D. Kevles, *The Physicists: The History of a Scientific Community in Modern America* (Cambridge, MA: Harvard University Press), pp. 344–60.

2 Harold Stein, *Disposal of the Aluminum Plants,* Inter-University Case Program, CPAC No. 6 (New York: Harcourt Brace & Co., 1952), p. 346. A number of patented processes, such as the Alclad process, that had been patented before the war continued to be royalty-bearing, but patents necessary to the operation of the newly transferred Defense Plant Corporation plants were either licensed royalty-free or bore a royalty negotiated with the government. That included a number of the machine patents. Interview with Edward B. Foote, former Alcoa patent attorney, in June, 1985 by Margaret B. W. Graham (hereafter cited as Foote Interview).

3 "Aluminum Reborn: Four Days Shook Aluminum into a Raucous New Industry," *Fortune,* 33(May 1946):105; T. E. Lloyd, "Alcoa, With Eye on Government, Girds for New Domestic and Future Canadian Competition," *Iron Age,* 158(3 October 1946):98–9; Stein, *Disposal of the Aluminum Plants,* p. 347.

4 According to Stein, *Disposal of the Aluminum Plants,* p. 328, Davis took that position in a July meeting among A. V. Davis, I. W. Wilson, Leon Hickman, and RFC Director Samuel Husbands.

5 See Francis Frary, "Quality Metal and Cost Reduction Mark History of

Aluminum Production," *Journal of Metals,* 7(August 1955):885–8. In 1984, Kent Van Horn, former vice-president of R&D, was still bitter about the patent giveaway: "We developed all the important alloys that are used in this country. We had to give them royalty free licenses thanks to F.D.R." Interview with Kent R. Van Horn, Aluminum Company of America, by George D. Smith and Margaret B. W. Graham, June 1984 (hereafter cited as Van Horn Interview).

6   "Wartime Progress in Alumina and Aluminum," *Chemical and Metallurgical Engineering,* 53(February 1946):157.

7   Frary, "Quality Metal and Cost Reduction," pp. 887.

8   Francis C. Frary, "History of Early Aluminum Research," transcript of a speech given in 1963, Historical Drawer, Alcoa Laboratories Archives, Alcoa Technical Center, Alcoa Center, PA (hereafter cited as ALA), pp. 25–6; G. H. Wagner, "Research at East St. Louis – A Brief History, 1923–1952," in "Alcoa Research Laboratories Histories." Vol. 2-B: "Histories of the Manufacturing Properties of the Aluminum Company of America, Affiliated Companies, and Defense Corporation Plants" (hereafter cited as Alcoa Plant Histories), p. B-140; Francis C. Frary et al., "History of Research and Development, Aluminum Company of America," a year-by-year summary of all research projects for 1888–1937, manuscript Historical Drawer, ALA.

9   Francis C. Frary, "Contributions of Aluminum Research Laboratories to the War Effort," memo to George R. Gibbons, 3 October 1944, ALA. While the plants were under construction, Alcoa built and operated at its own expense ($265,000) a semicommercial facility to test different types of equipment. It also absorbed all of the development and engineering costs, with no charge to the government for the know-how, and with no royalties.

10   "Wartime Progress in Alumina and Aluminum," p. 157; Frary, "History of Early Aluminum Research," pp. 25–6. The cost differential derived partly from the fact that there were no intermediate freight costs to the East St. Louis plant.

11   Frary, "Contributions of Aluminum Research Laboratories to the War Effort." The only other project that even reached pilot-plant scale was the Kalunite Company's process for treating alunite, of which very little was available.

12   Stein, *Disposal of the Aluminum Plants,* p. 349.

13   All these negotiations were between A. V. Davis, Alcoa's corporate counsel, Leon Hickman, and the U.S. assistant attorney general. See Stein, *Disposal of the Aluminum Plants,* pp. 350–2. See also George D. Smith, *From Monopoly to Competition: The Transformations of Alcoa, 1888–1986* (Cambridge University Press, 1988), pp. 237–42.

14   Stein, *Disposal of the Aluminum Plants,* p. 349.

15   Quoted in Stein, *Disposal of the Aluminum Plants,* p. 351.

16   Francis C. Frary, "Adventures with Alumina," *Industrial and Engineering Chemistry,* 38(February 1946):130.

17   Frary, "Adventures with Alumina," p. 131.

18   On the new mill at Davenport, see "From Pig to Sheet: How Aluminum Flows through Alcoa's New Rolling Mill at Davenport, Iowa," *Light Metal Age,* 8(June 1950):23–4.

19   As with a number of other processes, Alcoa's claim to have been the first

to discover the direct-chill process was disputed by European companies. Similar processes were being developed simultaneously, and largely independently, in Europe and Japan. See correspondence among W. T. Ennor, W. E. King, and F. C. Frary, September 1950, ALA.

20 Interviews with Walter Dean, former assistant director of research, Aluminum Company of America, by Margaret B. W. Graham, March 1985 (hereafter cited as Dean Interview), and John Hatch, former director of quality assurance and chief metallurgist for ingot and powder, by Margaret B. W. Graham, November 1984 (hereafter cited as Hatch Interview). One of the advantages Dean remembered about Cleveland was the wide variety of skills available to tackle problems. In alloy pouring, for instance, he worked with a former motion-picture director from the West Coast who photographed the molten metal as it flowed into the mold. That made possible the design of better molds.

21 Warren S. Peterson, "Cast Shop Technology and Reclamation: 100 Years of Progress," in Warren S. Peterson and Ronald E. Miller (eds.), *Hall-Héroult Centennial: First Century of Aluminum Process Technology, 1886–1986* (The Metallurgical Society, Inc., 1986), pp. 155–6.

22 Dean Interview (Dean had formerly worked under Joseph Nock at the experimental mill in New Kensington); S. P. Johnston to B. C. McFadden, 9 February 1929, discusses "side pouring of large ingots" at the Cleveland branch of the Research Bureau. The result was what they called the "bathtub ingot." Theodore Stay worked at Cleveland under Jeffries and Archer and later under their successor, Louis Kempf. Also see interview with Joseph Nock, 8 January 1985, by Margaret B. W. Graham (hereafter cited as Nock Interview).

23 The following account of direct-chill ingot development is drawn from W. T. Ennor, Alcoa Research Report No. 42592, "Progress Report – Ingot Development, Directly Chilled 12″ × 12″ Ingot," 30 April 1934, and Ennor, "Processes for Making Ingot for Working: Review and Present Status," a talk to the 1937 Alcoa metallurgists' meeting in New Kensington, 3 June 1937, ALA.

24 Ennor, "Process for Making Ingot."

25 Ibid.

26 John W. Hood to Richard L. Templin, "Strength of Cast Metal," 29 August 1935, and Templin to Hood, 13 September 1935, ALA.

27 R. G. Sturm to R. L. Templin, "Massena DC Ingots," 11 July 1935, ALA. Templin to Ennor, 12 July 1935, and Ennor to Templin, 22 July 1935, ALA, discuss that report and the ongoing exchange between Sturm and Ennor.

28 T. W. Bossert to W. T. Ennor, 13 August 1935.

29 Nagel to Templin, 20 September 1935, ALA.

30 Ennor to Nagel, "Directly Chilled Ingots," 15 January 1936, ALA: "It seems to me that Mr. Aber's results are based on actual stress data and must be accepted, that the calculation of stresses in an ingot from cooling data is much more complicated than is indicated in Mr. Sturm's memorandum, and that stresses in an ingot may be changed greatly and even be reversed from tension to compression by relatively small variations in casting conditions."

31 Templin to Nagel, 8 February 1936, ALA.

32 Sturm, report of 2 April 1936, and, on setting the meeting up, Nagel to Templin, 8 February 1936, ALA.

33 R. E. Sheffer to C. F. Nagel, Jr., 8 December 1936, ALA.

34 C. F. Nagel, Jr., speech to Alcoa metallurgists, New Kensington, 3 June 1937, ALA; Ennor, "Processes for Making Ingot"; Francis C. Frary, speech to the 1937 technical show, 16 December 1938, ALA.

35 See Bettye H. Pruitt and George D. Smith, "The Corporate Management of Innovation: Alcoa Research, Aircraft Alloys, and the Problem of Stress-Corrosion Cracking," in Richard S. Rosenbloom (ed.), *Research on Technological Innovation, Management and Policy,* Vol. 3 (Greenwich, CT: JAI Press, 1986), pp. 33–81. See also Nock Interview, and interview with Harold Y. Hunsicker, former technical advisor, Alloy Technology Division, Alcoa Laboratories, by Margaret B. W. Graham, January 1985.

36 E. H. Dix, Jr., "Acceleration of the Rate of Corrosion by High Constant Stresses," *Transactions of the American Institute of Mining and Metallurgical Engineers,* 143(1941):115; F. C. Frary to G. R. Gibbons, 3 October 1944, ALA. Prevention of stress-corrosion cracking of magnesium sheet was a related problem that was of particular concern to the Office of Scientific Research and Development (OSRD). Alcoa researchers cooperated with Professor Hunter, chairman of the OSRD committee on the subject, by giving him all the pertinent information they had and by fabricating "a great variety of magnesium sheet samples for his experiments." Hunter was a senior professor at Rensselaer who had taught and supervised a number of Alcoa researchers in their graduate work, including Walter Dean, later ARL assistant director. See Dean Interview and Nock Interview.

37 James T. Staley, "History of Wrought Aluminum Alloy Development," 7 February 1986, ALA, p. 16.

38 Fundamental work on DC casting in general had been going on at ARL since 1947, and information was being shared around the R&D system. See E. H. Dix, Jr., to W. T. Ennor, 8 August 1947, and E. C. Hartmann to R. L. Templin, 17 February 1947, ALA. A meeting to try to get at all the problems experienced with casting large 75S ingot was held by T. W. Bossert in October 1951. T. W. Bossert to W. T. Ennor, 17 October 1951, and J. H. Rowe to T. W. Bossert, 7 October 1951, ALA. See also W. A. Dean, "Re: Production of Large 75S Alloy Ingots," 26 October 1951, ALA. See further information about the difficulties with large-ingot casting in Hatch Interview.

39 Edgar H. Dix, Jr., "Aluminum-Zinc-Magnesium Alloys: Their Development and Commercial Production," the 1949 Edward De Mille Campbell Memorial Lecture, *Transactions of the American Society for Metals,* 42(1950):1125. Dix expressed doubt that much more could be gained from empirical testing of metal-mixing methods, "but the rewards of fundamental research are as great as ever."

40 W. T. Ennor to T. W. Bossert, "Re: Ingot Development – D.C. Coolants," 18 October 1945, ALA. See also B. C. McFadden to W. R. King, 21 September 1945, E. M. Kipp to McFadden, 25 September 1945, McFadden to Kipp, 29 October 1945, Ennor to McFadden, 30 October 1945, Kipp to McFadden, 31 October 1945, ALA.

41 Ennor to Bossert, 11 August 1945, ALA. Until that point, ARL's chief x-ray facility had been located in Cleveland, headed by Kent Van Horn.

42 E. H. Dix, Jr., to W. T. Ennor, 8 August 1947, Bossert to Ennor, 20 August 1945, ALA. It was agreed that much of the work Ennor wished to accomplish could not be done at Massena because it involved precise

measurements of temperatures of mold and metal during casting and follow-up examinations by both x-ray and microscopic examination of ingots produced. Another factor in the location of further casting research at the Laboratories was the transformation toward full-scale experimental equipment in the postwar era, which is discussed in Chapter 7; interview with Elbert Howarth, former associate director of Alcoa Laboratories, by Margaret B. W. Graham, 4 August 1987.

42 "That Familiar Alcoa Problem: War Assets, Antitrust Clash over Massena Plant Sale," *Fortune*, 36(January 1949):19; "Industrial News," *Chemical and Engineering News*, 26(15 November 1948):3416. Smith, *From Monopoly to Competition*, p. 240.

44 Crawford Greenewalt, speaking at a dedication of DuPont's expanded Experimental Station in 1957, pamphlet in the Harvard University Library. See David Hounshell and John K. Smith, *Science and Corporate Strategy: DuPont R&D, 1902–1980* (Cambridge University Press, 1988), pp. 358–83.

45 These changes were mentioned in the Van Horn Interview, in an interview with Philip Stroup, former chief chemist, Aluminum Company of America, by Margaret B. W. Graham, August 1983, in an interview with Ernest Hartmann, former director of Alcoa Laboratories, 29 January 1984, by Margaret B. W. Graham, and in the Dean Interview. Changes in patent policy specifically were addressed in the Foote Interview. Foote also recalled asking Junius Edwards if he thought competition had been harmful to Alcoa. Edwards replied: "I will say there has been more development."

CHAPTER 7

1 David P. Reynolds, "Reynolds Charts Postwar Aluminum Developments," *Iron Age*, 156(13 September 1945):102.

2 The argument behind that position was articulated by A. Bright and J. Exter, "War, Radar and the Radio Industry," *Harvard Business Review* (Winter 1947):255–72, and W. R. Maclaurin, "The Organization of Research in the Radio Industry after the War," *Proceedings of the I.R.E.* (1945):507–70. Recent scholarship has suggested that that stranglehold was illusory to some extent. David C. Mowery, "Firm Structure, Government Policy, and the Organization of Industrial Research: Great Britain and the United States, 1900–1950," *Business History Review*, 58(Winter 1984):504–31, found that while research performance certainly contributed to the long-term success of large firms, smaller firms increasingly participated in research as well and reaped similar benefits.

3 Margaret B. W. Graham, "Industrial Research in the Age of Big Science," in Richard S. Rosenbloom (ed.), *Research on Technological Innovation, Management and Policy*, Vol. 2 (Greenwich, CT: JAI Press, 1985), 47–79. See also Graham, "Corporate Research and Development: The Latest Transformation," *Technology in Society*, 7(1985):179–96. For a broader view of postwar relations between business and industry, see Louis Galambos and Joseph Pratt, *The Rise of the Corporate Commonwealth: United States Business and Public Policy in the 20th Century* (New York: Basic Books, 1988).

4 Graham, "Industrial Research in the Age of Big Science," p. 55.

5   William B. Harris, "The Splendid Retreat of Alcoa," *Fortune*, 52(October 1955):114–22. Many industry watchers predicted the postwar boom in aluminum. Manufacturers who previously had resisted using aluminum were becoming familiar with it and were open to adopting it if the price was right. Competition from Reynolds and Kaiser promised to help accelerate market expansion and would open some applications, such as in automobiles, that had previously been closed because Alcoa was the sole aluminum supplier. See "The Light Metals," *Business Week* (28 August 1943):57–8.

6   Interviews with Philip Stroup and Kent Van Horn covered the differences in the types of employees hired before and after World War II by the Laboratories: interview with Kent R. Van Horn, former vice-president for research and development, Aluminum Company of America, by George D. Smith and Margaret B. W. Graham, March 1984 (hereafter cited as Van Horn Interview); interview with Philip Stroup, former chief chemist, Aluminum Company of America, by Margaret B. W. Graham, August 1983 (hereafter cited as Stroup Interview).

7   Harris, "The Splendid Retreat of Alcoa," pp. 115, 118, 246. Harris touted the research program that had contributed so much to its rapid expansion: "Alcoa concentrates on the kind of basic work that results in new alloys or new processes for cutting primary refining and manufacturing costs." See also "From Pig to Sheet – How Aluminum Flows through Alcoa's New Rolling Mill at Davenport, Iowa," *Light Metal Age*, 8(June 1950):23–4. In that era, Alcoa's divergence from chemical-industry research practices became marked. In 1950, Alcoa's research expenditures amounted to 0.7 percent of sales revenues, versus an average of 2.7 percent spent by the chemical companies. In making that comparison, Frary pointed out, first, that it was not clear whether the figures cited in the article reflected research only or both research and development. If it was the latter, Frary noted, Alcoa's figure would be three times larger than what he had reported. Second, Frary noted that all of the chemical companies had been expanding rapidly into products derived from synthetic organic chemistry: detergents, dyes, fibers, plastics, antibiotics. "That kind of expansion into new fields naturally demands an excessive amount of research and development cost and produces a great increase in sales." See Francis C. Frary to I. W. Wilson, 5 June 1951, ALA.

8   Harris, "The Splendid Retreat of Alcoa," p. 122. One U.S. Steel Company executive reported, apparently with some excitement, that he had found a cast-iron vent pipe during a tour of the building on its opening day.

9   Francis C. Frary, "History of Early Aluminum Research," transcript of a speech given in 1963, Historical Drawer, Alcoa Laboratories Archives, Alcoa Technical Center, Alcoa Center, PA (hereafter cited as ALA), p. 35; Frary et al., "History of Research and Development, Aluminum Company of America," a year-by-year summary of all research projects for 1888–1937, manuscript, Historical Drawer, ALA.

10   Harris, "The Splendid Retreat of Alcoa," p. 117. Actually, the first such building was the Equitable Savings and Loan Association Building in Portland, Oregon, which used both castings and sheet on its exterior. That building was erected in 1947: "Review of Aluminum Markets," Alcoa press release, 31 December 1947, ALA.

11   T. E. Lloyd, "Alcoa, With Eye on Government, Girds for New Domestic and Future Canadian Competition," *Iron Age*, 158(3 October 1946):131, gives the prewar statistic; the postwar figure is from Alcoa's "Review of Aluminum Markets," p. 2.

12   Quoted in D. I. Brown, "Many Industrial Applications of Aluminum May Become Permanent," *Iron Age*, 160(13 November 1949):129. That was the second of two articles on the substitution of aluminum during the steel shortage of the late 1940s; the first was "Mushrooming Industrial Applications Brighten Aluminum Future," *Iron Age*, 160(6 November 1947):131–3.

13   Harris, "The Splendid Retreat of Alcoa," p. 117; Frary et al., "History of Research and Development," for years 1950–60. The Davenport works, which opened in 1948, was the first showcase for aluminum wiring: "Building a Showplace for Aluminum; Alcoa's Office Building in Davenport, Iowa," *Business Week* (9 July 1949):42.

14   Harris, "The Splendid Retreat of Alcoa," pp. 115, 148; "Aluminum Reborn: Four Days Shook Aluminum into a Raucous New Industry," *Fortune*, 33(May 1946):107.

15   W. L. Russell, "Alcoa's All-Aluminum Skyscraper to Go Up in Triangle Next Year," unidentified press clipping (2/3/49), ALA. On organizational changes, see George D. Smith, *From Monopoly to Competition: The Transformations of Alcoa, 1888–1983* (Cambridge University Press, 1988), pp. 257–61. The other new officers were Arthur P. Hall, vice-president for public relations and advertising, and Leon Hickman, Alcoa's first general counsel.

16   Van Horn Interview.

17   Career facts from *American Men of Science*, 8th ed. (1949), pp. 107, 626, 692, 2475, from *American Men and Women of Science*, 10th ed. (1960), Vol. 6, pp. 4196–7, and from "Alcoa Research Laboratories History." Vol. 2-B: "Histories of the Manufacturing Properties of the Aluminum Company of America, Affiliated Companies, and Defense Corporation Plants" (hereafter cited as Alcoa Plant Histories) in Alcoa Archives, Aluminum Company of America, Pittsburgh, PA (hereafter cited as AA). The general impression of the competition for director gained from those sources is corroborated by the Van Horn Interview and an interview with Allen S. Russell, former vice-president and chief scientist, Aluminum Company of America, by Margaret B. W. Graham, 8 January 1985 (hereafter cited as Russell Interview).

18   This paragraph and the next are based on the Van Horn Interview and Russell Interview.

19   Van Horn Interview; "Alcoa Research Laboratories History," Vol. 2-B, "Building and Personnel History" for 1944–60.

20   See Jeffrey F. Schoepf, "A Case Study of the Site Selection Process: ALCOA Technical Center," manuscript, 5 December 1981, and Schoepf, "Regarding Site Selection for Alcoa Laboratories," 13 November 1981, Historical Drawer, ALA. See also interview with Elbert Howarth, former assistant director, Alcoa Laboratories, 10 January 1985 and 4 August 1987, by Margaret B. W. Graham (hereafter cited as Howarth Interview).

21   "News from the American Institute of Management," 24 April 1956, ALA. The institute said further that Alcoa was conducting three-fourths

of all research in aluminum, although its share of the primary market was less than half.

22 I. W. Wilson to H. E. Bakken, 16 March 1944, ALA.

23 Van Horn Interview; Russell Interview.

24 Smelting accounted for 13 percent of the Laboratories' spending in 1928 and 1929, then fell to 11 percent in 1930 and 9 percent in 1931. The depression accelerated that trend. In 1932, expenditures for smelting R&D dropped sharply, to just 2 percent of the total for the Laboratories, hovering there until the start of the war, when it dropped still further, then crept back to 2 percent by 1945. Research Bureau and ARL annual reports, statements of expenditures, ALA.

25 "Alcoa Works History," Vol. 1, Alcoa Plant Histories, AA; "1948 Membership of General Committee, Technical Committee and Subcommittees of the Technical Committee," 1 July 1948, ALA. Smelting research was carried out at plant scale by the Metallurgical Department of the corporate Reduction Division, created after World War II. Like plant metallurgists in the fabricating area, this group was to be responsible for speeding development and transfer of innovations devised at ARL and for making their own improvements in the Hall-Héroult process based on operating experience.

26 Warren Haupin, "History of Electrical Consumption by Hall-Héroult Cells," in Warren S. Peterson and Ronald E. Miller (eds.), *Hall-Héroult Centennial: First Century of Aluminum Process Technology, 1886–1986* (The Metallurgical Society, Inc., 1986), pp. 106–13; B. J. Welch, "Gaining That Extra 2 Percent Current Efficiency," ibid., p. 129. The patterns of improvement in both these areas were similar: little improvement in current efficiency (from 70 to 74 percent) between 1893 and 1914, and none in power consumption; progress in both in the mid-1930s; progress again in the early 1950s, levelling off by 1956 at 87 percent currency efficiency and 14.5 kilowatt-hours per kilogram (6.6 kilowatt-hours per pound).

27 Alcoa Technical Committee, "Technical Budgets and Programs" (1951, 1954), Alcoa Archives, Records Storage Center, Boyers, PA (hereafter cited as AA-Boyers). Each year's "Technical Budget and Program" indicates both budgeted expenditures for the coming year and actual expenditures for the previous year for each R&D organization and within each category of work – for example, refining, reduction, alloy development.

28 That was the type of work that Bakken had advocated in his "sin of omission" memo before the war. The description of ARL projects in the following pages is based on Frary et al., "History of Research and Development," for the years 1945–60.

29 Quotations from Technical Committee minutes for 16 January 1952, ALA. See also C. F. Nagel, Jr., "Functions of the Aluminum Research Laboratories with respect to Plant Laboratories of the Castings, Fabricating, and Reduction Divisions," 25 July 1944, ALA.

30 "Aluminum Research Laboratories Annual Report for 1941," ALA; Frary, "History of Early Aluminum Research," pp. 32–4.

31 In his "Aluminum Research Laboratories Annual Report for 1951," ALA, Frary noted that the salary list for ARL showed a net loss for the second year in a row: "It has become increasingly difficult to keep competent technical employees against the competition of other companies and

to replace those that leave." In most years, ARL was able to offset losses with new hires.

32 Alcoa Technical Committee, "Technical Budget and Program" (1949), AA-Boyers.

33 E. H. Dix, Jr., to C. F. Nagel, Jr., 26 March 1953, ALA. Magee shared Nagel's desire to limit the number of alloys produced "to the absolute minimum necessary to sell the maximum profitable tonnage." F. L. Magee to H. E. Bakken, 6 July 1944, ALA.

34 "Aluminum Research Laboratories, Annual Report for 1949," ALA; Howarth Interview.

35 Alcoa Technical Committee, "Technical Budgets and Programs" (1960–70), AA-Boyers; interview with Robert Hampel, former vice-president for technical development, Aluminum Company of America, 4 March 1985, by Margaret B. W. Graham (hereafter cited as Hampel Interview).

36 Van Horn and Howarth Interviews.

37 "Technical Highlights Contributing to the Progress of Alcoa," manuscript (1979), ALA, pp. 24–5; on APDL budgets, see Alcoa Technical Committee, "Technical Budgets and Programs" (1958–9), AA-Boyers. Also see interview with Edwin H. Spuhler, former manager for applications engineering, Aluminum Company of America, by Bettye H. Pruitt, 20 March 1984 (hereafter cited as Spuhler Interview).

38 All of these reports are in ALA.

39 The five existing in 1945 were Ores and Mineral Materials; Alumina, Cryolite, and Chemical Products; Finishes; Metal Working; and Packaging. Those added by 1950 were Aluminum and Carbon; Metal Reclamation; Electrical Conductors; Oils and Lubricants; and Sand, Semi-Permanent and Permanent Mold Castings.

40 H. E. Bakken to H. V. Churchill et al., 15 November 1949, ALA.

41 H. E. Bakken to Francis C. Frary, 18 July 1950, AA-Boyers.

42 I. W. Wilson to F. C. Frary, 21 June 1951, ALA.

43 Frary noted that change in his own report for 1949 and said that henceforth he would merely summarize important developments: "Aluminum Research Laboratories Annual Report for 1949," ALA.

44 C. F. Nagel, Jr., to H. E. Bakken, 28 September 1949, ALA. The new categories of R&D work were Alumina, Cryolite and Aluminum Fluoride Investigations; Chemical Products Development; Power Development; Aluminum Reduction; Metal Melting and Ingot Casting Investigations; Aluminum Products – Alloy, Process, Product and Equipment Development; Magnesium Development Investigations; Sales Development Expenditures; and Development Expenditures of a General Nature.

45 "Aluminum Research Laboratories Annual Report for 1949," ALA.

46 E. H. Dix, Jr., to C. F. Nagel, Jr., 26 March 1953, ALA.

47 Van Horn Interview.

48 Van Horn Interview.

49 In June 1958, Magee reported the thinking of the Technical Policy Committee as follows: "It is quite possible that, in addition to the Alcoa Research Laboratories, there will be one or more development laboratories. These latter laboratories may be under the jurisdiction of the Director of Research, but reporting functionally to the Engineering, Metallurgical, Sales or some other Department. Alternatively, they might report completely to another department, and come under the jurisdiction of the

administrative policies established on the Merwin property. The details of the organization of these laboratories can be handled at the proper time." F. L. Magee, "Research and Technical Policy Committee," 30 June 1958, AA-Boyers.

50 "Alcoa, 1960: A Billion Dollar Baby," *Modern Metals,* 15(June 1959):30–2; "Alcoa Unveils Major Expansion," *Iron Age,* 180(18 July 1957):78; "Aluminum Looks Ahead," *Steel,* 141(19 August 1957):109.

51 Adding to the oversupply situation was the fact that Aluminium, Ltd., had also expanded and held a contract, negotiated during a period of shortage following the Korean War, to sell Alcoa 600,000 tons of aluminum over a period of years extending through 1961. "What the Price Cut Will Mean," *Modern Metals,* 14(April 1958):80; "Billion Dollar Baby," pp. 30–1; "Where All the Metal Is Going," *Business Week* (30 March 1957):192; "Aluminum Looks Ahead," p. 108; "Ordeal by Competition," *Forbes* (1 September 1965):18. Net profit fell from 10.4 percent of sales in 1956 to 5 percent in 1961, according to George Bookman, "Alcoa Strikes Back," *Fortune* (November 1962):114.

52 "Alcoa Strikes Back," pp. 114, 162.

53 "Billion Dollar Baby," pp. 32, 34.

54 See Walter A. McDougall, *The Heavens and the Earth: A Political History of the Space Age* (New York: Basic Books, 1985), pp. 74–89.

55 See "Alcoa Strikes Back," pp. 156–7, and "Aluminum's New, Widening World," *Iron Age* (3 November 1966):68–79.

56 That was the case at RCA, which, after settling an antitrust action similar to Alcoa's, chose to license heavily abroad: Margaret B. W. Graham, *RCA and the Videodisc: The Business of Research* (Cambridge University Press, 1986), pp. 68–75. See also the *Fortune* series on the electronics industry, 1957.

57 I. W. Wilson, "Research Policy Committee," 10 January 1957, AA, env. 1168. Welty was to be a member, along with M. M. Anderson, R. V. Davies, J. P. Haight, Van Horn, and Magee, the latter as chairman. The group was renamed the Research and Technical Policy Committee, and its responsibilities were enlarged to include providing "advice and counsel" to the Technical Committee on general policy matters.

58 G. D. Welty to F. L. Magee, 20 May 1958, AA-Boyers.

59 Ibid.

60 Van Horn accepted Welty's idea of a director of development in principle, but proposed "a refinement" of the idea that distinguished carefully among the many different development programs, some of which were highly proprietary and others of which were customer-oriented. In the end he suggested that there should be a director of process engineering, a manager of sales development, a director of product development, and a director of research. On deliberation, the Research and Technical Policy Committee decided simply to delegate authority for development to the chairman of the Technical Committee. Kent R. Van Horn to F. L. Magee et al., 24 June 1958, and F. L. Magee, "Research and Technical Policy Committee," 30 June 1958, AA-Boyers.

61 Its members were two executive vice-presidents, M. M. Anderson and L. Litchfield, Jr., T. W. Bossert (chief metallurgist), F. J. Close (vice-president for sales development), R. V. Davies (vice-president for sales), H. C. Erskine (vice-president for smelting and fabricating operations),

J. P. Haight (vice-president for engineering and purchasing), and Van Horn, who served as secretary.

62   R. V. Davies, "Research and Development Committee," 6 October 1958, AA, env. 1168. Bossert's title on the 1959 Alcoa organization chart (AA, env. 1059) was vice-president, chairman of the R&D Committee. He was presented to the world as vice-president for R&D: "Billion Dollar Baby," p. 34. The weight that Metallurgy carried in management circles was attributable in large part to "Dutch" Nagel and his long tenure on the Technical Committee. Bossert offered many of the same credentials as had Nagel. He had been with the Technical Direction Bureau in the 1920s as a plant metallurgist at Cleveland and had done a brief stint at ARL in New Kensington in 1929, working on ingot-casting problems. In the 1930s he had moved to Pittsburgh with Nagel to work in the central administration, as head of the Metallurgical Department of the Castings Division, and he had long been second in command in the expanded corporate Metallurgical Division.

63   F. L. Magee, "Reorganization of the Technical Policy Committee," 14 March 1960, AA, env. 1167. The quotation is from "Billion Dollar Baby," p. 36.

64   T. W. Bossert to members of Technical Committee, 22 September 1959, John H. Alden to members of Research and Development Committee, 7 October 1958 and 15 December 1958, and Bossert to K. R. Van Horn, 10 May 1960, ALA. See also Bossert to M. M. Anderson, 2 November 1960, AA, env. 1168.

65   Kent R. Van Horn, "ARL Organizational Changes," 27 June 1958, AA-Boyers. In the case of Mechanical Engineering, the problem was exacerbated by the appointment of its chief, Elbert Howarth, as project manager for development of the new technical center. Van Horn proposed that Howarth be appointed chief engineer of ARL and that his division be broken into two parts, one to continue research in engineering and metalworking processes, and the other to operate the machine shop, manage the physical plant, and provide drafting and design services to other divisions. He suggested that Howarth could run a similar division for the consolidated technical center when it was completed.

66   Van Horn, "ARL Organizational Changes."

67   On the level of funding for fundamental work, see Van Horn Interview and Van Horn, quoted in "New Division Expands Alcoa Research," *Industrial Laboratories*, 9(August 1958):16. On the evolution of metallurgy, see George J. Mills, "Future Developments in Aluminum Metallurgy," *Light Metal Age*, 16(April 1958):11–14.

68   Howarth Interview.

69   This was especially problematic at the time when engineering schools and science departments of many kinds had become quite theoretical and very antimanufacturing. See Michael Dertouzos, Richard Kloster, and Robert M. Solow, *Made in America: Regaining the Productive Edge* (Cambridge, MA: MIT Press, 1989), pp. 156–60, which notes this problem in retrospect.

70   W. E. King to W. T. Ennor, 12 September 1950, with handwritten marginal notes by Frary, ALA. Also see interview with Robert E. Spear, former technical director for casting R&D, Alcoa Laboratories, by Bettye H. Pruitt and Margaret B. W. Graham, 30 June 1988 (hereafter cited as

Spear Interview); Spear recalled the reaction to the nonpublication policy at Cleveland after the war, when younger researchers felt professionally inhibited as their senior colleagues had not been. In some instances they did not receive credit for things that were pioneered at Alcoa because they never published their work. That was true in Spear's field of metal melting and solidification and also in the area of precipitation hardening in high-strength alloys. See interview with Harold Y. Hunsicker, former technical advisor, Alloy Technology Division, Alcoa Laboratories, by Margaret B. W. Graham, 9 January 1985.

71 T. W. Bossert to Technical Policy Committee, 5 October 1960, Kent R. Van Horn to members of the Technical Policy Committee, 15 December 1960, E. C. Hartmann to T. W. Bossert, 14 September 1961, AA-Boyers.

72 John H. Alden, "Protection of Confidential Information," 10 June 1960, ALA.

73 "Billion Dollar Baby," pp. 34, 38.

74 E. S. Howarth, introduction to Harrison and Abramovitz, architects, "A Program for the Planning of the Alcoa Technical Center," manuscript (April 1960), ALA, p. 5. That introduction was clearly intended to express the views of the Technical Policy Committee and liberally quoted the remarks of Alcoa's top management. See also Schoepf interview with Elbert Howarth, "Regarding Site Selection for Alcoa Laboratories," Technical Policy Committee minutes for meetings of 4 June 1959, 6 August 1959, and 9 December 1959, AA-Boyers, and T. W. Bossert to R. V. Davies, 25 January 1960, AA-Boyers.

75 Howarth, introduction to "Program for the Planning of the Alcoa Technical Center," p. 8.

76 Van Horn Interview; Howarth Interview. At that time, APDL reported to Van Horn, as vice-president for R&D. See also Technical Policy Committee minutes for meeting of 17 October 1961, and K. R. Van Horn to members of the Technical Policy Committee, 11 June 1962, AA-Boyers.

77 "Ordeal by Competition," p. 18.

78 "Ordeal by Competition," pp. 21–2; Smith, *From Monopoly to Competition*, p. 320.

79 Harris, "The Splendid Retreat of Alcoa," p. 119; Van Horn to members of the Technical Policy Committee, 11 June 1962, AA-Boyers; interview with Frederick J. Close, former chairman, Aluminum Company of America, by George D. Smith, 24 August 1984. In 1959, Reynolds scored a coup in the transportation industry, securing a huge contract from Southern Railway with no competition from Alcoa. In its wake, Close reorganized Sales into industry groups, and Alcoa began to move away from its long-standing policy of leaving end-use markets entirely to its customers: "Alcoa Strikes Back," pp. 116, 118.

80 John D. Harper to E. C. Hartmann, 4 November 1963, ALA. The appointees to the R&D Committee in 1963 were as follows: B. J. Fletcher, chief engineer; John W. Hood, chief metallurgist; Ernest Hartmann, director of research; J. R. Fox, general manager, Refining Division; R. E. Sheffer, general manager, Fabricating Division; S. J. Simmons, Jr., vice-president, Industry and Product Sales; B. H. Sloane, general manager, Smelting Division; E. M. Strauss, Jr., manager, New Product Evaluation; J. H. Alden, Jr., secretary of the R&D Committee.

81 Van Horn Interview; interview with Ernest C. Hartmann, former director

of research, Aluminum Company of America, by Margaret B. W. Graham, 29 November 1984. Hartmann had become a research engineer at ARL in 1929 and had been an assistant director of research since 1955. See *American Men and Women of Science,* 11th ed. (1966), pp. 2146–7.

82   Harper to Hartmann, 4 November 1963, ALA.

83   See Smith, *From Monopoly to Competition,* pp. 342–7.

84   E. C. Hartmann to T. R. Gauthier, 21 July 1965, ALA. The figure for spending on fundamental research was calculated from expenditure data in Alcoa Technical Committee, "Technical Budgets and Programs," for 1965 and 1966, drawing on a statement by Robert G. Hampel in 1977 that, 10 years before (i.e., in 1967), 5 percent of total R&D expenditures had gone to basic research; by 1977 that figure was reduced to 2 percent: Robert G. Hampel to Edwin Mansfield, 21 November 1977, ALA. In 1966 the young executives in the Future Planning Committee agreed on the short-term focus of most subcommittees and expressed concern over the relative neglect of longer-range technical needs. Marvin Gantz, in the Pittsburgh office of the Fabrication Division, noted with "disgust" the annual technical-highlights document prepared by the subcommittees. He suggested that the developments cited by the Subcommittee on Extrusions, Tube, Wire, Rod, and Bar were "a testimonial to a pathetic lack of innovation in our extrusion R&D effort": E. M. Strauss to members of the Future Planning Committee, 9 June 1966, and M. B. Gantz, Jr., to K. B. Guiney, 13 June 1966, ALA.

85   E. M. Strauss to K. R. Van Horn, 4 August 1965, ALA. The "dictum" came down from Frank Magee, who was still chariman at that point in 1965, as quoted in "Billion Dollar Baby," p. 36.

86   As an example of DFR projects, the list of seven projects for 1965 included "Fundamental Studies of Oxide Films and Other Problems Relating to the Surfaces of Aluminum Products," "Development of Improved Corrosion Resistant Films," "New Alloying Techniques," "Reductions of Impurities in Alumina," and "Interactions of Metallic Elements in Food": Hartmann to Gauthier, 21 July 1965, ALA.

87   Interview with G. Keith Turnbull, manager for technology planning, Aluminum Company of America, by George D. Smith and Davis Dyer, 8 July 1983; interview with Eric A. Walker, former director and vice-president for science and technology, Aluminum Company of America, by Margaret B. W. Graham, 10 May 1985.

88   T. W. Bossert, "Research and Development Committee, Long Range Planning," 26 March 1960, and Kent R. Van Horn to E. C. Hartmann, 25 November 1965, ALA.

89   This statement is based on a review of indexes of Alcoa Laboratories correspondence showing that as much as 40 percent of the letters written by Van Horn to members of ARL in one year concerned these books.

90   Developments of the 1950s can be tracked in Frary et al., "History of Research and Development," for 1950–60. On continuous casting, see Spear Interview and "Continuous Casting of Aluminum May Pick Up," *Steel* (30 March 1961):132, 134. On powder metallurgy, see R. J. Towner, "Atomized Powder Alloys of Aluminum," *Metal Progress,* 73(May 1958):70–76.

91   John C. Churchill to R. L. LaBarge, 25 October 1968, ALA. Ford Motor Company had made professional marketing and finance the hallmarks of

managerial sophistication in the early 1960s. Ford managers were hired away by a number of American companies wishing to adopt a more professional management style in the 1950s. Within a few years of the time that Robert McNamara left Ford to run the Defense Department in the Kennedy administration, Archibald MacArdle and Jack Goldman went to Xerox, Chase Morsey to RCA, Robert White to First National City Bank, and the list goes on. In 1960, Theodore Levitt wrote a highly influential article advocating adoption of the "marketing concept": "Marketing Myopia," *Harvard Business Review* (July–August 1960):45–56. See also Graham, *RCA and the Videodisc*, pp. 104–27.

92 J. D. Harper, "Company Reorganization," 23 August 1968, ALA.

CHAPTER 8

1 Cliff Sands, "Alcoa Capabilities," 19 November 1968, Alcoa Laboratories Archives, Alcoa Technical Center, Alcoa Center, PA (hereafter cited as ALA).

2 "Can Market Battle Forces Basic Changes in Aluminum, Steel," *Iron Age* (5 March 1964):33, quotes R. B. Meneilly of U.S. Steel: "They'll have to get the cost of aluminum ingot down first. We know what it costs to roll and process metal to a finished article for can making." See also "Steel and Aluminum Vie for Containers," *Business Week* (13 October 1962):60, and "The Can Is Lighter If Not the Brew," *Business Week* (10 July 1965):90, which recounts the six-year struggle aluminum waged to capture steel's dominant share of the market for beer cans.

3 Allen S. Russell, "Pitfalls and Pleasures in New Aluminum Process Development," *AIME Metallurgical Transactions,* 12B(June 1981):204.

4 Louis B. Barnes of the Harvard Graduate School of Business Administration has conducted extensive interviews with retired Alcan executives as part of a research project. They show that Alcan's experience with its alternative smelting process was similar to Alcoa's. See J. G. Peacey and W. G. Davenport, "Evaluation of Alternative Methods of Aluminum Production," *Journal of Metals* (July 1974):25–8, who explain that despite all improvements, the conventional aluminum smelting process continues to be criticized because of its low energy efficiency, capital intensiveness, and scale.

5 P. T. Stroup, "Minutes of Aluminum and Carbon Subcommittee Meeting, January 15, 1952," 22 January 1952, and A. J. Rice to A. S. Russell, 22 September 1955, ALA.

6 P. T. Stroup to members of the Aluminum and Carbon Subcommittee, 4 April 1957, ALA; Aluminum Company of America, "Technical Budget and Program," 1957, 1958, in Alcoa Archives, Aluminum Company of America Records Storage Facility, Boyers, PA (hereafter cited as AA-Boyers); Francis C. Frary et al., "History of Research and Development, Aluminum Company of America," a year-by-year summary of all research projects for 1888–1937, 1956–7, manuscript, Historical Drawer, ALA.

7 A. J. Rice, "Meeting of the Subcommittee on Smelting," 3 October 1960, ALA. These are minutes of an important meeting reviewing the year's progress.

8 Ibid. Rice records that, "it was pointed out by Mr. Harper ... that it is

desirable to have developed and ready for use, if needed, a process which does not involve the use of fluorides."

9   Magee's dictum, from June 1960, is quoted in R&D Committee, "Minutes of Meeting of August 15, 1960," ALA. Steps in the evolution of top-down direction of R&D included Harper's calling for a joint meeting of the Technical Committee and its parent Research and Technical Policy Committee to review R&D and "develop a course of future action to insure the continuation of Alcoa's technical leadership in the aluminum industry." F. L. Magee to R. H. Brown, 12 September 1958, ALA. After that, every subcommittee had to rate its projects by priority and defer all those that were not at the top of the list. A. J. Rice to John H. Alden, 20 February 1959, ALA. Also significant, as described in Chapter 7, was Theodore Bossert's appointment to full-time chair of the Technical Committee (renamed the R&D Committee) and the change in its membership to include all subcommittee chairmen in 1958. After that, the higher-up Technical Policy Committee took up its long-unused power to have final authority over the budget. T. W. Bossert to the R&D Committee, 17 November 1960, ALA.

10   A. J. Rice to John H. Alden, 20 February 1959, and T. W. Bossert, "Memorandum," 24 March 1959, ALA.

11   G. T. Holmes to members of the Subcommittee on Smelting, "Minutes of Meeting of October 10–11," 17 October 1961, and W. E. Becker to A. S. Russell, 2 March 1961, ALA. The aluminum chloride process was pronounced "a standoff" with the Hall-Héroult process at 15.4 cents per pound, but Becker informed Russell that "on the basis of this cost analysis and the added consideration that this process was already partially developed by ARL, the chloride process was chosen for further development." See also interview with Kent Van Horn, former vice-president for R&D, Aluminum Company of America, by George D. Smith and Margaret B. W. Graham, March 1984 (hereafter cited as Van Horn Interview).

12   Lester L. Knapp to P. T. Stroup, 31 August 1961, and D. L. Wise to A. S. Russell, 12 December 1961, ALA. Wise described design modifications, made with the goal of capital reduction, through which they had decreased the number of reactors needed in a large plant from 44 to 6 by increasing the diameter of each reactor.

13   On the 1962 AIME annual meeting, see *Proceedings of the American Institute for Mining and Metallurgical Engineers*, April 1962, and "International Symposium on the Extractive Metallurgy of Aluminum, New York," *Journal of Metals*, 14(June 1962):442–6. On various alternative processes, see "Advance in Technology: Aluminum from Clay, Shale; Olin Matheson Chemical Corp. Acid Process," *Steel*, 148(27 March 1961):76, F. J. Starin, "New Aluminum Process Coming: Aluminium Limited," *Iron Age*, 186(22 December 1960):33, F. B. Domaas, "New Methods, New Ore Sources Attract Aluminum Industry Research Efforts," *Engineering and Mining Journal*, 162(October 1961):105–9, "Olin Research Moves One Step Closer to Aluminum from Clay," *Modern Metals*, 17(April 1961):59, "Aluminum Nears Direct Reduction, Extraction from Clays," *Engineering and Mining Journal*, 163(June 1962):180, H. H. Richardson et al., "New Aluminum Research Target: Better Ways to Produce for Less," *Steel*, 150(21 May 1962):125–8, and J. Glasser and W. E. Few, "Submerged-Arc Furnaces for Smelting Aluminum Ores: A Substitute for the Electrolytic Process?" *Journal of Metals*, 14(February 1962):126–8.

14   Subcommittee minutes for that meeting are in J. W. Dyer to G. T. Holmes, 31 May 1962, ALA.

15   P. T. Stroup to J. D. Harper, 20 July 1961, ALA. See also Van Horn Interview. Van Horn recalled that as soon as Alcan announced that they were pursuing an alternative to smelting that omitted the alumina step, "all the plants and the officers wanted to know what we were doing."

16   J. W. Dyer to G. T. Holmes, 31 May 1962, ALA.

17   J. W. Dyer to G. T. Holmes, "Minutes of Task Force on Potrooms," 10 June 1964, ALA. The Task Force on Potrooms had a two-day meeting at the Alcoa works. At that time Warren Haupin was the sole researcher working on Hall-Héroult problems, and he was working only half-time because of an illness that continued into 1965. The R&D Committee's "Technical Budget and Program for 1963" shows 1962 spending of $92,000 on Hall-Héroult and an initial 1963 budget of $110,000. That was crossed out and changed to $20,000, eliminating a six-part program related to current efficiency and optimum bath composition, except for consulting on those issues in the plants, and an entire program entitled "New Cell Design."

18   Quoted in "Minutes of the Meeting of October 10–11," G. T. Holmes to members of the Smelting Subcommittee, 17 October 1961, ALA.

19   Ibid.

20   G. T. Holmes to P. T. Stroup, 21 March 1962, ALA.

21   P. T. Stroup to G. T. Holmes, 4 April 1962, ALA.

22   G. T. Holmes, "New Hall Cell," 17 February 1963, and G. T. Holmes to members of the Smelting Subcommittee, 13 May 1963, ALA.

23   W. Haupin's work is discussed, and A. S. Russell is quoted, in Smelting Subcommittee minutes, in J. W. Dyer to G. T. Holmes, 10 June 1964, ALA.

24   B. H. Sloane to P. T. Stroup, 11 February 1964, and C. C. Cook, "Minutes of Meeting of Task Force on Potrooms, 25 and 26 February 1964," ALA.

25   C. C. Cook to members of the Task Force on Potrooms, 16 October 1970, ALA. G. T. Holmes to W. H. Krome George, 15 September 1965, ALA, warned that they were "near a critical point in manpower and money availability" and must begin to make choices. See also J. W. Dyer, "Minutes of the Smelting Subcommittee Meeting, October 7–8, 1965," 20 December 1965, ALA. Dyer recorded that "Mr. Holmes emphasized . . . the shortage of people throughout Alcoa, and particularly in the plants."

26   C. C. Cook to members of the Task Force on Potrooms, Smelting Subcommittee, 6 November 1969, ALA.

27   G. T. Holmes and J. R. Chapman, "Re: KWH Per Pound Versus Return on Investment," 5 July 1968, attached to J. W. Dyer to members of the Task Force on Potrooms, 29 July 1968, ALA. In the early 1970s, when the OPEC oil embargo altered energy costs radically, those conditions changed abruptly, but by then far better usage figures had been attained. On the Intalco smelter, see "Intalco: Highly Efficient Producer," *Light Metal Age*, 24(October 1966):10–12.

28   C. C. Cook to G. T. Holmes and A. S. Russell, 27 November 1962, ALA. Cook's report exhibited some of the limitations of the critical-path method when applied to a research project. He projected a target date for a prototype plant of February 1964, assuming they were at Event 8 on

the critical-path diagram. But he pointed out that previous steps had not been completed and that the steps were actually overlapping, not sequential, thus presumably invalidating the projected prototype date even as he set it.

29   G. T. Holmes to B. H. Sloane, 11 July 1963, ALA.

30   C. C. Cook, "Minutes of Meeting of the Task Force on Potrooms, June 29–30, 1966," ALA. That was the first meeting for which minutes of the discussion regarding development of the aluminum chloride process were typed on separate pages so that they could be distributed only on a need-to-know basis.

31   C. C. Cook, "Minutes of Meeting of the Task Force on Potrooms," June 29–30, 1966," ALA. Those minutes show that the Task Force on Potrooms decided at that point to leapfrog early 80,000-ampere versions of the bipolar cell at SPDL and focus on producing a 180,000-ampere version by the first quarter of 1967. On the see-through cell and other benefits to the Hall-Héroult process, see C. C. Cook to members of the Task Force on Potrooms and the Smelting Subcommittee, 14 May 1968 and 18 October 1968, and G. T. Holmes to members of the Smelting Subcommittee, 13 November 1967, ALA. Noel Jarrett reported to the committees that there was an increase in Hall-Héroult work during 1967. At the instigation of G. H. Traylor, chair of the Smelting Subcommittee, G. T. Holmes conducted a comparative evaluation of the aluminum chloride process and Hall-Héroult. He reported that the year's delay in moving up scale had been "well spent," and the outlook was good for both processes. As a result, the subcommittee solicited further ideas for Hall-Héroult process work.

32   "Minutes of the R&D Committee Meeting, November 24, 1965," transmitted in A. S. Russell and E. C. Hartmann to Kent Van Horn, 29 November 1965, ALA. The discussion at that meeting dealt with plans to expedite operating units in all possible ways. See also C. C. Cook to G. T. Holmes, 22 September 1969, ALA, reporting on a meeting with Russell, Jarrett, and Knapp, of the Smelting Division.

33   C. C. Cook to members of the Task Force on Potrooms and the Smelting Subcommittee, 18 October 1968, ALA, enclosing minutes of a meeting held 7–8 October.

33   C. C. Cook to members of the Task Force on Potrooms and the Smelting Subcommittee, 18 October 1968, ALA.

35   The 10-compartment cell was the next, intermediate-size version of the closed cell used in the aluminum chloride process. Its development answered a number of problems with the process design.

36   See C. C. Cook to members of the Task Force on Potrooms and the Smelting Subcommittee, 6 November 1969, ALA. Those meeting minutes show that Hall-Héroult work was being conducted in the plants and at ARL, where fundamental work was pushing ahead. See also L. L. Knapp, "Minutes of the Task Force on Potrooms," 19 March 1970, and C. C. Cook to A. S. Russell, 4 July 1970, ALA, which show that the task force was trying to redirect ARL back to ASP.

37   S. C. Jacobs to Noel Jarrett, 9 October 1973, and Jacobs, "Operational Results," 24 September 1973, ALA.

38   For problems at the pilot stage and the view that failure to seek outside advice in a timely fashion was a mistake, see interview with John Hatch,

former director of quality assurance and chief metallurgist for ingot and powder, Aluminum Company of America, by Margaret B. W. Graham, 7 January 1985. On the Alcan story, see "Alcan Pilots 2400/F Process Equipment," *Canadian Chemical Processing,* 51(February 1967):45–8, and "Recovery of Aluminum Is Tricky Step," *Canadian Chemical Processing,* 51(March 1967):75–8. Alcan had spent far more on its subhalide distillation process than Alcoa had. It is worth noting that the style of innovation management exhibited by Alcoa and Alcan during this period mirrored the approach that seems to have characterized many "blockbuster" projects of the period. Other cases of difficulty with "blockbuster" projects include DuPont's Kevlar and Eastman Kodak's disc camera. For Alcoa's later consultation with outside experts from the chemical industry, see Chapter 9, note 46.

39   G. T. Holmes to Noel Jarrett, C. C. Cook, L. K. King, and L. K. Hudson, 19 September 1975, ALA.

40   G. T. Holmes to C. Parry, 5 August 1975, ALA.

41   J. D. Dowd to K. R. Van Horn, 11 January 1962, ALA.

42   J. D. Dowd to K. R. Van Horn, 11 January 1962, ALA. At that time, Van Horn was still director of research, reporting to the vice-president for R&D, T. W. Bossert, and to the R&D Committee.

43   L. B. Sargent, Jr., to K. R. Van Horn, 12 January 1962, ALA.

44   F. J. Close, "The Steel Industry," 22 April 1964, ALA.

45   The episode of the Warrick plant, focusing on light-gauge sheet and providing the opportunity to install at short notice a number of new production technologies, offers an excellent example of the phenomenon Thomas Hughes has called "technological momentum." See Thomas P. Hughes, *Networks of Power: Electrification in Western Society, 1880–1930* (Baltimore: Johns Hopkins University Press, 1983), pp. 140–75. The pressure for productivity was especially high on Warrick because Alcoa had used a low-pricing strategy to compete with steel, pricing in anticipation of volume, with prices for can stock scaled well below those for regular aluminum sheet. See "Can Market Forces Basic Changes in Aluminum, Steel," *Iron Age* (5 March 1964):31–3.

46   Talk written by W. A. Woodburn for the Sheet, Plate and Foil Subcommittee presentation to the R&D Committee on April 19, 1966, forwarded in R. Couchman to H. J. Rowe, 21 April 1966, ALA. Interview with Robert E. Spear, former technical director, Alcoa Laboratories, by Bettye H. Pruitt and Margaret B. W. Graham, 30 June 1988 (hereafter cited as Spear Interview). According to R. T. Craig, "A.R.L. Horizontal (HDC) Casting Unit," 16 August 1960, ALA, ARL had a horizontal casting unit installed for experimental purposes in 1960. W. T. Ennor's last year in charge of casting research was 1958–9, and when Kenneth Brondyke took over, he quickly arranged to install experimental casting equipment. K. J. Brondyke to Subcommittee on Melting and Ingot Casting, 6 December 1960, ALA, shows that the original impetus for speedy adoption of horizontal DC casting came from publicity about the Reynolds installations of horizontal casting for extrusions in two of its plants. T. F. McCormick, "HDC Casting," 13 December 1960, ALA, shows that following that meeting, McCormick appointed a task group on HDC chaired by M. E. Gantz and including R. G. Hampel of AEDD and K. J. Brondyke of ARL. R. G. Hampel to R. W. Knapp, 30 January 1961, ALA, shows that

AEDD has been instructed to design and supply a production-scale HDC unit for Massena. M. E. Gantz, Jr., to Farquhar and N. Arbegast, 8 October 1963, ALA, lays out the concept of continuous casting, with several casting units, fed directly by molten metal, monitored by a control mechanism, and with the ingot produced conveyed mechanically to a stacking area.

47   M. E. Gantz, Jr., to R. N. Wagner, 3 February 1964, ALA. Wagner had raised the concern that they might not have explored steelmaking techniques vigorously enough, but Gantz argued that the priorities for aluminum production were different from those for steel – not so much on speed and productivity in the narrow sense as on scrap reduction and therefore rework reduction and metal recovery.

48   At that time, ingot casting came under the smelting side of the business; later it would move to the fabrication side of the business. According to Robert Spear, it was in a swing position and could go either way. Spear Interview.

49   On market pressures to bring Warrick on line, see H. J. Gersam, "Memorandum," 26 November 1963, ALA.

50   R. E. Spear and J. W. Foulke, "Methods for Producing Large Ingots," 20 December 1955, ALA, was a major progress report summarizing steps taken to modify the DC ingot-casting process to accommodate large-size ingots. The new method employed a peripheral distributor to allow flexibility in metal pouring and a wiper to remove water from the ingot surface below the mold. Further extensions of that technique resulted in the capability of casting extremely large ingots weighing over 40,000 pounds and measuring 50 inches diameter. See also John W. Alden, "Technical Highlights – 1961, Research and Development Committee," 11 October 1961, AA-Boyers, T. W. Bossert to W. E. King, 29 March 1949, ALA, and Spear Interview.

51   K. J. Brondyke, "Memo," 18 February 1964, and M. E. Gantz, Jr., to B. H. Sloane, 16 June 1964, ALA.

52   Ingot Manufacturing Department, "Continuous Casting Concepts," 20 February 1965, ALA.

53   Spear Interview.

54   H. J. Rowe, "R&D Committee Technical Highlights" for 1964, 1965, and 1966, ALA; W. A. Dean to E. C. Hartmann, 3 February 1964, ALA; M. E. Gantz, Jr., to T. F. McCormick, 30 June 1965, ALA.

55   R. E. Spear to K. J. Brondyke, 8 January 1968, ALA, reported on a conference in Brighton, England, showing that much fundamental work on mathematical modelling was taking place and that there was a good deal of competition for researchers in the area.

56   J. D. Dowd to L. B. Sargent, 27 October 1961, ALA.

57   E. C. Hartmann to W. A. Dean, 22 December 1961, ALA.

58   J. D. Dowd to L. B. Sargent, 9 April 1962, ALA. See Dowd's presentation to the Task Force on Automation in Rolling, 17 September 1962, ALA. On the transfer of the new lubricant system to the rolling mill at Alcoa, TN, see C. J. Walton to B. N. Peak, 6 April 1962, ALA, R. H. Brown to B. N. Peak, 9 April 1962, ALA, and T. R. Gauthier, "Memo," 15 October 1962, ALA. On Dowd's posting to Davenport, see Dowd to Sargent, 27 October 1961, ALA, and Dowd, "[Water-based Lubricant] Process at Dav-

enport," 6 November 1963, ALA. On Dean's struggle to create a subcommittee, see Dean to T. W. Bossert, "Job That Should Be Done on Subject of Rolling Aluminum," 24 November 1961, ALA, and Bossert's reply, 7 December 1961, ALA.

59 F. J. Close, "The Steel Industry," and Close, "Memo," 17 July 1964, ALA, which disclosed that John Hood would step down as chief metallurgist and would assist Close on a special project to coordinate a light-gauge-sheet expansion program.

60 R. P. Carter to Task Force on Water-Based Lubricants, 5 August 1966, ALA.

61 J. D. Dowd to Sheet, Plate and Foil Subcommittee members, 27 September 1965, minutes of August 17 meeting, ALA. For references to plant attitudes toward R&D-initiated projects, see E. C. Hartmann to W. A. Dean, 22 December 1961, ALA.

62 J. D. Dowd to J. Horne, 8 October 1965, ALA, discussed a meeting in Pittsburgh with ARL personnel to plan the expanded rolling program.

63 J. D. Dowd, R. Couchman, and R. S. Barker to W. A. Dean, 6 May 1963, ALA; R. Couchman to H. J. Rowe, 21 April 1966, ALA.

64 J. D. Dowd to members of Sheet, Plate and Foil Subcommittee, 1 July 1965, ALA, shows an entirely different situation from that discussed in correspondence between W. A. Dean and M. H. Brooks in May 1961. In 1961, ARL members were completely ignorant of rolling in practice, to the point that plant personnel saw no benefit in consulting them, whereas in 1965 they were giving seminars to plant personnel on rolling theory, having earned the respect of plant personnel.

65 J. D. Dowd to members of the Plate, Sheet and Foil Subcommittee, 1 July 1965, ALA.

66 Cliff Sands to S. J. Simmons, 20 September 1961, ALA. See also "Alcoa Aims Big Guns at Packaging Market," *Iron Age* (16 December 1965):117, in which Harper is quoted as saying "we want to [develop this market] by following our long-standing policy of working as suppliers to can manufacturers, not as competitors." See also "Master Marketing Plan, Can Sheet for Metal Cans," J. M. McKibbin to J. S. Hamilton, 6 March 1962, ALA.

67 In all, there were said to be eight different ways to make an aluminum can in the early 1960s, of which Alcoa was supporting research into at least five. See "Aluminum Takes Lid Off Can Goal," *Iron Age* (21 May 1965):45.

68 See, for example, "Steel and Aluminum Vie for Containers," *Business Week* (13 October 1962):62.

69 W. W. Nielson to T. R. Gauthier and C. F. Geisewitz, 16 March 1962, and R. Rolles to P. C. Althen, 16 March 1962, ALA; interview with J. Howard Dunn, former vice-president for R&D, Aluminum Company of America, by Margaret B. W. Graham, 4 August 1987 (hereafter cited as Dunn Interview); J. M. McKibbin to J. S. Hamilton, "Master Marketing Plan, Can Sheet for Metal Cans," 6 March 1962, ALA. McKibbin's memo indicates that in 1962, Alcoa was working on welded-seam technology, on data gathering for equipment development for coating coiled sheet, and on evaluating water-base lubricants that would meet FDA standards. They were marketing "Kold-Welded" ends to Minute Maid, but were

working on "Integral Rivet" easy-open ends as a replacement. APDL had developed a design for beer-can ends using lighter-gauge sheet, but that was on hold because Continental Can Company did not want to retool to adopt it until the aluminum can end had been accepted in the marketplace. Meanwhile, Alcoa was pursuing a request from Continental Can to develop fabricating practices for using Alclad sheet for cans.

70 "All Aluminum Beverage Cans Gain Popularity," *Iron Age* (21 August 1968):85; "The Can Is Lighter if Not the Brew," *Business Week* (10 July 1965):90–1.

71 J. A. Lake to P. C. Althen, 18 January and 2 September 1966, ALA, details successive progress reports on rigid containers. Both show that work continued on impact extrusion and wall iron can lines at AEDD, where they were developing equipment to support the can companies in their preferred methods.

72 Ellison L. Hazard to John D. Harper, 24 October 1964, ALA.

73 J. H. Alden to John Horne, 12 March 1964, ALA, announced that the informal group that had been meeting about can sheet would be formally constituted a Task Force on Can Sheet under the Sheet, Plate and Foil Subcommittee.

74 That was a big change from the strategy articulated in "Master Marketing Plan, Can Sheet for Metal Cans," J. M. McKibbin to J. S. Hamilton, 6 March 1962, ALA.

75 B. N. Peak to G. W. Shufelt, 6 May 1965 and 3 June 1965, ALA; B. N. Peak to W. F. Kneeland, 24 June 1966, ALA. Peak, quality assurance manager for the Warrick works, reported that 80,000 pounds of material had been rejected at Coors because of off-gauge problems. Peak was able to show that only three coils were off gauge, but there remained tool wear and cleaning problems. Through his contacts in the Packaging Institute, Philip Althen learned that users were reporting that Reynolds's product had had major rejections (300,000 pounds by American Can for excessive lubrication variation) and was showing microleakages through the can walls. See Wayne T. Chiappe (head of R&D, Continental Can Company) to Philip C. Althen, 3 January 1968, Althen to Chiappe, 10 January 1968, and W. C. Milz, "Memo," 13 July 1966, ALA. The Chiappe-Althen correspondence discussed taste problems arising from inadequate removal of lubricants from can-end stock. Milz, a member of the ARL technical staff who had visited Coors, reported that Alcoa's sheet performed worse than anybody else's because it was too clean and dry to draw well.

76 The quotation is from the task force's minutes, in E. T. Lenske to C. J. Walton, 23 August 1966, ALA. See also R. N. Wagner to R. O. Erickson, 4 March 1966, ALA. Wagner, a purchasing agent for Schlitz, complained at the progress of the project on the "Home Keg" for Schlitz beer that Alcoa was working to develop. To satisfy him, coatings, interior and exterior, and washing machines for the kegs all had to be developed in a very short time period. After visiting ARL in New Kensington, Wagner wrote: "It was also our opinion that the Alcoa personnel we talked to, while very knowledgeable and proficient in their own field, did not seem to be completely cohesive in pursuing a common goal in the time and manner that is absolutely necessary."

77 James J. Solomon to J. M. McKibbin, 7 June 1968, ALA. Solomon reported hearing from a reliable source of three separate developmental

programs for steel D&I cans. Two separate programs were still being pursued at the two different development divisions, APDL's Draw and Iron and AEDD's Impact Extrusion. A study group on impact and D&I cans formed in August to examine the relative merits of different container designs and to put together requests for appropriations for an entire in-house can-development effort.

78 P. C. Althen to J. A. Lake, 3 August 1966, ALA.

79 J. A. Lake to P. C. Althen, "Progress Report on Rigid Containers," 18 January 1966, ALA.

80 R. L. LaBarge to C. Sands, 3 September 1968, Sands to LaBarge, 9 September 1968, ALA. That correspondence contained an exchange about selling easy-open ends to captive can makers, who, LaBarge said, would not compete with Alcoa's existing large-can-company customers. Sands replied that Alcoa's capacity was already used up, and no relief in the form of additional capacity was planned to come on-stream until 1971.

81 James J. Rich to J. J. Solomon, 17 June 1968, ALA, contains the industry sales report concerning Anheuser-Busch.

82 J. J. Solomon to Cliff Sands, 5 July 1968, Sands to Solomon, 9 July 1968, ALA. Solomon warned: "They expect us to deliver limited volume of a production decorated or commercially finished can which will be filled and go through normal distribution channels for customer acceptance studies. They have made it clear that they will not accept less in evaluating whether they should produce an aluminum can."

83 Cliff Sands, "Statement of Policy," 22 July 1968, ALA.

84 K. R. Van Horn, "Aluminum Beer and Beverage Can Market," 25 November 1969, ALA. See also R. J. O'Brien to E. E. Rumberger and J. A. Lake, 15 September 1969, and O'Brien to W. W. Binger, 19 September 1969, ALA. That correspondence described the efforts of O'Brien, of APDL, to advance the position of the technical community that whereas the B-24 can line might be viewed "a necessary part of the marketing approach," it was very expensive, both in money and in manpower, and was "not a necessary technical expense required for the solution of this project." For the marketing side, see E. E. Rumberger, "Memorandum Re: Aluminum Beer and Beverage Can Market," 12 November 1969, ALA. On Alcan's "flatness capability," see J. S. Dowd to members of the Task Force on Water-based Lubricants, 4 March 1970, ALA.

85 J. J. Solomon to R. J. O'Brien, 30 April 1968, and J. A. Lake, APDL call report on 27 May 1968 visit to Anheuser-Busch, ALA.

86 K. R. Van Horn, "Aluminum Beer and Beverage Can Market," 25 November 1969, ALA.

87 E. E. Rumberger, "Memorandum Re: Aluminum Beer and Beverage Can Market," 12 November 1969, ALA. By 1971, J. A. Lake was projecting sale of an additional 154 million pounds of aluminum in the next five years attributable to the early completion of the can line. See J. A. Lake to Lloyd G. Dunn, "Re: B-24 Cans," 30 July 1971, ALA.

88 R. J. O'Brien, "Memo Re: Summary B-24 Lightweight Beer and Beverage Can Development," 19 November 1971, ALA.

89 Ibid.

90 W. E. Sicha to W. A. Dean, 28 April 1966, ALA. Sicha cited the VRC casting process and gave statistics for the huge tonnage of aluminum sold

in products made with the process – brake pistons, Ford rocker arms, and others. All this business, he argued, was created for Alcoa by the VRC process.

91 C. Sands, "Alcoa Capabilities," 19 November 1968, ALA. Sands was focusing on the amount Alcoa had contributed to the development of its customers' products and their unwillingness to pay any premium subsequently to Alcoa in the price of the sheet they purchased.

92 J. H. Dunn to W. W. Binger and R. L. LaBarge, 21 June 1968, ALA. Dunn suggested that APDL list aluminum radiators, D&I beer cans, and H-19 fin stock and that APDD list windows, low-rise bearing walls for buildings, and landing mats. He sent along a sample form for listing projects, with projected tonnage for each new product.

93 George E. Manners and Howard K. Nason, "The Decline in Industrial Research," *Research Management* (September 1978): 8–10; Margaret B. W. Graham, "Industrial Research in the Age of Big Science," in Richard S. Rosenbloom (ed.), *Research on Technological Innovation, Management, and Policy*, Vol. 2 (Greenwich, CT: JAI Press, 1985).

94 Heavily funded by government money, scientists in electronics and aeronautics firms often could run their own research programs much as they would have in universities, almost without reference to the preferences of the companies that employed them. The constituents they had to please were their peers in the scientific community and program officers for the government, not corporate operations or marketing managers. Alcoa researchers did not enjoy that kind of research autonomy at that time.

CHAPTER 9

1 Nathan Rosenberg, "A Historical Overview of the Evolution of Federal Investment in R&D since World War II," paper commissioned for a workshop on the federal role in research and development, 21–22 November 1985, summarizes the data and discusses their significance. See also George E. Manners and Howard K. Nason, "The Decline in Industrial Research – Causes and Cures," *Research Management* (September 1978):8–10. From 1966 to 1976, total U.S. spending for R&D was essentially static. The percentage of the research total performed by industry fell from over 60 percent to 40 percent. At the same time, the industry-funded portion of all basic research fell from 38 percent to 16 percent, while industry's portion of all applied research fell from 70 percent to 54 percent. Industry spending also shifted dramatically from research to development over that period, as the portion of all R&D spending devoted to research fell from 38 percent to 25 percent. See *National Patterns of R&D Resources: Funds and Manpower in the United States, 1953–1976*, National Science Foundation publication 76-310 (Washington, D.C.: NSF, 1977).

2 One example, and by no means an isolated example, of that behavior was RCA, previously the main company with a laboratory dedicated solely to electronics, which diversified into a range of service companies in the 1960s. See Margaret B. W. Graham, *RCA and the Videodisc: The Business of Research* (Cambridge University Press, 1986), pp. 104–9. There is an extensive literature on the trend toward diversification in the 1960s – the

so-called conglomerate movement. For a recent interpretation, see Louis Galambos and Joseph Pratt, *The Rise of the Corporate Commonwealth: United States Business and Public Policy in the 20th Century* (New York: Basic Books, 1988), pp. 158–71.

3 James Beizer, "Aluminum's New, Widening World," *Iron Age,* 198(3 November 1966):69. Before World War II, Alcan owned, wholly or in part, and operated smelters in six nations, including Japan, Norway, Britain, and Spain.

4 John D. Harper to J. W. Newsome, 17 September 1968, Alcoa Laboratories Archives, Alcoa Technical Center, Alcoa Center, PA (hereafter cited as ALA).

5 Quoted in Beizer, "Aluminum's New, Widening World," p. 75.

6 In the intensive self-examination that Alcoa Laboratories managers underwent between 1981 and 1983, they viewed the prevailing logic of much of the R&D program of the past decade as essentially "cashing in" on investments in technology rather than avoiding technological obsolescence. Robert Spear pointed out that although Alcoa had been doing a lot to keep the entire aluminum industry from complete obsolescence, all of the major processes were substantially the same as they had been since World War II. "Technological Obsolescence," Alcoa Laboratories' *Lab Log,* 7(April–May 1983):10. See also "New Roles, New Goals and a Sense of History," Alcoa Laboratories' *Lab Log,* 5(September–October 1981):2–6. On Alcoa's share of aluminum R&D, see Philip Farin et al., *Aluminum: Profile of an Industry* (New York: Metals Week, 1969), pp. 160–70.

7 On Pechiney R&D and achievements, see *One Hundred Years of Aluminum,* special issue of *La Technique Moderne,* 5–6(1986):12, 23, 73.

8 For example, Japanese aluminum producers applied the electronic controls they had developed for steel to modernization of aluminum production in the late 1970s and early 1980s. See "The World's Fastest Rolling Mills," *Esso Oilways International,* 30(1984):29–34, S. Echigo, H. Nagakura, K. Hayakawa, T. Miyanaga, T. Inoue, Y. Urakami, and T. Sakai, "Distributed Control System for Aluminum Hot Strip Mill at Nikko Works," *Furakawa Electrical Review,* 73(November 1981):121–34, K. Matsumiya, H. Ohshima, S. Kitagawa, M. Shimomura, and N. Tomimoto, "Automatic Flatness Control System for Aluminum Foil Rolling Mill," *Kobe Research Division Report,* 35(July 1985):115–17. They were also early to develop flexible manufacturing systems capable of producing a large range of fabricated products. See "Innovate Production Now: FMF (Flexible Manufacturing Factory) for Architectural Aluminum Materials," *Japanese Industrial Technology Bulletin,* 13(February 1986):2–4.

9 "Why Aluminum's Recovery Is only Temporary," *Business Week* (12 April 1976):76.

10 Interview with Eric A. Walker, former director and vice-president for science and technology, Aluminum Company of America, by Margaret B. W. Graham, 10 March 1985 (hereafter cited as Walker Interview). Walker stressed that new metals or other small-volume opportunities were viewed as trivia, not worthy of attention by Alcoa corporate managers of the 1960s and 1970s.

11 Facts on the moves and later reorganization are found in L. L. Grubb to Albert T. Jondro, 24 June 1970, A. S. Russell to J. W. Newsome, 23 April 1973, and R. G. Hampel to J. W. Newsome, 23 April 1973, ALA. See also

interviews with Elbert Howarth, former associate director of the Alcoa Technical Center, by Margaret B. W. Graham, 10 November 1984 and 5 September 1985 (hereafter cited as Howarth Interview).

12   On closing down Cleveland research, Van Horn recalled, "it killed me to shut it down. Harper was on my back." Interview with Kent R. Van Horn, former vice-president for research and development, Aluminum Company of America, by George D. Smith and Margaret B. W. Graham, June 1984 (hereafter cited as Van Horn Interview). See also interview with Walter A. Dean, former assistant director of research, Aluminum Company of America, by Margaret B. W. Graham, March 1985 (hereafter cited as Dean Interview). For more details about the consolidation and the clashes in style between the research and development organizations after they began to inhabit the same site, see Howarth Interview.

13   Van Horn Interview.

14   E. A. Walker and J. H. Dunn, "R&D Organization," 23 April 1973, ALA.

15   J. D. Harper to J. W. Newsome, 17 September 1968, ALA.

16   Interview with John Hatch, former quality assurance manager and chief metallurgist for ingot and powder, Aluminum Company of America, by Margaret B. W. Graham, 7 January 1985 (hereafter cited as Hatch Interview), who stressed that the postwar environment in New Kensington was especially problematic for innovation because of restrictive work rules limiting, among other things, the size of ingot that could be poured. Davenport, on the other hand, was, in Hatch's experience, a wonderful developmental plant because the work force was so much more technically involved. Information concerning lubricant formulations is from an interview with Joe Laemmle, senior technical supervisor, Fabricating Technology Division, Alcoa Laboratories, by Margaret B. W. Graham, 5 April 1984.

17   The meetings were recorded by J. H. Dunn, "Memorandum," 10 March 1969, ALA.

18   L. K. Hudson to R. J. O'Brien, 5 February 1970, and J. H. Dunn and T. R. Gauthier to J. W. Newsome and R. G. Hampel, 2 November 1970, ALA, give details of the Project Evaluation System. The new categories for R&D expenditures were Primary Products (Raw Materials, Refining, Chemicals, Smelting, Ingot Production, Powders and Pigments) and Mill Products (Product and Industry). For the auto-body-sheet program, see William F. Lewis, "The Alcoa Automotive Body Sheet Program," July 1971, and R. G. Hampel to M. E. Gantz, Jr., "Re: Auto Body Sheet," 22 September 1976, ALA. The former explains the plan to concentrate on selling General Motors and Ford, noting that the auto companies expect to have aluminum at a cost competitive with steel if they are to adopt it. The latter reports on a project team headed by James Dowd that reported on such matters as improved alloys, recycling, materials, energy, producibility, formability, strength, joining, finishing, repairability, and marketability. In both cases the aim was to develop alloy systems that would replace steel primarily on a price basis, but in the second, aluminum's unique and superior performance qualities were to be taken into account.

19   "How Alcoa Sweetens Its Success," Business Week (18 January 1969):46.

20   J. H. Dunn and J. W. Newsome, "Memorandum," 5 June 1969, ALA.

21   H. Y. Hunsicker to Dr. J. L. Brandt et al., 24 April 1969, ALA.

22   Dunn and Newsome, "Memorandum," 5 June 1969, and H. Y. Hunsicker to A. S. Russell, 19 August 1969, ALA; interview with H. Y. Hunsicker, former technical advisor, Alcoa Laboratories, by Margaret B. W. Graham, 9 January 1985 (hereafter cited as Hunsicker Interview).

23   Newsome is quoted in minutes of the meeting, in John King to members of the Future Planning Committee, 27 January 1966, ALA. See also E. M. Strauss to members of the Future Planning Committee, 9 September 1966, ALA.

24   W. F. Lewis to R. J. O'Brien, 18 February 1970, ALA. Dunn's remarks are from Dunn to Van Horn, 5 March 1969, ALA; the ranking of reform objectives at the 1969 R&D managers' meeting is given in Dunn, "Memorandum," 10 March 1969, ALA.

25   "He Was Graduated from the Halls of Ivy to Big Business," *Chemical Week* (21 October 1970):104; Walker Interview.

26   Walker Interview. See also announcements of his appointment, in John D. Harper to J. W. Newsome, 29 June 1970, and Harper to Newsome, 1 July 1970, ALA. During the first few months of 1970, Walker received a crash course in Alcoa's diverse operations. His agenda for a trip to East St. Louis, including seven half-hour lectures on refining and related research, then an hour-and-a-half tour of the ESL laboratory, is described in L. K. Hudson to A. S. Russell, 9 January 1970, ALA.

27   Walker to J. H. Dunn, 18 May 1971, and Walker to J. H. Dunn, R. G. Hampel, and J. W. Newsome, 25 May 1971, ALA. See also C. J. Walton to J. W. Newsome, 5 April 1971, and J. W. Clark to Newsome, 30 July 1971, ALA. Walker also asked for proposals for research that Alcoa would like to see conducted in universities. He recommended that those who were charged with contact with the universities be not more than 10 years out of university themselves, a stipulation that was unpopular because many of the older people were more appropriate choices to follow the work. On Walker's mandate, see J. D. Harper to staff meeting attendees, 17 February 1971, ALA; Walker Interview.

28   J. W. Newsome to J. H. Dunn, 15 April 1971, ALA, conveys the list of project areas, including exploration, alumina and related chemical products, refining, smelting, alloy development, melting practices and molten-metal quality, dynamic solidification of aluminum alloys, deformation of aluminum alloys, aluminum powder and pigment products, quality-control methods (analytical, mechanical property, nondestructive testing, x-ray, etc.), finishing of aluminum products, anodic coatings (oxide films), mechanisms of corrosion processes, durability of aluminum products, and electrical conductors. On the request for "half-baked ideas" and others, see J. L. Evankovich to E. A. Walker, 25 January 1971, and the reply, 1 February 1971, ALA.

29   Walker to Newsome, paraphrased in Newsome to Dunn, 15 April 1971, ALA.

30   Newsome to Dunn, 15 April 1971, ALA; Walker to members of the Corporate R&D Committee, 5 October 1972, Alcoa Archives, Alcoa Records Storage Center, Boyers, PA (hereafter cited as AA-Boyers); Walker Interview. E. S. Howarth to J. G. Kaufman et al., 21 June 1971, ALA, includes a request for proposals for DFR from ARL division chiefs and department heads, the work to be funded by money added to the research budget for that purpose. Howarth also noted remarks by Walker

to the effect that the funding for such research would be increased again in 1972.

31   For a positive view of the functioning of the subcommittee system and its evolution in that period, see Hatch Interview; for more political perspective, see interviews with Keith Turnbull by George D. Smith and Davis Dyer, July 1983, and by George D. Smith and Margaret B. W. Graham, November 1984 (hereafter cited as Turnbull Interviews 1 & 2), and interview with Peter Bridenbaugh by Margaret B. W. Graham, May 1983 (hereafter cited as Bridenbaugh Interview). Bridenbaugh recalled that a rolling-mill project at Warrick was made considerably easier for him because the works production manager, knowing of his occasional returns to the Laboratories to attend subcommittee meetings that also included Fred Resch (manager in charge of mill-products manufacturing), mistakenly concluded that Bridenbaugh had a direct line to Resch.

32   W. H. Krome George, "R&D Committee Organization," 1 May 1972, and J. W. Newsome to ARL assistant directors and budget-makers, 1 September 1972, AA-Boyers. P. Bridenbaugh recalled that Walker also made significant amounts of money available in discretionary funds for in-plant R&D projects, including one that Bridenbaugh had at his disposal when he was working on rolling-mill productivity projects at Warrick in the early 1970s. Bridenbaugh Interview.

33   R&D expenditure figures are from R. E. Spear to P. R. Bridenbaugh et al., "Population and Budget History," 15 December 1987, ALA, and Earl G. Huber to A. S. Russell, "Relation of Technical Budget Expenditures to Consolidated Net Revenues and Operating Margin, 1957–79," 10 April 1979, AA-Boyers.

34   J. W. Newsome to ARL directors and budget-makers, 1 September 1972, AA-Boyers.

35   J. Harper to J. W. Newsome, 24 July 1970, ALA.

36   "How to Get Extra Return on R&D," *Chemical Week* (15 March 1972):37; "Expertise for Sale," *Wall Street Journal* (12 June 1972). The Van Horn Interview indicated that the decision to sell Alcoa's technology came from the top, a statement corroborated by former Alcoa patent attorney Edward B. Foote, interviewed by Margaret B. W. Graham, 17 June 1985 (hereafter cited as Foote Interview).

37   J. D. Harper to J. W. Newsome, 24 July 1970, ALA. On Anaconda's growth on the eve of that announcement, see Farin et al., *Aluminum: Profile of an Industry*, p. 30.

38   J. Dunn to W. W. Binger, 15 April 1969, AA-Boyers. The Sales Department point of view was expressed in Peter Broockmen to S. J. Simmons, Jr., 4 October 1967, AA-Boyers. Also see D. M. Naser to K. Van Horn, 22 August 1969, AA-Boyers, for opposition to licensing of filtering and degassing processes for ingot casting: "From a commercial standpoint, it seems far more advisable to regain our research and development investment through revenues on a share of ingot sales rather than outright sale of the technology."

39   J. H. Dunn to E. C. Hartmann, 12 February 1968, AA-Boyers. On the questionnaire, see K. R. Van Horn to J. H. Dunn, E. C. Hartmann, A. H. Schmeltz, and R. N. Wagner, 13 March 1968, and P. T. Stroup to K. R. Van Horn, 27 May 1968, AA-Boyers. Dunn's tabulation showed that the numbers of patents granted to Reynolds, Kaiser, and Alcoa in 1965 were

31, 22, and 8, respectively; the figures for 1967 were 33, 16, and 12 (Dunn to Hartmann, 12 February 1968).

40   C. F. Billhardt to W. L. Crawford, 5 October 1970, K. J. Brondyke, "Processes and Know-How," 8 October 1970, and R. G. Hampel to R. W. Callahan, 8 October 1970, ALA.

41   J. D. Harper to Eric Walker, 9 October 1970, ALA.

42   Noel Jarrett to A. S. Russell, 17 December 1970, J. W. Clark to E. S. Howarth, 21 January 1971, E. S. Howarth to J. W. Newsome, 25 January 1971, ALA. See also Billhardt to Crawford, 5 October 1970, and Hampel to Callahan, 8 October 1970, ALA.

43   R. G. Hampel to Task Force on Sale of Know-How, 15 October 1971, ALA. See also J. W. Newsome to ARL directors, division chiefs, and department heads, 3 March 1971, E. A. Walker to J. W. Newsome, 12 July 1971, and Verne C. Koch to D. J. George, 13 August 1971, ALA.

44   J. H. Dunn to J. D. Harper and W. H. Krome George, 18 December 1970 and 10 November 1971, and J. D. Harper, "Patent Policy and Patent Committee," 17 November 1971, AA-Boyers.

45   E. A. Walker to Task Force on Sale of Know-How, 7 January 1972 and 7 February 1972, ALA. On TMD revenues, see S. A. Earnest, "Memorandum," 10 October 1974, and E. C. Lighthiser to Roger C. Sharp, 19 December 1975 and 23 December 1976, ALA.

46   W. H. Krome George to E. A. Walker, 11 September 1973, and Noel Jarrett to J. W. Newsome et al., 10 October 1973, ALA. The group known as the "Ad Hoc Group on Lummus" disbanded in September 1975 when the ASP Subcommittee was established under the chairmanship of G. T. Holmes. R. G. Hampel, "Smelting Research and Development," 3 September 1975, AA-Boyers.

47   W. H. Krome George to Noel Jarrett, 4 September 1974, ALA. In announcing the new assignment for TMD, George stated that "the rapid advancement of technology and the need to concentrate our R&D efforts indicate that there will be an acceleration of this type of activity."

48   W. H. Krome George, "Memo," 22 March 1974, AA-Boyers.

49   W. C. Woodward to L. P. Favorite, 24 April 1963, ALA; Bettye H. Pruitt, conversation with D. J. George, R&D contracts manager, Alcoa Laboratories; Hunsicker Interview.

50   E. A. Walker to F. L. Abernathy et al., 12 August 1971, ALA; J. H. Dunn to members of the R&D Committee, 18 August 1971, ALA. For the characteristics of "big science" in the postwar era, see Margaret B. W. Graham, "Industrial Research in the Age of Big Science," in Richard S. Rosenbloom, (ed.), *Research on Technological Innovation, Management, and Policy,* Vol. 2 (Greenwich, CT: JAI Press, 1986); pp. 47–97.

51   E. A. Walker to F. L. Abernathy et al., 12 August 1971, ALA.

52   Bridenbaugh Interview. Government R&D work posed similar issues for other companies. See "Review of Industrial Innovation Urged," *Chemical and Engineering News* (27 February 1978):18–19. In an unusual joint Senate-House hearing at the AAAS meeting held to explore how lagging R&D investment by industry was affecting the U.S. economy, Bruce Hannay of Bell Laboratories pointed out that the government policy requiring free availability of patents arising out of contract R&D benefited no one. In the absence of an exclusive license, he explained, "what belongs to everyone is usually of interest to nobody." On the requirements for de-

fense contractors, see *Technology Transfer between Air Force Contractors,* report of the COCAM Committee of the Manufacturing Studies Board, National Research Council (Washington, D.C.: NRC, 1979).

53 W. H. Krome George's election to the position of president at Alcoa was treated by the news media as selection of a technical person, but despite George's chemical engineering background, his first love was the financial and accounting aspects of the business: "Alcoa Puts an Engineer on Top," *Chemical Week* (1 July 1970):15. For his changes in the subcommittee system and its control of R&D resource allocation, see W. H. Krome George to staff meeting attendees, 22 September 1975, AA-Boyers. By 1978, R&D expenses would be allocated directly by the business units. For practice in other companies, see George E. Manners and Howard K. Nason, "The Decline in Industrial Research," p. 8. Over 40 percent of the member firms of the Industrial Research Institute in 1976 reported having a top-level R&D policy committee, which, it was stated, was a "virtually non-existent practice as recently as 10 years ago." See also David M. Kiefer, "New Challenges Facing Industrial Research," *Chemical and Engineering News* (15 December 1975):38–45. Kiefer referred to the trend toward strategic emphasis on R&D and the closer ties between research and the operating arms of companies such as Celanese, Rohm and Haas, and Diamond Shamrock.

54 W. H. Krome George to staff meeting attendees, 22 September 1975, Huber to A. S. Russell, "Relation of Technical Budget Expenditures to Consolidated Net Revenues and Operating Margin, 1957–79," 10 April 1979, and Spear to Bridenbaugh et al., "Population and Budget History," AA-Boyers. R&D spending continued to grow in dollar amounts, but in real terms it leveled off, and in relation to corporate revenues it declined steadily until 1980. See Figures 9.6, 9.7, and 9.10.

55 W. H. Krome George to staff meeting attendees, 22 September 1975, AA-Boyers. On the problems cited by other companies, see Manners and Nason, "The Decline in Industrial Research," pp. 9–10, and Kiefer, "New Challenges Facing Industrial Research," p. 38.

56 W. C. Woodward, "R&D Subcommittees," 12 February 1976, R. G. Hampel to subcommittee chairmen and secretaries, 17 February 1976, and Hampel, "Operation Plan for Subcommittee System," 4 March 1976, AA-Boyers. Other sources were the Hatch and Hunsicker Interviews.

57 R. G. Hampel, "Operation Plan for Subcommittee System," 4 March 1976, AA-Boyers.

58 R. G. Hampel, "Committee on Corporate R&D Projects," 16 June 1978, AA-Boyers.

59 R. A. Kochera and M. M. Ball to N. W. Nielsen, 11 November 1977, ALA.

60 Interview with Robert E. Spear and James D. Dowd, former technical director for fabricating R&D, Alcoa Laboratories, by Margaret B. W. Graham and Bettye H. Pruitt, 26 May 1988 (hereafter cited as Spear-Dowd Interview). Perhaps the most significant change took place when the decision was made no longer to have R&D personnel chair subcommittees in the early 1980s. The R&D people remember that as forgoing what had become a heavy administrative burden for a technical staff spread too thinly. According to Keith Turnbull, however, that change reflected a serious loss of confidence in the leadership capability of Alcoa's technical community. G. K. Turnbull to C. K. Ligon, "Re: Russ Ackoff Visit – 1983 May 24," 16 May 1983, AA-Boyers.

61   J. G. Kaufman to Norm Cochran, July 1977, ALA.

62   R. G. Hampel, "Technical Development Department," 5 June 1980, AA-Boyers. In a letter to the authors dated 21 July 1985, R. G. Hampel noted that one of the activities he had pushed that had been successful, after disappointing beginnings, was systematic technology assessment. In 1976 a Technology Assessment and Forecasting Study Group was formed comprising R. G. Hampel, R. C. Hatfield, and F. J. Resch. It used cold-rolling technology as a test effort, comparing Alcoa's Flat Rolled Products facilities with those of its competitors and with the best practice in steel. A year-long study culminated in a report that established reliable benchmarks against which to measure Alcoa's further improvements in rolling. See J. R. Archibald to T. I. Stephenson et al., "Re: Technology Assessment and Forecasting Study Group," 13 October 1976, ALA, asking plant cooperation in data gathering, and James D. Dowd to Steering Committee (Fetterolf, Hampel, and Hatfield), "Re: Cold Rolling Technology Assessment," 23 February 1978, ALA, forwarding the final report and recommending a coordinated effort to follow up on the opportunity for major improvement that it presented. Another activity that took a longer time to bear fruit was the New Ventures Task Force, composed of Charles Ligon, Paul Abernathy, and Peter Bridenbaugh, which concerned itself with the type of diversification Alcoa should be pursuing. Though its main function seemed to be to delay closure on the subject of diversification, the task force served as a vehicle through which the technical community represented by Bridenbaugh could convince the rest of the company that technical relatedness was an important strategic principle for Alcoa to keep in mind when diversifying. That may have had some influence on Krome George, leading him to bound Alcoa's diversification, saying that "we want no bluejeans factories in Taiwan." Bridenbaugh Interview.

63   M. E. Gantz, Jr., "Technical Policy Committee," 29 July 1982, and C. P. Yohn to members of S/C Corporate R&D, 2 November 1982, AA-Boyers. The subcommittee, said Gantz, "should at least 'plant some stakes' which can be used as a guide for long range diversification."

64   Robert Spear, former technical director for castings R&D, interview with Margaret B. W. Graham and Bettye H. Pruitt, 30 June 1988; Spear-Dowd Interview.

65   Spear-Dowd Interview; William B. Renner, "Technical Planning – Major Projects Search," 6 August 1979, AA-Boyers. It was during that period that Renner and others in senior management took a look at succession planning for the technical community and sent a few key second-tier technical managers to broaden their exposure to other parts of Alcoa. G. K. Turnbull went to Pittsburgh in Planning, W. Sleppy went to Alcoa's Australian operations, and P. R. Bridenbaugh went to Alcoa, Tennessee, as manager of quality assurance.

66   Interview with Allen S. Russell by Margaret B. W. Graham, 8 January 1985 (hereafter cited as Russell Interview); C. P. Yohn, "Five-Year Summary and Assessment of R&D Major Accomplishment Evaluations," 14 August 1981, and "Environmental Goals and Objectives," 1982, AA-Boyers. See also R. E. Spear, "Memo," 3 February 1970, ALA, which includes subcommittee minutes indicating that in response to growing pressure from state governments for pollution control, the Arnold casting facility was working on skim reclamation technologies and improved burners and remelt furnaces.

67 "New Products and Processes, Better Fundamental Understanding and No Illusions about the Technical Challenges to Get Us There," Alcoa Laboratories' *Lab Log,* 7(February 1983):4. The controversy surrounding the "Mature Industry" research concept shows up even in the sanitized minutes of the subcommittee meetings of the mid-1970s. To researchers in the RCS program who had unfunded projects with payoffs expected in the range of two to five years, the mature-industry forecast and its consequences for Alcoa's competitive outlook in RCS were disheartening and frightening. A concluding comment on the "critical 2–5 year period" warned that "all competition is working to get where we are – we should address the problem of maintaining or improving market positions over next *several* years through research." J. K. McBride memo, "Re: Subcommittee on Alloy Development Task Force B – RCS Alloys, Minutes of June 15, 1976 Meeting," 23 July 1976, ALA.

68 Alcoa Laboratories' *Lab Log* coverage at the time showed how much the reorganization efforts at the Laboratories were viewed with suspicion as the centrally imposed and bureaucratic measures of nontechnical managers who might be putting new emphasis on technology as a strategic imperative, but were not viewed as effective managers of technology. See "Brondyke Responds to Lab Alcoans' Questions," special issue of *Lab Log* (reports on 10 April 1981 speech by K. Brondyke), and Spear-Dowd Interview. G. K. Turnbull noted in 1983 that the past three vice-presidents for science and technology had all had marketing and production backgrounds and that that tended to create a climate that precluded major business enhancement through technology. G. K. Turnbull to C. K. Ligon "Re: Russ Ackoff Visit – 1983 May 24," 16 May 1983, AA-Boyers.

69 A. S. Russell to T. H. Kerry, 17 August 1976, ALA.

70 A. S. Russell to C. F. Fetterolf, 19 November 1976, ALA. The minutes of the Alloy Development Subcommittee of 15 June 1976 show that Brondyke was understating the case: People were very upset at the opportunities being forgone because of the mature-market assumptions on which the 1977 budget was supposed to be based. J. K. McBride memo, "Re: Subcommittee on Alloy Development Task Force B – RCS Alloys, Minutes of June 15, 1976 Meeting," 23 July 1976, ALA.

71 Hampel to Edwin Mansfield, 21 November 1977, ALA.

72 Manners and Nason, "The Decline in Industrial Research," pp. 9–10.

73 R. G. Hampel to J. A. McGowan, AA-Boyers, which reported that current planning indicated it would be desirable to have a commercial plant ready for operation in 1980. What was proposed, therefore, was a demonstration plant constructed on a schedule that would allow for no mistakes in technical matters, decision making, or construction.

74 "Subcommittee on Primary Metals," 4 November 1975, AA-Boyers; Noel Jarrett to members of the ASP Subcommittee, 17 November 1975, ALA.

75 Interview with W. H. Krome George, former chairman and CEO, Alcoa, by George David Smith and Margaret B. W. Graham, 28–29 August 1983.

76 G. T. Holmes to C. W. Parry, 5 August 1975, ALA.

77 Noel Jarrett to M. H. Brown et al., 15 April 1974, ALA; M. J. Bruno, "Re: 14B219 Budget," 31 October 1977, shows that the Federal Energy Research and Development Agency (ERDA) contracted to fund 67 percent of this research in the first year.

78 C. F. Fetterolf, "Subcommittee on ASP Task Force Structure"; Noel Jarrett, minutes of ASP Subcommittee meeting, 20 June 1979, and C. C. Cook, minutes of ASP Subcommittee meetings, 22–23 January 1980, 24–25 April 1980, 14–15 July 1980, 2 March 1981, 13 July 1981, and 7 January 1982, AA-Boyers.

79 R. J. Ormesher to R. J. Logan, 8 October 1969, and B. Thompson to R. E. Spear, 10 March 1969, ALA. Thompson reported the first operation of a recycling unit at Arnold capable of continuous metal circulation.

80 Spear Interview, and "A Visionary with Strong Links to Alcoa's Technological History," *Lab Log* (June–July 1985):12–14.

81 The minutes of the subcommittee for corporate R&D (C. P. Yohn to members of the Subcommittee for Corporate R&D, 2 November 1982, ALA) show that there was a strong faction in favor of looking to outside consultants to generate ideas for long-range R&D. For an account of the Broner mill-control installations, based on interviews of R. J. Ebert, R. Fanning, D. Nolan, J. Sanders, F. Stewart, and M. D. Waltz, see Margaret B. W. Graham, "The Broner Mill Control: Technology Transfer between Multiple Plant Sites," manuscript, ALA. See also J. C. Sanders to Dr. G. K. Turnbull, "Re: Cost Breakdown on Broner Control Work," 31 July 1983, and Richard J. Ebert to H. R. Powers amd D. H. Levisay, "Re: Transfer of . . . Technology to Warrick and Davenport Continuous Hot Mills," 22 September 1982, ALA. By January 1983 it was reported that a total investment of just under $1.2 million had realized savings of $5.4 million per year.

82 R. A. Kelsey to P. A. Haas, 15 September 1981, AA-Boyers.

83 Data on levels of contract work were supplied by D. J. George, R&D contracts manager, Alcoa Laboratories. On the effort to build relationships with contracting agencies, see G. Barthold, "Government Market Development Profile," 18 December 1974, and J. H. Dunn "Government R&D Contracts," 3 June 1974, ALA.

84 J. W. Evancho to A. C. Sheldon, 16 January 1981, AA-Boyers.

85 On the navy's support of alloy development, see Chapter 10. On the work for the air force, see F. R. Billman to P. A. Haas, 18 September 1981, AA-Boyers.

86 Yohn, "Five-Year Summary," 14 August 1981.

87 C. F. Fetterolf to W. B. Renner, 27 March 1981, ALA; Alcoa organization charts, AA, env. 1059.

88 Yohn's presentations to the committee are found in Roger Haddon, "R&D Budgeting and Planning through the Subcommittee System," 12 May 1980, AA-Boyers, and J. W. Evancho to members of the Subcommittee for Corporate R&D, 12 February 1982, ALA. Yohn reported that between 1980 and 1982 Alcoa's R&D portfolio had moved in the prescribed direction: support for existing businesses and new process development down, work on new products and new ventures up.

89 A. C. Sheldon to members of the Technical Policy Committee, 5 February 1981, AA-Boyers. Slagle broadcast his message outside the committee via memos: Robert F. Slagle to W. B. Renner et al., 15 October 1980, and "Technology Sharing in the Aluminum Industry," 13 February 1982, AA-Boyers.

90 "OVA: Alcoa's Introspection," *Lab Log* (June–July 1982). Although handled with far more consultation than the abrupt 1962 layoff had been, OVA still had devastating effects on Laboratory morale.

91 *Lab Log,* 6(January 1982), *Lab Log,* 6(March 1982), and reorganization special issue of *Lab Log* (undated).

92 *Lab Log* reorganization special issue. The technical directors were Noel Jarrett for chemical engineering R&D, James Dowd for fabricating R&D, and Robert Spear for casting R&D.

93 W. H. Krome George and Charles W. Parry, *Responses to a Changing World,* Alcoa annual report for 1982 (February 17 1983), pp. 9, 17.

94 Charles W. Parry, "New Directions in Aluminum Research," *Journal of Metals,* 35(May 1983):47.

95 On the mature-market mentality, see David Olive, "Alcan's Still Tops in Aluminum, but the Heat's on from R&D-Happy American Producers," *Canadian Business,* 57(January 1984):19, in which Alcoa's president, Fetterolf, is quoted as saying that "after aluminum replaced steel in the U.S. Beverage can market in the 1970s, we somehow let ourselves think we'd found every practical use for aluminum. Lately we've realized that aluminum is still a wonder metal and that we've many more mountains to climb." The words were encouraging for advocates of a more aggressive technical posture, but the reality was much harder to achieve.

CHAPTER 10

1 Robert R. Irving, "It's Time for a Change in Aircraft Materials," *Iron Age,* 217(29 March 1976):33–8; J. T. Staley, "Threats to the Continued Use of Aluminum in the Aerospace Industry," 7 January 1977, Alcoa Laboratories Archives, Alcoa Technical Center, Alcoa Center, PA (hereafter cited as ALA).

2 E. H. Dix, Jr., "Aluminum-Zinc-Magnesium Alloys; Their Development and Commercial Production," the 1949 Edward De Mille Campbell Memorial Lecture, *Transactions of the American Society for Metals,* 42(1950):1124.

3 Interview with Edwin H. Spuhler, former manager for applications engineering, Aluminum Company of America, by Bettye H. Pruitt, 20 March 1984 (hereafter cited as Spuhler Interview); interview with Harold Hunsicker, former technical advisor, Alloy Technology Division, Alcoa Laboratories, by Margaret B. W. Graham, 9 January 1985 (hereafter cited as Hunsicker Interview).

4 Hunsicker Interview.

5 Variations in temperature and timing during the processes of heat treatment, quenching, and age hardening that produce high-strength alloys result in metals of different "tempers" – that is, with different final properties. For the T73 temper, the age-hardening process is accelerated by a slight increase in temperature, and it is allowed to continue *beyond* the point at which the alloy achieves maximum strength, in order to create maximum resistance to SCC. For a more complete discussion of these issues, see Bettye H. Pruitt and George D. Smith, "The Corporate Management of Innovation: Alcoa Research, Aircraft Alloys, and the Problem of Stress-Corrosion Cracking," in Richard S. Rosenbloom (ed.), *Research on Technological Innovation, Management and Policy,* Vol. 3 (Greenwich, CT: JAI Press, 1986), pp. 50–4.

6 J. T. Staley, "History of Wrought Aluminum Alloy Development," manuscript, ALA, pp. 17–18.

7   H. Y. Hunsicker and H. C. Stumpf, "History of Precipitation Harden-
    ing," in Cyril S. Smith (ed.), *The Sorby Centennial Symposium on the History of
    Metallurgy* (New York: Gordon & Breach, 1965), pp. 306–7.
8   Interview with Kent R. Van Horn, former vice-president for research
    and development, Aluminum Company of America, by George D. Smith
    and Margaret B. W. Graham, June 1984 (hereafter cited as Van Horn
    Interview), interview with Robert E. Spear, former technical director for
    casting R&D, Alcoa Laboratories, by Bettye H. Pruitt and Margaret B. W.
    Graham, 30 June 1988 (hereafter cited as Spear Interview), and inter-
    view with Walter A. Dean, former assistant director of research, Alumi-
    num Company of America, by Margaret B. W. Graham, March 1985
    (hereafter cited as Dean Interview).
9   A more detailed account of the development of these alloys can be found
    in Pruitt and Smith, "Corporate Management of Innovation, pp. 62–76.
10 Spear Interview.
11 Schmidt to Aerospace Industries Association of America, Inc., 19 March
    1974, copy in Alcoa Archives, Records Storage Center, Boyers, PA (here-
    after cited as AA-Boyers).
12 Harold Hunsicker to Margaret B. W. Graham, 10 January 1985, and
    J. T. Staley to G. Barthold, 29 November 1971, ALA; J. T. Staley, "Pro-
    posal to Develop an Al-Mg-Li Alloy for High Performance Aircraft," 4
    May 1972, ALA; J. W. Evancho, "Development of An Al-Mg-Li Alloy,"
    final report, Naval Air Development Center contract N62269-73-C-0219
    (28 June 1974), ALA, pp. 5–6.
13 E. H. Spuhler, A. H. Knoll, and J. G. Kaufman, "Lithium in Aluminum –
    X2020," *Metal Progress,* 77(June 1960):80–2; C. L. Burton, L. W. Mayer,
    and E. H. Spuhler, "Aircraft and Aerospace Applications," in Kent R.
    Van Horn (ed.), *Aluminum. Vol. II: Design and Application* (Metals Park,
    OH: American Society for Metals, 1967), p. 417; James T. Staley, "Re-
    search on High-Strength Aerospace Aluminum Alloys," *Canadian Aero-
    nautics and Space Journal,* 31(March 1985):14–29; Staley, "History of
    Wrought Aluminum Alloy Development," p. 9. Alloy 2020 was patented
    by I. M. LeBaron, "Aluminum Alloy," U.S. Patent 2,381,219, August
    1945.
14 Staley, "History of Wrought Aluminum Alloy Development," p. 9; W. A.
    Anderson to Subcommittee on Alloy Development, 23 August 1973, AA-
    Boyers. Publications that mentioned problems with alloy 2020 included
    Spuhler, Knoll, and Kaufman, "Lithium in Aluminum," pp. 81–2, and
    Burton, Mayer, and Spuhler, "Aircraft and Aerospace Applications," p.
    430.
15 J. W. Evancho and J. T. Staley, "Technical Proposal, Development of an
    Al-Mg-Li Alloy for High Performance Aircraft," 3 May 1972, and J. W.
    Evancho, "Development of an Al-Mg-Li Alloy, Final Report," 28 June
    1974, pp. 1–2, 6, ALA. Alcoa was able to track Soviet research in this
    field through the work of William F. Marley, Jr., a metallurgist with the
    U.S. Army Foreign Science and Technology Center who was responsible
    for monitoring foreign alloy development. See W. F. Marley to Allen S.
    Russell, 9 September 1974, and "Soviet Development of Aluminum-
    Lithium Alloys," 28 February 1978, in John R. Ramm to T. H. Sanders,
    12 May 1978, ALA.
16 Evancho, "Development of an Al-Mg-Li Alloy, Final Report," 28 June

1974, pp. 27–8; Evancho to G. B. Barthold, 26 April 1974 and 20 June 1974, ALA.

17 Evancho to G. B. Barthold, 22 November 1974, and attached proposal, "Work to Determine Reasons for Low Toughness of Li-Containing Alloys, Technical Proposal," 22 November 1974, ALA. See also G. B. Barthold to J. T. Staley, J. W. Evancho, and E. H. Spuhler, 10 September 1974, ALA.

18 "Proposed Extension of Naval Air Development Center Contract No. N62269-76-C0271," in T. H. Sanders to J. R. Ramm, 23 March 1977, ALA.

19 G. B. Barthold to J. T. Staley, 28 October 1976, with attached "Navy Manufacturing Technology Project Proposal Brief," 12 October 1976, ALA. Balmuth noted a Lockheed study that showed that use of Al-Li in a particular L-1011 part could save 160 pounds, as compared with 200 pounds for graphite, but the Al-Li alloy would be considerably more cost-effective.

20 Barthold to Staley, 28 October 1976, ALA. On the attitude of the subcommittee, see W. A. Anderson to Subcommittee on Alloy Development, 23 August 1973 and 23 April 1974, AA-Boyers. In 1975, Alcoa had rejected the opportunity to purchase Soviet know-how related to production of the Al-Mg-Li alloy 01420, even with government funding. H. Y. Hunsicker to R. Schmidt, 28 October 1976, ALA.

21 Staley, "Threats to the Continued Use of Aluminum in the Aerospace Industry," 7 January 1977, ALA.

22 D. M. Naser to J. T. Staley, 30 May 1978, ALA. This contrasts with the fact that almost none of the Laboratories' other work was done under government auspices. See also J. G. Kaufman to R. G. Hampel, 29 April 1977, Kaufman to Hampel and A. S. Russell, 2 May 1977, and A. S. Russell to J. G. Kaufman, 2 May 1977, ALA. On the government policy of fostering competition in R&D, see National Academy of Sciences, *Innovation and Technology Transfer of U.S. Air Force Manufacturing Technology*, a publication by the COCAM Committee of the Manufacturing Studies Board (Washington, D.C.: National Academy Press, 1981).

23 D. J. George to John R. Ramm, 17 May 1978, and John R. Ramm, "Naval Air Systems Command," 28 June 1978 and 3 October 1978, ALA.

24 Gregory B. Barthold to J. P. Lyle, 2 April 1979, ALA; William F. Marley, Jr., "Soviet Development of Aluminum-Lithium Alloys," letter report, U.S. Army Foreign Science and Technology Center, 28 February 1978, in John R. Ramm to T. H. Sanders, 12 May 1978, ALA.

25 J. T. Staley to Edward L. Crouse, 7 November 1977, John E. Haygood to J. W. Evancho, 25 May 1973, and Haygood to Staley, 5 March 1974, ALA.

26 Editor, *Metallurgical Transactions*, to H. Y. Hunsicker, 18 June 1979, ALA.

27 Thomas H. Sanders, Jr., and Edgar A. Starke, Jr., to F. R. Billman, 29 May 1980, ALA. The Fifth International Al-Li Conference was held in March 1989 in Virginia.

28 Gregory B. Barthold, "Memo," 9 February 1979, Barthold to D. L. Mauney, 23 March 1979, and Barthold to R. A. Bonewitz, 19 October 1979, ALA.

29 N. W. Nielson to Technology Audit Team, 11 April 1980, P. J. Wright,

Jr., to J. P. Lyle, 11 June 1980, Allen S. Russell to K. J. Brondyke, 24 June 1980, ALA. See also Staley, "History of Wrought Aluminum Alloy Development," p. 6.

30 J. G. Kaufman, "Minutes of Meeting – 1978 August 30," 6 September 1978, ALA. In that meeting the Task Force on Aerospace Alloys of the Subcommittee on Alloy Development had approved a budget sufficient to support a single metallurgist on a small program of fundamental work and experimentation with alternate heat treatment to improve the properties of alloy 2020. But the vote had been split on whether or not to assign that work a priority rating high enough to protect it from subsequent budget cuts.

31 J. P. Lyle, "Subcommittee on Alloy Development, Minutes of Meeting – 80 April 23," 25 April 1980, ALA. See also D. O. Sprowls, "Subcommittee on Alloy Development, Task Force on Aerospace Alloys, Minutes of Meeting – 80 April 4," 17 April 1980, ALA.

32 Spear Interview.

33 A. K. Vasudevan, "Report," 27 July 1979, ALA.

34 Staley to J. P. Lyle, 14 May 1980, ALA.

35 P. J. Wright, Jr., to E. W. Johnson, 15 August 1980, and William B. Renner, "Memo," 28 February 1980, ALA. Spear Interview.

36 J. T. Staley to R. E. Miller and N. E. Lawson, 13 March 1981, A. K. Vasudevan to N. W. Nielson, 23 December 1980, ALA. Staley's earlier roadmap had called for a full year of continuing work on the fracture-toughness problem before beginning a program on ingot casting.

37 W. H. Hunt, Jr., to J. T. Staley, 18 May 1981, ALA. As project manager, Staley was designated to act as the critical communications link between the team and "the outside." Jacoby was responsible for developing both lab- and plant-scale melting and ingot-casting technology at ATC and for assisting in its transfer to the plants. Scott's assignment was to develop heat treatment and fabricating practices for the new alloys and to help implement them in production. Vasudevan was the principal researcher in the area of fundamentals. His primary charge was to continue his work, at an accelerated pace, "consistent with the timing and goals of the project." He was also asked to give a tutorial for the other team members, to bring them up to speed on the fundamentals of Al-Li alloys. Hunt's role was to "implement" the information generated by Vasudevan in the production of experimental alloys in various forms and tempers for evaluation and to oversee technical transfer to the plants, arrangements for testing and evaluation of candidate materials, development of information on potential applications other than aerospace, and handling the project's administrative details.

38 Staley to Miller and Lawson, 13 March 1981, ALA.

39 W. H. Hunt, Jr., to J. T. Staley, 11 May 1981, ALA.

40 W. H. Hunt, Jr., to Al-Li Project Team members, 13 August 1981, ALA.

41 W. H. Hunt, Jr., "Minutes of Al-Li Project Team Meeting," 11 May 1981 and 11 August 1981, ALA.

42 G. Edward Graddy, Jr., to Thomas L. Francis, 31 August 1981, ALA.

43 Seymour G. Epstein to Safety Committee, Task Group on Molten Metal Explosions, 9 October 1981, and James A. Demmler to J. B. Fulmer, 27 October 1981, ALA; W. H. Hunt, Jr., "Minutes of Al-Li Project Team

Meetings of 1981 September 30, 1981 October 16, and 1981 October 26," 29 October 1981, ALA.

44   Hunt, "Minutes of Al-Li Project Team Meetings," 29 October 1981, ALA; J. C. Kuli, "Basic Operating Procedures for [Verona-type] Casting," 8 November 1982, ALA; S. J. Cieslak to S. J. Jack, 21 July 1982, ALA.

45   W. S. Cebulak to N. W. Nielsen, 8 October 1982 and 17 May 1983, S. J. Cieslak to S. J. Jack, 21 July 1982, ALA. The story about the tree was recounted by Del M. Naser in an interview for Jay C. Lowndes, "Alcoa Producing Lighter Lithium Alloy," *Aviation Week and Space Technology*, 68(27 February 1984):68–71.

46   Cebulak to Nielson, 8 June 1982, ALA.

47   J. A. Shockey to P. R. Bridenbaugh, 14 April 1983, ALA.

48   K. J. Brondyke to M. E. Gantz, Jr., 1 February 1982; Daniel E. Sands, "Future Aircraft Materials, A Report Prepared for the Aluminum Company of America" (September 1981); N. W. Nielson to P. R. Bridenbaugh, 15 January 1982; M. E. Gantz, Jr., to K. J. Brondyke, 18 January 1982; Walter S. Cebulak to D. M. Naser, N. W. Nielson, and G. B. Scott, 15 April 1982, ALA.

49   Walter S. Cebulak to Kenneth J. Brondyke, 20 January 1982, ALA.

50   Ibid.; Cebulak to Brondyke, 10 February 1982, ALA.

51   D. M. Naser to W. S. Cebulak, "Aluminum-Lithium I/M Alloys, Boeing/Alcoa Development Agreement"; Naser to T. J. Taylor and R. R. Hoffman, 20 May 1982, ALA.

52   D. M. Naser to R. R. Hoffman et al., 30 March 1982, ALA.

53   This paragraph and the next are based on W. H. Hunt, Jr., "Development of Aluminum-Lithium Alloys for Aircraft Applications," 22 March 1982, ALA.

54   Walter S. Cebulak to Robert E. Spear, 12 October 1982; Cebulak to N. W. Nielsen, 12 November 1982, ALA.

55   R. R. Sawtell to N. W. Nielson, 24 June 1983, ALA.

56   R. L. Burns to R. J. Kegarise, 21 July 1983, ALA.

57   R. R. Sawtell, "Al-Li Alloy Development – Interaction with Boeing Commercial Airplane Company," 5 April 1982, ALA.

58   D. M. Naser to E. H. Spuhler, 16 December 1983, ALA.

59   D. M. Naser to N. W. Nielsen, 10 January 1984, ALA.

60   For example, see S. Suresh, A. K. Vasudevan, M. Tosten, and P. R. Howell, "Microscopic and Macroscopic Aspects of Fracture in Lithium-Containing Aluminum Alloys," *Acta Metallurgia*, 35(1987):25–46.

61   J. T. Staley, memo, 6 March 1981, ALA.

62   Advertisement enclosed in R. H. Graham to D. M. Naser and N. W. Neilsen, 9 November 1982, ALA.

63   D. M. Naser to N. W. Nielsen et al., 25 April 1983; R. H. Graham to D. M. Naser and N. W. Nielsen, 9 November 1982, ALA.

64   Article in D. M. Naser, 25 April 1983; see note 63.

65   N. W. Nielsen, "Aluminum-Lithium Alloy Development – Competitive Situation," 2 November 1982, ALA; British Aluminium advertisement enclosed in R. H. Graham letter, cited in note 63; the quotation below is from an article enclosed in D. M. Naser, 25 April 1983, cited in note 63.

66   W. D. Coker, "Aerospace Aluminum Industry Strategy Assessment Meeting 1983 September 13–15," 19 September 1983, ALA.

EPILOGUE

1   Having first introduced it in Alcoa's annual report of 1983, Parry presented a more developed version of his strategy to the shareholders at the 1986 annual meeting.

2   See David Landes, *The Unbound Prometheus: Technological Change and Industrial Development in Western Europe from 1750 to the Present* (Cambridge University Press, 1968) p. 260. In what Landes calls the common economic phenomenon of "the Indian summer of growth and achievement in obsolescence" a technology derives resilience from one or more of three factors: (1) a creative technological response to the challenge of a new competitor, (2) a compression of cost and elimination of waste in the struggle for survival, and (3) demand created by a new technique. All three factors could be applied to aluminum in the late 1980s, and the company's increasing attention to technology as a competitive weapon made an extended Indian summer a real possibility.

3   "Director's Notebook," Alcoa Laboratories' *Lab Log,* 9(February–March 1985), and interview with Charles Fletcher, operations director for primary products, by Margaret B. W. Graham, February 1984.

4   *Alcoa Laboratories 1986 Overview,* internal confidential report of the Laboratories. The goal of 75 percent advanced degrees was later revised in light of changes to the Laboratories' mission. For the new emphasis on project management and the issues it posed, see R. R. Sawtell, "Memorandum Re: Project Management – An Example, Al-Li," and interviews by Margaret B. W. Graham with R. R. Sawtell, Rolf Rolles, and R. Snodgrass in January 1986.

5   Bridenbaugh defined four major objectives for the Laboratories under his leadership: to support and build the existing aluminum business, with special emphasis on new products and new processes; to build a technology base in new materials; to explore new technologies that would lead to new businesses; to conduct fundamental research. See "Director's Notebook, 1986" and Bridenbaugh's "State of the Laboratories" speech entering the centennial year, Alcoa Laboratories' *Lab Log,* 12(January–February 1988).

6   Ron Hoffman, group vice-president for packaging systems, explained, in "Ron Hoffman: Alcoa Poised to Meet the Challenges of a Changed Packaging Industry," Alcoa Laboratories' *Lab Log,* 11(March 1987):10–13, that it was a critical period when many food producers were contemplating changing their packaging and when either the can companies would change or the food producers would integrate into container production. Metal Box brought to the venture with Alcoa its packaging expertise, and Alcoa brought its capabilities in polymers and coatings. The goal, according to Ron Hoffman, was to marry the two research efforts to produce "high-barrier plastics" that could provide long shelf life.

7   The auto-body-sheet program received its biggest external impetus from federal regulation of vehicle weight that followed the mid-1970s energy crisis, and its fortunes tended to rise and fall with the broader interest in energy conservation. See *Automotive Industries,* 1 December 1977, for the prediction that aluminum would continue to replace steel at a steady pace during the 1980s.

8   "ARALL Laminates Come of Age," Alcoa Laboratories' *Lab Log*, 11(December 1987):3–7.

9   The Laboratories' internal awards program recognized patents, best published papers, best internal reports, community service, educational accomplishments, and outstanding job performance.

10 See "Patently Clear," Aloca Laboratories' *Lab Log*, 10(May–July 1986):14–17, containing a joint interview with Alcoa's patent counsel, David Brownlee, and associate patent counsel, Carl Lippert.

11 "New Group Vice Presidents Comment on Their Businesses, Expectations of the Labs," Alcoa Laboratories' *Lab Log*, 10(November–December 1986):14–15.

12 "Advanced Manufacturing: Bringing the Factory of the Future into the Present," Alcoa Laboratories' *Lab Log*, 11(May 1987):22–3, reported on a trip by Alcoa President Fred Fetterolf and a group of Alcoa executives, including Peter Bridenbaugh, Ron Hoffman, and Vince Scorsone, to Japan, where they witnessed aluminum plants comparable to their own, with much higher productivity rates owing to such practices as "Just-in-Time," "Total Quality Commitment," and "Single Minute" exchange of dies. Peter Bridenbaugh reflected on the importance of integration among materials development, the design function, and the manufacturing process, which was possible and necessary once process control had been fully realized: "Director's Notebook" Alcoa Laboratories' *Lab Log*, 12(May–June 1988), entitled the "Corporate R&D Budget."

13 "Advanced Manufacturing," Alcoa Laboratories' *Lab Log*, 11(May 1987).

14 "The Quiet Coup at Alcoa," *Business Week* (27 June 1988):58–65.

15 "Alcoa Committed to Technology with Added Emphasis on Implementation," Alcoa Laboratories' *Lab Log*, 12(May–June 1988):10–12, an interview with C. Fred Fetterolf, Alcoa president and chief operating officer.

16 "Customer Demand, Value Potential, Should Drive R&D Priorities," Alcoa Laboratories' *Lab Log*, 12(August–September 1988):3–7, an interview with Alcoa Chairman Paul O'Neill.

17 "Customer Demands," Alcoa Laboratories' *Lab Log*, 12(August–September 1988).

18 "The Corporate R&D Budget," "Director's Notebook," Alcoa Laboratories' *Lab Log*, 12(May–June 1988):28–9.

CONCLUSION

1   See Lester Thurow, "A Weakness in Process Technology," *Science* (December 1987):1659–63.

2   For a discussion of Alcoa's strategy and structure, see George D. Smith, *From Monopoly to Competition: The Transformations of Alcoa, 1888–1986* (Cambridge University Press, 1988), pp. 53–5.

3   Few American companies confronted with that dilemma in the postwar era chose the third alternative that has more recently been adopted by Japanese companies: increasing the prior education and skill levels of its operations personnel to match the sophistication of the technology.

4   See, for instance, Michael Dertouzos, Richard Kloster, and Robert M. Solow, *Made in America: Regaining the Productive Edge* (Cambridge, MA: MIT Press, 1989), pp. 72–4.

5 David C. Mowery, "Industrial Research and Firm Size, Survival and Growth in American Manufacturing, 1921–1946: An Assessment," *Journal of Economic History*, 43(December 1983):953–80.

6 Alfred D. Chandler, Jr., and Herman Daems (eds.), *Managerial Hierarchies: Comparative Perspectives on the Rise of the Modern Industrial Enterprise* (Cambridge, MA: Harvard University Press, 1977), pp. 152–5.

7 These are questions that have been raised concerning the long-term efficacy of the large hierarchical structure that was such an important feature of the triumph of the modern firm in the twentieth century. See Oliver E. Williamson, "Emergence of the Visible Hand: Implications for Industrial Organization," in Chandler and Daems (eds.), *Managerial Hierarchies*, p. 198.

8 When only one core technology had to be mastered, as at Bayer and other chemical companies, it was diversification that brought stimulus. When multiple core technologies were involved, it took a considerably longer time to master the technologies, especially when the interactive effects created problems of their own.

9 Marianne Jellinek, *Institutionalization of Innovation: The Case of Texas Instruments* (Lexington, MA: Ballinger, 1978).

10 Thomas Hughes, in his essay "The Evolution of Large Technological Systems," in Wiebe Bijker, Thomas P. Hughes, and Trevor Pinch (eds.), *The Social Construction of Technological Systems* (Cambridge, MA: MIT Press, 1987), notes that system builders often create not only the components of their systems but also their contexts. The problem is that once in place, both the institutions and the infrastructure thus created can outlast their usefulness and interfere with the necessary evolution of the technology itself.

Index

Index 643